Organizational Behavior

Fifth Edition

Richard M. Steers
Kazumitsu Shiomi Professor of
Management and International Studies
University of Oregon

J. Stewart Black
Associate Professor of
International Management
American Graduate School of
International Management

HarperCollins*CollegePublishers*

Acquiring Editor: Melissa Rosati
Developmental Editor: Olive Collen
Project Coordination, Text and Cover Design: PC&F, Inc.
Cover Illustration: Franklin Hammond
Photo Researcher: Carol Parden
Production Manager: Valerie A. Sawyer
Compositor: PC&F, Inc.
Printer and Binder: R.R. Donnelley & Sons Company
Cover Printer: The Lehigh Press, Inc.

Photo Credits: p. 3: Pascal Della Zuana/Sygma; *p. 29:* George Rost/Gamma Liaison; *p. 43:* Courtesy Diamond-Star Motor Corporation; *p. 63:* Tim Brown/Tony Stone Images; *p. 99:* Lincoln Potter/Gamma Liaison; *p. 107:* Courtesy General Motors; *p. 131:* Chuck Keeler/Tony Stone Images; *p. 146:* Courtesy General Motors; *p. 160:* Bruce Ayres/Tony Stone Images; *p. 163:* Jeff Greenberg/PhotoEdit; *p. 199:* Jim Pickerell/Tony Stone Images; *p. 227:* Courtesy the State of Oregon; *p. 241:* PhotoEdit; *p. 271:* Courtesy General Motors; *p. 279:* Chuck Keeler/Tony Stone Images; *p. 292:* Courtesy General Mills; *p. 297:* Courtesy Motorola; *p. 301:* Courtesy Diamond-Star Motor Corporation; *p. 321:* Peter Correz/Tony Stone Images; *p. 327:* Courtesy San Diego State University; *p. 359:* Tim Brown/Tony Stone Images; *p. 391:* Courtesy Motorola; *p. 401:* Chuck Keeler/Tony Stone Images; *p. 421:* Courtesy NeXT Inc.; *p. 435:* Mel Lindstrom/Tony Stone Images; *p. 443:* Courtesy Hyatt Hotels Corporation; *p. 473:* Frank Herholt/Tony Stone Images; *p. 521:* Blake J. Discher/Sygma; *p. 553:* Jim Graham/Gamma Liaison; *p. 566:* Courtesy Intel; *p. 587:* Ian o'Leary/Tony Stone Images; *p. 629:* Philip & Karen Smith/Tony Stone Images; *p. 675:* UPS and UPS in shield design are registered trademarks of United Parcel Service of America, Inc. Used by permission.

Organizational Behavior, **Fifth Edition**

Library of Congress Cataloging-in-Publication Data

Steers, Richard M.
    Organizational behavior / Richard M. Steers, J. Stewart Black.—5th ed.
        p.   cm.
    Revised ed. of: Introduction to organizational behavior. 4th ed. 1991.
    Includes bibliographical references and indexes.
    ISBN 0-673-46830-5
    1. Organizational behavior.   2. Industrial management.
3. Psychology, Industrial.   I. Black, J. Stewart.
II. Steers, Richard M.   Introduction to organizational behavior.
III. Title.
HD58.7.S74   1993
658'.001'9—dc20

93-11767
CIP

93 94 95 96 9 8 7 6 5 4 3 2 1

*Dedicated,
with love and appreciation,
to Sheila and Kathleen Steers
and to Janet, Jared, Nathaniel,
and Kendra Black*

Contents

Chapter 4

Chapter 5

Chapter 6

Chapter 7

Part Three Groups and Organization Design 239

Chapter 11

◼ **Environment, Technology, and Organization Design**   358

Part Four   Organizational Processes   399

Chapter 12

◼ **Leadership and Group Performance**   400

Chapter 15

Chapter 16

Chapter 17

■ Stress and Well-Being 586

Close Up
Performance Pressures and Stress at Food
Lion 586
Problems of Work Adjustment 588
Work-Related Stress 589
SELF-ASSESSMENT 17.1: How Stressful Is
Your Job? 591
Organizational Influences on
Stress 592
IN PRACTICE: Are the Japanese Working
Themselves to Death? 598
Personal Influences on Stress 600
SELF-ASSESSMENT 17.2: Are You a
Type A? 603
IN PRACTICE: Executive Stress Around
the World 604
SELF-ASSESSMENT 17.3: How Stable Is
Your Life? 605
Buffering Effects on Work-Related
Stress 605
IN PRACTICE: Stress Management in the
Army 606
Consequences of Work-Related
Stress 607
IN PRACTICE: Time Out at Tandem
Computers 612
SELF-ASSESSMENT 17.4: Are You
Suffering from Burnout? 613
Coping with Work-Related Stress 614
IN PRACTICE: Health Promotion at
Control Data 618
Pulling It All Together 618
Summary of Key Points 619
Key Words 619
Questions for Discussion 620
Notes 620

Part Five Employee and Organization
Development 627

Chapter 18

■ Careers and Employee
Development 628

Close Up
The Double Edge of Overseas Career
Moves 628
The Employment Relationship 630
Organizational Entry 633
IN PRACTICE: Realistic Job Previews at
Nissan-USA 638
Socialization and Employee
Adaptation 639
Careers in Organizations 643
SELF-ASSESSMENT 18.1: What Are Your
Career Anchors? 645
IN PRACTICE: Perpetual Careers at Asahi
Breweries 648
Mentoring 649
Managing a Diverse
Work Force 651
SELF-ASSESSMENT 18.2: How Important
Is Success to You? 653
IN PRACTICE: Mommy Track, Daddy
Track 654
Pulling It All Together 654
Summary of Key Points 655
Key Words 656
Questions for Discussion 656
Notes 656

Chapter 19

■ Organizational Change and Development 664

Preface

The field of management and organizational behavior exists today in a constant state of evolution and change. Even a casual review of such periodicals as *Business Week, Fortune,* and the *Wall Street Journal* illustrates the dynamic nature of organizations in today's ever-changing business environment. We see articles about increased industrial competitiveness, takeovers and acquisitions, new government regulations, stockholder revolts, the need for increased industrial competitiveness, and so forth. As organizations change in response to these pressures, however, so too do their employees, their organization structures, their core technologies, their corporate cultures, and their approaches to management. This book is about these changes and what effective managers can do to understand and anticipate such changes and respond accordingly.

Objectives for This Book

This is the fifth edition of *Organizational Behavior.* As we approached this revision, the publisher and the authors both felt strongly that, in view of the emergent trends in the business environment, this edition had to meet at least three objectives.

First, the book had to be current. As a result, we committed ourselves to a *major revision* of the text that went well beyond what can be found in a typical textbook revision. Over half of the material presented in this fifth edition represents entirely new or updated information. New material on negotiation behavior, cross-cultural and international management, managing diversity, ethical behavior, and career management has been added. New theories and research findings have been integrated into the text, where they contribute to improving the reader's understanding of the practice of management. Throughout, an effort has been made to incorporate only the latest and most useful material for a better understanding of organizational behavior.

Second, the book had to be both *interesting* and *relevant.* It is easy to write a theoretical book, but more difficult to explain to others how such theories apply in the real world. We invested considerable time and energy in incorporating practical examples into the text to show how the concepts work. And implications for management can be found throughout the book. Finally, considerable effort was spent on improving the readability of the text, on the assumption that we learn better when we are interested in what we are reading.

Third, we wanted a *fully integrated and comprehensive learning package.* That is, we felt that in order to master the field of organizational behavior and learn how to apply its concepts on the job, the student had to be presented with a comprehensive package of instructional materials. This was done in several ways. Within the text itself, students will find extensive cross-referencing to tie various aspects of the field together. Moreover, each topic is discussed from an integrative standpoint. For example, while everyone agrees that international management and ethics are important topics, there are no separate chapters on these topics in this book. This was intentional. Instead, these and other important topics are discussed in many places throughout the text as they pertain to the various topics treated. In this way, the student can see how material presented in each chapter actually applies.

In addition to having an integrated text, this book is accompanied by an integrated learning package of supplemental materials described below. Taken together, the package offers an educational experience that we hope will be valuable to the consumer in the years ahead.

New Developments in the Field

As we look around us, we can identify at least five emerging trends in the field of organizational behavior that affect contemporary managers. In preparing this book, we have tried to address these trends in a comprehensive and authoritative way. Consider the following trends and how they are addressed throughout the text.

1. Changes in the business environment. Today's managers face increased pressures from a constantly changing and turbulent business environment. Mergers, acquisitions, bankruptcies, hostile takeovers, and new ventures are all prominent features on the business landscape, and each affects organizations in profound ways. Contemporary managers must be aware of such changes and be capable of responding appropriately. We deal with the impact of these changes throughout this book. For example, the ways in which companies restructure themselves in response to environmental challenges is discussed at length in Chapters 10 and 11. Elsewhere, in Chapter 19, we focus on how organizations can implement efforts to change in order to continue to adapt to external developments. And in Chapter 13, changes in communication patterns brought about as a result of our technological revolution are discussed.

2. Increasing international pressure for competitiveness. A second trend in organizations is the increasing tendency toward internationalization. We see this in several ways, including foreign acquisition and management of local companies, foreign manufacturing facilities established in this country, increased globalization of markets, intense races to develop and utilize new technologies, and so forth. In point of fact, most successful companies today require managers who can understand and act effectively in a global context rather than just a national one. Hence, a major portion of this book is devoted to developing an awareness and understanding of the international dimensions of organizational behavior. This includes understanding how cultural variations affect employee selection and adaptation (Chapter 2), employee motivation (Chapter 6), leadership and decision making (Chapters 12 and 14), communication and information processing (Chapter 13), and business negotiations (Chapter 16). Throughout, an effort is made to show how the material in the text relates to how managers deal with foreign workers or fellow managers.

3. A shift from manufacturing to service industries. As foreign manufacturing increases, the economies of North America are increasingly focusing on the service sector. With this change come special organizational problems. Organizing and managing a service company is quite different from managing an industrial firm, and managers must understand these differences. While examples are found throughout this book, this topic is dealt with in detail in Chapter 11.

4. Increasing diversity in the work force. A fourth emerging trend in organizational behavior is the increasing diversity to be found among the work force. More women, minorities, and handicapped individuals are entering the labor force. With them come special concerns about equality of opportunity and how to accommodate the special needs associated with such diversity. In view of the need for companies to make the best use of all of their human resources, this topic is of utmost concern. Problems and opportunities associated with managing diversity are discussed at length in Chapter 18, although examples relating to this issue are found throughout the text.

5. A renewed emphasis on ethical conduct in management. Finally, more and more executives and government officials are learning the value of conducting business and management in an ethical fashion. Litigation and prosecution aimed at curbing corporate excess and exploitation—whether by an individual or a company—have increased dramatically in recent years. Civil and criminal penalties for such misconduct as sexual harassment, job discrimination, insider trading, mismanagement of funds, and marketing unsafe products are now commonplace. Today's manager realizes that such infringements on others are not only unethical, but also bad business.

The ethics of management are dealt with throughout this book in several ways. The topic is introduced in Chapter 2. The role of ethics is then discussed as it relates to performance appraisals and rewards (Chapter 7), leadership (Chapter 12), decision making (Chapter 14), power in organizations (Chapter 15), and negotiation (Chapter 16). Finally, management ethics is the theme of many of the exercises and cases found throughout the book, in which the topic is put to students in the form of various dilemmas to be resolved.

Pedagogical Considerations

In writing this book, we have incorporated several pedagogical tools designed to enhance the learning experience. These include the following:

"Close Ups." Each chapter presents the reader with a real-life example of a management problem or experience to set the stage for the concepts that follow. For example, we look at the cross-cultural management challenges at Euro Disney, new education and training initiatives at Motorola, how to motivate fast trackers when the pace of advancement slows, new team approaches at Corning, the downsizing challenges at IBM, and the power play in GM's board room that pushed out the CEO, Roger Stempel. In each case, these chapter openers provide a useful frame of reference for better understanding and applying the materials that follow.

"In Practice" examples. Throughout the text, there are numerous in-depth management examples to show how the topics presented in each chapter relate to the practice of management. Many sections in this new edition feature international and ethical challenges. For example, we look at

Japan's attempt to reduce its work week, at how to be effective overseas, of Japan's hell camps, assessment centers at British Telecom, Mazda's innovative success with the Miata, and team building at British Petroleum. In examining ethical issues, we look at the ethics of such issues as influencing a salesperson's behavior using insider information. Through examples such as these, a direct link is established between the conceptual material and actual managerial behavior and performance.

"Self-Assessment" exercises.   This edition contains a series of "Self-Assessment" exercises enabling students to see firsthand how the subjects under discussion relate to them. For example, when we consider the topic of values, students can complete a questionnaire assessing their own values. When we discuss leadership style in Chapter 12, students can actually assess their own leadership styles, thereby adding relevance to the discussion. Other Self-Assessment exercises deal with locus of control, motivational levels, stress, group relations, job design, communication patterns, decision making, conflict, and career issues. All told, this book contains 34 such exercises, specifically designed for students. Scoring procedures and interpretations are presented in Appendix B.

Chapter summaries.   Each chapter concludes with a paragraph designed to help students integrate material from the chapter ("Pulling It All Together") and with a detailed summary designed to highlight the major points covered.

"Key Words."   All key words are listed at the end of each chapter. For easy reference, these words are italicized in the text where their definitions appear.

Discussion questions.   Discussion questions are presented at the end of each chapter to help students organize their thoughts about what they have read. Typically, they focus on understanding the larger, more complicated issues involved in managing organizational behavior.

"Experiential Exercises."   Each chapter is followed by an "Experiential Exercise" in which students are given an opportunity to experience firsthand how organizations work. These exercises may ask the student to make a management decision, to collect data on some management activity, or to design a small organization. In each case, the focus is on applying what students have learned to the real world. Fifteen of these exercises are new to this edition.

"Management Dilemma" cases.   Finally, each chapter concludes with a "Management Dilemma" case. These cases present the student with problems to be solved. What should a manager do with an employee whose performance has fallen off? What should a manager do when an employee claims discrimination in his or her performance appraisal? What should one do when a company's organization and management no longer suit environmental realities? In each case, there is no right or wrong answer, only a real-life problem to be solved. The student's job is to assume managerial responsibility and seek out the facts necessary to make a fair and reasonable decision under difficult conditions.

Organization of the Text

There are many ways to structure a book on organizational behavior. After considerable discussion and analysis, we determined that the most effective way to explore this topic was to take a "building block" approach. That is, we begin with rudimentary topics and build to a consideration of more complex concepts. Thus, Chapter 1 begins by defining basic concepts such as work and management. The characteristics of the workplace are introduced and a model of organizational behavior is discussed.

On the basis of this general introduction in Part One, we turn in Part Two to an analysis of the role of individual behavior in organizations. Included here are discussions of individual differences, perception, job attitudes, learning processes, employee motivation and performance, and appraisal systems. Taken together, these chapters form the basis for developing an understanding of the larger issues of groups and organization-wide behavior and performance.

In Part Three, we focus on group behavior and organization design. First, intra- and intergroup relations are discussed. This is followed by a look at job design as it affects group performance. Finally, we look at the structure of organizations, including design issues and the ways organizations respond to environmental challenges.

Part Four examines organizational processes. Included here are such topics as leadership, communication and information processing, decision making, power and politics, conflict and negotiation, and stress and well-being. Finally, in Part Five, we look at employee and organization development, including an examination of career processes and organizational change.

Hence, as we progress through the book, we start from an individual perspective, build up to a group perspective, and end with an organizational perspective. Theory, research, and practice are integrated throughout. All theoretical materials are grounded in real-life practical examples to facilitate the learning experience.

For students who are interested in learning more about how behavioral research is done in organizations, Appendix A reviews the basics of organizational research. This appendix represents a nontechnical introduction to the subject and shows how we have learned what we know about individuals and groups in organizational settings.

Supplements

In addition to the text, we have developed a supplemental package of instructional materials designed to complement the learning experience. These include the following:

Instructor's Manual. Any commitment to excellence in education requires that instructors be fully prepared to guide student learning. One key to this is the availability of a well-documented instructor's manual. The author and publisher have worked closely with Bob Giacolone of the University of Richmond to develop a comprehensive handbook for instructors. This manual includes overviews, teaching notes, essay questions, key word definitions, supplemental instructional materials, and a film guide designed to enhance student learning. We hope that the manual will provide sufficient depth of coverage to add to the intellectual richness of the classroom experience.

Student Guide.   Working with Robert Giacolone of the University of Richmond, we have developed a student guide to accompany this text. This guide includes self-testing material for each chapter, along with expanded chapter outlines, crossword puzzles, and a case analysis section.

HarperCollins Videos.   A selection of videos prepared exclusively for HarperCollins are available to qualified adopters of *Organizational Behavior.*

Transparencies.   This text is accompanied by a set of more than 100 transparencies reproducing important figures and graphs. These transparencies are available free to adopters.

Test Bank.   This text is accompanied by a comprehensive test bank. Included here are over 2,000 multiple-choice, essay, and true-false questions. These questions are also available on *HarperTest*, a computerized test bank available for the IBM PC and compatibles and the Apple Macintosh computer. This computerized test bank allows the instructor to scramble questions, add new questions, and select questions on the basis of level of difficulty. Essay questions and short quizzes with accompanying answer sheets from the Instructor's Manual are also available.

Grades.   HarperCollins offers to adopters a computerized grade-keeping and classroom management package, for use on IBM PC or compatibles, that maintains data for up to 200 students.

Acknowledgments

Clearly, no book is the product of a single person. For a book to be effective, a collaborative effort of many persons is required, and this book is no exception. As we began the revision process, input and advice were sought from many quarters.

To begin with, the text itself was reviewed and re-reviewed by many instructors from both large and small universities and colleges, and to these people we are most grateful. Among those who participated in this review process and offered numerous suggestions for improvements are the following:

Peggy A. Anderson, University of Wisconsin-Whitewater
Terry R. Armstrong, University of West Florida
Jane Burman-Holtom, University of Florida
Stephen J. Carroll, University of Maryland at College Park
Daniel R. Cillis, Long Island University
Diana L. Deadrick, Vanderbilt University
James J. Freiburger, New Hampshire College
Gregory O. Ginn, Stephen F. Austin State University
Brian Graham-Moore, University of Texas at Austin
William F. Grossnickle, East Carolina University
Nell Tabor Hartley, Robert Morris College
Y. Paul Huo, Washington State University
Peter G. Kirby, Our Lady of the Lake University
Janina C. Latack, The Ohio State University

Bronston T. Mayes, California State University, Fullerton
Bonnie L. McNeely, Murray State University
Edward B. Parks, Marymount University
C. Glenn Pearce, Virginia Commonwealth University
Daniel J. Rowley, University of Northern Colorado
Paul L. Starkey, Delta State University
Dianna L. Stone, SUNY Albany
Harry E. Stucke, Long Island University

We also wish to thank the editorial staff at HarperCollins, who helped improve the manuscript at every stage. These include Melissa Rosati, Pam Wilkie, Arianne Weber, and freelance editor Olive Collen. Lyman W. Porter, Consulting Editor for the HarperCollins management texts, was always available with advice and counsel as the project developed. Carolyn Steller at Dartmouth College was also a great help with this revision. The quality of the finished product is largely due to the diligence and dedication of these professionals.

We owe a special debt of gratitude to doctoral students at the University of Oregon and to colleagues at both Oregon and Dartmouth College. No intellectual endeavor prospers for long without supportive colleagues and friends like these.

Finally, we wish to express special thanks to our families—to Rick's wife, Sheila, and his daughter, Kathleen, and to Stewart's wife, Janet, and his children Jared, Nathaniel, and Kendra for their support, patience, and encouragement throughout the many long hours of research and writing. It is to these special people that this book is dedicated.

RICHARD M. STEERS
J. STEWART BLACK

About the Authors

Richard M. Steers is the Kazumitsu Shiomi Professor of Management and International Studies in the Graduate School of Management at the University of Oregon. The author of fifteen books and numerous research publications, Professor Steers is widely known for his work on employee motivation and performance, turnover and absenteeism, and organizational effectiveness. He is a Past President and a Fellow of the Academy of Management, and a Fellow of both the American Psychological Association and the American Psychological Society. He has served on several editorial boards, including *Administrative Science Quarterly, Academy of Management Journal, Academy of Management Review, Journal of Management Inquiry,* and the *Asia Pacific Journal of Management.* Professor Steers received his Ph.D. from the University of California, Irvine, and has taught at the University of California, Irvine; Oxford University (England); the Nijenrode School of Business (Netherlands); and the University of Cape Town (South Africa). His three most recent books are *The Chaebol: Korea's New Industrial Might* (Harper & Row, 1989), *Managing Employee Absenteeism* (Addison-Wesley, 1990), and *Motivation and Work Behavior*, Fourth Edition (McGraw-Hill, 1991).

J. Stewart Black is Associate Professor of International Management at Thunderbird (American Graduate School of International Management). Black spent five years on the faculty of the Amos Tuck School of Business Administration of Dartmouth College where much of the effort for this revision was undertaken. He has published over 30 articles in both academic and practitioner journals and is known for his work on international human resource management. He is currently the director of Thunderbird's Japan Center and has served for two years on the executive committee of the international division of the Academy of Management. Professor Black received his Ph.D. from the University of California, Irvine, and has taught at Dartmouth College and the International University of Japan. His most recent book is *Global Assignments: Successfully Expatriating and Repatriating International Managers* (Jossey-Bass, 1992). Professor Black has also consulted with a variety of U.S. and Japanese multinational firms.

Part One

The Managerial Challenge

1

Management and Organizational Behavior

The Management Challenge

- To understand the meaning of work in a societal context.
- To recognize and meet the challenge facing managers in the 1990s.
- To understand what is expected of a manager.
- To understand the role of the behavioral sciences in management and organizations.

CLOSE UP

The Management Challenge at Euro Disney

Despite big hopes and dreams, the $4 billion Euro Disney theme park got off to a difficult start. The park lost 188 million francs in 1992 and was expected to lose money again in 1993. In fact, some analysts projected a loss of 750 million francs in 1993.

Amid these troubles, chairman of Euro Disney, Robert Fitzpatrick, resigned as head of the operation. Although selected for his knowledge of the French country and culture (he is married to a French woman and speaks French fluently), Mr. Fitzpatrick was the lighting rod for continual charges of "cultural imperialism" as Disney tried to duplicate the magic of the Magic Kingdom as it had successfully done in Orlando and Tokyo. In fact, the protest from many French became so strong that during a news conference just prior to the opening of the park, Disney chairman, Michael Eisner, was pelted by rotten eggs by an angry crowd.

With Mr. Fitzpartick's departure, Philippe Bourguignon, a Frenchman, was promoted from president to chairman of Euro Disney. As the new head of Euro Disney, Mr. Bourguignon faced not only the looming financial difficulties of an operation losing money, but also the challenge of motivating a workforce that was as diverse as the people expected to visit the park. A third of the employees were Americans; another third were French; and the rest were assorted Europeans. The diversity of the workforce was designed to meet the diversity of the customers.

Unlike the parks in America or Japan in which a single culture represents a large majority of the customers, Euro Disney has customers from a wide variety of nationalities. Despite its location near Paris, only one third of the customers were French during the summer of 1992. This diversity of customers makes even the simplest of things like the "proper" behavior for waiting in line problematic. In certain cultures the normal distance between two people ("personal space") is much smaller than other cultures, and the norms of "waiting in line" versus "moving ahead in line" also differ substantially. These difference are not trivial when the wait can be over an hour.

Because Euro Disney is listed on the French stock exchange, Mr. Bourguignon not only has to satisfy the diverse customers and employees of Euro Disney, but he also has to keep his boss, Disney Chairman Michael Eisner, happy as well as the stockholders. Think about yourself in Mr. Bourguignon's shoes; the organizational challenges are nearly overwhelming.[1]

Examples like that of Euro Disney highlight the fundamental challenge facing contemporary managers: How do companies achieve their productivity goals while maintaining employee commitment and satisfaction? At Euro Disney, this was complicated by the fact that employees came from different countries and had different expectations. The example of Euro Disney is illustrative of what is happening in the workplace all around the globe. Contemporary managers are witnessing changes in technologies, markets, competition, work force demographics, employee expectations, and ethical standards. At the heart of these changes is the issue of how to manage people effectively. To attain corporate objectives, each manager must discover how to develop and maintain a work force that can meet today's needs while getting ready for tomorrow's challenges. As a result, managers are asking questions such as:

How can we meet the international competition?
How can we make this organization more effective?
How can we better utilize our human resources?
How can we create a more satisfying and rewarding work environment for all employees?
How can we improve the quality of our products?
How can we improve communication and decision-making processes at work?
How should we evaluate and reward performance?
How can we develop the company leaders of tomorrow?

Questions such as these point to the issue of effective management. That is, what can managers do to improve both organizational and employee performance? This is the focus of a business or management education. Effective management requires an in-depth knowledge of financial management, marketing research and consumer behavior, accounting and control practices, manufacturing and production techniques, and quantitative methods. In addition, however, effective management requires "people skills." That is, a good manager must be able to motivate his or her employees, to lead skillfully, to make appropriate and timely decisions, to communicate effectively, to organize work, to deal with organizational politics, and to work to develop both employees and the organization as a whole. These issues constitute the subject of this book. We shall examine principles of the behavioral sciences that can help managers improve both their own skills and abilities and those of their subordinates in order to enhance organizational performance and effectiveness.

THE NATURE OF WORK

As a prelude to this analysis, we begin with a brief look at the natures of work and of management. Contemporary challenges are discussed. Next, we consider a model of organizational behavior that will serve as a guide throughout this book. We begin with an examination of work.

The Meaning of Work

What is work, and how do people feel about the work they do? These questions may be answered from several perspectives. Perhaps one of the best ways to understand how people feel about their jobs is simply to ask them. A number of years ago Chicago writer Studs Terkel did exactly that. How did the people he interviewed feel about their jobs? Here are some excerpts from his book *Working:*[2]

I'm a dying breed. . . . A laborer. Strictly muscle work . . . pick it up, put it down, pick it up, put it down . . . you can't take pride any more. You remember when a guy could point to a house he built, how many logs he stacked. He built it and he was proud of it.

—Steelworker [p. 1]

I changed my opinion of receptionists because now I'm one. It wasn't the dumb broad at the front desk who took telephone messages. She had to be something else because I thought I was something else. I was fine until there was a press party. We were having a fairly intelligent conversation. Then they asked me what I did. When I told them, they turned around to find other people with name tags. I wasn't worth bothering with. I wasn't being rejected because of what I said or the way I talked, but simply because of my function.

—Receptionist [p. 57]

People ask me what I do, I say, "I drive a garbage truck for the city." . . . I have nothing to be ashamed of. I put in my eight hours. We make a pretty good salary. I feel I earn my money. . . . My wife's happy; this is the big thing. She doesn't look down at me. I think that's more important than the white-collar guy looking down at me.

—Sanitation Truck Driver [p. 149]

I'm human. I make mistakes like everybody else. If you want a robot, build machines. If you want human beings, that's what I am.

—Policeman [p. 186]

I usually say I'm an accountant. Most people think it's somebody who sits there with a green eyeshade and his sleeves rolled up with a garter, poring over books, adding things—with glasses. I suppose a certified public accountant has status. It doesn't mean much to me. Do I like the job or don't I? That's important.

—Accountant [p. 351]

The boss . . . lost his secretary. She got promoted. So they told this old timekeeper she's to be his secretary-assistant. Oh, she's in her glory. No more money or anything and she's doing two jobs all day long. She's rushin' and runnin' all the time, all day. She's a nervous wreck. And when she asked him to write her up for an award, he refused. That's her reward for being so faithful, obedient.

—Process Clerk [p. 461]

Examples such as these—and there are many, many more—show how some employees view their jobs and the work they perform. Obviously, some jobs are more meaningful than others, and some individuals are more easily satisfied than others. Some people live to work, while others simply work to live. In any case, people clearly have strong feelings about what they do on the job and about the people with whom they work. In our study of behavior in organizations, we shall examine what people do, what causes them to do it, and how they feel about what they do. As a prelude to this analysis, however, we should first consider the basic unit of analysis in this study: work itself. What is work, and what functions does it serve in today's society?

Work has a variety of meanings in contemporary society. Often we think of work as paid employment—the exchange of services for money. Although this definition may suffice in a technical sense, it does not adequately describe why work is necessary. Perhaps *work* could be more meaningfully defined as an activity that produces something of value for other people. This definition broadens the scope of work and emphasizes the social context in which the wage-effort bargain transpires. It clearly recognizes that work has purpose—it is productive. Of course, this is not to say that work is necessarily interesting or rewarding or satisfying. On the contrary, we know that many jobs are dull, repetitive, and stressful. Even so, the activities performed do have utility for society at large. One of the challenges of management is to discover ways of transforming necessary yet distasteful jobs into more meaningful situations that are more satisfying and rewarding for individuals and that still contribute to organizational productivity and effectiveness.

Functions of Work

We know why work activities are important from an organization's viewpoint. Without work there is no product or service to provide. But why is work important to individuals? What functions does it serve?

First, work serves a rather obvious economic function. In exchange for labor, individuals receive necessary income with which to support themselves and their families. But people work for many reasons beyond simple economic necessity.

Second, work also serves several social functions. The workplace provides opportunities for meeting new people and developing friendships. Many people spend more time at work with their co-workers than they spend at home with their own families.

Third, work also provides a source of social status in the community. One's occupation is a clue to how one is regarded on the basis of standards of importance prescribed by the community. For instance, in the United States a corporate president is generally accorded greater status than a janitor in the same corporation. In China, on the other hand, great status is ascribed to peasants and people from the working class, whereas managers are not so significantly differentiated from those they manage. In Japan, status is first a function of the company you work for and how well known it is, and then the position you hold. It is important to note here that the status associated with the work we perform often transcends the boundaries of our organization. A corporate president or a university president may have a great deal of status in the community at large because of his or her position in the organization. Hence, the work we do can simultaneously represent a source of social differentiation and a source of social integration.

Fourth, work can be an important source of identity and self-esteem and, for some, a means for self-actualization. It provides a sense of purpose for individuals and clarifies their value or contribution to society. As Freud noted long ago, "Work has a greater effect than any other technique of living in binding the individual more closely to reality; in his work he is at least securely attached to a part of reality, the human community."[3] Work contributes to self-esteem in at least two ways. First, it provides individuals with an opportunity to demonstrate competence or mastery over themselves and their environment. Individuals discover that they can actually *do* something. Second, work reassures individuals that they are carrying out activities that produce something of value to others—that they have something significant to offer. Without this, the individual feels that he or she has little to contribute and is thus of little value to society.

We clearly can see that work serves several useful purposes from an individual's standpoint. It provides a degree of economic self-sufficiency, social interchange, social status, self-esteem, and identity. Without this, individuals often experience sensations of powerlessness, meaninglessness, and normlessness—a condition called *alienation*. In work, individuals have the possibility of finding some meaning in their day-to-day activities—if, of course, their work is sufficiently challenging. When employees are not involved in their jobs because the work is not challenging enough, they usually see no reason to apply themselves, which, of course, jeopardizes productivity and organizational effectiveness. This self-evident truth has given rise to a general concern among managers about declining productivity and work values. In fact, concern about this situation has caused many managers to take a renewed interest in how the behavioral sciences can help them solve many of the problems of people at work.

THE CHANGING WORKPLACE: TOWARD THE YEAR 2000

It has often been said that the only constant in life is change, and nowhere is this more true than in the workplace. As one recent survey concluded, "Over the past decade, the U.S. corporation has been battered by foreign competition, its own out-of-date technology and out-of-touch management and, more recently, a flood of mergers and acquisitions. The result has been widespread streamlining of the white-collar ranks and recognition that the old way of doing business is no longer possible or desirable."[4] As the twenty-first century approaches, companies face a variety of changes and challenges that will have a profound impact on organizational dynamics and performance. In fact, in many ways, these changes will determine who will survive and prosper into the next century and who will not. Among these challenges are the following:

The Challenge of International Competition

Until the 1980s, many American firms had little in the way of serious international competition. As a result, there was little incentive to innovate and remain efficient and competitive. Many companies became lazy and lost touch with their customers. This situation changed abruptly as companies in Asia and Western Europe developed more sophisticated products and marketing systems and gained significant market shares in home electronics, automobiles, medical equipment, telecommunications, and shipbuilding, to name a few areas. As a result, American companies lost considerable clout—and profitability.

If we examine corporate behavior during the 1980s, it is not difficult to see some of the reasons for the demise. In short, many North American firms lost their *industrial competitiveness;* that is, they lost their capacity to compete effectively in global markets. Consider the following examples:[5]

During the last decade, Japan experienced a 5.5 percent *annual growth rate in manufacturing productivity.* This is a measure of how efficient industries are becoming. Great Britain, France, and Italy all had close to 4 percent increases. At the same time, however, the United States barely had a 3 percent annual increase (and Canada had a 1.5 percent increase).

During the same period, Japan and Europe both increased their *annual expenditures for factory automation* by an average of 17 percent, while the United States increased its expenditures by about 12 percent.

Finally, the number of products that were *invented in the United States* but are now primarily *manufactured overseas* has increased dramatically (see Exhibit 1.1). There has been a significant decline in our manufacturing sector. Although many American companies have made significant headway during the past several years, the average firm and industry often lag far behind.

Consider several indicators of the relative industrial competitiveness of Japanese firms and American firms between 1975 and 1988 (see Exhibit 1.2). The United States is far behind Japan on all six of these dimensions. However

Exhibit 1.1
Products Invented in the U.S., Manufactured Elsewhere

U.S.-Invented Technology	U.S. Producers' Domestic Market Share				
	1970	1975	1980	1985	1990
Phonographs	90%	40%	30%	1%	1%
Color televisions	90	80	60	10	7
Audiotape recorders	40	10	10	0	0
Videotape recorders	10	10	1	1	1
Machine tools	99	97	79	35	20
Telephones	99	95	88	25	15
Semiconductors	89	71	65	64	40
Computers	—	97	96	74	55

Source: Based on data from Council on Competitiveness, U.S. Department of Commerce, as reported in Otis Port, "Innovation in America," *Business Week,* 1989 Special Issue, pp. 12–34.

Exhibit 1.2
Indicators of Industrial Competitiveness in the U.S. and Japan

Indicators	U.S.	Japan
Working stock and inventory	Up to 9 mos.	Under 2 mos.
Time from order to shipment	5–6 months	1–2 months
Quality defects and rework	8%–10%	1% or less
Average age of equipment	17 years	10 years
Annual investment per worker	$2,600	$6,500
Change in average investment per worker since 1975	+25%	+90%

Source: From "The Productivity Paradox," reprinted from the June 6, 1988, issue of *Business Week* by special permission. Copyright 1988 by McGraw-Hill, Inc.

we look at it, the challenge of industrial competitiveness remains to be met. North American companies are simply not investing the money, time, or effort to catch up with or surpass the competition, and, as a result, our industrial growth rate—and standard of living—remains lower than many would like.

In terms of organizational survival, here lies what is perhaps management's biggest challenge: how to become more competitive. Greater competitiveness requires an understanding of individuals, groups, and entire organizational systems. Throughout this book, we shall see numerous examples of how companies from around the world—including the United States and Canada—have met the challenge of industrial competitiveness. Particular emphasis will be placed on management practices in other countries as a point of comparison.

The Challenge of New Technologies

Although it is common to think of "high tech" as applying only to the aerospace and telecommunications industries, advanced technologies can be found throughout most industries. For example, most of us are familiar with the explosive growth in microcomputing. Both hardware and software change so rapidly that it is difficult for many companies to keep up. In personal computers (PCs), the 80286 and 80386 chips are being replaced with 486 and Pentium® chips, each faster than its predecessor. We see increases in both random access memory (RAM) and fixed-disk (hard disk) storage capabilities. Dot matrix printers are being replaced with laser and color laser printers. CGA color monitors are being replaced with VGA and SVGA color, each with increased resolution. Software is increasingly complex but increasingly user-friendly. And the use of PC networks has increased eightfold from 1986 to 1990.[6] More and more companies are using computer-based systems and equipment—such as E-mail, fax machines, and cellular phones—for communications. As a result, the way in which employees and managers communicate and make decisions is changing dramatically, and the importance of educated and knowledgeable workers is increasing rapidly.

Technological changes also can be seen in the increased use of robotics, expert systems, and computer-integrated manufacturing systems, which have changed the way many products are manufactured today. Such changes affect not only production efficiency and product quality but also the nature of jobs. In many industries, the first-line supervisors are disappearing and being replaced by self-managing work teams who assume responsibility for production scheduling, quality control, and even performance appraisals. All of these technological changes require managers who are capable of effectively implementing technological change in the workplace—managers who can adapt to the technological imperative while still maintaining and developing the organization's human resources. We will examine the role of technology as it relates to organization structure, job design, communication, decision making, and work- related stress. We will see how some companies successfully adapted to technological change in a way that benefited all parties concerned.

The Challenge of Increased Quality

The challenge of industrial competitiveness incorporates several interrelated factors, including an appropriate product mix, manufacturing efficiency, effective cost controls, investment in research and development, and so forth. Not to be ignored in this pursuit is the quest for increased quality control of the products and services offered in the marketplace. Total Quality Management (TQM) is a term often used to describe comprehensive efforts to monitor and improve all aspects of quality within a firm. BMW established and continues to maintain its reputation in part because customers have come to respect its high level of quality. Quality is also a major reason for the success of many Japanese products in North America. Simply put, if North America is to compete, renewed efforts must be devoted to enhanced quality assurance. This, too, is a management challenge. How can managers get employees to care about the products they produce or the services they offer? In this book, we will consider both the issue of quality control (what is it?) and mechanisms of ensuring improved product quality (how do we get it?).

Moreover, quality control includes several organizational issues. For instance, how can managers get parties who are traditionally independently associated with a product to work together to build a better product? That is, how can they get the design staff, manufacturing engineers, workers, suppliers—and potential customers—to come together and cooperate in developing and manufacturing a superior product? Later in the book we will examine several instances in which such teamwork played a major role in quality improvement.

The Challenge of Employee Motivation and Commitment

A major hurdle in the pursuit of industrial competitiveness is the traditional adversarial relationship between management and workers. Whether a company is unionized or not, we see situations in which the average employee simply sees no reason to increase output or to improve the quality of existing outputs. Frequently, the company's reward system restricts, rather than increases, performance. At other times, rewards encourage employees to increase quantity at the expense of quality. Furthermore, North American companies often view their work force as a variable expense (in contrast to Japan, where the work force is viewed as a fixed expense) and lay workers off

Exhibit 1.3
Characteristics Desired
in a Job

Characteristic	% ranking it as very important
Good health insurance and benefits	81
Interesting work	78
Job security	78
Opportunity to learn new skills	68
A week or more of vacation	66
Being able to work independently	64
Recognition from co-workers	62
Being able to help others	58
High income	56

Source: C. Caggiano, "What Do Workers Want?" *Inc.,* November 1992, p. 101.

when they are not needed for short-run activities. As a result, many employees see little reason to be committed or loyal to their employers. Turnover and absenteeism rates are often unreasonably high, further eroding performance efficiency and effectiveness.

If companies are to succeed in an increasingly turbulent environment, managers must discover better ways to develop and motivate employees. A company's human resources often represent its biggest single asset, and failing to properly nurture this asset leads to suboptimal return on an organization's resources. Part of solving this problem involves knowing and understanding today's employees. Exhibit 1.3 illustrates the various characteristics people consider important in a job. In addition, as Exhibit 1.4 illustrates, the workforce in the United States has changed dramatically over the last 40 years.

This problem is made all the more difficult by the changing nature of occupations. As shown in Exhibit 1.5, the year 2000 will see a sharp increase in the number of technicians, service workers, and sales workers. Growth

Exhibit 1.4
Changes in the U.S.
Labor Force

Characteristic	Year 1951	Year 1991
Gender: (Ratio of male to female workers)	2:1	1.22:1
Education:		
Less than high school	58%	12%
4 years of high school	28%	39%
At least 4 years of college	8%	28%
Average Annual Earnings: (1991 dollars)	$16,000	$22,000
Skills: (Ratio of less skilled to skilled)	2:1	1.13:1
Employment:		
Manufacturing	24%	16%

Source: Reprinted from the May 4, 1992 issue of *Fortune* by special permission.

Exhibit 1.5
The Fastest-Growing Occupations

Occupation	1990 Employment	Projected Percent Change 1990-2005
Computer systems analyst	463,000	79
Operations researcher	57,000	73
Travel agent	132,000	62
Management consultant	151,000	52
Marketing/PR manager	427,000	47
Health service manager	257,000	42
Accountant/auditor	985,000	34
Lawyer/judge	633,000	34
Electrical engineer	426,000	34
Construction contractor	183,000	33
Financial manager	701,000	28
College faculty	712,000	19
Chemical engineer	48,000	12
Bank teller	517,000	− 5
Farmer	1,223,000	−16
Telephone operator	325,000	−32

Source: Based on data from Jay M. Berman and Theressa A. Cosca, "The Job Outlook in Brief 1990–2005," *Occupational Outlook Quarterly,* 1992, 36(1), pp. 6-40.

also can be expected in engineering and managerial positions. These changes require a new look at how such employees are motivated. For example, do we motivate an engineer the same way we motivate a sales representative? How do we motivate senior executives as opposed to junior managers? In this book, we shall touch on these issues when we examine approaches to employee motivation. Managers have at their disposal several ways in which to increase employee motivation and performance, and an effective manager learns how and when to use each approach.

The Challenge of Managing a Diverse Work Force

Historically, the American economy has been dominated by white males. They have filled the vast majority of managerial positions and many of the more important blue-collar jobs, becoming skilled craftsmen. Traditionally, women filled lower-paying clerical positions and often left the work force to raise their families. Minorities of both genders found considerable barriers to entering the labor market at the higher (and higher-paying) levels. Now, things are changing, and the pace of this change is accelerating. Among other changes, the twenty-first century will also bring major changes in terms of work force demographics. We will see changes in gender, race, and age.

For example, the year 2000 will see a drop in the percentage of white American-born male workers in the workplace. Only 15 percent of the new entrants will be white males.[7] The percentages for nonwhites and immigrants of both genders will increase (see Exhibit 1.6). In general, there will be more women in positions of responsibility in both the public and private sectors and more opportunities for minorities. Some predict that the coming labor shortage will cause many companies to try to retain older workers for longer periods of time, beyond the traditional retirement age. Additionally, the belief that mentally or physically challenged individuals can play productive roles at work is increasing. Such changes bring opportunities for companies but also potential problems of adjustment if not managed intelligently. We will examine several of these issues when we discuss careers and employee development.

The Challenge of Ethical Behavior

Finally, the future will bring a renewed concern with maintaining high standards of ethical behavior in business transactions and in the workplace. Many executives and social scientists see unethical behavior as a cancer working on the fabric of society both in business and beyond. Many are concerned that we face a crisis of ethics in the West that is undermining our competitive strength. This crisis involves business, government, customers, and employees. Especially worrisome is unethical behavior among employees at all levels of the organization. For example, a recent study found that employees accounted for a higher percentage of retail thefts than did customers.[8] The study estimated that one in every fifteen employees steals from his or her employer.

In addition, we hear about illegal and unethical behavior on Wall Street, pension scandals in which disreputable executives gamble on risky business ventures with employee retirement funds, companies that expose their workers to hazardous working conditions, and blatant favoritism in hiring and promotion practices. Although such practices occur throughout the world, their presence nonetheless serves to remind us of the challenge we face.

This challenge is especially difficult because standards for what constitutes ethical behavior lie in a "grey zone" where clear-cut right-or-wrong answers may not always exist. For example, if you were a sales representative for an American company abroad and your foreign competitors used bribes to get business, what would you do? In the United States such behavior is illegal, yet it is perfectly acceptable in other countries. What is ethical

Exhibit 1.6
Projected Demographic
Changes in the Work Force,
1985–2000

Composition of Labor Force	1985*	2000
U.S.-born white males	47%	15%
U.S.-born white females	36	42
U.S.-born nonwhite males	5	7
U.S.-born nonwhite females	5	13
Immigrant males	4	13
Immigrant females	3	10

Figures for 1985 represent the total work force; projections for 2000 represent new entrants only.

Source: Based on data from *Statistical Abstract of the United States,* 1992 and Bruce Nussbaum, "Needed: Human Capital," *Business Week,* September 19, 1988, pp. 100–103.

here? Similarly, in many countries women are systematically discriminated against in the workplace; it is felt that their place is in the home. In the United States, again, this practice is illegal. If you ran an American company in one of these countries, would you hire women in important positions? If you did, your company might be isolated in the larger business community, and you might lose business. If you did not, you might be violating what most Americans believe to be fair business practices.

Effective managers must know how to deal with ethical issues in their everyday work lives; therefore, we will devote parts of this book to the role of ethics in decision making, the exercise of power, performance appraisals and reward systems, and so forth. In fact, in many of the Management Dilemmas at the end of each chapter, you will be asked to make a decision or solve a problem that involves an ethical dimension. These exercises should provide opportunities to consider how you would make decisions in this grey zone of ethical behavior.

THE NATURE OF MANAGEMENT

If organizations are to be successful in meeting these challenges of the coming decade, it will be their managements who must lead the way. With effective management, contemporary companies can accomplish a great deal toward becoming more competitive in the global environment. On the other hand, ineffective management dooms the organization to mediocrity and sometimes outright failure. Because of this, we turn now to a look at the nature of management. However, we want to point out that even though our focus is on managers, what we discuss is also relevant to the actions of non-managers. On the basis of this examination, we should be ready to begin our analysis of what managers can learn from the behavioral sciences to improve their effectiveness in a competitive environment.

What Is Management?

Many years ago, Mary Parker Follett defined management as "the art of getting things done through people." A manager coordinates and oversees the work of others to accomplish ends he or she could not attain alone. Today this definition has been broadened. *Management* is generally defined as the process of planning, organizing, directing, and controlling the activities of employees in combination with other resources to accomplish organizational objectives. In a broad sense, then, the task of management is to facilitate the organization's effectiveness and long-term goal attainment by coordinating and efficiently utilizing available resources. Based on this definition, it is clear that the topics of effectively managing individuals, groups, or organizational systems is relevant to anyone who must work with others to accomplish organizational objectives.

Management exists in virtually all goal-seeking organizations, whether they are public or private, large or small, profit-making or not-for-profit, socialist or capitalist. For many, the mark of an excellent company or organization is the quality of its managers.

Managerial Responsibilities

An important question often raised about managers is: What responsibilities do managers have in organizations? According to our definition, managers are involved in planning, organizing, directing, and controlling. A survey of 600 managers in a large electronics manufacturing organization provided detailed insight into managerial responsibilities.[9] Responding to questions about their activities, managers described responsibilities that suggested nine major types of activity. These include:

1. *Long-range planning.* Managers occupying executive positions are frequently involved in strategic planning and development.
2. *Controlling.* Managers evaluate and take corrective action concerning the allocation and use of human, financial, and material resources.
3. *Environmental scanning.* Managers must continually watch for changes in the business environment and monitor business indicators such as returns on equity or investment, economic indicators, business cycles, and so forth.
4. *Supervision.* Managers continually oversee the work of their subordinates.
5. *Coordinating.* Managers often must coordinate the work of others both inside the work unit and out.
6. *Customer relations and marketing.* Certain managers are involved in direct contact with customers and potential customers.
7. *Community relations.* Contact must be maintained and nurtured with representatives from various constituencies outside the company, including state and federal agencies, local civic groups, and suppliers.
8. *Internal consulting.* Some managers make use of their technical expertise to solve internal problems, acting as inside consultants for organizational change and development.
9. *Monitoring products and services.* Managers get involved in planning, scheduling, and monitoring the design, development, production, and delivery of the organization's products and services.

As we shall see, not every manager engages in all of these activities. Rather, different managers serve different roles and carry different responsibilities, depending upon where they are in the organizational hierarchy. We will begin by looking at several of the variations in managerial work.

Variations in Managerial Work

Although each manager may have a diverse set of responsibilities, including those mentioned above, the amount of time spent on each activity and the importance of that activity will vary considerably. The two most salient perceptions of a manager are (1) the manager's level in the organizational hierarchy and (2) the type of department or function for which he or she is responsible. Let us briefly consider each of these.

Management by Level.   We can distinguish three general levels of management: executives, middle management, and first-line management (see Exhibit 1.7). Executive managers are at the top of the hierarchy and are responsible for

Exhibit 1.7
Levels in the
Management Hierarchy

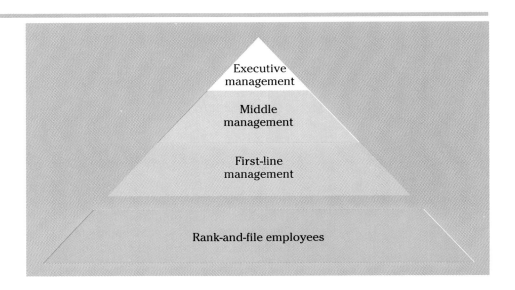

the entire organization, especially its strategic direction. Middle managers, who are at the middle of the hierarchy, are responsible for major departments and may supervise other lower-level managers. Finally, first-line managers supervise rank-and-file employees and carry out day-to-day activities within departments.

Exhibit 1.8 shows differences in managerial activities by hierarchical level. The higher a number in the table is, the more importance it has for managers at a given level. For example, top managers rate high on such activities as long-range planning, monitoring business indicators, coordinating, and internal consulting. Lower-level managers, by contrast, rate high on supervising because their responsibility is to accomplish tasks through rank-and-file employees. Middle managers rate near the middle for all activities.

These findings suggest that the skills required of managers change as the managers move up the hierarchy and acquire greater responsibility. We can distinguish three types of managerial skills:[10]

Exhibit 1.8
Importance of Management
Activities by Level

Managerial Activities	Management Level		
	First-Line	**Middle**	**Executive**
Long-range planning	25	45	84
Controlling	38	50	61
Monitoring business indicators	30	49	74
Supervising	65	50	33
Coordinating	31	52	70
Customer relations/marketing	27	49	69
External contact	38	45	57
Consulting	30	52	70
Products and services	33	50	58

Source: Luis Gomez-Mejia, Joseph E. McCann, and Ronald C. Page, "The Structure of Managerial Behaviors and Rewards," *Industrial Relations,* 24 (1985), 147–154. Used with permission.

1. *Technical skills.* Managers must have the ability to use the tools, procedures, and techniques of their special areas. An accountant must have expertise in accounting principles, whereas a production manager must know operations management. These skills are the mechanics of the job.
2. *Human relations skills.* Human relations skills involve the ability to work with people and understand employee motivation and group processes. These skills allow the manager to become involved with and lead his or her group.
3. *Conceptual skills.* These skills represent a manager's ability to organize and analyze information in order to improve organizational performance. They include the ability to see the organization as a whole and to understand how various parts fit together to work as an integrated unit. These skills are required to coordinate the departments and divisions successfully so that the entire organization can pull together.

As shown in Exhibit 1.9, different levels of these skills are required at different stages of the managerial hierarchy. That is, success in executive positions requires far more conceptual skill and less use of technical skills in most (but not all) situations, whereas first-line managers generally require more technical skills and fewer conceptual skills. Note, however, that human or people skills remain important for success at all three levels in the hierarchy.

Management by Department or Function. In addition to level in the hierarchy, managerial responsibilities also differ with respect to the type of department or function. Exhibit 1.10 illustrates differences for quality assurance, manufacturing, marketing, accounting, and personnel departments. In this exhibit, the higher the number, the more important the activity in the manager's job. Manufacturing department managers rate high on products and services, controlling, and supervising. Marketing managers, in comparison, rate low on planning, coordinating, and consulting but high on customer relations and external contact. Managers in both accounting and personnel departments rate high on long-range planning and low on products. As the exhibit shows, managers in accounting are also concerned with controlling

Exhibit 1.9
Differences in Skills Required for Successful Management According to Level in the Hierarchy

Executive Managers	Middle Managers	First-Line Managers
Conceptual	Conceptual	Conceptual
Human	Human	Human
Technical	Technical	Technical

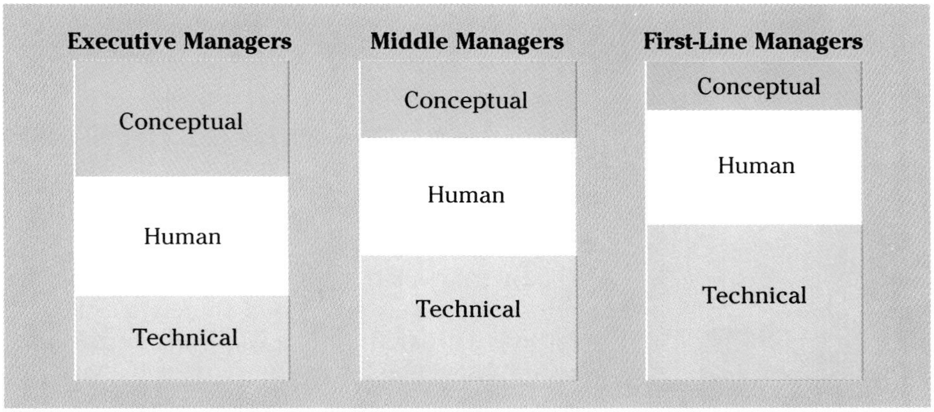

Exhibit 1.10
Importance of Management
Activities by Department

Management Activities	QA	Mfg.	Mktg.	Acctg.	HRM
			Department		
Long-range planning	21	39	21	68	72
Controlling	66	70	53	80	48
Monitoring business indicators	21	30	62	73	32
Supervising	51	65	50	40	44
Coordinating	42	38	22	51	71
Customer relations/marketing	25	31	93	39	22
External contact	34	31	61	42	67
Consulting	32	41	26	61	80
Products and services	66	70	52	19	20

Source: Luis Gomez-Mejia, Joseph E. McCann, and Ronald C. Page, "The Structure of Managerial Behaviors and Rewards," *Industrial Relations,* 24 (1985), 147–154. Used with permission.

and with monitoring performance indicators, while personnel managers provide consulting expertise, coordination, and external contacts. Thus, Exhibit 1.10 illustrates that the emphasis on and intensity of managerial activities varies considerably by the department the manager is assigned to.

At a personal level, knowing that the mix of conceptual, human, and technical skills changes over time and that different functional areas require different levels of specific management activities can serve at least two important functions. First, if you choose to become a manager, knowing that the mix of skills changes over time can help you avoid a common complaint that often young employees want to think and act like a CEO before they have mastered being a first line supervisor. Second, knowing the different mix of management activities by functional area can facilitate your selection of an area or areas that best match your skills and interests.

In many firms managers are rotated through departments as they move up in the hierarchy. In this way they obtain a well-rounded perspective on the responsibilities of the various departments. In their day-to-day tasks they must emphasize the right activities for their departments and their managerial levels. Knowing what types of activity to emphasize is the core of the manager's job. In any event, we shall return to this issue when we address the nature of individual differences in the next chapter.

The Twenty-first Century Executive

We discussed above many of the changes and challenges facing organizations as they approach the twenty-first century. Because of changes such as these, the managers and executives of tomorrow will have to change their approaches to their jobs if they are to succeed in meeting the new challenges. In fact, their profiles may even look somewhat different than they often do today. Consider a prediction from *The Wall Street Journal* concerning what successful executives will be like in the year 2000 compared to what they are like today. For the past several decades, executive profiles have typically looked like this:

He started out as a finance man with an undergraduate degree in accounting. He methodically worked his way up through the company from the controller's office in a division, to running that division, to the top job. His military background shows. He is used to giving orders—and to having them obeyed. As head of the United Way drive, he is a big man in his community. However, the first time he travelled overseas on business was as chief executive. Computers make him nervous.[11]

Now compare this with predictions about what a twenty-first-century executive will look like:

His [or her] undergraduate degree is in French literature, but he also has a joint MBA/engineering degree. He started in research and was quickly picked out as a potential CEO. He zigzagged from research to marketing to finance. He proved valuable in Brazil by turning around a failing joint venture. He speaks Portuguese and French and is on a first-name basis with commerce ministers in half a dozen countries. Unlike his predecessor's predecessor, he isn't a drill sergeant. He is first among equals in a five-person Office of the Chief Executive.[12]

Clearly, the future holds considerable excitement and promise for future managers and executives who are properly prepared to meet the challenges. How do we prepare them? One study suggested that the manager of the future must be able to fill at least the following four roles:[13]

Global strategist.   Executives of the future must understand world markets and think internationally. They must have a capacity to identify unique business opportunities and then move quickly to exploit them.

Master of technology.   Executives and managers of the future must be able to get the most out of emerging technologies, whether these technologies are in manufacturing, communications, marketing, and so forth.

Politician par excellence.   The successful executive of the future will understand how to cut through red tape to get a job done, how to build bridges with key people from highly divergent backgrounds and points of view, and how to make coalitions and joint ventures work.

Leader-motivator.   Finally, the executive of tomorrow must understand group dynamics and how to counsel, coach, and command work teams and individuals so they perform at their best. Future organizations will place greater emphasis on teams and coordinated efforts, requiring managers to understand participative management techniques.

Great communicator.   To this list of four, we would add that managers of the future must be great communicators. They must be able to communicate effectively with an increasingly diverse set of employees as well as customers, suppliers, community and government leaders.

Whether these predictions are completely accurate is difficult to know. Suffice it to say that most futurists agree that the organizational world of the twenty-first century will likely resemble, to some extent, the portrait described here. The task for future managers, then, is to attempt to develop these requisite skills to the extent possible so they will be ready for the challenges of the next decade.

A MODEL OF MANAGEMENT AND ORGANIZATIONAL BEHAVIOR

A major responsibility—perhaps *the* major responsibility—of managers is to make organizations operate effectively. Bringing about effective performance, however, is no easy task. As Nadler and Tushman note:

> Understanding one individual's behavior is challenging in and of itself; understanding a group that's made up of different individuals and comprehending the many relationships among those individuals is even more complex. Imagine, then, the mind-boggling complexity of a large organization made up of thousands of individuals and hundreds of groups with myriad relationships among these individuals and groups.[14]

Despite this difficulty, however, organizations must be managed. Nadler and Tushman continue:

> Ultimately the organization's work gets done through people, individually or collectively, on their own or in collaboration with technology. Therefore, the management of organizational behavior is central to the management task—a task that involves the capacity to *understand* the behavior patterns of individuals, groups, and organizations, to *predict* what behavioral responses will be elicited by various managerial actions, and finally to use this understanding and these predictions to achieve *control.*[15]

The work of society is accomplished largely through organizations, and the role of management is to see to it that organizations perform this work. Without it, the wheels of society would soon grind to a halt.

What Is Organizational Behavior?

The study of the behavior of people in organizations is typically referred to as *organizational behavior.* Here, the focus is on applying what we can learn from the social and behavioral sciences so we can better understand and predict human behavior at work. We examine such behavior on three levels—the individual, the group, and the organization as a whole. In all three cases, we seek to learn more about what causes people—individually or collectively—to behave as they do in organizational settings. What motivates people? What makes some employees leaders and others not? Why do groups often work in opposition to their employer? How do organizations respond to changes in their external environments? How do people communicate and make decisions? Questions such as these constitute the domain of organizational behavior and are the focus of this book.

To a large extent, we can apply what has been learned from psychology, sociology, and cultural anthropology. In addition, we can learn from economics and political science. All of these disciplines have something to say about life in organizations. However, what sets organizational behavior apart is its particular focus on the organization (not the discipline) in organizational analysis (see Exhibit 1.11). Thus, if we wish to examine a problem of employee motivation, for example, we can draw upon economic theories of wage structures in the workplace. At the same time, we can also draw on the psychological theories of motivation and incentives as they relate to work. We can bring in sociological treatments of social forces on behavior, and we can make use of anthropological studies of cultural influences on individual performance. It is this conceptual richness that establishes organizational behavior as a unique applied discipline. And throughout our analyses, we are continually concerned with the implications of what we learn for the quality of working life and organizational performance. We always look for management implications so the managers of the future can develop more humane and more competitive organizations for the future.

For convenience, we often differentiate between micro- and macro-organizational behavior. *Micro*-organizational behavior is primarily concerned with the behavior of individuals and groups, while *macro*-organizational behavior (also referred to as organization theory) is concerned with organization-wide issues, such as organization design and the relations between an organization and its environment. Although there are times when this distinction is helpful, it is always important to remember that in most instances we learn the most when we take a comprehensive view of organizational behavior and integrate these two perspectives. That is, issues such as organization structure can influence employee motivation. Hence, by keeping these two realms separate we lose valuable information that can help us better understand how to manage organizations.

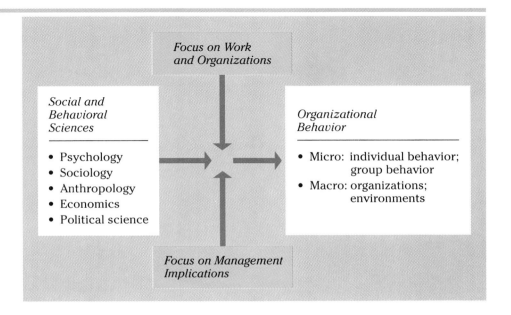

Exhibit 1.11
Origins of
Organizational Behavior

Focus on Work
and Organizations

Social and
Behavioral
Sciences

- Psychology
- Sociology
- Anthropology
- Economics
- Political science

Organizational
Behavior

- Micro: individual behavior; group behavior
- Macro: organizations; environments

Focus on Management
Implications

Building Blocks of Organizations

Understanding the behavior of people at work is fundamental to the effective management of an organization. Obviously, a number of factors come together to determine this behavior and its organizational consequences. In order to understand the origins and characteristics of these factors, it is necessary to have a model that organizes and simplifies the variables involved. We offer such a model here in the hope that it will bring some order to the study of this subject. The model can be considered in two parts (see Exhibit 1.12).

The first part of the model is the simple recognition of organizational inputs and outcomes. That is, organizations receive inputs from the external

Exhibit 1.12
A Model of Management and
Organizational Behavior

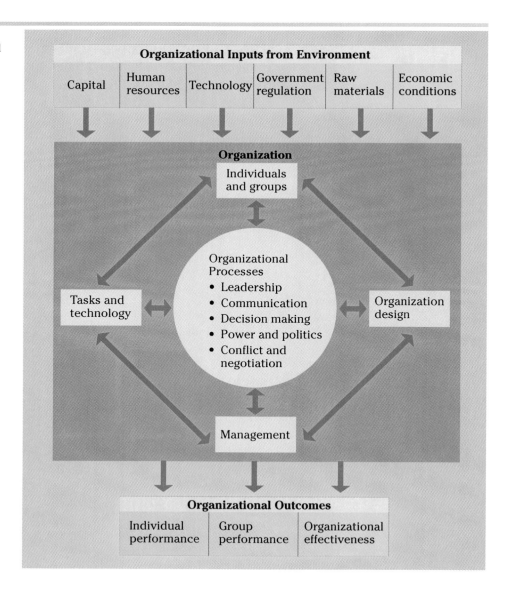

environment in the form of capital, raw materials, labor, community or government support, and so forth. In addition, organizations experience or produce certain outcomes, including (1) organizational goal attainment, (2) group performance and effectiveness, and (3) individual performance and effectiveness. Thus, organizations and the people in them exist in a constant state of flux, receiving and transforming inputs from the environment and returning those transformed inputs in the form of finished goods and services, return on stockholders' equity, salaries that are paid to employees, and so forth. It is, in short, a dynamic system.

The second aspect of the model is the organization itself and all of its parts. One way to understand the complexity of organizations is to think of them simply as a set of building blocks, including:

Individuals and groups.   Organizations are collectives of individuals and groups working to pursue common objectives. Their members come from various backgrounds and have varying abilities and skills, differing motivational levels, and different ambitions. Within the organizational context, these people must communicate, make decisions, show leadership, and handle power and organizational politics as they carry out their assigned activities.

Tasks and technology.   In addition to variations among individuals and groups, we must recognize variations in the technology of the workplace. That is, how does the work actually get done? Technology includes both the actual design of jobs and the tools and techniques used in manufacture (e.g., robotics and expert systems).

Organization design.   Putting together these factors—individuals and groups and tasks—is the subject of organization design. That is, how do we structure an organization so it effectively coordinates and controls employee behavior to facilitate performance?

Organizational processes.   In addition to people, machines, and structure, we must recognize a series of organizational processes, such as leadership, communication, decision making, power and politics, and so forth. The processes largely determine the nature and quality of interpersonal and intergroup relations within the workplace and, as such, influence ultimate organizational performance.

Management.   Finally, the glue that holds these building blocks together is the character of management. Throughout this text, we shall see numerous examples of how the degree of managerial effectiveness and prowess have determined the success or failure of a venture. We shall take a managerial view throughout our survey of organizational behavior.

These five variables, then, will constitute the primary ingredients of this book. We shall proceed sequentially, beginning with individual behavior and moving to group and intergroup behavior and finally to organization design and structure. On the basis of this, we will turn to a consideration of several of the more important organizational processes. Finally, we will look to the future and examine ways that organizations can continue to develop and improve their work forces and the organization as a whole. Throughout, the roles of technology and management will be considered. Also throughout, we will blend theory with research and practice.

PULLING IT ALL TOGETHER

Work will almost inevitably be a large part of your life. An understanding of organizational behavior will aid you in making that part of life more productive and enjoyable for yourself as well those you are in a position to influence. Over the course of this book, our objective is to provide sound and relevant insights concerning individuals, groups, and overall organizational systems that will be helpful to you not just as an executive or CEO but also when you are a lower-level employee or subordinate.

SUMMARY OF KEY POINTS

- The fundamental challenge facing managers is how to achieve performance goals while simultaneously providing for employee welfare and satisfaction.

- Work may be defined as an activity that produces something of value for other people. Work serves several functions, including economic, social, status, self-esteem, and self-actualization.

- As managers approach the year 2000, several challenges arise, including international competition, new technologies, increased quality, employee motivation and commitment, a diverse work force, and ethical behavior. These challenges must be met by managers concerned about survival and competitiveness in the future.

- Management is the process of planning, organizing, directing, and controlling the activities of employees in combination with other resources to accomplish organizational goals.

- Managerial responsibilities include long-range planning, controlling, environmental scanning, supervision, coordination, customer relations, community relations, internal consulting, and monitoring of products and services.

- These responsibilities differ by level in the organizational hierarchy and by department or function.

- The twenty-first-century manager will differ from most current managers in four ways. In essence, he or she will be a global strategist, a master of technology, a good politician, and a premier leader-motivator.

- Organizational behavior is the study of people in organizations. It can be studied on a micro level, which focuses on individual or group behavior, or on a macro level, which focuses on organization-wide actions and events.

- A model of organizational behavior is presented, consisting of five building blocks: individuals and groups, tasks and technology, organization design, organizational processes, and management.

KEY WORDS

alienation
ethics
executive management
first-line management

industrial competitiveness
long-range planning
macro-organizational behavior
management

micro-organizational behavior
middle management
organization design
organization theory
organizational behavior

organizational processes
technology
theory
work

QUESTIONS FOR DISCUSSION

1. Define *work.*
2. What functions does work serve in modern society?
3. Describe the extent and nature of the challenges facing the workplace in the next decade. What can be done about these challenges?
4. Define *management.* How does the nature of management change according to one's level and function in the organization?
5. Discuss the role of management in the larger societal context. What do you think the managers of the future will be like?
6. Identify what you think are the critical issues facing contemporary management. Explain.

NOTES

1. D. J. Jefferson and B. Colemen,"American Quits Chairman Post at Euro Disney." *Wall Street Journal,* January 18, 1993. pp. B1, B3.
2. S. Terkel, *Working* (New York: Pantheon, 1974).
3. S. Freud, Lecture XXXIII, *New Introductory Lectures on Psychoanalysis* (New York: Norton, 1933), p. 34.
4. Cited in *U.S. News & World Report,* January 16, 1989, p. 42.
5. O. Port, "The Productivity Paradox," *Business Week,* June 6, 1988, pp. 100–114.
6. W. Bulkely, "Fighting Back Against Data Overload," *Wall Street Journal,* October 20, 1989, p. B–1.
7. B. Nussbaum, "Needed: Human Capital," *Business Week,* September 19, 1988, pp. 100–103.
8. S. Silverstein, "One in 15 Employees in Study Caught Stealing," *Los Angeles Times,* December 2, 1989, p. D–1.
9. L. Gomez-Mejia, J. McCann, and R. Page, "The Structure of Managerial Behaviors and Rewards," *Industrial Relations,* 1985, pp. 147–154.
10. R. Katz, "Skills of an Effective Administrator," *Harvard Business Review,* September-October 1974, pp. 34–56.
11. A. Bennett, "Going Global: The Chief Executives in the Year 2000 Are Likely to Have Had Much Foreign Experience," *Wall Street Journal,* February 27, 1989, p. A–4.
12. Ibid.
13. C. Work, "The Twenty-first Century Executive," *U.S. News & World Report,* March 7, 1988, pp. 48–51; E. Ehrlich, "How The Next Decade Will Differ," *Business Week,* September 25, 1989, pp. 142–156.
14. D. Nadler and M. Tushman, "A Model for Diagnosing Organizational Behavior," *Organizational Dynamics,* 1980, p. 35.
15. Ibid.

Part Two

Individual Behavior at Work

2

Individual and Cultural Differences

The Management Challenge

- To be able to appropriately select individuals for particular jobs and/or organizations.
- To take people with different abilities, skills, and personalities and build effective work teams.
- To cope effectively with individual differences in the workplace.
- To foster a work environment that allows employees an opportunity to develop and grow.
- To know how to get the best from each employee.
- To understand the role of ethical behavior in managerial actions.
- To be able to manage and do business with people from different cultures.

CLOSE UP · Stanley Gold, Turnaround Specialist

Stanley Gold, 49, is a hard-charging executive and consistently shows up at UCLA's track at 5:45 for his morning run. He also takes a no-nonsense approach to running a business. Some say his personality is particularly suited to the tough job of turnarounds. Mr. Gold has his opportunity with L.A. Gear.

L.A. Gear burst on the American shoe scene in the mid-1980s with trendy designs that grabbed the attention of teenagers and, more importantly, grabbed their pocketbooks. However, fashion is fickle, especially teen fashions, and soon L.A. Gear was in deep financial trouble.

In 1991, Trefoil Capital Investors LP paid $100 million for a one-third stake in the company and put Stanley Gold in as CEO. Within a few short months, Gold replaced nearly a dozen of L.A. Gear's top executives. He also slashed inventory and tried to get back into the men's athletic shoe market where the firm had stumbled in the 80s because of poor shoe quality.

For those who say that L.A. Gear needs big changes fast in order to survive, Stanley Gold seems to be the type of person for whom quick and decisive action is natural.[1]

INDIVIDUAL AND CULTURAL FACTORS IN EMPLOYEE PERFORMANCE

As we can see in the example of Stanley Gold, our unique personal characteristics can have a dramatic influence on both individual behavior and the behavior of those around us. To succeed in any managerial position, it is necessary to have the appropriate skills and abilities for the situation. Moreover, when selecting subordinates, managers have similar concerns. In short, individual differences can play a major role in how well someone performs on the job. They can even influence whether someone gets the job in the first place. Because of this, we begin this section of the book with a look at individual differences in the workplace.

Several factors can be identified that influence employee behavior and performance. One early model of job performance argued simply that performance was largely a function of *ability* and *motivation*.[2] Using this simple model as a guide, we can divide our discussion of individual factors in performance into two categories: those that influence our *capacity to respond* and those that influence our will or *desire to respond*. The first category includes such factors as mental and physical abilities, personality traits, perceptual capabilities, and stress-tolerance levels. The second category includes those variables dealing with employee motivation. Both of these sets of factors are discussed in this part of the book as a prelude to more complex analyses of overall organizational performance.

Specifically, we begin our analysis in this chapter with a look at individual differences, including employee abilities and skills, personality variables, and work values. We will also examine the nature of culture and cultural diversity as it affects behavior in organizations both at home and abroad. Next, in Chapter 3 we look at perception and job attitudes, and in Chapter 4 we review basic learning and reinforcement techniques. In Chapter 5 basic theories of employee motivation are introduced, including the concept of employee needs. More complex cognitive models of motivation are examined in Chapter 6. Finally, in Chapter 7, we review contemporary approaches to performance appraisals and reward systems in organizations. All told, this section of the book aims to introduce the reader to the more salient aspects of individual behavior as they relate to organizational behavior and effectiveness.

EMPLOYEE ABILITIES AND SKILLS

We begin with a look at *employee abilities and skills.* Abilities and skills generally represent those physical and intellectual characteristics that are relatively stable over time and that help determine an employee's capability to respond. Recognizing them is important in understanding organizational behavior, because they often bound an employee's ability to do the job. For example, if a clerk-typist simply does not have the manual dexterity to master the fundamentals of typing or keyboard entry, his or her performance will likely suffer. Similarly, a sales representative who has a hard time with simple numeric calculations will probably not do well on the job.

Mental Abilities

It is possible to divide our discussion of abilities and skills into two sections: mental abilities and physical abilities. *Mental abilities* are an individual's intellectual capabilities and are closely linked to how a person makes decisions and processes information. Included here are such factors as verbal comprehension, inductive reasoning, and memory. A summary is shown in Exhibit 2.1.

From a managerial standpoint, a key aspect of mental ability is cognitive complexity. *Cognitive complexity* represents a person's capacity to acquire and sort through various pieces of information from the environment and organize them in such a way that they make sense. People with high cognitive complexity tend to use more information—and to see the relationships between aspects of this information—than people with low cognitive complexity. For example, if a manager was assigned a particular problem, would he have the capacity to break the problem down into its various facets and understand how these various facets relate to one another? A manager with low cognitive complexity would tend to see only one or two salient aspects of the problem, whereas a manager with higher cognitive complexity would understand more of the nuances and subtleties of the problem as they relate to each other and to other problems.

People with *low* cognitive complexity typically exhibit the following characteristics:[3]

They tend to be categorical and stereotypic. Cognitive structures that depend upon simple fixed rules of integration tend to reduce the possibility of thinking in terms of degrees.

Internal conflict appears to be minimized with simple structures. Since few alternative relationships are generated, closure is quick.

Behavior is apparently anchored in external conditions. There is less personal contribution in simple structures.

Fewer rules cover a wider range of phenomena. There is less distinction between separate situations.

Exhibit 2.1
Dimensions of
Mental Abilities

- *Verbal comprehension.* The ability to understand the meanings of words and their relations to each other.
- *Word fluency.* The ability to name objects or use words to form sentences that express an idea.
- *Number aptitude.* The ability to make numerical calculations speedily and accurately.
- *Inductive reasoning.* The ability to discover a rule or principle and apply it to the solution of a problem.
- *Memory.* The ability to remember lists of words and numbers and other associations.
- *Spatial aptitude.* The ability to perceive fixed geometric figures and their relations with other geometric figures.
- *Perceptual speed.* The ability to perceive visual details quickly and accurately.

On the other hand, people with *high* levels of cognitive complexity are typically characterized by the following:[4]

Their cognitive system is less deterministic. Numerous alternative relationships are generated and considered.

The environment is tracked in numerous ways. There is less compartmentalization of the environment.

The individual utilizes more internal processes. The self as an individual operates on the process.

Research on cognitive complexity has focused on two important areas from a managerial standpoint: leadership style and decision making. In the area of leadership, it has been found that managers rated high on cognitive complexity are better able to handle complex situations, such as rapid changes in the external environment. Moreover, such managers also tend to use more resources and information when solving a problem and tend to be somewhat more considerate and consultative in their approach to managing

Exhibit 2.2
Dimensions of
Physical Abilities

Physical Abilities

- *Dynamic strength.* The ability to exert muscular force repeatedly or continuously for a period of time.
- *Trunk strength.* The ability to exert muscular strength using the back and abdominal muscles.
- *Static strength.* The amount of continuous force one is capable of exerting against an external object.
- *Explosive strength.* The amount of force one is capable of exerting in one or a series of explosive acts.
- *Extent flexibility.* The ability to move the trunk and back muscles as far as possible.
- *Dynamic flexibility.* The ability to make rapid and repeated flexing movements.
- *Gross body coordination.* The ability to coordinate the simultaneous actions of different parts of the body.
- *Equilibrium.* The ability to maintain balance and equilibrium in spite of disruptive external forces.
- *Stamina.* The ability to continue maximum effort requiring prolonged effort over time; the degree of cardiovascular conditioning.

Psychomotor Abilities

- *Control precision.* The ability to make fine, highly controlled muscular movements needed to adjust a control mechanism.
- *Multilimb coordination.* The ability to coordinate the simultaneous movement of hands and feet.
- *Response orientation.* The ability to make an appropriate response to a visual signal indicating a direction.
- *Rate control.* The ability to make continuous anticipatory motor adjustments in speed and direction to follow a continuously moving target.
- *Manual dexterity.* The ability to make skillful and well-directed arm-hand movements in manipulating large objects quickly.
- *Finger dexterity.* The ability to make skillful and controlled manipulations of small objects.
- *Arm-hand steadiness.* The ability to make precise arm-hand movements where steadiness is extremely important and speed and strength are relatively unimportant.
- *Reaction time.* How quickly a person can respond to a single stimulus with a simple response.
- *Aiming.* The ability to make highly accurate, restricted hand movements requiring precise eye-hand coordination.

their subordinates.[5] In the area of decision making, fairly consistent findings show that individuals with high cognitive complexity (1) seek out more information for a decision, (2) actually process or use more information, (3) are better able to integrate discrepant information, (4) consider a greater number of possible solutions to the problem, and (5) employ more complex decision strategies than individuals with low cognitive complexity.[6]

Physical Abilities

The second set of variables relates to someone's *physical abilities*. Included here are both basic physical abilities (for example, strength) and psychomotor abilities (such as manual dexterity, eye-hand coordination, and manipulation skills). These factors are summarized in Exhibit 2.2.[7] Considering both mental and physical abilities helps one understand the behavior of people at work and how they can be better managed. The recognition of such abilities—and the recognition that people have *different* abilities—has clear implications for employee recruitment and selection decisions; it brings into focus the importance of matching people to jobs. For example, Florida Power has a 16-hour selection process that involves 12 performance tests. Over the test period of a couple of years, 640 individuals applied for "lineperson" jobs. Of these 259 were hired. As a consequence of the new performance tests and selection process, turnover went from 43 percent to 4.5 percent, and the program saved net $1 million.[8] In addition to selection, knowledge of job requirements and individual differences is also useful in evaluating training and development needs. Because human resources are important to management, it is imperative that managers become more familiar with the basic characteristics of their people.

PERSONALITY: AN INTRODUCTION

The second individual difference variable deals with the concept of personality. We often hear people use and misuse the term *personality*. For example, we hear that someone has a "nice" personality. For our purposes, we will examine the term from a psychological standpoint as it relates to behavior and performance in the workplace. To do this, let us start with a more precise definition of the concept.

Definition of Personality

Personality can be defined in many ways. Perhaps one of the more useful definitions for purposes of organizational analysis is offered by Salvatore Maddi, who defines *personality* as follows:

. . . a stable set of characteristics and tendencies that determine those communalities and differences in the psychological behavior (thoughts, feelings, and actions) of people that have continuity in time and that may not be easily understood as the sole result of the social and biological pressures of the moment.[9]

Several aspects of this definition should be noted. First, personality is best understood as a constellation of interacting characteristics; it is necessary to look at the whole person when attempting to understand the phenomenon and its effects on subsequent behavior. Second, various dimensions of personality are relatively stable across time. Although changes—especially evolutionary ones—can occur, seldom do we see major changes in the personality of a normal individual. And third, the study of personality emphasizes both similarities and differences across people. This is important for managers to recognize as they attempt to formulate actions designed to enhance performance and employee well-being.

Influences on Personality Development

Early research on personality development focused on the issue of whether heredity or environment determined an individual's personality. Although a few researchers are still concerned with this issue, most contemporary psychologists now feel this debate is fruitless. As noted long ago by Kluckhohn and Murray:

The two sets of determinants can rarely be completely disentangled once the environment has begun to operate. The pertinent questions are: (1) which of the various genetic potentialities will be actualized as a consequence of a particular series of life-events in a given physical, social, and cultural environment? and (2) what limits to the development of this personality are set by genetic constitution?[10]

In other words, if the individual is viewed from the whole-person perspective, the search for the determinants of personal traits focuses on both heredity and environment as well as the interaction between the two over time. In this regard, five major categories of determinants of personal traits may be identified: physiological, cultural, family and social group, role, and situational determinants.

Physiological Determinants.   Physiological determinants include factors such as stature, health, and sex that often act as constraints on personal growth and development. For instance, tall people often tend to become more domineering and self-confident than shorter people. Traditional sex-role stereotyping has served to channel males and females into different developmental patterns. For example, males have been trained to be more assertive, females more passive.

Cultural Determinants.   Because of the central role of culture in the survival of a society, there is great emphasis on instilling cultural norms and values in children growing up. For instance, in capitalist societies, where individual responsibility is highly prized, emphasis is placed on developing achievement-oriented, independent, self-reliant people, whereas in socialistic societies, emphasis is placed on developing cooperative, group-oriented individuals who place the welfare of the whole society ahead of individual needs. Cultural determinants affect personal traits. As Mussen notes, "The child's cultural group defines the range of experiments and situations he is likely to encounter and the values and personality characteristics that will be reinforced and hence learned."[11] Consider, for example, how Japanese society develops its world-renowned work ethic.

Family and Group Determinants.   Perhaps the most important influences on personal development are family and social group determinants. For instance, it has been found that children who grow up in democratic homes tend to be more stable, less argumentative, more socially successful, and more sensitive to praise or blame than those who grow up in authoritarian homes.[12] One's immediate family and peers contribute significantly to the socialization process, influencing how individuals think and behave through an intricate system of rewards and penalties.

Role Determinants.   People are assigned various roles very early in life because of factors such as sex, socioeconomic background, and race. As one grows older, other factors, such as age and occupation, influence the roles we are expected to play. Such role determinants often limit our personal growth and development as individuals and significantly control acceptable behavior patterns.

Situational Determinants.   Finally, personal development can be influenced by situational determinants. These are factors that are often unpredictable, such as a divorce or death in the family. For instance, James Abegglen studied 20 successful male executives who had risen from lower-class childhoods and discovered that in three-fourths of the cases these executives had experienced some form of severe separation trauma from their fathers. Their fathers (and role models) had either died, been seriously ill, or had serious financial setbacks. Abegglen hypothesized that the sons' negative identification with their fathers' plights represented a major motivational force for achievement and success.[13]

PERSONALITY AND WORK BEHAVIOR

Personality theories that utilize the trait approach have proven popular among investigators of employee behavior in organizations. There are several reasons for this. To begin with, trait theories focus largely on the normal, healthy adult, in contrast to psychoanalytic and other personality theories that focus largely on abnormal behavior. Trait theories identify several characteristics that describe people. Allport insisted that our understanding of individual behavior could progress only by breaking behavior patterns down into a series of elements (traits).[14] "The only thing you can do about a *total* personality is to send flowers to it," he once said. Hence, in the study of people at work, we may discuss an employee's dependability, emotional stability, or cognitive complexity. These traits, when taken together, form a large mosaic that provides insight into individuals. A third reason for the popularity of trait theories in the study of organizational behavior is that the traits that are identified are measurable and tend to remain relatively stable over time. It is much easier to make comparisons among employees using these tangible qualities rather than the somewhat mystical psychoanalytic theories or the highly abstract and volatile self theories.

The number of traits people are believed to exhibit varies according to which theory we employ. In an exhaustive search, over 17,000 can be identified. Obviously, this number is so large as to make any reasonable analysis of the effects of personality in the workplace impossible. In order for us to make any sense out of this, it is necessary for us to concentrate on a small number of personality variables that have a direct impact on work behavior. If we do this, we can identify six traits that seem to be relatively important for our purposes here. It will be noted that some of these traits (for example, self-esteem or locus of control) have to do with how we see ourselves, whereas other traits (for example, introversion-extroversion or dependability) have to do with how we interact with others. Moreover, these traits are largely influenced by one's personality development and, in turn, influence actual attitudes and behaviors at work, as shown in Exhibit 2.3.

Self-Esteem

One trait that has emerged recently as a key variable in determining work behavior and effectiveness is an employee's self-esteem. *Self-esteem* can be

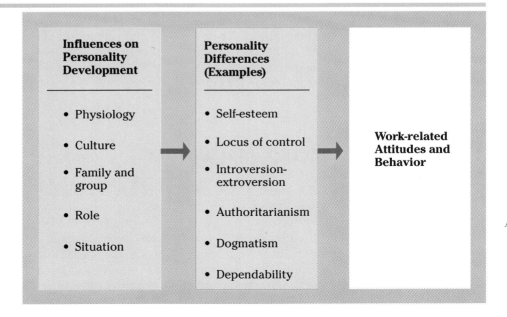

Exhibit 2.3
Relation of Personality to
Attitudes and Behavior

Influences on Personality Development

- Physiology
- Culture
- Family and group
- Role
- Situation

Personality Differences (Examples)

- Self-esteem
- Locus of control
- Introversion-extroversion
- Authoritarianism
- Dogmatism
- Dependability

Work-related Attitudes and Behavior

defined as one's opinion or belief about one's self and self-worth. It is how we see ourselves as individuals. Do we have confidence in ourselves? Do we think we are successful? Attractive? Worthy of others' respect or friendship?

Research has shown that high self-esteem in school-age children enhances assertiveness, independence, and creativity. People with high self-esteem often find it easier to give and receive affection, set higher goals for personal achievement, and exert energy to try to attain goals set for them. Moreover, individuals with high self-esteem will be more likely to seek higher-status occupations and will take more risks in the job search. For example, one study found that students possessing higher self-esteem were more highly rated by college recruiters, received more job offers, and were more satisfied with their job search than students with low self-esteem.[15] Hence, personality traits such as this one can affect your job and career even before you begin work!

Locus of Control

Locus of control refers to the tendency among individuals to attribute the events affecting their lives either to their own actions or to external forces; it is a measure of how much you think you control your own destiny. Two types of individual are identified. People with an *internal* locus of control tend to attribute their successes—and failures—to their own abilities and efforts. Hence, a student would give himself credit for passing an examination; likewise, he would accept blame for failing.

In contrast, people with an *external* locus of control tend to attribute things that happen to them as being caused by someone or something else. They give themselves neither credit nor blame. Hence, passing an exam may be dismissed by saying it was "too easy," whereas failing may be excused by convincing oneself that the exam was "unfair."

If you want to determine your own locus of control, fill out Self-Assessment 2.1. This is an abbreviated version of the scale originally developed by Rotter. When you have finished, refer to Appendix B for scoring procedures.

Recent research on locus of control suggests that people with an internal locus of control (1) exhibit greater work motivation, (2) have stronger expectations that effort will lead to actual high job performance, (3) perform better on tasks requiring learning or problem solving, (4) typically receive higher salaries and salary increases, and (5) exhibit less job-related anxiety than externals.[16] Locus of control has numerous implications for management. For example, consider what would happen if you placed an "internal" under tight supervision or an "external" under loose supervision. The results probably would not be very positive. Or what would happen if you placed both internals and externals on a merit-based compensation plan? Who would likely perform better? Who might perform better under a piece-rate system?

Introversion-Extroversion

The third personality dimension we should consider focuses on the extent to which people tend to be shy and retiring or socially gregarious. *Introverts* tend to focus their energies inwardly and have a greater sensitivity to

SELF-ASSESSMENT 2.1
What Is Your Locus of Control?

Instructions: This instrument lists several pairs of statements concerning the possible causes of behavior. For each pair, circle the letter (*A* or *B*) that better describes your own beliefs. Remember: there are no right or wrong answers.

1. **A.** In the long run, the bad things that happen to us are balanced by the good ones.
   B. Most misfortunes are the result of lack of ability, ignorance, laziness, or all three.
2. **A.** I have often found that what is going to happen will happen.
   B. Trusting to fate has never turned out as well for me as making a decision to take a definite course of action.
3. **A.** Many of the unhappy things in people's lives are partly due to bad luck.
   B. People's misfortunes result from the mistakes they make.
4. **A.** Without the right breaks one cannot be an effective leader.
   B. Capable people who fail to become leaders have not taken advantage of their opportunities.
5. **A.** Many times I feel I have little influence over the things that happen to me.
   B. It is impossible for me to believe that chance or luck plays an important role in my life.
6. **A.** Most people don't realize the extent to which their lives are controlled by accidental happenings.
   B. There really is no such thing as "luck."
7. **A.** Unfortunately, an individual's worth often passes unrecognized no matter how hard he tries.
   B. In the long run, people get the respect they deserve.

abstract feelings, whereas *extroverts* direct more of their attention to other people, objects, and events. Research evidence suggests that both types of people have a role to play in organizations.[17] Extroverts more often succeed in first-line management roles, where only superficial "people skills" are required; they also do better in field assignments—for example, as sales representatives. Introverts, on the other hand, tend to succeed in positions requiring more reflection, analysis, and sensitivity to people's inner feelings and qualities. Such positions are included in a variety of departments within organizations, such as accounting, personnel, and computer operations. In view of the complex nature of modern organizations, both types of individual are clearly needed.

Authoritarianism and Dogmatism

Authoritarianism refers to an individual's orientation toward authority. More specifically, an authoritarian orientation is generally characterized by an overriding conviction that it is right and proper for there to be clear status and power differences among people.[18] According to T. W. Adorno, a high authoritarian is typically (1) demanding, directive, and controlling of his or her subordinates; (2) submissive and deferential toward superiors; (3) intellectually rigid; (4) fearful of social change; (5) highly judgmental and categorical in reactions to others; (6) distrustful; and (7) hostile in response to restraint. Nonauthoritarians, on the other hand, generally believe that power and status differences should be minimized, that social change can be constructive, and that people should be more accepting and less judgmental of others.

In the workplace, the consequences of these differences can be tremendous. Research has shown, for example, that employees who are high in authoritarianism often perform better under rigid supervisory control, whereas those rated lower on this characteristic perform better under more participative supervision.[19] Can you think of other consequences that might result from these differences?

Related to this authoritarianism is the trait of dogmatism. *Dogmatism* refers to a particular cognitive style that is characterized by closed-mindedness and inflexibility.[20] This dimension has particularly profound implications for managerial decision making; it is found that dogmatic managers tend to make decisions quickly, based on only limited information and with a high degree of confidence in the correctness of their decisions.[21] Do you know managers (or professors) who tend to be dogmatic? How does this behavior affect those around them?

Dependability

Finally, people can be differentiated with respect to their behavioral consistency, or *dependability*. Individuals who are seen as self-reliant, responsible, consistent, and dependable are typically considered to be desirable colleagues or group members who will cooperate and work steadfastly toward group goals.[22] Personnel managers often seek a wide array of information concerning dependability before hiring job applicants. Even so, contemporary managers often complain that many of today's workers simply lack the feeling of personal responsibility necessary for efficient operations. Whether this is a result of the personal failings of the individuals or a lack of proper motivation by superiors remains to be determined.

Obviously, personality factors such as those discussed here can play a major role in determining work behavior both on the shop floor and in the executive suite. A good example of this can be seen in the events leading up to the demise of one of America's largest and oldest architectural firms. Observe the role of personality in the events that follows.

IN PRACTICE
Personality Clash: Design vs. Default

Philip Johnson, at age 86, was considered the dean of American architecture and known for such landmarks as the AT&T building in New York and the Pennzoil Center in Houston; but he was also forced out of the firm that he built only to watch it fall into default and bankruptcy.

In 1969, Mr. Johnson invited John Burgee, who was just 35, to become his sole partner to handle the management side of the business and thereby allow him to focus on the creative side. "I picked John Burgee as my right-hand man. Every design architect needs a Burgee. The more leadership he took, the happier I was." Mr. Burgee's personality was perfectly suited to the nuts-and-bolts tasks of managing the firm and overseeing the projects through construction.

For all his management effort, Mr. Burgee felt that only Mr. Johnson's name ever appeared in the press. "It was always difficult for me, being a younger man and less flamboyant," commented Mr. Burgee. Eventually, Mr. Burgee was able to get Mr. Johnson to change the name of the firm first to Philip Johnson & John Burgee Architects, then to Johnson/Burgee Architects, and finally to John Burgee Architects, with Philip Johnson. Although Burgee wanted to be involved in all aspects of the business, Johnson was unwilling to relinquish control over design to Burgee.

In 1988, Burgee sent a four-page memo to Johnson in which he listed each of the firm's 24 projects and outlined the ones for which Johnson could initiate designs, initiate contact with clients, or work on independently at home. Burgee also instructed Johnson not to involve himself with the younger architects or advise them on their drawings.

The clash of the creative personality of Johnson and the controlling personality of Burgee came to a climax when Burgee asked Johnson to leave the firm. Unfortunately, Burgee underestimated the reaction of clients and lost many key contracts. Eventually, Burgee had to file for Chapter 11, and Johnson continued working on his own, including a project for Estée Lauder.[23]

PERSONALITY AND ORGANIZATION: A BASIC CONFLICT?

Most theories of personality stress that an individual's personality becomes complete only when the individual interacts with other people; growth and development do not occur in a vacuum. Human personalities are the individual expressions of our culture, and our culture and social order are the group expressions of individual personalities. This being the case, it is important to understand how work organizations influence the growth and development of the adult employee.

A model of person-organization relationships has been proposed by Chris Argyris.[24] This model, called the *basic incongruity thesis,* consists of three parts: what individuals want from organizations, what organizations want from individuals, and how these two potentially conflicting sets of desires are harmonized.

Argyris begins by examining how healthy individuals change as they mature. On the basis of previous work, Argyris suggests that as people grow to maturity, seven basic changes in needs and interests occur:

1. People develop from a state of passivity as infants to a state of increasing activity as adults.
2. People develop from a state of dependence upon others to a state of relative independence.
3. People develop from having only a few ways of behaving to having many diverse ways of behaving.
4. People develop from having shallow, casual, and erratic interests to having fewer, but deeper, interests.
5. People develop from having a short time perspective (i.e., behavior is determined by present events) to having a longer time perspective (behavior is determined by a combination of past, present, and future events).
6. People develop from subordinate to superordinate positions (from child to parent or from trainee to manager).
7. People develop from a low understanding or awareness of themselves to a greater understanding of and control over themselves as adults.

Although Argyris acknowledges that these developments may differ among individuals, the general tendencies from childhood to adulthood are believed to be fairly common.

Next, Argyris turns his attention to the defining characteristics of traditional work organizations. In particular, he argues that in the pursuit of efficiency and effectiveness, organizations create work situations aimed more at getting the job done than at satisfying employees' personal goals. Examples include increased task specialization, unity of command, a rules orientation, and other things aimed at turning out a standardized product with standardized people. In the pursuit of this standardization, Argyris argues, organizations often create work situations with the following characteristics:

1. Employees are allowed minimal control over their work; control is often shifted to machines.
2. They are expected to be passive, dependent, and subordinate.
3. They are allowed only a short-term horizon in their work.
4. They are placed on repetitive jobs that require only minimal skills and abilities.
5. On the basis of the first four items, people are expected to produce under conditions leading to psychological failure.

Hence, Argyris argues persuasively that many jobs in our technological society are structured in such a way that they conflict with the basic growth needs of a healthy personality. This conflict is represented in Exhibit 2.4. The

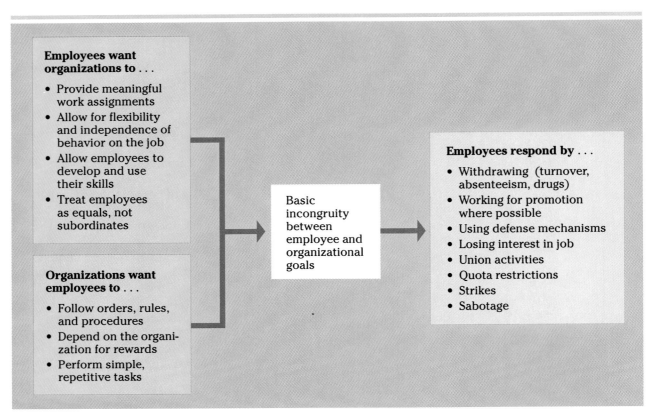

Employees want organizations to . . .

- Provide meaningful work assignments
- Allow for flexibility and independence of behavior on the job
- Allow employees to develop and use their skills
- Treat employees as equals, not subordinates

Organizations want employees to . . .

- Follow orders, rules, and procedures
- Depend on the organization for rewards
- Perform simple, repetitive tasks

Basic incongruity between employee and organizational goals

Employees respond by . . .

- Withdrawing (turnover, absenteeism, drugs)
- Working for promotion where possible
- Using defense mechanisms
- Losing interest in job
- Union activities
- Quota restrictions
- Strikes
- Sabotage

Exhibit 2.4
Basic Conflict Between
Employees and Organizations

magnitude of this conflict between personality and organization is a function of several factors. The strongest conflict can be expected under conditions where employees are very mature; organizations are highly structured, and rules and procedures are formalized; and jobs are fragmented and mechanized. Hence, we would expect the strongest conflict to be at the lower levels of the organization, among blue-collar and clerical workers. Managers tend to have jobs that are less mechanized and tend to be less subject to formalized rules and procedures.

Where strong conflicts between personalities and organizations exist, or, more precisely, where strong conflicts exist between what employees and organizations want from each other, employees are faced with difficult choices. They may choose to leave the organization or to work hard to climb the ladder into the upper echelons of management. They may defend their self-concepts and adapt through the use of defense mechanisms. Disassociating themselves psychologically from the organization (e.g., losing interest in their work, lowering their work standards, etc.) and concentrating instead on the material rewards available from the organization is another possible response. Or they may find allies in their fellow workers and, in concert, may further adapt *as a group* by such activities as quota restrictions, unionizing efforts, strikes, and sabotage.

Unfortunately, although such activities may help employees feel that they are getting back at the organization, they do not alleviate the basic situation that is causing the problem. To do this, one has to examine the nature of the job and the work climate. This we do in Chapter 9. Personality represents a powerful force in the determination of work behavior and must be recognized before meaningful change can be implemented by managers to improve the effectiveness of their organizations.

IN PRACTICE

Integrating Employee and Organizational Goals at Diamond-Star

In many ways the above scenario paints a bleak portrait of the relationship of many workers to their employers. However, it should be noted that many companies are trying to change this relationship and create a partnership between employees and company in which the goals of both are realized. In doing so, however, these companies are careful to select and hire only those employees who have the potential to fit in with the company's unique culture. A case in point is Diamond-Star Motors Corporation, in Normal, Illinois. Diamond-Star began as a joint venture between Chrysler and Mitsubishi, but became a subsidary of Mitsubishi when Chrysler sold its shares of the auto assembly plant in October of 1991.

At Diamond-Star, employee selection is critical. Over a fourth of all applicants wash out during the company's written, medical, and drug tests. About 40 percent of those who pass the first stage fail the company's screening and training process. Still, Diamond-Star ended up with 100,000 qualified applicants for the 2,500 positions initially being filled. The company spent over $40 million—roughly $13,000 per employee—to staff and train the associates at the plant. This is almost ten times what the average U.S. firm spends on staffing. As the company's human resource management director explained, "We want employees who are not only good at their jobs, but who also have growth potential."

What kind of employee are they looking for in this manufacturing firm? Interpersonal skills are in; rugged individualism is out. The company seeks employees who demonstrate dedication and commitment and have an aptitude for teamwork. In this way, Diamond-Star hopes to secure a work force they can retain and develop for the long run. And in doing so, the company hopes to offer its employees a work environment that allows for considerable personal growth and need-satisfaction. In short, the company aims to reduce the possibility of a basic incongruity developing between employee and organizational goals.[25]

PERSONALITY AND EMPLOYEE SELECTION

Recent years have seen an increased interest in the use of pre-employment screening tests. Several key assumptions underlie the use of personality tests as one method of selecting potential employees: (1) individuals have different personalities and traits, (2) these differences affect their behavior and performance, and (3) different job have different requirements. Consequently, tests can be used to select individuals who match the overall company as well as match particular types of people to specific jobs. However, mangers must be careful in their use of these selection instruments. Legally all selection tests must meet the guidelines for nondiscrimination set forth in the Equal Employment Opportunity Commission's Uniform Guidelines on Employee Selection Procedures. Specifically, in 1971 the Supreme Court ruled (Griggs *v.* Duke Power Company) that "good intent or the absence of discriminatory intent does not redeem . . . testing mechanisms that operate as built-in 'headwinds' for minority groups and are unrelated to measuring job capability." This ruling led to two important cases in which discrimination might apply to selection practices. First, "disparate treatment" involves the intentional discrimination against an individual based on race, color, gender, religion or national origin. Second, "disparate impact" involves the adverse affect of selection practices (as well as other practices) on minorities regardless of whether these practices were intended to have an adverse impact or not. Consequently, although personality tests can be an important means of selecting potential employees as well as matching them to appropriate jobs, care must be taken to demonstrate that the characteristics measured actually predict job performance.

PERSONAL VALUES AND ETHICS

A factor that has surprised many business leaders is the alarming rise in accusations of unethical or disreputable behavior in today's companies. We hear with increasing regularity of stock market manipulations, disregard of environmental hazards, bribes, and kickbacks. To understand these behaviors, we must examine the role of values and personal ethics in the workplace. We begin with the concept of values.

A *value* may be defined as "an enduring belief that a specific mode of conduct or end-state of existence is personally or socially preferable to an opposite or converse mode of conduct or end-state of existence."[26] In other words, a value represents a judgment by an individual that certain things are "good" or "bad," "important" or "unimportant," and so forth. As such, values serve a useful function in providing guidelines or standards for choosing one's own behavior and for evaluating the behavior of others.

Characteristics of Values

The values people have tend to be relatively stable over time. The reason for this lies in the manner in which values are acquired in the first place. That is, when we first learn a value (usually at a young age), we are taught that such-and-such behavior is *always* good or *always* bad. For instance, we may be taught that lying or stealing is always unacceptable. Few people are taught that such behavior is acceptable in some circumstances but not in others. Hence, this definitive quality of learned values tends to secure them firmly in our belief systems. This is not to say that values do not change over time. As we grow, we are increasingly confronted with new and often conflicting situations. Often, it is necessary for us to weigh the relative merits of each and choose a course of action. Consider, for example, the worker who has a strong belief in hard work but who is pressured by her colleagues not to outperform the group. What would you do in this situation?

Rokeach has identified two fundamental types of value: instrumental and terminal.[27] *Instrumental values* represent those values concerning the way we approach end-states. That is, do we believe in ambition, cleanliness, honesty, or obedience? What factors guide your everyday behavior? *Terminal values,* on the other hand, are those end-state goals that we prize. Included here are such things as a comfortable life, a sense of accomplishment, equality among all people, and so forth. Both sets of values have significant influence on everyday behavior at work.

You can assess your own instrumental and terminal values by completing Self-Assessment 2.2. Simply rank-order the two lists of values, and then refer to Appendix B for scoring procedures.

Role of Values and Ethics in Organizations

Personal values represent an important force in organizational behavior for several reasons. In fact, at least three purposes are served by the existence of personal values in organizations: (1) values serve as standards of behavior for determining a correct course of action; (2) values serve as guidelines for decision making and conflict resolution; and (3) values serve as an influence on employee motivation. Let us consider each of these functions.

Standards of Behavior.   First, values help us determine appropriate standards of behavior. They place limits on our behavior both inside and outside the organization. In such situations, we are referring to what is called *ethical behavior.* Employees at all levels of the organization have to make decisions concerning what to them is right or wrong, proper or improper. For example, would you conceal information about a hazardous product made by your company, or would you feel obliged to tell someone? How would you respond to petty theft on the part of a supervisor or co-worker in the office? To some extent, ethical behavior is influenced by societal values. Societal norms tell us it is wrong to engage in certain behaviors. In addition, however, individuals must often determine for themselves what is proper and what is not. This is particularly true when people find themselves in "grey zones"—situations where ethical standards are ambiguous or unclear. In many situations, a particular act may not be illegal. Moreover, one's colleagues and friends may disagree about what is proper. In such circumstances, people have to determine their own standards of behavior.

SELF-ASSESSMENT 2.2
Which Values Are Most Important to You?

Instructions: People are influenced by a wide variety of personal values. In fact, it has been argued that values represent a major influence on how we process information, how we feel about issues, and how we behave. In this exercise, you are given an opportunity to consider your own personal values. Below are listed two sets of statements. The first list presents several instrumental values, while the second list presents several terminal values. For each list you are asked to rank the statements according to how important each is to you personally. In the list of instrumental values, place a "1" next to the value that is most important to you, a "2" next to the second most important, and so forth. Clearly, you will have to make some difficult decisions concerning your priorities. When you have completed the list for instrumental values, follow the same procedure for the terminal values. Please remember that this is not a test—there are no right or wrong answers—so be completely honest with yourself.

Instrumental Values

_____ Assertiveness; standing up for yourself
_____ Being helpful or caring toward others
_____ Dependability; being counted upon by others
_____ Education and intellectual pursuits
_____ Hard work and achievement
_____ Obedience; following the wishes of others
_____ Open-mindedness; receptivity to new ideas
_____ Self-sufficiency; independence
_____ Truthfulness; honesty
_____ Being well-mannered and courteous toward others

Terminal Values

_____ Happiness; satisfaction in life
_____ Knowledge and wisdom
_____ Peace and harmony in the world
_____ Pride in accomplishment
_____ Prosperity; wealth
_____ Lasting friendships
_____ Recognition from peers
_____ Salvation; finding eternal life
_____ Security; freedom from threat
_____ Self-esteem; self-respect

Ethical Challenge

IN PRACTICE
Two Cultures' Perspectives of Straight Talk

Yukiko Tanabe, a foreign exchange student from Tokyo, Japan, was both eager and anxious about making new friends during her one-year study abroad in the United States. After a month-long intensive course in English over the summer, she began her studies at the University of California. Yukiko was in the same psychology class as Jane McWilliams. Despite Yukiko's somewhat shy personality, it did not take long before she and Jane were talking before and after class and studying together.

Part of the way through the term, the professor asked for volunteers to be part of an experiment on personalities and problem solving. The professor also offered extra credit for participation in the experiment and asked interested students to stay after class to discuss the project in more detail.

When class was over, Jane asked Yukiko if she wanted to stay after and learn more about the project and the extra credit. Yukiko hesitated and then said that she was not sure. Jane replied that it would only take a few minutes to listen to the explanation, and so the two young women went up to the front of the class, along with about 20 other students, to hear the details.

The project would simply involve completing a personality questionnaire and then attempting to solve three short case problems. In total, it would take about one hour of time and would be worth 5 percent extra credit. Jane though it was a great idea and asked Yukiko if she wanted to participate. Yukiko replied that she was not sure. Jane responded that they could go together, that it would be fun, and that 5 percent extra credit was a nice bonus. To this Yukiko made no reply, so Jane signed both of them up for the project and suggested that they meet at the "quad" about 10 minutes before the scheduled beginning of the experiment.

On the day of the experiment, however, Yukiko did not show up. Jane found out later from Yukiko that she did not want to participate in the experiment. "Then why didn't you just say so?" asked Jane. "Because I did not want to embarrass you in front of all your other friends by saying no," explained Yukiko.[28]

Guidelines for Decision Making and Conflict Resolution. In addition, values serve as guidelines for making decisions and for attempting to resolve conflicts. Managers who value personal integrity are less likely to make decisions they know to be injurious to someone else. Relatedly, values can influence how someone approaches a conflict. For example, if your boss asks your opinion about a report she wrote that you don't like, do you express your opinion candidly or be polite and flatter her? We shall return to this issue in Chapters 14 and 16.

An interesting development in the area of values and decision making involves integrity or honesty tests. These tests are designed to measure an individual's level of integrity or honesty based on the notion that honest or dishonest behavior and decisions flow from a person's underlying values. Today over 5000 firms use these tests some of which use direct questions while others use camouflaged questions. Although the reliability of the most common tests seem good, their validity (i.e., the extent to which they can accurately predict dishonest behavior) is more open to question.[29] Nevertheless, because they do not cost much (typically $10 per person) and the fact that they are less intrusive than drug or polygraph testing, integrity tests are increasingly used to screen potential employees.

Influence on Motivation.   Values affect employee motivation by determining what rewards or outcomes are sought. Employees are often offered overtime work and the opportunity to make more money at the expense of free time and time with their families. Which would you choose? Would you work harder to get a promotion to a perhaps more stressful job or "lay back" and accept a slower and possibly less rewarding career path? Value questions such as these confront employees and managers every day.

Prominent among work-related values is the concept of the *work ethic*. Simply put, the work ethic refers to the strength of one's commitment and dedication to hard work, both as an end in itself and as a means to future rewards. Much has been written lately concerning the relative state of the work ethic in North America. It has been repeatedly pointed out that one reason for our trouble in international competition lies in our rather mediocre work ethic. This is not to say that many Americans do not work hard; rather, it is to say that others (most notably those in East Asia) simply work harder.

There are many ways to assess these differences, but perhaps the simplest way is to look at actual hours worked on average in different countries both in Asia and Western Europe. Looking at Exhibit 2.5, you may be surprised to discover that although the average American works 1934 hours (and takes an average of 19.5 vacation days) per year, the average Korean works 2833 hours per year (and takes only 4.5 days of vacation)![30] The typical Japanese worker works 2180 hours per year and takes 9.6 days of vacation. Meanwhile, Western Europeans work fewer hours and take more vacation days. Thus, although Americans may work longer hours than many Europeans, they fall far behind many in East Asia.

IN PRACTICE
Japan Tries to Reduce Its Workweek

What does a country do when its people are overmotivated? Consider the case of Japan. On the basis of Japan's newfound affluence and success in the international marketplace, many companies—and the government—are beginning to be concerned that perhaps Japanese employees work too hard and should slow down. They may be too motivated for their own good. As a result, the Japanese Department of Labor has initiated a drive to shorten the workweek and encourage more Japanese employees to take longer holidays. The effort is focusing on middle-aged and older employees, because their physical stamina may be less than that of their more junior colleagues. Many companies are following this lead and are beginning to reduce the workweek. This is no easy task in a land where such behavior may be seen by employees as showing disloyalty toward the company. It requires a fundamental change in employee attitudes.

Exhibit 2.5
Average Hours Worked and
Vacation Taken per Year for
Male Industrial Workers

Country	Average Hours Worked per Year	Vacation Days Actually Taken
Korea	2,833	4.5
Japan	2,180	9.6
United States	1,934	19.5
Great Britain	1,941	22.5
West Germany	1,652	30.2
France	1,649	25.0

Source: From Richard M. Steers, Yoo Keun Shin, and Gerardo R. Ungson, *The Chaebol: Korea's New Industrial Might* (Philadelphia: Ballinger, 1989). Reprinted by permission of HarperBusiness, a division of HarperCollins Publishers.

At the same time, among younger employees, cracks are beginning to appear in the fabled Japanese work ethic. Younger workers are beginning to express increased frustration with dull jobs and routine assignments, and job satisfaction appears to be at an all-time low. Young Japanese are beginning to take longer lunch periods and look forward to Friday and the coming weekend. Whether this is attributable to increasing affluence in a changing society or simply the emergence of a new generation, things are changing—however slowly—in the East.[31]

CULTURAL DIFFERENCES

The final topic we will discuss in this chapter is the role of culture and cultural diversity in organizational behavior. Cultural diversity can be analyzed in many ways. For instance, we can compare cultural diversity *within* one country or company, or we can compare cultures *across* units. That is, we can look inside a particular North American firm and see employees who are Asian, black, Latino, American Indian, white, and so forth. Clearly, these individuals have different cultural backgrounds, frames of reference, traditions, and so forth. Or we can look more globally and compare a typical American firm with a typical Mexican, Italian, or Chinese firm and again see significant differences in culture.

We can also analyze cultural diversity by looking at different patterns of behavior. For instance, Americans often wonder why Japanese or Korean businesspeople always bow when they meet; this seems strange to some. Likewise, many Asians wonder why Americans always shake hands, a similarly strange behavior. Americans often complain that Japanese executives say "yes" when they actually mean something else, while Japanese executives claim many Americans promise things they know they cannot deliver. Many of these differences result from a lack of understanding concerning the various cultures and how they affect behavior both inside and outside the workplace. As the marketplace and economies of the world merge ever closer, it is increasingly important that we come to understand more about cultural variations as they affect our world.

What Is Culture?

Simply put, *culture* may be defined as "the collective programming of the mind which distinguishes the members of one human group from another; the interactive aggregate of common characteristics that influences a human group's response to its environment."[32] More to the point, culture is the "collective mental programming of a people."[33] It is the unique characteristics of a people. As such, culture is:

■ Something that is shared by all or most of the members of a society.

■ Something that older members of a society attempt to pass along to younger members.

■ Something that shapes our view of the world.

The concept of culture represents an easy way to understand a people, albeit on a superficial level. Thus, we refer to the Chinese culture or the American culture. This is not to say that every member within a culture behaves in exactly the same way. On the contrary, every culture has diversity, but members of a certain culture tend to exhibit similar behavioral patterns that reflect where and how they grew up. A knowledge of a culture's patterns should help us deal with its members.

Culture affects the workplace because it affects what we do and how we behave. As shown in Exhibit 2.6, cultural variations influence our values, which in turn affect attitudes and, ultimately, behaviors. For instance, a culture that is characterized by hard work (e.g., the Korean culture discussed above) would exhibit a value or ethic of hard work. This work ethic would be reflected in positive attitudes toward work and the workplace; people would feel that hard work is satisfying and beneficial—they might feel committed to their employer; they might feel shame if they do not work long hours. This, in

Exhibit 2.6
Relationship of Culture to Values, Attitudes, and Behavior

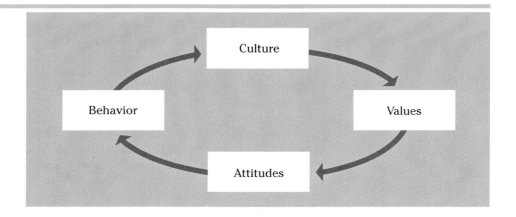

turn, would lead to actual high levels of work. This behavior, then, would serve to reinforce the culture and its value, and so on.

To see how this works, consider the results of a survey of managerial behavior by French researcher Andre Laurent.[34] He asked managers how important it was for managers to have precise answers when asked a question by subordinates. The results, shown in Exhibit 2.7, clearly show how culture can influence very specific managerial behavior. In some countries, it is imperative for the manager to "know" the answer (even when he or she really doesn't), whereas in other countries it made little difference. Thus, if we want to understand why someone does something in the workplace, at least part of the behavior may be influenced by his or her cultural background.

Dimensions of Culture

There are several ways to distinguish different cultures from one another. Kluckholm and Strodtbeck have identified six dimensions that are helpful in understanding such differences.[35] These are as follows:

1. *How people view humanity.* Are people basically good, or are they evil? Can most people be trusted or not? Are most people honest? What is the true nature of humankind?
2. *How people see nature.* What is the proper relationship between people and the environment? Should people be in harmony with nature, or should they attempt to control or harness nature?
3. *How people approach interpersonal relationships.* Should one stress individualism or membership in a group? Is the person more or less important than the group? What is the "pecking order" in a society? Is it based on seniority or on wealth and power?
4. *How people view activity and achievement.* Which is a more worthy goal: activity (getting somewhere) or simply being (staying where one is)?
5. *How people view time.* Should one focus on the past, the present, or the future? Some cultures are said to be living in the past, whereas others are looking to the future.
6. *How people view space.* How should physical space be used in our lives? Should we live communally or separately? Should important people be physically separated from others? Should important meetings be held privately or in public?

To see how this works, examine Exhibit 2.8, which differentiates four countries (Mexico, Germany, Japan, and the United States) along these six dimensions. Although the actual place of each country on these scales may be argued, the exhibit does serve to highlight several trends that managers should be aware of as they approach their work. For example, although managers in all four countries may share similar views on the nature of people (good versus bad), significant differences are noted on such dimensions as people's relation to nature and interpersonal relations. This, in turn, can affect how managers in these countries approach contract negotiations, the acquisition of new technologies, and the management of employees.

Exhibit 2.7
Appropriate Managerial
Behavior in Different
Countries

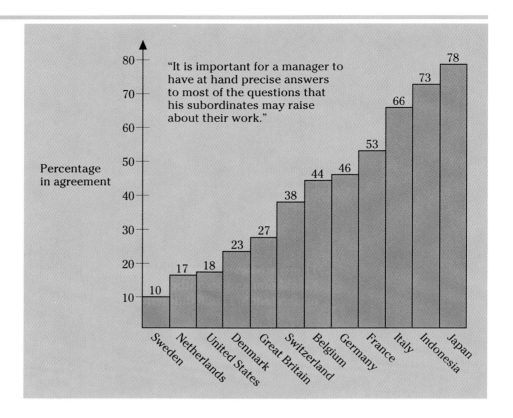

"It is important for a manager to have at hand precise answers to most of the questions that his subordinates may raise about their work."

Percentage in agreement

Sweden 10, Netherlands 17, United States 18, Denmark 23, Great Britain 27, Switzerland 38, Belgium 44, Germany 46, France 53, Italy 66, Indonesia 73, Japan 78

Exhibit 2.8
Cultural Differences Among
Managers in Four Countries

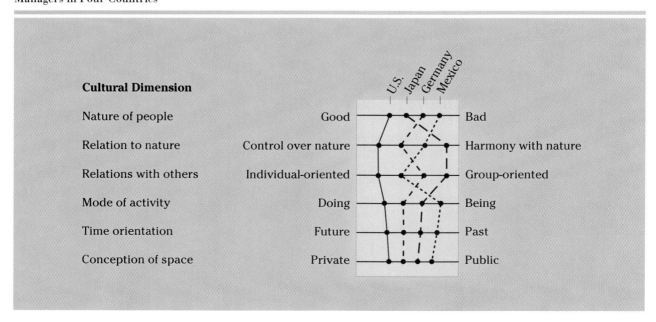

Cultural Dimension		U.S. Japan Germany Mexico	
Nature of people	Good		Bad
Relation to nature	Control over nature		Harmony with nature
Relations with others	Individual-oriented		Group-oriented
Mode of activity	Doing		Being
Time orientation	Future		Past
Conception of space	Private		Public

Dimensions such as these help us frame any discussion about how people differ. We can say, for example, that most Americans are individualistic, activity-oriented, and present/future-oriented. We can further say that they value privacy and want to control their environment. In another culture, perhaps the mode is past-oriented, reflective, group-oriented, and unconcerned with achievement. In Japan we hear that "the nail that sticks out gets hammered down"—a comment reflecting a belief in homogeneity within the culture and the importance of the group. In the United States, by contrast, we hear "Look out for Number One" and "A man's home is his castle"—comments reflecting a belief in the supremacy of the individual over the group. Neither culture is "right" or "better." Instead, each culture must be recognized as a force within individuals that motivates their behaviors within the workplace. However, even within the U.S. workforce, we must keep in mind that there are subcultures that can influence behavior. For example, recent work has shown that the Hispanic culture within the U.S. places a high value on groups compared to individuals and as a consequence takes a more collective approach to decision making.[36] As we progress through this book, we shall continually build upon these differences as we attempt to understand behavior in the workplace.

International Challenge

IN PRACTICE
Can a Serbian Trust a Canadian Working in Sweden?

One of the dimensions discussed above is people's beliefs concerning human nature. Can most people be trusted, or not? This dimension of culture is illustrated in the following true account of a Canadian business student who found a summer job working in a Serbian restaurant in Sweden:

A young Canadian in Sweden found summer employment working in a restaurant owned by Serbians. As the Canadian explained, "I arrived at the restaurant and was greeted by an effusive Serbian man who set me to work at once washing dishes and preparing the restaurant for the June opening.

"At the end of the first day, I was brought to the back room. The owner took an old cash box out of a large desk. The Serb owner counted out my wages for the day and was about to return the box to the desk when the phone rang in the front room. The owner hesitated: should he leave me sitting in the room with the money or take it with him? Quite simply, could he trust me?

"After a moment, the man got up to answer the phone, leaving me with the open money box. I sat there in amazement; how could he trust me, someone he had known for less than a day, a person whose last name and address he didn't even know?"[37]

This incident contrasts perceptions of individuals as good or evil. The Serbian manager saw individuals as good and inherently trustworthy. For this reason, he could leave the employee alone with the money without worrying that it would be gone when he returned. The employee's surprise that this stranger trusted him with the money is a reflection of a North American's values orientation toward individuals. Believing that people are capable of both good and evil, North Americans are cautious. If the Canadian were in the owner's shoes, he probably would have taken the cash box with him to the other room to answer the telephone, fearing that the money would be stolen.

PULLING IT ALL TOGETHER

Because people enter organizations with preset dispositions, it is important to be able to analyze important individual characteristics, effectively select individuals, and appropriately match them to their jobs. However, this must be done carefully in light of both ethical and legal issues that face managers today.

SUMMARY OF KEY POINTS

▮ Ability refers to one's capacity to respond, whereas motivation refers to one's desire to respond. Abilities can be divided into mental abilities and physical abilities.

▮ Personality represents a stable set of characteristics and tendencies that determines the psychological behavior of people.

▮ Personality development is influenced by several factors, including physiological, cultural, family and group, role and situational determinants.

▮ Self-esteem represents opinions and beliefs concerning oneself and one's self-worth.

▮ Locus of control is a tendency for people to attribute the events affecting their lives either to their own actions (referred to as internal locus of control) or to external forces (referred to as external locus of control).

▮ Authoritarianism represents an individual's orientation toward authority and is characterized by an overriding conviction that it is appropriate for there to be clear status and power differences between people.

▮ Dogmatism refers to a cognitive style characterized by closed-mindedness and inflexibility.

▮ The basic incongruity thesis asserts that individuals and organizations exist in a constant state of conflict because each has different goals and expectations from the other. Employees want organizations to provide more autonomy and meaningful work, while organizations want employees to be more predictable, stable, and dependable.

▮ A value is an enduring belief that one specific mode of conduct or end-state is preferable to others. Instrumental values are beliefs concerning the most appropriate ways to pursue end-states, whereas terminal values are beliefs concerning the most desirable end-states themselves.

▮ Ethics are important to individuals because they serve as (1) standards of behavior for determining a correct course of action, (2) guidelines for decision making and conflict resolution, and (3) influences on employee motivation.

▨ The work ethic refers to someone's belief that hard work and commitment to a task are both ends in themselves and means to future rewards.

▨ Culture refers to the collective mental programming of a group or people that distinguishes them from others. It (1) is shared by the members of the group, (2) is passed on from older members to younger members, and (3) shapes our view of the world.

▨ Six dimensions of culture can be identified: (1) how people see themselves, (2) how people see nature, (3) how people approach interpersonal relationships, (4) how people view activity and achievement, (5) how people view time, and (6) how people view space.

KEY WORDS

authoritarianism
basic incongruity thesis
cognitive complexity
culture
dependability
dogmatism
ethics
extroversion
instrumental values
introversion

locus of control
mental abilities
personal values
personality
physical abilities
psychomotor abilities
self-esteem
terminal values
work ethic

QUESTIONS FOR DISCUSSION

1. Why is it important for managers to understand individual differences at work?
2. Which employee abilities seem to be most important in determining job performance? Explain.
3. Define *personality*. Which personality traits are most relevant to understanding organizational behavior? Why?
4. Explain how the concept of *locus of control* works. Provide an example.
5. Describe the basic incongruity thesis. Do you agree with this thesis? Under what circumstances might the thesis be most likely to be true? Least likely to be true? Explain.
6. Why is it important for managers to understand ethical standards in the workplace? How do ethics affect our behavior at work?
7. How should managers handle the "grey zones" that are common to ethical dilemmas in organizations? Explain.
8. Define *culture*. How do culture and cultural variations affect work behavior and job performance? Provide examples to show why a knowledge of such differences is important for managers.

NOTES

1. Michael O'Neal and Thane Peterson. "25 Executives to Watch." *The 1992 Business Week 1000* (New York: McGraw-Hill, 1992)
2. V. H. Vroom, *Work and Motivation* (New York: Wiley, 1964).
3. R. J. Ebert and T. R. Mitchell, *Organization Decision Processes: Concepts and Analysis* (New York: Crane, Russak, 1975), p. 81.
4. Ibid.
5. T. R. Mitchell, "Cognitive Complexity and Leadership Style," *Journal of Personality and Social Psychology,* 1970, *16,* pp. 166–174.
6. H. M. Schroder, M. H. Driver, and S. Streufert, *Human Information Processing* (New York: Holt, Rinehart and Winston, 1967).
7. E. J. McCormick and J. Tiffin, *Industrial Psychology* (Englewood Cliffs, N.J.: Prentice-Hall, 1976).
8. Dale Feuer & Chris Lee. 1988. The Kaizen Connection: How Companies Pick Tomorrow's Workers. Training. May, 23–35.
9. S. R. Maddi, *Personality Theories: A Comparative Analysis* (Homewood, Ill.: Dorsey, 1980), p. 10.
10. C. Kluckholn and H. Murray, *Personality in Society and Nature,* (New York: Knopf, 1953).
11. P. H. Mussen, *The Psychological Development of the Child* (Englewood Cliffs, N.J.: Prentice-Hall, 1963).
12. Ibid.
13. J. C. Abegglen, "Personality Factors in Social Mobility: A Study of Occupationally Mobile Businessmen," *Genetic Psychology Monographs,* August 1958, pp. 101–159.
14. G. W. Allport, *Pattern and Growth in Personality* (New York: Holt, Rinehart and Winston, 1961).
15. R. A. Ellis and M. S. Taylor, "Role of Self-Esteem within the Job Search Process," *Journal of Applied Psychology,* 1983, *68,* pp. 632–640.
16. P. Spector, "Behavior in Organizations as a Function of Locus of Control," *Psychological Bulletin,* May 1982, pp. 482–497; P. Nystrom, "Managers' Salaries and Their Beliefs About Reinforcement Control," *Journal of Social Psychology,* August 1983, pp. 291–292.
17. L. R. Morris, *Extroversion and Introversion: An Interactional Perspective* (New York: Hemisphere, 1979), p. 8.
18. T. W. Adorno, E. Frenkel-Brunswik, and D. J. Levinson, *The Authoritarian Personality* (New York: Harper & Row, 1950).
19. V. H. Vroom, *Some Personality Determinants of the Effects of Participation* (Englewood Cliffs, N.J.: Prentice-Hall, 1960).
20. M. Rokeach, *The Open and Closed Mind* (New York: Basic Books, 1960).
21. R. N. Taylor and M. D. Dunnette, "Influence of Dogmatism, Risk-Taking Propensity, and Intelligence on Decision-Making Strategies for a Sample of Industrial Managers," *Journal of Applied Psychology,* 1974, *59,* pp. 420–423.
22. R. Stogdill, "Personal Factors Associated with Leadership: A Survey of the Literature," *Journal of Psychology,* 1948, *25,* pp. 35–71; F. L. Greer, *Small Group Effectiveness* (Philadelphia: Institute for Research on Human Relations, 1955).
23. Mitchelle Pacelle, "Design Flaw." *Wall Street Journal,* September 2, 1992, p. A1, A5.
24. C. Argyris, "Personality and Organization Theory Revisited," *Administrative Science Quarterly,* 1973, *18,* pp. 141–167.
25. W. Hampton, "How Does Japan Inc. Pick Its American Workers?" *Business Week,* October 3, 1988, pp. 84–88.
26. M. Rokeach, *The Nature of Human Values* (New York: Free Press, 1973), p. 5.
27. Ibid.
28. Personal communication. Names have been disguised.

29. Paul R. Sackett, Laura R. Burris, and Christine Callahan. 1989. Integrity Testing for Personnel Selection. Personnel Psychology, *42*, 491–529.
30. R. M. Steers, Y. K. Shin, and G. R. Ungson, *The Chaebol: Korea's New Industrial Might* (New York: Harper & Row, 1989), p. 96.
31. L. Smith, "Cracks in the Japanese Work Ethic," *Fortune,* May 14, 1984, pp. 162–168; K. Van Wolferen, *The Enigma of Japanese Power* (New York: Knopf, 1989).
32. G. Hofstede, *Culture's Consequence,* (Beverly Hills, Calif.: Sage, 1980), p. 25.
33. Ibid.
34. A. Laurent, "The Cultural Diversity of Western Conceptions of Management," *International Studies of Management and Organization,* XIII, 1–2, Spring-Summer 1983, pp. 75–96.
35. F. Kluckholm and F. Strodtbeck, *Variations in Value Orientations* (Evanston, Ill.: Row, Peterson, 1961).
36. T. Cox, et al., "Effects of Ethnic Group Cultural Differences on Cooperative and Competitive Behavior on a Group Task," Academy of Management J., *34,* pp. 827–847.
37. S. Gruman, cited in N. Adler, *International Dimensions of Organizational Behavior* (Boston: PWS/Kent, 1986), pp. 13–14.

EXPERIENTIAL EXERCISE 2

New York Trading Company and the Foreign Corrupt Practices Act

New York Trading Company (NYTC) is an American company headquartered in New York City. The company recently entered into a trading agreement with a company in Pakistan. The Pakistani company has agreed to act as representative for NYTC on the basis of the product information provided by your company, as well as government incentives provided by the Pakistani government. One of NYTC's vice-presidents for international sales has been sent to Pakistan to ensure the success of the project. Upon arrival, the vice-president is surprised to find that the initial shipment has been held up in customs because government import restrictions have not been complied with owing to insufficient data. This information was supplied previously by NYTC to the local company. The information is vital to the implementation of the agreement.

When asked why this information has not been forwarded to customs, a junior clerk in the local company quietly explains that his predecessor was very disorganized and that the material has probably been misfiled. The clerk is very apologetic and suggests that if he were to work overtime he could probably find the material. However, the local company does not pay for overtime. The clerk suggests that he could probably find the missing documents quickly if he were appropriately compensated for his time.

NYTC needs this venture to succeed. The senior executive back in New York expects the vice-president to get the job done but also expects behavior of a high ethical standard. The future career with the company of the vice-president may be affected by this problem is handled.

In 1977 the U.S. congress passed the Foreign Corrupt Practices Act (FCPA). The FCPA makes it illegal for US companies to influence corruptly foreign officials, to make payments to officials, or to have "reason to know" that payments will be made to officials. Penalties include up to $1 million in fines to companies and $10,000 and 5 years in jail for individuals found guilty of violating FCPA. A legal distinction has been made between bribes and facilitating payments. Essentially a bribe is defined as a payment made to procure special and unjustified favors, whereas facilitating payments are made to induce officials to perform functions that they are obliged to perform as their normal duties. The FCPA was designed to punish firms and individuals who utilized bribes as a means of securing large contracts.

Role Play

Below four roles are described and the key thoughts of each individual are provided. Read and think about your assigned role. Articulate in your mind and/or on paper key arguments, positions, and counterarguments concerning the situation described above. After you have spent 5 minutes or so preparing, assume the role that you have been assigned and play out a discussion of whether or not payments should be made to the clerk.

CEO: You are very busy and cannot be intimately involved in all the day-to-day operations of the company. You understand that things are done differently in Pakistan, but one critical test of potential top executives is their ability to handle difficult problems.

Legal Counsel #1:   When asked about this situation, you are of the opinion that the potential payment if it were made would be of a very small size and would constitute a "facilitating payment" rather than a bribe. Consequently, you are not that worried about violating the FCPA.

Legal Counsel #2:   When asked about this situation, you are of the opinion that legally it is not clear if the payment would constitute a bribe or a facilitating payment. Consequently, you are very worried about the potential consequences to both the firm and the individual vice-president if the payment does constitute a bribe.

Vice-President: You know this is an important contract to your firm and that your potential for future top executive positions is being evaluated based on how you handle the current problem and especially the results you achieve.

MANAGEMENT DILEMMA 2

Hangul-Biogenics: Clashing Perspectives and Culture

Biogenics, Inc., is one of the largest biotechnology firms in the United States and has extensive international operations. Its competitive position depends heavily on research and development. Sales activity in Korea of Biogenics' early products began in the early 1970s through a distributorship arrangement with the Hangul Group, a major producer of drugs and chemicals in Korea. To prepare itself for increasingly keen competition from Korean and other competitors, Biogenics decided to undertake local production of some of its product lines in Seoul. In 1980, the company formed a joint venture with the Hangul Group called Hangul-Biogenics to manufacture its products.

With the combined efforts of both partners, Hangul-Biogenics soon began to manufacture sufficiently broad lines of products to fill the general demands of the Korean market. Production levels also allowed for some export to countries in Southeast Asia. Hangul-Biogenics also invested heavily in research and development; these efforts were coordinated through a joint committee of both partners to avoid unnecessary duplication of efforts. Several successful new products emerged from this endeavor. Biogenics, Inc., considered the Korean operation to be one of the most successful of its international ventures. It felt that the company's future prospects were quite promising, especially since there was steady improvement in Korea's standard of living.

The Korean joint venture was headed by an executive from the Hangul Group (the son of the group's founder), but day-to-day operations were managed by Andrew Shapiro, vice-president and general manager. He was assisted by Alan Bird, executive assistant to Shapiro, and several Korean managing directors. Although several other Americans were assigned to the venture, they were concerned with R&D and held no overall management responsibilities.

Shapiro arrived in Korea two years ago to replace the former general manager, who had been in Korea since 1981. Shapiro was an experienced international executive, having spent most of his 27-year career with the company in its international divisions. He had served in Indonesia, France, and Argentina and had spent several years in the home office's international division. He was delighted with the challenge to expand the Korean operations. Shapiro was also pleased with the progress the company had made under his leadership and felt a sense of accomplishment in developing a smooth-running operation. However, he had become concerned in recent months with the notable changes in Alan Bird's attitude and thinking. Shapiro felt that Bird had absorbed and internalized the Korean culture to such a point that he had lost the American point of view. Bird had "gone native," and this change resulted in a substantial loss of his administrative effectiveness, according to Shapiro.

Bird was born and raised in Seattle, Washington. Although he was a business major at the University of Washington, he also studied Korean language and culture. After graduation, he entered the army and was stationed in Korea. He made many Korean friends, fell in love with Korea, and vowed to return there to live. When he was discharged from the army, he returned to the United States and went to work for Biogenics. When the company started the Korean joint venture, Bird was a natural person to send to Seoul to help with the venture.

Bird was pleased to return to Korea, not only because of his love for the country, but also for the opportunity to improve the "ugly American" image abroad. Because of his language ability and interest in Korea, he was able to intermingle with broad segments of the local population. He noted that

Americans had a tendency to impose their value systems, ideals, and thinking patterns upon the Koreans in the belief that anything American was universally right and applicable. He felt indignant about American attitudes on numerous occasions and was determined to do something about it. At Hangul-Biogenics, Bird's responsibilities included troubleshooting with major Korean customers, attending trade meetings, negotiating with government officials, conducting marketing research projects, and helping with day-to-day administration. He reported directly to Shapiro, who initially sought his advice on many difficult and complex administrative problems.

But in Shapiro's mind, Bird had changed. Shapiro recounted several examples of what he meant by Bird's "complete emotional involvement" with the culture of Korea. To begin with, Bird had met and married a Korean woman from Yonsei University. He had moved to a strictly Korean neighborhood. He relaxed in a kimono at home, used the public bath, and was invited to weddings, neighborhood parties, and even funerals. Although Biogenics had a policy of granting two months' home leave every two years with paid transportation for the employee and his or her family, Bird declined his trips, preferring to visit remote parts of Korea with his wife.

In the office, Bird had assumed many characteristics of a typical Korean executive. He spent a great deal of time listening to the personal problems of his subordinates, maintained close social ties with many of the men in the organization, and had even helped arrange marriages for some of the young employees. Consequently, many employees sought Bird's advice and attention to register their complaints or concerns with management. For example, many employees complained to Bird about the personnel policy that Shapiro had installed. This involved a move away from promotion based on seniority to one based on superiors' evaluation of subordinates. The employees asked Bird to intercede on their behalf. He did so and insisted that their demands were fully justified in view of traditional practices.

Although Shapiro found it helpful to learn the feelings of middle managers from Bird, he resented having to deal with Bird as an adversary rather than an ally. Shapiro became reticent to ask Bird's opinion because he invariably raised objections to changes that were contrary to Korean norms and customs. Shapiro believed that there were significant changes emerging in Korean customs and culture, and he was confident that many of the points Bird objected to were not tied to existing cultural patterns as rigidly as Bird seemed to think. This view was bolstered by the fact that many Korean subordinates were more willing to try out new ideas than Bird was. Shapiro further thought that there was no point in a progressive American company's merely copying the local customs. He felt that the company's real contribution to Korean society was in introducing new ideas and innovations.

Other events had raised some doubts in Shapiro's mind as to the soundness of Bird's judgment, which Shapiro had never before questioned. For instance, when Shapiro wanted to dismiss a manager who, in his opinion, lacked initiative, leadership, and general competency, Bird defended the manager, noting that the company had never before fired a manager. Bird also argued that the manager had been loyal and honest and that the company was partially at fault for having kept him on for the last five years without spotting the incompetency. But Shapiro fired the manager anyway, only to discover two weeks later that Bird had interceded on behalf of the fired manager and had gotten another Hangul Group company to hire him. When confronted, Bird simply said that he had done what was expected of a superior in any Korean company.

Shapiro concluded that these incidents were symptomatic of a serious problem. Bird had been an effective and efficient manager. His knowledge of the language and the people had proved invaluable. On numerous occasions, his American friends envied Shapiro for having a man of Bird's qualifications as an assistant. Shapiro also knew that Bird had received several outstanding offers to go with other companies in Korea. Shapiro felt that Bird would be far more effective if he could take a more emotionally detached attitude toward Korea. In Shapiro's view, the best international executive was one who retained a belief in the fundamentals of the U.S. point of view while also understanding foreign attitudes. This understanding, of course, should be thorough or even instinctive, but it also should be objective, characterized neither by disdain nor by strong emotional attachment. First and foremost, a good executive should remain true to American values and ideals. On the basis of this information, what would you do?

1. How would you contrast the perceptions of Bird and Shapiro concerning the definition of good management and the implementation of U.S. personnel policies in the Korean operations?
2. What are the major reasons for these differences in perceptions?
3. If you were in Biogenics' corporate management and the conflict between Bird and Shapiro came to your attention, what would you do? Be sure to identify some alternatives, and then make a recommendation.

3

Perception and Job Attitudes

The Management Challenge

- ■ To understand how differences in perception affect employee behavior and performance.
- ■ To minimize the negative impact of stereotypes and other barriers to accurate social perception in interpersonal relations.
- ■ To understand how people attribute credit and blame for organizational events.
- ■ To create a work environment characterized by positive work attitudes.
- ■ To facilitate the development of a committed work force.

CLOSE UP

Kevin Rockford's Job Decision

There were no prices on the menu, and that alone impressed Kevin Rockford. Kevin was having dinner with the college recruiting officer, the southwest district manager, and the vice-president of marketing of a large consulting firm. Kevin had spent two days interviewing at the firm and was seriously considering a job offer that had been extended to him.

The position offered to Kevin was in sales, and the offer included a competitive salary, a generous moving allowance, and a performance bonus that could be as high as 30 percent of his base salary. It also had the promise of providing a clear path onto the sales and marketing fast track.

During his tour through the headquarters, Kevin had noticed the large and attractively decorated offices that all the managers seemed to have and that the young woman whose promotion had opened the position offered him had just bought a new Mustang convertible. Kevin was also struck by how well dressed and in shape every one of the managers and corporate staff seemed to be. In fact, he could not remember seeing a more attractive group of people in a corporate setting before. Also, he couldn't help noticing that most of the young male managers were quite similar to him: six feet tall, athletic, clean-cut, wearing white shirts, contemporary ties, and wing-tip shoes. It also struck him that all of the senior executives had secretaries who surely must have been models before joining the firm.

Kevin, however, paid much less attention to a number of other aspects of the people and environment. He really didn't notice that people described their competitors as enemies and the competition as a war, or that they used similar metaphors to describe the internal culture and environment of the company. Kevin also paid little attention to the comment by the woman whose position he had been offered that she had virtually no social life outside of work because she simply didn't have the time. Nor did he pay much attention to the crude locker-room jokes that the younger male managers often told with great enthusiasm in front of the female staff.

In the end, Kevin decided to take the job, only later to decide that he had made a serious mistake and that the culture of the company simply did not fit his expectations. He wondered how he could have been so blind.

What happened to Kevin is not uncommon. Just as Kevin's decision was based on what he noticed or did not notice, how you perceive a situation or another person has a tremendous impact on your subsequent decisions and behaviors. For example, whether you decide to accept a firm's salary offer may be a function of your perception of other aspects of working in that organization or how honest and fair you feel the other side has been throughout the negotiations. Obviously, your perception may be correct or mistaken; yet, even if incorrect, it will have a strong influence on your decisions. These issues form the basis of this chapter. We begin by looking at perceptual processes in organizations. On the basis of this analysis, we move to an exploration of job attitudes. When taken together, these two factors should go a long way toward explaining what happened to Kevin Rockford.[1]

THE PERCEPTUAL PROCESS

By *perception* we mean the process by which one screens, selects, organizes, and interprets stimuli to give them meaning.[2] It is a process of making sense out of the environment in order to make an appropriate behavioral response. Perception does not necessarily lead to an accurate portrait of the environment, but rather to a unique portrait, influenced by the needs, desires, values, and disposition of the perceiver. As described by Kretch and associates,[3] an individual's perception of a given situation is not a photographic representation of the physical world; it is a partial, personal construction in which certain objects, selected out by the individual for a major role, are perceived in an individual manner. Every perceiver is, as it were, to some degree a non-representational artist, painting a picture of the world that expresses an individual view of reality.

The multitude of objects that vie for attention are first selected or screened by individuals. This process is called *perceptual selectivity.* Certain of these objects catch our attention, while others do not. Once individuals notice a particular object, they then attempt to make sense out of it by organizing or categorizing it according to their unique frame of reference and their needs. This second process is termed *perceptual organization.* When meaning has been attached to an object, individuals are in a position to determine an appropriate response or reaction to it. Hence, if we clearly recognize and understand we are in danger from a falling rock or a car, we can quickly move out of the way.

Because of the importance of perceptual selectivity for understanding the perception of work situations, we will examine this concept in some detail before considering the topic of social perception.

Perceptual Selectivity: Seeing What We See

As noted above, *perceptual selectivity* refers to the process by which individuals select objects in the environment for attention. Without this ability to focus on one or a few stimuli instead of the hundreds constantly surrounding us, we would be unable to process all the information necessary to initiate behavior. In essence, perceptual selectivity works as follows (see Exhibit 3.1). The individual is first exposed to an object or stimulus—a loud noise, a new car, a tall building, another person, and so on. Next, the individual focuses

Exhibit 3.1
The Process of
Perceptual Selectivity

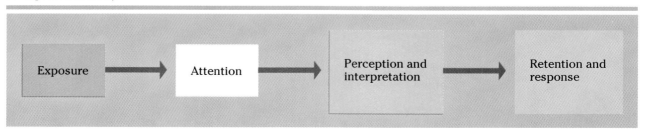

attention on this one object or stimulus, as opposed to others, and concentrates his or her efforts on understanding or comprehending the stimulus. For example, while conducting a factory tour, two managers came across a piece of machinery. One manager's attention focused on the stopped machine; the other manager focused on the worker who was trying to fix it. Both managers simultaneously asked the worker a question. The first manager asked why the machine was stopped, and the second manager asked if the employee thought that she could fix it. Both managers were presented with the same situation, but they noticed different aspects. This example illustrates that once attention has been directed, individuals are more likely to retain an image of the object or stimulus in their memory and to select an appropriate response to the stimulus. These various influences on selective attention can be divided into external influences and internal (personal) influences (see Exhibit 3.2).

External Influences on Selective Attention

External influences consist of the characteristics of the observed object or person that activate the senses. Most external influences affect selective attention because of either their physical properties or their dynamic properties.

Physical Properties.   The physical properties of the objects themselves often affect which objects receive attention by the perceiver. Emphasis here is on the unique, different, and out of the ordinary. A particularly important physical property is *size*. Generally, larger objects receive more attention than smaller ones. Advertising companies use the largest signs and billboards allowed to capture the perceiver's attention. However, when most of

Exhibit 3.2
Major Influences on
Selective Attention

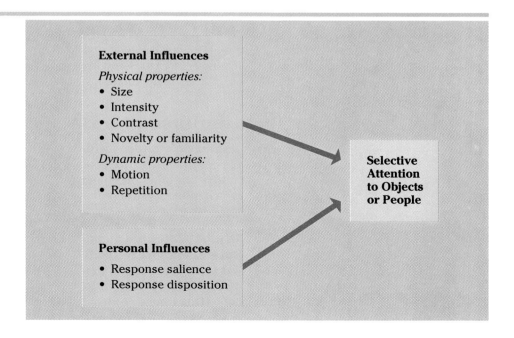

the surrounding objects are large, a small object against a field of large objects may receive more attention. In either case, size represents an important variable in perception. Moreover, brighter, louder, and more colorful objects tend to attract more attention than objects of less *intensity*. For example, when a factory foreman yells an order at his or her subordinates, it will probably receive more notice (although it may not receive the desired response) from workers. It must be remembered here, however, that intensity heightens attention only when compared to other comparable stimuli. If the foreman always yells, employees may stop paying much attention to the yelling. Objects that *contrast* strongly with the background against which they are observed tend to receive more attention than less contrasting objects. An example of the contrast principle can be seen in the use of plant and highway safety signs. A terse message such as "Danger" is lettered in black against a yellow or orange background. A final physical characteristic that can heighten perceptual awareness is the *novelty* or *unfamiliarity* of the object. Specifically, the unique or unexpected seen in a familiar setting (an executive of a conservative company who comes to work in Bermuda shorts) or the familiar seen in an incongruous setting (someone in church holding a can of beer) will receive attention.

Dynamic Properties. The second set of external influences on selective attention are those that either change over time or derive their uniqueness from the order in which they are presented. The most obvious dynamic property is *motion*. We tend to pay attention to objects that move against a relatively static background. This principle has long been recognized by advertisers, who often use signs with moving lights or moving objects to attract attention. In an organizational setting, a clear example is a rate-buster, who shows up his or her colleagues by working substantially faster, attracting more attention.

Another principle basic to advertising is *repetition* of a message or image. Work instructions that are repeated tend to be received better, particularly when they concern a dull or boring task on which it is difficult to concentrate. This process is particularly effective in the area of plant safety. Most industrial accidents occur because of careless mistakes during monotonous activities. Repeating safety rules and procedures can often help keep workers alert to the possibilities of accidents.

Personal Influences on Selective Attention

In addition to a variety of external factors, several important personal factors are also capable of influencing the extent to which an individual pays attention to a particular stimulus or object in the environment. The two most important personal influences on perceptual readiness are *response salience* and *response disposition*.

Response Salience. This is a tendency to focus on objects that relate to our *immediate* needs or wants. Response salience in the work environment is easily identified. A worker who is tired from many hours of work may be acutely sensitive to the number of hours or minutes until quitting time. Employees negotiating a new contract may know to the penny the hourly wage of workers doing similar jobs across town. Managers with a high need

SELF-ASSESSMENT 3.1
Can You Understand This Passage?

Instructions: The procedure is actually quite simple. First you arrange things into different groups. Of course, one pile may be sufficient depending on how much there is to do. If you have to go somewhere else due to lack of facilities that is the next step, otherwise you are pretty well set. It is important not to overdo things. That is, it is better to do too few things at once than too many. In the short run this may not seem important but complications can easily arise. A mistake can be expensive as well. At first the whole procedure will seem complicated. Soon, however, it will become just another facet of life. It is difficult to foresee any end to the necessity for this task in the immediate future, but then one never can tell. After the procedure is completed one arranges the materials into different groups again. Then they can be put into their appropriate places. Eventually they will be used once more and the whole cycle will then have to be repeated. However, that is part of life.

Comprehensive Scale

Very incomprehensive		Neutral		Very comprehensive
1	2	3	4	5

Source: From "Contextual Prerequisites for Understanding: Some Investigations of Comprehension and Recall" by John D. Bransford and Marcia K. Johnson, in *Journal of Verbal Learning and Verbal Behavior,* December 1972, p. 722. Reprinted by permission of Academic Press and John D. Bransford.

to achieve may be sensitive to opportunities for work achievement, success, and promotion. Finally, female managers may be more sensitive than many male managers to condescending male attitudes toward women. Response salience, in turn, can distort our view of our surroundings. For example, as Ruch notes:

> Time spent on monotonous work is usually overestimated. Time spent in interesting work is usually underestimated. . . . Judgment of time is related to feelings of success or failure. Subjects who are experiencing failure judge a given interval as longer than do subjects who are experiencing success. A given interval of time is also estimated as longer by subjects trying to get through a task in order to reach a desired goal than by subjects working without such motivation.[4]

In order to understand how response salience works, you may want to complete Self-Assessment 3.1. Read the passage, and rate it on its comprehensibility. Does it make sense to you? Next, look at the appropriate frame of reference given in note 5 at the end of the chapter. Now read the passage again, and rate it for its comprehensibility. Does it make more sense now that you have a specific frame of reference?

Response Disposition.   Whereas response salience deals with immediate needs and concerns, *response disposition* is the tendency to recognize familiar objects more quickly than unfamiliar ones. The notion of response disposition carries with it a clear recognition of the importance of past learning on what we perceive in the present. For instance, in one study, a group of individuals was presented with a set of playing cards with the colors and symbols reversed—that is, hearts and diamonds were printed in black, and spades and clubs in red. Surprisingly, when subjects were presented with these cards for brief time periods, individuals consistently described the cards as they expected them to be (red hearts and diamonds, black spades and clubs) instead of as they really were. They were predisposed to see things as they always had been in the past.[6]

Thus, the basic perceptual process is in reality a fairly complicated one. Several factors, including our own personal makeup and the environment, influence how we interpret and respond to the events we focus on. Although the process itself may seem somewhat complicated, it in fact represents a shorthand to guide us in our everyday behavior. That is, without perceptual selectivity we would be immobilized by the millions of stimuli competing for our attention and action. The perceptual process allows us to focus our attention on the more salient events or objects and, in addition, allows us to categorize such events or objects so that they fit into our own conceptual map of the environment. Kevin Rockford noticed aspects of the environment and people of the consulting firm that he was predisposed to focus on and that contrasted with other firms, were familiar, and were important to him.

International Challenge

IN PRACTICE
Which Car Would You Buy?

When General Motors teamed up with Toyota to form California-based New United Motor Manufacturing, Inc. (NUMMI), they had a great idea. NUMMI would manufacture not only the popular Toyota Corolla but would also make a GM car called the Geo Prizm (formerly called the Chevrolet Nova). Both cars would be essentially identical except for minor styling differences. Economies of scale and high quality would benefit the sales of both cars. Unfortunately, General Motors forgot one thing. The North American consumer holds a higher opinion of Japanese-built cars than American-made ones. As a result, from the start of the joint venture, Corollas have sold rapidly, while sales of Geo Prizms have languished.

With hindsight, it is easy to explain what happened in terms of perceptual differences. That is, the typical consumer simply perceived the Corolla to be of higher quality (and perhaps higher status) and bought accordingly. Not only was the Prizm seen more skeptically by consumers, but General Motors' insistence on a whole new name for the product left many buyers unfamiliar with just what they were buying. As a result, General Motors lost $80 million on the Prizm in its first year of sales. Meanwhile, demand for the Corolla exceeded supply.

The final irony here is that no two cars could be any more alike than the Prizm and the Corolla. They are built on the same assembly line by the same workers to the same design specifications. They are, in fact, the same car. The only difference is in how the consumer's perceive the two cars—and these perceptions obviously are radically different.[7]

SOCIAL PERCEPTION IN ORGANIZATIONS

Up to this point, we have focused on an examination of basic perceptual processes—how we see objects or attend to stimuli. Based on this discussion, we are now ready to examine a special case of the perceptual process—*social perception* as it relates to the workplace. Social perception consists of those processes by which we perceive other people.[8] Particular emphasis in the study of social perception is placed on how we interpret other people, how we categorize them, and how we form impressions of them.

Clearly, social perception is far more complex than the perception of inanimate objects such as tables, chairs, signs, and buildings. This is true for at least two reasons. First, people are obviously far more complex and dynamic than tables and chairs. More careful attention must be paid in perceiving them so as not to miss important details. Second, an accurate perception of others is usually far more important to us personally than are our perceptions of inanimate objects. The consequences of misperceiving people are great. Failure to accurately perceive the location of a desk in a large room may mean we bump into it by mistake. Failure to perceive accurately the hierarchical status of someone and how the person cares about this status difference might lead you to inappropriately address the person by their first name or use slang in their presence and thereby significantly hurt your chances for promotion if that person is involved in such decisions. Consequently, social perception in the work situation deserves special attention.

We will concentrate now on the three major influences on social perception: the characteristics of (1) the person being perceived, (2) of the particular situation, and (3) of the perceiver. When taken together, these influences are the dimensions of the environment in which we view other people. It is important for students of management to understand the way in which they interact (see Exhibit 3.3).

Characteristics of the Person Perceived

The way in which we are evaluated in social situations is greatly influenced by our own unique sets of personal characteristics. That is, our dress, talk, and gestures determine the kind of impressions people form of us. In particular, four categories of personal characteristics can be identified: (1) physical appearance, (2) verbal communication, (3) nonverbal communication, (4) ascribed attributes.

Physical Appearance.   A variety of physical attributes influence our overall image. These include many of the obvious demographic characteristics

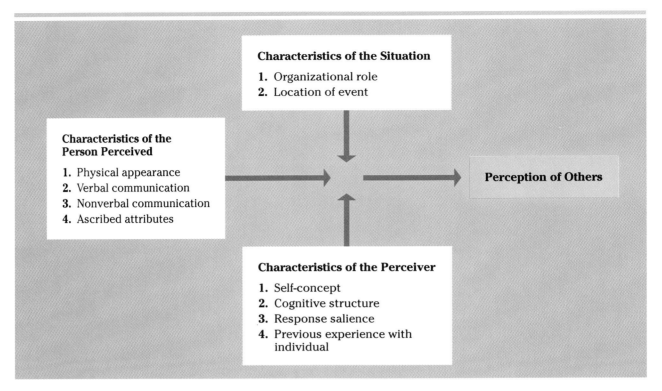

Characteristics of the Situation

1. Organizational role
2. Location of event

Characteristics of the Person Perceived

1. Physical appearance
2. Verbal communication
3. Nonverbal communication
4. Ascribed attributes

Perception of Others

Characteristics of the Perceiver

1. Self-concept
2. Cognitive structure
3. Response salience
4. Previous experience with individual

Exhibit 3.3
Major Influences on Social
Perception in Organizations

such as age, sex, race, height, and weight. A study by Mason found that most people agree on the physical attributes of a leader (i.e., what leaders *should* look like), even though these attributes were not found to be consistently held by actual leaders. However, when we see a person who appears to be assertive, goal-oriented, confident, and articulate, we infer that this person is a natural leader.[9] Another example of the powerful influence of physical appearance on perception is clothing. People dressed in business suits are generally thought to be professionals, whereas people dressed in work clothes are assumed to be lower-level employees.

Verbal and Nonverbal Communication.   What we say to others—as well as how we say it—can influence the impressions others form of us. Several aspects of verbal communication can be noted. First, the *precision* with which one uses language can influence impressions about cultural sophistication or education. An *accent* provides clues about a person's geographic and social background. The *tone of voice* used provides clues about a speaker's state of mind. Finally, the *topics* people choose to converse about provide clues about them.

Impressions are also influenced by nonverbal communication—how people behave. For instance, facial expressions often serve as clues in forming impressions of others. People who consistently smile are often thought to have positive attitudes.[10] A whole field of study that has recently emerged is *body language,* the way in which people express their inner feelings subconsciously through physical actions: sitting up straight versus being relaxed, looking people straight in the eye versus looking away from people.

These forms of expressive behavior provide information to the perceiver concerning how approachable others are, how self-confident they are, or how sociable they are.

Ascribed Attributes.   Finally, we often ascribe certain attributes to a person before or at the beginning of an encounter; these attributes can influence how we perceive that person. Three ascribed attributes are status, occupation, and personal characteristics. We ascribe *status* to someone when we are told that he or she is an executive, holds the greatest sales record, or has in some way achieved unusual fame or wealth. Research has consistently shown that people attribute different motives to people they believe to be high or low in status, even when these people behave in an identical fashion.[11] For instance, high-status people are seen as having greater control over their behavior and as being more self-confident and competent; they are given greater influence in group decisions than low-status people. Moreover, high-status people are generally better liked than low-status people. *Occupations* also play an important part in how we perceive people. Describing people as salespersons, accountants, teamsters, or research scientists conjures up distinct pictures of these various people before any first-hand encounters. In fact, these pictures may even determine whether there can be an encounter.

IN PRACTICE
Would You Hire an Image Consultant?

Whether we are selecting new employees, new CEOs, or political candidates, physical appearance can have a lot to do with how we perceive such people. It can also have a lot to do with who ultimately gets hired, promoted, or elected. As recently as 15 years ago, image consulting was virtually unheard of as an avocation. According to Jacqueline Thompson, the New York-based publisher of the *Directory of Image Consultants,* there were a scant 37 people in the field in 1978. Today, the *Directory* lists over 250 consultants who coach executives in everything from business protocol to scarf-tying. The variety of specializations is staggering: speech consultants teach you how to appease angry stockholders; communications consultants help you cope with corporate politics; psychologists fine-tune your self-esteem and self-perception.

Most image consultants, however, tend to concentrate on the basics, i.e., outward appearance—evaluating a client's wardrobe, hair, and (for women) makeup. Then they either recommend new purchases or set aside clothing in the stores, later accompanying the client on a shopping trip and fitting.

Michael R. Solomon, chairman of the marketing department at Rutgers University in New Brunswick, N.J., divides people who use image consultants into two categories: those who utilize them for their "legs" and those who utilize them for their "heads." In other words, image consultants can either function as shoppers (legs) or, more commonly, as stylists (heads).

Kathleen McGrath, CFO of Implemented Software Solutions, Inc. in Long Island City, N.Y. is one example of an executive who opted to hire an image consultant's "head" for a full-blown overhaul. "Because we work for attorneys," she explains, "there's a certain look that needs to be maintained."

At an image consultant's suggestion, McGrath paired her gray suits with blouses in warm, cheerful colors and discarded her out-of-date pieces. She spent about $1,500 on new suits, dresses, shoes, and accessories. Although McGrath says she was "very satisfied" with the image consultant's services she acknowledges that there are some risks. "You're introducing someone else's tastes and preferences into your own appearance, which is a very personal thing," she says.

Despite the fact that "You never get a second chance to make a first impression," some feel that what's inside, the real person, is being given short shrift in favor of what an image consultant *perceives* your image should be.

Of course deciding to hire an image consultant for yourself is one thing. Breaking the news to an unsuspecting employee is quite another. Besides being prepared to shell out the consultant's hourly fee, you'll be faced with the horrific task of advising valued employees that their image isn't quite up to snuff. That in itself is enough to make any manager want to crawl under a desk and forget the whole idea. After all, employees don't wake up in the morning and decide not to look their best. But there are more important questions to be asked here: Do managers have the right to demand a specific kind of image from their employees? Where do we draw the line between corporate image and personal freedom?[12]

Characteristics of the Situation

The second major influence on how we perceive others is the situation in which the perceptual process occurs. Two situational influences can be identified: (1) the organization and the employee's place in it, and (2) the location of the event.

Organizational Role.   An employee's place in the organizational hierarchy can also influence his or her perceptions. A classic study of managers by Dearborn and Simon emphasizes this point. In this study, executives from various departments (accounting, sales, production) were asked to read a detailed and factual case about a steel company.[13] Next, each executive was asked to identify the major problem a new president of the company should address. The findings showed clearly that the executives' perceptions of the most important problems in the company were influenced by the departments in which they worked. Sales executives saw sales as the biggest problem, whereas production executives cited production issues. Industrial relations and public relations executives identified human relations as the primary problem in need of attention.

In addition to perceptual differences emerging horizontally across departments, such differences can also be found when we move vertically up or down the hierarchy. The most obvious difference here is seen between managers and unions, where the former see profits, production, and sales as vital areas of concern for the company, whereas the latter place much greater emphasis on wages, working conditions, and job security. Indeed, our views of managers and workers are clearly influenced by the group to which we belong. The positions we occupy in organizations can easily color how we view our work world and those in it. Consider the results of a classic study of

Exhibit 3.4
Differences in Perception
between Supervisors
and Subordinates

Types of Recognition	Frequency with Which Supervisors Give Various Types of Recognition for Good Performance	
	As Seen by Supervisors	**As Seen by Subordinates**
Gives privileges	52%	14%
Gives more responsibility	48	10
Gives a pat on the back	82	13
Gives sincere and thorough praise	80	14
Trains for better jobs	64	9
Gives more interesting work	51	5

Source: Adapted from R. Likert, *New Patterns in Management* (New York: McGraw-Hill, 1961), p. 91. Used by permission of McGraw-Hill, Inc.

perceptual differences between superiors and subordinates.[14] Both groups were asked how often the supervisor gave various forms of feedback to the employees. The results, shown in Exhibit 3.4, demonstrate striking differences based on one's location in the organizational hierarchy.

Location of Event.   Finally, how we interpret events is also influenced by where the event occurs. Behaviors that may be appropriate at home, such as taking off one's shoes, may be inappropriate in the office. Acceptable customs vary from country to country. For instance, assertiveness may be a desirable trait for a sales representative in the United States, but it may be seen as being brash or coarse in Japan or China. Hence, the context in which the perceptual activity takes place is important.

Characteristics of the Perceiver

The third major influence on social perception is the personality and viewpoint of the perceiver. Several characteristics unique to our personalities can affect how we see others. These include (1) self-concept, (2) cognitive structure, (3) response salience, and (4) previous experience with the individual.[15]

Self-Concept.   Our self-concept represents a major influence on how we perceive others. This influence is manifested in several ways. First, when we understand ourselves (i.e., can accurately describe our own personal characteristics), we are better able to perceive others accurately. Second, when we accept ourselves (i.e., have a positive self-image), we are more likely to see favorable characteristics in others. Studies have shown that if we accept ourselves as we are, we broaden our view of others and are more likely to view people uncritically. Conversely, less secure people often find faults in others. Third, our own personal characteristics influence the characteristics we notice in others. For instance, people with authoritarian tendencies (see Chapter 2) tend to view others in terms of power, whereas secure people tend to see others as warm rather than cold.[16] From a management standpoint, these findings emphasize how important it is for administrators to understand themselves; they also provide justification for the human relations training programs that are popular in many organizations today.

Cognitive Structure.   Our cognitive structures also influence how we view people. People describe each other differently. Some use physical characteristics such as tall or short, whereas others use central descriptions such as deceitful, forceful, or meek. Still others have more complex cognitive structures and use multiple traits in their descriptions of others; hence, a person may be described as being aggressive, honest, friendly, *and* hardworking. (See the discussion in Chapter 2 on cognitive complexity.) Ostensibly, the greater our cognitive complexity—our ability to differentiate between people using multiple criteria—the more accurate our perception of others. People who tend to make more complex assessments of others also tend to be more positive in their appraisals.[17] Research in this area highlights the importance of selecting managers who exhibit high degrees of cognitive complexity. These individuals should form more accurate perceptions of the strengths and weaknesses of their subordinates and should be able to capitalize on their strengths while ignoring or working to overcome their weaknesses.

Response Salience.   This refers to our sensitivity to objects in the environment as influenced by our particular needs or desires. Response salience can play an important role in social perception because we have a tendency to see what we *want* to see. A company personnel manager who has a bias against women, minorities, or handicapped persons would tend to be adversely sensitive to them during an employment interview. This focus may cause the manager to look for other potentially negative traits in the candidate to confirm his biases. The influence of positive arbitrary biases is called the *halo effect* where as the influence of negative biases is often called the *horn effect.* Another personnel manager without these biases would be much less inclined to be influenced by these characteristics when viewing prospective job candidates.

Previous Experience with the Individual.   Our previous experiences with others often will influence the way in which we view their current behavior. When an employee has consistently received poor performance evaluations, a marked improvement in performance may go unnoticed because the supervisor continues to think of the individual as a poor performer. Similarly, employees who begin their careers with several successes develop a reputation as fast-track individuals and may continue to rise in the organization long after their performance has leveled off or even declined. The impact of previous experience on present perceptions should be respected and studied by students of management. For instance, when a previously poor performer earnestly tries to perform better, it is important for this improvement to be recognized early and properly rewarded. Otherwise, employees may give up, feeling that nothing they do will make any difference.

Together, these factors determine the impressions we form of others (see Exhibit 3.3 on page 70). With these impressions, we make conscious and unconscious decisions about how we intend to behave toward people. Our behavior toward others, in turn, influences the way they regard us. Consequently, the importance of understanding the perceptual process, as well as factors that contribute to it, is apparent for managers. A better understanding of ourselves and careful attention to others leads to more accurate perceptions and more appropriate actions.

BARRIERS TO ACCURATE SOCIAL PERCEPTION

In the perceptual process, several barriers can be identified that inhibit the accuracy of our perception. These barriers are (1) stereotyping, (2) selective perception, and (3) perceptual defense. Each of these will be briefly considered as it relates to social perception in work situations (see Exhibit 3.5).

Stereotyping

One of the most common barriers in perceiving others at work is *stereotyping*. A stereotype is a widely held generalization about a group of people. Stereotyping is a process in which attributes are assigned to people solely on the basis of their class or category. It is particularly likely to occur when one meets new people, since very little is known about them at that time. On the basis of a few prominent characteristics such as sex, race, or age we tend to place people into a few general categories. We ascribe a series of traits to them based upon the attributes of the category in which we have put them. We assume that older people are old-fashioned, conservative, obstinate, and, perhaps, senile. We view professors as absentminded, impractical, idealistic, or eccentric.

One explanation for the existence of stereotypes has been suggested by Triandis.[18] He argues that stereotypes may be to some extent based upon fact. People tend to compare other groups with their own group, accentuating minor differences between groups to form a stereotype. For example, older people as a group may indeed be more conservative or more old-fashioned. These traits then become emphasized and attributed to particular older individuals.

At least three types of stereotype can be found in organizations: those dealing with age, race, and gender. Age stereotypes can be found throughout

Exhibit 3.5
Barriers to Accurate
Perception of Others

Barrier	Definition
Stereotyping	A tendency to assign attributes to people solely on the basis of their class or category.
Selective perception	A process by which we systematically screen out or discredit information we don't wish to hear and focus instead on more salient information.
Perceptual defense	A tendency to distort or ignore information that is either personally threatening or culturally unacceptable.

organizations. A study by Rosen and Jerdee[19] found that some business students have clear stereotypes of older employees. They are thought to be (1) more resistant to organizational change, (2) less creative, (3) less likely to take calculated risks, (4) lower in physical capacity, (5) less interested in learning new techniques, and (6) less capable of learning new techniques. When asked to make personnel decisions concerning older people, the business students generally followed several trends. First, they gave older people lower consideration in promotion decisions. Older people also received less attention and fewer resources for training and development. Finally, older people tended to be transferred to other departments instead of confronted by their superiors when a problem with their performance emerged.

Similar problems arise for people from different racial or cultural backgrounds and for gender. A particular problem in many companies today is that of attitudes toward women as managers or executives. Although to succeed in a managerial position is always difficult, the job is all the harder if your co-workers, superiors, or subordinates are not supportive. As an exercise, you may want to complete Self-Assessment 3.2, which will illuminate your own attitudes toward women as executives. After you have completed the ten items, refer to Appendix B.

IN PRACTICE
To See Ourselves As Others See Us

International Challenge

In considering stereotyping in organizations, it may be interesting to examine how people in different countries and cultures see others around the world. Specifically, we should note that "foreigners" often hold certain stereotypes of what a "typical" American looks and acts like. Look, for example, at Exhibit 3.6. This table shows how people in seven countries around the globe view the typical American. Note the sizable differences in perceptions. Moreover, in a separate study, people from six other countries were asked to describe an average American. Exhibit 3.7 shows the terms most (and least) frequently used to describe us.

When examining these exhibits, consider the extent to which you think these perceptions and stereotypes are accurate or inaccurate. Why do people in different countries form such divergent opinions of our country? How do their perceptions color the behavior and effectiveness of American managers working abroad? On the basis of this assessment, you might want to reassess your own stereotypes of people in different countries. How accurate do you think your own stereotypes have been?

Selective Perception

Selective perception is the process by which we systematically screen out information we don't wish to hear, focusing instead on more salient information. Saliency here is obviously a function of our own experiences, needs, and orientations. The example of the Dearborn and Simon[20] study of managers described earlier provides an excellent glimpse of selective perception.

SELF-ASSESSMENT 3.2
How Do You Feel About Women Executives?

Instructions: This instrument focuses on your attitudes toward women in executive positions. For each item, circle the number that best represents your feelings concerning women executives in organizations. Be completely honest with yourself in responding.

		Strongly Disagree				Strongly Agree
1.	It is high time we had more women in executive positions.	1	2	3	4	5
2.	Women make just as good managers as men.	1	2	3	4	5
3.	Women often fail to have the same level of technical competence as men.	1	2	3	4	5
4.	Women executives should receive the same respect and trust as their male counterparts.	1	2	3	4	5
5.	Men tend to be better suited for managerial positions than women.	1	2	3	4	5
6.	Women are too emotional to succeed in top-level management.	1	2	3	4	5
7.	Women have a hard time supervising the work of male subordinates.	1	2	3	4	5
8.	I would prefer not to work for a female manager.	1	2	3	4	5
9.	Success as an executive has nothing to do with one's gender.	1	2	3	4	5
10.	Many women executives get to the top either because of affirmative action pressure or connections.	1	2	3	4	5

Production managers focused on production problems to the exclusion of other problems. Accountants, personnel specialists, and sales managers were similarly exclusive. Everyone saw his or her own specialty as more important in the company than other specialties.

Another example of selective perception in groups and organizations is provided by Miner.[21] Miner summarizes a series of experiments dealing with groups competing on problem-solving exercises. Consistently, the groups tended to evaluate their own solutions as better than the solutions proposed by others. Such findings resemble a syndrome found in many research organizations. There is a frequent tendency for scientists to view ideas or products originating outside their organization or department as inferior and to judge

Exhibit 3.6
Foreign Observations
of Americans

The following are quotations from foreign visitors to the United States:

India: "Americans seem to be in a perpetual hurry. Just watch the way they walk down the street. They never allow themselves the leisure to enjoy life; there are too many things to do."

Kenya: "Americans appear to us rather distant. They are not really as close to other people—even fellow Americans—as Americans overseas tend to portray. It's almost as if an American says, 'I won't let you get too close to me.' It's like building a wall."

Turkey: "Once we were out in a rural area in the middle of nowhere and saw an American come to a stop sign. Though he could see in both directions for miles and no traffic was coming, he still stopped!"

Colombia: "The tendency in the United States to think that life is only work hits you in the face. Work seems to be the one type of motivation."

Indonesia: "In the United States everything has to be talked about and analyzed. Even the littlest thing has to be 'Why, Why, Why?' I get a headache from such persistent questions."

Ethiopia: "The American is very explicit; he wants a 'yes' or 'no.' If someone tries to speak figuratively, the American is confused."

Iran: "The first time . . . my [American] professor told me, 'I don't know the answer, I will have to look it up,' I was shocked. I asked myself, 'Why is he teaching me?' In my country a professor would give the wrong answer rather than admit ignorance."

Source: J. Feig and G. Blair, *There Is a Difference,* 2nd ed., (Washington: Meridian House International). Reprinted by permission. Meridian House International is an organization that conducts intercultural training for visitors to the U.S. and for Americans going abroad.

Exhibit 3.7
Characteristics Most Often
Associated with Americans

*Characteristics most often associated with Americans by the populations of:**

France	Japan	West Germany	Great Britain	Brazil	Mexico
Industrious	Nationalistic	Energetic	Friendly	Intelligent	Industrious
Energetic	Friendly	Inventive	Self-indulgent	Inventive	Intelligent
Inventive	Decisive	Friendly	Energetic	Energetic	Inventive
Decisive	Rude	Sophisticated	Industrious	Industrious	Decisive
Friendly	Self-indulgent	Intelligent	Nationalistic	Greedy	Greedy

*Characteristics least often associated with Americans by the same populations:**

Lazy	Industrious	Lazy	Lazy	Lazy	Lazy
Rude	Lazy	Sexy	Sophisticated	Self-indulgent	Honest
Honest	Honest	Greedy	Sexy	Sexy	Rude
Sophisticated	Sexy	Rude	Decisive	Sophisticated	Sexy

From a list of fourteen characteristics.

Source: "A Newsweek Poll: How Others See Americans," *Newsweek,* July 11, 1983. Copyright © 1983, Newsweek, Inc. All rights reserved. Reprinted by permission.

other researchers as less competent and creative than themselves. This is often referred to as the "Not-Invented-Here" syndrome. Similar patterns of behavior can be found among managers, service workers, and secretaries.

Perceptual Defense

A final barrier to social perception is *perceptual defense*.[22] Perceptual defense is founded on three related principles:

1. Emotionally disturbing or threatening stimuli have a higher recognition threshold than neutral stimuli;
2. such stimuli are likely to elicit substitute perceptions that are radically altered so as to prevent recognition of the presented stimuli;
3. these critical stimuli arouse emotional reactions even though the stimuli are not recognized.

In other words, through perceptual defense we tend to distort or ignore information that is either personally threatening or culturally unacceptable. Because emotionally disturbing stimuli have a higher recognition threshold, people are less likely to fully confront or acknowledge the threat. Instead, they may see entirely different or even erroneous stimuli that are safer. Even so, the presence of the critical stimulus often leads to heightened emotions despite the lack of recognition. For instance, suppose that during a contract negotiation for an assembly plant, word leaked out that because of declining profits, the plant might have to close down permanently. Anxious workers might ignore this message and instead choose to believe the company management is only starting false rumors to increase their leverage during wage negotiations. Even if the leverage claim is accepted by the workers as truth, strong emotional reactions against the company can be expected.

One effect of perceptual defense is to save us from squarely facing events that we either do not wish to handle or may be incapable of handling. We dissipate our emotions by directing our attention to other (substitute) objects and hope the original event that distressed us will eventually disappear.

Perceptual defense is especially pronounced when people are presented with a situation that contradicts their long-held beliefs and attitudes. In a classic study of perceptual defense among college students, Haire and Grunes presented the students with descriptions of factory workers. Included in these descriptions was the word *intelligent*. Because the word was contrary to the students' beliefs concerning factory workers, they chose to reject the description by using perceptual defenses.[23] Four such defense mechanisms can be identified:[24]

1. *Denial.* A few of the subjects denied the existence of intelligence in factory workers.
2. *Modification and distortion.* This was one of the most frequent forms of defense. The pattern was to explain away the perceptual conflict by joining intelligence with some other characteristics; for instance, "He is intelligent but doesn't possess initiative to rise above his group."

3. *Change in perception.* Many students changed their perception of the worker because of the intelligence characteristic. Most of the change, however, was very subtle; for example, "cracks jokes" became "witty."
4. *Recognition, but refusal to change.* A very few students explicitly recognized the conflict between their perception of the worker and the characteristic that was confronting them. For example, one subject stated, "The trait seems to be conflicting . . . most factory workers I have heard about aren't too intelligent."

Perceptual defense makes any situation in which conflict is likely to be present more difficult. It creates blind spots causing us to fail to hear and see events as they really are. The challenge for managers is to reduce or minimize the perception of threat in a situation so these defenses are not immediately called into play. This can be accomplished by reassuring people that things that are important to them will not be tampered with, or by accentuating the positive.

ATTRIBUTIONS: INTERPRETING THE CAUSES OF BEHAVIOR

A major influence on how people behave is the way they interpret the events around them. People who feel they have control over what happens to them are more likely to accept responsibility for their actions than those who feel control of events is out of their hands. The cognitive process by which people interpret the reasons or causes for their behavior is described by *attribution theory.*[25] Specifically, "attribution theory concerns the process by which an individual interprets events as being caused by a particular part of a relatively stable environment."[26]

Attribution theory is based largely on the work of Fritz Heider. Heider argues that behavior is determined by a combination of internal forces (e.g., abilities or effort) and external forces (e.g., task difficulty or luck). Following the cognitive approach of Lewin and Tolman, he emphasizes that it is *perceived* determinants, rather than actual ones, that influence behavior. Hence, if employees perceive that their success is a function of their own abilities and efforts, they can be expected to behave differently than they would if they believed job success was due to chance.

The Attribution Process

The underlying assumption of attribution theory is that people are motivated to understand their environment and the causes of particular events. If individuals can understand these causes, they will then be in a better position to influence or control the sequence of future events. This process is diagrammed in Exhibit 3.8. Specifically, attribution theory suggests that particular behavioral events (e.g., the receipt of a promotion) are analyzed by individuals to determine their causes. This process may lead to the conclusion that the promotion resulted from the individual's own effort or, alternatively, from some other cause, such as luck. Based on

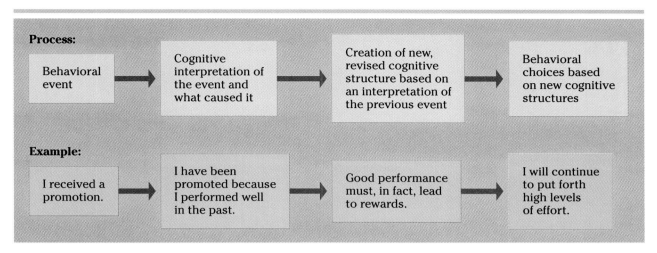

Exhibit 3.8
The General
Attribution Process

such cognitive interpretations of events, individuals revise their cognitive structures and rethink their assumptions about causal relationships. For instance, an individual may infer that performance does indeed lead to promotion. Based on this new structure, the individual makes choices about future behavior. In some cases, the individual may decide to continue exerting high levels of effort in the hope that it will lead to further promotions. On the other hand, if an individual concludes that the promotion resulted primarily from chance and was largely unrelated to performance, a different cognitive structure might be created, and there might be little reason to continue exerting high levels of effort. In other words, the way in which we perceive and interpret events around us significantly affects our future behaviors.

Internal and External Causes of Behavior

Building upon the work of Heider, Harold Kelley attempted to identify the major antecedents of internal and external attributions.[27] He examined how people determine—or, rather, how they actually perceive—whether the behavior of another person results from internal or external causes. Internal causes include ability and effort, whereas external causes include luck and task ease or difficulty.[28] Kelley's conclusion, illustrated in Exhibit 3.9, is that people actually focus in on three factors when making causal attributions:

1. *Consensus.* The extent to which you believe that the person being observed is behaving in a manner that is consistent with the behavior of his or her peers. High consensus exists when the person's actions reflect, or are similar to, the actions of the group; low consensus exists when the person's actions do not.
2. *Consistency.* The extent to which you believe that the person being observed behaves consistently—in a similar fashion—when confronted

Exhibit 3.9
Causes of Internal and
External Attributions

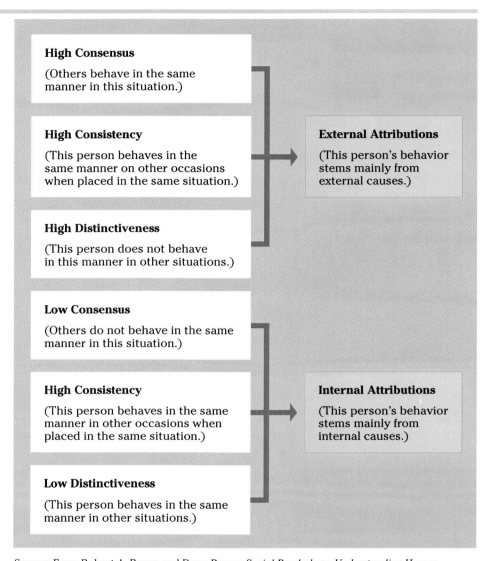

High Consensus

(Others behave in the same
manner in this situation.)

High Consistency

(This person behaves in the
same manner on other occasions
when placed in the same situation.)

High Distinctiveness

(This person does not behave
in this manner in other situations.)

External Attributions

(This person's behavior
stems mainly from
external causes.)

Low Consensus

(Others do not behave in the same
manner in this situation.)

High Consistency

(This person behaves in the same
manner in other occasions when
placed in the same situation.)

Low Distinctiveness

(This person behaves in the same
manner in other situations.)

Internal Attributions

(This person's behavior
stems mainly from
internal causes.)

Source: From Robert A. Baron and Donn Byrne. *Social Psychology: Understanding Human
Interaction.* Fifth Edition. Copyright © 1987 by Allyn and Bacon. Reprinted with permission.

on other occasions with the same or similar situations. High consistency
exists when the person repeatedly acts in the same way when faced with
similar stimuli.

3. *Distinctiveness.* The extent to which you believe that the person being
observed would behave consistently when faced with different situations. Low distinctiveness exists when the person acts in a similar manner in response to different stimuli; high distinctiveness exists when the
person varies his or her response to different situations.

How do these three factors interact to influence whether one's attributions are internal or external? According to the exhibit, under conditions of

high consensus, high consistency, and high distinctiveness, we would expect the observer to make external attributions about the causes of behavior. That is, the person would attribute the behavior of the observed (say, winning a golf tournament) to good fortune or some other external event. On the other hand, when consensus is low, consistency is high, and distinctiveness is low, we would expect the observer to attribute the observed behavior (winning the golf tournament) to internal causes (the winner's skill).

In other words, we tend to explain the reasons behind the success or failure of others to either internal or external causes according to how we interpret the underlying forces associated with the others' behavior. Consider the example of the first female sales manager in a firm to be promoted to an executive rank. How do you explain her promotion—luck and connections or ability and performance? To find out, follow the model. If she, as a sales representative, had sold more than her (male) counterparts (low consensus in behavior), consistently sold the primary product line in different sales territories (high consistency), and was also able to sell different product lines (low distinctiveness), we would more than likely attribute her promotion to her own abilities. On the other hand, if her male counterparts were also good sales representatives (high consensus) and her sales record on secondary products was inconsistent (high distinctiveness), people would probably attribute her promotion to luck or connections, regardless of her sales performance on the primary product line (high consistency).

Attributional Bias

One final point should be made with respect to the attributional process. In making attributions concerning the causes of behavior, people tend to make certain errors of interpretation. Two such errors, or biases, should be noted here. The first is called the *fundamental attribution error.* This error is a tendency to *underestimate* the effects of external or situational causes of behavior and to *overestimate* the effects of internal or personal causes. Hence, when a major problem occurs within a certain department, we tend to blame people rather than events or situations.

The second error in attribution processes is generally called the *self-serving bias.* There is a tendency, not surprisingly, for individuals to attribute success on an event or project to his or her own actions while attributing failure to others. Hence, we often hear sales representatives saying "*I* made the sale," but "*They* stole the sale from me" rather than "I lost it." These two biases in interpreting how we see the events around us help us understand why employees looking at the same event often see substantially different things.

ATTITUDES AND BEHAVIOR

Closely related to the topic of perception and attribution—indeed, largely influenced by it—is the issue of attitudes. An *attitude* can be defined as a predisposition to respond in a favorable or unfavorable way to objects or persons in one's environment.[29] When we like or dislike something, we are, in effect, expressing our attitude toward the person or object.

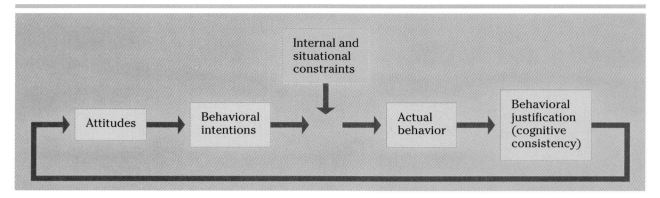

Exhibit 3.10
Relationship Between
Attitudes and Behavior

Three important aspects of this definition should be noted. First, an attitude is a hypothetical construct; that is, although its consequences can be observed, the attitude itself cannot. Second, an attitude is a unidimensional concept: An attitude toward a particular person or object ranges on a continuum from very favorable to very unfavorable. We like something or we dislike something (or we are neutral). Something is pleasurable or unpleasurable. In all cases, the attitude can be evaluated along a single evaluative continuum. And third, attitudes are believed to be related to subsequent behavior. We will return to this point later in the discussion.

An attitude can be thought of as composed of three highly interrelated components: (1) a *cognitive* component, dealing with the beliefs and ideas a person has about a person or object; (2) an *affective* component, dealing with a person's feelings toward the person or object; and (3) an *intentional* component, dealing with the behavioral intentions a person has with respect to the person or object.[30]

Now that we know what an attitude is, let us consider how attitudes are formed and how they influence behavior. A general model of the relationship between attitudes and behavior is shown in Exhibit 3.10. As can be seen, attitudes lead to behavioral intentions, which, in turn, lead to actual behavior. Following behavior, we can often identify efforts by the individual to justify his or her behavior. Let us examine each of these components of the model separately, beginning with the process of attitude formation.

How Are Attitudes Formed?

There is considerable disagreement about this question. One view offered by psychologist Barry Staw and others is the *dispositional approach*,[31] which argues that attitudes represent relatively stable predispositions to respond to people or situations around them. That is, attitudes are viewed almost as personality traits. Thus, some people would have a tendency—a predisposition—to be happy on the job, almost regardless of the nature of the work itself. Others may have an internal tendency to be unhappy, again almost regardless of the actual nature of the work. Evidence in support of this approach can be found in a series of studies that found that attitudes change very little among people before and after they make a job change. To the extent that these findings are correct, managers may have little influence over improving job attitudes short of trying to select and hire only those with appropriate dispositions.

A second approach to attitude formation is called the *situational approach*. This approach argues that attitudes emerge as a result of the uniqueness of a given situation. They are situationally determined and can vary in response to changing work conditions. Thus, as a result of experiences at work (a boring or unrewarding job, a bad supervisor, etc.), people react by developing appropriate attitudes. Several variations on this approach can be identified. Some researchers suggest that attitudes result largely from the nature of the job experience themselves. That is, an employee might reason: "I don't get along well with my supervisor; therefore, I become dissatisfied with my job." To the extent that this accurately describes how attitudes are formed, it also implies that attitudes can be changed relatively easily. For example, if employees are dissatisfied with their job because of conflicts with supervisors, either changing supervisors or changing the supervisors' behavior may be viable means of improving employee job attitudes. In other words, if attitudes are largely a function of the situation, then attitudes can be changed by altering the situation.

Other advocates of the situational approach suggest a somewhat more complicated process of attitude formation—namely, the *social-information-processing approach*. This view, developed by Pfeffer and Salancik, asserts that attitudes result from "socially constructed realities" as perceived by the individual (see Exhibit 3.11).[32] That is, the social context in which the individual is placed shapes his or her perceptions of the situation and hence his or her attitudes.

Here is how it works. Suppose a new employee joins a work group consisting of people who have worked together for some time. The existing group already has opinions and feelings about the fairness of the supervisor, the quality of the workplace, the adequacy of the compensation, and

Exhibit 3.11
A Social-Information-Processing View of Attitudes

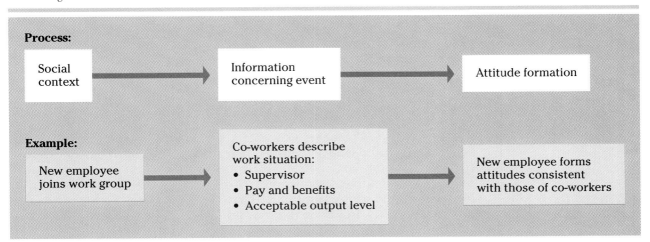

Process:

Social context → Information concerning event → Attitude formation

Example:

New employee joins work group → Co-workers describe work situation:
• Supervisor
• Pay and benefits
• Acceptable output level
→ New employee forms attitudes consistent with those of co-workers

so forth. Upon arriving, the new worker is fed socially acceptable cues from co-workers about acceptable attitudes toward various aspects of the work and company. Thus, due in part to social forces, the new employee begins to form attitudes based on externally provided bits of information from the group instead of objective attributes of the workplace. If the social-information-processing perspective is correct, changing the attitudes of one person will be difficult unless the individual is moved to a different group of co-workers or unless the attitudes of the current co-workers are changed.

Which approach is correct? In point of fact, research indicates that both the dispositional and the social-information-processing views have merit, and it is probably wise to recognize that socially constructed realities and dispositions interact to form the basis for an individual's attitudes at work. The implication of this combined perspective for changing attitudes is that efforts should not assume that minor alterations in the situation will have significant impacts on individual attitudes but that systematic efforts focusing on groups and interconnected social systems are likely required for successful changes in attitudes.

Behavioral Intentions and Actual Behavior

Regardless of how the attitudes are formed (either through the dispositional or social-information-processing approach), the next problem we face is understanding how resulting behavioral intentions guide actual behavior (return to Exhibit 3.10). Clearly, this relationship is not a perfect one. Despite one's intentions, various internal and external constraints often serve to modify an intended course of action. Hence, even though you decide to join the union, you may be prevented from doing so for a variety of reasons. Similarly, a person may have every intention of coming to work but may get the flu. Regardless of intent, other factors that also determine actual behavior often enter the picture.

Behavioral Justification

Finally, people often feel a need to ensure that their behaviors are consistent with their attitudes toward the event (see Exhibit 3.10). This tendency is called *cognitive consistency*.[33] When people find themselves acting in a fashion that is inconsistent with their attitudes—when they experience *cognitive dissonance*—they experience tension and attempt to reduce this tension and return to a state of cognitive consistency.

For example, a manager may hate her job but be required to work long hours. Hence, she is faced with a clear discrepancy between an attitude (dislike of the job) and a behavior (working long hours) and will probably experience cognitive dissonance. In order to become cognitively consistent, she can do one of two things. First, she can change her behavior and work fewer hours. However, this may not be feasible. Alternatively, she can change her attitude toward the job to a more positive one. She may, for example, convince herself that the job is really not that bad and that working long hours may lead to rapid promotion. In doing so, she achieves a state of cognitive consistency. Failure to do so will more than likely lead to increased stress and withdrawal from the job situation.

WORK-RELATED ATTITUDES

When we apply the concept of attitudes to work settings, we have to specify which attitude we are concerned with. Although a variety of work-related attitudes can be identified, the one receiving most attention is job satisfaction. As this is one of the most widely studied concepts in organizational behavior, we will examine it here in some detail.

Job Involvement and Organizational Commitment

First, however, we should introduce two job attitudes that should also be recognized: job involvement and organizational commitment. *Job involvement* refers to the extent to which a person is interested in and committed to assigned tasks. This is not to say that the person is "happy" (or satisfied) with the job, only that he or she feels a certain responsibility toward ensuring that the job itself is done correctly and with a high standard of competence. Here the focus of the attitude is the job itself.[34]

Organizational commitment, on the other hand, represents the relative strength of an individual's identification with and involvement in an organization.[35] Commitment can be characterized by three factors: (1) a strong belief in and acceptance of the organization's goals and values, (2) a willingness to exert considerable effort on behalf of the organization, and (3) a strong desire to maintain membership in the organization. When viewed this way, commitment represents something beyond mere passive loyalty to the company. Instead, it involves an active relationship with the organization in which individuals are willing to give something of themselves in order to help the company succeed and prosper. A careful reading of the research on keys to the success of many Japanese firms will highlight the importance played by a committed work force. Now we turn to the third work attitude of job satisfaction.

Job Satisfaction

Job satisfaction may be defined as "a pleasurable or positive emotional state resulting from the appraisal of one's job or job experience."[36] It results from the perception that an employee's job actually provides what he or she values in the work situation.

Several characteristics of the concept of job satisfaction follow from this definition. First, satisfaction is an emotional response to a job situation. It can be fully understood only by introspection. As with any attitude, we cannot observe satisfaction; we must infer its existence and quality either from an employee's behavior or verbal statements.

Second, job satisfaction is perhaps best understood in terms of discrepancy. Several writers have pointed to the concept of job satisfaction as being a result of how much a person wants or expects from the job compared to how much he or she actually receives.[37] People come to work with varying levels of job expectations. These expectations may vary not only in quality (different people may value different things in a job), but also in intensity. On the basis of work experiences, people receive outcomes (rewards) from the job. These include not only extrinsic rewards, such as pay and promotion, but also a variety of intrinsic rewards, such as satisfying co-worker relations and meaningful work. To the extent that the outcomes received by an employee meet or exceed expectations, we would expect the employee to be satisfied with the job and wish to remain. On those occasions when outcomes actually surpass expectations, we would expect employees to reevaluate their expectations and probably raise them to meet available outcomes. However, when outcomes do not meet expectations, employees are dissatisfied and may prefer to seek alternative sources of satisfaction, either by changing jobs or by placing greater value on other life activities, such as outside recreation.

Dimensions of Job Satisfaction. It has been argued that job satisfaction actually represents several related attitudes. So, when we speak of satisfaction, we must specify "satisfaction with what?" Research has suggested that five job dimensions represent the most salient characteristics of a job about which people have affective responses. These five are:

1. *Work itself.* The extent to which tasks performed by employees are interesting and provide opportunities for learning and for accepting responsibility.
2. *Pay.* The amount of pay received, the perceived equity of the pay, and the method of payment.
3. *Promotional opportunities.* The availability of realistic opportunities for advancement.
4. *Supervision.* The technical and managerial abilities of supervisors, the extent to which supervisors demonstrate consideration for and interest in employees.
5. *Co-workers.* The extent to which co-workers are friendly, technically competent, and supportive.

Although other dimensions of job satisfaction have been identified, these five dimensions are used most often when assessing various aspects of job attitudes in organizations.

Measurement of Job Satisfaction. Probably the most common attitude surveys in organizations today focus on job satisfaction. Satisfaction is

SELF-ASSESSMENT 3.3
Are You Satisfied with Your Job?

Instructions: Answer each of the ten questions by circling the numbers that best describe how satisfied or dissatisfied you are with the particular item. Then sum your results for questions 1–5 and 6–10 separately.

	Very Dissatisfied				Very Satisfied
1. The way I am noticed when I do a good job	1	2	3	4	5
2. The way I get full credit for the work I do	1	2	3	4	5
3. The recognition I get for the work I do	1	2	3	4	5
4. The way they usually tell me when I do my job well	1	2	3	4	5
5. The praise I get for doing a good job	1	2	3	4	5
6. The amount of pay for the work I do	1	2	3	4	5
7. The chance to make as much money as my friends	1	2	3	4	5
8. How my pay compares with that for similar jobs in other companies	1	2	3	4	5
9. My pay and the amount of work I do	1	2	3	4	5
10. How my pay compares with that of other workers	1	2	3	4	5

Source: Adapted from David J. Weiss, Rene V. Dawis, George W. England, and Lloyd H. Lofquist, *Manual for the Minnesota Satisfaction Questionnaire* (Minneapolis: Industrial Relations Center, University of Minnesota, 1967). Used with permission.

considered by many managers to be an important indicator of organizational effectiveness, and, therefore, it is regularly monitored to assess employee feelings toward the organization. By far the most common means of assessing satisfaction is the rating scale. Rating scales represent direct verbal self-reports concerning employee feelings; they have been widely used in companies since the 1930s. Several job satisfaction scales exist. One of the most popular is the Minnesota Satisfaction Questionnaire (MSQ). This instrument uses a Likert-response format to generate satisfaction scores on 26 scales, including satisfaction with compensation, promotion opportunities, co-workers, recognition, and so forth.

Examples of the MSQ for two of these scales (compensation and recognition) can be seen in Self-Assessment 3.3. If you wish to complete this sample questionnaire, simply refer to a (paid or unpaid) job that you have had and answer the questionnaire. To score the instrument, refer to Appendix B.

The MSQ and similar rating scales have several advantages for evaluating levels of job satisfaction. First, they are relatively short and simple and can be completed by large numbers of employees quickly. Second, because of the generalized wording of the various terms, the instruments can be administered to a wide range of employees in various jobs. It is not necessary to alter the questionnaire for each job classification. Finally, extensive normative data (or norms) are available. These norms include summaries of the scores of thousands of people who have completed the instruments. Hence, it is possible for employers in other organizations to determine relative standings.

However, although rating scales have many virtues compared to other techniques, at least two drawbacks must be recognized. First, as with any self-report inventory, it is assumed that respondents are both willing and able to describe their feelings accurately. As noted by several researchers,[38] people often consciously or unconsciously distort information that they feel is damaging and enhance information that they feel is beneficial. For example, it is possible that employees who think their supervisors may see the results of their questionnaire may report overly favorable job attitudes.

A second problem with rating scales is the underlying assumption that questionnaire items mean the same thing to all people. There may, in fact, not be a common interpretation across individuals. Even so, rating scales have proved to be helpful in assessing satisfaction in various aspects of the job situation. Managers can use the results to identify potential problem areas and to generate discussions and action plans of how to correct aspects of jobs or the organization that are causing unacceptable levels of dissatisfaction.

IN PRACTICE
How Satisfied Are Employees?

Managers often discuss ways of improving job attitudes in the workplace. Central to these discussions is the question of how satisfied employees are with their work. Through a variety of means, companies are continually attempting to assess this variable. Most often, companies or industrial groupings use anonymous attitude surveys among random samples to see how people actually feel about their jobs.

"[The notion] of work hard, do a good job, and you will be rewarded has been flushed down a U.S.A. toilet," asserts a California middle manager.

Across the U.S., in companies large, small, and in-between, ranks of smiling employees are about as rare as a blizzard in Phoenix. Only among senior executives surveyed—chairmen, presidents, and CEOs—do smiles outnumber scowls. But even in executive offices, nearly one-fifth of the occupants these days find no joy on the job, indicates an Industry Week survey conducted during late August and early September of 1992.

Significantly, among middle managers and first-line supervisors, sourpusses are more common now than in late 1990. Nearly 70% of all middle managers in this survey find no fun at work. In contrast, only 63% of a similar group surveyed in 1990 were scowling.

Employees most frequently cite the absence of teamwork as their reason for job dissatisfaction. Suggesting that actions lag well behind all the words about team-building, nearly 61 percent of all respondents claim there's something akin to a "dog-eat-dog" atmosphere where they work. Among middle managers and first-line supervisors, 57 percent of respondents in the current survey decry the absence of teamwork, compared with 49 percent of the group surveyed in late 1990. Comparing only middle managers and first-line supervisors, scowls stemming from an absence of praise are eight percentage points more numerous now (38.5 percent) than in late 1990 (30 percent).

Is it fun where you work?	1992 data	1990 data
No	67%	63%
Yes	33%	37%

Who's not having fun?	
Vice presidents	61.3%
Middle management	63.1%
First-line supervisors	77.6%
Non-management	74.8%

However we look at it, companies have to put their money where their mouths are; if they want increased commitment and improved motivation, they have to provide the necessary incentives. As most employees will note, working for a company represents an exchange relationship in which both partners must give something. We shall say more about this subject in Chapters 5 and 6.[39]

PULLING IT ALL TOGETHER

One of the key determinants of people's behavior in organizations is how they see and interpret situations and people around them. It is vital for anyone (manager or subordinate) who desires to be more effective to understand the critical aspects of context, object, and perceiver that influence perceptions and interpretations and the relationship between these and subsequent attitudes, intentions, and behaviors. This understanding will not only facilitate the ability to correctly understand and anticipate behaviors but it will also enhance the ability to change or influence that behavior.

SUMMARY OF KEY POINTS

- Perception is the process by which individuals screen, select, organize, and interpret stimuli in order to give them meaning.

- Perceptual selectivity is the process by which individuals select certain stimuli for attention instead of others. Selective attention is influenced by both external factors (e.g., physical or dynamic properties of the object) and personal factors (e.g., response salience).

- Social perception is the process by which we perceive other people. It is influenced by the characteristics of the person perceived, the perceiver, and the situation.

- Stereotyping is a tendency to assign attributes to people solely on the basis of their class or category.

- Selective perception is a process by which we systematically screen or discredit information we don't wish to hear and instead focus on more salient information.

- Perceptual defense is a tendency to distort or ignore information that is either personally threatening or culturally unacceptable.

- Attribution theory concerns the process by which individuals attempt to make sense of the cause-effect relationships in their life space. Events are seen as being either internally caused (that is, by the individual) or externally caused (that is, by other factors in the environment). In making causal attributions, people tend to focus on three factors: consensus, consistency, and distinctiveness.

- The fundamental attribution error is a tendency to underestimate the effects of external or situational causes of behavior and overestimate the effects of personal causes.

- The self-serving bias is a tendency for people to attribute success on a project to themselves while attributing failure to others.

- An attitude can be defined as a predisposition to respond in a favorable or unfavorable way to objects or persons in one's environment.

- There are two theories concerning the manner in which attitudes are formed. The first, called the dispositional approach, asserts that attitudes are fairly stable tendencies to respond to events in certain ways, much like personality traits. Thus, some people may be happy on almost any job regardless of the nature of the job. The second, called the situational approach, asserts that attitudes result largely from the particular situation in which the individual finds himself or herself. Thus, some jobs may lead to more favorable attitudes than others.

- The social-information-processing approach to attitudes is a situational model that suggests that attitudes are strongly influenced by the opinions and assessments of co-workers.

- Cognitive consistency is a tendency to think and act in a predictable manner. Cognitive dissonance occurs when our actions and our attitudes are in conflict. This dissonance will motivate us to attempt to return to a state of cognitive consistence, where attitudes and behaviors are congruent.

■ Job involvement refers to the extent to which an individual is interested in his or her assigned tasks.

■ Organizational commitment refers to the relative strength of an individual's identification with and involvement in a particular organization.

■ Job satisfaction is a pleasurable or positive emotional state resulting from the appraisal of one's job or job experience.

KEY WORDS

affect
attitude
attributional bias
attribution theory
behavioral justification
body language
cognition
cognitive consistency
cognitive dissonance
dispositional approach
fundamental attribution error
halo effect
job involvement
job satisfaction

organizational commitment
perception
perceptual defense
perceptual organization
perceptual selectivity
response disposition
response salience
selective perception
self-serving bias
situational approach
social-information-processing approach
social perception
stereotyping

QUESTIONS FOR DISCUSSION

1. Describe how the basic perceptual process works. Why should managers understand this process?
2. How can variations in social perception affect everyday work behavior? Provide an example to illustrate.
3. What can managers do to reduce the incidences of stereotyping in the workplace?
4. How does the attributional process work? Provide an example to show why this process is so important in understanding organizational behavior.
5. How do attributional biases work? What can managers do to reduce such biases?
6. What are the differences between job involvement, organizational commitment, and job satisfaction? Are all three influenced by the same factors?
7. What are the major reasons for job satisfaction? What are the primary consequences of dissatisfaction? Explain.

NOTES

1. Personal communication.
2. M. W. Levine and J. M. Shefner, *Fundamentals of Selection and Perception* (Reading, Mass.: Addison-Wesley, 1981).
3. D. Kretch, R. S. Crutchfield, and E. L. Ballachey, *Individual in Society* (New York: McGraw-Hill, 1962).
4. F. L. Ruch, *Psychology and Life* (Glenview: Scott, Foresman, 1983).
5. The appropriate frame of reference for reading the passage in Self-Assessment 3.1 is *washing clothes.*
6. J. S. Bruner and L. Postman, "On the Perception of Incongruity: A Paradigm," *Journal of Personality,* 1949, *18,* pp. 206–223.
7. R. Hof, "This Team-Up Has It All—Except Sales," *Business Week,* August 14, 1989, p. 35.
8. S. T. Fiske and S. E. Taylor, *Social Cognition* (Reading, Mass.: Addison-Wesley, 1984).
9. D. J. Mason, "Judgements of Leadership Based on Physiognomic Cues," *Journal of Abnormal and Social Psychology,* 1957, *54,* pp. 273–274.
10. P. F. Secord, "The Role of Facial Features in Interpersonal Perception," in R. Tagiuri and L. Petrullo, eds., *Person Perception and Interpersonal Behavior* (Palo Alto: Stanford University Press, 1958), pp. 300–315.
11. J. W. Thibaut and H. W. Riecker, "Authoritarianism, Status, and the Communication of Aggression," *Human Relations,* 1955, *8,* pp. 95–120.
12. B. Wiesendanger. "Do You Need An Image Consultant?" *Sales & Marketing Management,* May 1992, *144(*5), pp.30–36.
13. D. C. Dearborn and H. A. Simon, "Selective Perception: A Note on Departmental Identification of Executives," *Sociometry,* 1958, *21,* p. 142.
14. R. Likert, *New Patterns of Management* (New York: McGraw-Hill, 1961).
15. Levine and Shefner, op. cit.
16. Ibid.
17. K. J. Frauenfelder, "A Cognitive Determinant of Favorability of Impression," *Journal of Social Psychology,* 1974, *94,* pp. 71–81.
18. H. C. Triandis, *Attitude and Attitude Change* (New York: Wiley, 1971).
19. B. Rosen and T. Jerdee, "Influence of Sex-Role Stereotype on Personnel Decisions," *Journal of Applied Psychology,* 1974, *59,* pp. 9–14.
20. Dearborn and Simon, op. cit.
21. J. B. Miner, *The Management Process: Theory, Research, and Practice* (New York: Macmillan, 1973).
22. Levine and Shefner, op. cit.
23. M. Haire and W. Grunes, "Perceptual Defenses: Processes Protecting an Organized Perception of Another's Personality," *Human Relations,* 1950, *3,* pp. 403–412.
24. Ibid., p. 409.
25. H. H. Kelley, "The Process of Causal Attributions," *American Psychologist,* February 1973, pp. 107-128; F. Forsterling, "Attributional Retraining: A Review," *Psychological Bulletin,* November 1985, pp. 495-512; B. Weiner, *Human Motivation* (New York: Holt, Rinehart and Winston, 1980).
26. Kelley, op. cit., p. 193.
27. Ibid.
28. Ibid.
29. Based on G. W. Allport, "Attitudes," in C. Murchison, ed., *Handbook of Social Psychology* (Worcester: Clark University Press, 1935).
30. H. C. Triandis, op. cit.
31. B. M. Staw and J. Ross, "Stability in the Midst of Change: A Dispositional Approach to Job Attitudes," *Journal of Applied Psychology,* 1985, *70,* pp. 469–480.

32. G. Salancik and J. Pfeffer, "A Social Information Processing Approach to Job Attitudes and Task Design," *Administrative Science Quarterly,* 1978, *23,* pp. 224–253.

33. L. Festinger, *A Theory of Cognitive Dissonance* (Palo Alto: Stanford University Press, 1957).

34. T. Lodahl and M. Kejner, "The Definition and Measurement of Job Involvement," *Journal of Applied Psychology,* 1965, *49,* pp. 24–33.

35. R. T. Mowday, L. W. Porter, and R. M. Steers, *Employee-Organization Linkages: The Psychology of Employee Commitment, Absenteeism and Turnover* (New York: Academic Press, 1982).

36. E. A. Locke, "The Nature and Causes of Job Satisfaction," in M. D. Dunnette, ed., *Handbook of Industrial and Organizational Psychology* (Chicago: Rand McNally, 1976).

37. L. W. Porter and R. M. Steers, "Organizational, Work, and Personal Factors in Employee Turnover and Absenteeism," *Psychological Bulletin,* 1973, *80,* pp. 151–176.

38. B. M. Staw, *Intrinsic and Extrinsic Motivation* (Morristown, N.J.: General Learning Press, 1976).

39. J. S. McClenahen. "On the Job: Lean & Mean." *Industry Week,* November 2, 1992, pp. 30–34.

EXPERIENTIAL EXERCISE 3

Perceptions of an Ideal Manager

Half the class should write down 10 ideal personal or physical characteristics that Brenda should have to be an effective manager.

Half the class should write down 10 ideal personal or physical characteristics that Brent should have to be an effective manager.

MANAGEMENT DILEMMA 3

North American Shipping: Perceptions and Reality

If today's middle managers feel threatened, they might well feel nearly extinct as corporations approach the twenty-first century. It is predicted that within 20 years, the typical corporation will employ no more than a third of its current managers, with fewer than half the levels of management. Most at risk in this change are middle managers who lack operating responsibilities—those who advise, counsel, or coordinate. Headquarters staffs could virtually disappear with the rise of information networks that will supply and analyze data. As a result, the classic pyramidal form of the large corporation is being replaced by organization designs that are flatter in shape, with fewer layers and fewer people. Some have even suggested that tomorrow's corporate structure will look like an hourglass—with the fewest managers in the middle. Throughout this evolution, what happens to the middle manager currently on the job? Consider the case of North American Shipping, a real company with a disguised name.

North American Shipping is riding the crest of an industry boom. Before the year is out, analysts expect the company to post record earnings and revenues. But Sherry Summer, a middle manager at corporate headquarters in Chicago offers a different perspective, having spent more than 15 years with the company. His story follows:

When I first came here, I just never paid attention to titles. I worked for an executive. We disagreed a lot, but we respected each other and could talk. Everything went fine until mid-1985, when we moved to Chicago from Los Angeles and my boss retired. All of a sudden, our department fell apart. We didn't have any leadership. Other officers and our consultants recommended me for the job. But we got a new guy from outside, and then came what I call the Mafia, because he brought all these guys with him. I found myself explaining really elementary stuff to them.

When the new executive arrived, I said, "Here are the problems." But, instead of listening to me, he spent more time complaining about the past administration than cleaning up the problems we faced. From day one, he insisted upon a complete divorce from the past—and of course I was a part of that past. It happens to a lot of middle managers. They go only so far, particularly where you have a change of administration.

We had another executive who retired. He had an assistant who had helped run the department. He got passed over, and all of a sudden he retired. There was nothing left for him. They had another guy who had been brought up, who I felt was almost incompetent. He trained for six months, then all of a sudden they decided no, they wouldn't give him the job, either. Now they're looking outside. They've passed over five or six good guys.

If it wasn't for my particular expertise, I'd probably be fired. I would take early retirement today if I could live off of it. You just realize there is nothing in the future. I feel like I've just hit a wall. I uprooted my family for the move, and so I really don't want to leave the area now. And I'm old enough so that a move would be very difficult. I'm obsolete, I'm at a dead end. There's no way up. No way down. And no way out.

The company gives us a rose on our birthdays. I just threw it away. We get a bonus in a good year. And last year I got the biggest bonus I've ever gotten, and the money was nice. But it didn't make me feel good. Nothing I did affected my bonus because it's based on overall corporate earnings. There is a mathematical formula that I couldn't describe to anybody, and they made a great to-do of it. As long as the fifty-first floor is prepared to give me $60,000, I'll take it. Did I work any harder, or less hard? No. The industry just went up. We just happen to be here at the right time.

Our benefits have been cut back. They changed the retirement plan. The old formula was not the best, but not too bad. Do you know what they replaced it with? I figured it out for myself, and my retirement income turned into a significant drop. Our VP for employee relations two years ago wanted to count Labor Day as vacation time if you take the day off. He got his ears burned off.

Despite cutbacks, we're still not lean, either. We have more make-work executive or middle management-type jobs than we need. We've got a lot more junior executives than we know what to do with. They just sit around reading the *Wall Street Journal.* I think we've made a lot of jobs that aren't jobs. And how do you bring managers up when they aren't doing anything? Now, we've got great plant management, real dedicated people. It's the secret of the company. But when you get down to it, we just aren't lean and mean.

If you were in charge of human resource management for North American Shipping, what courses of action would you take to remedy the present situation?

1. What is influencing Sherry Summer's perception of the situation?
2. Who is really seeing reality—insiders, like Sherry, or outsiders, like her new boss?
3. What would you realistically do to resolve the dilemma? What is your plan of action?
4. What roadblocks would you expect if you tried to implement your plan?
5. Who in the organization would need to support your actions for you to be successful?

Chapter 4

Learning and Reinforcement

The Management Challenge

- To offer appropriate rewards in a timely fashion.
- To know how best to train employees in new job skills.
- To know how to reduce undesirable employee behavior while reinforcing desirable behavior.
- To encourage employees to assume more responsibility for self-improvement and job performance.
- To create a work environment characterized by continual self-learning and employee development.

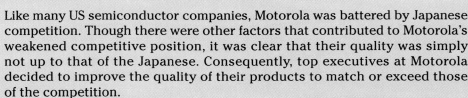

CLOSE UP   Basic Training at Motorola University

Like many US semiconductor companies, Motorola was battered by Japanese competition. Though there were other factors that contributed to Motorola's weakened competitive position, it was clear that their quality was simply not up to that of the Japanese. Consequently, top executives at Motorola decided to improve the quality of their products to match or exceed those of the competition.

One of the first tasks undertaken was to training people in the concept of high quality. The quality standard they set out after was "six sigma." Six sigma is a term used by statisticians and engineers that represents six standard deviations from a mean. This translates into 3.4 defects per million or production that is 99.99966 percent perfect. Motorola decided that if manufacturing was going to strive for six sigma, then all aspects of the firm ought to be held to the same standard. Consequently, employees from the research labs to the kitchen were trained in the concept of six sigma. For the chef, this meant that only 3 out of a million muffins baked could get burned.

Unfortunately, top executives at first assumed that everyone would want to learn about the new quality standard and how to measure defects, compute defect ratios, and so on. Executives quickly discovered that the "lifetime employment" practice of the past did not serve as an incentive for people to learn new techniques. They also discovered that nearly 60 percent of their blue collar workforce had difficulty with simple arithmetic. Motorola was planning to introduce new sophisticated equipment to help get them to six sigma, but many of the future operators could not calculate decimals, fractions, and percentages. As they investigated further, they found that part of the reason for these mathematical mistakes was due to the person's inability to read beyond the second- or third-grade level, which was particularly true of older workers.

Rather than simply fire many of these older workers, Motorola turned a $7 million training budget into a $120 million annual investment in education. It joined forces with universities and community colleges to design classes from basic reading to advanced statistical process control. The company established time frames within which individuals would need to make progress with their education in order to retain their jobs, and it set up recognition awards for those who completed the designed curriculum. In plants in which the programs were fully implemented, Motorola calculated that they were getting $33 return for every dollar spent, including the cost of wages paid while people were in class.[1]

The example of Motorola demonstrates the importance of learning and of understanding the fundamentals of the learning process as they apply to organizational behavior. Among other factors, we must recognize that learning is a prerequisite for most forms of behavior, including behavior on the job. Managers, clerical workers, skilled craftspeople—every employee—must learn certain skills that are necessary for good job performance. Understanding how learning takes place and how it influences subsequent behavior is extremely useful. Thus, although six sigma quality programs may be a means of competitive advantage in the future, the fundamentals of learning and training are often at the heart of these type of new programs. In fact, many U.S. companies may find, as Motorola did, that they need to spend considerable sums on training and developing their employees. To the extent that such efforts are based on a sound understanding of the principles of learning, their chances for success are enhanced.

Just as personality and motivation are related, so too are learning and motivation. A knowledge of learning processes is helpful in understanding employee motivation. This connection is particularly evident in recent efforts to use behavior modification or behavioral self-management techniques in organizations. These applications of learning theory are gaining popularity among managers as a strategy for improving employee performance. Without a thorough understanding of the mechanisms underlying such efforts, managers run the risk of inappropriately applying the techniques, to the detriment of performance and organizational effectiveness.

Finally, a major responsibility of managers is to evaluate and reward their subordinates. If managers are to maximize the impact of available (and often limited) rewards, a thorough knowledge of reinforcement techniques is essential. We shall devote this chapter to developing a detailed understanding of learning processes in organizations. We begin by looking at basic models of learning.

BASIC MODELS OF LEARNING

Learning may be defined, for our purposes, as a relatively permanent change in behavior that occurs as a result of experience. That is, someone is said to have learned something when he or she consistently exhibits a new behavior over time. Several aspects of this definition are noteworthy.[2] First, learning involves a change in an attitude or behavior. This change does not necessarily have to be an improvement, however, and can include such things as learning bad habits or forming prejudices. In order for learning to occur, the change that takes place must be relatively permanent. So changes in behavior that result from fatigue or temporary adaptation to a unique situation would not be considered examples of learning. Next, learning typically involves some form of practice or experience. For example, the change that results from physical maturation, as when a baby develops the physical strength to walk, is in itself not considered learning. Third, this practice or experience must be reinforced over time for learning to take place. Where reinforcement does not follow practice or experience, the behavior will eventually diminish and disappear ("extinction"). Finally, learning is an inferred process; we cannot observe learning directly. Instead, we must infer the existence of learning from observing changes in overt behavior.

We can best understand the learning process by looking at four stages in the development of research on learning (see Exhibit 4.1). Scientific interest in learning dates from the early experiments of Pavlov and others around the turn of the century. The focus of this research was on stimulus-response relationships and the environmental determinants of observable behaviors. This was followed by the discovery of the law of effect, experiments in operant conditioning, and, finally, the formulation of social learning theory.

Classical Conditioning

Classical conditioning is the process whereby a stimulus-response bond is developed between a conditioned stimulus and a conditioned response through the repeated linking of a conditioned stimulus with an unconditioned stimulus. This process is shown in Exhibit 4.2. The classic example of Pavlov's experiments illustrates the process. Pavlov was initially interested in the digestive processes of dogs but noticed that the dogs started to salivate at the

Exhibit 4.1
The Development of Modern Behavioral Learning Theory

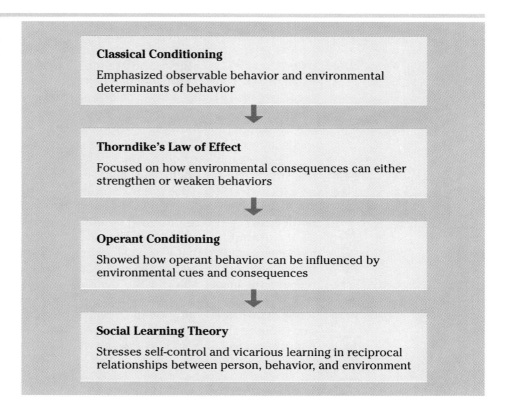

Classical Conditioning

Emphasized observable behavior and environmental determinants of behavior

Thorndike's Law of Effect

Focused on how environmental consequences can either strengthen or weaken behaviors

Operant Conditioning

Showed how operant behavior can be influenced by environmental cues and consequences

Social Learning Theory

Stresses self-control and vicarious learning in reciprocal relationships between person, behavior, and environment

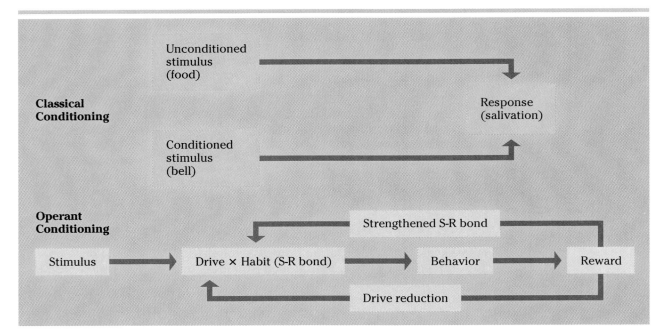

Exhibit 4.2
Classical Versus
Operant Conditioning

first signal of approaching food. On the basis of this discovery, he shifted his attention to the question of whether animals could be trained to draw a causal relationship between previously unconnected factors. Specifically, using the dogs as subjects, he examined the extent to which the dogs could learn to associate the ringing of a bell with the act of salivation. The experiment began with unlearned, or *unconditioned,* stimulus-response relationships. When a dog was presented with meat (unconditioned stimulus), the dog salivated (unconditioned response). No learning was necessary here, as this relationship represented a natural physiological process.

Next, Pavlov paired the unconditioned stimulus (meat) with a neutral one (the ringing of a bell). Normally, the ringing of the bell by itself would not be expected to elicit salivation. However, over time, a learned linkage developed for the dog between the bell and meat, ultimately resulting in an S-R bond between the conditioned stimulus (the bell) and the response (salivation) without the presence of the unconditioned stimulus (the meat). Evidence emerged that learning had occurred and that this learning resulted from conditioning the dogs to associate two normally unrelated objects, the bell and the meat.

Although Pavlov's experiments are widely cited as evidence of the existence of classical conditioning, it is necessary from the perspective of organizational behavior to ask how this process relates to people at work. Ivancevich, Szilagyi, and Wallace provide one such work-related example of classical conditioning:

An illustration of classical conditioning in a work setting would be an airplane pilot learning how to use a newly installed warning system. In this case the behavior to be learned is to respond to a warning light that indicates that the plane has dropped below a critical altitude on an assigned glide path. The proper response is to increase the plane's altitude. The pilot already knows how to appropriately respond to the trainer's warning to increase altitude (in this case we would say the trainer's warning is an unconditioned stimulus and the corrective action of increasing altitude is an unconditioned response). The training session consists of the trainer warning the pilot to increase altitude every time the warning light goes on. Through repeated pairings of the warning light with the trainer's warning, the pilot eventually learns to adjust the plane's altitude in response to the warning light even though the trainer is not present. Again, the unit of learning is a new S-R connection or habit.[3]

Although classical conditioning clearly has applications to work situations, particularly in the area of training and development, it has been criticized as explaining only a limited part of total human learning. Psychologist B. F. Skinner argues that classical conditioning focuses on respondent, or reflexive, behaviors; that is, it concentrates on explaining largely involuntary responses that result from stimuli.[4] More complex learning cannot be explained solely by classical conditioning. As an alternative explanation, Skinner and others have proposed the operant conditioning model of learning.

Operant Conditioning

The major focus of operant conditioning is on the effects of reinforcements, or rewards, on desired behaviors. One of the first psychologists to examine such processes was J. B. Watson, a contemporary of Pavlov, who argued that behavior is largely influenced by the rewards one receives as a result of actions.[5] This notion is best summarized in Thorndike's *law of effect*. This law states that of several responses made to the same situation, those which are accompanied or closely followed by satisfaction [reinforcement] will be more likely to occur; those which are accompanied or closely followed by discomfort [punishment] will be less likely to occur.[6]

In other words, it posits that behavior that leads to positive or pleasurable outcomes tends to be repeated, whereas behavior that leads to negative outcomes or punishment tends to be avoided. In this manner, individuals learn appropriate, acceptable responses to their environment. If we repeatedly dock the pay of an employee who is habitually tardy, we would expect that employee to learn to arrive early enough to receive a full day's pay.

A basic operant model of learning is presented in Exhibit 4.2. There are three important concepts of this model:

Drive.   A drive is an internal state of disequilibrium; it is a felt need. It is generally believed that drive increases with the strength of deprivation. A drive, or desire, to learn must be present for learning to take place. For example, not currently being able to afford the house you want, is likely to lead to a drive for more money to buy your desired house. Living in a run-down shack is likely to increase this drive compared to living in a nice apartment.

Habit.   A habit is the experienced bond or connection between stimulus and response. For example, if a person learns over time that eating satisfies hunger, a strong stimulus-response (hunger-eating) bond will develop. Habits thus determine the behaviors, or courses of action, we choose.

Reinforcement or reward.   This represents the feedback individuals receive as a result of action. For example, if as a salesperson you are given a bonus for greater sales and plan to use the money to buy the house you have always wanted, this will reinforce the behaviors that you believed led to greater sales, such as smiling at customers, repeating their name during the presentation, and so on.

A stimulus activates an individual's motivation through its impact on drive and habit. The stronger the drive and habit (S-R bond), the stronger the motivation to behave in a certain way. As a result of this behavior, two things happen. First, the individual receives feedback that reduces the original drive. Second, the individual strengthens his or her belief in the veracity of the S-R bond to the extent that it proved successful. That is, if one's response to the stimulus satisfied one's drive or need, the individual would come to believe more strongly in the appropriateness of the particular S-R connection and would respond in the same way under similar circumstances.

An example will clarify this point. Several recent attempts to train chronically unemployed workers have used a daily pay system instead of weekly or monthly systems. The primary reason for this is that the workers, who do not have a history of working, can more quickly see the relationship between coming to work and receiving pay. An S-R bond develops more quickly because of the frequency of the reinforcement, or reward.

Operant Versus Classical Conditioning

Operant conditioning can be distinguished from classical conditioning in at least two ways.[7] First, the two approaches differ in what is believed to cause changes in behavior. In classical conditioning, changes in behavior are thought to arise through changes in stimuli—that is, a transfer from an unconditioned stimulus to a conditioned stimulus. In operant conditioning, on the other hand, changes in behavior are thought to result from the *consequences* of previous behavior. When behavior has been rewarded, we would expect it to be repeated; when behavior has not been rewarded or has been punished, we would not expect it to be repeated.

Second, the two approaches differ in the role and frequency of rewards. In classical conditioning, the unconditioned stimulus, acting as a sort of reward, is administered during every trial. In contrast, in operant conditioning the reward results only when individuals choose the correct response. That is, in operant conditioning, individuals must correctly operate on their environment before a reward is received. The response is instrumental in obtaining the desired reward.

Social Learning Theory

The last model of learning we should examine is noted psychologist Albert Bandura's social learning theory. *Social learning* is defined as the process of molding behavior through the reciprocal interaction of a person's cognitions, behavior, and environment.[8] This is done through a process that Bandura calls *reciprocal determinism*. This concept implies that people control their own environment (for example, by quitting one's job) as much as the environment controls people (for example, being laid off). Thus, learning is seen as a more active, interactive process in which the learner has at least some control.

Social learning theory shares many of the same roots as operant conditioning. Like Skinner, Bandura argues that behavior is at least in part controlled by environmental cues and consequences, and Bandura uses observable behavior (as opposed to attitudes, feelings, etc.) as the primary unit of analysis. However, unlike operant conditioning, social learning theory posits that cognitive or mental processes affect our response to the environmental cues.

Social learning theory has four central elements: attention, retention, reproduction, and incentives. Before someone can learn something, they must notice or pay attention to the thing that is to be learned. For example, you probably would not learn much as a student in any class unless you paid attention to information conveyed by the text or instructor. Retention is the process by which what you have noticed is encoded into your memory. Reproduction involves the translation of what was recorded in your mind into overt actions or behaviors. Obviously, the higher the level of attention and the greater the retention, the better the reproduction of what was learned. Finally, incentives can influence all three processes. For example, if you are rewarded (say, praised) for paying attention, you will pay more attention. If you are rewarded for remembering what you studied (say good grades), you will retain more. If you are rewarded for reproducing what you learned (say, a promotion for effectively motivating your subordinates), you will produce that behavior more.

Central to this theory is the concept of vicarious learning. *Vicarious learning* is learning that takes place through the imitation of other role models. That is, we observe and analyze what another person does and the resulting consequences. As a result, we learn without having to experience the phenomenon firsthand. Thus, if we see a fellow employee being disciplined or fired for being disruptive in the workplace, we might learn not to be disruptive ourselves. If we see that gifts are usually given with the right hand in the Middle East, we might give gifts in that manner ourselves.

A model of social learning processes is shown in Exhibit 4.3. As can be seen, three factors—the person, the environment, and the behavior—interact through such processes as vicarious learning, symbolic representations, and self-control to cause actual learned behaviors.

Major Influences on Learning.   On the basis of this work, it is possible by way of summary to identify several general factors that can enhance our learning processes. An individual's desire to learn, background knowledge of a subject, and the length of the learning period are some of the components of a learning environment. Filley, House, and Kerr identify five major influences on learning effectiveness.[9]

Drawn largely from behavioral science and psychology literature, substantial research indicates that learning effectiveness is increased considerably when individuals have high *motivation to learn*. We sometimes

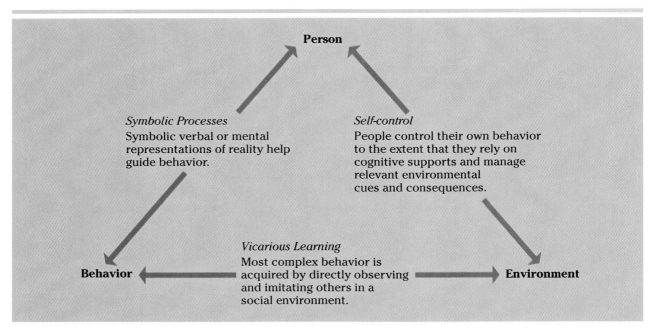

Exhibit 4.3
A Basic Model of
Social Learning

Source: From "A Social Learning Approach to Behavioral Management: Radical Behaviorists 'Mellowing Out,'" by Robert Kreitner et al. Reprinted, by permission of the publisher, from *Organizational Dynamics,* Autumn 1984, © 1984 American Management Association, New York. All rights reserved.

encounter students who work day and night to complete a term paper that is of interest to them, whereas writing an uninteresting term paper may be postponed until the last possible minute. Maximum transfer of knowledge is achieved when a student or employee is motivated to learn by a high need to know.

Considerable evidence also demonstrates that we can facilitate learning by providing individuals with feedback on their performance. A *knowledge of results* serves a gyroscopic function, showing individuals where they are correct or incorrect and furnishing them with the perspective to improve. Feedback also serves as an important positive reinforcer that can enhance an individual's willingness or desire to learn. Students who is told by their professor how they performed on an exam and what they could do to improve next time are likely to study harder.

In many cases, *prior learning* can increase the ability to learn new materials or tasks by providing needed background or foundation materials. In math, multiplication is easier to learn if addition has been mastered. These beneficial effects of prior learning on present learning tend to be greatest when the prior tasks and the present tasks exhibit similar stimulus-response connections. For instance, most of the astronauts selected for the space program have had years of previous experience flying airplanes. It is assumed that their prior experience and developed skill will facilitate learning to fly the highly technical, though somewhat similar, vehicles.

Another influence on learning concerns whether the materials to be learned are presented in their entirety or in parts—*whole versus part learning*.[10] Available evidence suggests that when a task consists of several distinct and unrelated duties, part learning is more effective. Each task should be learned separately. However, when a task consists of several integrated and related parts (such as learning the components of a small machine), whole learning is more appropriate, because it ensures that major relationships among parts, as well as proper sequencing of parts, is not overlooked or underemphasized.

The final major influence on learning highlights the advantages and disadvantages of concentrated as opposed to distributed training sessions. Research suggests that *distribution of practice*—short learning periods at set intervals—is more effective for learning motor skills than for learning verbal or cognitive skills (see Chapter 2).[11] Distributed practice also seems to facilitate learning of very difficult, voluminous, or tedious material. It should be noted, however, that concentrated practice appears to work well where insight is required for task completion. Apparently, concentrated effort over short durations provides a move synergistic approach to problem solving.

Although there is general agreement that these influences are important (and are under the control of management in many cases), they cannot substitute for the lack of an adequate reinforcement system. In fact, reinforcement is widely recognized as the key to effective learning. If managers are concerned with eliciting desired behaviors from their subordinates, a knowledge of reinforcement techniques is essential.

International Challenge

IN PRACTICE
Learning to be Effective Overseas

General Motors has learned by experience that it pays not to have managers learn only by experience how to function effectively while working in foreign countries. Consequently, GM spends nearly $500,000 a year to help about 150 Americans and their families learn about the country and culture to which they are being sent prior to their stepping on the airplane.

These training programs involve a wide variety of teaching methods. Factual information may be conveyed through lectures or printed material. More subtle information is learned through role plays, case studies, and simulations.

The research on cross-cultural training suggests that the more involved participants are in the training the more they learn and that the more they practice or simulate new behaviors that they need to master in the foreign environment, the more effective they will be in actual situations.

The results for GM have been impressive. Most companies that do not provide cross-cultural training for their employees sent on international assignments experience failure rates of about 25 percent, and each failure or early return costs the company on average $150,000. GM has a failure rate of less than 1 percent. Also, in GM's case, the training has been extended to the manager's family and has helped reluctant spouses and children more readily accept, if not embrace, the foreign assignment.[12]

REINFORCEMENT AND BEHAVIORAL CHANGE

A central feature of most approaches to learning is the concept of reinforcement. This concept dates from Thorndike's law of effect which, as mentioned earlier, states that behavior that is positively reinforced tends to be repeated, whereas behavior that is not reinforced will tend not to be repeated. Hence, *reinforcement* can be defined as anything that causes a certain behavior to be repeated or inhibited.

Reinforcement Versus Motivation

It is important to differentiate reinforcement from the concept of employee motivation. Motivation, as described in the next chapter, represents a primary psychological process that is largely cognitive in nature. Thus, motivation is largely internal—it is *experienced* by the employee, and we can see only subsequent manifestations of it in actual behavior. Reinforcement, on the other hand, is typically observable and most often externally administered. A supervisor may reinforce what he or she considers desirable behavior without knowing anything about the underlying motives that prompted it. For example, a supervisor who has a habit of say, "That's interesting" whenever he or she is presented with a new idea may be reinforcing innovation on the part of the subordinates without the supervisor really knowing why this result is achieved. The distinction between theories of motivation and reinforcement should be kept in mind when we examine behavior modification and behavioral self-management later in this chapter.

Strategies for Behavioral Change

From a managerial standpoint, several strategies for behavioral change are available to facilitate learning in organizational settings. At least four different types should be noted: (1) positive reinforcement; (2) avoidance learning, or negative reinforcement; (3) extinction; and (4) punishment. Each type plays a different role in both the manner in which and extent to which learning occurs. Each will be considered separately here.

Positive Reinforcement. Positive reinforcement consists of presenting someone with an attractive outcome following a desired behavior. As noted by Skinner, "A positive reinforcer is a stimulus which, when added to a situation, strengthens the probability of an operant response."[13] A simple example of positive reinforcement is supervisory praise for subordinates when they perform well in a certain situation. That is, a supervisor may praise an employee for being on time consistently (see Exhibit 4.4). This behavior-praise pattern may encourage the subordinate to be on time in the future in the hope of receiving additional praise.

In order for a positive reinforcement to be effective in facilitating the repetition of desired behavior, several conditions must be met. First, the

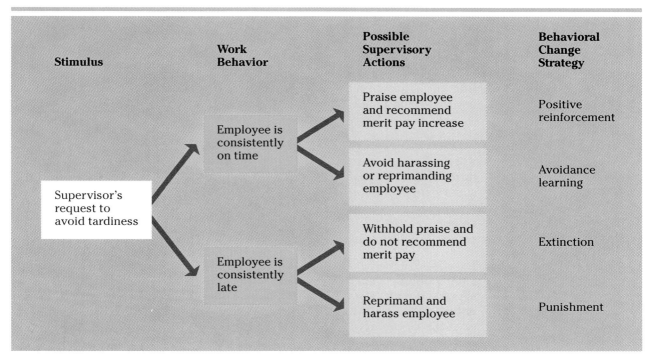

Stimulus	Work Behavior	Possible Supervisory Actions	Behavioral Change Strategy
Supervisor's request to avoid tardiness	Employee is consistently on time	Praise employee and recommend merit pay increase	Positive reinforcement
		Avoid harassing or reprimanding employee	Avoidance learning
	Employee is consistently late	Withhold praise and do not recommend merit pay	Extinction
		Reprimand and harass employee	Punishment

Exhibit 4.4
Strategies for
Behavioral Change

reinforcer itself (praise) must be valued by the employee. It would prove ineffective in shaping behavior if employees were indifferent to it. Second, the reinforcer must be strongly tied to the desired behavior. Receipt of the reinforcer by the employee must be directly contingent upon performing the desired behavior. "Rewards must result from performance, and the greater the degree of performance by an employee, the greater should be his reward."[14] It is important to keep in mind here that "desired behavior" represents behavior defined by the supervisor, not the employee. Thus, for praise to be a reinforcer, not only must it be valued by the employee but it must directly follow the desired behavior and should be more intense as the behavior is closer to the ideal the supervisor has in mind. Praise thrown out at random is unlikely to reinforce the desired behavior. Third, there must be ample occasion for the reinforcer to be administered following desired behavior. If the reinforcer is tied to certain behavior that seldom occurs, then individuals will seldom be reinforced and will probably not associate this behavior with a reward. For example, if praise is only provided for truly exceptional performance, then it is unlikely to have a powerful impact on the desired behavior. It is important that the performance-reward contingencies be structured so that they are easily attainable.

Avoidance Learning.   A second method of reinforcement is avoidance learning, or negative reinforcement. Avoidance learning refers to seeking to avoid an unpleasant condition or outcome by following a desired behavior.

Employees learn to avoid unpleasant situations by behaving in certain ways. If an employee correctly performs a task or is continually prompt in coming to work (see Exhibit 4.4), the supervisor may refrain from harassing, reprimanding, or otherwise embarrassing the employee. Presumably, the employee learns over time that engaging in correct behavior diminishes admonishion from the supervisor. In order to maintain this condition, the employee continues to behave as desired.

Extinction.   The principle of extinction suggests that undesired behavior will decline as a result of a lack of positive reinforcement. If the perpetually tardy employee in the example in Exhibit 4.4 consistently fails to receive supervisory praise and is not recommended for a pay raise, we would expect this nonreinforcement to lead to an "extinction" of the tardiness. The employee may realize, albeit subtly, that being late is not leading to desired outcomes, and he or she may try coming to work on time.

Punishment.   Finally, a fourth strategy for behavior change used by managers and supervisors is punishment. Punishment is the administration of unpleasant or adverse outcomes as a result of undesired behavior. An example of the application of punishment is for a supervisor to publicly reprimand or fine an employee who is habitually tardy (see Exhibit 4.4). Presumably, the employee would refrain from being tardy in the future in order to avoid such an undesirable outcome. The most frequently used punishments (along with the most frequently used rewards) are shown in Exhibit 4.5.

The use of punishment is indeed one of the most controversial issues of behavior change strategies. Although punishment can have positive work outcomes—especially if it is administered in an impersonal way and as soon as possible after the transgression—negative repercussions can also result when employees either resent the action or feel they are being unfairly treated. These negative outcomes from punishment are shown in Exhibit 4.6. Thus, although punishment represents a potent force in corrective learning,

Exhibit 4.5
Frequently Used Rewards and Punishments

Rewards	Punishments
Pay raise	Oral reprimands
Bonus	Written reprimands
Promotion	Ostracism
Praise and recognition	Criticism from superiors
Awards	Suspension
Self-recognition	Demotion
Sense of accomplishment	Reduced authority
Increased responsibility	Undesired transfer
Time off	Termination

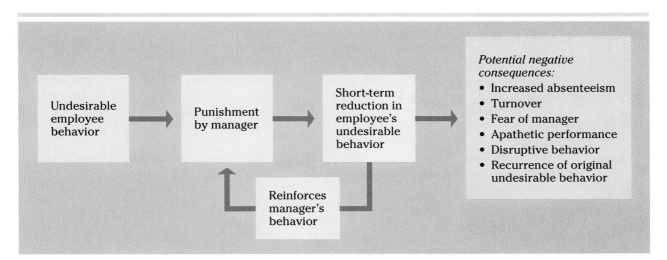

Exhibit 4.6
Potential Negative
Consequences of Punishment

its use must be carefully considered and implemented. In general, for punishment to be effective the punishment should "fit the crime" in severity, should be given in private, and should be explained to the employee.

IN PRACTICE
Shaping a Salesperson's Behavior

Ethical Challenge

Sharon Johnson worked for a publishing company based in Nashville, Tennessee that sold a line of children's books directly to the public through a door-to-door sales force. Sharon had been a very successful salesperson and was promoted first to district and then to regional sales manager after just four years with the company. Sales bonuses were fixed and a fixed dollar bonus was tied to every $1000 in sales over a specific minimum quota. However, there were a wide variety of rewards, from praise to gift certificates, that were left to Sharon's discretion.

Sharon knew from her organizational behavior class that giving out praise to those who liked it and gifts to those who preferred them was an important means of reinforcing desired behavior, and she had been quite successful in implementing this principle. She also knew that if you reinforced a behavior that was "on the right track" to the ideal behavior you wanted out of a salesperson, eventually you could shape their behavior, almost without their realizing it.

Sharon had one particular salesperson, Lyle, that she thought had great potential, yet his weekly sales were somewhat inconsistent and often lower than she thought possible. When Lyle was questioned about his performance, he indicated that sometimes he felt that the families he approached could not afford the books he was selling and so he did not think it was right to push the sale too hard. Although Sharon argued that it was not Lyle's place to decide for others what they could or could not afford, Lyle still felt uncomfortable about utilizing his normal sale approach with these families.

Sharon believed that through subtle reinforcement of certain behaviors she could shape Lyle's behavior and that over time he would increasingly use his typical sales approach with the families he thought could not afford the books. For example, she knew that in the cases of families Lyle thought could not afford the books, he spent only 3.5 minutes in the house compared to 12.7 minutes in homes of families he judged able to afford the books. Sharon believed that if she praised Lyle when the average time he spent in each family's home was quite similar that Lyle would increase the time he spent in the homes of families he judged unable to afford the books. She believed that the longer he spent in these homes, the more likely Lyle was to utilize his typical sales approach. This was just one of several ways Sharon thought she could shape Lyle's behavior without trying to change his mind about pushing books onto people he thought could not afford them.

Sharon saw no ethical issues in this case until she told a friend about it and the friend questioned whether it was ethical to utilize learning and reinforcement techniques to change people's behavior "against their will" even if they did not realize that this was happening.[15]

In summary, positive reinforcement and avoidance learning focus on bringing about the *desired* response from the employee. With positive reinforcement the employee behaves in a certain way in order to gain desired rewards, whereas with avoidance learning the employee behaves in order to avoid certain unpleasant outcomes. In both cases, however, the behavior desired by the supervisor is enhanced. In contrast, extinction and punishment focus on supervisory attempts to reduce the incidence of *undesired* behavior. That is, extinction and punishment are typically used to get someone to stop doing something the supervisor doesn't like. It does not necessarily follow that the individual will begin acting in the most desired, or correct, manner.

Often students have difficulty seeing the distinction between avoidance and extinction or in understanding how either could have a significant impact on behavior. Two factors are important to keep in mind. The first we will simply call the "history effect." Not being harassed could reinforce an employee's prompt arrival at work if in the past the employee had been harassed for being late. Arriving on time and thereby avoiding the past harassment would reinforce arriving on time. This same dynamic would hold true for extinction. If the employee had been praised in the past for arriving on time, then arrived late and was not praised, this would serve to weaken the tendency to arrive late. The second factor we will call the "social effect." For example, if you see others harassed when they arrive late and then you are not harassed when you arrive on time, this could reinforce your arriving at work on time. Again, this same dynamic would hold true for extinction. If you had observed others being praised for arriving on time, then not receiving praise when you arrived late would serve to weaken the tendency to arrive late.

From a managerial perspective, questions arise about which strategy of behavioral change is most effective. Advocates of behavioral change strategies, such as Skinner, answer that positive reinforcement combined with extinction is the most suitable way to bring about desired behavior. There are several reasons for this focus on the positive approach to reinforcement. First, although punishment can inhibit or eliminate undesired behavior, it often does not provide information to the individual about how or in which direction to change. Also, the application of punishment may cause the individual to become alienated from the work situation, thereby reducing the chances that useful change can be effected. Similarly, avoidance learning tends to emphasize the negative; that is, people are taught to stay clear of certain behaviors, such as tardiness, for fear of repercussions. In contrast, it is felt that combining positive reinforcement with the use of extinction has the fewest undesirable side effects and allows individuals to receive the rewards they desire. A positive approach to reinforcement is believed by some to be the most effective tool management has to bring about favorable changes in organizations.

Schedules of Reinforcement

Having examined four distinct strategies for behavioral change, we now turn to an examination of the various ways, or *schedules,* of administering these techniques. As noted by Costello and Zalkind, "The speed with which learning takes place and also how lasting its effects will be is determined by the timing of reinforcement."[16] Thus, a knowledge of the types of schedules of reinforcement is essential to managers if they are to know how to choose rewards that will have maximum impact on employee performance. Although there are a variety of ways in which rewards can be administered, most approaches can be categorized into two groups: continuous and partial (or intermittent) reinforcement schedules. A *continuous* reinforcement schedule rewards desired behavior every time it occurs. For example, a manager could praise (or pay) employees every time they perform properly. With the time and resource constraints most managers work under, this is often difficult, if not impossible. So, most managerial reward strategies operate on a partial schedule. A *partial* reinforcement schedule rewards desired behavior at specific intervals, not every time desired behavior is exhibited. Compared to continuous schedules, partial reinforcement schedules lead to slower learning but stronger retention. Thus, learning is generally more permanent. Four kinds of partial reinforcement schedules can be identified: (1) fixed-interval, (2) fixed-ratio, (3) variable-interval, and (4) variable-ratio (see Exhibit 4.7).

Fixed-Interval Schedule.   A fixed-interval reinforcement schedule rewards individuals at specified intervals for their performance, as with a biweekly paycheck. If employees perform even minimally, they are paid. This technique generally does not result in high or sustained levels of performance, because employees know that marginal performance usually leads to the same level of reward as high performance. Thus, there is little incentive for high effort and performance. Also, when rewards are withheld or suspended, extinction of desired behavior occurs quickly. Many of the recent job redesign efforts in organizations were prompted by recognition of the need for alternate strategies of motivation rather than paying people on fixed-interval schedules.

Schedule of Reinforcement	Nature of Reinforcement	Effects on Behavior When Applied	Effects on Behavior When Terminated	Example
Fixed interval	Reward on fixed time basis	Leads to average and irregular performance	Quick extinction of behavior	Weekly paycheck
Fixed ratio	Reward consistently tied to output	Leads quickly to very high and stable performance	Quick extinction of behavior	Piece-rate pay system
Variable interval	Reward given at variable intervals around some average time	Leads to moderately high and stable performance	Slow extinction of behavior	Monthly performance appraisal and reward at random times each month
Variable ratio	Reward given at variable output levels around some average output	Leads to very high performance	Slow extinction of behavior	Sales bonus tied to selling X accounts, but X constantly changes around some mean

Exhibit 4.7
Schedules of
Partial Reinforcement

Fixed-Ratio Schedule.   The second fixed schedule is the fixed-ratio schedule. Here the reward is administered only upon the completion of a given number of desired responses. In other words, rewards are tied to performance in a ratio of rewards to results. A common example of the fixed-ratio schedule is a piece-rate pay system, whereby employees are paid for each unit of output they produce. Under this system, performance rapidly reaches high levels. In fact, according to Hamner, "The response level here is significantly higher than that obtained under any of the interval (time-based) schedules."[17] On the negative side, however, performance declines sharply when the rewards are withheld, as with fixed-interval schedules.

Variable-Interval Schedule.   Using variable reinforcement schedules, both variable-interval and variable-ratio reinforcements are administered at random times that cannot be predicted by the employee. The employee is generally not aware of when the next evaluation and reward period will be. Under a variable-interval schedule, rewards are administered at intervals of time that are based on an average. For example, an employee may know that *on the average* his or her performance is evaluated and rewarded about once a month, but he or she does not know when this event will occur. He or she does know, however, that it will occur sometime during the interval of a month. Under this schedule, effort and performance will generally be high and fairly stable over time because employees never know when the evaluation will take place.

Variable-Ratio Schedule.   Finally, a variable-ratio schedule is one in which rewards are administered only after an employee has performed the desired behavior a number of times, with the number changing from the administration of one reward to the next but averaging over time to a certain *ratio* of number of performances to rewards. For example, a manager may determine that a salesperson will receive a bonus for every fifteenth new account sold.

However, instead of administering the bonus every fifteenth sale (as in a fixed-interval schedule), the manager may vary the number of sales that is necessary for the bonus, from perhaps ten sales for the first bonus to twenty for the second. On the average, however, the 15:1 ratio prevails. If the employee understands the parameters, then the "safe" level of sales or the level of sales most likely to result in a bonus is in excess of 15. Consequently, the variable-ratio schedule typically leads to high and stable performance. Moreover, extinction of desired behavior is slow.

Which of these four schedules of reinforcement is superior? In a review of several studies comparing the various techniques, Hamner concludes:

> The necessity for arranging appropriate reinforcement contingencies is dramatically illustrated by several studies in which rewards were shifted from a response-contingent (ratio) to a time-contingent (interval) basis. During the period in which rewards were made conditional upon occurrence of the desired behavior, the appropriate response patterns were exhibited at a consistently high level. When the same rewards were given based on time and independent of the worker's behavior, there was a marked drop in the desired behavior. The reinstatements of the performance-contingent reward schedule promptly restored the high level of responsiveness.[18]

In other words, the performance-contingent (or ratio) reward schedules generally lead to better performance than the time-contingent (or interval) schedules, regardless of whether such schedules are fixed or variable. We will return to this point in a subsequent chapter on performance appraisal and reward systems.

International Challenge

IN PRACTICE
In Japan's Hell Camp

There is a saying in Japan that "the nail that sticks up gets hammered down." This means that in corporate Japan employees are supposed to act together and move in unison. Individuality is not encouraged. Although Japanese companies use many techniques to train their employees to work hard and overcome adversity as a group, one rather notable approach that is used by many companies is known as Hell Camp.

The purpose of Hell Camp is to develop employees so they can "concentrate under difficulty." Representing something of a blend of Outward Bound and assertiveness training, Hell Camp is designed to toughen employees by putting them through numerous humiliating exercises (e.g., making them shout their company song outside the local train station). If they pass each exercise (for example, if they shout loud enough and with sufficient emotion), they are allowed to remove one of several "badges of shame." Criteria for removing a badge are left vague, so, in essence, the program uses a variable-ratio reinforcement system. The employee never quite knows when the trainer will say he has succeeded; therefore, the most likely level of performance that will result in the removal of shame badges is that at the higher end of the spectrum of performance. If the employee succeeds, during the week-long program, in removing all of the badges and shows his sincerity and commitment, he graduates. If not, he must repeat the program.

It is estimated that over 50,000 Japanese managers have gone through the program. Companies like it because they see it as a way to keep managers from getting soft. As one executive notes, "Companies have been getting very soft, very weak in their way of demanding excellence." It is thought that the harassment received during Hell Camp and the reinforcement following satisfactory task accomplishment instill character, and Japanese companies show no sign of losing interest in the program.[19]

BEHAVIOR MODIFICATION IN ORGANIZATIONS

When the above principles and techniques are applied to the workplace, we generally see one of two approaches: *behavior modification* and *behavioral self-management*. Both approaches rest firmly on the principles of learning described above. Because both of these techniques have wide followings in corporations, we shall review them here. First, we look at the positive and negative sides of behavior modification.

Behavior modification is the use of operant conditioning principles to shape human behavior to conform to desired standards defined by superiors. In recent years, behavior modification has been applied in a wide variety of organizations. In most cases, positive results are claimed. For example, in one of the first examples of the use of behavior modification, Emery Air Freight found that the technique cut its operating costs by $1 million during its first three years of operation. The 3M Company estimated that the technique saved them $3.5 million in one year alone. And in the accounting department of Collins Foods International, behavior modification led to a reduction in the error rate in accounts payable from 8 percent to 0.2 percent.[20] Examples such as these stimulate interest in the technique as a management tool to improve performance and reduce costs.

Because of its emphasis on shaping behavior, it is more appropriate to think of behavior modification as a technique for motivating employees rather than as a theory of work motivation. It does not attempt to provide a comprehensive model of the various personal and job-related variables that contribute to motivation. Instead, its managerial thrust is how to motivate, and it is probably this emphasis that has led to its current popularity among some managers. Even so, we should be cautioned against the unquestioned acceptance of any technique until we understand the assumptions underlying the model. If the underlying assumptions of a model appear to be uncertain or inappropriate in a particular situation or organization, its use is clearly questionable.

Assumptions of Behavior Modification

The foundation of behavior modification as a technique of management rests on three ideas.[21] First, advocates of behavior modification believe that individuals are basically passive and reactive (instead of proactive). They tend to respond to stimuli in their environment rather than assuming personal responsibility in initiating behavior. This assertion is in direct contrast to cognitive theories of motivation (such as expectancy/valence theory, discussed in Chapter 6), which hold that individuals make conscious decisions about their present and future behaviors and take an active role in shaping their environment.

Second, advocates of behavior modification focus on observable and measurable behavior instead of on unobservable needs, attitudes, goals, or motivational levels. In contrast, cognitive theories focus on both observable and unobservable factors as they relate to motivation. Social learning theory, in particular, argues that individuals can change their behavior simply by observing others and noticing the punishments or rewards that the observed behaviors produce.

Third, behavior modification stresses that permanent changes can be brought about only as a result of reinforcement. Behaviors that are positively reinforced will be repeated (that is, learned), whereas behaviors not so reinforced will diminish (according to the law of effect, discussed earlier in this chapter).

Designing a Behavior Modification Program

If behavior modification techniques are to work, their application must be well designed and systematically applied. Systematic attempts to implement these programs typically go through five phases (see Exhibit 4.8).

Exhibit 4.8
Steps in Implementing a Behavior Modification Program

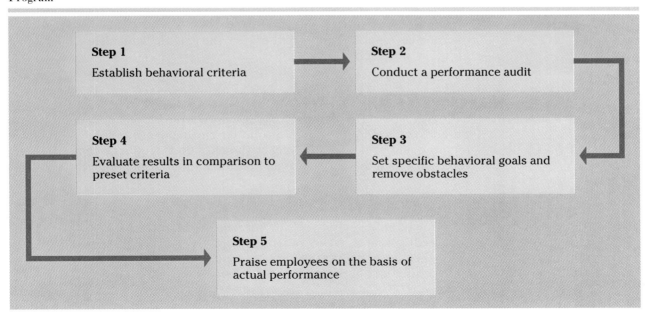

Step 1
Establish behavioral criteria

Step 2
Conduct a performance audit

Step 4
Evaluate results in comparison to preset criteria

Step 3
Set specific behavioral goals and remove obstacles

Step 5
Praise employees on the basis of actual performance

Establishing Clear Behavioral Criteria.　First, management attempts to define and clearly specify the behavioral aspects of acceptable performance. Management must be able to designate what constitutes acceptable behavior in terms that employees can understand, and this specification must be in objective, measurable terms. Examples of behavioral criteria include good attendance, promptness in arriving for work, and completing tasks on schedule. Sometimes it is difficult to determine suitable objective indicators of successful performance. For instance, as a training director of a major airline asked, "How do you quantify what a flight attendant does?" Even so, there are many situations and work behaviors that do lend themselves to clear specification.

Conducting a Performance Audit.　Once acceptable behavioral criteria have been specified, a performance audit can be done. Because management is concerned about the extent to which employees are successfully meeting the behavioral criteria, the audit is aimed at pinpointing trouble spots where desired behaviors are not being carried out. For instance, a review of attendance records of various departments may reveal a department in which absenteeism or tardiness is unusually high. Action can then be taken to focus on the problem area. In short, the performance audit aims to identify discrepancies between what management sees as desired or acceptable behavior and actual behavior.

Setting Specific Behavioral Goals.　Third, specific behavioral goals must be set for each employee. Failure to specify concrete behavioral goals is a primary reason for the failure of many behavior modification programs. Examples of such goals are decreasing absenteeism or tardiness, reducing product defects on an assembly line, and meeting production schedules. The goals should be both realistic (that is, reasonably achievable by the employees) and acceptable to them. Otherwise, the goals lack relevance, and resulting effort will diminish.

Evaluating Results.　Next, employees and supervisors keep track of the employee's performance record as compared to the preset behavioral criteria and goals. Discrepancies are noted and discussed. For example, the record could provide employees with continuous feedback concerning the extent to which they are on target in meeting their defect reduction goals.

Administering Feedback and Rewards.　Finally, on the basis of the assessment of the employee's performance record, the supervisor administers feedback and, where warranted, praise. For example, praise could strengthen the employees' efforts to reduce defects (positive reinforcement). The withholding of praise for defect levels deemed less than adequate or below established goals could cause employees to stop behavior that was contributing to defects or work harder to reduce defects (extinction).

Central to this phase of the process is the notion of *shaping.* Shaping is the process of improving performance incrementally, step by step. Suppose that an employee is absent 30 percent of the time during one month. To improve attendance, we would set a goal of being absent only 5 percent of the time. After implementing the above procedure, we find that absenteeism falls to 20 percent in the second month. Although this is not at goal level, it is clearly an improvement and, as such, is rewarded. The next month, absenteeism falls to 15 percent, and, again, we reward the incremental improvement. Hence, by this incremental approach, the employee gets ever closer to the desired level of behavior. In other words, we have "shaped" his or her behavior.

IN PRACTICE
Behavior Modification on the Shop Floor

There are many ways to see how the principles of behavior modification can be applied in organizational settings. Perhaps one of the best examples can be found in a classic study carried out by Luthans and Kreitner.[22] These researchers carried out a field experiment in a medium-sized light manufacturing plant. Two separate groups of supervisors were used in the study. In one group (the experimental group—see Appendix A), the supervisors were trained in the techniques of behavior modification. This program was called "behavioral contingency management," or BCM. Included here were ten 90-minute lectures conducted over ten weeks on behavioral change strategies. The second group of supervisors (the control group) received no such training. Following this, the trained supervisors were asked to implement what they had learned among their groups; obviously, the control group supervisors were given no such instructions.

After ten weeks, group performance was examined for all groups. Two types of data were collected. First, the researchers were interested in any possible behavioral changes among the various workers in the experimental groups (compared to the control groups) as a result of the behavior modification efforts. Significantly, the following changes were noted for these groups in areas that were targeted for change: (1) the frequency of complaints among group members declined; (2) the scrap rates declined; (3) group quality indicators increased; and (4) the frequency of individual performance problems declined. No such changes were recorded for the control groups not exposed to behavior modification. The second measure taken focused on the overall performance rates for the various groups. This was calculated as a measure of direct labor effectiveness for each group. Again, overall group performance—that is, labor effectiveness ratings—improved significantly in the experimental groups but remained unchanged in the control groups. This can be seen in Exhibit 4.9. The researchers concluded that the introduction of the behavioral modification program led to substantive improvements in factory performance.

Exhibit 4.9
Intergroup Comparison of
Performance Using BCM

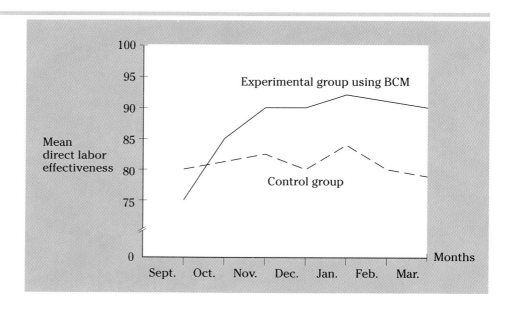

BEHAVIORAL SELF-MANAGEMENT

The second managerial technique for shaping learned behavior in the workplace is *behavioral self-management* (or BSM). Behavioral self-management is the process of modifying one's own behavior by systematically managing cues, cognitive processes, and contingent consequences.[23] BSM is an approach to learning and behavioral change that relies on the individual to take the initiative in controlling the change process. The emphasis here is on "behavior" (because our focus is on changing behaviors), not attitudes, values, or personality. Although similar to behavior modification, BSM differs in one important respect: there is a heavy emphasis on cognitive processes, reflecting the influence of Bandura's social learning theory.

The Self-Regulation Process

Underlying BSM is a firm belief that individuals are capable of self-control; if they want to change their behavior (whether it is to come to work on time, quit smoking, lose weight, etc.), it is possible through a process called *self-regulation,* as depicted in Exhibit 4.10.[24] According to the model, people tend to go about their day's activities fairly routinely until something unusual or unexpected occurs. At this point, the individual initiates the self-regulation process by entering into *self-monitoring* (Stage 1). In this stage, the individual tries to identify the problem. For example, if your supervisor told you that your choice of clothing was unsuitable for the office, you would more than likely focus your attention on your clothes.

Next, in Stage 2, or *self-evaluation,* you would consider what you should be wearing. Here, you would compare what you have on to acceptable standards

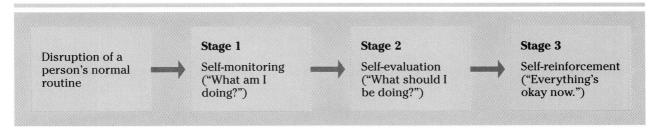

Exhibit 4.10
Kanfer's Model
of Self-Regulation

that you learned from colleagues, other relevant role models, and advertising, for example. Finally, after evaluating the situation and taking corrective action if necessary, you would assure yourself that the disruptive influence had passed and everything was now fine. This phase (Stage 3) is called *self-reinforcement.* You are now able to return to your normal routine. This self-regulation process forms the foundation for BSM.

Self-Management in Practice

When we combine the above self-regulation model with social learning theory (discussed earlier), we can see how the self-management process works. As shown in Exhibit 4.11, four interactive factors must be taken into account. These are *situational cues, the person, behaviors,* and *consequences.*[25] (Note that the arrows in this diagram go in both directions to reflect the two-way process among these four factors.)

Situational Cues.   In attempting to change any behavior, people respond to the cues surrounding them. One reason it is so hard for some people to give up smoking is the constant barrage of advertisements on billboards, in magazines, and so forth. There are too many cues reminding people to smoke. However, situational cues can be turned to our advantage when using BSM. That is, through the use of six kinds of cue (shown in Exhibit 4.11, column 1),

Exhibit 4.11
A Social Learning Theory
Model of Self-Management

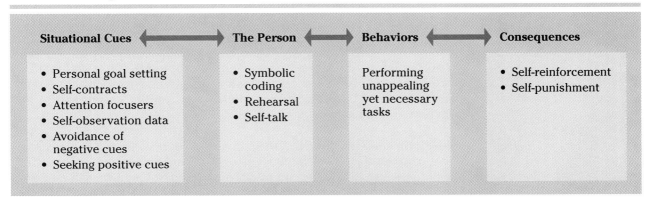

people can set forth a series of positive reminders and goals concerning the desired behaviors. These reminders serve to focus our attention on what we are trying to accomplish. Hence, a person who is trying to quit smoking would (1) avoid any contact with smokers or smoking ads, (2) seek information on the hazards of smoking, (3) set a personal goal of quitting, and (4) keep track of cigarette consumption. These activities are aimed at providing the right situational cues to guide behavior.

Cognitive Supports.   Next, the person makes use of three types of cognitive support to assist with the self-management process. Cognitive supports represent psychological (as opposed to environmental) cues. Three such supports can be identified:

1. *Symbolic Coding.* First, people may use symbolic coding, whereby they try to associate verbal or visual stimuli with the problem. For example, we may create a picture in our mind of a smoker who is coughing and obviously sick. Thus, every time we think of cigarettes, we would associate it with illness.
2. *Rehearsal.* Second, people may mentally rehearse the solution to the problem. For example, we may imagine how we would behave in a social situation without cigarettes. By doing so, we develop a self-image of how it would be under the desired condition.
3. *Self-Talk.* Finally, people can give themselves "pep talks" to continue their positive behavior. We know from behavioral research that people who take a negative view of things ("I can't do this") tend to fail more than people who take a more positive view ("Yes, I can do this"). Thus, through self-talk, we can help convince ourselves that the desired outcome is indeed possible.

Behavioral Dilemmas.   Obviously, self-management is used almost exclusively to get people to do things that may be unappealing; we need little incentive to do things that are fun. Hence, we use self-management to get individuals to stop procrastinating on a job, attend to a job that may lack challenge, assert themselves, and so forth. These are the "behavioral dilemmas" referred to in the model (Exhibit 4.11). In short, the challenge is to get people to substitute what have been called low-probability behaviors (e.g., adhering to a schedule or forgoing the immediate gratification from one cigarette) for high-probability behaviors (e.g., procrastinating or contracting lung cancer). In the long run, it is better for the individual— and his or her career—to shift behaviors, because failure to do so may lead to punishment or worse. As a result, people often use self-management to change their short-term dysfunctional behaviors into long-range beneficial ones. This short- versus long-term conflict is referred to as a behavioral dilemma.

Self-Reinforcement.   Finally, the individual can provide *self-reinforcement.* People can, in effect, pat themselves on the back and recognize that they accomplished what they set out to do. According to Bandura, self-reinforcement requires three conditions if it is to be effective: (1) clear performance

SELF-ASSESSMENT 4.1
Designing Your Own Behavioral Self-Management Program

Instructions: Think of a personal problem that you would like to overcome. This problem could be to stop smoking, improve your grades, stop a certain habit, and so forth. With this problem in mind, design your own behavioral self-management program using the procedures and principles previously outlined in this chapter. After you have designed and started the program, monitor your performance over time and see how effective you are both in following the program and in meeting your objectives. In light of your experience, how do you feel about the potential of behavioral self-management programs in the industrial setting? (See Appendix B.)

standards must be set to establish both the quantity and quality of the targeted behavior; (2) the person must have control over the desired reinforcers; and (3) the reinforcers must be administered only on a conditional basis—that is, failure to meet the performance standard must lead to denial of the reward.[26] Thus, through a process of working to change one's environment and taking charge of one's own behavior, self-management techniques allow individuals to improve their behavior in a way that can help them and those around them.

In order to understand better how behavioral self-management programs operate, you might want to complete Self-Assessment 4.1 and design your own self-management program. This exercise allows you to see firsthand how these programs can be applied to a wide array of problems. It also highlights the advantages and drawbacks of such programs. Refer to Appendix B when you are finished in order to evaluate your results.

IN PRACTICE
Reducing Absenteeism Through Self-Management

In a recent study, efforts were made to reduce employee absenteeism using some of the techniques found in behavioral self-management. The employees were unionized state government workers with a history of absenteeism. Self-management training was given to these workers. Training was carried out over eight one-hour sessions for each group, along with eight 30-minute one-on-one sessions with each participant.

Included in these sessions were efforts to (1) teach the participants how to describe problem behaviors (e.g., disagreements with co-workers) that led to absences; (2) identify the causes creating and maintaining the behaviors;

and (3) develop coping strategies. Participants set both short-term and long-term goals with respect to modifying their behaviors. In addition, they were shown how to record their own absences in reports including their frequency and the reasons for and consequences of them. Finally, participants identified potential reinforcers and punishments that could be self-administered contingent upon goal attainment or failure.

When, after nine months, the study was concluded, results showed that the self-management approach had led to a significant reduction in absences (compared to a control group). The researchers concluded that such an approach has important applications to a wide array of behavioral problems in the workplace.[27]

PULLING IT ALL TOGETHER

People learn both through direct experience and vicarious experience. What is retained and produced as behavior is a function of the positive and negative consequences either directly experience by individuals or observed as the result of the actions of others. Often, managers and trainers underestimate the power of vicarious learning. Also, keep in mind that reinforcement that has some variability in its application (variable ratio or interval) has the strongest and longest-lasting impact on desired learned behaviors.

SUMMARY OF KEY POINTS

■ Learning is a relatively permanent change in behavior that occurs as a result of experience.

■ Thorndike's law of effect notes that behavior that is rewarded is likely to be repeated, whereas behavior that is punished is unlikely to be repeated.

■ Operant conditioning can be distinguished from classical conditioning in two ways: (1) it asserts that changes in behavior result from the consequences of previous behaviors instead of changes in stimuli, and (2) it asserts that desired behaviors result only when rewards are tied to correct responses instead of when unconditioned stimuli are administered after every trial.

■ Social learning is the process of altering behavior through the reciprocal interaction of a person's cognitions, previous behavior, and environment. This is done through a process of reciprocal determinism.

■ Vicarious learning is learning that takes place through observation and imitation of others.

■ Learning is influenced by (1) a motivation to learn, (2) knowledge of results, (3) prior learning, (4) the extent to which the task to be learned is presented as a whole or in parts, and (5) distribution of practice.

■ Reinforcement causes a certain behavior to be repeated or inhibited. Positive reinforcement is the practice of presenting someone with an attractive outcome following a desired behavior.

■ Avoidance learning occurs when someone attempts to avoid an unpleasant condition or outcome by behaving in a way desired by others.

■ Punishment is the administration of an unpleasant or adverse outcome following an undesired behavior.

■ Reinforcement schedules may be continuous or partial. Among the partial reinforcement schedules are (1) fixed-interval, (2) fixed-ratio, (3) variable-interval, and (4) variable-ratio.

■ Behavior modification is the use of operant principles to shape human behavior to conform to desired standards as defined by superiors. A behavior modification program follows five steps: (1) establish clear objectives; (2) conduct a performance audit; (3) set specific goals and remove obstacles; (4) evaluate results against preset criteria; and (5) administer feedback and praise where warranted.

■ Behavioral self-management is the process of modifying one's own behavior by systematically managing cues, cognitions, and contingent consequences. BSM makes use of the self-regulation process.

KEY WORDS

avoidance learning	partial reinforcement
behavior modification	performance audit
behavioral criteria	positive reinforcement
behavioral dilemmas	punishment
behavioral self-management	reciprocal determinism
classical conditioning	reinforcement
conditioned response	self-regulation
continuous reinforcement	self-reinforcement
drive	self-talk
extinction	shaping
habit	social learning theory
law of effect	symbolic coding
learning	unconditioned response
operant conditioning	vicarious learning

QUESTIONS FOR DISCUSSION

1. Define learning. Why is an understanding of learning important for managers?
2. Compare and contrast operant conditioning with classical conditioning. Provide examples of each.
3. What is social learning theory? Describe how this process works.

4. What implications of social learning theory for management can you identify?
5. Identify four strategies for reinforcement, and provide an example of each.
6. Describe the four different schedules of reinforcement, and show how their use by managers can vary.
7. How might you design a simple behavior modification program for a group of employees? Explain.
8. What are some problems in trying to implement a behavioral self-management program? How can managers attempt to overcome these problems?

NOTES

1. W. Wiggenhorn, "Motorola U: When Training Becomes an Education," *Harvard Business Review,* July-August, 1990 pp. 71–83.
2. G. A. Kimble and N. Garmezy, *Principles of General Psychology* (New York: Ronald Press, 1963).
3. J. M. Ivancevich, A. D. Szilagyi, and M. Wallace, *Organizational Behavior and Performance* (Glenview, Ill.: Scott, Foresman, 1977), p. 80.
4. B. F. Skinner, "Operant Behavior," *American Psychologist,* 1963, *18,* pp. 503–515.
5. J. B. Watson, Behavior: An *Introduction to Comparative Psychology* (New York: Holt, Rinehart and Winston, 1914).
6. E. L. Thorndike, *Animal Intelligence* (New York: Macmillan, 1911), p. 244.
7. F. Luthans, *Organizational Behavior* (New York: McGraw-Hill, 1988).
8. A. Bandura, *Social Learning Theory* (Englewood Cliffs, N.J.: Prentice-Hall, 1977).
9. A. Filley, R. J. House, and S. Kerr, *Managerial Process and Organizational Behavior* (Glenview, Ill.: Scott, Foresman, 1975).
10. E. J. McCormick and J. Tiffin, *Industrial Psychology* (Englewood Cliffs, N.J.: Prentice-Hall, 1976).
11. B. M. Bass and J. Vaughn, *Training in Industry: The Management of Learning* (Belmont, Ca.: Wadsworth, 1966); G. P. Latham, "Human Resource Training and Development," in M. Rosenzweig and L. W. Porter, eds., *Annual Review of Psychology* (Palo Alto: Annual Reviews, 1988), pp. 545–581.
12. J. Lublin. "Companies Use Cross-Cultural Training to Help Their Employees Adjust Abroad." *Wall Street Journal,* August 4, p. B1.
13. B. F. Skinner, *Science and Human Behavior* (New York: Macmillan, 1953), p. 73.
14. W. C. Hamner, "Reinforcement Theory," in H. L. Tosi and W. C. Hamner, eds., *Organizational Behavior and Management: A Contingency Approach* (Chicago: St. Clair, 1977), p. 98.
15. This ethical challenge is based on a true but disguised case observed by the second author.
16. T. W. Costello and S. S. Zalkind, *Psychology in Administration: A Research Orientation* (Englewood Cliffs, N.J.: Prentice-Hall, 1963), p. 193.
17. Hamner, op. cit., p. 105.
18. Ibid.
19. R. Phalon, "Hell Camp," *Forbes,* June 18, 1984, pp. 56–58.
20. "Productivity Gains from a Pat on the Back," *Business Week,* January 23, 1978, pp. 56–62.
21. B. F. Skinner, *Beyond Freedom and Dignity* (New York: Knopf, 1971).

22. F. Luthans and R. Kreitner, *Organizational Behavior Modification* (Glenview, Ill.: Scott, Foresman, 1975), pp. 150–159.

23. F. Luthans and R. Davis, "Behavioral Self-Management—The Missing Link in Managerial Effectiveness," *Organizational Dynamics,* Summer 1979, p. 43; F. Luthans and R. Kreitner, *Organizational Behavior Modification and Beyond: An Operant and Social Learning Approach* (Glenview, Ill.: Scott, Foresman, 1985).

24. F. H. Kanfer and A. P. Goldstein, *Helping People Change: A Textbook of Methods* (New York: Pergamon Press, 1980).

25. C. C. Manz, The Art of Self-Leadership (Englewood Cliffs, N.J.: Prentice-Hall, 1983).

26. A. Bandura, "Self-Reinforcement: Theoretical and Methodological Considerations," *Behaviorism,* Fall 1976, pp. 135–155; Luthans and Kreitner, *Organizational Behavior Modification and Beyond.*

27. G. Latham and C. Fayne, "Self-Management Training for Increasing Job Attendance," *Journal of Applied Psychology,* 1989, pp. 411–416.

EXPERIENTIAL EXERCISE 4

Designing a Training Program for the Customer Service Department

The Customer Service Department of a major public utility is responsible for handling customer complaints and requests for service. The company is keenly aware that this department is the primary interface between them and their customers. Because of recent deregulation, the company is also aware that their customers can take their business elsewhere if they are not satisfied with the level or quality of service they receive.

The department contains 30 clerical workers. Most of these are women ranging in age from 19 to 57. The office operates only on a day shift from 8:00 to 5:00. It is important that the phones and front desk are staffed adequately during these periods.

Recently, top management has become concerned with what they believe to be excessive tardiness and absenteeism among the workers in the department. At 8:10 on a recent day, for example, management counted only half the workers present; more straggled in during the next ten minutes. Moreover, on any given day absence runs around 20 percent, far higher than the industry average. Because of these problems, the company has had to hire more employees than should be needed just to keep the department running smoothly. As a result, personnel costs have risen to an unacceptable level, and management has determined to take corrective action.

You are the personnel manager for this company. It is important to you that this problem of tardiness and absenteeism be solved so that customer service (and profitability) does not suffer. However, these employees are valuable to the company, and you do not want to alienate them unduly. Terminating employees would be a very grave decision for this company and would probably lead to legal action by the employees. Because of current budget cuts, there is no money with which to entice the employees to improve their attendance records.

Group A: Use the ideas of operant conditioning to design a program that would reduce the problems of tardiness and absenteeism.

Group B: Use the ideas of behavior modification and reinforcement to design a program to reduce these problems.

Group C: Use the ideas of social learning theory to design a program that would reduce the problems of tardiness and absenteeism.

MANAGEMENT DILEMMA 4

Jim Preston's Declining Performance

Ever since the Atlas Electrical Supply Co. was bought out by Carey and Co., Jim Preston had been in a sales slump. A leading salesman for Atlas for the past twenty-eight years, Preston had enjoyed handsome monthly bonuses, thanks to the company's incentive pay system. He had always been proud of the extra money, both as a symbol of his value to the company and for the practical uses to which he had applied it. He often boasted that the bonuses had helped him complete his mortgage several years early as well as finance his daughter's education at the University of Toronto. In the four months since the new managment had taken over, however, Jim's sales had fallen off sharply, along with his enthusiasm and company spirit, even though the bonus system was still being used. In fact, he had not collected a bonus in months. Sarah Powell, Jim's new supervisor since the takeover, was concerned. She held a series of informal discussions with Jim and several other sales personnel to try to get to the bottom of Jim's problems.

Mrs. Powell learned from her meetings that Jim resented being supervised by a woman who was younger than his own daughter—now a college graduate. He blew up at her during one of their meetings, yelling, "All of you new brass are the same—always trying to squeeze more out of the little guy. You think you know everything about selling! I was selling electrical parts and supplies before you or any of the other Carey supervisors were old enough to know what they are. Now you're telling me how to do my job. Why don't you get off my back? It's my business if I don't earn any bonuses!"

Sarah was startled by Preston's outburst and concerned by his apparent resentment and hostility toward her. She learned that several of Preston's fellow salesmen, who were mostly younger than he, also resented his resistance to the recent attempt to unionize the office staff. Several of them claimed that he was "a real company man," even though his sales figures didn't reflect it. She also learned that Jim was periodically receiving sales directives from Stan Campbell, Jim's former boss who had been moved laterally at the time of the takeover. Jim claimed he was never told clearly who his new supervisor was, now that the companies had merged.

Also attending a luncheon meeting on job redesign, Sarah tried to "motivate" higher sales from Jim by adding to the product lines he carried, giving him a larger district to cover, and letting him move upstairs into a slightly larger office. She hoped that the changes would arouse new energy in Preston, who, to her added frustration, seemed increasingly more preoccupied with his imminent retirement to a country town. Finally, Sarah asked Jim if he would like to retire early. He declined the offer, but Sarah recommended to her boss that they give old Jim "the golden handshake." Nothing else had worked.

Assume you are Sarah Powell.

1. On the basis of the materials presented in this chapter, how would you explain Jim Preston's behavior?
2. What course of action would you take to turn Preston around into a more motivated employee if your boss declined your suggestion to fire him?

Source: C. C. Pinder, *Work Motivation: Theory, Issues, and Applications* (Glenview, Ill.: Scott, Foresman and Company, 1984). Reprinted by permission of Scott, Foresman and Company.

Employee Motivation:
Basic Concepts

The Management Challenge

- To understand what motivates employees and why they behave as they do in organizational settings.
- To motivate employees to contribute their best for the organization.
- To know how to identify employee needs and aspirations and respond accordingly.
- To match people to jobs in a way that maximizes individual contributions to overall organizational success.
- To stimulate creativity and "intrapreneurship" within a group.

CLOSE UP

How to Motivate Fast Trackers During Decline?

Edgar J. Woolard, 56, took 32 years and 22 jobs to become the CEO of Du Pont. In fact, in his race to the top, Woolard never spent more than three years in any one position. In the 1980s, Du Pont cut nearly 10 percent of its workforce. Unlike the past, most of these cuts were achieved by eliminating management positions. As a result, Du Pont is a much flatter organization.

Unfortunately, for those who would also like to take a similar track to the top, it is likely to be a much slower trip. First, the competitive pressures in the 1980s that led many corporations, including Du Pont, to trim or even slash their workforce resulted in fewer management positions into which fast trackers could be promoted. Second, this reduction in middle management positions could not have come at a worse time. Now in their thirties and forties, the 81 million baby boomers are clogging the management ranks.

So how can firms keep these "go-getters" going? Most of these "boomers" were raised in a time of growing prosperity, and many earned MBAs from top schools whose faculty and administrators reinforced their ambitions of racing to the top. In a survey of 700 managers, Korn/Ferry International found that 70 percent of the managers were dissatisfied both with their responsibilities and attainments. "There is a grudging awareness and acknowledgment that there is a slowing down, that organizations are flatter, and that there are fewer levels to go to," noted Harold E. Johnson, a Korn/Ferry managing vice-president.

Will it be fear of being next to hit the unemployment line, broader responsibilities but slower advancement and pay increases, more lateral moves, more overseas transfers, or will the Du Ponts, GEs, IBMs, and GMs of the world find it impossible to motivate the former fast trackers who are now stuck?[1]

To understand this question, it is necessary to explore the subject of employee motivation as it relates to job performance. Such is the topic of this and the next chapters. As any manager will tell you, a thorough knowledge of basic motivational processes is essential for understanding organizational dynamics. Managerial and organizational effectiveness cannot be achieved without a motivated work force. Hence, we need to understand why people behave as they do on the job. What causes good or bad performance? Why do people skip work or leave the company altogether? The answers to questions such as these can only be found by comprehending what motivates the employee.

It is also important to have a clear grasp of the topic of employee needs. A knowledge of how employees differ can help the manager better understand his or her employees and, as a result, take actions aimed at facilitating employee satisfaction. Consider, for instance, the implications for employee selection and placement. As we shall see, certain types of employees are likely to be more successful in sales positions, whereas others are likely to excel in staff positions (such as personnel administration). Understanding these differences can be useful in making decisions concerning who is placed in which positions.

The concept of employee needs also has clear implications for reward practices. Because employees respond differently to different rewards, an awareness of differences in needs can help the manager design appropriate reward systems. The recognition that employees pursue different goals also helps the manager understand, to some extent, why different employees behave as they do. For instance, an employee with a high need for achievement is likely to pursue task-related activities with vigor, whereas an employee with a high need for affiliation may devote more attention to developing social relationships on the job.

BASIC MOTIVATIONAL PROCESSES

The word *motivation* is derived from the ancient Latin *movere,* which means "to move." As the word is used in the study of employee motivation in work settings, however, this definition is clearly inadequate. A more comprehensive approach defines motivation as that which energizes, directs, and sustains human behavior.

This more complete definition emphasizes three distinct aspects of motivation that are important. First, motivation represents an energetic force that *drives* people to behave in particular ways. Second, this drive is directed *toward* something. In other words, motivation has strong goal orientation. Third, the idea of motivation is best understood within a *systems* perspective. That is, to understand human motivation, it is necessary to examine the forces within individuals and their environments that provide them with feedback and reinforce their intensity and direction.

Before considering the various models of employee motivation that are currently in use, we will examine the nature of the underlying motivational process. Although the models of motivation may sometimes differ in certain aspects, they all tend to share basic assumptions about how behavior is

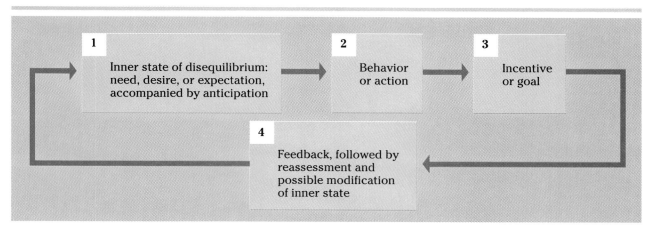

Exhibit 5.1
A Model of Basic
Motivational Processes

energized, directed, and sustained through time. A generalized model of the *basic motivational process* is shown in Exhibit 5.1. As can be seen in this exhibit, there are four basic components of the process: (1) needs or expectations, (2) behavior, (3) goals, and (4) feedback.[2]

At any point in time, employees have a constellation of needs, desires, and expectations. For instance, one worker may have a strong need for achievement, a desire for monetary gain, and an expectation that doing his job well will, in fact, lead to the receipt of desired rewards. When such needs, desires, and expectations are present, people experience a state of inner disequilibrium. This disequilibrium, in turn, may cause behavior that is directed toward specific goals. Having these goals facilitates a return to a state of homeostasis, or balance. The resulting behavior activates a series of cues (either within the individual or from the external environment) that feed messages back to the individuals concerning the impact of their behavior. This feedback may serve to reassure individuals that the behavior is correct (that is, that it satisfies their needs), or it may tell them that their present course of action is incorrect and should be modified.

Consider the following example. A young sales representative has a high need for personal achievement. She experiences an inner state of disequilibrium because a need exists that has not been met. On the basis of the strength or potency of this need, the representative engages in behavior that she believes will lead to feelings of personal accomplishment. For instance, she may attempt to outsell her colleagues, thereby receiving recognition for a job done well. On the basis of this goal-directed behavior, she receives feedback both from her own assessment of her behavior and from others. The feedback may tell her that she has indeed accomplished something important or worthwhile, returning her (at least temporarily) to a state of homeostasis with respect to this particular need.

Although this simple model obviously does not take into account all influences on human motivation, it is illustrative of the basic nature of the process. Moreover, it emphasizes the cyclical nature of motivation. It shows that people are in a continual state of disequilibrium, constantly striving to satisfy a variety of needs. Once one need has been adequately met, another need or desire emerges to stimulate further action. In this way, people direct and redirect their energies as they attempt to adapt to changing needs and a changing environment.

EARLY THEORIES OF MOTIVATION

The topic of motivation has long been of concern to both managers and psychologists. However, until recently, the emphases and approaches of these two groups differed sharply. In order to gain a clearer understanding of how contemporary models evolved, it is necessary to touch on the developmental sequences of both psychological and managerial models of motivation. Because much of the work by managers is based on previous psychological studies, we begin with the corpus of psychological research.

Psychological Approaches to Motivation

We can identify four stages in the psychological research on motivational processes: (1) hedonism, (2) instinct theory, (3) reinforcement theory, and (4) cognitive theory. As we will see, although psychologists originally approached the topic of motivation from a quite different perspective than did management theorists, the contemporary positions of both groups have apparently converged to a considerable extent. This convergence is shown in Exhibit 5.2.

Exhibit 5.2
Evolution of Approaches
to Motivation

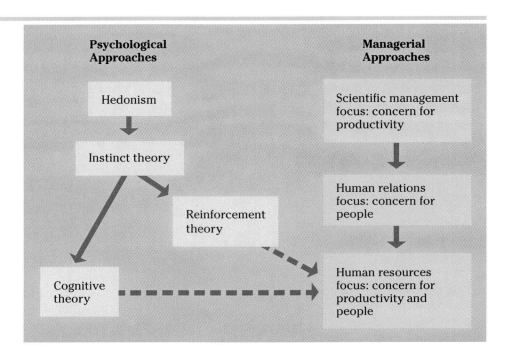

Hedonism.   The first coherent documentation of the principle of *hedonism* dates from the time of the early Greeks. It later reemerged in the eighteenth and nineteenth centuries as a popular explanation of behavior among such philosophers as Locke, Bentham, and Mill. Briefly, the principle of hedonism implies that individuals will tend to seek pleasure and avoid pain. It is assumed that individuals are likely to do those things that bring them some kind of satisfaction and to avoid those that are less satisfying.

Although the concept of hedonism is still pervasive throughout our current models of motivation, it is far too simplistic to represent a comprehensive explanation of motivated behavior. Moreover, it fails to account for those instances when people engage in various activities even though they may be unpleasant. Hence, more complete explanations of behavior are needed. The next such theory that evolved was instinct theory.

Instinct Theory.   The first psychological theory of motivation emerged late in the nineteenth century (around 1890) as a result of the work of James, Freud, and McDougall. These theorists argued that a large portion of human behavior is not conscious and rational, as hedonism suggests. Instead, behavior was thought to be largely influenced by instincts. An *instinct* was defined as an inherited biological tendency toward certain objects or actions.[3] Included in the list of instincts were locomotion, curiosity, love, fear, jealousy, and sympathy. These instincts were thought to be the primary determinants of behavior.

Although instinct theory was fairly widely accepted during the first quarter of this century, in the 1920s it came under increasing attack on several grounds.[4] Among other things, the list of instincts continued to grow, ultimately reaching almost 6000. With so many variables, it became exceedingly difficult to develop a cogent explanation of human behavior. Moreover, there was no acceptable explanation concerning which of the many instincts would be stronger influences on performance. As a result, in the absence of a solid conceptual framework, it was difficult to predict behavior. Also, a number of research studies found only a very weak relationship between an instinct and subsequent behavior. Other factors in addition to the instincts under study were apparently also influencing behavior. Finally, it was argued by some psychologists that instincts are not inherited, but rather represent *learned* behavior. This last criticism was advanced by those who subsequently suggested a quite different theory of motivation: reinforcement theory.

Reinforcement Theory.   As we saw in the previous chapter, reinforcement theory, beginning with the early work of Thorndike, Woodworth, and Hull, emerged in the 1920s as a widely accepted systematic explanation of behavior. Reinforcement theory assumes that people make decisions about their current behavior on the basis of consequences or rewards of past behavior. When past actions lead to positive consequences or rewards, individuals are likely to repeat them. On the other hand, when past actions lead to negative consequences or punishment, individuals are likely to avoid repeating them. This contention, known as the *law of effect* (see Chapter 4), emphasizes the role of learning on human behavior. Past learning and previous stimulus-response connections are viewed as the major causes of behavior. Today, as we have seen, reinforcement still remains a popular explanation of human behavior.

Cognitive Theory. The most recent psychological approach (arising in the early 1940s) to understanding motivation is cognitive theory. In contrast to reinforcement theory, in which emphasis is placed on the influence of past rewards and reinforcements, cognitive models emphasize future expectations and beliefs. That is, individuals are viewed as rational beings who make conscious decisions about their present and future behavior on the basis of what they believe will happen.[5] In other words, they use their cognitive processes. Past behavior influences these decisions only to the extent that the individual believes that past cause-effect relationships affect future events. For example, if you do not believe that your boss will reward you for extra effort because he has not rewarded you in the past, you are unlikely to put in extra time and energy beyond that which is required. Behavior, therefore, is seen as purposeful, goal-directed, and based on the conscious behavioral intentions of individuals. Significantly, it is this emphasis on reasoning and anticipation that sets cognitive models apart from other models of motivation.

The influence of cognitive theories is pervasive and can be seen in several models of employee effort and performance that are discussed in Chapter 6. In particular, equity theory, goal-setting theory, and expectancy/valence theory all draw heavily from the basic cognitive model.

Managerial Approaches to Motivation

The evolution of management thought concerning employee motivation has also passed through several relatively distinct stages—the traditional approach, the human relations approach, and the human resources approach.[6] It is interesting to note that as managerial thinking evolved through these three phases, the focus of managerial motivation efforts also shifted—from concern for production to concern for people and finally to concern for both production and people.

Traditional Model: Concern for Production. With the emergence of the industrial revolution in the late 1800s, it became necessary for managers to redefine both their conception of the nature of work and the social relationships between people in various levels in organizations. A need existed for a new philosophy of management that was consistent with the prevailing managerial beliefs of the times. These beliefs held that the average worker was basically lazy and was motivated almost entirely by money. Moreover, it was felt by many managers that few workers wanted or could handle a high degree of autonomy or self-direction on their jobs. These assumptions are summarized in Exhibit 5.3. The underlying focus of this approach was to discover ways to increase production; improving conditions of work or employee well-being was of secondary concern.

On the basis of these assumptions, it was felt that the best way to motivate employees was to pay them using a piece-rate system, then redesign their jobs to maximize the amount of output of the average worker. This job redesign, which was at the heart of the *scientific management* movement, was aimed not at enrichment but at job simplification and fractionization. The simpler the task, it was reasoned, the greater the output. The original advocates of scientific management (such as Frederick Taylor) saw this approach

Traditional Model	Human Relations Model	Human Resources Model
Assumptions		
1. Work is inherently distateful to most people.	1. People want to feel useful and important.	1. Work is not inherently distateful. People want to contribute to meaningful goals that they have helped establish.
2. What they do is less important than what they earn for doing it.	2. People desire to belong and to be recognized as individuals.	
3. Few want or can handle work that requires creativity, self-direction, or self-control.	3. These needs are more important than money in motivating people to work.	2. Most people can exercise far more creative, responsible self-direction and self-control than their present jobs demand.
Policies		
1. The manager's basic task is to closely supervise and control subordinates.	1. The manager's basic task is to make each worker feel useful and important.	1. The manager's basic task is to make use of "untapped" human resources.
2. He or she must break tasks down into simple, repetitive, easily learned operations.	2. He or she should keep subordinates informed and listen to their objections to his or her plans.	2. He or she must create an environment in which all members may contribute to the limits of their ability.
3. He or she must establish detailed work routines and procedures and enforce these firmly but fairly.	3. The manager should allow subordinates to exercise some self-direction and self-control on routine matters.	3. He or she must encourage full participation on important matters, continually broadening subordinates self-direction and control.
Expectations		
1. People can tolerate work if the pay is decent and the boss is fair.	1. Sharing information with subordinates and involving them in routine decisions will satisfy their basic needs to belong and to feel important.	1. Expanding subordinates' influence, self-direction, and self-control will lead to direct improvements in operating efficiency.
2. If tasks are simple enough and people are closely controlled, they will produce up to standard.	2. Satisfying these needs will improve morale and reduce resistance to formal authority; subordinates will "willingly cooperate."	2. Work satisfaction may improve as a "by-product" of subordinates' making full use of their resources.

Exhibit 5.3
General Patterns of
Managerial Approaches
to Motivation

as being far from exploitative in nature, but rather as being in the best interest of the worker, because workers' pay increased with output. It was felt that in exchange for increased income, workers would tolerate the fractionated and routine jobs of the factory.

Human Relations Model: Concern for People. As the scientific management movement gained momentum, several problems began to emerge. First, it became increasingly apparent that factors other than money had motivating potential. This is not to say that money was unimportant—only that it was not the sole influence on employee effort. Second, managers became aware that many employees were self-starters and did not need to be closely supervised and controlled. Finally, some managers attempted to use the job simplification techniques of scientific management without tying resulting output to pay increases. This practice led to employee distrust of management as wages fell behind productivity and more workers were laid off because of increased efficiency. The result was often reduced effort by workers, accompanied by drives for unionization. Thus, managers learned that the human factor had to be taken into account if long-term productivity was to be maintained.

This emphasis on the human factor in employee performance—that is, concern for people—began around 1930 and became known as the *human relations* movement. With this added perspective, the basic assumptions about the nature of people at work changed. It was now known that people wanted to feel useful and important at work; they wanted to be recognized as individuals. Such needs were seen to be as important as money (see Exhibit 5.3). Hence, managerial approaches to motivation were characterized by a strong social emphasis. Attention shifted away from the study of man-machine relations toward a better understanding of the nature of interpersonal and group relations on the job. The clearest example of this new emphasis was the Hawthorne study by Harvard psychologists Roethlisberger and Dickson, who found that the failure to treat employees as human beings was largely responsible for problems such as low morale and poor performance.[7]

In order to overcome these problems, managers were told to make employees feel important and involved. Morale surveys emerged as a popular index of employee discontent. Moreover, increased efforts were directed at opening new communication channels within organizations. Departmental meetings, company newspapers, and seminars on improving communications effectiveness all emerged to ensure that employees felt they were involved and were important to the organization. Finally, supervisory training programs were begun to train managers to understand the nature of group dynamics and how the forces that operate within them could be used for the benefit of the organization.

Two features carried through from the traditional theories of motivation. First, the basic goal of management under human relations was still to secure employee compliance with managerial authority; changed, however, were the strategies for accomplishing this (namely, there was increased concern for social dynamics in the workplace). Second, throughout the human relations movement, almost no attention was given to changing the nature of the job itself. Instead, emphasis was placed on making employees more satisfied (and, it was hoped, more productive) primarily through interpersonal strategies.

Human Resources Model: Concern for People and Productivity. More recently, it has become increasingly apparent that the assumptions underlying the human relations model represented an incomplete statement of human behavior at work. More contemporary models view motivation in more complex terms, assuming that *many* factors are capable of influencing behavior. These factors may include the nature of the incentive system; social influences; the nature of the job; supervisory style; and employee needs, values, and perceptions of the work environment. In addition, the newer models recognize clearly that performance and productivity gains cannot be ignored by managers. Thus, efforts must be made to tap human potential in such a way that employees can grow at work while simultaneously maximizing their contribution to workplace effectiveness. Given the realities of global competition, nothing less is acceptable.

This newer approach also assumes that different employees want different rewards from their jobs, that many employees sincerely want to contribute, and that employees by and large have the capacity to exercise a great deal of self-direction and self-control at work (see Exhibit 5.3). In short, many contemporary managerial views of motivation focus on employees as potential human resources. Given this assumption, it becomes management's responsibility to find ways to tap these resources so that the needs and goals of employees and organizations alike are served.

Better utilization of an organization's human resources can be accomplished in a variety of ways. First, attempts can be made to fit the person to the job so employees can most fully use their talents. Efforts can be made to integrate personal goals with organizational goals so employees can satisfy their own needs while working toward organizational objectives. The popular practice of paying sales representatives a commission or bonus based on level of sales is a good example of such goal integration (see Chapter 7). In addition, some organizations have increasingly turned to various forms of participative decision making to better utilize the talents, ideas, and suggestions of their employees in solving organizational problems (see Chapter 14). Contemporary managerial approaches to employee motivation thus take a more complex and comprehensive approach to understanding employee motivation and performance, as we will see in the following chapters.

IN PRACTICE
Why Do Japanese Want to Work at Kyocera?

International Challenge

What company do the Japanese admire most for innovation? Sony? Honda? Toyota? Guess again. In four surveys of 15,000 Japanese over the past five years top honors have gone to an outfit called Kyocera Corporation.

Why are the Japanese so motivated to work for Kyocera? It is its decidedly un-Japanese emphasis on innovation through highly original research. Company officials estimate that 90% of their products originated in their own labs. Kyocera is a pioneer. It has transformed the ancient craft of ceramics into an exciting technology that spans office machines, industrial cutting and grinding tools, and prosthetic devices such as artificial teeth and hips.

Kyocera's founder Kazuo Inamori acts more like the proprietor of a Silicon Valley startup than a conventional, conservative Japanese CEO. Twice since 1983 Inamori has been named the country's most effective manager by *Nikkei Business,* a leading magazine. Like his company, Inamori does un-Japanese things. He is an autocrat, yet he encourages grassroots enterprise and independence inside the company. Highly creative himself, he spends hours encouraging young engineers "to do things no one has done before."

In contrast, the company's reward system, is distinctly Japanese. In a booklet describing his philosophy, Inamori writes, "We don't think in terms of individual rewards. We don't buy individuals' loyalty with monetary incentives or titles. Rather, we believe that individuals who are endowed with superior capabilities should contribute their capabilities for the good of the entire group." Consequently, in Kyocera, an outstanding leader gets no extra money, at least not right away, but scores extra points toward promotion. In keeping with Inamori's belief in spiritual rewards, employees are offered no stock options.

Despite a lack of obvious extrinsic rewards, Kyocera has little difficulty attracting or motivating employees. One interesting means of motivating and instilling team spirit is by encouraging employees to take on one another in intramural sports during off-hours.[8]

CONCEPTUAL APPROACHES TO WORK MOTIVATION

We have traced the early developments in the study of employee motivation. On the basis of this analysis, we are in a position to consider several contemporary theories of motivation in both this chapter and the next. First, however, we should recognize the various types of theories. There are two common ways to categorize them. The first way is to distinguish between whether the model focuses on content or process. *Content theories* attempt to identify those factors that tend to cause a person to behave as he or she does. We are, in essence, looking for "things" that motivate behavior. Little or no analysis of sequential or interactive dynamics occurs. Some content theories, such as need theories, focus almost exclusively on the characteristics and inner drives of the person; these may also be called "person theories."[9] Hence, when we look at need theories, we are, in effect, asking which needs within a particular person are causing a certain kind of behavior. Other content theories focus largely on environmental influences on motivation. These theories include behavior modification and the basic reinforcement model discussed in the previous chapter. Reinforcement theory looks simply at ways of shaping behavior, not understanding it. This is why many people do not consider reinforcement theory a true theory of motivation, as discussed in Chapter 4.

Process theories, on the other hand, attempt to explain the psychological processes underlying behavior. As we shall see in the next chapter, this approach takes a systems perspective and looks for patterns of interactions in which many variables come together to jointly determine behavior. In a sense, process theories focus on the person-environment interaction.[10] Heavy emphasis is placed on understanding the decision processes within the person that underlie behaviors.

A second way to differentiate between the various theories of motivation is to distinguish between cognitive and acognitive models. That is, some theories of motivation are largely *acognitive,* or noncognitive, in the sense that they rely on overt observable behavior, not internal processes such as attitudes or feelings. A good example here is the basic reinforcement model discussed above and in the previous chapter. In fact, as shown in Exhibit 5.4, reinforcement theory is both an acognitive model (it ignores thought processes) and a content model (it looks simply at factors that influence motivation, not the underlying processes). *Cognitive* theories of motivation, on the other hand, focus on better understanding the feelings and thought processes people go through when making decisions concerning work behavior.

We examined an acognitive model in Chapter 4, and we will introduce several new cognitive models in Chapter 6. First, however, it will be useful for us to examine the concept of employee needs as they relate to motivation

Exhibit 5.4
Conceptual Approaches to
Work Motivation

Content Theories	**Need Theories**
(What factors influence motivation?)	• Need hierarchy theory • Manifest needs theory
	Acognitive Theories • Reinforcement theory
Process Theories (What are the underlying processes that cause motivation? How do they work?)	**Cognitive Theories** • Social learning theory • Equity theory • Goal-setting theory • Expectancy/valence theory

and behavior. The two models presented here, by Maslow and Murray, focus primarily on the interrelationship between individual motives or needs and subsequent behavior. Both of these *need theories* provide a useful foundation for understanding the more complex models that follow.

NEED HIERARCHY THEORY

Perhaps the most widely known theory of individual needs and motivation is the need hierarchy proposed by Abraham Maslow.[11] Maslow was a clinical psychologist who, in the 1940s, began his early developmental work on this theory among children with mental or emotional problems. On the basis of his observations, he attempted to develop a model of how the healthy personality grows and develops over time and how personality manifests itself in terms of motivated behavior. During the 1960s the theory was popularized among managers and organization analysts primarily through the work of Douglas McGregor.[12]

Basic Premises of the Need Hierarchy Model

The need hierarchy model consists of two basic premises. First, people are seen as being motivated by a desire to satisfy several different types of need (for example, needs for security, social interaction, self-esteem). Second, it is postulated that these needs are arranged in hierarchical form and that people attend to these needs in a sequential fashion, moving from the bottom of the hierarchy toward the top as their needs are satisfied. For example, if you are hungry because you have not eaten for a while, you will likely want to satisfy that need before worrying about satisfying your needs to belong to and be accepted by a group.

Maslow argues that there are two basic kinds of needs: deficiency needs and growth needs.[13] *Deficiency needs* are needs that must be satisfied if the individual is to be healthy and secure. "Needs for safety, the feeling of belonging, love and respect (from others) are all clearly deficits."[14] To the extent that these needs are not met, the individual will fail to develop a healthy personality. *Growth needs,* on the other hand, refer to those needs that relate to the development and achievement of one's potential. Maslow notes that the concept of growth needs is vague: "Growth, individuation, autonomy, self-actualization, self-development, productiveness, self-realization are all crudely synonymous, designating a vaguely perceived area rather than a sharply defined concept."[15]

Maslow goes further, suggesting that people are motivated by five rather general needs and that these needs are arranged in a hierarchy. In order of ascendance they are:

Deficiency Needs

1. *Physiological needs.* These needs are the most basic and include the needs for food, water, and sex.
2. *Safety needs.* The second level of needs centers around the need to provide a safe and secure physical and emotional environment—one that is free from threats to existence.
3. *Belongingness needs.* The third level consists of those needs relating to one's desire to be accepted by one's peers, to have friendships, and to be loved.

Growth Needs

4. *Esteem needs.* These needs focus on one's desire to have a worthy self-image and to receive recognition, attention, and appreciation from others for one's contributions.
5. *Self-actualization needs.* The highest need category is the need for self-fulfillment. Here the individual is concerned with developing his or her full potential as an individual and becoming all that it is possible to become.

Individuals are believed to move up the hierarchy by a process of *deprivation* and *gratification.* That is, when a particular need is unfulfilled (i.e., when the person is "deprived"), this need will emerge to dominate the individual's consciousness. Hence, a person concerned about physical safety will ignore other higher-order needs and devote all of his or her efforts to securing a safer environment. Once this need is gratified, however, that need submerges in importance and the next needs up the hierarchy are activated (in this case, belongingness needs). This dynamic cycle of alternating deprivation, domination, gratification, and activation continues throughout the various need levels until the individual reaches the self-actualization level.

Maslow, in his later writings, suggested that gratification of the need for self-actualization tends to cause an *increase* in the potency of this need instead of a decline. In other words, self-actualization is a process of *becoming;* this process is intensified, as well as sustained, as one gradually approaches self-fulfillment. Although Maslow did not believe that growth needs could be defined precisely, he did suggest, on the basis of his clinical observations, some characteristics exhibited by individuals manifesting such needs. These include the following:[16]

Superior perception of reality
Increased acceptance of self, of others, and of nature
Increased spontaneity
Increase in problem-centering
Increased detachment and desire for privacy
Increased autonomy and resistance to enculturation
Greater freshness of appreciation and richness of emotional reaction
Higher frequency of peak experiences
Increased identification with the human species
Changed (the clinician would say, improved) interpersonal relations
More democratic character structure
Greatly increased creativity

This constellation of factors, taken together, describes the rather abstract idea Maslow referred to as self-actualization. Although it is nice in theory, some have disagreed about the genuineness of this need.

Research Evidence on Need Hierarchy Theory

Maslow's work has prompted a good deal of research into the utility of the theory in organizational settings. For instance, it has been found that managers in higher echelons of organizations are generally more able to satisfy their growth needs than lower-level managers.[17] Such a finding follows from the fact that upper-level managers tend to have more challenging, autonomous jobs, where it is possible to seriously pursue growth needs. Lower-level managers, on the other hand, tend to have more routine jobs, which makes it more difficult to satisfy these needs.

However, although it is possible to differentiate between jobs that facilitate growth need satisfaction and those that inhibit it, it is much more difficult to establish the validity of the need hierarchy itself. In fact, after an extensive review of the research findings on the need hierarchy concept, Wahba and Bridwell conclude: "Maslow's need hierarchy theory presents the student of work motivation with an interesting paradox: The theory is widely accepted, but there is little research evidence to support it."[18]

Even so, the conclusion that does appear to stand empirical testing is the notion of two distinct need levels. That is, people generally attempt to satisfy deficiency needs before attending to growth needs. Ultimately, Maslow's need hierarchy model has proved useful in generating ideas about the basic nature of human motives and in providing a conceptual framework for understanding the diverse research findings about people at work.

Implications for Management

Maslow's needs hierarchy theory has proved to be particularly popular among managers, probably because of its simplicity as a conceptual framework in the discussion of motivation. When it is applied to organizations, clear recommendations for management emerge. The theory suggests that managers have a responsibility to create a work climate in which employees can satisfy their needs. Assuming that most employees have largely met their deficiency needs (i.e., they are free from hunger and threat and have established sufficient social relationships), managers can focus on creating a work climate that is aimed at satisfying growth needs. For instance, the proper climate may include opportunities for greater variety, autonomy, and responsibility so that employees can more fully realize their potential. Failure to provide such a climate would logically lead to increased employee frustration, poorer performance, lower job satisfaction, and increased withdrawal from work activities.

ERG Theory: A Reformulation

A modification of Maslow's original theory has been proposed by Clayton P. Alderfer.[19] Alderfer's reformulation was suggested largely in response to the failure of Maslow's five-level hierarchy to hold up to empirical validation. Alderfer reformulates Maslow's five need levels into three more general need levels:

1. *Existence needs.* Those needs required to sustain human existence, including both physiological and safety needs.
2. *Relatedness needs.* Those needs concerning how people relate to their surrounding social environment, including the need for meaningful social and interpersonal relationships.
3. *Growth needs.* Those needs relating to the development of human potential, including the needs for self-esteem and self-actualization. Growth needs are thought to be the highest need category.

Alderfer's model is similar to Maslow's earlier formulation in that both models posit that individuals move up the hierarchy one step at a time. The model differs from Maslow's, however, in two important regards. First, according to Maslow, individuals progress up the hierarchy as a result of the satisfaction of the lower-order needs. In contrast, Alderfer's ERG theory suggests that in addition to this satisfaction-progression process, there is also a frustration-regression process (see Exhibit 5.5). Hence, when an individual is

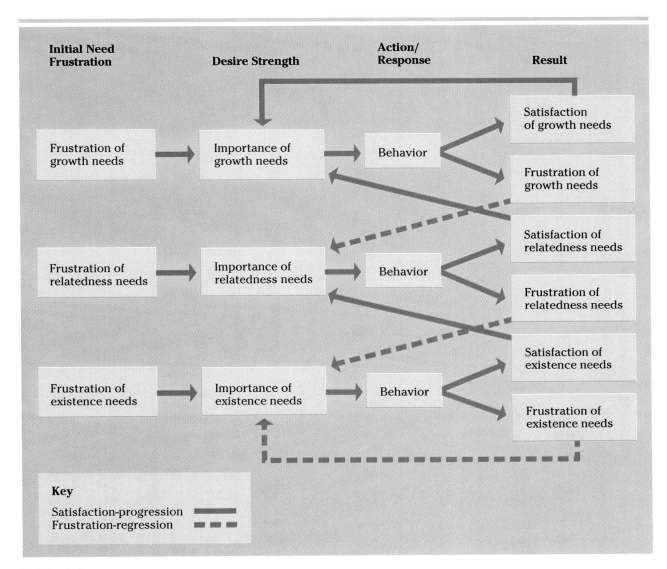

Exhibit 5.5
Satisfaction-Progression and
Frustration-Regression
Components of ERG Theory

continually frustrated in his or her attempts to satisfy growth needs, related-ness needs will reemerge as a primary motivating force, and the individual is likely to redirect his or her efforts toward lower-level needs.

Second, whereas Maslow's model has individuals focusing on one need at a time, Alderfer's model suggests that more than one need may be operative (or activated) at the same time. Thus, Alderfer's model is less rigid, allowing for greater flexibility in describing human behavior.

To get a rough idea of how you stand in need satisfaction according to the ERG need theory, you may wish to complete Self-Assessment 5.1. Simply answer the 12 items, and then score your questionnaire according to the pro-cedures described in Appendix B.

SELF-ASSESSMENT 5.1
Where Are You in the Need Hierarchy?

Instructions: For each of the items listed below, circle the number that best represents how important the item is to you when considering a job. Remember: be honest with yourself in your responses; everything can't be "very important" to you.

	Unimportant			Very Important	
1. Working harmoniously with my fellow workers.	1	2	3	4	5
2. Gaining additional job-related skills.	1	2	3	4	5
3. Receiving a high salary for my efforts.	1	2	3	4	5
4. Being accepted and appreciated by my fellow workers.	1	2	3	4	5
5. Maintaining my independence on the job.	1	2	3	4	5
6. Getting regular pay raises at work.	1	2	3	4	5
7. Having close friends at work.	1	2	3	4	5
8. Believing in myself.	1	2	3	4	5
9. Receiving good fringe benefits from the company.	1	2	3	4	5
10. Being open and honest with my co-workers.	1	2	3	4	5
11. Having opportunities for personal growth and development on the job.	1	2	3	4	5
12. Feeling secure from personal threat or harm.	1	2	3	4	5

Source: Based on the research of Clayton P. Alderfer, as reported in *Existence, Relatedness, and Growth: Human Needs in Organizational Settings* (New York: The Free Press, 1972).

IN PRACTICE
Needs Hierarchies at GM

Advocates of need theories in organizations suggest that people are primarily motivated by whatever needs are most prominent at a given time. What happens, then, when a company has to reduce its workforce to remain competitive in a global marketplace? GM encountered that question when it announced that over a period of three to four years it would need to reduce its workforce by 74,000 employees. This announcement followed a year in which it was estimated that its North American automobile operations lost over $8 billion.

Although the United Auto Workers (UAW) had in the past often focused collective bargaining talks on issues of wages increases and benefits, the focus after the announced layoffs was firmly on job security. To drive home their concern, the UAW ordered a strike of a strategic metal stamping plant that provided stamped metal fixtures such as doors and hoods for some of GM's most profitable lines, including its new Saturn line of cars. This strategic strike soon required the temporary stoppage of work at a number of other factories and assembly plants.

The uncertainty about future employment levels had redirected the UAW's focus to job security issues and forced them to consider trade-offs of salary and benefits in exchange for greater security.

MANIFEST NEEDS THEORY

The final need theory of motivation was developed by Henry A. Murray and is called the *manifest needs theory* (or the need-press model). Although the initial formulations were developed by Murray in the 1930s and 1940s, the model has been considerably developed and extended by David McClelland and John Atkinson.[20]

Basic Premises of the Manifest Needs Model

Murray felt, as Maslow had, that individuals could be classified according to the strengths of various needs. People were thought to possess at any one time a variety of divergent and often conflicting needs that influence their behavior, where a *need* is a "recurrent concern for a goal state."[21] Each need was deemed to be composed of two components: (1) a qualitative, or directional, component that includes the object toward which the need is directed; and (2) a quantitative, or energetic, component that consists of the strength or intensity of the need toward the object. Needs were thus viewed as the central motivating force for people in terms of both direction and intensity.

Overall, Murray posited that individuals possess about two dozen needs, including the needs for achievement, affiliation, power, and so forth. Examples of some of these needs and their definitions are shown in Exhibit 5.6. Murray believed that needs are mostly learned, rather than inherited, and are activated by cues from the external environment. For example, an employee with a high need for achievement would be expected to pursue that need (that is, to try to achieve something) only when the environment conditions were appropriate (e.g., when he was given a challenging task). Only then would the need become manifest. When the need was not cued, the need was said to be latent, or not activated.

Exhibit 5.6
Examples of Murray's
Manifest Needs

Need	Characteristics
Achievement	Aspires to accomplish difficult tasks; maintains high standards and is willing to work toward distant goals; responds positively to competition; willing to put forth effort to attain excellence.
Affiliation	Enjoys being with friends and people in general; accepts people readily; makes efforts to win friendships and maintain associations with people.
Autonomy	Tries to break away from restraints, confinement, or restrictions of any kind; enjoys being unattached, free, not tied to people, places, or obligations; may be rebellious when faced with restraints.
Power	Attempts to control the environment and to influence or direct other people; expresses opinions forcefully; enjoys the role of leader and may assume it spontaneously.

Maslow vs. Murray

The manifest needs theory resembles Maslow's model in that both theories suggest a set of needs and goals toward which behavior is directed. The two models differ, however, in two important respects. First, Murray does not suggest that needs are arranged in hierarchical form, as does Maslow. And second, Murray's model allows for more flexibility in describing people. Maslow's need hierarchy model places individuals on one level at a time in the hierarchy (e.g., esteem needs). Using Murray's manifest needs model, on the other hand, we can describe an individual as having high needs for achievement and autonomy and low needs for affiliation and power—all at the same time. Hence, we are able to be more specific in describing people instead of merely claiming they have "higher-order need strengths" as Maslow did.

Need for Achievement

Whereas the manifest needs model encompasses an entire set of needs, most research in organizational settings has focused on the needs of achievement, affiliation, autonomy, and power. These four needs seem to be particularly important for understanding people at work. Therefore, we shall consider each of these needs as it relates to work settings.

Basic Concepts.   By far the most prominent need from the standpoint of studying organizational behavior is the need for achievement (also known as *n Ach*). Need for achievement is defined as "behavior toward competition with a standard of excellence."[22] High need for achievement is characterized by (1) a strong desire to assume personal responsibility for finding solutions to problems, (2) a tendency to set moderately difficult achievement goals and take calculated risks, (3) a strong desire for concrete feedback on task performance, and (4) a single-minded preoccupation with task and task accomplishment. Low need for achievement, on the other hand, is typically characterized by a preference for low risk levels and shared responsibility on tasks.

Need for achievement is an important motive in organizations because many managerial and entrepreneurial positions require such drive in order to be successful. Thus, when a manager who has a high *n Ach* is placed on a difficult job, the challenging nature of the task serves to cue the achievement motive, which, in turn, activates achievement-oriented behavior. However, it is important to point out that when high need achievers are placed on routine or unchallenging jobs, the achievement motive will probably not be activated. Hence, there would be little reason to expect them to perform in a superior fashion under such conditions.[23]

The concept of need for achievement is important not only for understanding human behavior in its own right, but also for understanding how people respond to the work environment. Thus, the concept has important implications for job design. Enriching an employee's job by providing greater amounts of variety, challenge, and responsibility would probably enhance performance only for those employees who were excited by such a job (that is, high need achievers). Low need achievers, on the other hand, might be frustrated by the increased personal responsibility for task accomplishment and, thus, might perform poorly or might even withdraw from the situation. We shall examine this phenomenon further in Chapter 9 when we explore job design.

Achievement Motivation and Economic Development.   McClelland has applied the notion of *n Ach* to the study of economic development in underdeveloped countries. These studies are described in an interesting book entitled The Achieving Society.[24] From several years of study, two general findings emerged. First, according to McClelland, there is a fairly consistent correlation between a country's current state of economic development and measurable mean levels of *n Ach* in that country. Higher mean levels of *n Ach* are found in more prosperous nations, whereas lower levels are found in the less prosperous. Second, when McClelland examined the literature of ancient cultures for references to achievement-oriented aspirations and behaviors, he found some evidence that increases in the achievement motive preceded subsequent economic development in those civilizations.

On the basis of these findings, McClelland argues that economic development and prosperity at a national level can be influenced to some extent by the achievement strivings of a nation's people. Such findings have important implications for current efforts to assist underdeveloped nations or even underdeveloped segments within developed nations, because they suggest that in addition to giving economic aid, we must foster the achievement motive in the population in order to facilitate development.

Developing Achievement Motivation.   Need for achievement, like other needs, is apparently learned at an early age and is influenced largely by the independence training given children by their parents. As Sanford and Wrightsman point out, "The relatively demanding parent who clearly instigates self-reliance in the child and who then rewards independent behavior is teaching the child a need for achievement."[25] Because it is estimated that only about 10 percent of the population are high need achievers, it is logical to ask how one can become a high need achiever. McClelland's answer to this question is that achievement motivation can be taught to adults with moderate success. Achievement motivation training consists of four steps:[26]

1. Teach participants how to think, talk, and act like persons with high need achievement.
2. Stimulate participants to set higher, but carefully planned and realistic, work goals for themselves.
3. Give the participants knowledge about themselves.
4. Create a group *esprit de corps* by having group members learn about each others' hopes and fears and successes and failures and by having them go through an emotional experience together.

To date, the evidence appears to support the usefulness of such training programs for increasing *n Ach*. With few exceptions, managers in various countries who attended such programs received more rapid promotions, made more money, and expanded their businesses more quickly after completing the course than did control groups. It is important to note here, however, that the managers studied were consistently chosen from entreprenurial-type jobs thought to be most suited for high need achievers. The success of such programs on employees who perform routine, clerical, or automated tasks remains very doubtful, because such jobs are not designed to activate the achievement motive.

IN PRACTICE
The Young Entrepreneurs

A characteristic trait of high achievers is a strong desire to take risks and accomplish important goals. Nowhere is this better witnessed than in the behavior of young entrepreneurs. Consider the following examples:

At the age of 28, Nolan Bushnell created Pong, the nation's first video game. To market his invention, he formed his own company, which he called Atari. Within 5 years, he sold his interest in Atari for $28 million. Another young entrepreneur, Frederick W. Smith, sketched out plans for an air-delivery service while still a student at Yale. After graduation, he founded his dream company—Federal Express—and by the time he was 37, his company was grossing $600 million a year. And then there was Steven Jobs who, along with Stephen Wozniak, founded Apple Computer at the age of 26. After being forced out of Apple (as a multimillionaire), he began again with NEXT. Perhaps the ultimate wonderboy was William Gates, co-founder of Microsoft. Along with Paul Alan, Gates started Microsoft before he was 20. At age 36, Gates' 30.5 percent stake in Microsoft was worth an estimated $5.9 billion and the company had a market value nearly that of General Motors.

What is it that creates young entrepreneurs? Research suggests that risk takers typically exhibit strong self-confidence, a driving vision of what they want to accomplish, and a need to control their own destinies, in other words they have high need for achievement. Most gain some experience with major companies but soon leave these large organizations in order to pursue their own goals. Moreover, it also has been found that most entrepreneurs get started between the ages of 25 and 35. After this, people tend to get too concerned about their own careers or their vested interests in a company or their lifestyles.

Interestingly, the Europeans and the Japanese, who have proven to be formidable competitors to North American firms, have been no match in terms of revolutionary new ventures. A Steven Jobs in Europe probably would find start-up capital unavailable and in Japan would be expected to focus on the corporate needs of his employer. In such circumstances, the young entrepreneur would probably become discouraged.

The success of young entrepreneurs in the United States has implications far beyond the corporate halls. It has been estimated that small emerging businesses will account for most of the new jobs in the next decade. Thus, it appears that America's economic and social future may be closely tied to the rise of the young entrepreneurs.[27]

Need for Affiliation

In contrast to the need for achievement, relatively little is known about the behavioral consequences of the need for affiliation, despite the fact that this need has been widely recognized since early in this century.[28] The need for affiliation *(n Aff)* may be defined as an "attraction to another organism in order to feel reassured from the other that the self is acceptable."[29] This need should not be confused with being sociable or popular; instead, it is the need for human companionship and reassurance.

People with a high need for affiliation are typified by the following: (1) a strong desire for approval and reassurance from others, (2) a tendency to conform to the wishes and norms of others when pressured by people whose friendship they value, and (3) a sincere interest in the feelings of others. High *n Aff* individuals tend to take jobs characterized by a high amount of interpersonal contact such as sales, teaching, public relations, and counseling. How does *n Aff* influence employee behavior? Some evidence suggests that individuals with a high need for affiliation have better attendance records than those with a low *n Aff.*[30] Moreover, some research suggests that high *n Aff* employees perform somewhat better in situations where personal support and approval are tied to performance. Support for this position comes from French, who found in a laboratory experiment that, although high *n Aff* individuals perform better when given *task-related* feedback, they also perform better when given *supportive* feedback.[31] In addition, effort and performance for those high in *n Aff* can be enhanced somewhat under a cooperative work norm, where pressure for increased output is exerted only by one's *friends*. The implications of such findings for leadership or supervisory behavior are fairly clear. To the extent that supervisors can create a cooperative, supportive work environment where positive feedback is tied to task performance, we would expect high *n Aff* employees to be more productive. The reason for this is simple: working harder in such an environment would lead to the kinds of satisfaction desired by those high in *n Aff.*

Need for Autonomy

Need for autonomy *(n Aut)* is a desire for independence and for freedom from any kind of constraint. Individuals with a high need for autonomy prefer situations where they work alone, control their own work pace, and are not hampered by excessive rules or procedures.[32]

The effects of a high need for autonomy on employee behavior can be significant. For instance, it has been found that high *n Aut* individuals tend not to respond to external pressures for conformity to group norms, tend to be poor performers unless they are allowed to participate in the determination of their tasks, and are not committed to the goals and objectives of the organization. They are typically found among craft and tradespeople and lower-echelon employees, not managers.[33] This last finding may be explained by the fact that managerial success is in large measure determined by a person's ability to interact successfully with others, to cooperate, and to compromise. Individuals with a high need for autonomy typically do not do this.

Need for Power

A final need that has proved important for understanding organizational behavior is an individual's need for power (or dominance). Need for power represents a desire to influence others and to control one's environment. It has a strong social connotation, in contrast to *n Aut,* in that a high *n Pow* employee will try to control or lead those around him. Interest in the power motive dates from the early work (in the 1930s) of Alfred Adler, who believed that power was the major goal of all human activity. Adler saw human development as a process by which people learn to exert control over the forces that have power over them. Hence, a person's ultimate satisfaction comes with his or her ability to have influence over the environment. Although Murray, McClelland, and others do not see power as an all-consuming drive as Adler did, they nevertheless view it as an important need.

People with a high need for power may be described as follows: They usually attempt to influence others directly—by making suggestions, by giving their opinions and evaluations, and by trying to talk others into things. They seek positions of leadership in group activities; whether they become leaders or are seen only as "dominating individuals" depends on other attributes such as ability and sociability. They are usually verbally fluent, often talkative, sometimes argumentative.[34]

Additional research demonstrates that employees with high needs for power tend to be superior performers, have above-average attendance records, tend to be in supervisory positions, and are rated by others as having good leadership abilities.[35]

McClelland notes that the power needed can take two forms among managers: personal power and institutionalized power.[36] Employees with a *personal power* orientation strive for dominance almost for the sake of dominance. Personal conquest is very important to them. Moreover, such individuals tend to reject institutional responsibilities. McClelland likens personal-power types to *conquistadors* or feudal chieftains; that is, they attempt to inspire their subordinates to heroic performance but want those subordinates to be responsible to their leader, not to the organization.

The *institutionalized power* manager, on the other hand, is far more concerned with problems of the organization and what he or she can do to facilitate goal attainment. Institutionalized-power types may be described as follows: (1) they are organization-minded and feel personal responsibility for building up the organization; (2) they enjoy work and getting things done in an orderly fashion; (3) they seem quite willing to sacrifice some of their own self-interest for the welfare of the organization; (4) they have a strong sense of justice or equity; and (5) they are more mature (i.e., they are less defensive and more willing to seek expert advice when necessary).

If you are interested in seeing how you score on the four needs for achievement, affiliation, autonomy, and power, simply complete Self-Assessment 5.2. In answering this questionnaire, you should use a work environment as a frame of reference. And remember, be completely honest with yourself. When you are done, you may score the instrument using the procedure outlined in Appendix B.

Manifest Needs and Managerial Effectiveness

On the basis of the foregoing discussion of various needs, questions are logically raised concerning the influence these manifest needs have on managerial behavior and effectiveness. Is it possible to build a profile of a successful manager on the basis of these needs? Research by McClelland suggests that it is possible to do so on a very general level. The argument begins by asking what we mean by managerial success:

> Almost by definition, a good manager is one who, among other things, helps subordinates feel strong and responsible, who rewards them properly for good performance, and who sees that things are organized in such a way that subordinates feel they know what they should be doing. Above all, managers should foster among subordinates a strong sense of team spirit, of pride in working as part of a particular team. If a manager creates and encourages this spirit, his subordinates certainly should perform better.[37]

On the basis of this description, what type of manager is most suited to the tasks of managing? A manager with a high need for achievement, affiliation, or power? McClelland argues persuasively that the best manager is one who has a high need for power! Let's examine why.

Managers who have a high need for *achievement* concentrate their efforts on personal accomplishment and improvement. They tend to be highly independent individuals who want to assume responsibility and

SELF-ASSESSMENT 5.2
Which Needs Are Most Important to You?

Instructions: Think of a job assignment on which you have worked—a paid or volunteer job or some other form of work experience. With this job in mind, answer the following questions by circling the number that most closely agrees with how you feel about the item.

	Strongly Disagree				Strongly Agree
1. I do my best work when my job assignments are fairly difficult.	1	2	3	4	5
2. I try very hard to improve on my past performance at work.	1	2	3	4	5
3. I take moderate risks and stick my neck out to get ahead.	1	2	3	4	5
4. I try to avoid any added responsibilities on my job.	5	4	3	2	1
5. I try to outperform my co-workers.	1	2	3	4	5
6. When I have a choice, I prefer to work in a group instead of by myself.	1	2	3	4	5
7. I pay a good deal of attention to the feelings of others at work.	1	2	3	4	5
8. I prefer to do my own work and let others do theirs.	5	4	3	2	1
9. I express my disagreements with others openly.	5	4	3	2	1
10. I often find myself talking to those around me about nonwork matters.	1	2	3	4	5
11. In my work assignments, I try to be my own boss.	1	2	3	4	5
12. I go my own way at work, regardless of the opinions of others.	1	2	3	4	5
13. I often disregard rules and policies that hamper my personal freedom.	1	2	3	4	5
14. I consider myself a team player at work.	5	4	3	2	1
15. I try my best to work along on a job.	1	2	3	4	5
16. I seek an active role in the leadership of a group.	1	2	3	4	5
17. I avoid trying to influence those around me to see things my way.	5	4	3	2	1
18. I often find myself showing others how to do their jobs better.	1	2	3	4	5
19. I often work to gain more control over the events around me.	1	2	3	4	5
20. I strive to be in charge when I am working in a group.	1	2	3	4	5

Source: Adapted from R. Steers and D. Braunstein, "A Behaviorally Based Measure of Manifest Needs in Work Settings," *Journal of Vocational Behavior,* 1976, *9,* p. 254.

credit for task accomplishment and who want short-term, concrete feedback on their performance so they know how well they are doing. These characteristics are often closely associated with entrepreneurial success, as shown in the previous In Practice example. However, these same characteristics can be detrimental where an individual has to manage others. In complex organizations, managers obviously cannot perform all the tasks necessary for success—teamwork is necessary. Moreover, feedback on the group's effort and performance is often vague and delayed. Hence, the managerial environment is not totally suitable to stimulate the achievement motive in managers.

Managers who have a high need for *affiliation* fare no better. Affiliative managers have a strong need for group acceptance and, partly as a result of this, they often tend to be indecisive in decision making for fear of alienating one faction or another. Moreover, this concern for maintaining good interpersonal relationships often results in their attention being focused on keeping subordinates happy instead of on work performance. McClelland summed up his research findings on the affiliative manager by noting:

> The manager who is concerned about being liked by people tends to have subordinates who feel that they have very little personal responsibility, that organizational procedures are not clear, and that they have little pride in their work groups.[38]

In contrast, managers with a high need for *institutionalized power* were found to supervise work groups that were both more productive and more satisfied than other managers. (Note: managers high in need for *personal power* were far less successful managers than those with a need for institutionalized power.) Several reasons exist for the success of the n Power manager. One explanation is suggested by Zaleznik:

> Whatever else organizations may be (problem-solving instruments, sociotechnical systems, reward systems, and so on), they are political structures. This means that organizations operate by distributing authority and setting a stage for the exercise of power. It is no wonder, therefore, that individuals who are highly motivated to secure and use power find a familiar and hospitable environment in business.[39]

In other words, power-oriented managers, when truly concerned about the organization as a whole (instead of themselves), provide the structure, drive, and support necessary to facilitate goal-oriented group behavior. In this sense, they fit very nicely into the definition of managerial success noted above. However, it should be noted that a power-oriented manager pays a price in terms of personal health. In a study of need for power among a group of Harvard graduates over a 20-year period, it was found that 58 percent of those rated high in power either had high blood pressure or had died of heart failure![40]

One final point needs to be discussed before we leave the topic of needs and managerial success. This concerns the interactive effects of the various needs on performance. In particular, a study by Andrews looked at both *n Pow* and *n Ach* in two Mexican companies.[41] Company A was a dynamic and rapidly growing organization characterized by high employee morale and enthusiasm. Company B, on the other hand, had shown almost no growth despite large initial investments and a favorable market; moreover, Company B had serious problems of employee dissatisfaction and turnover. An assessment of the various need strengths among managers in both companies revealed several interesting findings. To begin with, the upper management of Company A (the more dynamic firm) rated much higher on *n Ach* than did managers in Company B. The presidents of both companies were extremely high in *n Pow*. However, in Company A, the president's *n Pow* was combined with a moderately high *n Ach*. This was not the case in the less successful Company B. Hence, on the basis of these findings, it would appear that the most successful managers may be those who combine a power orientation with an achievement orientation.

This chapter has presented an important part of the motivation picture. In the next chapter we expand upon this foundation and more directly look at the relationship between motivation and performance.

PULLING IT ALL TOGETHER

Needs and the drive to fulfill them are two of the cornerstones of motivation. Although some common needs can be identified, the intensity of these needs, their priority, and therefore the impact they have on behavior can be different between people of different cultures and even between individuals within a culture. Understanding your own needs can be an important step in selecting appropriate jobs or careers; understanding the needs of others can be critical in your attempts to motivate and influence them.

SUMMARY OF KEY POINTS

■ A motivation is something that energizes, directs, and sustains behavior. Components of the basic motivational process are: unmet needs or expectations, behavior directed toward specific goals, and feedback concerning the extent to which the original needs or expectations have been met.

■ Scientific management was an effort to enhance worker productivity through job analysis and job simplification.

■ The human relations movement, begun in the 1930s, represented an attempt to satisfy employees' social needs in the workplace.

■ The human resources model asserts that employees are motivated by several interrelated factors, including the need to develop their potential to the fullest.

■ *Intrapreneurship* is the process of encouraging innovation and new ventures within groups or departments of an organization.

■ Content theories of work motivation focus on identifying the factors that motivate employees; process theories focus on understanding the processes and interrelationships underlying motivation.

■ Cognitive theories focus on understanding employee thought processes and decisions as they relate to behavior and performance. Acognitive theories focus on observable behaviors (instead of cognitive processes) and emphasize the role of reinforcements for desired behaviors.

■ Maslow's needs hierarchy model asserts that people all pursue a set of needs and that these needs are pursued in a hierarchical, or sequential, fashion. Included here are physiological, safety, belongingness, esteem, and self-actualization needs.

■ Alderfer's ERG theory distilled Maslow's model down to three needs (existence, relatedness, and growth), although these three are still believed to be arranged in a hierarchy.

■ Murray's manifest needs model sees motivation as caused by a series of human needs including achievement, affiliation, autonomy, and power. No hierarchy is proposed. The primary focus of Murray's needs in the workplace is on the need for achievement, defined as the pursuit of goals with a standard of excellence.

KEY WORDS

acognitive
cognitive
cognitive theory
content theory
deficiency needs
ERG theory
growth needs
hedonism
human relations model
human resources model
instinct theory
institutionalized power
intrapreneurship
law of effect

manifest needs theory
motivation
need
need for achievement
need for affiliation
need for autonomy
need for power
need hierarchy theory
personal power
process theory
reinforcement theory
scientific management
self-actualization
stimulus-response bond

QUESTIONS FOR DISCUSSION

1. Define motivation.
2. Describe the basic motivational process.
3. Review the development of management thought concerning approaches to motivation. How does this compare to the development of psychological approaches to motivation?
4. What is the basic difference between the human relations approach to management and motivation and the human resources approach?
5. Compare and contrast Maslow's need hierarchy theory and Murray's manifest needs theory. Which model would you follow as a manager?
6. Describe Maslow's deprivation-gratification cycle.

7. What changes did Alderfer's ERG theory make in Maslow's original formulation of the needs hierarchy theory?
8. Review the research evidence on Maslow's needs hierarchy theory.
9. Discuss the role of achievement motivation in economic development.
10. How is need for achievement developed?
11. What impact does need for affiliation have on employee performance?
12. Describe the two faces of power and the impact of each on organizational performance.
13. What kind of need set combination makes the best manager?

NOTES

1. J. Weber. "Farewell, Fast Track," *Business Week,* December 10, 1990, pp. 192–200.
2. M. D. Dunnette and W. K. Kirchner, *Psychology Applied to Industry* (New York: Appleton-Century-Crofts, 1965).
3. W. McDougall, *An Introduction to Social Psychology* (London: Methuen, 1908).
4. E. Hilgard and J. Atkinson, *Introduction to Psychology* (New York: Harcourt, Brace, and World, 1967).
5. K. Lewin, *The Conceptual Representation and Measurement of Psychological Forces* (Durham, N.C.: Duke University Press, 1938); E. Tolman, "Principles of Purposive Behavior," in S. Koch ed., *Psychology: A Study of Science,* vol. 2 (New York: McGraw-Hill, 1959).
6. R. E. Miles, L. W. Porter, and J. A. Craft, "Leadership Attitudes Among Public Health Officials," *American Journal of Public Health,* 1966, *56,* pp. 1990–2005.
7. F. Roethlisberger and W. Dickson, *Management and the Worker* (Cambridge, Mass.: Harvard University Press, 1939).
8. G. Bylinsky. "The Hottest High-Tech Company in Japan." *Fortune,* 121 (1), January 1, 1990, pp. 82–88. D. Whiteside, "How One Owner Avoids the `Economic Rape' of His Workers," *International Management,* November 1986, pp. 74–79.
9. R. M. Steers and L. W. Porter, *Motivation and Work Behavior,* 5th ed. (New York: McGraw-Hill, 1991).
10. Ibid.
11. A. Maslow, *Motivation and Personality* (New York: Harper & Row, 1954).
12. D. McGregor, *The Human Side of Enterprise* (New York: McGraw-Hill, 1960).
13. A. Maslow, *Toward a Psychology of Being* (New York: Van Nostrand, 1968).
14. A. Maslow, *Motivation and Personality,* p. 10.
15. A. Maslow, *Toward a Psychology of Being,* p. 24.
16. Ibid., p. 25.
17. L. W. Porter, "A Study of Perceived Need Satisfaction in Bottom and Middle Management Jobs," *Journal of Applied Psychology,* 1961, *45,* pp. 1–10.
18. M. A. Wahba and L. G. Bridwell, "Maslow Reconsidered: A Review of Research on the Need Hierarchy Theory," *Organizational Behavior and Human Performance,* 1976, *1576,* pp. 212–240.
19. C. Alderfer, *Existence, Relatedness, and Growth* (New York: Free Press, 1972).
20. H. A. Murray, *Explorations in Personality* (New York: Oxford University Press, 1938); D. C. McClelland, *Assessing Human Motivation* (New York: General Learning Press, 1971); J. W. Atkinson, *An Introduction to Motivation* (Princeton, N.J.: Van Nostrand, 1964).
21. McClelland, op. cit., p. 13.
22. D. C. McClelland et al., *The Achievement Motive* (New York: Appleton-Century-Crofts, 1953).
23. D. C. McClelland, *The Achieving Society* (New York: Van Nostrand, 1961).

24. Ibid.
25. F. Sanford and L. Wrightsman, *Psychology* (Monterey, Calif.: Brooks/Cole, 1970), p. 212.
26. D. C. McClelland, "Toward a Theory of Motive Acquisition," *American Psychologist,* 1965, pp. 321–333.
27. Based on "Striking It Rich," *Time,* February 15, 1982, pp. 36–44.
28. W. Trotter, *Instincts of the Herd in Peace and War* (New York: Macmillan, 1916).
29. D. Birch and J. Veroff, *Motivation: A Study of Action* (Monterey, Calif.: Brooks/Cole, 1966), p. 65.
30. R. M. Steers and D. N. Braunstein, "A Behaviorally Based Measure of Manifest Needs in Work Settings," *Journal of Vocational Behavior,* 1976, *9,* pp. 251–266.
31. E. French, "Effects of the Interaction of Motivation and Feedback on Task Performance," in J. Atkinson ed., *Motives in Fantasy, Action, and Society* (Princeton, N.J.: Van Nostrand, 1958), pp. 400–408.
32. Birch and Veroff, op. cit.
33. See, for example, V. Vroom, *Work and Motivation* (New York: Wiley, 1964).
34. G. Litwin and R. Stringer, *Motivation and Organizational Climate* (Boston: Division of Research, Graduate School of Business Administration, Harvard University, 1966), p. 18.
35. Steers and Braunstein, op. cit.
36. D. C. McClelland and D. H. Burnham, "Power Is the Great Motivator," *Harvard Business Review,* 1976, *54,* pp. 100–110.
37. Ibid., p. 102.
38. Ibid., p. 104.
39. A. Zaleznik, "Power and Politics in Organizational Life," *Harvard Business Review,* 1970, p. 47.
40. McClelland and Burnham, "Power is the Great Motivator," op. cit.
41. J. Andrews, "The Achievement Motive and Advancement in Two Types of Organizations," *Journal of Personality and Social Psychology,* 1967, *6,* pp. 163–168.

EXPERIENTIAL EXERCISE 5

What Motivates You?

This exercise focuses on which factors motivate workers to perform on the job and also on the opinions of union leaders and executives with respect to the relative importance of such motivating factors.

Look at the picture on page 160 for just a moment (10–15 seconds) and then write a brief story about the picture. The instructions for how to analyze the content of your story will be provided by your instructor.

MANAGEMENT DILEMMA 5

Motivating Raymond Hargrove

Craig Johnson was debating whether he should simply fire Raymond Hargrove, assign him to a new sales area, or have another talk with him. Unfortunately, none of the alternatives had much appeal.

After six years in the Navy where he had achieved the rank of lieutenant, Raymond became a salesman for the fertilizer division of Northwest Industries about four year ago and had reported to Craig Johnson, the district

sales manager, from the beginning. Raymond's father, a wealthy businessman who had passed away while he was in the Navy, was a close friend of the CEO and founder of Northwest Industries, Mr. Gerold Simon. After Raymond got out of the Navy, his mother mentioned her son to Mr. Simon, who then arranged for Raymond to be interviewed for a job.

Raymond was a tall, handsome, well-built, and well-dressed man of 31. After completing the company training program he was given a sales area in Oregon. The sales area was large and required his being away from home two to three nights per week. The person who had the area before Raymond had done well enough to be promoted to district sales manager of another but related division.

Raymond enjoyed his home in Oregon and spent many hours taking care of his lawn and garden. He also had made several additions and modifications to the home. His wife and young sons also enjoyed the area and liked living in the country. In particular, Raymond liked the different geological formations that could be found in the area, and he often spent weekends either fishing or just exploring the area.

At first, Raymond's performance was about average with an occasional period in which he would rise into the top 20 group, or the top 20 percent of salesman for the division. However, over the last two years his performance had gradually declined.

When Craig first approached Raymond about his declining performance, Raymond simply responded that he must be getting lazy but that he would try harder in the future. However, he failed to properly fill out the sales reports unless specifically directed to do so. About the only project in which Raymond had exceeded what was required of him was a marketing research study that Craig had not had time to complete.

About a year before Raymond's sales reached the bottom, he had written a report in which he described an accident in which he had been involved. On his way back from a sales call, a little boy had suddenly run out from behind a bush right in front of Raymond's car. Because the accident occurred out in the country, he had rushed the boy and his mother to the nearest hospital. The boy was not seriously hurt and had only minor cuts and bruises. When Craig talked with Raymond on the phone about the accident, it was once of the few times Raymond had seemed unsettled.

About three months after the accident, Raymond and his family went to San Francisco to spend the holidays with his mother and the family's "downtown" home on Nob Hill. After the vacation, Craig noticed a significant drop in Raymond's performance. Before long his was the bottom salesperson in Craig's district. Craig estimated that while the performance bonus for the top salesperson in his district would be roughly 10 percent of base salary, Raymond was unlikely to make any bonus at all. At the monthly sales meetings, some of the other salespeople joked about Raymond being from money so there was no need for him to work hard.

In an effort to think of some reason for Raymond's poor performance, Craig took advantage of a lunch with the CEO to ask him about Raymond's background and see if Mr. Simon had any advice. Mr. Simon said that he was sure Raymond would eventually come around and that he was not to be disciplined without Mr. Simon's review of the case. He also told Craig that Raymond's mother had asked him to see if he could get Raymond to write to her more frequently, and asked Craig to pass the message on to Raymond.

Raymond had invited Craig to go on one of their frequent fishing trips next week, and Craig was determined to take advantage of the situation. What he still had to decide was what to do.*

1. Using the concepts of need for achievement, affiliation, autonomy, and power, how would you describe Raymond Hargrove?
2. How would you explain Raymond's behavior and performance?
3. What course of action would you take if you were Craig Johnson?

This case was inspired by John Hennessey.

Chapter 6

Motivation and Performance

The Management Challenge

- ■ To understand how individual decision-making processes affect motivation and performance.
- ■ To see employee motivation as a complex phenomenon requiring a multi-faceted approach by managers.
- ■ To recognize how individual differences, beliefs, and values can affect work motivation.
- ■ To make effective use of goal-setting techniques to enhance performance.
- ■ To understand the relationship between job attitudes and performance.
- ■ To reduce unwanted absenteeism and turnover.

CLOSE UP

Two Strikes Against Worker Motivation in Russia

Some have argued that *glasnost* and *perestroika* were critical to the breakup of the Soviet Union. Yet even in Russia where Boris Yeltsin continued these ideas raised by Mikhail Gorbachev, it has become clear that political changes far surpass the economic ones. That is, although some amount of democracy is creeping into the fabric of everyday life in Russia, the basic economy remains locked in the past despite efforts to change things. First Gorbachev and then Yeltsin proposed introducing numerous forms of incentive programs into the factories to improve productivity and offer Russian workers greater pay for greater performance. Yet, repeatedly, these proposals are vigorously resisted by the average Russian worker.

This problem is most vividly demonstrated on the factory floors, where workers routinely refuse to make any effort to change their jobs or productivity levels. And in a land where the custom—called *uravnilovka*—is to pay the same wages to the industrious and the lazy, there is little incentive to work. A case in point is Tanya, a 35-year-old single mother who works as a meatcutter in a Moscow canning plant. When asked about the economic reforms, she says only, "I don't want to work like an American. The Soviet Union is a good place because if you don't want to work hard you don't have to." In short, Tanya is grateful for one freedom that Soviet society appears to provide in abundance: the freedom to loaf.

Recent efforts to change Russia into a more "market economy" have resulted in high inflation as old artificial price levels and subsidies are removed. Food and product shortages combined with ever rising prices also works against worker motivation. After all, how attractive can working harder be if it is not seen a a viable means of "getting ahead"?

In combination, the past history of not rewarding differences in individual performance coupled with the current belief by many workers that extra effort will not help them improve their standard of living serves to seriously reduce the motivation level of individual workers. If the recent efforts to revitalize Russia are to succeed, managers and political leaders must formulate with ways to increase the motivational levels of the average Soviet worker. If such workers fail to see any reason to produce at higher levels, economic reforms—and ultimately, political reforms—may not endure. Clearly, Russia has a motivation problem.[1]

The topic of employee motivation—whether in Russia, North America, or anywhere else—is clearly one of the most important topics for managers. Indeed, one of the most persuasive arguments for studying motivation is advanced by Katz and Kahn in their classic book *The Social Psychology of Organizations.*[2] They note that organizations have three *behavioral requirements* for the people who work in them. These are:

1. People must be enticed into joining the organization and remaining with it.
2. People must dependably perform the tasks for which they were hired.
3. People must transcend dependable role performance and engage in some form of creative, spontaneous, and innovative behavior at work.

All three of these behavioral requirements deal squarely with motivation. Motivational techniques must be employed not only to encourage employees to join and remain with an organization, but also to perform in a dependable fashion and to think and take advantage of unique opportunities.

Because of ever-tightening constraints placed on organizations by unions, government agencies, and increased foreign and domestic competition, companies must find ways to improve efficiency and effectiveness in the workplace. Much of the organizational slack and many of the excess resources that were relied on in the past have diminished; this requires that all resources, including human resources, be utilized to their maximum. In recent years, increased attention has been devoted to developing employees as future resources—a sort of talent bank—from which organizations can draw as they grow and develop. Examples of these efforts can be seen in the increase in management development programs, manpower planning, and job redesign. Motivation is the foundation upon which these efforts are built.

From the individual's standpoint, motivation is a key to a productive and useful life. Work consumes a sizable portion of our waking hours. If this time is to be meaningful and contribute toward the development of a healthy personality, the individual must be willing to devote effort toward task accomplishment. Motivation plays a central role in this.

REASONS FOR HIGH AND LOW PRODUCTIVITY

A major complaint of managers in both private and public organizations is lack of productivity or job performance among the work force. This problem is especially acute in industries facing global competitive forces or where resources are in short supply. In such cases, enhancing productivity can mean the difference between survival and extinction. To set the stage for our discussion of cognitive models of motivation and performance, let us see how the cognitive approach can be used to analyze the forces that facilitate or inhibit good (and bad) performance. Using the cognitive model, we will consider several reasons why employees may feel that it is not in their best interest to maximize their performance on the job. On the basis of this analysis, we will turn to three models of motivation that should help us understand what managers can do to enhance performance.

To begin with, employees often place different values on different outcomes. Some employees want added income, for example, whereas others prefer extra time off or an opportunity to enter a training program. Thus, if employees of a particular company find that the *rewards offered by the organization are unappealing,* they are unlikely to increase their efforts. Employees must place a high value on the rewards available to them in order to justify increasing their performance. Rewards that are not valued will not merit special effort. Some employees may regularly take work home at night to maximize job performance in hope of getting a raise or promotion. However, other employees elect to take home no work and instead spend the evening hours with their families, even when it slows their career progress.

Sometimes the problem is not that the rewards themselves are unappealing, but that there is a *weak performance-reward linkage.* That is, employees may fail to see a strong connection between increased performance and receipt of additional rewards. And the employees are not necessarily wrong—the failure to see a linkage is often because there is none. It is difficult to measure performance accurately, especially at the managerial level. As a result, opportunities for inequity emerge in the reward system, and good performance may not be rewarded to the extent it should be. When employees fail to see a good relationship between performance and subsequent rewards, a major motivating force is lost.

A third reason employees might restrict their productivity is their *distrust of management.* Workers may feel that increased performance can only result in undesired outcomes such as increases in the quotas or production rates required. Such distrust, which can be particularly strong among blue-collar workers, tends to neutralize the incentive system. In addition, workers at times feel that increased performance will lead to a reduction in the work force (that is, they may work themselves out of a job). These fears lead to group pressures to maintain acceptable, moderate performance levels and to punish rate-busters as threats to the well-being of the group.

On an individual level, one cause of restricted output is the *desire to have control over one's job.* In order to resist being a cog in the wheel, employees often attempt to leave sufficient slack in their work schedules (by intentional underproduction) so they can vary their work methods. By doing so, they reassure themselves that they still have some mild degree of control over their own behavior and therefore count as people. Such behavior increases individuals' feelings of self-worth and independence by increasing their freedom of action.

Another restriction of individual motivation may be insufficient knowledge, training, skills, tools or abilities. If employees do not believe they have the knowledge or skills necessary to perform the task well, even if they tried as hard as they could, they are unlikely to be motivated to put forth much effort.

Finally, a sixth reason for output restriction may be a *lack of job involvement* due simply to dislike of the job (see Chapter 3). If an employee is not interested in a job and would really prefer to do something else, he or she will find it difficult to concentrate and focus energy on the immediate task at hand. Employees may demonstrate their lack of involvement through absenteeism or other forms of withdrawal (such as alcoholism), thus reducing performance levels even further.

One way to understand how these factors influence or inhibit productivity is to use a *force field analysis.* As developed by Kurt Lewin, a force field analysis is a pictorial representation of the forces (or pressures) promoting or discouraging a certain course of action. For example, we can develop a fairly simple force field analysis of influences on productivity by comparing various factors that promote production with factors that may inhibit production, as shown in Exhibit 6.1.

At least six forces against productivity can be identified, as noted above. These are shown in the right half of Exhibit 6.1. Opposing these is a series of positive performance forces. These positive forces can include having valued rewards contingent upon performance, strong personal work values and goals, employee perceptions of equitable treatment by peers and management, role clarity, and a good match between employees and the abilities and traits necessary to do the job. Of course, these are only a few examples of many of the forces in favor of productivity. However, these examples do illustrate how the employee weighs positive and negative forces to determine how much effort to devote to performance.

Problems resulting from poor motivation are commonplace in contemporary work organizations. If managers intend to remedy this condition, they must make an effort to understand the causes underlying these problems and how the nature of the job and the work environment affect them. One way is to develop models of employee motivation that focus on the way individuals react to work situations. Examples of such complex models are discussed here. A review of three major cognitive models of motivation will shed light both on *why* employees do or do not produce and on *what* managers can do to facilitate employee performance and job satisfaction. The first model to be considered focuses on social comparison processes and perceived equity.

We have seen that theories of motivation can be divided into cognitive and acognitive approaches. Acognitive models of motivation assert that it is possible to predict behavior without an understanding of internal thought processes. They stress instead the relationship between external stimuli and behavior and do not explore the effects of internal mechanisms. People are seen as being largely reactive to environmental stimuli, which makes it unnecessary, according to this view, to examine internal processes. Acognitive models were discussed in detail in Chapter 4. On the other hand, cognitive models of motivation, such as those presented in this chapter, rest on the assumption that individuals often make conscious decisions about their

Exhibit 6.1
A Force Field Analysis
of Pressures For and
Against Productivity

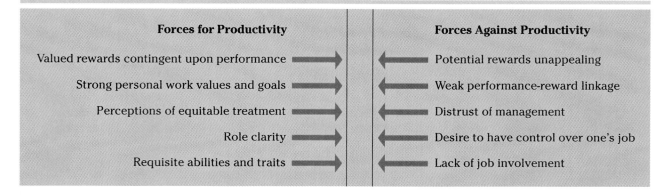

Forces for Productivity	Forces Against Productivity
Valued rewards contingent upon performance ⟹	⟸ Potential rewards unappealing
Strong personal work values and goals ⟹	⟸ Weak performance-reward linkage
Perceptions of equitable treatment ⟹	⟸ Distrust of management
Role clarity ⟹	⟸ Desire to have control over one's job
Requisite abilities and traits ⟹	⟸ Lack of job involvement

behavior and that this decision process must be clearly understood in order to understand human behavior. Cognitive theories emphasize the how and why of behavior by focusing on internal mechanisms. Individuals are seen as active organisms in their environment. They are proactive as well as reactive to environmental forces.

Although these two basic approaches to understanding human behavior are not entirely incompatible, they do represent distinct differences in emphasis and assumptions about the nature of people. These distinctions should become clear as we examine three complex cognitive theories of employee motivation: equity theory, goal-setting theory, and expectancy/valence theory. Each theory rests on the assumption that people are reasoning (if not reasonable) creatures who make conscious choices from among alternative forms of behavior. All three models emerge from and are unified by the role of cognitions in human behavior. Following this examination, we will conclude this chapter by considering several of the more prevalent outcomes or consequences of motivated behavior: job satisfaction, attendance or absenteeism, and turnover.

EQUITY THEORY

One of the more popular cognitive explanations of human behavior in work organizations is equity theory. Equity theory, as first advanced by Adams and Weick,[3] is the most popular of the *social comparison theories* of motivation. Social comparison theories focus on individuals' feelings about and perceptions of how fairly they are being treated as compared to others.

Equity theory rests on two assumptions about human behavior.[4] First, it assumes that individuals engage in a process of evaluating their social relationships much as they would evaluate economic transactions in the marketplace. Social relationships are viewed as an *exchange process* in which individuals make contributions or investments and expect certain outcomes in return. March and Simon's inducements-contributions theory is one such early example.[5] We expect individuals to have expectations about the outcomes of their contributions of time and effort. The social comparison process is a function of perceptions of one's own and other's situation. As discussed in Chapter 3, people's perceptions are not always accurate, but if they believe them, they act as if their perception is reality.

Second, it assumes that people do not assess the equity of an exchange in a vacuum. Instead, they *compare* their own situations with those of others to determine the relative balance. Determining the extent to which an exchange is satisfactory is thus influenced by what happens to oneself compared to what happens to others.

In this section, we will examine the basic components of equity theory and discuss the consequences of inequity. Next, a brief summary of the research on equity theory will be presented, followed by a discussion of the managerial implications of the model. Throughout, be aware of the central role played by cognitions in the process.

Antecedents of Inequity

Social comparison processes, such as those involved in equity theory, are typically based on the relationship between two variables: inputs and outcomes. *Inputs,* or investments, represent those things an individual contributes to an exchange. In a work situation, inputs include items such as previous work experience, education, and level of effort on the job. *Outcomes* are items that an individual receives from the exchange. Outcomes include pay, fringe benefits, accrued status, seniority, and positive feedback.

In order for an input or outcome to be a factor in evaluating exchange relationships, two conditions must be met. First, the existence of an input or outcome must be *recognized* by one or both parties in the exchange. The major outcome from a particular job is irrelevant unless at least one of the parties involved considers it a major outcome. Second, an input or outcome must be considered *relevant,* or have marginal utility, to the exchange. Unless both conditions—recognition and relevance—are met, potential inputs or outcomes will not be considered in determining the degree of equity in the exchange.

According to the theory, individuals assign weights to the various inputs and outcomes on the basis of their perceived importance. This is not to say that people are highly precise in these weighing processes, but that they roughly differentiate between more important and less important inputs and outcomes. Intuitively, people arrive at a ratio of their outcomes to inputs *as compared to* the ratio of another individual's or group's outcomes to inputs. The other may be any of the following: people with whom we engage in direct exchanges, others engaged in exchanges with a common third party, or persons in a previous or hypothetical work situation. This referent other becomes the point of comparison for people in determining the degree to which they feel equitably treated.

A state of perceived equity exists whenever the ratio of a person's outcomes to inputs is equal to the ratio of others' outcomes to inputs. This state is represented below, where *p* represents the ratio of the person and *o* represents the ratio of the comparison other:

$$\frac{O_p}{I_p} = \frac{O_o}{I_o}$$

A state of perceived inequity exists whenever these two ratios are unequal:

$$\frac{O_p}{I_p} < \frac{O_o}{I_o} \quad or \quad \frac{O_p}{I_p} > \frac{O_o}{I_o}$$

In this approach to the concept of equity in social exchange, several aspects of the model must be emphasized. To begin, the conditions necessary to produce a state of equity or inequity are based on a person's *perceptions* of inputs and outcomes. If an individual has a highly distorted view of the major factors involved in an exchange (e.g., thinks that co-workers are earning far more than is actually the case), these distortions will be incorporated into the person's calculations of equity or inequity.

Second, inequity is a *relative* phenomenon. That is, inequity does not exist simply because a person has high inputs and low outcomes, so long as the comparison other also has a similar ratio. Employees may be fairly satisfied with a job demanding high effort and offering low rewards if their frame of reference is a similar situation.

SELF-ASSESSMENT 6.1
How Fair Is Your Employer?

Instructions: Think of your present job or a former job, and answer each of the following questions as honestly as possible.

Item	Strongly Disagree						Strongly Agree
1. My supervisor shows considerable favoritism toward some of my co-workers.	7	6	5	4	3	2	1
2. In this company, pay is clearly based on performance.	1	2	3	4	5	6	7
3. This company treats everyone according to the same policies and rules.	1	2	3	4	5	6	7
4. Everyone has an equal chance to get ahead in this organization.	1	2	3	4	5	6	7
5. Job assignments are allocated on the basis of whom you know, not your ability.	7	6	5	4	3	2	1

My company's score is _____.

Third, it is important to note that inequity occurs when people are relatively underpaid *or overpaid.* Available research suggests that the threshold for underpayment is lower than it is for overpayment.[6] People are more willing to accept overpayment in an exchange relationship than underpayment. Even so, both theory and research observe that people who experience overpayment will sometimes be motivated to reduce the exchange imbalance by working harder. The ways people strive to reduce inequities in exchange are discussed below.

In order to better understand how this model works, you are encouraged to complete Self-Assessment 6.1. You may apply this to your current job, if you are working, or to a previous full- or part-time job. After you have answered the five questions, see Appendix B for scoring procedures.

Consequences of Inequity

The implications of equity theory in motivation follow from the hypothesized consequences of perceived inequity. As formulated by Stacy Adams, the major postulates of the theory are as follows: (1) perceived inequity (underpayment or overpayment) creates tension within individuals; (2) the tension is proportionate to the magnitude of the inequity; (3) the tension experienced by individuals will motivate them to attempt to reduce it; and (4) the strength of the motivation or drive to reduce it is proportional to the perceived inequity.[7] Thus, if, after comparing one's situation with a "relevant other," we determine we are in a state of equity, we are motivated to continue our present course of action: everything is all right. On the other hand, if we determine that an inequity exists *vis-à-vis* the other person, the resulting tension would motivate us to attempt change. This process is shown in Exhibit 6.2.

In this process, individuals are faced with the problem of *how* to reduce perceived inequity. Six resolution strategies are suggested:

1. *People may alter their inputs.* People may increase or decrease their inputs, depending upon whether the inequity is advantageous or disadvantageous. For instance, underpaid people may reduce their level of effort on the job or increase absenteeism, whereas overpaid people may increase effort.

2. *People may alter their outcomes.* Similarly, it is possible for individuals to increase or decrease outcomes received on the job. One clear example of increasing outcomes can be seen in union efforts to improve wages, hours, and working conditions without parallel increases in employee effort (or input).

3. *People may cognitively distort their inputs or outcomes.* For instance, people who feel inequitably treated may artificially increase the status outcomes attached to their jobs ("This is really an important job") or may decrease perceived effort ("I really don't work that hard on this job"). By doing so, the input-outcome ratios become more favorable by comparison, and people are more content.

4. *People may cognitively distort the inputs and outcomes of others.* In the face of injustice, people may cognitively distort the ratio of the referent. For instance, people may come to believe that the referent others actually work harder than they do, and thereby deserve greater rewards. Or, they may reduce the perceived benefits of others' outcomes ("The promotion she got is no big deal; it really is just going to bring more headaches").

Exhibit 6.2
Consequences of Perceived
Equity and Inequity

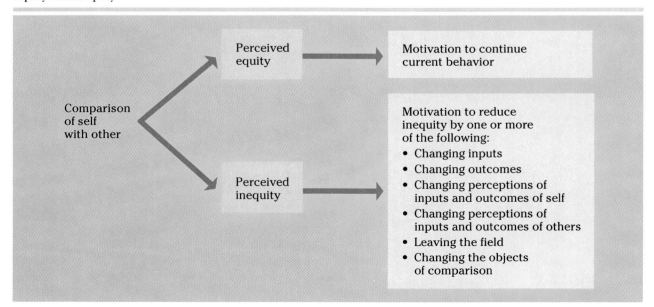

5. *People may leave the field.* Simply put, individuals who feel inequitably treated may decide to leave the situation by transferring to other jobs or departments or by quitting. In doing so, they apparently hope to find a more favorable balance of inputs to outcomes.

6. *People may change objects of comparison.* Finally, people may decide that their referent others are not the most suitable points of comparison and may select others who will yield more favorable balances in the social exchange process. For instance, if the others receive salary increases while the individuals do not, they may decide that the others now belong to a different level in the organization hierarchy, thereby justifying the need to select more relevant others.

Through these techniques, individuals attempt to cope with situations they believe are unfair or inequitable. Their efforts and motivations are aimed at returning to a state of equity and reduced tension. Equity theory, like other cognitive theories of motivation, views individuals as existing in a constant state of flux. They continually try to understand their environment and to act on it in a way that satisfies their more pressing needs, desires, and expectations.

International Challenge

IN PRACTICE
Do U.S. CEOs Make Too Much?

When Apple laid off more than 400 employees, John Sculley, Chairman, President, and CEO, took a pay cut. Somehow, it didn't generate much sympathy, though: His cash pay dropped to $2.25 million from $2.48 million.

"The ever-widening gap between CEOs and their workers is causing resentment and the loss of a true middle class," asserts Bob Roush, a manufacturing engineer in Portland, OR. "We've become a nation of industrial slaves, and the CEOs are the masters of the plantation."

In fact, the average CEO of a large U.S. company makes 35 times (and in some cases, 1,000 times) as much as the average U.S. manufacturing employee. In Japan, this ratio is only 15-to-1 and in Europe 20-to-1. In Japan, the average CEO of a large firm makes about $352,000 in pay, benefits, and perks, reports Towers, Perrin, Forsters & Crosby (TPF&C), a New York–based consulting firm. French and German CEOs take home salaries in the range of $300,000. Compare this with the mind-boggling figures recently revealed in U.S. proxy statements: total 1989 remuneration—including salary, bonus, stock options, restricted shares, and other types of long-term incentive opportunities—of the average CEO in one of the nation's 100 largest companies leaped 20 percent in 1989 to a staggering $3.3 million, says Pearl Meyer & Partners, a New York consulting firm. The CEOs of mid-sized companies ($200 million to $5 billion in sales) who had some catching up to do, Pearl Meyers observes, cleaned up even more. Their total remuneration skyrocketed 29 percent to an average of $2.1 million. To put this in perspective, at a minimum wage of $4.25 an hour, a worker would have needed to have started working about the time Columbus discovered America in order to earn what the average U.S. CEO makes in a year in a large firm.

It is no surprise that corporations are starting to hear rumblings from below. Dr. Elaine Sloan, a vice president for executive services at Personnel

Decisions, Inc., a Minneapolis consulting firm, cites a Carnegie Mellon University study that found that fully 55 percent of all workers don't trust top management. "Some feel very personally devalued and depressed. They see a superman getting so much more and begin to feel they've failed," she says.

"We expect more potential for unionization," Dr. Sloan notes. "At the very least, middle managers won't be as likely to stand in the way of unionization and might not be willing to act as a credible mouthpiece for the organization to deflect it." Also some employees become cynical. "They'll stick around, but they'll be a drain on the motivation of others," the industrial psychologist says.

Interestingly, negative reactions are also seen in the executives who make these 'outrageous' salaries. "If they feel they're getting paid too much and they're not totally callous and corrupted, they may feel guilty and avoid contact with the rest of the workforce," Dr. Sloan says.

If you violate an employee's sense of equity by failing to link pay with performance, employees look for what does not affect pay. Many play politics since they conclude "it's who you know that counts." Others become more likely to steal from the company or lie on expense accounts.

It also becomes difficult for executives to use extrinsic motivation to reward worker performance. "How can you ask someone to do something for the sheer satisfaction of doing the work if you're not doing the same?" rhetorically asks Dr. Sloan.

Is it right for U.S. CEOs to be paid so much more than their counterparts in other countries? Is right for them to be paid so much more than the lower-level employees whose hands actually run the machines and make the products? In any case, where perceived inequity is high, you can be sure employees will try to find ways to reduce it.[8]

Managerial Implications of Equity Theory

A great deal of research generated over the past two decades focuses on the validity and utility of equity theory.[9] From the standpoint of work-related behaviors, the most relevant research has focused on equity theory predictions of employee reactions to pay. These predictions generally distinguish between two conditions of pay inequity (underpayment and overpayment) and two methods of compensation (hourly and piece rate). The specific predictions of each interaction are shown in Exhibit 6.3.

Available evidence tends to support many equity theory predictions, particularly concerning underpayment, as they relate to expected behaviors under various compensation and equity conditions. The findings are not unanimous. Following a recent review, Richard Mowday concluded:

> In summary, predictions from Adams' theory about employee reactions to wage inequities have received some support in the research literature. Research support for the theory appears to be strongest for predictions about underpayment inequity. Although there are fewer studies of underpayment than of overpayment, results of research on underpayment are relatively consistent and subject to fewer alternative explanations. There are both theoretical and empirical grounds for being cautious in generalizing the results of research on overpayment inequity to employee

	Underpayment	Overpayment
Hourly payment	Subjects underpaid by the hour produce less or poorer-quality output than equitably paid subjects.	Subjects overpaid by the hour produce more or higher-quality output than equitably paid subjects.
Piece-rate payment	Subjects underpaid by piece rate will produce a large number of low-quality units in comparison with equitably paid subjects.	Subjects overpaid by piece rate will produce fewer units of higher quality than equitably paid subjects.

Exhibit 6.3
Behavioral Consequences of
Inequitable Payment

Source: R. T. Mowday, "Equity Theory Predictions of Behavior in Organizations," in *Motivation and Work Behavior,* 4th ed., ed. R. M. Steers and L. W. Porter (New York: McGraw-Hill, 1987). Reprinted by permission.

behavior in work organizations. Where such studies have manipulated perceived inequity by challenging subjects' qualifications for the job, observed differences in performance can be explained in ways that have little to do with inequity. Where other methods of inducing overpayment inequity are used, considerably less support is often found for the theory. Predicted differences in productivity and satisfaction due to overpayment inequity are often in the predicted direction but fail to reach acceptable levels of statistical significance.[10]

Equity theory does make a contribution toward a better understanding of work behavior in organizations. Perceived states of equity affect our responses to the work environment as well as our intentions and behavior on the job. Although equity theory is not a complete explanation of employee motivation, it does describe several important motivationally relevant processes that managers should understand. As a result, several implications for management can be identified.

From a managerial standpoint, perhaps the most obvious implication is the necessity for managers to be continually alert to social comparison processes in organizations and, as a consequence, to view motivation in dynamic and changing terms. For example, redesigning someone's job may not increase subsequent motivation and performance if the changes do not alter the inputs-outcomes balance. If employees still think they are being inequitably treated, they are unlikely to provide optimal effort. Hence, as much as possible, managers have a responsibility to ensure that employees feel they are equitably treated.

Employers and managers must also recognize the importance of perception in employee motivation. If employees *perceive* that they are being inequitably treated, they will act accordingly—even if they are in fact overcompensated for their level of effort. Managers view the workplace differently from workers and often fail to understand this critical point. Consequently, managers may have to target people's perceptions of their own or other's inputs and outputs in order to resolve feelings of inequity.

Equity theory attaches much importance to monetary rewards and the manner in which they are distributed. Money is one of the few rewards that people clearly see and measure. As a result, it often becomes a major focal point in employee assessments of their own equity.

Finally, equity theory requires managers to evaluate (and reevaluate) the bases on which they distribute available rewards. Leventhal identifies three general types of *distribution rules:* (1) distribution of rewards based on equity or contribution, (2) distribution of rewards based on feelings of social responsibility, and (3) distribution of rewards based on equality, with equal outcomes given to all participants.[11] Managers tend to select one or more of these ways according to the nature of the situation and certain factors known at the time. It should be clear that the manager's choice of distribution rule in no small way affects employees' perceptions of their own state of equity and their willingness to respond and participate.

GOAL-SETTING THEORY

A second cognitive theory of motivation is *goal-setting theory.* Goal-setting theory lies at the heart of performance-based motivational programs—such as management by objectives—and plays a central role in facilitating organizational effectiveness. In fact, most major business firms use some form of goal-setting process to ensure the efficient use of limited resources for task accomplishment. The chief proponents of this model are Edwin A. Locke and Gary P. Latham.[12] In this section, we will examine several aspects of the goal-setting process, including how it works, how to establish a goal-setting program, and major influences on goal-setting effectiveness. Finally, we review managerial implications.

How Does Goal Setting Work?

According to Locke and his associates, goal setting affects motivation in four ways (see Exhibit 6.4).[13] First, the setting of goals for an employee serves to focus attention on a particular task or objective. In sports, we often see teams with a goal of winning a state or national championship; this goal spurs the team on through each of its games and often leads to higher actual performance because of increased effort. This leads us to the second function of goals: they serve to regulate or increase effort. We simply try harder when we have a goal in front of us.

Next, goals help us keep going in the face of adversity; they enhance persistence on a task. If we have a goal in front of us, it serves as a continual reminder of where we are going and how important goal accomplishment is. Finally, goals—if they are accepted—encourage people to look for ways of attaining them. We become more creative in trying to *develop new strategies and action plans* for reaching our desired destination. That is, if we truly want to achieve a goal—whether it be to lose weight, attain a personal best in running, or sell more than our co-workers—we tend to spend time figuring out ways to bring this about. Thus, goal-setting processes in organizations help us in many ways to achieve on the job. Perhaps this explains why the technique has proved so popular in today's corporations.

Exhibit 6.4
Goal Setting
and Performance

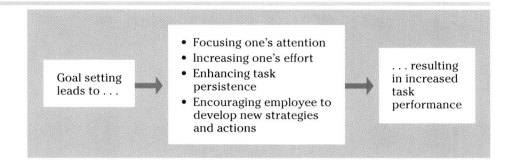

Designing a Goal-Setting Program

Making goal-setting techniques work properly requires considerable effort and commitment on the part of management. To implement such an approach, it is desirable to work through three phases, as shown in Exhibit 6.5. These three phases, when taken together, should ensure that goals are properly set, accepted by the employees, and reinforced with proper training and reward systems.[14]

Step 1: Set appropriate goals. Initially, it is vital that managers establish goals that are task-specific yet reasonable to employees. To the extent that the established goals are specific, quantifiable, and challenging, employees should have a clearer idea of what is expected of them. As a result, wasted or misdirected efforts are reduced or minimized.

Several important points should be made here. To begin with, research has shown that in general, *difficult goals* fairly consistently lead to better performance than easy goals or no goals.[15] However, we must be clear that in the employee's mind the goal is, in fact, difficult but not impossible. As we see in Exhibit 6.6, effort tends to increase as goals become more difficult, only to diminish when the employee feels the task is simply impossible. We must remember here that difficulty level is in the eyes of the employee, not the supervisor (see the discussion on perception in Chapter 3). Thus, what may appear easy to the supervisor may appear quite difficult to the employee.

Next, research has also shown that *specific quantifiable goals* lead to higher performance levels than less specific qualitative goals. This should not be

Exhibit 6.5
Three Stages in Implementing
a Goal-Setting Program

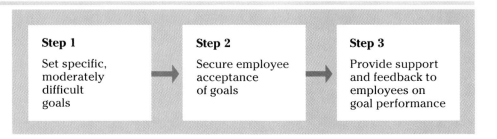

Exhibit 6.6
Relationship Between Goal
Difficulty and Performance

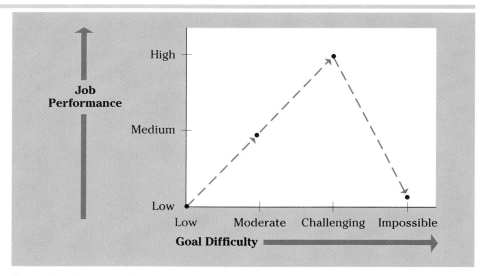

Source: Based on research reported by E. A. Locke and G. P. Latham in *A Theory of Goal Setting and Task Performance* (Englewood Cliffs, N.J.: Prentice Hall, 1990).

surprising. When we have a clear road map and we know exactly what is expected of us, our available energies are more focused. For example, a reasonable approach for an automotive dealership may be to tell its sales representative to sell nine cars this month rather than "outsell everyone in the county." The goal (nine cars) is specific, and, assuming that nine cars is a "challenging" goal, it should be of sufficient difficulty to provide the necessary motivation to spur effort.

In setting such goals, it is important to recognize the role played by *individual differences* (see Chapters 2 and 5). All employees are clearly not capable of the same performance levels. Research has shown, for example, that employees with high achievement needs respond favorably to moderately difficult goals and perform better under such circumstances. Employees with low achievement needs, on the other hand, may experience considerable anxiety working under difficult goals, and their performance may actually decline.[16]

Finally, managers must be cognizant of various *situational factors* that may affect the goal-setting process. For example, managers might want to avoid setting very difficult goals when employees are embarking on a new task or project, because doing so might serve to increase both anxiety and resistance. In such cases, it is better to gradually increase the goal levels as employee skill level and confidence rise.[17] Furthermore, there are times when qualitative goals should take precedence over quantitative ones; this is also a situational factor. It has been argued, for example, that one factor that led to the *Challenger* space shuttle disaster was the preoccupation with making a set number of launches in the year, thereby possibly overlooking qualitative requirements. Other examples can be seen where companies push quotas on the production line and ignore quality. In such cases, one must question whether the goal-setting process is working properly.

Step 2:   Secure goal acceptance from employees. Once reasonable goals have been set, it is important that employees—those we expect to achieve the goals—accept the stated objectives as a reasonable work schedule. Otherwise, significant resistance can emerge that will jeopardize the entire program. Goal acceptance is crucial to program effectiveness. As noted by Locke:

> It is not enough to know that an order or request was made; one has to know whether or not the individual heard it and understood it, how he appraised it, and what he decided to do about it before its effects on his behavior can be predicted and explained.[18]

Goal acceptance can be encouraged in several ways, including explaining the rationale behind the goals to employees, allowing participation in the actual goal-setting process, tying rewards to goal attainment, and providing a supportive work environment that is conducive to goal effort. However it is done, it must be remembered that goal-setting processes work best when the employees accept the goals as *their* goals, not just the company's.

Step 3:   Provide support and feedback to employees. Finally, employees must be given continuous feedback concerning the results of their efforts. in fact, as Latham and Locke point out, "Motivation without knowledge is useless."[19] Employees must know what they are doing right and what they are doing wrong. Such feedback provides the cybernetic function necessary to enhance goal-directed effort. In addition, employees must be provided with sufficient job-related skills to work effectively toward the goals. Hence, training, feedback, and reinforcement emerge as key variables in any attempt to successfully implement goal-setting programs in organizations.

IN PRACTICE
Setting Goals at Johnsonville Sausage

Johnsonville Sausage was a regional producer whose national competitors could out-muscle it through advertising and pricing and had local and regional competitors who were more nimble and customer-oriented. Realizing he was in a tight spot, CEO Ralph Stayer decided that the organizations needed some new goals. He wanted to create an organization that was like a flock of geese, flying in a unified "V", with a common goal, each individual pulling his or her own weight, taking turns leading, and adjusting to the environment as it changed.

His first step was a survey to determine how satisfied workers were and what their attitudes were toward the company and their jobs. He was disappointed to find out, and at first rejected the results, that indicated that his workers were no happier than those in some big, impersonal conglomerate. Mr. Stayer wanted employees to commit to a company goal, but they saw little to commit to.

Stayer then began to focus on specific issues and problems rather than trying to address all of the issues of the corporation at once. He found that in one plant workers disliked working on weekends. He also discovered that machine downtime was between 30 percent and 40 percent. Employees accepted the goal of reducing downtime so that they did not have to work on the weekends. Within three weeks, employees had cut machine downtime to less than 10 percent and had the weekends off.

Stayer involved another group of employees in tackling the problem of vacuum-packed plastic packages of sausages that leaked air. This leakage shortened the shelf life of the product. A goal was set and agreed upon to reduce the leakage problem by half or more. Within a short time, workers had reduced leakage problems from 5 percent to 0.5 percent.

Stayer's conclusion from all this: "Nothing matters more than a goal."[20]

Managerial Implications of Goal-Setting Theory

The concept of goal setting and management by objectives (MBO) is very rich in terms of the implications for management. For example, managers give greater consideration to the precise nature of the task-goal attributes of each employee. That is, managers have a responsibility not simply to assign goals to their subordinates but also to see to it that these goals are specified so that they have maximum motivational potential.

In addition, managers pay more attention to how different types of employees react to their assigned goals. For instance, it has been found that high- and low-need achievers each perform better under different conditions. Such findings suggest that managers have a responsibility to tailor goals to individual needs as much as possible and to create an optimal performance environment for each employee. Increased attention can also be paid to how situational variables influence performance effectiveness. Differences in leadership style, technology, and group structure often influence the impact of various task-goal attributes on performance.

It is important to be aware of the possible negative job attitudes that might result from certain aspects of MBO programs. Recent research has indicated that although goal-setting techniques often lead to improved performance, this performance is at times achieved at the expense of job satisfaction. Where goals are seen by employees as being far too rigid, the credibility of the program itself may be jeopardized, which will lead to poor effort and performance. Care must be taken to ensure that the general parameters of the program are widely accepted by program participants.

Where MBO programs are used, it is advisable to monitor both performance and attitudes among employees as an early-warning system against possible trouble spots. Some research has indicated that MBO programs can lose their potency as motivating forces over time. Continuous monitoring systems can help identify trends and suggest remedies where needed.

Finally, consideration must be given to reinforcing contingencies, thereby improving the motivating potential of the program. Where employees can clearly see personal rewards to be gained from directing effort toward goal attainment, effort and performance should be enhanced.

In summary, available evidence on the effectiveness of goal-setting techniques clearly shows that the relative success of these techniques is largely a result of management's ability to assess problems comprehensively. Consideration must be given not only to the feasibility of task goals and their applicability to the large issue of organizational objectives, but also to the role played by individual and situational differences as they relate to performance. When all of these factors are jointly considered, program effectiveness is enhanced, and the rate of goal failure is diminished.

EXPECTANCY/VALENCE THEORY

The third major cognitive model of employee motivation is *expectancy/valence theory.* This theory, sometimes simply called expectancy theory, dates from the early work of Kurt Lewin and Edward Tolman during the 1930s and 1940s. Early investigators rejected many of the notions of reinforcement theory and instead argued that much of human behavior results from interaction between the characteristics of individuals (their personality traits, attitudes, needs, and values) and the perceived environment.

According to the basic model, individuals make conscious choices about present and future behavior. They are not seen as inherently motivated or unmotivated, as many earlier noncognitive models suggest. Instead, motivational level depends on the particular work environment people find themselves in. To the extent that this environment is compatible with their needs, goals, and expectations, they are motivated. This point will become clearer as we examine the major parts of the theory.

The first systematic formulation of expectancy theory as it relates to work situations was presented by Victor Vroom in his classic book *Work and Motivation.*[21] This was followed closely by extensions and refinements of the model, most notably by Lyman Porter and Edward Lawler.[22] According to Porter and Lawler, a useful way to understand expectancy theory is to break it down into its various components. Expectancy theory attempts to answer two basic questions: (1) What causes motivation? and (2) What causes performance?

What Causes Motivation?

According to expectancy theory, motivation is determined by expectancies and valences. In simple terms, an *expectancy* is a belief about the likelihood that a particular act (such as working harder) will lead to a particular outcome (such as a pay raise). The degree of this belief can vary from 0, where an individual sees no chance that the behavior will lead to the outcome, to 1.0, where an individual is absolutely certain that the behavior will lead to the outcome. In other words, we view expectancies much like probability statements. And of course, most expectancies fall somewhere in between these two extremes. For example, what are your expectancies of passing this class? 0.5? 0.8? 1.0?

On the other hand, *valence* refers to the value an individual places on the expected outcomes or rewards. A valence can range from +1.0 to -1.0 depending upon whether the outcome is highly prized by the employee (e.g., passing the course, money, etc.) or highly undesirable (e.g., failing the course, being fired, etc.). In other words, valence simply says how much you want the outcome to happen. Now let's get a little more complicated by looking more closely at these concepts.

E→P Expectancies.   Expectancies can be divided into two types: (1) *effort-performance* (or E→P) expectancies and (2) *performance-outcome* (or P→O) expectancies. An E→P expectancy is an individual's belief that effort will, in fact, lead to performance. For example, an employee may feel that working overtime will lead to a higher level of output. These expectancies are influenced by several factors, including the employee's level of *self-esteem* (see Chapter 2), past experiences in similar situations (e.g., "Was I able to do it last time?"), and perceptions of the actual situation.

P→O Expectancies.   A *performance-outcome expectancy* (or P→O expectancy) is the belief that if a person performs well in a given situation, certain outcomes will follow. For instance, an employee may believe that a higher level of output will result in a pay raise. Conversely, the same employee may also believe that increased performance might lead to a layoff as he works himself out of a job. Performance-outcome expectancies are influenced by a variety of factors, including past experience in similar situations, the attractiveness of the various outcomes available, the extent of internal locus of control and belief in an ability to control the environment (see Chapter 2), the person's E→P expectancies, and his or her perception of the actual situation.

Valence.   Valence, as noted above, is the value individuals place on available outcomes or rewards. If employees truly do not value the rewards offered by an organization, they will not be motivated to perform. The valence attached to certain outcomes can vary widely. For instance, some employees do not want to be promoted into positions of increased responsibility and stress, whereas others welcome such opportunities. Hence, rewarding employees with a promotion will not necessarily be well received. (Consider the detrimental effects of the up-or-out promotional policies of many large companies.) On the other hand, some rewards, such as money, are consistently valued in their own right or because of their instrumental value in leading to the acquisition of other outcomes such as a house, a new car, or new clothes.

One way to understand the concept of valence is to see how it relates to you. To see which outcomes you value most in a job, you may wish to complete Self-Assessment 6.2. Refer to Appendix B when you have finished for comments.

Putting It All Together: An Example.   Having identified the major variables that influence motivation in expectancy theory, we can consider how they fit together. As shown in Exhibit 6.7, these three variables are believed to influence an employee's motivational level in a multiplicative fashion. According to expectancy theory, employee motivation (not to be confused with actual performance) is a result of an employee's E→P expectancies *times* the P→O expectancies *times* the valences for the outcomes.

A simple example will illustrate how this process works. If a salesperson believes that the chances are good (say 9 out of 10, or 0.9) that increased effort in selling leads to higher sales, we say the person has a high E→P expectancy. Moreover, if this individual further believes (also at a 0.9 level of probability) that such sales increases would lead to a bonus or a pay raise, we say that he or she has a high P→O expectancy. Finally, let's assume the salesperson places a high value on this bonus or pay raise

SELF-ASSESSMENT 6.2
What Do You Want Most in a Job?

Instructions: Below are listed ten possible outcomes that people may receive from their jobs. Please rank these ten outcomes in terms of which you value most, giving a "1" to your most preferred, a "2" to your second most preferred, and so on. Remember: there are no right answers; this exercise is designed so you can better understand what you want out of a job.

_____ A good salary and fringe benefits
_____ Opportunities for promotion and advancement
_____ Interesting and supportive co-workers
_____ Recognition for a job well done
_____ Help with personal problems
_____ Interesting and challenging work
_____ Job security
_____ Good working conditions
_____ Company loyalty to employees
_____ Being consulted on decisions affecting my job

(say $+0.8$ on a scale from -1.0 to $+1.0$). When these three factors are combined in a multiplicative fashion ($0.9 \times 0.9 \times 0.8 = 0.65$), it becomes clear that the salesperson has a reasonably high motivational force. On the other hand, if expectancies were high (0.9 and 0.9, respectively) but the salesperson preferred to have more free time away from the job and genuinely had little desire for additional income (say a valence of $+0.1$ instead of $+0.9$), the motivational force would be considerably lower ($0.9 \times 0.9 \times 0.1 = 0.08$). Hence, for an employee to be highly motivated, *all three* factors must be high. In the absence of one of the factors, we do not expect to see high motivational levels.

Exhibit 6.7
A Model of Expectancy/Valence Theory of Motivation and Performance

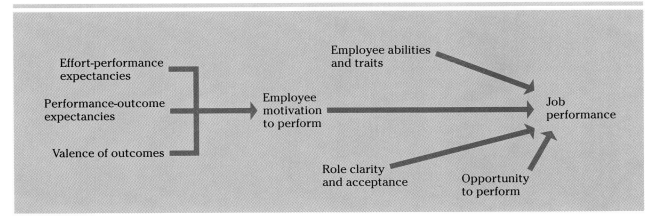

What Causes Performance?

Although an understanding of the determinants of employee motivation is obviously important, the concepts of motivation and performance are not synonymous. Motivation represents an employee's desire to perform, or level of effort, whereas *performance* is the extent to which an someone can successfully accomplish a task or achieve a goal. Performance, as a concept, includes not only the production of certain tangible units of output but also of less tangible outputs, such as effectively supervising others, thinking in a creative way, inventing a new product, resolving a conflict between others, or selling goods or a service. In many ways, effective employee performance is the ultimate criterion by which managers are judged. As can be seen in Exhibit 6.7, performance is influenced by several factors. Clearly, motivation is a central influence. But in addition to motivation at least three factors are involved: (1) abilities and traits, (2) role clarity and acceptance, and (3) opportunity to perform.[23]

Abilities and Traits. The abilities and traits that employees bring to the job largely determine their *capacity* to perform, as opposed to employee motivation, which is concerned with an employee's *will* or *desire* to perform. Abilities and traits are believed to be enduring and stable over time, although some changes are possible as a result of outside intervention, such as employee training (see Chapter 2).

Job performance can be influenced by employee abilities and traits in several ways. For example, it has been shown that managerial effectiveness is modestly related to intellectual capabilities—such as verbal comprehension, inductive reasoning, and memory—and that these capabilities grow in importance as individuals move up the managerial hierarchy into increasingly responsible positions.[24] Abilities and skills such as typing or knowing a trade are also obviously important for the successful performance of clerical or blue-collar employees. Finally, several personal traits (such as cognitive complexity) have been shown to influence performance.

These findings have clear implications in the recruitment, selection, and placement of new employees *as long as* managers are willing to fit individuals to jobs that match their skills. Placing highly intelligent employees with a high need for achievement in jobs that lack challenge or interest would not only inhibit their level of motivation and performance, it would probably hasten their leaving the organization altogether. Thus, a major responsibility for managers is to ensure that they select employees who are suitable to the tasks to be done.

Role Clarity and Acceptance. Being motivated to perform and having the requisite abilities do not ensure good job performance. Employees must also understand and accept the requirements of the job. Providing employees with greater role clarity increases the amount of energy that is directed specifically toward work goals and decreases the amount of energy that is wasted on other activities. For instance, if supervisors know that they bear primary responsibility for reducing shop floor accidents, they will be likely to devote effort to accomplishing this goal. On the other hand, if clarity is lacking, supervisors may take a "let the employee worry about it" attitude, with negative results. Role clarity has also been found to lead to increased goal commitment, work group cohesiveness, job involvement, and job satisfaction.[25] In one sense, goal setting can be thought of as a particularly effective means of clarifying what is expected of employees.

Opportunity to Perform.   Finally, a point that is often overlooked in a consideration of employee motivation is that employees must have an opportunity to perform in order to achieve job success.[26] If a salesperson is asked to sell a product that nobody wants, such as buggy whips, or if a production manager is given an unrealistic deadline for producing a certain product, the chances of successful job performance are low—even if the employee is motivated, has the requisite abilities, and possesses a clear picture of the task.

A similar problem is faced by personnel managers who are asked to develop programs to improve employee motivation *without* affecting production levels, changing jobs substantially, or changing the compensation and reward system. Under such circumstances, it is not surprising that managers are unable to improve motivational levels substantially—they simply do not have the opportunity to perform.

Another example of the lack of opportunity to perform can be seen in assembly line jobs where the pace of production is determined by machines. Where technology controls production, improved motivation can do little to increase quantity of output, although it may influence quality of output in some cases.

In summary, the model outlined in Exhibit 6.7 suggests four primary influences on job performance: (1) employee motivation, (2) employee abilities and skills, (3) role clarity and acceptance, and (4) opportunity to perform. These four factors together suggest that successful job performance is determined jointly by individuals and their environment. Individuals can contribute to job performance through their motivation to perform and the skills and abilities they bring to the workplace. Managers, on the other hand, can contribute to job performance by ensuring that reward systems encourage motivation and that job requirements are clear and precise. In addition, managers can attempt to create work assignments in which employees really have opportunities to perform. The more control employees have over their performance environment, the greater the impact of their motivation on subsequent job performance.

IN PRACTICE
Merit Pay at Johnsonville Sausage

Remember Johnsonville Sausage and how the CEO, Ralph Stayer, used goals to increase motivation and performance? His changes in the compensation system at Johnsonville Sausage (JS) reflect important principles of expectancy theory. Expectancy models of motivation suggest that employees' effort and performance are heavily influenced by their belief that effort will lead to performance and that performance will lead to desired rewards.

Stayer was eager to change the compensation policy at JS to better motivate employees to perform well. The old policy essentially compensated people for tenure in the firm rather than their performance. Now, every six months the performance of every employee is evaluated both by the employee and supervisor. Employees are rated on a scale of 1 to 9 relative to 17 areas grouped into performance, teamwork, and personal development. The total score on all 17 issues for the employee and supervisor must be within 9 points. If the gap cannot be narrowed to 9 points, an arbitration group will review and make a decision, though this group has never been needed.

A specified portion of pretax profits are set aside for performance bonuses. An individual performance bonus is tied directly to performance ratings. A significant difference between top performers and bottom performers even within a job or position is maintained through a fixed distribution of bonuses. For example, only 5 percent of the workers can be classified as superior performers. Consequently, people feel that if they try, that effort is likely to be reflected in performance evaluations (since the evaluation also includes their own personal rating); people feel that superior performance will be rewarded with significant performance bonuses; and people in this organization value these monetary bonuses.[27]

Managerial Implications of Expectancy Theory

Given the somewhat complicated nature of expectancy theory, we might think that the model has little to say to managers concerned with real organizational problems. This is not the case, however. In fact, expectancy theory provides a rich conceptual framework for managers interested in understanding how motivation and performance can be improved. Included in managerial implications are the following:

1. *Clarify E→P expectancies.* Employee beliefs that effort will lead to performance can be enhanced in several ways, including the use of training programs, coaching, supervisory support, guidance, and participation in job-related decisions. Through such assistance, employees will feel that high levels of performance are actually within reach.
2. *Clarify P→O expectancies.* One of the most important functions of management is to design reward systems that are based on actual performance. Increasing performance-reward contingencies lets employees know exactly what they can expect in exchange for high levels of performance. Such contingencies add equity to the reward system.
3. *Match rewards to employee desires.* Different employees often want different rewards or outcomes from their jobs. Although some employees may place a high valence on receiving additional income, others may prefer time off either for vacation or for receiving additional training for a future promotion. Managers can improve motivational levels by offering a variety of rewards for employees. "Cafeteria," or flexible, fringe benefit plans have been used successfully by organizations such as Steelcase, TRW, and the Educational Testing Service (see Chapter 7).
4. *Try to influence valences.* Often valences are based on perceptions rather than unchangeable values or needs. For example, someone might view a promotion as a negative outcome because they perceive that the promotion

will involve lots of paperwork and take them away from productive activities. To the extent that this perception is incorrect or inflated, the manager may be able to change the perception of the employee and change a negative valence to a positive one. Similarly, managers might be successful in reducing the strength of negative valences (even if they can't change them into positive ones) or increase the strength of existing positive valences. Valences may be fixed and unchangeable, but managers should explore the extent to which they might effectively influence existing valences.

5. *Recognize conscious behavior.* A major tenet of expectancy theory is that individuals often make conscious decisions about their present and future behavior on the basis of the outcomes they expect for various behaviors. This is not to say that people make conscious decisions before every act. Instead, people periodically evaluate and reevaluate what they are doing and why they are doing it. For example, a job applicant confronted with two job offers typically weighs the positive and negative aspects of each job in deciding which to accept. Once on the job, employees often reassess the jobs they hold in comparison to alternative options. In short, managers should acknowledge that employees often do not accept the status quo for very long, a situation that forces circumstances and managers to change and adapt over time.

6. *Select people who are equipped for the job.* The role of employee abilities and traits in performance should not be minimized. All too often employees are hired, promoted, transferred, or fired on the basis of personality rather than ability.

7. *Clarify role expectations.* Sometimes people are hired into ambiguous jobs and given little guidance about what is expected of them. We hear the comment, "I want to see what he can *make* out of the job." Such attitudes can lead to wasted efforts while employees search for answers. If managers instead spend the necessary time to clarify job objectives (as in management-by-objectives programs), less search behavior and more task-related behavior takes place.

8. *Provide opportunities to perform.* If employees are placed on impossible jobs or in situations where probability of success is small, they will see little reason to perform. An example is the frustration experienced by local branch managers in banks. Although they are held accountable for improving such performance indicators as deposits on account, these indicators are often more a function of the location of the branch than of the manager's effort. An encyclopedia salesperson in a poor neighborhood experiences similar frustration if no one in the territory can afford the product. If we want people to perform, they must be placed in situations where high performance is possible.

The expectancy model of motivation points to several concrete guidelines for managers seeking to increase performance. The majority of these suggestions are not simply ways to manipulate employees. Instead, they often lead to improved situations for employees. In this sense, the implications suggested here represent a strategy for integrating employee needs, desires, and goals with those of the organization.

MOTIVATION IN PRACTICE: KEYS TO SUCCESS

Now that we have reviewed three contemporary models of employee motivation, it is useful to pause and compare these models. There are obvious differences in the various implications each model suggests for management. As noted in earlier discussions, the three models emphasize quite different aspects of persons and work situations as primary motivators.

In addition to differences in application, distinct differences can also be noted in theory. For instance, equity theory suggests that people make motivational decisions almost exclusively by comparing their own situations to those of others. Expectancy theory, on the other hand, recognizes the importance of peer influence but allows for situations where individuals make decisions irrespective of others. Expectancy theory is more individual in orientation.

Whereas equity theory and expectancy theory both emphasize the role of future rewards in motivation and behavior, goal-setting theory focuses on the nature of task-goals (and whether they are accepted) and is relatively silent about the role of rewards. Even so, goal-setting theory might have clearer applications for managers than the other two models.

Several similarities across the three models should also be recognized. To begin, all three models recognize individual and situational differences, although this recognition is more pronounced in expectancy theory and goal-setting theory. All three models focus on the motivational *process,* the steps leading up to behavior. This is important in order to better understand employee behavior at work. Finally, the models are in agreement in their predictions of human behavior. In fact, it has been argued that equity considerations and goal-setting processes could be subsumed under the more general expectancy theory framework.

Which is the "best" theory of motivation? This question is basically unanswerable, because each theory might at some time be most appropriate, depending upon the situation and the people involved. Rather than attempting to select the one best model, it is probably far more useful to ask what managers can learn from a review of cognitive models of motivation in general and try to integrate the models.

If we start with expectancy theory, there are three critical questions to which employees must answer yes in order to be motivated. First, if I try do I believe I can perform? Although skills, abilities, training, and knowledge can all have an impact the answer to this question, so to can the clarity of performance expectations. The critical steps discussed concerning effective goal setting can be a very useful means of clarifying performance expectations. Second, if I perform well what outcomes are likely to result? Third, how positively or negatively do I value these outcomes? Managers can increase motivation by strengthening the relationship between performance and positive outcomes and weakening the relationships between negative outcomes as well as trying to influence perceptions of particular outcomes. However, managers should keep notions of equity in mind and remember that not only will employees be motivated by the relationship between their performance and subsequent outcomes, but they will also be influenced by the comparisons they make between themselves and others concerning performance and outcomes. Thus, they must not only believe that positive outcomes are highly probable if they perform well, but they must also believe that these outcomes are equitable when compared to those of others.

Perhaps most important, managers must understand that if they are truly concerned with improving performance and work attitudes, they must take an active role in *managing* motivational processes on the job. Managing motivation represents a conscious attempt by managers to participate actively in creating proper work environments and matching people to jobs. Managers cannot sit back and simply complain about unmotivated workers; motivating employees requires work.

Managers' efforts to improve employee motivation and performance should be preceded by examination of their own strengths and weaknesses. Do they really understand their own needs, aspirations, and expectations? Are their self-perceptions consistent with the perceptions others have of them? Failure to understand oneself does not facilitate motivation in others.

The need to recognize and deal with individual differences in the work environment has emerged consistently throughout our discussion of motivational processes. Managers must recognize that employees possess different abilities, expectations, and valences. An awareness of these differences allows managers to utilize more effectively the diversity of talent among subordinates and, within policy limitations, acknowledge good performance with rewards most valued by employees.

It is important for managers to establish clear performance-reward contingencies. Managers need to know their subordinates well enough to recognize good performance when it occurs (and not be unduly influenced by stereotypes or halo effects). Once such performance occurs, rewards should be forthcoming in a way clearly recognized by employees as having resulted from performance. This contention argues against compensation systems that fail to recognize individual merit.

Questions of motivation ultimately come to rest on the nature of the job or task that employees are asked to perform. Although the issue of job design is reserved for Chapter 9, we can point out here the obvious need to design jobs that employees will find meaningful and personally satisfying. When this cannot be done, greater management creativity is called for; managers will have to compensate for less desirable jobs with other rewards. Managers should give attention to improving the overall quality of the work environment. What effects do group processes, supervisory style, or working conditions have on employee morale and the desire to participate actively in organizational activities?

Efforts can be made to monitor employee attitudes periodically and discover general trends. When attitudes begin to decline, managers are alerted to potential problems that can be solved before they adversely affect employee performance or retention.

Finally, managers can recognize the simple fact that without employee cooperation and support, a great deal of managerial energy can be wasted. It is important to involve employees as much as possible in decisions affecting their jobs. Employees have a major stake in what happens to an organization and are often willing to contribute beyond what is asked (or allowed) of them. In short, managers can recognize that employees represent a human resource for which they are responsible. A major criterion for evaluating managerial effectiveness is the extent to which managers efficiently make use of these resources.[28]

CONSEQUENCES OF MOTIVATION AND WORK BEHAVIOR

We have spent most of this chapter examining factors that enhance or reduce employee performance, emphasizing the relationship between motivation and job performance. Now we will briefly consider several additional *consequences* of motivated behavior. Specifically, we will consider three topics: job satisfaction, attendance, and turnover. We begin with job satisfaction.

Performance and Job Satisfaction: Is There a Relationship?

In Chapter 3, we discussed the nature of job attitudes. On the basis of this discussion and what we have now learned about motivated behavior, let us consider the relationship that exists between performance on the job and job satisfaction. For many years, managers believed that "a happy worker is a productive worker," and considerable energies were invested in finding ways to make employees "happy" at work. This assumption can be seen in the recommendations of the human relations movement discussed in the previous chapter.

More recently, however, research has demonstrated that the causal relationship may, in fact, be just the opposite, if certain conditions are met. That is, job satisfaction may result from good job performance so long as the rewards received by the employee are believed to be fair and commensurate with the level of job performance.[29] As shown in Exhibit 6.8, job performance leads to the receipt of a given level of rewards. If the employee feels that the rewards are equitable (that is, fair, given his or her level of performance), the employee should feel a certain amount of satisfaction.

For example, if an employee worked particularly hard on a project and received a bonus or some form of recognition, we would expect that employee to be satisfied. Moreover, he or she would probably be motivated to continue to work hard in the belief that future rewards would follow. On the other hand, if the employee worked hard but failed to receive what he or she considered to be a fair reward, we would expect that employee to be

Exhibit 6.8
Relationship of Job
Performance to
Job Satisfaction

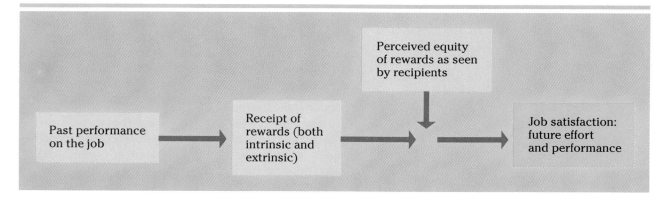

dissatisfied. Hence, satisfaction is largely influenced by the degree of perceived equity in administering rewards based on job performance. We will return to this point in the next chapter when we examine reward systems.

Employee Absenteeism

Throughout this chapter, we have focused our attention of factors that motivate people to perform. There is an equally important question—namely, how do we motivate people to participate? As was noted at the beginning of the chapter, organizations have to meet three behavioral requirements, and one of these is the ability to get people to join and remain with the organization. If we cannot secure an acceptable level of participation—if we cannot get employees to come to work and stay on the job—organizational effectiveness is severely diminished.

As with theories of job performance, it is possible to examine issues such as employee absenteeism and turnover using the cognitive approach. That is, we can look at cognitive processes to consider how people make conscious—and sometimes unconscious—decisions concerning coming to work or remaining with the corporation. First, let us look at employee attendance. Any way we look at it, employee absenteeism is expensive. One study estimates that average absenteeism in the United States is about 4.7 percent.[30] This means that on any given day, almost 5 percent of the work force is not present. The productivity implications of this are obvious. Moreover, absenteeism is expensive. It has been estimated that absenteeism costs U.S. industry over $40 billion per year and Canadian industry $12 billion.[31] Clearly, managers interested in improving effectiveness should be interested in this problem.

If we try to understand what influences employee attendance, the model presented in Exhibit 6.9 should help.[32] According to this model, actual *attendance* is influenced by two primary factors: an employee's *attendance motivation* (that is, how motivated is the employee to try to come to work?) and an employee's *ability to attend* (that is, can the employee actually get to work regardless of motivational level?). To understand this better, let us look at the roots of each of these factors.

Attendance Motivation.   An employee's desire to come to work is influenced by several factors. These include the prevailing *absence culture,* or the prevailing norms the group and organization have concerning what constitutes an acceptable level of attendance. We all know of some organizations where a degree of absenteeism is tolerated and even encouraged, and some where it is not. Beyond this, management can influence attendance motivation through the kind of people it selects and hires, company absence control policies, and so forth. Finally, employee attitudes, values, and goals play a part in determining motivational levels. People who are dissatisfied with their jobs will more than likely not be eager to come to work.

These factors, in turn, exist within a societal and economic milieu. That is, while American absence rates hover around 5 percent, the comparable rates in Japan and Korea are less than a tenth of that figure. Clearly, different societal norms concerning what is acceptable behavior play a part here. Moreover, economic conditions can affect attendance motivation in several

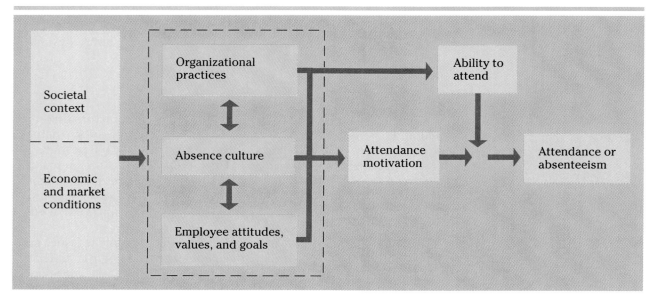

Exhibit 6.9
A Diagnostic Model of
Employee Attendance

Source: Adapted from Figure 3.5 in S. R. Rhodes and R. M. Steers, *Managing Employee Absenteeism* (Reading, Mass.: Addison-Wesley, 1990). © 1990 by Addison-Wesley Publishing Co., Inc., Reading, Massachusetts. Reprinted with permission of the publisher.

ways. For example, during periods of economic prosperity, people tend to take more days off, whereas during poor economic conditions, attendance actually increases (possibly because people are afraid of losing their jobs). Thus, several factors interact to cause attendance motivation.

Ability to Attend.   However, as we noted above, being motivated is not enough. The employee must be able to come to work. Here, three factors seem to influence ability to attend. First, managers interested in reducing absenteeism sometimes forget that people do get sick; clearly, illness affects attendance. In addition, people sometimes have transportation problems (their cars break down, there is a snowstorm, etc.). And, finally, an employee's family responsibilities sometimes interfere with attendance. If a child is sick, one parent may have to stay home with the child and thereby miss a day's work. Although companies can *assist* with the employee's ability to attend (through wellness programs, car pools, and company-sponsored day-care centers), this ability still moderates actual attendance levels.

Employee Turnover

The second form of withdrawal from the organization is more severe—actually leaving the company. As is the case with absenteeism, turnover represents a sizable cost for most companies, and efforts to understand and reduce turnover of a company's most valued employees represents time well spent. Using the cognitive framework, we again approach this problem from the standpoint of understanding the thought or decision processes relating to the decision to stay or leave an organization.

An abbreviated model of the turnover process is shown in Exhibit 6.10.[33] Following the behavioral intention model outlined in Chapter 4, we can see that *job attitudes* (which are influenced by a host of individual and organizational factors, such as unmet job expectations, perceived inequitable rewards, poor supervisory relations, etc.) combine with *nonwork influences* (e.g., one's desire to stay home to raise a family, the transfer of one's spouse) to determine an employee's desire to stay or leave the organization. If the employee desires to remain, we would normally expect continued job performance. On the other hand, if the employee feels the need to leave, we would expect turnover if the employee has available alternatives. If not, we might see the employee engage in a series of efforts to accommodate his or her inability to leave. These may include efforts to improve the work situation (e.g., to get along better with his or her supervisor, to form a union) or perhaps efforts to retaliate against the company through sabotage or other destructive means. Absenteeism and other forms of withdrawal may also follow. Whatever the means, employees will generally attempt to develop an accommodation strategy that allows them to accept their situation.

Clearly, the full decision process involved in leaving organizations is very complex and varies with the individuals and situations involved. Even so, the above outline should serve to highlight several of the typical factors that can affect our staying or leaving. As with employee absenteeism, the more managers understand about factors that entice or force people away from the organization—either temporarily or permanently—the more they can take corrective actions to retain valued employees.

Exhibit 6.10
Influences on
Employee Turnover

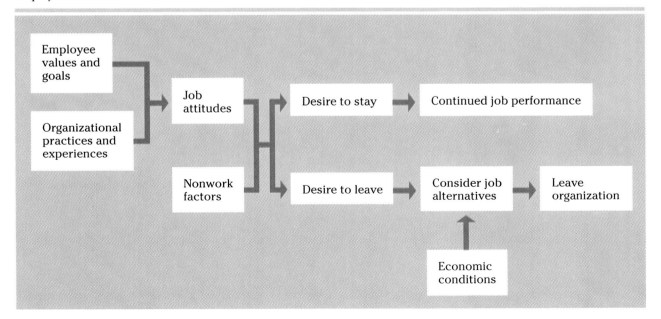

Source: Adapted from R. M. Steers and R. T. Mowday, "Employee Turnover and Post-Decision Accommodation Processes," in *Research in Organizational Behavior* by L. L. Cummings and B. M. Staw (eds.), Vol. 3. Copyright © 1981 JAI Press Inc. Reprinted by permission of the publisher.

PULLING IT ALL TOGETHER

People's motivation is a function of their understanding of what performance is expected and their beliefs that they can perform well and that good performance will be rewarded equitably. The actual outcomes of performance (rewards or punishments) also have a significant impact on their motivation and performance. Because motivation plays a critical role in performance, managers must understand the motivation process, but they must also consider the role of other factors such as ability and opportunity to perform.

SUMMARY OF KEY POINTS

■ Organizations need three things from their employees. These are referred to as behavioral requirements and include (1) commitment to remaining with the organization, (2) dependable role performance, and (3) spontaneous and innovative behavior.

■ Low productivity in organizations is often the result of the following factors: (1) unappealing rewards for good performance, (2) weak performance-reward linkages, (3) distrust of management, (4) desire to have control over one's job, and (5) lack of job involvement.

■ Equity theory of work motivation asserts that people view their work experience as a social exchange process; they compare their own inputs and outcomes with those of a referent other. If the exchange is unequal, individuals will be motivated to resolve the inequity.

■ Employees may attempt to resolve an inequity by changing inputs or outcomes, changing their perceptions of inputs or outcomes for themselves or others, leaving the organization, or changing the comparison other.

■ Goal-setting theory asserts that motivation and performance are enhanced to the extent that employees pursue realistic, task-oriented goals. These goals serve to focus attention, increase effort, enhance task persistence, and encourage the development of new strategies for goal attainment.

■ A goal-setting program consists of (1) setting difficult but attainable goals, (2) securing employee acceptance of these goals, and (3) providing support and feedback to employees on task performance.

■ Expectancy/valence theory focuses on how employees develop expectations concerning the relationship between effort and rewards and the extent to which they value the available rewards. Motivation is seen as a function of employee beliefs that effort will lead to performance and that performance will lead to desired rewards. Actual job performance, on the other hand, is a function of motivation combined with employee abilities and skills, role clarity and acceptance, and opportunity to perform.

■ Job satisfaction is believed to be influenced by the degree to which performance is followed by the receipt of what employees consider equitable rewards.

▨ Employee absenteeism is largely determined by an employee's motivation to attend combined with his or her ability to attend.

▨ Employee turnover typically results when employee job dissatisfaction leads to a desire to leave and a search for better job alternatives. When a better position becomes available, termination is likely to follow. However, if dissatisfaction is very intense, the employee may depart even without an alternative job.

KEY WORDS

absence culture
absenteeism
acognitive
attendance motivation
behavioral requirements
cognitive
distribution rules
effort-performance expectancy
equity theory
expectancy/valence theory

force field analysis
goal difficulty
goal specificity
goal-setting theory
performance-outcome expectancy
role acceptance
role clarity
social comparison theory
turnover
valence

QUESTIONS FOR DISCUSSION

1. What do Katz and Kahn mean when they argue that every organization must meet three behavioral requirements?
2. Discuss several reasons for employee restriction of output.
3. Contrast cognitive and acognitive theories of employee motivation.
4. What are the basic premises of equity theory? How do these premises differ from those of goal-setting theory and expectancy/valence theory?
5. Describe the process by which perceptions of equity or inequity result.
6. How can an employee resolve feelings of inequity on the job?
7. Does existing research support equity theory?
8. Describe how the various task-goal attributes influence performance under goal-setting conditions. Which task-goal attributes are most powerful in determining performance?
9. What individual and situational influences serve to moderate the influence of task-goal attributes on performance?
10. According to expectancy theory, what causes motivation? What causes performance?
11. Compare and contrast the various managerial implications of the three theories of motivation.
12. Describe the relationship between satisfaction and performance.
13. Describe the major influences on employee attendance. What can managers do to increase attendance?
14. What causes employee turnover? Why would managers want to be careful in trying to reduce company turnover rates?

NOTES

1. M. D'Anastasio, "Soviet Workers Resist Gorbachev Plan to Link Wage Levels and Performance," *Wall Street Journal,* June 3, 1987, p. A-27.
2. D. Katz and R. Kahn, *The Social Psychology of Organizations* (New York: Wiley, 1978).
3. J. S. Adams, "Injustice in Social Exchange," in L. Berkowitz, ed., *Advances in Experimental Social Psychology,* vol. 2 (New York: Academic Press, 1965); K. Weick, "The Concept of Equity in the Perception of Pay," *Administrative Science Quarterly,* 1966, *11,* pp. 414–439.
4. R. T. Mowday, "Equity Theory Predictions of Behavior in Organizations," in R. M. Steers and L. W. Porter, eds., *Motivation and Work Behavior,* 4th ed. (New York: McGraw-Hill, 1987).
5. J. G. March and H. A. Simon, *Organizations* (New York: Wiley, 1958).
6. Mowday, op. cit.
7. Adams, op. cit.
8. J. Nelson-Horchler. "The Pay Revolt Brews." *Industry Week,* June 18, 1990, pp. 28–36; "What CEOs Really Make," *Fortune,* June 15, 1992, pp. 94–99.
9. V. D. Wall and L. L. Nolan, "Perceptions of Inequity, Satisfaction, and Conflict in Task-oriented Groups," *Human Relations,* November 1986, pp. 1033–1052; R. C. Huseman, J. D. Hatfield, and E. W. Miles, "A New Perspective on Equity Theory: The Equity Sensitivity Concept," *Academy of Management Review,* April 1987, pp. 222–234.
10. Mowday, op. cit., p. 100.
11. G. S. Leventhal, "Fairness in Social Relationships," in J. Thibaut and R. Carson, eds., *Contemporary Topics in Social Psychology* (Morristown, N.J.: General Learning Press, 1976).
12. E. A. Locke and G. P. Latham, *Goal-Setting—A Motivational Technique That Works* (Englewood Cliffs, N.J.: Prentice-Hall, 1984).
13. Ibid. See also E. A. Locke, K. N. Shaw, L. M. Saari, and G. P. Latham, "Goal-Setting and Task Performance: 1969–1980," *Psychological Bulletin,* July 1981, p. 126.
14. G. P. Latham and E. A. Locke, "Goal-Setting: A Motivational Technique That Works," *Organizational Dynamics,* Autumn 1979, pp. 68-80.
15. Locke et al., op. cit.
16. R. M. Steers, "Task-Goal Attributes, n Achievement, and Supervisory Performance," *Organizational Behavior and Human Performance,* 1975, 13, pp. 392–403.
17. L. A. Taylor, "Decision Quality and Commitment within a Probabilistic Environment," *Organizational Behavior and Human Decision Processes,* April 1987, pp. 203–227.
18. E. A. Locke, "Toward a Theory of Task Performance and Incentives," *Organizational Behavior and Human Performance,* 1968, 3, pp. 157–189.
19. Locke and Latham, op. cit.
20. R. Stayer, "How I Learned to Let My Workers Lead." *Harvard Business Review,* 1990, Nov.-Dec., 66–83.
21. V. H. Vroom, *Work and Motivation* (New York: Wiley, 1964).
22. L. W. Porter and E. E. Lawler, *Managerial Attitudes and Performance* (Homewood, Ill.: Irwin, 1968).
23. Ibid.; Steers and Porter, op. cit.
24. E. E. Ghiselli, Explorations in Managerial Talent (Santa Monica, Calif.: Goodyear, 1966).
25. Steers and Porter, op. cit.
26. J. Campbell and R. Pritchard, "Motivation Theory in Industrial and Organizational Psychology," in M. D. Dunnette ed., *Handbook of Industrial and Organizational Psychology* (Chicago: Rand McNally, 1976), pp. 63–130.
27. R. Stayer, op. cit.

28. Steers and Porter, op. cit.

29. Porter and Lawler, op. cit.

30. B. W. Klein, "Missed Work and Hours Lost," *Monthly Labor Review,* November 1986, pp. 26–30.

31. S. R. Rhodes and R. M. Steers, *Managing Employee Absenteeism* (Reading, Mass.: Addison-Wesley, 1990).

32. Ibid.

33. R. M. Steers and R. T. Mowday, "Employee Turnover and Post-Decision Accommodation Processes," in L. L. Cummings and B. M. Staw eds., *Research in Organizational Behavior* (Greenwich, Conn.: JAI Press, 1979), pp. 237–249.

EXPERIENTIAL EXERCISE 6

What Are Your Career Goals?

What would you like to accomplish in your lifetime? Most of us daydream about the answer to this question, but few think through and write out career goals. This exercise is one in which the more time and effort you put into it, the more you will get out of it.

To start, write down as many goals *in 5 minutes* as possible concerning such issues as job, finances, family, spiritual life, etc. Next, spend 5 more minutes refining these goals. Once you have finished this task, then repeat the process for a period of the next five years and the next 12 months. After you have these three sets of goals, see if there are any conflicts or inconsistencies. Also, see if clear priorities emerge.

Next, focus on your career goals. Assume that you must make a career decision soon. Take a stab at determining your "best possible" decision. Also, what would be your "worst possible" decision? What are some of the important consequences concerning your career, family, social life, etc. under each of these decisions.

Now look at what you have recorded under your life goals and under your career deicision. What patterns emerge? What insights can you glean? What would someone who knows you well think of your lists?

MANAGEMENT DILEMMA 6

Understanding the Motivation of Pamela Jones

Pamela Jones enjoyed banking. She had taken a battery of personal aptitude and interest tests that suggested that she might like and do well in either banking or librarianship. Since the job market for librarians was poor, she applied for employment with a large chartered bank, the Bank of Winnipeg, and was quickly accepted.

Her early experiences in banking were almost always challenging and rewarding. She was enrolled in the bank's management development program because of her education (a B.A. in languages and some postgraduate training in business administration), her previous job experience, and her obvious intelligence and drive.

During her first year in the training program, Pamela attended classes on banking procedures and policies, and worked her way through a series of low-level positions in her branch. She was repeatedly told by her manager that her work was above average. Similarly, the training officer who worked out of the main office and coordinated the development of junior officers in the program frequently told Pamela that she was "among the best three" of her cohort of twenty trainees.

Although she worked hard and frequently encountered discrimination from senior bank personnel (as well as customers) because of her sex, Pamela developed a deep-seated attachment to banking in general, and to her bank and branch, in particular. She was proud to be a banker and proud to be a member of the Bank of Winnipeg. After one year in the management development program however, Pamela found she was not learning anything new about banking or her employer. She was shuffled from one job to another at her own branch, cycling back over many positions several times to help meet temporary problems caused by absences, overloads, and turnover. Turnover—a rampant problem in banking—amazed Pamela. She couldn't understand, for many months, why so many people started careers "in the service" of banking, only to leave after one or two years.

After her first year, the repeated promises of moving into her own position at another branch started to sound hollow to Pamela. The training officer claimed that there were no openings suitable for her at other branches. On two occasions when openings did occur, the manager of each of the branches in question rejected Pamela, sight unseen, presumably because she hadn't been in banking long enough.

Pamela was not the only unhappy person at her branch. Her immediate supervisor, George Burns, complained that because of the bank's economy drive, vacated customer service positions were left unfilled. As branch accountant, Burns was responsible for day-to-day customer service. As a result, he was unable to perform the duties of his own job. The manager told Burns several times that customer service was critical, but that Burns would have to improve his performance on his own job. Eventually, George Burns left the bank to work for a trust company, earning seventy dollars a month more for work similar to that he had been performing. This left Pamela in the position of having to supervise the same tellers who had trained her only a few months earlier. Pamela was amazed at all the mistakes the tellers made but found it difficult to do much to correct their poor work habits. All disciplinary procedures had to be administered with the approval of Head Office.

After several calls to her training officer, Pamela was finally transferred to her first "real" position in her own branch. Still keen and dedicated, Pamela was soon to lose her enthusiasm.

At her new branch, Pamela was made "assistant accountant." Her duties included the supervision of the seven tellers, some customer service and a great deal of paper work. The same economy drive that she had witnessed at her training branch resulted in the failure to replace customer service personnel. Pamela was expected to "pick up the slack" at the front desk, neglecting her own work. Her tellers seldom balanced their own cash, so Pamela stayed late almost every night to find their errors. To save on overtime, the manager sent the tellers home while Pamela stayed late, first to correct the tellers' imbalances, then to finish her own paperwork. He told Pamela that as an officer of the bank, she was expected to stay until the work of her subordinates, and her own work, were satisfactorily completed. Pamela realized that most of her counterparts in other B. of W. branches were willing to give this sort of dedication; therefore, so should she. This situation lasted six months with little sign of change in sight.

One day, Pamela learned from a phone conversation with a friend at another branch that she would be transferred to Hope, British Columbia, to fill an opening that had arisen. Pamela's husband was a professional, employed by a large corporation in Vancouver. His company did not have an office in Hope; moreover, his training was very specialized, and he could probably find employment only in large cities anyway.

Accepting transfers was expected of junior officers who wanted to get ahead. Pamela inquired at Head Office and learned that the rumor was true. Her training officer told her, however, that Pamela could decline the transfer if she wished, but he couldn't say how soon her next promotion opportunity would come about. Depressed, annoyed, disappointed, and frustrated, Pamela quit the bank.

1. First, let us try to understand what is happening. Use expectancy/valence theory to explain Pamela's behavior at the bank.
2. Does equity theory help explain Pamela's behavior? If so, why?
3. What concrete steps could be taken to ensure that people like Pamela do not leave their positions?

Source: C. C. Pinder, *Work Motivation: Theory, Issues, and Applications* (Glenview, Ill.: Scott, Foresman and Company, 1984), pp. 317–318. Reprinted by permission of Scott, Foresman and Company.

Chapter 7

Performance Appraisal and Rewards

The Management Challenge

- To make effective use of performance appraisals to improve individual job performance.
- To know the limitations inherent in the use of various appraisal systems.
- To choose the best appraisal system for a particular organization.
- To know how to give effective feedback to subordinates.
- To use incentives and rewards effectively to secure the best possible performance from subordinates.

CLOSE UP

Two Performance Appraisal Interviews

"Janet, thanks for coming in. As you know, it's that time of year again. I've been going over this performance appraisal form and have written in my evaluation. I'd like you to look it over and then sign it."

Janet looked over her ratings which were nearly all in the "satisfactory" range. Even the category of dependability was marked "satisfactory," yet, it was Janet who came in on three different occasions to cover for workers in her group who were absent for one reason or another. Janet mentioned this issue to her boss, Ken.

"Well, Janet, you're right and that's exactly what I expect of my employees. You know this is your first year here and you can't expect to reach the top in one jump. But I like your style and if you keep it up, who knows how far you'll go."

Twenty-four minutes after the interview began, Janet left, bewildered and disappointed. She had worked hard during her first year; in fact, she had gone the extra mile on a few occasions, and now she was more confused than ever about what was expected of her and what constituted good performance. "Maybe it just doesn't pay to work hard."

Two weeks before their scheduled interview, Mary asked Ron to review his goals and accomplishments for the last six months and to note any major changes in his job that had taken place during that period. In the meantime, Mary pulled out her file in which she had periodically recorded both positive and negative specific incidents over the last six months concerning Ron's performance. She also reviewed the goals they had jointly set at the end of the last review and thought carefully about not only the possible goals for the next six months but longer-term development needs and goals that might be appropriate for Ron.

On the day of the interview, both Mary and Ron came well prepared to review the past six months as well as to think about and plan for the next performance period and beyond. The interview took nearly two hours. After candidly discussing Ron's past performance and the extent to which both sides felt he had or had not accomplished the goals for that period, they began to focus on what should be accomplished in the future. The discussion caused both sides to made changes in their original evaluations and ideas about targets for the future. When it was over, Ron left more motivated than before and confident that even though he had areas in which he could improve he had a bright future ahead of him if he continued to be motivated and work hard.

PERFORMANCE APPRAISAL SYSTEMS

Performance appraisals are one of the most important and often one of the most mishandled aspects of management. Typically, we think of performance appraisals as involving a boss evaluating a subordinate. However, performance appraisals increasingly involve subordinates appraising bosses,[1] customers appraising providers, and peers evaluating co-workers.

Whether appraisals are done by subordinates, peers, customers, or superiors, the process itself is vital to the lifeblood of the organization. Performance appraisal systems provide a means of systematically evaluating employees across various performance dimensions to ensure that organizations are getting what they pay for. They provide valuable feedback to employees and managers, and they assist in identifying promotable people as well as problems. However, such appraisals are meaningless unless they are accompanied by an effective feedback system that ensures that the employee gets the right messages concerning performance.

Reward systems represent a powerful motivational force in organizations, but this is true only when the system is fair and tied to performance. Because a variety of approaches to appraising performance exists, managers should be aware of the advantages and disadvantages of each. In turn, an understanding of reward systems will help managers select the system best suited to the needs and goals of the organization.

Performance appraisal systems serve a variety of functions of central importance to employees. Appraisal techniques practiced today are not without problems, though. Managers should keep abreast of recent developments in compensation and reward systems so they can modify existing systems when more appropriate alternatives become available.

A key management responsibility has always been to oversee and develop subordinates. In fact, it has been said that every manager is a human resource manager. Nowhere is this more true than with regard to evaluating and rewarding subordinates. Managers are consistently involved with employee training and development, monitoring employee performance, providing job-related feedback, and administering rewards.

In this chapter we examine three interrelated aspects of the performance appraisal and reward process. As Exhibit 7.1 shows, this process moves from evaluating employee performance to providing adequate and constructive feedback to determining discretionary rewards. Where effort and performance are properly evaluated and rewarded, we would expect to see more stable and consistent job performance. On the other hand, where such performance is only evaluated intermittently or where the appraisal and review process is poorly done, we would generally see less consistent performance. We begin our discussion with a look at the nature of appraisals.

We begin by examining three aspects of performance appraisal systems: (1) the uses of performance appraisals, (2) problems found in performance appraisals, and (3) methods for reducing errors in the appraisal system. This overview will provide a foundation for studying specific techniques of performance appraisal. Those interested in more detailed information on performance appraisal systems may wish to consult books on personnel administration or compensation.

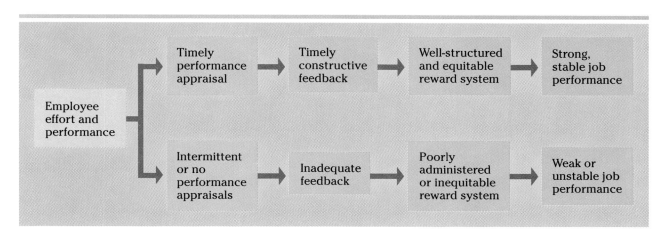

Exhibit 7.1
The Performance Appraisal
and Reward Process

Uses of Performance Appraisals

In most work organizations, performance appraisals are used for a variety of reasons. These reasons range from improving employee productivity to developing the employees themselves. This diversity of uses is well documented in a study of why companies use performance appraisals.[2] As shown in Exhibit 7.2, compensation and performance feedback have been the most prominent reasons organizations use performance appraisals.

Feedback to employees.   Performance appraisals provide feedback to employees about quantity and quality of job performance. Without this information, employees have little knowledge of how well they are doing their jobs and how they might improve their work.

Self-development.   Performance appraisals can also serve as an aid to employee self-development. Individuals learn about their strengths and weaknesses as seen by others and can initiate self-improvement programs (see discussion on behavioral self-management programs in Chapter 4).

Reward systems.   In addition, appraisals may form the bases of organizational reward systems—particularly merit-based compensation plans.

Personnel decisions.   Performance appraisals serve personnel-related functions as well. In making personnel decisions, such as those relating to promotions, transfers, and terminations, they can be quite useful. Employers can make choices on the basis of information about individual talents and shortcomings. In addition, appraisal systems help management evaluate the effectiveness of its selection and placement functions. If newly hired employees generally perform poorly, managers should consider whether the right kind of people are being hired in the first place.

Exhibit 7.2
Primary Uses of Appraisals

Use	Small Organizations (Percent)	Large Organizations (Percent)
Compensation	80.6	62.2
Performance improvement	49.7	60.6
Feedback	20.6	37.8
Promotion	29.1	21.1
Documentation	11.4	10.0
Training	8.0	9.4
Transfer	7.4	8.3
Manpower planning	6.3	6.1
Discharge	2.3	2.2
Research	2.9	0.0
Layoff	0.6	0.0

Source: Alan H. Locher and Kenneth S. Teel, "Performance Appraisal—A Survey of Current Practices," *Personnel Journal,* May 1977. Copyright May 1977. Reprinted with the permission of *Personnel Journal,* Costa Mesa, California; all rights reserved.

Training and development.   Finally, appraisals can help managers identify areas in which employees lack critical skills for either immediate or future performance. In these situations, new or revised training programs can be established to further develop the company's human resources.

It is apparent that performance appraisal systems serve a variety of functions in organizations. In light of the importance of these functions, it is imperative that the accuracy and fairness of the appraisal be paramount considerations in the evaluation of a system. Many performance appraisal systems exist. It is the manager's job to select that technique or combination of techniques that best serves the particular needs (and constraints) of the organization. Before considering these various techniques, let us look at some of the more prominent problems and sources of error that are common to several of them.

Problems with Performance Appraisals

A number of problems can be identified that pose a threat to the value of appraisal techniques. Most of these problems deal with the related issues of the validity and reliability of the instruments or techniques themselves. *Validity* is the extent to which an instrument actually measures what it intends to measure, whereas *reliability* is the extent to which the instrument consistently yields the same results each time it is used. Ideally, a good performance appraisal system will exhibit high levels of both validity and reliability. If not, serious questions must be raised concerning the utility (and possibly the legality) of the system.

It is possible to identify several common sources of error in performance appraisal systems. These include: (1) central tendency error, (2) strictness or leniency error, (3) halo effect, (4) recency error, and (5) personal biases. Many of these problems are linked to barriers to accurate perceptions discussed in Chapter 3.

Central Tendency Error.   It has often been found that supervisors rate most of their employees within a narrow range. Regardless of how people actually perform, the rater fails to distinguish significant differences among group members and lumps everyone together in an "average" category. This is called central tendency error and is shown in Exhibit 7.3. In short, the central tendency error is the failure to recognize either very good or very poor performers.

Strictness or Leniency Error.   A related rating problem exists when a supervisor is overly strict or overly lenient in evaluations (see Exhibit 7.3). In college classrooms, we hear of professors who are "tough graders" or, conversely, "easy A's." Similar situations exist in the workplace, where some supervisors see most subordinates as not measuring up to their high standards, whereas other supervisors see most subordinates as deserving of a high rating. As with central tendency error, strictness or leniency error fails to distinguish adequately between good and bad performers and instead relegates almost everyone to the same or related categories.

Halo Effect.   The halo effect exists where a supervisor assigns the same rating to each factor being evaluated for an individual. For example, an employee rated above average on quantity of performance may also be rated

Exhibit 7.3
Examples of Strictness,
Central Tendency, and
Leniency Errors

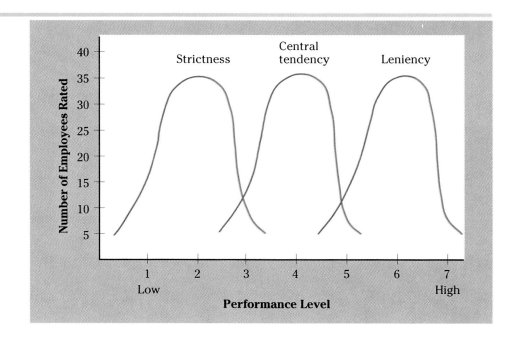

above average on quality of performance, interpersonal competence, attendance, and promotion readiness. In other words, the supervisor cannot effectively differentiate between relatively discrete categories and instead gives a global rating.

A good example of the halo effect in operation can be seen in a description of performance appraisal systems at General Motors.[3] A former GM executive claims that so much emphasis was placed on cost cutting in the company that other important areas of managerial accountability went almost unnoticed in evaluations. For instance, the Tarrytown, New York, assembly division once had the dubious distinction of producing the poorest-quality cars of all 22 U.S. GM plants. (Note: Tarrytown no longer has this reputation. Indeed, recent work redesign efforts have dramatically improved product quality.) During this time, some trucks were so poorly built that dealers refused to accept them. Even so, the plant had the lowest manufacturing costs in GM. As a result, the plant manager at Tarrytown received one of the largest bonuses of all the assembly divisions while building the worst cars in the company. Clearly, the manager's evaluation concerning costs overshadowed considerations of product quality.

Recency Error.   Oftentimes evaluators focus on an employee's most recent behavior in the evaluation process. This is known as the recency error. That is, in an annual evaluation, a supervisor may give undue emphasis to performance during the past months—or even weeks—and ignore performance levels prior to this. This practice, if known to employees, leads to a situation where employees may "float" for the initial months of the evaluation period and then overexert themselves in the last few months or weeks prior to evaluation. This practice leads to uneven performance and contributes to the attitude of "playing the game."

Personal Biases.   Finally, it is not uncommon to find situations in which supervisors allow their own personal biases to influence their appraisals. Such biases include like or dislike for someone, as well as racial and sexual biases. Personal biases can interfere with the fairness and accuracy of an evaluation and are illegal in many situations.

Reducing Errors in Performance Appraisals

A number of suggestions have been advanced recently to minimize the effects of various biases and errors on the performance appraisal process.[4] When errors are reduced, more accurate information is available for personnel decisions and personal development. These methods for reducing error include:

■ Ensuring that each dimension or factor on a performance appraisal form represents a single job activity instead of a group of job activities.

■ Avoiding terms such as "average," because different evaluators define the term differently.

■ Ensuring that raters observe subordinates on a regular basis throughout the evaluation period. It is even helpful if the rater takes notes for future reference.

■ Keeping the number of persons evaluated by one rater to a reasonable number. When one person must evaluate many subordinates, it becomes difficult to discriminate. Rating fatigue increases with the number of ratees.

■ Ensuring that the dimensions used are clearly stated, meaningful, and relevant to good job performance.

■ Training raters so they can recognize various sources of error and understand the rationale underlying the evaluation process.

■ Using mechanisms like these, better employee ratings that can have greater meaning both for the individual employee and the organization will result.

TECHNIQUES OF PERFORMANCE APPRAISAL

Organizations use numerous methods to evaluate personnel. We will summarize several popular techniques. Although countless variations on these themes can be found, the basic methods presented provide a good summary of the commonly available techniques. Following this review, we will consider the various strengths and weaknesses of each technique. Six techniques are reviewed here: (1) graphic rating scales, (2) critical incident technique, (3) behaviorally anchored rating scales, (4) behavioral observation scales, (5) management by objectives, and (6) assessment centers.

Graphic Rating Scales

Certainly, the most popular method of evaluation used in organizations today is the *graphic rating scale.* One study found that 57 percent of the organizations they surveyed used rating scales, and another study found the figure to be 65 percent.[5] Although this method appears in many formats, the supervisor or rater is typically presented with a printed form that contains both the employee's name and several evaluation dimensions (quantity of work, quality of work, knowledge of job, attendance). The rater is then asked to rate the employee by assigning a number or rating on each of the dimensions. An example of a graphic rating scale is shown in Exhibit 7.4.

By using this method, if we assume that evaluator biases can be minimized, it is possible to compare employees objectively. It is also possible to examine the relative strengths and weaknesses of a single employee by comparing scores on the various dimensions.

However, one of the most serious drawbacks of this technique is its openness to central tendency, strictness, and leniency errors. It is possible to rate almost everyone in the middle of the scale or, conversely, at one end of the scale. In order to control for this, some companies have assigned required percentage distributions to the various scale points. Supervisors may be allowed to rate only 10 percent of their people outstanding and are required to rate 10 percent unsatisfactory, perhaps assigning 20 percent, 40 percent, and 20 percent to the remaining middle categories. By doing this, a

	Outstanding	Good	Satisfactory	Fair	Unsatisfactory
Name _____ Dept. _____ Date _____					

Quantity of work
  Volume of acceptable work under
    normal conditions
  Comments:
	☐	☐	☐	☐	☐

Quality of work
  Thoroughness, neatness, and
    accuracy of work
  Comments:
	☐	☐	☐	☐	☐

Knowledge of job
  Clear understanding of the facts or
    factors pertinent to the job
  Comments:
	☐	☐	☐	☐	☐

Personal qualities
  Personality, appearance,
    sociability, leadership, integrity
  Comments:
	☐	☐	☐	☐	☐

Cooperation
  Ability and willingness to work
    with associates, supervisors,
    and subordinates toward
    common goal
  Comments:
	☐	☐	☐	☐	☐

Dependability
  Conscientious, thorough,
    accurate, reliable with respect
    to attendance, lunch periods,
    reliefs, etc.
  Comments:
	☐	☐	☐	☐	☐

Initiative
  Earnestness in seeking
    increased responsibilities
  Self-starting, unafraid to
    proceed alone
  Comments:
	☐	☐	☐	☐	☐

Exhibit 7.4
A Typical Graphic
Rating Scale

Source: From *Personnel: A Diagnostic Approach,* Third Edition, by W. F. Glueck. Business Publications, 1982. Reprinted by permission of Richard D. Irwin, Inc.

SELF-ASSESSMENT 7.1
How Would You Rate Your Supervisor?

Instructions: Think of your current supervisor or one for any job you have held, and evaluate him or her on the following dimensions. Give a "1" for very poor, a "3" for average, a "5" for outstanding, etc.

		Very Poor		**Average**		**Outstanding**
1.	Your boss's knowledge of the job.	1	2	3	4	5
2.	Your boss's leadership skills.	1	2	3	4	5
3.	Your boss's communication skills.	1	2	3	4	5
4.	Your boss's ability to motivate subordinates.	1	2	3	4	5
5.	Your boss's attendance and promptness.	1	2	3	4	5
6.	Your boss's commitment to the organization.	1	2	3	4	5
7.	Your boss's long-term potential for promotion.	1	2	3	4	5
8.	What is your overall assessment of your supervisor?	1	2	3	4	5

distribution is forced within each department. However, this procedure may penalize a group of truly outstanding performers or reward a group of poor ones. For an example of the graphic rating system, refer to Self-Assessment 7.1. When you are finished, see Appendix B for scoring procedures and interpretation.

Critical Incident Technique

With the *critical incident technique* of performance appraisal, supervisors record incidents, or examples, of each subordinate's behavior that led to either unusual success or unusual failure on some aspect of the job. These incidents are recorded in a daily or weekly log under predesignated categories (planning, decision making, interpersonal relations, report writing). The final performance rating consists of a series of descriptive paragraphs or notes about various aspects of an employee's performance (see Exhibit 7.5).

The critical incident method provides useful information for appraisal interviews, and managers and subordinates can discuss specific incidents. Good qualitative information is generated. However, because little quantitative data emerge, it is difficult to use this technique for promotion or

The following performance areas are designed to assist you in preparing this appraisal and in discussing an individual's performance with him or her. It is suggested that areas of performance that you feel are significantly good or poor be documented below with specific examples or actions. The points listed are suggested as typical and are by not means all-inclusive. Examples related to these points may be viewed from either a positive or negative standpoint.

1. Performance on Technology of the Job

   A. *Safety Effectiveness*—possible considerations:
   1. Sets an excellent safety example for others in the department by words and action.
   2. Trains people well in safety areas.
   3. Gains the cooperation and participation of people in safety.
   4. Insists that safety be designed into procedure and processes.
   5. Is instrumental in initiating departmental safety program.
   6. Accepts safety as a fundamental job responsibility.

   Item   Related Examples
   _____
   _____
   _____

   B. *Job Knowledge*—Technical and/or Specialized—possible considerations:
   1. Shows exceptional knowledge in methods, materials, and techniques; and applies in a resourceful and practical manner.
   2. Stays abreast of development in field and applies to job.
   3. "Keeps up" on latest material in his or her special field.
   4. Participates in professional or technical organizations pertinent to his or her activities.

   Item   Related Examples
   _____
   _____
   _____

2. Performance on Human Relations

   A. *Ability to Communicate*—possible considerations:
   1. Gives logical, clear-cut, understandable instructions on complex problems.
   2. Uses clear and direct language in written and oral reporting.
   3. Organizes presentations in logical order and in order of importance.
   4. Provides supervisor and subordinates with pertinent and adequate information.
   5. Tailors communications approach to group or individual.
   6. Keeps informed on how subordinates think and feel about things.

   Item   Related Examples
   _____
   _____

   B. *Results Achieved Through Others*—possible considerations:
   1. Develops enthusiasm in others that gets the job done.
   2. Has respect and confidence of others.
   3. Recognizes and credits skills of others.
   4. Coordinates well with other involved groups to get the job done.

   Item   Related Examples
   _____
   _____

Exhibit 7.5
An Example of Critical
Incident Evaluation

Source: R. Daft and R. Steers, *Organizations: A Micro/Macro Approach* (Glenview, Ill.: Scott, Foresman and Company, 1986), p. 129.

salary decisions. The qualitative output here has led some companies to combine the critical incident technique with one of the quantitative techniques, such as the rating scale, to provide different kinds of feedback to the employees.

Behaviorally Anchored Rating Scales

An appraisal system that has received increasing attention in recent years is the behaviorally anchored rating scale (BARS). This system requires considerable work prior to evaluation but, if the work is carefully done, can lead to highly accurate ratings with high inter-rater reliability. Specifically, the BARS technique begins by selecting a job that can be described in observable behaviors. Managers and personnel specialists then identify these behaviors as they relate to superior or inferior performance.

An example of this is shown in Exhibit 7.6, where the BARS technique has been applied to the job of college professor. As shown, as one moves from extremely poor performance to extremely good performance, the performance descriptions, or behavioral anchors, increase. Oftentimes, six to ten scales are used to describe performance on the job. Exhibit 7.6 evaluates the professor's organizational skills. Other scales could relate to the professor's teaching effectiveness, knowledge of the material, availability to students, and fairness in grading. Once these scales are determined, the evaluator has only to check the category that describes what he or she observes on the job, and the employee's rating is simultaneously determined. The BARS technique has several purported advantages. In particular, many of the sources of error discussed earlier (central tendency, leniency, halo) should be significantly reduced, because raters are considering verbal descriptions of specific behaviors instead of general categories of behaviors such as those used in graphic rating scales. In addition, the technique focuses on job-related behaviors and ignores less relevant issues such as the subordinate's personality, race, or gender. This technique should also lead to employees being less defensive during performance appraisals, because the focus of the discussion would be actual measured behaviors, not the person. Finally, BARS can aid in employee training and development by identifying those domains needing most attention.

On the negative side, as noted above, considerable time and effort in designing the forms are required before the actual rating. Because a separate BARS is required for each distinct job, it is only cost-efficient on common jobs. Finally, because the technique relies on observable behaviors, it may have little applicability for such jobs in such areas as research science (and sometimes management), where much of the work is mental and relevant observable behaviors are difficult to obtain.

Behavioral Observation Scales

The *behavioral observation scale* (BOS) is similar to BARS in that both focus on identifying observable behaviors as they relate to performance. It is, however, less demanding of the evaluator. Typically, the evaluator is asked to rate

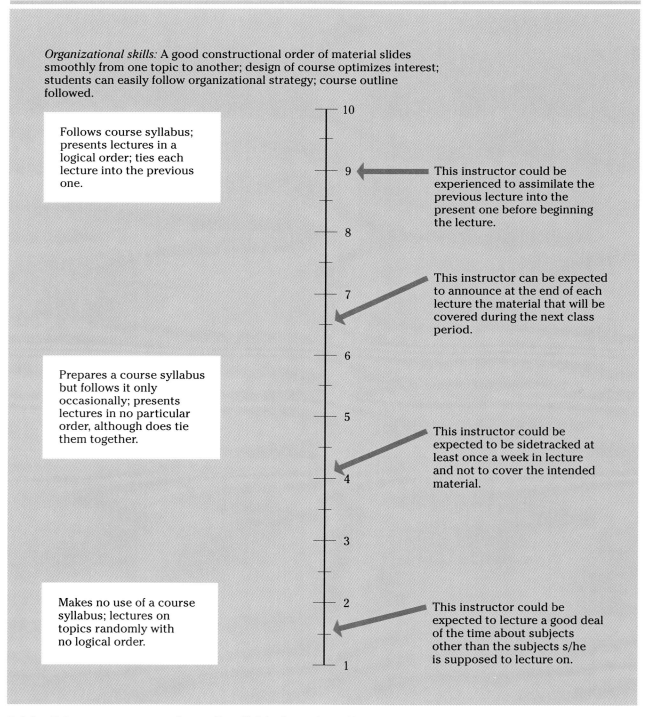

Organizational skills: A good constructional order of material slides smoothly from one topic to another; design of course optimizes interest; students can easily follow organizational strategy; course outline followed.

Follows course syllabus; presents lectures in a logical order; ties each lecture into the previous one.

This instructor could be experienced to assimilate the previous lecture into the present one before beginning the lecture.

This instructor can be expected to announce at the end of each lecture the material that will be covered during the next class period.

Prepares a course syllabus but follows it only occasionally; presents lectures in no particular order, although does tie them together.

This instructor could be expected to be sidetracked at least once a week in lecture and not to cover the intended material.

Makes no use of a course syllabus; lectures on topics randomly with no logical order.

This instructor could be expected to lecture a good deal of the time about subjects other than the subjects s/he is supposed to lecture on.

Exhibit 7.6
A Behaviorally Anchored
Scale For Rating
College Professors

Source: From H. John Bernardin and Richard W. Beatty, *Performance Appraisal: Assessing Human Behavior at Work* (Boston: Kent Publishing Company, 1984) Reprinted by permission of H. John Bernardin.

		Almost **Never**				**Almost** **Always**
1.	Describes the details of the change to subordinates.	1	2	3	4	5
2.	Explains why the change is necessary.	1	2	3	4	5
3.	Discusses how the change will affect the employee.	1	2	3	4	5
4.	Listens to the employee's concerns.	1	2	3	4	5
5.	Asks the employee for help in making the change work.	1	2	3	4	5
6.	If necessary, specifies the date for a follow-up meeting to respond to employee's concerns.	1	2	3	4	5
	Total =					

6–10	11–15	16–20	21–25	26–30
Below adequate	Adequate	Full	Excellent	Superior

Exhibit 7.7
Example of a Behavioral Observation Scale for Managers: Overcoming Resistance to Change

Source: G. Latham and K. Wexley, *Increasing Productivity Through Performance Appraisal,* Figure 3.8, p. 56, © 1981, Addison-Wesley Publishing Company, Inc., Reading, Massachusetts. Reprinted with permission of the publisher.

each behavior on a scale from 1 to 5 to indicate the frequency with which the employee exhibits the behavior. Evaluation of an employee's performance on a particular dimension is derived by summing the frequency ratings for the behaviors in each dimension.

For example, in Exhibit 7.7 we can see an example of a form to evaluate a manager's ability to overcome resistance to change. The rater simply has to circle the appropriate numbers describing observed behaviors and get a summary rating by adding the results. The BOS technique is easier to construct than the BARS and makes the evaluator's job somewhat simpler. Even so, this is a relatively new technique that is only now receiving some support in industry.

Management by Objectives

A popular technique for evaluating employees who are involved in jobs that have clear quantitative output is *management by objectives* (MBO). Although the concept of MBO encompasses much more than just the appraisal process (incorporating an organization-wide motivation, performance, and control system), we will focus here on its narrower application to evaluating employee performance. MBO is closely related to the goal-setting theory of motivation discussed in Chapter 6.

Exhibit 7.8
MBO Evaluation Report for
Sales Representative

Goals Categories	Goal	Actual Performance	Variance
1. Number of sales calls	40	38	95%
2. Number of new customers contacted	10	10	100%
3. Number of customer complaints	5	10	50%
4. Sales of product #1	10,000 units	11,000 units	110%
5. Sales of product #2	15,000 units	14,000 units	93%
6. Sales of product #3	25,000 units	30,000 units	120%

Under MBO, individual employees work with their supervisor to establish goals and objectives for which they will be responsible during the coming year. These goals are stated in clear language and relate to tasks that are within the domain of the employee. An example of these goals for a sales representative is shown in Exhibit 7.8. Following a specified period of time, the employee's performance is compared to the preset goals to determine the extent to which the goals have been met or exceeded.

Several advantages of MBO have been observed. These include the ability to do better planning; improved motivation, because of knowledge of results; fairer evaluations, done on the basis of results rather than personality; improved commitment through participation; and improved supervisory skills in such areas as listening, counseling, and evaluating. On the negative side, however, MBO has been criticized because it emphasizes quantitative goals at the expense of qualitative goals and often creates too much paperwork. It is difficult to compare performance levels among employees, because most are responsible for different goals. Sometimes the implementation of MBO goals are autocratic and therefore ineffective or even counterproductive. As discussed in Chapter 6, goals must be accepted to be effective. Finally, in order to succeed, MBO must have constant attention and support from top management; it does not run itself. In the absence of this support, the technique loses legitimacy and often falls into disrepair.

Assessment Centers

A relatively new method of evaluation is the *assessment center*. Assessment centers are unique among appraisal techniques in that they focus more on evaluating employee long-range potential to an organization than on performance over the past year. They are also unique in that they are used almost exclusively among managerial personnel.

An assessment center consists of a series of standardized evaluations of behavior based on multiple inputs. Over a two- or three-day period (away from the job) trained observers make judgments on managers' behavior in response to specially developed exercises. These exercises may consist of in-basket exercises, role playing, and case analyses, as well as personal interviews and psychological tests. An example of an assessment center program is shown in Exhibit 7.9.

On the basis of these exercises, the trained observers make judgments on employees' potential for future managerial assignments in the organization. More specifically, information is obtained concerning employees' interpersonal skills, communication ability, creativity, problem-solving skills, tolerance for stress and ambiguity, and planning ability. This technique has been used successfully by some of the largest corporations in the United States, including AT&T; Sears, Roebuck and Company; J. C. Penney; IBM; and General Electric.

Results from a series of assessment center programs appear promising, and the technique is growing in popularity as a means of identifying future managerial potential. For example, Coca-Cola USA experimented with using assessment centers to select its managerial personnel. After a detailed study, the company found that those selected in this way were only one-third as likely to leave the company or be fired than those selected in the traditional way. Although the assessment center approach added about 6 percent to the cost of hiring, the lower turnover rate led to an overall savings of over $700,000.[6]

Some problems with the technique have been noted. In particular, because of the highly stressful environment created in assessment centers, many otherwise good managers may simply not perform up to their potential. Moreover, the results of a poor evaluation in an assessment center may be far-reaching; individuals may receive a "loser" image that will follow them for a long time. And, finally, there is some question concerning exactly how valid and reliable assessment centers really are in predicting future managerial success.[7] Despite these problems, assessment centers remain a popular vehicle in some companies for developing and appraising managerial potential.

Exhibit 7.9
Example of Two-Day
Assessment Center Schedule

Day #1		Day #2	
8:00 – 9:00 A.M.	Orientation session	8:00 – 10:30 A.M.	In-basket exercise
9:00 – 10:30 A.M.	Psychological testing	10:30 – 10:45 A.M.	Coffee break
10:30 – 10:45 A.M.	Coffee break	10:45 – 12:30 P.M.	Role-playing exercise
10:45 – 12:30 P.M.	Management simulation game	12:30 – 1:30 P.M.	Lunch
12:30 – 1:30 P.M.	Lunch	1:30 – 3:15 P.M.	Group problem-solving exercise
1:30 – 3:15 P.M.	Individual decision-making exercise	3:15 – 3:30 P.M.	Coffee break
3:15 – 3:30 P.M.	Coffee break	3:30 – 4:30 P.M.	Debriefing by raters
3:30 – 4:30 P.M.	Interview with raters		

International Challenge

IN PRACTICE
Assessment Centers at British Telecom

British Telecom is roughly Great Britain's equivalent to America's AT&T before deregulation. For decades it basked in a completely regulated environment and saw no reason to become more efficient. In the mid-1980s, however, the conservative British government felt it was time for a change. Pressure was put on the company to improve both efficiency and effectiveness. As a result, British Telecom management embarked on a long-range program to assess managerial deficiencies and enhance managerial performance.

The overall objective of the program was to help future senior-level managers develop broad-based managerial skills for the telecommunications industry of the future. The company had outside consultants interview and survey managers to identify the nature and extent of the problem and to refine the company's operating definition of managerial effectiveness. Thirteen training priorities were identified. On the basis of this information, an assessment center program was established in which several job-relevant skills were simulated. Exercises included union negotiation, meeting with customers, handling service problems, and so forth.

The company emphasized that the aim of the program was to benefit the employees and that participation was voluntary. Managers had to nominate themselves for the program, and confidentiality of results was assured. The assessment center was carried out over a two-day period and included tests, exercises, and job simulations. Each manager's results were carefully analyzed, and a specific individual development plan was designed. As a result, British Telecom was able to develop a corps of executives capable of meeting the telecommunications challenges of the 1990s and beyond. Efficiency and effectiveness ratings improved significantly, and efforts were made to continue a version of the program for future managers.[8]

Comparison of Appraisal Techniques

It is important to consider which appraisal technique or set of techniques may be most appropriate for a given situation. Although there is no simple answer to this question, we can consider the various strengths and weaknesses of each technique. This is done in Exhibit 7.10. It is important to keep in mind that the appropriateness of a particular appraisal technique is in part of function of the purpose for the appraisal. For example, if the purpose of the appraisal is to identify high potential executives, then assessment centers are more appropriate than rating scales.

As would be expected, the easiest and least expensive techniques are also the least accurate. They are also the least useful for purposes of personnel decisions and employee development. Once again, it appears that managers and organizations get what they pay for. If performance appraisals represent an important aspect of organizational life, clearly the more sophisticated—and more time-consuming—techniques are preferable. If,

	Rating Scales	Critical Incidents	BARS	BOS	MBO	Assessment Centers
Meaningful dimensions	Sometimes	Sometimes	Usually	Usually	Usually	Usually
Amount of time required	Low	Medium	High	Medium	High	High
Development costs	Low	Low	High	Medium	Medium	High
Potential for rating errors	High	Medium	Low	Low	Low	Low
Acceptability to subordinates	Low	Medium	High	High	High	High
Acceptability to superiors	Low	Medium	High	High	High	High
Usefulness for allocating rewards	Poor	Fair	Good	Good	Good	Fair
Usefulness for employee counseling	Poor	Fair	Good	Good	Good	Good
Usefulness for identifying promotion potential	Poor	Fair	Fair	Fair	Fair	Good

Exhibit 7.10
Major Strengths
and Weaknesses of
Appraisal Techniques

on the other hand, it is necessary to evaluate employees quickly and with few resources, techniques such as the graphic rating scale may be more appropriate. Managers must make cost-benefit decisions about the price (in time and money) they are willing to pay for a quality performance appraisal system.

FEEDBACK

It was pointed out in the previous chapter that feedback represented a critical variable in determining the success or failure of the goal-setting process. The same applies to the performance appraisal process. Without effective knowledge of results, the motivational impact of the appraisal process is lost. To better understand how feedback in work settings affects employee behavior, consider the model shown in Exhibit 7.11.[9]

Feedback comes from many sources, including the task at hand, the supervisor, co-workers, and oneself. This input is then cognitively evaluated by the employee, who considers such factors as the perceived *accuracy* of the feedback (e.g., does the employee consider the information to be correct?); the *credibility of the source* of the feedback (e.g., does the employee trust the supervisor's opinion?); the employee's opinion concerning the *fairness* of the evaluation process; the extent to which the feedback met the employee's *expectations* (e.g., does the employee think he or she could have done better?); and the *reasonableness* of the performance standards.

If one or more of these evaluations prove negative (for example, the employee believes he or she is being unfairly evaluated), the credibility of the feedback is dismissed, and the employee may increase his or her resistance to task effort. On the other hand, where the feedback is accepted, it

Exhibit 7.11
Effects of Feedback on
Job Performance

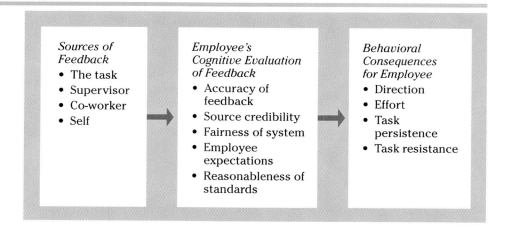

reinforces the employee's direction, effort on the task, and persistence on the task. Thus, although feedback is essential, it is the nature and quality of the feedback that determines ultimate employee response.

To see how this works, you may wish to complete Self-Assessment 7.2. Think of a current or previous job, and evaluate the source and quality of the feedback you received from your supervisor. When you are through, refer to Appendix B for scoring procedures.

International Challenge

IN PRACTICE
Providing Feedback in Different Countries

Americans often forget that cultural differences can have a profound effect on how performance evaluations, criticism, negotiations, and feedback are handled by managers.[10] To see how these differences work, consider the following two examples.

In most European countries, senior managers would not dare to propose that they evaluate their subordinates as frequently or rigorously as they do in the United States or Canada. European managers seldom look to their boss or their subordinates to find out how well they are doing on the job. It is simply inappropriate. This contrasts sharply with typical Americans, who expect considerable feedback concerning their performance. In fact, in the United States, it is difficult to demote or fire someone unless the company can prove clearly that it has provided substantial warnings concerning deteriorating performance.[11]

And in many Asian countries (e.g., Korea, Taiwan, and Japan), managers would not dream of telling subordinates they were doing a terrible job. Nor would they ever say "no" to a subordinate's request. Instead, they would simply avoid saying anything. They might ask a counter-question, evade the question, promise an answer in the future, or simply change the subject. To the attentive subordinate, however, the message would be clear. In

SELF-ASSESSMENT 7.2
How Much Feedback Are You Getting from Your Job?

Instructions: Think of a current or previous job. With this in mind, answer the following questions as accurately as possible.

Item	Strongly Disagree						Strongly Agree
1. My boss lets me know when I make a mistake.	1	2	3	4	5	6	7
2. My co-workers help me improve on the job.	1	2	3	4	5	6	7
3. I receive formal evaluations from the company on my job.	1	2	3	4	5	6	7
4. My boss always tells me when I do a good job.	1	2	3	4	5	6	7
5. This company really appreciates good performance.	1	2	3	4	5	6	7
6. When I do something especially well, I receive a "thanks" from my boss.	1	2	3	4	5	6	7
7. My co-workers are very appreciative when I do a good job.	1	2	3	4	5	6	7
8. My co-workers compliment me on the quality of my work.	1	2	3	4	5	6	7
9. My co-workers are very supportive of my efforts.	1	2	3	4	5	6	7
10. I know when I have done a good job.	1	2	3	4	5	6	7
11. My job provides me with solid feedback on my performance.	1	2	3	4	5	6	7
12. I can see the results when I learn to do something better.	1	2	3	4	5	6	7

fact, in Korea and Japan, the mark of a good manager—and subordinate—is to be able to "read someone's face, to look into their eyes and know what they are trying to tell you. Why do they do this? To some extent this evasive approach "saves face" (that is, avoids embarrassment) for both parties. It is important to preserve harmony at almost any cost in many Asian countries, and an evasive answer serves this purpose while at the same time allowing the manager to remain honest and get his message across to those capable of deciphering it.[12]

REWARD SYSTEMS IN ORGANIZATIONS

After a company has designed and implemented a systematic performance appraisal system and provided adequate feedback to employees, the next step is to consider how to tie available corporate rewards to the outcomes of the appraisal. Behavioral research consistently demonstrates that performance levels are highest when rewards are contingent upon performance. Thus, in this section, we will examine five aspects of reward systems in organizations: (1) functions served by reward systems, (2) bases for reward distribution, (3) intrinsic versus extrinsic rewards, (4) the relationship between money and motivation, and, finally, (5) pay secrecy.

Functions of Reward Systems

Reward systems in organizations are used for a variety of reasons. It is generally agreed that reward systems influence the following:

■ *Job effort and performance.* Following expectancy theory, employees' effort and performance would be expected to increase when they felt that rewards were contingent upon good performance. Hence, reward systems serve a very basic motivational function.

■ *Attendance and retention.* Reward systems have also been shown to influence an employee's decision to come to work or to remain with the organization. This was discussed in the previous chapter.

■ *Employee commitment to the organization.* It has been found that reward systems in no small way influence employee commitment to the organization, primarily through the exchange process.[13] That is, employees develop ties with organizations when they perceive that the organization is interested in their welfare and willing to protect their interests. This exchange process is shown in Exhibit 7.12. To the extent that employee needs and goals are met by the company, we would expect commitment to increase.

■ *Job satisfaction.* Job satisfaction has also been shown to be related to rewards, as discussed in the previous chapter. Edward E. Lawler, a well-known researcher on employee compensation, has identified four conclusions concerning the relationship between rewards and satisfaction: (1) satisfaction with a reward is a function of both how much is received and how much the individual feels should have been received; (2) satisfaction is influenced by comparisons with what happens to others, especially one's co-workers; (3) people differ with respect to the rewards they value; and (4) some rewards are satisfying because they lead to other rewards.[14]

■ *Occupational and organizational choice.* Finally, the selection of an occupation by an individual, as well as the decision to join a particular organization within that occupation, are influenced by the rewards that are thought to be available in the occupation or organization. To prove this, simply look at the classified section of your local newspaper and notice how many jobs highlight beginning salaries.

Exhibit 7.12
The Exchange Process
Between Employee
and Organization

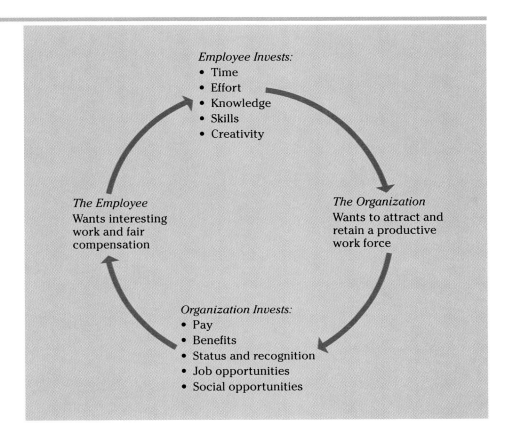

Reward systems in organizations have far-reaching consequences for both individual satisfaction and organizational effectiveness. Unfortunately, cases can easily be cited where reward systems have been distorted to punish good performance or inhibit creativity. Consider, for example, the Greyhound Bus Company driver who was suspended for 10 days without pay for breaking a company rule against using a CB radio on his bus. The bus driver had used the radio to alert police that his bus, with 32 passengers on board, was being hijacked by an armed man. The police arrested the hijacker, and the bus driver was suspended for breaking company rules.[15] Such incidents hardly encourage employees to focus their efforts on responsible performance.

Bases for Reward Distribution

A common reality in many contemporary work organizations is the inequity that exists in the distribution of available rewards. One often sees little correlation between those who perform well and those who receive the greatest rewards. At the extreme, it is hard to understand how a company could pay its president $10 to $20 million per year (as many large corporations do) while it pays its secretaries and clerks less than $15,000. Each works approximately 40 hours per week, and both are important for organizational performance. Is it really possible that the president is 1000 times more important than the secretary, as the salary differential suggests?

How do organizations decide on the distribution of available rewards? At least four mechanisms can be identified. In more cases than we choose to admit, rewards go to those with the greatest *power* (either market power or personal power). In many of the corporations whose presidents earn eight-figure incomes, we find that these same people are either major shareholders in the company or have certain abilities, connections, or status that the company wants. Indeed, a threat of resignation from an important or high-performing executive often leads to increased rewards.

A second possible basis for reward distribution is *equality*. Here, all individuals within one job classification would receive the same, or at least similar, rewards. The most common example here can be found among unionized workers, where pay rates are established and standardized with little or no reference to actual performance level. Instead of ability or performance, these systems usually recognize seniority as the key factor in pay raises or promotions.

The basis for the social welfare reward system in this country is need. In large part, the greater the need, the greater the level of support. It is not uncommon to see situations in business firms where need is taken into account in layoff situations—where an employee is not laid off because he or she is the sole support of a family.

A fourth mechanism used by organizations in allocating rewards is *distributive justice*. Under this approach, employees receive (at least a portion of) their rewards as a function of their level of contribution to the organization. The greater the contribution (such as performance), the greater the reward. This mechanism is most prominent in merit-based incentive programs, where pay and bonuses are determined by performance levels.

Extrinsic and Intrinsic Rewards

The variety of rewards that employees can receive in exchange for their contributions of time and effort can be classified as either *extrinsic* or *intrinsic* rewards. *Extrinsic rewards* are external to the work itself. They are administered externally—that is, by someone else (usually management). Examples of extrinsic rewards include wages and salary, fringe benefits, promotions, and recognition and praise from others.

On the other hand, *intrinsic rewards* represent those rewards that are related directly to performing the job. In this sense, they are often described as "self-administered" rewards, because engaging in the task itself leads to their receipt. Examples of intrinsic rewards include feelings of task accomplishment, autonomy, and personal growth and development that come from the job.

In the literature on employee motivation, there is considerable controversy concerning the possible interrelationship of these two kinds of reward. It has been argued (with some research support) that extrinsic rewards tend to drive out the positive effects of some intrinsic rewards.[16] Consider, for example, the child next door who begs you to let her help you wash your car. For a young child, this task can carry considerable excitement (and intrinsic motivation). Now, consider what happens on a Saturday afternoon when you need your car washed but the child has other options. What do you do? You offer to pay her this time to help wash your car. What do you think will happen the next time you ask the neighbor to help you wash the car for free? In other words, when extrinsic rewards such as pay are tied closely to performance (called performance-reward contingency), *intrinsic motivation*—the desire to do a task because you enjoy it—can decrease.

Also, it is important to keep in mind that because extrinsic rewards are administered by sources external to the individual, their effectiveness rests on accurate and fair monitoring, evaluating, and administration. Implementation can be expensive, and the timing of performance and rewards may not always be close. For example, you may perform well on a task, but unless there is a way for that to be noticed, evaluated, recorded, and rewarded within a reasonable time frame, an extrinsic reward may not have a significant impact. Intrinsic rewards are a function of self-monitoring, evaluation, and administration; consequently, these rewards often are less costly and more effectively administered. For example, even if no one else notices or rewards you for superior performance on a task, you can still reward yourself with a mental pat on the back for a job well done or a sense of satisfaction for overcoming a challenge. The implications of this finding will become apparent when we discuss efforts to enrich employees' jobs (see Chapter 9).

IN PRACTICE
Racing Ahead with Motivation

Three days a week, Joe Amato, 47, races dragsters. He was the National Hot Rod Association's 1990 Top Fuel Champion, the heavyweight champ of professional drag racing. The other four days, he runs the company he built from a scratch: Keystone Automotive Warehouse, a $125 million (1990 sales) distributor of automotive parts.

Joe is just as successful at motivating his employees by using a variety of rewards as he is at accelerating from 0 to 300 miles per hour in about 4 seconds. "Joe has developed a very loyal core of people who will do just about anything for him," says Amato's longtime friend, Eugene Mariotti. "He pays them well, but mostly he does it by earning their respect." One way is by not being afraid to roll up his sleeves. For example, Raymond Labosky, who supervises construction and maintenance at Keystone's facilities, can remember Amato mixing concrete with him.

Amato is also quick to reward key people with perks like cruises and flexible work schedules. Keystone paid for Leonard Ross, the company's computer expert, to spend a month at Pritikin, a medically supervised health spa. And James Chebala, the Chief Financial Officer, doesn't like to get up in the morning, so he works from 11 to 7.

Perhaps most the important reward Amato uses to motivate his employees is sharing credit with them. The walls of Keystone's offices are covered with sales awards and pictures of employees. In post-race press conferences, says Amato, "I always mention the players behind the man. You've got to share the glory."[17]

Money and Motivation: A Closer Look

A recurring debate among managers focuses on the issue of whether money is a primary motivator. Some argue that most behavior in organizational settings is motivated by money (or at least monetary factors), whereas others argue that money is only one of many factors that motivate performance. Whichever group is correct, we must recognize that money can have important motivational consequences for many people in many situations. In fact, money serves several important functions in work settings.[18] These include serving as (1) a goal or incentive, (2) a source of satisfaction, (3) an instrument for gaining other desired outcomes, (4) a standard of comparison for determining relative standing or worth, and (5) a conditional reinforcer where its receipt is contingent upon a certain level of performance. Even so, experience tells us that the effectiveness of pay as a motivator varies considerably. Sometimes there seems to be an almost direct relationship between pay and effort, whereas at other times no such relationship is found. Why? Lawler suggests that certain conditions must be present in order for pay to act as a strong motivator:[19]

■ Trust levels between managers and subordinates must be high.

■ Individual performance must be able to be accurately measured.

■ Pay rewards to high performers must be substantially higher than those to poor performers.

■ Few, if any, negative consequences for good performance must be perceived.

Under these conditions, a climate or culture is created where employees have reason to believe that significant performance-reward contingencies truly exist. Given this perception (and assuming the reward is valued), we would expect performance to be increased.[20]

Pay Secrecy

Secrecy about pay rates seems to be a widely accepted practice in work organizations, particularly among managerial personnel. It is argued that salary is a personal matter and we should not invade another's privacy. Available evidence, however, suggests that pay secrecy may have several negative side effects. To begin, it has been consistently found that in the absence of actual knowledge, people have a tendency to *over*estimate the pay of co-workers and those above them in the hierarchy. As a result, much of the motivational potential of a differential reward system is lost.[21] Even if an employee receives a relatively sizable salary increase, he or she may still perceive an inequity compared to what others are receiving. This problem is highlighted in the results of a study by Lawler. In considering the effects of pay secrecy on motivation, Lawler noted:

> Almost regardless of how well the individual manager was performing, he felt he was getting less than the average raise. This problem was particularly severe among high performers, since they believed that they were doing well yet received minimal reward. They did not believe that pay was

in fact based upon merit. This was ironic, since their pay did reflect performance. . . . Thus, even though pay was tied to performance, these managers were not motivated because they could not see the connection.[22]

Pay secrecy also affects motivation via feedback. Several studies have shown the value of feedback in motivating performance (see previous discussion). The problem is that for managers, money represents one of the most meaningful forms of feedback. Pay secrecy eliminates the feedback.

When salary information is open (or at least when the range of percentage increases within a job classification are made known to the people in that group), employees are generally provided with more recognition for satisfactory performance and are often more motivated to perform on subsequent tasks. It is easier to establish feelings of pay equity and trust in the salary administration system. On the other hand, publicizing pay rates and pay raises can cause jealousy among employees and create pressures on managers to reduce perceived inequities in the system. There is no correct position concerning whether pay rates should be secret or open. The point is that managers should not assume a priori that pay secrecy—or pay openness—is a good thing. Instead, careful consideration should be given to the possible consequences of either approach in view of the particular situation in the organization at the time.

INDIVIDUAL AND GROUP INCENTIVE PLANS

We now turn to an examination of various employee incentive programs used by organizations. First, we consider the relative merits of individual versus group incentive programs. Next, we focus on several relatively new approaches to motivation and compensation. Finally, we suggest several guidelines for effective incentive systems.

Individual Versus Group Incentives

Companies usually have choices among various compensation plans and must make decisions about which is most effective for its situation. Incentive systems in organizations are usually divided into two categories on the basis of whether the unit of analysis—and the recipient of the reward—is the individual or a group. Among individual incentive plans, several approaches can be identified, including merit-based compensation (commonly known as merit compensation), piece-rate incentive programs (where people are paid according to the quantity of output), bonus systems of various sorts, and commissions. In each case, rewards are tied fairly directly to the performance level of the individual.

Although individual incentive systems often lead to improved performance, some reservations have been noted. In particular, these programs may at times lead to employees competing with one another, with undesirable results. For instance, department store salespeople on commission may fight over customers, thereby chasing the customers away. After all, customers don't care who they deal with, only that the service is good. Second, these plans typically are resisted by unions, which prefer compensation to be based on seniority or job classification. Third, where quality control systems are lax, individual incentives such as piece rates may lead employees to maximize units of output while sacrificing quality. And, finally, in order for these programs to be successful, an atmosphere of trust and cooperation is necessary.

In order to overcome some of these shortcomings, many companies have turned to group or organizational incentive plans. Group incentive programs base at least some of an employee's rewards on group or organization performance. Hence, employees are encouraged to cooperate with each other and with the corporation so that all employees can benefit. Programs such as profit-sharing or gain-sharing plans (discussed below) are designed to tie the employees' future rewards and prosperity to that of the company and reduce the age-old antagonism between the two. The results are often dramatic.

Creative Pay Practices

Recently, we have seen several innovations in the way corporations approach reward systems. These efforts are designed to facilitate the integration of employee and company interests in a way that maximizes both productivity and quality of working life. Five such creative pay practices should be noted: (1) gain-sharing plans, (2) skills-based incentives, (3) lump-sum pay increases, (4) participative pay decisions, and (5) flexible benefits programs. These approaches, along with their major advantages and drawbacks, are summarized in Exhibit 7.13.

Gain-Sharing Plans. Giving executives and senior managers bonuses to reflect their contributions to organizational effectiveness is commonplace. In fact, in some companies executive bonuses are often larger than salaries. Recently, companies have increasingly applied this same principle to all employees in the form of *gain-sharing* (profit-sharing) plans. Here, employees

Exhibit 7.13
Advantages and
Disadvantages of
New Pay Practices

Pay Practice	Advantages	Disadvantages
Gain sharing	Ties pay to performance; encourages group cooperation	Plans that focus exclusively on productivity may lead employees to ignore other important objectives, such as quality.
Skills-based incentives	More flexible and skilled work force; increased satisfaction	Higher training and salary costs
Lump-sum increase	Greater visibility of pay increases; increased pay satisfaction	Cost of administration
Participative pay decisions	Increased trust in a satisfaction with pay decisions; better pay decisions	Time-consuming
Flexible benefits	Increased satisfaction with pay and benefits	Cost of administration

are given a chance to share in corporate productivity gains through increased earnings. The greater the productivity gains, the greater the earnings. Several variations on this theme can be found, including the Scanlon Plan, IMPROSHARE, the Ruker Plan, and the Lincoln Electric Plan (see below). Regardless of the title, the basic plan is similar.

For example, under the Scanlon Plan (probably the oldest such program), three operating guidelines are used: (1) each department or division is treated as a business unit for purposes of performance measurement; (2) specific cost measures associated with the production process are identified and agreed to by all parties; and (3) bonuses are paid to all employees according to a predetermined formula tying the amount of the bonus to the actual cost savings realized during the time period. Under such a plan, it is clearly in the employees' best interest to contribute to cost savings, thereby increasing their own incomes.

IN PRACTICE
Gain Sharing at Lincoln Electric

While many U.S. companies are currently in search of new and effective ways to motivate their employees, the Lincoln Electric Company of Cleveland is still successfully running a motivation program that was put into effect when the United States was just seven years into the twentieth century.[23]

The basis of Lincoln's effective program is pay incentives. Most of its 2,500 employees are paid on a piecework system, with an annual bonus tacked on. The bonus is a result of the employees' performance, and it can exceed their regular pay. However, an employee's mistake can lead to a deduction in his or her bonus. Because this method seems pressure-packed, one might find it hard to believe that Lincoln's turnover rate is a mere 0.3 percent a month, which indicates its employees' satisfaction with this system.

The company was founded by John C. Lincoln in 1895 to produce electric motors. (Along with the three-phase industrial motor they now produce, Lincoln has become the world's leading manufacturer of arc-welding equipment.) By 1907 his brother James joined on and began employing worker motivation programs reinforced with the idea that workers benefit when the company prospers. They made stock available for purchase at book price to employees, encouraging worker pride and participation.

Employees are solely responsible for the quality of their work. They inspect their own parts and, if a flaw exists, they remain to fix it on their own time. The company keeps track of workers by recording the names of the persons working on each piece of equipment. If a defect slips by an employee, but is spotted by one of Lincoln's quality-control people (Lincoln was recognized by *Quality Magazine,* August 1983, for outstanding product quality), or complained about by a customer, the employee involved has his bonus, pay, or merit rating reduced. Merit ratings are based on points accumulated throughout the year. Acquiring points can create tension within groups since only a specific amount of points is allocated to each department. But not all merit points come from within the group. In fact, a company spokesman says that only the first 10 points above 100 come from the group. Everything beyond that is from a pool of points set aside especially for rewarding outstanding achievements in the company.

Because of the poor industrial market [in the early 1980s], most employees average a 30-hour work week. However, due to the incentive program, the average pay in 1982 was still above $30,000. According to the spokesman, there are instances where an employee will work up to or beyond 50 hours a week, but he attributes this to Lincoln's cautious hiring plan—instead of hiring new employees in a boom economy, the company asks existing workers to take on additional hours, thus enabling Lincoln to guarantee 30-hour work weeks for employees with the company for two or more years. And Lincoln has not laid anyone off in over 30 years. The rigorous demands on the employees can be bothersome. Besides the unfriendly competition sometimes generated from merit points, workers also face a fast-paced environment that can be both mentally and physically draining. Lincoln has no unions, no seniority system, and all promotions are done from within. If an employee desires a position outside the piecework factory environment, he must apply for a job posted on bulletin boards throughout the company and compete for that position with other employees, both old and new. And while some employees have gripes about the program, Lincoln's overall results speak for themselves. Last year's [1983] recession cut earnings by 42 percent and sales by 28 percent as compared with 1981 figures. However, volume and profit have increased. Over a seven-year period ending in 1981, sales escalated to a record $526.9 million, up from $232.8 million, and earnings during that period advanced to $39.7 million, also a record.

Skills-Based Incentives.   Typical compensation programs are tied to job evaluations. In these, jobs are analyzed to assess their characteristics, and then salary levels are assigned to each job on the basis of such factors as job difficulty and labor market scarcity. In other words, pay levels are set on the basis of the job, not the individual. This approach fails to encourage employees to improve their skills on the job, because there is no reward for the improvement. This thinking also keeps all employees in their places and minimizes the possibility of inter-job transfers.

Under the *skills-based incentive program,* employees are paid according to their skills level (that is, the *number* of jobs they can perform), regardless of the actual tasks they are allowed to perform. This approach has proved successful in organizations such as Procter & Gamble and General Foods. Employees are encouraged to learn additional skills and are appropriately rewarded. The organization is provided with a more highly trained and more flexible work force. However, training and compensation costs are necessarily increased, so the program is appropriate only in some situations. The technique is most often seen as part of a larger quality-of-working-life program, where it is associated with job redesign efforts.

Lump-Sum Pay Increases.   Another technique that has received some attention is to allow employees to decide how (that is, in what amounts) they wish to receive their pay raises for the coming year. Under the traditional program, pay raises are paid in equal amounts in each paycheck over the year. Under the alternate plan, employees can elect to receive equal amounts during the year, or they can choose to take the entire raise in one *lump sum.* This plan allows employees greater discretion over their own financial matters. If an employee wants to use the entire pay raise for a vacation, it can be paid in a lump sum in June. Then, if the employee quits before the end of the year, the unearned part of the pay raise is subtracted from the final paycheck. This plan increases the visibility of the reward to the employee. That is, the employee receives, for example, a $600 pay raise (a rather sizable amount) instead of twelve $50 monthly pay raises. As with the flexible rewards system discussed below, however, the administration costs of the lump-sum plan are greater than those of the traditional method.

Participative Pay Decisions.   In addition, a concern to many managers is the extent to which employees should be involved in decisions over pay raises. This is the issue of *participative pay decisions.* Recently, several organizations have been experimenting with involving employees in pay raise decisions, and the results seem to be quite positive. By allowing employees to participate either in the design of the reward system or in actual pay raise decisions (perhaps through a committee), it is argued that decisions of higher quality are made on the basis of greater information. Also, employees then have greater reason to place confidence in the fairness of the decisions. On the negative side, this approach requires considerably more time for both the manager and the participating subordinates. Costs must be weighed against benefits to determine which approach is most suitable for the particular organization and its goals.

Flexible Benefits Systems.   A typical fringe benefit package provides the same benefits—and the same number of benefits—to all employees. As a result, individual differences or preferences are largely ignored. Studies by Lawler indicate variations in benefit preferences.[24] For instance, young unmarried men prefer more vacation time, whereas young married men prefer to give up vacation time for higher pay. Older employees want more retirement benefits, whereas younger employees prefer greater income. Through a *flexible benefits program* (also called a "cafeteria benefits program"), employees are allowed some discretion in the determination of their own packages and can make trade-offs, within certain limits. Organizations such as Pepsico, TRW, and the Educational Testing Service already use such programs. Although certain problems of administration exist with the programs, efforts in this direction can lead to increased need satisfaction among employees.

IN PRACTICE
Flexible Benefits for Oregon State Employees

Flexible reward systems come in a variety of forms. Some of the more adventuresome plans allow employees to choose, for example, between more money or more time off. More conservative efforts focus specifically on fringe benefits. One such example can be seen among state employees in Oregon. In 1989, Oregon changed its approach to health care benefits and began offering employees a choice of how their health care dollars were spent. The goal of the plan was to contain rising health care costs while at the same time providing employees with the individual coverage they desired.

To start, all employees were given a certain number of health care "dollars" (really credit in their health care accounts), which they could allocate among the different medical, dental, vision care, disability, and life insurance plans. Thus, one family might choose a bare-bones health plan with a low co-payment or deductible, and another family might choose a more comprehensive plan at greater cost. Some might choose to carry maternity benefits, and others might not. Some might want a large life insurance policy, and others might not. All policies are costed out for the employees. Plan A costs this, and plan B costs that. Once employees have selected their desired level of coverage, they use their "dollars" to pay the premiums. If the premiums for the various policies exceed their allotted budgets, the employees pay the difference from payroll deductions. In this way, employees are given a major voice in how their health care dollars are spent.

We have seen a number of different creative solutions to the compensation dilemma. Which approaches are most effective in motivating employees? This is obviously a difficult question to answer. However, one way to get relevant information on this question is to see what corporations actually use. One such study asked major employers which of a variety of approaches had been used with a high success level. The results are shown in Exhibit 7.14. As can be seen, skills-based compensation, earned time off, and gain sharing all received high marks from personnel executives, although other programs are also widely supported. It would appear from these results that many approaches can be useful; the choice of which one to use would depend upon the circumstances and goals of a particular organization.

Guidelines for Effective Incentive Programs

Whatever incentive plan is selected, care must be taken to ensure that the plan is appropriate for the particular organization and work force. In fact, a simple test of the effectiveness of an incentive plan would be as follows:[25]

▨ *Does the plan capture attention?* Do employees discuss the plan and take pride in their early successes?

▨ *Do employees understand the plan?* Can employees explain how the plan works, and do they understand what they must do to earn the incentive?

▨ *Does the plan improve communication?* As a result of the plan, do employees understand more about corporate mission, goals, and objectives?

▨ *Does the plan pay out when it should?* Are incentives being paid for desired results, and are they withheld for undesirable results?

▨ *Is the company performing better as a result of the plan?* Are profits or market share up or down? Have any gains resulted in part from the incentive plan?

If a new (or existing) pay plan can meet these tests, it is probably fairly effective in motivating employee performance and should be retained by the

Exhibit 7.14
Companies Successfully Using
Creative Incentive Plans

Type of Incentive	Percent of Companies Reporting Success
Skills-based compensation	89%
Earned time off	85
Gain-sharing plans	81
Small-group incentives	75
Individual incentives	73
All-salaried work force	67
Lump-sum bonus	66

Source: Data from J. Horn, *Psychology Today,* July 1987, pp. 54–57.

organization. If not, perhaps some other approach should be tried. On the basis of such a test, several specific guidelines can be identified to increase the effectiveness of the programs. These include the following:[26]

■ Any reward system or incentive plan should be as *closely tied to actual job performance* as possible. This point was discussed earlier in this chapter.

■ If possible, incentive programs should *allow for individual differences.* They should recognize that different people want different outcomes from a job. Flexible benefits programs such as the ones discussed here make an effort to accomplish this.

■ Incentive programs should *reflect the type of work that is done* and the structure of the organization. This simply means that the program should be tailored to the particular needs, goals, and structures of a given organization. Individual incentive programs, for example, would probably be less successful among unionized personnel than would group programs such as the Scanlon plan. This point has been clearly demonstrated in research by Lawler, who points out that organizations with traditional management and those with more participative management might approach reward systems quite differently in order to be effective.[27] As shown in Exhibit 7.15, both types of company can be effective as long as their reward systems are congruent with their overall approach to management.

■ The incentive program should *be consistent with the culture* and constraints of the organization. Where trust levels are low, for example, it may take considerable effort to get any program to work. In an industry already characterized by high levels of efficiency, basing an incentive system on increasing efficiency even further may have little effect, because employees may see the task as nearly impossible.

■ Finally, incentive programs should *be carefully monitored over time* to ensure that they are being fairly administered and that they accurately reflect current technological and organizational conditions. For instance, it may be appropriate to offer sales clerks in a department store an incentive to sell outdated merchandise, because current fashion items sell themselves. Responsibility falls on managers not to select the incentive

Reward System	Traditional	Participative
Fringe benefits	Vary according to organizational level	Cafeteria—same for all levels
Promotion	All decisions made by top management	Open posting for all jobs; peer group involvement in decision process
Status symbols	A great many, carefully allocated on the basis of job position	Few present, low emphasis on organization level
Pay type	Hourly and salary	All salary
Base rate	Based on job performed; high enough to attract job applicants	Based on skills; high enough to provide security and attract applicants
Incentive plan	Piece-rate	Group and organization-wide bonus, lump-sum increase
Communication policy	Very restricted distribution of information	Individual rates, salary survey data, all other information made public
Decision-making locus	Top management	Close to location of person whose pay is being set

Exhibit 7.15
Matching Reward Systems
to Management Style

Source: E. E. Lawler, *The Design of Effective Reward Systems,* Technical Report (Los Angeles: University of Southern California, 1983), p. 52.

program that is in vogue or used "next door," but rather to consider the unique situations and needs of their own organizations. Then, with this understanding, a program can be developed and implemented that will facilitate goal-oriented performance.

PULLING IT ALL TOGETHER

If performance is to be changed or improved, it must be rewarded. To be rewarded, it must be measured. However, great care must be taken (1) to measure important behaviors and outcomes (individual, group, or organizational) and not just those that are easy to measure; (2) to measure them with the appropriate technique(s); and (3) to tie appropriate rewards to the desired behaviors and outcomes.

SUMMARY OF KEY POINTS

■ Organizations use performance appraisals for several reasons: (1) to provide feedback to employees, (2) to allow for employee self-development, (3) to allocate rewards, (4) to gather information for personnel decisions, and (5) to guide them in developing training and development efforts.

■ Performance appraisals are subject to several problems, including central tendency error, strictness or leniency error, halo effect, recency error, and personal biases.

■ Among the most common appraisal systems are graphic rating scales, critical incident technique, behaviorally anchored rating scales, behavioral observation scales, management by objectives, and assessment centers. Assessment centers represent a special case of evaluations in that they focus on assessing an employee's long-term potential to an organization.

■ Rewards serve several functions, including (1) stimulating job effort and performance, (2) reducing absenteeism and turnover, (3) enhancing employee commitment, (4) facilitating job satisfaction, and (5) facilitating occupational and organizational choice.

■ Rewards may be distributed on the basis of power, equality, need, or distributive justice. Distributive justice rests on the principle of allocating rewards in proportion to employee contribution.

■ Intrinsic rewards represent those outcomes that are administered by the employee (e.g., a sense of task accomplishment), whereas extrinsic rewards are administered by others (e.g., wages).

■ Gain-sharing incentive plans base some of the employees' pay on corporate profits or productivity. As a result, employees are generally more interested in facilitating corporate performance.

■ Skills-based incentives reward employees on the basis of the skills they possess, not the skills they are allowed to use at work. As a result, employees are encouraged to continually upgrade their skill levels.

■ A lump-sum salary increase simply provides employees with their pay raises at one time (possibly shortly before summer vacation or a major holiday).

■ Participative pay decisions allow employees some input in determining their pay raises.

■ Flexible benefits allow employees to choose the fringe benefits that best suit their needs.

■ A good reward system (1) is closely tied to performance, (2) allows for individual differences, (3) reflects the type of work that is being done, (4) is consistent with the corporate culture, and (5) is carefully monitored over time.

KEY WORDS

assessment center
behaviorally anchored rating scale
behavioral observation scale
central tendency error
critical incident technique
distributive justice
extrinsic rewards
feedback
flexible benefits system
gain sharing
graphic rating scale
halo effect

intrinsic motivation
intrinsic rewards
leniency error
lump-sum pay increase
management by objectives
participative pay decisions
performance appraisal
recency error
reliability
skills-based incentives
strictness error
validity

QUESTIONS FOR DISCUSSION

1. Identify the various functions of performance appraisals. How are appraisals used in most work organizations?
2. What are some problems associated with performance appraisals?
3. Define *validity* and *reliability*. Why are these two concepts important from a managerial standpoint?
4. How can errors in appraisals be reduced?
5. Critically evaluate the advantages and disadvantages of the various techniques of performance appraisal.
6. Discuss the role of feedback in employee performance.
7. What is the difference between intrinsic and extrinsic rewards?
8. Identify the major bases of reward distribution.
9. How does money influence employee motivation?
10. Discuss the relative merits of individual and group incentive programs.
11. Describe the benefits and drawbacks of several of the new approaches to reward systems. Which ones do you feel would be most effective in work organizations?

NOTES

1. W. Kiechel, "When Subordinates Evaluate the Boss," *Fortune,* June 19, 1989, pp. 201–202.
2. C. J. Fombrum and R. L. Laud, "Strategic Issues in Performance Appraisal Theory and Practice." *Personnel,* 601(6), pp. 23–31.
3. P. Wright, *On a Clear Day You Can See General Motors* (New York: Avon Books, 1979).
4. W. Cascio, *Managing Human Resources* (New York: McGraw-Hill, 1989).
5. A. H. Locher and K. S. Teel, "Performance Appraisal: Current Practices and Techniques," *Personnel,* May-June 1984, pp. 57–59.
6. L. Slavenski, "Matching People to Jobs," *Training and Development Journal,* August 1986, pp. 54–57.
7. F. D. Frank, D. W. Bracken, and M. R. Smith, "Beyond Assessment Centers," *Training and Development Journal,* March 1988, pp. 65–67.
8. D. Rogers and C. Mabey, "BT's Leap Forward from Assessment Centers," *Personnel Management,* July 1987, pp. 32–35.
9. M. S. Taylor, C. D. Fisher, and D. R. Ilgen, "Individuals' Reactions to Performance Feedback in Organizations: A Control Theory Perspective," in K. M. Rowland and G. R. Ferris, eds., *Research in Personnel and Human Resources Management,* vol. 2 (Greenwich, Conn.: JAI Press, 1984), pp. 81–124.
10. P. Thorne and B. Meyer, "The Care and Feeding of Your American Management," *International Management,* October 1987, p. 114.
11. Ibid.
12. R. M. Steers, Y. K. Shin, and G. R. Ungson, *The Chaebol: Korea's New Industrial Might* (New York: Harper & Row, 1989).
13. R. T. Mowday, L. W. Porter, and R. M. Steers, *Employee-Organization Linkages: The Psychology of Employee Commitment, Absenteeism, and Turnover* (New York: Academic Press, 1982).
14. E. E. Lawler, "New Approaches to Pay Administration," *Personnel,* 1976, *5,* pp. 11–23.
15. Cited in *Eugene Register-Guard,* July 15, 1980, p. B1.
16. A. Kohn, "Incentives Can Be Bad for Business," *Inc.,* January 1988, pp. 93–94.
17. C. Palmeri. "Motorhead." *Forbes, 148*(4) August 19, 1991, p. 128.
18. R. L. Opsahl and M. D. Dunnette, "The Role of Financial Compensation in Industrial Motivation," *Psychological Bulletin,* 1966, 66, pp. 94–96.

19. E. E. Lawler, *Pay and Organizational Effectiveness* (New York: McGraw-Hill, 1971).
20. R. M. Steers and L. W. Porter, *Motivation and Work Behavior* (New York: McGraw-Hill, 1991).
21. Lawler, *Pay and Organizational Effectiveness,* op. cit.
22. Ibid., p. 174.
23. "Lincoln Electric's Past Enhances Its Future," *Management Review,* January 1984, pp. 40–41.
24. Lawler, "New Approaches to Pay Administration," op. cit.
25. M. Wallace, cited in N. Perry, "Here Come Richer, Riskier Pay Plans," *Fortune,* December 19, 1988, pp. 50–58.
26. Perry, op. cit.; Cascio, op. cit.
27. E. E. Lawler, "The Design of Effective Reward Systems," Technical Report, University of Southern California, April 1983.

EXPERIENTIAL EXERCISE 7

Granville Manufacturing Company: Allocating Pay Raises

The Granville Manufacturing Company is a small manufacturing company located in San Antonio, Texas. The company is not unionized and manufactures clinical analyzers and other health care products for sale to hospitals, clinical laboratories, and physicians. A little over a year ago, Granville instituted a pay-for-performance merit compensation system. Each division was asked to establish specific performance objectives and reward employees on the basis of their performance against these goals.

You are the division manager for the assembly division for the clinical analyzers. You have six supervisors reporting to you, each of whom is responsible for one work team. As part of the new system, you have established three performance goals for the supervisors in your division: (1) reduce raw material waste rates by 12 percent; (2) increase overall production by 10 percent; and (3) decrease the number of quality rejects by 15 percent. You have made it clear to your supervisors that the degree to which each one met or exceeded these goals would be one of the major determinants of his or her merit pay increase for the year.

The six team supervisors worked on similar production lines. Each team was about the same size, and the skill levels of the average worker in each group were similar. In fact, the groups often saw themselves in friendly competition with each other to achieve their production goals. A profile of each supervisor is as follows:

Terry O'Leary: age 25, white, male, married with no children. Has been with Granville for a little over a year since graduating from University of Texas, San Antonio. First full-time job since graduation. O'Leary is well liked by all employees and has exhibited a high level of enthusiasm for his work.

Wendy Mitchell: age 28, white, single. Mitchell has been with the company for three years since receiving her degree from Arizona State University. She recently received a job offer from another company for a similar position that would provide her with a 15-percent raise over her current salary. Granville does not want to lose Wendy because her overall performance has been excellent. The job offer would require her to move to another state, which she views unfavorably. Thus, Granville could probably retain her if it could come close to matching her salary offer.

Jesse Smith: age 32, black, married with three children. Smith has been with Granville for over four years since his graduation from high school. He started community college but dropped out after a year and a half to support his family. He is one of the most stable and steady supervisors. However, his subordinates are known to be unfriendly and uncooperative with him and other employees.

Alexander Wilenski: age 33, white, married with four children. Wilenski has a high school equivalent education and one year with the company. He immigrated to this country seven years ago from Poland and has recently become a U.S. citizen. He is a steady worker and is well liked by his co-workers but has had difficulty learning English. As a result, certain problems of communication within his group and with other groups have developed.

Inge Swensen: age 27, white, divorced with two children. Swensen has been with the company for two years and received a technical associate arts degree (a two-year college degree) in her native Sweden before coming to the United States. Since her divorce two years ago, her performance has begun to improve. Prior to that, her performance has very erratic, with frequent absences. She is the sole support of her two children.

Angelo Scarpelli: age 29, white, single. He has been with Granville for over two years and graduated from the University of Alabama. Scarpelli is one of the best-liked employees at the company. However, he has shown a lack of initiative and ambition on the job. He often appears to be preoccupied with his social life. However, no one at the company has ever complained to him about this preoccupation on the job.

Either individually or in small groups, your assignment is to assume you are the division manager responsible for allocation of the six pay raises. Exhibit 7A summarizes the performance data for each of the six supervisors' groups for the past year. This table also shows their current salaries and your own recent performance evaluation for each. The budget for the upcoming year provides a total of $12,000 for pay raises for the six supervisors in your division. Top management has indicated that at least some of the salary increase money should be given across the board as a cost-of-living raise and that part should be given on the basis of performance. The actual percentage raises given is completely up to you. However, in making the merit pay increase decisions, you should keep the following points in mind:

■ Your salary decisions will likely set a precedent for future salary and merit increase considerations.

■ No salary increase should be excessive but should be representative of the supervisor's performance during the past year. It is hoped that the supervisors develop a clear perception that performance will lead to monetary rewards and that this will serve to motivate them to even better performance.

		Annual Performance Review				Goal Performance*		
Name	Current Salary	Job Effort	Knowledge of Job	Attitude and Cooperativeness	Human Relations Skills	Waste Rates	Quality Rejects	Overall Production
Terry O'Leary	$28K	Outstanding	Good	Outstanding	Good	10%	16%	12%
Wendy Mitchell	$29K	Outstanding	Outstanding	Outstanding	Outstanding	12%	12%	14%
Jesse Smith	$29K	Good	Good	Outstanding	Good	6%	4%	3%
Alexander Wilenski	$28K	Outstanding	Average	Good	Average	4%	12%	5%
Inge Swensen	$27K	Average	Good	Average	Average	12%	8%	10%
Angelo Scarpelli	$27K	Average	Average	Average	Average	7%	4%	10%

*Goal performance was calculated as the percent *reduction* in waste rate and quality rejects and the percent *increase* in overall productivity.

Exhibit 7A
Salaries, Annual Reviews, and Goal Performance for Supervisors

■ Your decisions should be concerned with equity; that is, they ought to be consistent with one another.

■ Granville does not want to lose any of these experienced supervisors to other firms. The top management of this company not only wants the supervisors to be satisfied with their salary increases but also wants to further develop the feeling that Granville is a good company for advancement, growth, and career development.

With these constraints in mind, you (or your group) should do the following:

1. Calculate (in dollars and percentages) the pay raises to be given to each of the six supervisors.
2. Provide a rationale to the class, outlining the reasons behind your allocation decision.
3. Identify any negative consequences associated with your allocation decisions. What might you do to soften these negative repercussions?

MANAGEMENT DILEMMA 7

Performance Appraisal Problems at Central Catholic Hospital

Jayne Burroughs and John Watson are both employed as technicians in the pathology lab of Central Catholic Hospital, a major medical center in the core of a major city. They both hold specialist degrees and are licensed pathologist's assistants. Both have been employed in their jobs for five years.

Last month Dr. Clarence Cutter, the chief pathologist and supervisor of the lab, decided to reorganize his operation. He decided that supervising the work of both assistants was taking up too much of his time. He reasoned that if he were to promote one of them to midlevel supervisory position, he could reduce the time he spent in direct supervision. Dr. Cutter presented his argument to Fred Wunderlich, the hospital's director of personnel. Wunderlich agreed and added that Dr. Cutter could probably use even more help in the lab. He suggested that either Burroughs or Watson be promoted to a new job titled administrative assistant to the pathologist and that a new person be hired to fill the vacated lab technician position. Thus, a new structure was developed for the department in which two lab technicians reported to an administrative assistant, who in turn reported to the chief pathologist.

The next task for Dr. Cutter was to decide which of his lab technicians to promote to the new position. To make the decision, he pulled the latest six-month performance evaluations he had made on Burroughs and Watson. Exhibit 7B reproduces their performance reviews. On the basis of the reviews, Dr. Cutter promoted John Watson to the administrative assistant position.

On learning of Watson's promotion, Burroughs went to Dr. Cutter and demanded that he explain why he had promoted Watson instead of her. He told her that he was not obligated to present a justification to her, that he was perfectly within his rights as chief pathologist to make such a decision, and that she should rest assured that his decision was made on grounds that were fair and equitable to her and Watson.

Exhibit 7B
Six-Month Performance
Reviews for Burroughs
and Watson

Employee: *Jayne Burroughs*   Supervisor: *Dr. Cutter*
Department: *Pathology*   Date: *11-28-86*

Work Quantity		Work Quality		Cooperation	
Far below average	☐	Far below average	☐	Far below average	☐
Below average	☒	Below average	☐	Below average	☒
Average	☐	Average	☒	Average	☐
Above average	☐	Above average	☐	Above average	☐
Far above average	☐	Far above average	☐	Far above average	☐

Employee: *John Watson*   Supervisor: *Dr. Cutter*
Department: *Pathology*   Date: *12-24-86*

Work Quantity		Work Quality		Cooperation	
Far below average	☐	Far below average	☐	Far below average	☐
Below average	☐	Below average	☐	Below average	☐
Average	☒	Average	☐	Average	☐
Above average	☐	Above average	☒	Above average	☐
Far above average	☐	Far above average	☐	Far above average	☒

This explanation did not satisfy Burroughs, and she filed a formal complaint alleging sex discrimination in a promotion decision with John Wunderlich, the personnel manager, and Robyn Payson, the hospital's Equal Employment Opportunity officer.

A hearing was scheduled by Wunderlich to resolve the issues. Wunderlich and Payson constituted the review board at the hearing, and Cutter and Burroughs were invited to present their cases. Burroughs opened the hearing by presenting her formal complaint: Both she and Watson had identical credentials for their jobs and had equal tenure on the job (five years). In addition, she believed she and Watson had performed equivalently during this period of time. Therefore, according to Burroughs' charge, the only reason Dr. Cutter could possibly have had for promoting Watson over her would be her sex. She noted that such a decision was in clear violation of Title VII of the Civil Rights Act of 1964, which reads in part:

> It shall be an unlawful employment practice for an employer to fail or refuse to hire or to discharge or otherwise to discriminate against any individual with respect to his compensation terms, conditions, or privileges of employment because of such individual's race, color, religion, sex, or national origin (Title VII, Sec. 703, Par. a-1 of the Civil Rights Act of 1964, as amended by P.L. 92-261, effective March 24, 1972).

Dr. Cutter countered by justifying his decision on the basis of actual performance review data. He argued that sex had nothing to do with his decision. Rather, he presented the latest six-month performance evaluations, which showed Watson to be performing better than Burroughs on three performance dimensions: work quantity; work quality; and cooperation.

The performance results angered Burroughs further. She asked that the hearing be adjourned and reconvened after she had had a chance to review the results and prepare her case further. Wunderlich and Payson agreed and scheduled a second hearing two weeks later.

At the second hearing, Burroughs presented the following list of grievances with regard to the promotion decision and the information on which it was based:

1. The decision was still in violation of Title VII of the Civil Rights Act because the way the performance evaluation was carried out discriminated against her on the basis of sex. Her reasoning on this point included the following charges:
   a. Dr. Cutter was biased against women, and this caused him to rate men in general above women in general.
   b. Dr. Cutter and Watson were in an all-male poker group that met on Friday nights, and she had systematically been excluded. Thus, ties of friendship had developed along sex lines, which created a conflict of interest for Dr. Cutter.
   c. Dr. Cutter had told her and others on several occasions that he doubted women could carry out managerial tasks because they had to constantly be concerned with duties at home and they get pregnant.
2. The measuring device itself failed to include a number of activities Burroughs carried out that were critical to the functioning of the lab. For example, while Dr. Cutter and Watson talked over coffee, she frequently

cleaned up the lab. She said that, although Watson's work was good, he tended to concentrate on visible outcomes and left much of the "invisible work," like cleaning up, to her.

3. The timing of the performance review was bad. Burroughs charged it was unfair to her to base the decision on only one six-month evaluation. Dr. Cutter had ten performance reviews for each employee. Why hadn't he based his decision on all ten, rather than just the latest review?

4. Also with respect to timing, Burroughs pointed out that her review had been made a month earlier than Watson's. She noted that December 24 was Christmas Eve and the day of the lab's office party. She charged that the spirits of the occasion (liquid and other) tended to shade Dr. Cutter's judgment in favor of Watson.

Put yourself in the position of Mr. Wunderlich and Ms. Payson. Decide whether there is any merit to Ms. Burroughs' charges, or if Dr. Cutter is justified in his decision. In making your decision, address yourself to the following questions:

1. Are issues of reliability involved in this case? If so, what sources of error must you consider in making a judgment?

2. Are issues of validity involved in this case? If so, what sources of error must you consider in making a judgment?

3. Is the measuring instrument itself at issue in this case?

4. If your answer to question 3 is yes, what recommendations would you make for changing the instrument?

5. Are problems of administration an issue in this case?

6. If your answer to question 5 is yes, what changes in administration would you recommend?

7. Do you think the problem would have arisen had Dr. Cutter adopted and followed a policy of open feedback on performance review results?

Source: Reprinted from A. Szilagyi and M. Wallace, *Organizational Behavior and Performance,* 4th ed. (Glenview, Ill.: Scott, Foresman, 1987), pp. 458-460. Reprinted by permission.

Part Three

Groups and Organization Design

Chapter 8

Group and Intergroup Relations

The Management Challenge

- To manage group and intergroup processes effectively.
- To understand how group norms, roles, and status systems affect employee behavior and performance.
- To develop group cohesiveness, which facilitates organizational goal attainment.
- To recognize barriers to intergroup cooperation and to take action to minimize such impediments.
- To get the most out of the collective actions of groups in organizations in order to enhance industrial competitiveness.

Teaming for Success at Corning

The source of Corning's past strength had been manufacturing technology. However, in the 1980s, foreign competitors had gained access to these technologies and could operate at lower cost. Corning concluded after a six-month study that improving inventory control and automating more production would not be enough to maintain a competitive position. The study concluded that a new team-oriented approach to production was also critical.

In 1987, Corning had the opportunity to expand production of ceramic "substrates," the filters that serve as the core of catalytic converters in cars. They decided to reopen a closed plant and start from scratch. The new plant did have 50 percent fewer production steps, but it also had only two levels of management and workers who were divided into 14-member teams. After sorting through 8,000 job applications, Plant Manager Robert D. Hoover and his team selected 150 employees who had the highest problem-solving ability and willingness to work in a team setting. The new plant was opened in 1989.

In preparation for the opening, team members were trained in multiple production skills and job classification were lowered from 47 to 4 to facilitate rotation and the use of multiple skills. Team members were also trained in group dynamics and effective group problem solving.

What resulted was a cohesive set of productive teams. For example, the teams at the reopened Blacksburg, Va. plant could retool a line to produce a different type of filter in only 10 minutes, which was six times faster than workers in a traditional filter plant. This greater cohesiveness and flexibility is a key factor in the plant's $2 million profit instead of the $2.3 million loss that was projected to the startup period.

The team approach has worked so well in Blacksburg that Corning is thinking of transplanting the approach to its 27 other factories around the country.[1]

Companies such as Corning, with its Blacksburg unit, clearly demonstrate the importance of group and intergroup relations as aspects of organizational dynamics and industrial competitiveness. But a knowledge of groups alone is not sufficient. In addition, we must understand how jobs or tasks are organized so they can be performed efficiently and effectively. What kind of job design was used in Blacksburg plant? And we must understand how groups and tasks are integrated to form entire organizations. How did the Blacksburg plant relate to the rest of the company? Questions such as these constitute the focus of Part Three.

On the basis of our analysis of individual behavior in Part Two, we are now in a position to consider what happens when individuals are placed in work units to perform their tasks. We do this in the next four chapters. The nature of groups and intergroup relations is discussed in this chapter. The topics of job design and productivity are discussed in Chapter 9. Organization design and effectiveness are discussed in Chapters 10 and 11. Taken together, the chapters in Part Three provide a solid understanding of organization *structure*—that is, how people and work units are put together for purposes of task accomplishment. Following this, we turn our attention, in Part Four, to a look at organizational *processes* (such as leadership, decision making, communication, etc.) and the social dynamics among people as they perform their jobs.

WORK GROUPS: BASIC CONSIDERATIONS

Available research on group dynamics demonstrates rather conclusively that individual behavior is highly influenced by co-workers in a work group. For instance, we see many examples of individuals who, when working in groups, intentionally set limits on their own incomes so they earn no more than the other group members. We see other situations where individuals choose to remain on undesirable jobs because of their friends in the plant, even though preferable jobs are available elsewhere. In summarizing much research on the topic, Hackman and Morris concluded the following:

> There is substantial agreement among researchers and observers of small task groups that something important happens in group interaction which can affect performance outcomes. There is little agreement about just what that "something" is—whether it is more likely to enhance or depress group effectiveness, and how it can be monitored, analyzed, and altered.[2]

In order to gain a clearer understanding of this "something," we must first consider in detail what we mean by a *group,* how groups are formed, and how various groups differ.

What Is a Group?

The literature of group dynamics is a very rich field of study and includes many definitions of work groups. For example, we might conceive of a group in terms of *perceptions;* that is, if individuals see themselves as a group, then a group exists. Or, we can view a group in *structural* terms. For instance, McDavid and Harari define a group as "an organized system of two or more individuals who are interrelated so that the system performs some function, has a standard set of role relationships among its members, and has a set of norms that regulate the function of the group and each of its members."[3] Groups can also be defined in *motivational* terms as "a collection of individuals whose existence as a collection is rewarding to the individuals."[4] Finally, a group can be viewed with regard to *interpersonal interaction*—the degree to which members communicate and interact with one another over time.[5]

By integrating these various approaches to defining groups, we may conclude for our purposes here that a *group* is a collection of individuals who share a common set of norms, who generally have differentiated roles among themselves, and who interact with one another toward the joint pursuit of common goals (the definitions of roles and norms is provided later in this chapter). This definition assumes a dynamic perspective and leads us to focus on two major aspects of groups: group structure and group processes. Group structure is the topic of this chapter, and group processes will be discussed in later chapters.

Types of Groups

There are two primary types of groups: formal and informal. Moreover, within these two types, groups can be further differentiated on the basis of their relative degree of permanence. The resulting four types are shown in Exhibit 8.1.

Formal Groups.   *Formal groups* are work units that are prescribed by the organization. Examples of formal groups include sections of departments (such as the accounts receivable section of the accounting department), committees, or special project task forces. These groups are set up by management on either a temporary or permanent basis to accomplish prescribed tasks. When the group is permanent, it is usually called a *command group* or *functional group*. An example would be the sales department in a company. When the group is less permanent, it is usually referred to as a *task group*. An example here would be a corporate-sponsored task force on improving affirmative action efforts. In both cases, the groups are formal in that they are both officially established by the company to carry out some aspect of the business.

Informal Groups.   In addition to formal groups, all organizations have a myriad of *informal groups*. These groups evolve naturally out of individual and collective self-interest among the members of an organization and are not the result of deliberate organizational design. People join informal groups

Exhibit 8.1
Types of Groups

	Relatively Permanent	Relatively Temporary
Formal	Command group	Task group
Informal	Friendship group	Interest group

because of common interests, social needs, or simply friendship. Informal groups typically develop their own norms and roles and establish unwritten rules for their members. Studies in social psychology have clearly documented the important role of these informal groups in facilitating (or inhibiting) performance and organizational effectiveness. Again on the basis of their relative degree of permanence, informal groups can be divided into *friendship groups* (people you like to be around) and *interest groups* (e.g., a network of working women or minority managers). Friendship groups tend to be long lasting, whereas interest groups often dissolve as people's interests change.

One of the more interesting aspects of group processes in organizations is the interaction between informal and formal groups. Both groups establish norms and roles, goals and objectives, and both demand loyalty from their members. When an individual is a member of many groups—both formal and informal—a wide array of potentially conflicting situations emerge that have an impact upon behavior in organizations. We will focus on this interplay throughout the next few chapters.

Reasons for Joining Groups

People join groups for many reasons. Often, joining a group serves several purposes at once. In general, at least six reasons can be identified for joining groups:

1. *Security.* Most people have a basic need for protection from external threats, real or imagined. These threats include the possibility of being fired or intimidated by the boss, the possibility of being embarrassed in a new situation, or simply the anxiety of being alone. Groups can be a primary source of *security* against such threats. We have often heard that there is "safety in numbers."
2. *Social Needs.* In addition, as discussed in previous chapters, basic theories of personality and motivation emphasize that most individuals have relatively strong *social needs.* They need to interact with other people and develop meaningful relationships. People are clearly social creatures. Groups provide structured environments in which individuals can pursue friendships.
3. *Self-Esteem.* Similarly, membership in groups can assist individuals in developing self-esteem. People often take pride in being associated with prestigious groups; note such examples as professors elected to membership in the National Academy of Sciences or salespersons who qualify for a million dollar club as a reward for sales performance.
4. *Economic Self-Interest.* People often associate with groups to pursue their own *economic self-interest.* Labor unions are a prime example of this phenomenon, as are various professional and accrediting agencies, such as the American Bar Association. These organizations often attempt to limit the supply of tradespeople or professionals in order to maintain employment and salaries.
5. *Mutual Interest.* Some groups are formed to pursue goals that are of *mutual interest* to group members. Included here are bridge clubs, company-sponsored baseball teams, and literary clubs. By joining together, individuals can pursue group goals that are typically not feasible alone.

6. *Physical Proximity.* Finally, many groups form simply because people are located in close *physical proximity* to one another. In fact, office architecture and layout can have considerable influence over the development of social networks and groups. Consider, for example, two floors in the same building. On the first floor, all the managers have private offices arranged in a long row, with their secretaries arranged in a similar row in front of them. This horizontal pattern of offices does not allow for frequent interaction between either the managers or the secretaries, and as a result group formation may be slowed. On the second floor, however, suppose all the managers' offices are arranged in a cluster surrounding a similar cluster of secretaries. The result would be more frequent social interaction among employees. This is not to say that one arrangement is superior to the other; rather, it is simply to point out how variations in office arrangements can have an impact on group formation.

Stages in Group Development

Before we begin a comprehensive examination of the structure of groups, consider briefly the stages of group development. How do groups grow and develop over time? Tuckman has proposed one model of group development that consists of four stages through which groups generally proceed.[6] These four stages are referred to by the deceptively simple titles *forming, storming, norming,* and *performing* (see Exhibit 8.2).

1. *Forming.* In the first stage of development, when group members first come together, emphasis is usually placed on making acquaintances, sharing information, testing each other, and so forth. This stage is referred to as forming. Group members attempt to discover which interpersonal behaviors are acceptable or unacceptable in the group. In this process of sensing out the environment, a new member is heavily dependent upon others for providing cues to acceptable behavior.

2. *Storming.* In the second stage of group development, a high degree of intergroup conflict (storming) can usually be expected as group members attempt to develop a place for themselves and to influence the development of group norms and roles. Issues are discussed more openly, and efforts are made to clarify group goals.

3. *Norming.* Over time, the group begins to develop a sense of oneness. Here, group norms emerge *(norming)* to guide individual behavior. Group members come to accept fellow members and develop a unity of purpose that binds them.

4. *Performing.* Once group members agree on basic purposes, they set about developing separate roles for the various members. In this final stage, role differentiation emerges to take advantage of task specialization in order to facilitate goal attainment. The group focuses its attention on the task *(performing)*. As we consider this simple model, it should be emphasized that Tuckman does not claim that all groups proceed through this sequence of stages. Rather, this model provides a generalized conceptual scheme to help us understand the processes by which groups form and develop over time.

Exhibit 8.2
Stages in Group Development

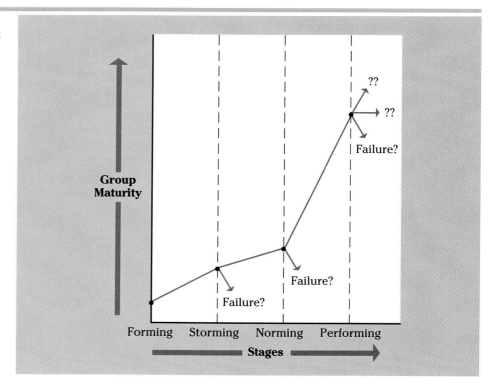

To begin linking some of this material, think about the reasons for joining a group and the development stages groups often go through. For example, at the storming stage, what differences might you expect between groups formed for economic self-interest and groups formed for mutual self-interest?

WORK GROUP STRUCTURE

Work group structure can be characterized in many different ways. We examine several characteristics that are useful in describing and understanding what makes one group different from another. This matrix of variables will, when taken together, paint a portrait of work groups in terms of relatively enduring group properties. The aspects of group structure to be considered are (1) work roles, (2) work group size, (3) work group norms, (4) status relationships, and (5) work group cohesiveness. Each of these factors has been shown to influence group processes, as shown in Exhibit 8.3. Thus, the material presented here will be important when we focus on group processes later in the text.

Work Roles

In order to accomplish its goals and maintain its norms, a group must differentiate the work activities of its members. One or more members assume leadership positions, others carry out the major work of the group, and still others serve in support roles. This specialization of activities is commonly referred to as role differentiation. More specifically, a *work role* is an expected behavior pattern assigned or attributed to a particular position in the organization. It defines individual responsibilities on behalf of the group.

It has been suggested that within organizational settings, work roles can be divided into three types on the basis of the nature of the activities that encompass the role.[7] These are:

1. *Task-oriented roles.* These roles focus on task-related activities aimed at achieving group performance goals.
2. *Relations-oriented roles.* These roles emphasize the further development of the group, including building group cohesiveness and consensus, preserving group harmony, looking after group member welfare, and so forth.
3. *Self-oriented roles.* These roles emphasize the specific needs and goals of individual members, often at the expense of the group.

As we might expect, individual group members often perform several of these roles simultaneously. A group leader, for example, must focus group attention on task performance while at the same time preserving group harmony and cohesiveness. To see how this works, consider your own experience. You may be able to recognize the roles you have played in groups you have been a member of. In your experience, have you played multiple roles or single roles? To assist in your analysis, you may wish to complete Self-Assessment 8.1. Simply think of a group you have belonged to, and answer each question as honestly as possible. When you are through, refer to Appendix B for interpretation.

Perhaps the best way to understand the nature of work roles is to examine a *role episode*. A role episode is an attempt to explain how a particular role is learned and acted upon. As can be seen in Exhibit 8.4, a role episode begins with members' expectations about what one person should be doing in a particular position (Stage 1). These expectations are then communicated to the individual (Stage 2), causing the individual to perceive the expectations about the expected role (Stage 3). Finally, the individual decides to act upon the role in terms of actual role-related behavior (Stage 4). In other words, Stages 1 and 2 deal with the *expected* role; whereas Stage 3 focuses on the *perceived* role; and Stage 4 focuses on the *enacted* role.

Exhibit 8.3
Group Structure and Process

Group Structure
- Work roles
- Group size
- Norms
- Status systems
- Cohesiveness

Group Processes
- Leadership
- Communication
- Decision making
- Power and politics
- Conflict and negotiation

SELF-ASSESSMENT 8.1
How Do You Behave in a Group?

Instructions: Think of a typical group situation in which you often find yourself (e.g., a club, study group, small work group), and answer the following items as accurately as possible.

In a group, how often do you:	Never	Seldom	Fairly Often	Frequently
1. Keep the group focused on the task at hand?	1	2	3	4
2. Help the group clarify the issues?	1	2	3	4
3. Pull various ideas together?	1	2	3	4
4. Push the group to make a decision or complete a task?	1	2	3	4
5. Support and encourage other groups members?	1	2	3	4
6. Try to reduce interpersonal conflicts?	1	2	3	4
7. Help the group reach a compromise?	1	2	3	4
8. Assist in maintaining group harmony?	1	2	3	4
9. Seek personal recognition from other group members?	1	2	3	4
10. Try to dominate group activities?	1	2	3	4
11. Avoid unpleasant or undesirable group activities?	1	2	3	4
12. Express your impatience or hostility with the group?	1	2	3	4

Consider the following simple example. A group may determine that its newest member is responsible for getting coffee for group members during breaks (Stage 1). This role is then explained to the incoming member (Stage 2), who becomes aware of his or her expected role (Stage 3). On the basis of these perceptions (and probably reinforced by group norms), the individual then would probably carry out the assigned behavior (Stage 4).

Several aspects of this model of a role episode should be noted. First, Stages 1 and 2 are initiated by the group and directed at the individual. Stages 3 and 4, on the other hand, represent thoughts and actions of the individual receiving the stimuli. In addition, Stages 1 and 3 represent cognitive and perceptual evaluations, whereas Stages 2 and 4 represent actual behaviors. The sum total of all the roles assigned to one individual is called the *role set*.

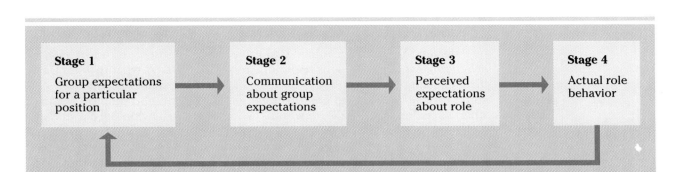

Exhibit 8.4
A Simplified Model
of a Role Episode

Source: Developed from D. Katz and R. Kahn, *The Social Psychology of Organizations,* 2nd ed. (New York: Wiley, 1978).

Although the role episode presented here seems straightforward, in reality we know that it is far more complicated. For instance, individuals typically receive multiple and sometimes conflicting messages from various groups, all attempting to assign them a particular role. This can easily lead to *role conflict.* Messages sent to an individual may sometimes be unclear, leading to *role ambiguity.* Finally, individuals may simply receive too many role-related messages, contributing to *role overload.* Discussion of these topics is reserved for Chapter 17, where we will examine several important aspects of psychological adjustment to work.

Work Group Size

Obviously, work groups can be found in various sizes. Early management theorists spent considerable time and effort to no avail attempting to identify the right size for the various types of work groups. There is simply no right number of people for most group activities. They did, however, discover a great deal about what happens as group size increases.[8] A number of relevant size-outcome relationships are summarized in Exhibit 8.5.

Exhibit 8.5
Effects of Group Size
on Group Dynamics

Factor	Size of Group	
	Small	**Large**
Group interaction	Increased	Decreased
Group cohesiveness	Higher	Lower
Job satisfaction	Higher	Lower
Absenteeism	Lower	Higher
Turnover	Lower	Higher
Social loafing	Lower	Higher
Productivity	No clear relation	No clear relation

Group Interaction Patterns. First, we will consider the effects of variations in group size on group interaction patterns. A series of classic studies by Bales and Borgatta examined this issue using a technique known as *interaction process analysis.*[9] This technique records who says what to whom, and through using it Bales and his colleagues found that smaller groups (2–4 persons) typically exhibited greater tension, agreement, and opinion seeking, whereas larger groups (13–16 persons) showed more tension release and giving of suggestions and information. This suggests that harmony is crucial in smaller groups and that people in them have more time to develop their thoughts and opinions. On the other hand, individuals in larger groups must be more direct because of the increased competition for attention.

Job Attitudes. Increases in work group size are fairly consistently found to be inversely related to satisfaction, although the relationship is not overly strong.[10] That is, people working in smaller work units or departments report higher levels of satisfaction than those in larger units. This finding is not surprising in view of the greater attention one receives in smaller groups and the greater importance group members typically experience in such things as their role set.

Absenteeism and Turnover. Available research indicates that increases in work group size and absenteeism are moderately related among blue-collar workers, although no such relationship exists for white-collar workers.[11] One explanation for these findings is that increased work group size leads to lower group cohesiveness, higher task specialization, and poorer communication. As a result, it becomes more difficult to satisfy higher-order needs on the job, and job attendance becomes less appealing. This explanation may be more relevant in the case of blue-collar workers, who typically have little job autonomy and control. White-collar workers typically have more avenues available to them for need satisfaction. Similar findings exist for employee turnover.[12] Turnover rates are higher in larger groups.[12] Again it can be hypothesized that because larger groups make need satisfaction more difficult, there is less reason for individuals to remain with the organization.

Productivity. No clear relationship has been found between group size and productivity.[13] There is probably good reason for this. Unless we take into consideration the type of task that is being performed, we really cannot expect a clear or direct relationship. Mitchell explains it as follows:

> Think of a task where each new member adds a new independent amount of productivity (certain piece-rate jobs might fit here). If we add more people, we will add more productivity. . . . On the other hand, there are tasks where everyone works together and pools their resources. With each new person the added increment of new skills or knowledge decreases. After a while increases in size will fail to add much to the group except coordination and motivation problems. Large groups will perform less well than small groups. The relationship between group size and productivity will therefore depend on the type of task that needs to be done.[14]

However, when we look at productivity and group size, it is important to recognize the existence of a unique factor called *social loafing,*[15] a tendency for individual group members to reduce their effort on a group task. This phenomenon occurs (1) when people see their task as being unimportant or simple, (2) when group members think their individual output is not identifiable, and (3) when group members expect their fellow workers to loaf. Social loafing is more prevalent in larger groups than in smaller groups, presumably because the above three factors are accentuated. From a managerial standpoint, this problem can be reduced by providing workers with greater responsibility for task accomplishment and more challenging assignments. This issue is addressed in the following chapter, on job design.

Work Group Norms

The concept of work group norms represents a complex topic with a history of social psychological research dating back several decades. In this section we will highlight several of the essential aspects of norms and how they relate to people at work. We will consider the characteristics and functions of work group norms as well as conformity with and deviance from them.

Characteristics of Work Group Norms.   A *work group norm* may be defined as a standard that is shared by group members and that regulates member behavior within an organization. An example of a norm can be seen in a typical classroom situation when students develop a norm against speaking up in class too often. It is believed that students who are highly visible improve their grades at the expense of others. Hence, a norm is created that attempts to govern acceptable classroom behavior. We see similar examples in the workplace. There may be a norm against producing too much or too little, against getting too close to the supervisor, against being late for work, and so forth.

Work group norms may be characterized by at least five factors:[16]

1. Norms summarize and simplify group influence processes. They denote the processes by which groups regulate and regularize member behavior.
2. Norms apply only to behavior, not to private thoughts and feelings. Although norms may be based on thoughts and feelings, they cannot govern them. That is, private acceptance of group norms is unnecessary, only public compliance.
3. Norms are generally developed only for behaviors that are viewed as important by most group members.
4. Norms usually develop gradually, but the process can be quickened if members wish. Norms usually are developed by group members as the need arises, such as when a situation occurs that requires new ground rules for members in order to protect group integrity.
5. All norms do not apply to all members. Some norms, for example, apply only to young initiates (such as getting the coffee), whereas others are based on seniority, sex, race, or economic class.

Functions of Work Group Norms.   Most all groups have norms, although some may be more extensive than others. To see this, examine the norms that exist in the various groups to which you belong. Which groups have more fully developed norms? Why? What functions do these norms serve? Several efforts have been made to answer this question. In general, work group norms serve four functions in organizational settings:[17]

1. *Norms facilitate group survival.* When a group is under threat, norms provide a basis for ensuring goal-directed behavior and rejecting deviant behavior that is not purposeful to the group. This is essentially a "circle the wagons" phenomenon.
2. *Norms simplify expected behaviors.* Norms tell group members what is expected of them—what is acceptable and unacceptable—and allows members to anticipate the behaviors of their fellow group members and to anticipate the positive or negative consequences of their own behavior.
3. *Norms help avoid embarrassing situations.* By identifying acceptable and unacceptable behaviors, norms tell group members when a behavior or topic is damaging to another member. For example, a norm against swearing signals group members that such action would be hurtful to someone in the group and should be avoided.
4. *Norms help identify the group and express its central values to others.* Norms concerning clothes, language, mannerisms, and so forth help tell others who belongs to the group and, in some cases, what the group stands for. Norms often serve as rallying points for group members.

Conformity and Deviance.   Managers often wonder why employees comply with the norms and dictates of their work group even when they seemingly work against their best interests. This concern is particularly strong when workers intentionally withhold productivity that could lead to higher incomes. The answer to this question lies in the concept of conformity to group norms. Situations arise when the individual is swept along by the group and acts in ways that he or she would prefer not to.

To see how this works, consider the results of a classic study of individual conformity to group pressures that was carried out by Solomon Asch.[18] Asch conducted a laboratory experiment in which a naive subject was placed in a room with several confederates. Each person in the room was asked to match the length of a given line (*X*) with that of one of three unequal lines (*A, B,* and *C*). This is shown in Exhibit 8.6. Confederates, who spoke first, were all instructed prior to the experiment to identify line *C* as the line most like *X*, even though *A* was clearly the answer. The results were startling. In over one-third of the trials in the experiment, the naive subject denied the evidence of his own senses and agreed with the answers given by the unknown confederates. In other words, when confronted by a unanimous answer from others in the group, a large percentage of individuals chose to go along with the group rather than express a conflicting opinion, even though these individuals were confident their own answers were correct.

What causes such conformity to group norms? And, under what conditions will an individual deviate from these norms? Conformity to group norms is believed to be caused by at least three factors.[19] First, personality plays a major role. For instance, negative correlations have been found between conformity and intelligence, tolerance, and ego strength, whereas authoritarianism was found to be positively related. Essentially, people who have a strong self-identity are more likely to stick to their own norms and deviate from those of the group when a conflict between the two exists. Second, the initial stimulus

Exhibit 8.6
Asch's Experiment in
Group Pressure and
Individual Judgment

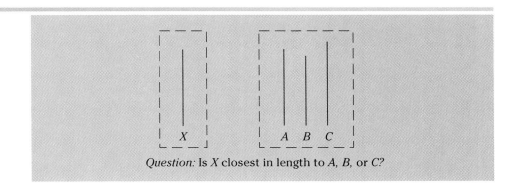

Question: Is *X* closest in length to *A, B,* or *C?*

that evokes responses can influence conformity. The more ambiguous the stimulus (e.g., a new and confusing order from top management), the greater the propensity to conform to group norms ("I'm not sure what the new order from management really means, so I'll just go along with what others think it means."). In this sense, conformity provides a sense of protection and security in a new and perhaps threatening situation. Finally, group characteristics themselves can influence conformity to group norms. Factors such as the extent of pressure exerted on group members to conform, the extent to which a member identifies with the group, and the extent to which the group has been successful in achieving previous goals can influence conformity.

What happens when someone deviates from group norms? Research indicates that groups often respond by increasing the amount of communication directed toward the deviant member.[20] This communication is aimed at bringing the deviant into the acceptable bounds set by the group. A good example of this process can be seen in Janis's classic study of the group processes leading up to the abortive Bay of Pigs invasion in Cuba.[21] At one meeting, Arthur Schlesinger, an advisor to President Kennedy, expressed opposition to the plan even though no one else expressed similar doubts. After listening to his opposition for a while, Robert Kennedy took Schlesinger aside and said, "You may be right or you may be wrong, but the President has his mind made up. Don't push it any further. Now is the time for everyone to help him all they can." Janis elaborated on this group decision-making process and termed it "groupthink." This issue is discussed in detail in Chapter 14.

When a deviant member refuses to heed the message and persists in breaking group norms, group members often respond by rejecting or isolating the deviant. They tell the deviant, in essence, that they will no longer tolerate such behavior and prefer to reconstitute the group. If the deviant is not expelled, the group must continually confront behavior that conflicts with what it holds to be true. Rather than question or reexamine its beliefs, the group finds it simpler—and safer—to rid itself of dangerous influence.

Status Systems

A fourth characteristic, or structural property, of work groups is the status system. *Status systems* serve to differentiate individuals on the basis of some criterion or set of criteria. There are five general bases on which status differentiations are made: birth, personal characteristics, achievement, possessions, and formal authority. All five bases can be seen as establishing status in work groups. For example, an employee may achieve high status because he is the boss's son (birth), the brightest or strongest member of the group (personal characteristics), the best performer (achievement), the richest or highest paid (possessions), or the foreman or supervisor (formal authority).

Reasons for Status Systems. Status systems can be seen throughout most organizations. We differentiate between blue-collar and white-collar employees (and even pink and gold collar), skilled tradespersons and unskilled workers, senior and junior managers, high achievers and low achievers, and popular and unpopular employees. Why do we do this? In essence, status differentiation in organizations (and their related status symbols) serves four purposes:[22]

Motivation. We ascribe status to persons as rewards or incentives for performance and achievement. If high achievement is recognized as positive behavior by an organization, individuals are more willing to exert effort.

Identification. Status and status symbols provide useful cues to acceptable behavior in new situations. In the military, for example, badges of rank quickly tell members who has authority and who is to be obeyed. Similarly, in business, titles serve the same purpose.

Dignification. People are often ascribed status as a means of signifying respect that is due them. A clergyman's attire, for instance, identifies a representative of the church.

Stabilization. Finally, status systems and symbols facilitate stabilization in an otherwise turbulent environment by providing a force for continuity. Authority patterns, role relationships, and interpersonal interactions are all affected and, indeed, defined by the status system in effect. As a result, much ambiguity in the work situation is reduced.

Status can be conferred on an individual in many different ways. One way common in organizations is through the assignment and decoration of offices. John Dean, counsel to former President Nixon, provides the following account concerning status in the White House:[23]

> Everyone [on the White House Staff] jockeyed for a position close to the President's ear, and even an unseasoned observer could sense minute changes in status. Success and failure could be seen in the size, decor, and location of offices. Anyone who moved into a smaller office was on the way down. If a carpenter, cabinetmaker, or wallpaper hanger was busy in someone's office, this was the sure sign he was on the rise. Every day, workmen crawled over the White House complex like ants. Movers busied themselves with the continuous shuffling of furniture from one office to another as people moved in, up, down, or out. We learned to read office changes as an index of the internal bureaucratic power struggles. The expense was irrelevant to Haldeman. . . . He once retorted when we discussed whether we should reveal such expense, "This place is a national monument, and I can't help it if the last three Presidents let it go to hell."

Actually, the costs had less to do with the fitness of the White House than with the need of its occupants to see tangible evidence of their prestige.[23]

More recently, we can see status symbols at work in the office decor of some of Hollywood's most prestigious directors and producers.[24] When an executive moves from one studio to another, it is not uncommon to spend between $20,000 and $150,000 simply to redecorate his or her office. For example, when Leonard Goldberg became president of Fox, the studio spent over $100,000 to remodel his office; the renovation included a working fireplace of gold-veined black marble. When you enter Mr. Goldberg's office, he wants you to know who he is.

Status Incongruence. An interesting aspect of status systems in organizations is the notion of *status incongruence.* This situation exists when a person is high on certain valued dimensions but low on others, or when a person's characteristics seem inappropriate for a particular job. Examples of status incongruence include the college student who takes a janitorial job during the summer (usually referred to as the "college kid" by the other janitors), the president's son who works his way up through the organizational hierarchy (at an accelerated rate, needless to say), or the young fast-track manager who is promoted to a level typically held by older employees.

Status incongruence presents problems for everyone involved. The individual may become the target of hostility and jealousy from co-workers who feel the individual has risen above his or her station. The co-workers, on the other hand, may be forced to acknowledge their own lack of success or achievement. One might ask, for example, "Why has this youngster been promoted over me when I have more seniority?" At least two remedies for this conflict are available to managers: (1) an organization can select or promote only those individuals whose characteristics are congruent with the job and work group, and (2) an organization can attempt to change the values of the group. Neither of these possibilities seems realistic or fair. Hence, dynamic organizations that truly reward high achievement (instead of seniority) must accept some level of conflict resulting from status incongruence.

IN PRACTICE
Status Systems in Japanese Business

International Challenge

In Japan, etiquette is not simply a prescription for appropriate social responses, it is a complete guide to conducting oneself in all social interactions. At the root of this system of social interaction is one's status within the organization and society.

The effects of status in Japan can be seen in many ways. For example, when two businessmen meet for the first time, they exchange business cards—before they even say hello to each other. After carefully reading the cards, each knows precisely the other's rank (and status) in the organizational hierarchy and, thus, how to respond. The person with the lower status must bow lower than the person with the higher status.

Moreover, when four managers get into a car, status determines where each will sit. This is shown in Exhibit 8.7, where it can be seen that the most important (highest-status) manager will sit in the backseat, directly behind the driver. Similarly, when four managers enter an elevator, the least senior

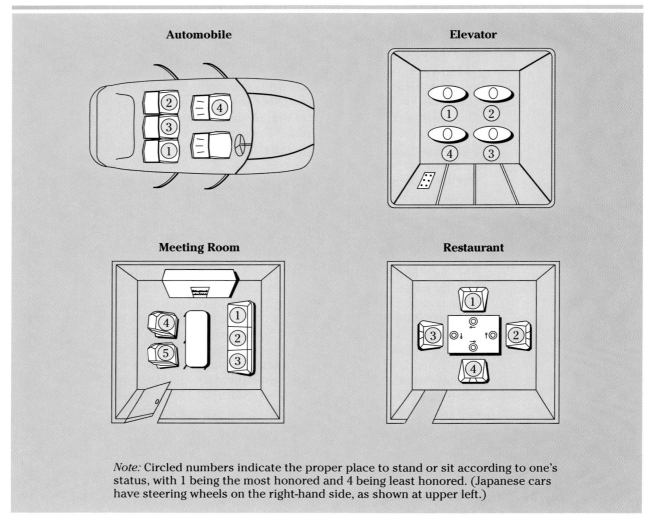

Automobile

Elevator

Meeting Room

Restaurant

Note: Circled numbers indicate the proper place to stand or sit according to one's status, with 1 being the most honored and 4 being least honored. (Japanese cars have steering wheels on the right-hand side, as shown at upper left.)

Exhibit 8.7
The Place of Honor in Japan

stands in front of the elevator controls, with the most senior behind. In a meeting room or in a restaurant, the most honored seat is farthest from the door, whereas the least honored is nearest the door. Even within the meeting room itself, a sofa is considered higher in rank than armchairs.

Clearly, status plays an important role in Japanese (and several other East Asian) societies. Status recognizes age (an important cultural variable in these societies) and tells everyone involved how to behave. Though such prescriptive practices may seem strange to many Westerners, it is quite natural in Japan. In fact, many Japanese feel such guidelines are helpful and convenient in defining social relationships, avoiding awkward situations, and making business transactions more comfortable and productive. Whether or not this perception is accurate, status systems are a fact of life that must be recognized by Western managers attempting to do business in Asia. Failure to understand such social patterns puts the Western manager at a distinct disadvantage.[25]

Group Cohesiveness

A fifth characteristic of work groups is group cohesiveness. We have all come in contact with groups whose members feel a high degree of camaraderie, group spirit, and unity. In these groups, individuals seem to be concerned about the welfare of other group members as well as that of the group as a whole. There is a feeling of "us against them" that creates a closeness among them. This phenomenon is called group cohesiveness. More specifically, *group cohesiveness* may be defined as the extent to which individual members of a group are motivated to remain in the group. According to Shaw, "Members of highly cohesive groups are more energetic in group activities, they are less likely to be absent from group meetings, they are happy when the group succeeds and sad when it fails, etc., whereas members of less cohesive groups are less concerned about the group's activities."[26]

We shall consider two primary aspects of work group cohesiveness. First, we look at major causes of cohesiveness. Following this, we examine its consequences.

Determinants of Group Cohesiveness.   Why do some work groups develop a high degree of group cohesiveness whereas others do not? To answer this question, we have to examine both the composition of the group and several situational variables that play a role in determining the extent of cohesiveness. The major factors that influence group cohesiveness are shown in Exhibit 8.8.[27] These include the following:

Exhibit 8.8
Determinants and
Consequences of
Group Cohesiveness

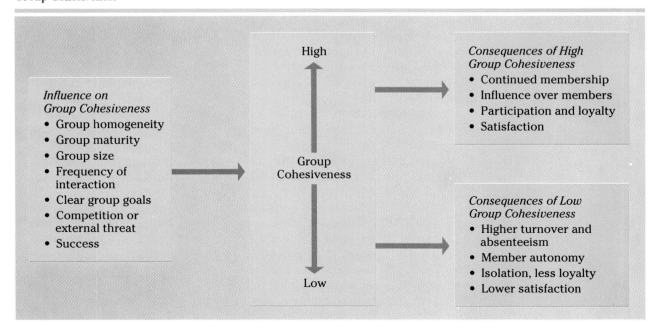

▓ *Group homogeneity.* The more homogeneous the group—that is, the more members share similar characteristics and backgrounds—the greater the cohesiveness.

▓ *Group maturity.* Groups tend to become more cohesive simply as a result of the passage of time. Continued interaction over long periods of time helps members develop a closeness born of shared experiences.

▓ *Group size.* Smaller groups have an easier time developing cohesiveness, possibly because of the less complex interpersonal interaction patterns.

▓ *Frequency of interaction.* Groups that have greater opportunities to interact on a regular or frequent basis tend to become more cohesive than groups that meet less frequently or whose members are more isolated.

▓ *Clear group goals.* Groups that know exactly what they are trying to accomplish develop greater cohesiveness, in part because of a shared sense of mission and the absence of conflict over mission.

▓ *Competition or external threat.* When groups sense external threat or hostility, they tend to band together more closely. There is, indeed, "safety in numbers."

▓ *Success.* Group succe on a previous task often facilitates increased cohesiveness and a sense of "we did it together."

In other words, a wide variety of factors can influence work group cohesiveness. The precise manner in which these processes occur is not known. Even so, managers must recognize the existence of certain forces of group cohesiveness if they are to unllderstand the nature of group dynamics in organizations. The second aspect of group cohesiveness that must be understood by managers relates to their consequences.

Consequences of Group Cohesiveness. As shown in Exhibit 8.8, several consequences of group cohesiveness can also be identified. The first and most obvious consequence is *maintenance of membership.* If the attractiveness of the group is sufficiently stronger than the attractiveness of alternative groups, then we would expect the individual to remain in the group. Hence, turnover rates should be low.

In addition, high group cohesiveness typically provides the group with considerable *power over group members.* The power of a group over members depends upon the level of outcomes members expect to receive from the group compared to what they could receive through alternate means. When the group is seen as being highly instrumental to achieving personal goals, individuals will typically submit to the will of the group.

Third, members of highly cohesive groups tend to exhibit greater *participation and loyalty.* Several studies have shown that as cohesiveness increases, there is more frequent communication among members, a greater degree of participation in group activities, and less absenteeism. Moreover, members of highly cohesive groups tend to be more cooperative and friendly and generally behave in ways designed to promote integration among members.

Fourth, members of highly cohesive groups generally report high levels of *satisfaction.* In fact, the concept of group cohesiveness almost demands all this be the case, because it is unlikely that members will feel like remaining with a group with which they are dissatisfied.

Finally, what is the effect of group cohesiveness on *productivity?* No clear relationship exists here. Instead, research shows that the extent to which cohesiveness and productivity are related is moderated by the extent to which group members accept organizational goals. This is shown in Exhibit 8.9. Specifically, when cohesiveness and acceptance of organizational goals are high, performance will probably be high. When acceptance is high but cohesiveness is low, group performance will typically be moderate. Finally, performance will generally be low when goal acceptance is low regardless of the extent of group cohesiveness. In other words, high performance is most likely to result when highly cohesive teams accept the goals of the organization. At this time, both forces for performance are congruent.

IN PRACTICE
Group Cohesiveness at AT&T Credit

AT&T Credit Corporation was established to provide financing for customers who lease AT&T equipment. Typically, finance companies represent the ultimate in the electronic assembly line, providing jobs that are dull and repetitive. But from the beginning, AT&T Credit decided to do it differently. The job fractionization typical of the industry would be replaced by integrated work teams that would be responsible for work flow, quality checks, and productivity.

The new president of the company was confident that if management trusted the employees and worked with them "as advisors, not dictators," the employees would respond. And they did. Productivity under the new system stands at twice that found in the industry. Employee morale is high, and the company is growing by 40 percent per year, in part because of the productivity yields of the employees.

Why is this happening? According to both managers and employees, the combination of the new integrated work team concept (where groups of employees are responsible for a wide array of tasks instead of each employee being responsible for only one task) and management's trust in the groups has led to a situation in which a high degree of team spirit and group cohesiveness has developed. Team members help each other. Moreover, because

Exhibit 8.9
Group Cohesiveness,
Goal Agreement,
and Performance

		Agreement with Organizational Goals	
		High	Low
Degree of Group Cohesiveness	High	High performance	Low performance
	Low	Moderate performance	Low performance

team members see the organization as a friend, and because the reward system provides incentives for productivity, this group cohesiveness is focused on increasing performance instead of restricting it. The goals of the group and those of the company are largely congruent, which results in higher group effort and productivity. Now the company is considering expanding the team concept to other parts of the organization.[28]

MANAGING EFFECTIVE WORK GROUPS

We have examined in detail the nature and structure of work groups, noting that work groups differ along such dimensions as size, norms, and roles. Some groups are more cohesive than others. In view of these differences, it is interesting to ask how managers can facilitate increased work group effectiveness. To answer this question, we will make use of Hackman's model of group effectiveness.[29] According to this model, illustrated in Exhibit 8.10, the effectiveness of a work group is influenced by environmental factors, design factors, and task-related interpersonal processes. These three factors combine to influence what are called the "intermediate criteria," which, in turn, combine with the nature of the work technology to determine ultimate group effectiveness.

Exhibit 8.10
Determinants of Work
Group Effectiveness

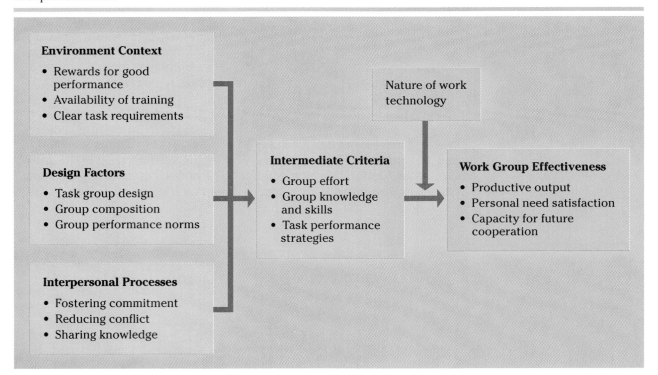

Source: From *Managing Organizational Behavior* by David A. Nadler, J. Richard Hackman, and Edward E. Lawler III (Boston: Little, Brown, 1979). Reprinted by permission of David A. Nadler.

What Is Work Group Effectiveness?

The first question to raise concerning work group effectiveness is what we mean by the concept itself. According to Hackman's model, effectiveness is defined in terms of three criteria:

1. *Productive output.* The productive output of the group must meet or exceed the quantitative and qualitative standards defined by the organization.
2. *Personal need satisfaction.* Groups are effective if membership facilitates employee need satisfaction.
3. *Capacity for future cooperation.* Effective groups employ social processes that maintain or enhance the capacity of their members to work together on subsequent tasks. Destructive social processes are avoided so members can develop long-term cohesiveness and effectiveness.

To see how group effectiveness works, try Self-Assessment 8.2. Choose a work group (or groups) to which you belong (or did belong in the past). If you wish, you may choose student groups organized in your class for class assignments. Once your group is selected, simply answer the items on the questionnaire by checking either "mostly yes" or "mostly no." When you have finished, refer to Appendix B for scoring.

Determinants of Work-Group Effectiveness

Group effectiveness is largely determined by three factors that have been called *intermediate criteria.* These factors are as follows:

1. *Group effort.* The amount of effort group members exert toward task accomplishment.
2. *Group knowledge and skill.* The amount of knowledge and skills possessed by group members that are available for group effort and performance.
3. *Task performance strategies.* The extent to which the group's strategies for task performance (that is, how it analyzes and attempts to solve problems) are appropriate.

Although the relative importance of each of these three intermediate factors may vary, all three are important. Without considerable group effort, appropriate skills and knowledge, and a clear strategy for task completion, groups are unlikely to be effective.

An important influence on the relative importance of these three variables is the nature of *work technology.* This includes the equipment and materials used in manufacture, the prescribed work procedures, and the physical layout of the work site. For example, if jobs are highly routinized, individual skills and knowledge may be somewhat less important than simple effort. On more complex tasks, however, such as research and development, effort alone will be of little help without concomitant skills and knowledge. Hence, although the relative importance of these three variables may vary with the job technology, all should be considered in any effort to understand determinants of work group effectiveness in a particular situation.

SELF-ASSESSMENT 8.2
How Effective Is Your Work Group?

Instructions: Select a group to which you belong, and use this group to answer the following questions. Check "mostly yes" or "mostly no" to answer each question.

		Mostly Yes	Mostly No
1.	The atmosphere is relaxed and comfortable.	_____	_____
2.	Group discussion is frequent, and it is usually pertinent to the task at hand.	_____	_____
3.	Group members understand what they are trying to accomplish.	_____	_____
4.	People listen to each others' suggestions and ideas.	_____	_____
5.	Disagreements are tolerated, and an attempt is made to resolve them.	_____	_____
6.	There is general agreement on most courses of action taken.	_____	_____
7.	The group welcomes frank criticism from inside and outside sources.	_____	_____
8.	When the group takes action, clear assignments are made and accepted.	_____	_____
9.	There is a well-established, relaxed working relationship among the members.	_____	_____
10.	There is a high degree of trust and confidence among the leader and subordinates.	_____	_____
11.	The group members strive hard to help the group achieve its goal.	_____	_____
12.	Suggestions and criticisms are offered and received with a helpful spirit.	_____	_____
13.	There is a cooperative rather than a competitive relationship among group members.	_____	_____
14.	The group goals are set high but not so high as to create anxieties or fear of failure.	_____	_____
15.	The leaders and members hold a high opinion of the group's capabilities.	_____	_____
16.	Creativity is stimulated within the group.	_____	_____
17.	There is ample communication within the group of topics relevant to getting the work accomplished.	_____	_____
18.	Group members feel confident in making decisions.	_____	_____
19.	People are kept busy but not overloaded.	_____	_____
20.	The leader of the group is well suited for the job.	_____	_____

Source: A. J. DuBrin, *Contemporary Applied Management,* (Plano, TX.: Business Publications, Inc. [Richard D. Irwin, Inc.], 1985), pp. 169–170. As adapted by A. J. DuBrin from *The Human Side of Enterprise* (New York: McGraw-Hill, 1960).

Finally, it must be recognized that these determinants of effectiveness are themselves influenced by three sets of factors (shown at the left-hand side of Exhibit 8.10). First, we must recognize a series of *environmental context* factors, such as the company's reward system, training programs, job descriptions, and so forth. Second are several *design factors,* including group structure, member composition, and performance norms. Finally, the role of *interpersonal processes*—such as efforts among group members and management to reduce conflict, foster commitment, and share knowledge—must be recognized. These three sets of factors, then, are largely responsible for determining the so-called intermediate criteria which, in turn, combine with appropriate job technologies to determine work group effectiveness.

Implications for Group Management

On the basis of this analysis of group processes in work organizations, we can identify several actions managers can take in order to help groups to be more effective.

Increased Managerial Awareness.   To begin, managers can make themselves more aware of the nature of groups and the functions groups perform for individuals. By learning why individuals join groups, for example, managers should be able to better understand the motivational implications of group dynamics. Is high group cohesiveness in a particular group a result of high commitment to the organization and its goals, or is it a result of alienation from the organization?

Sensitivity to Group Norms.   Managers can be sensitive to group norms and the extent to which they facilitate or inhibit group and organizational performance. The potency of group norms has been clearly established. It has also been shown that company actions can increase or decrease the likelihood that norms will work to the benefit of the organization. Much of the thrust of current organizational development efforts (see Chapter 19) is to use process consultation techniques to develop group norms that are compatible with company goals.

Understanding Pressures for Conformity.   Much has been said in the research literature about the effects of groups on individual conformity and deviance. Groups often place significant pressures on individuals to conform, and they punish deviants by such means as ostracism. From a managerial standpoint, conformity can represent a mixed blessing. On one hand, there are many work situations in which managers typically want workers to conform to standard operating procedures (this is called *dependable role performance*). On the other hand, employees must be sufficiently free to take advantage of what they believe to be unique or important opportunities on behalf of the organization *(innovative and spontaneous behavior)*. If pressures toward conformity are too strong, this spontaneity may be lost, along with unique opportunities for the organization.

Harnessing Group Cohesiveness.   Where it is desirable to develop highly cohesive groups, managers can show employees how group members can help one another by working together. It is important to note, however, that group cohesiveness by itself does not guarantee increased group effectiveness. Instead, managers must take the lead in showing group members why they benefit from working toward organizational goals. One way to accomplish this is through the reward systems used by the organization.

In short, there are several lessons for managers here concerning the effects of group dynamics on performance and effectiveness. The lesson is clear: managers must be sensitive to and deal with group processes in the workplace. Without doing so, the manager and the company are destined at best to achieve mediocre results.

IN PRACTICE
Improving Team Effectiveness at Federal Express

Federal Express has found great success in using high-involvement teams in its back-office operations in Memphis. Fedex began organizing its workers into teams in the late 1980s and early 1990s. One of the first groups organized were the clerical workers, who were responsible for literally millions of bills. Fedex began by organizing them into teams of five to ten people and giving them authority over their own management.

One day at a weekly team meeting, a clerk discovered a billing problem. Couriers were not always making sure that the proper weight was being marked on packages when picked up from customers. The team uncovered who in Fedex's 30,000-person courier network were not properly checking packages when they picked them up. They created a tracking system for invoices and in one year saved the company $2.1 million. Other team-driven changes resulted in a 13 percent decrease in incorrect bills.

While you might think that the workers at Fedex would be clamoring for a share of the millions they saved the company, Fedex found that sincere recognition and the self-satisfaction enjoyed within teams were what workers wanted first and foremost for their efforts.[30]

INTERGROUP BEHAVIOR AND PERFORMANCE

We are now ready to move on to an examination of intergroup behavior. That is, what happens when one group in an organization must interact with another? Clearly, in any corporation, a high degree of intergroup interaction is vital to organizational success. Even in small companies the production group must interact with the sales group, and both must accommodate the finance and accounting groups. Without smooth intergroup relations, organizational effectiveness and industrial competitiveness are virtually impossible.

Determinants of Intergroup Performance

To understand how groups interact with one another, it is important to identify the primary variables that characterize intergroup behavior.[31] We can do this by suggesting a model of intergroup performance. This model is outlined in Exhibit 8.11. As shown, intergroup behavior occurs when two groups intersect. Each group has its own characteristics and uniqueness, but both operate within the larger confines of organizational policies, culture, reward systems, and so forth. Within this context, performance is largely influenced by three types of *interaction requirements:* interdependence requirements, information flow requirements, and integration requirements. The quality of intergroup performance is affected by the extent to which all parties to the interaction can meet these requirements.

Exhibit 8.11
A Model of Intergroup
Behavior and Performance

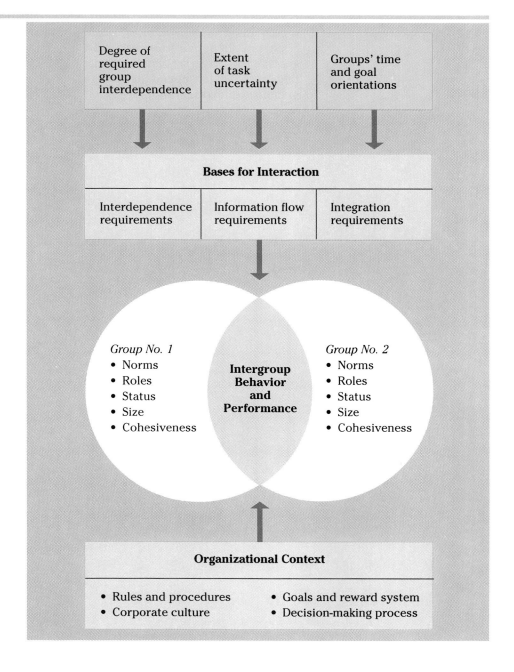

Interdependence Requirements.   *Interdependence requirements* relate to the frequency and quality of interactions among groups; high-quality interaction is required for successful task accomplishment. To successfully achieve corporate objectives, organizations must achieve enough intergroup interaction to coordinate resource allocation and utilization. The amount of interaction required is determined by the extent and nature of the groups' interdependence. Group interdependence takes three primary forms (see Exhibit 8.12):

1. *Pooled interdependence.* This occurs when various groups are largely independent of each other, even though each contributes to and is supported by the larger organization. For example, although the physics and music departments may not interact frequently, both contribute to the larger goals of the university, and both use university resources. In a factory setting, pooled interdependence can be seen in a company with two distinct manufacturing divisions, one for consumer products and one for industrial

Exhibit 8.12
Three Types of
Group Interdependence

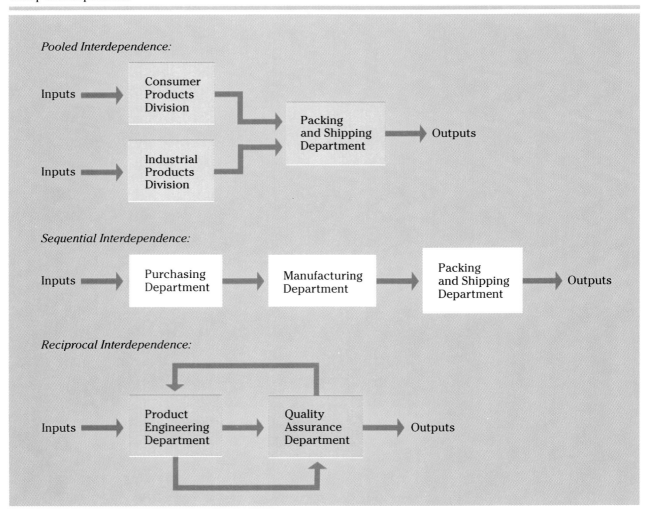

products. Although produced separately, both kinds of products come together in the shipping department, and both represent products of the same company.

2. *Sequential interdependence.* This exists when the outputs of one unit or group become the inputs for another. For example, the manufacturing department in a company is clearly dependent on the purchasing department for the success of its own operation, whereas the purchasing department is much less dependent on manufacturing.

3. *Reciprocal interdependence.* This occurs when two or more groups depend on one another for inputs. For example, without product engineering, the marketing department would have nothing to sell. On the other hand, without consumer information from marketing, product engineering might not know what to manufacture. The two units are highly dependent on each other, thereby requiring a high degree of interaction.

In summary, the type of interdependence determines in large part the degree of interrelationship that develops among two or more groups. High interdependence typically requires high intergroup interaction, whereas low interdependence typically requires relatively low intergroup interaction.

Information Flow Requirements.   The second requirement for successful intergroup performance is optimal *information flow.* To be successful, groups need the appropriate amount of information. Information flow is influenced to a large degree by the extent of *task uncertainty.* When groups are working on highly uncertain tasks (e.g., a new product, an experiment, or an old product in a new environment), the need for communication increases. When task uncertainty is low, less information is typically needed.

Task uncertainty, in turn, is influenced by two factors. The first, *task clarity,* is the extent to which the requirements and responsibilities of the group are clearly understood. The use of standard operating procedures in organizations is an example of a group requirement. The other consideration is *task environment,* those factors inside and outside the organization that can affect the group's performance. The task environment has two aspects: the number of groups that must be dealt with and the relative stability of the environment. Obviously, the more groups that must interact and the more dynamic the environment, the greater the task uncertainty. In a dynamic environment, groups tend to expand their information-gathering efforts to detect and cope with environmental changes. Hence, the greater the task uncertainty, the greater the need for comprehensive information flow systems.

Integration Requirements.   The final requirement for successful intergroup performance is integration. *Integration requirements* focus on the extent of collaboration, cooperation, or structural relationships among groups needed to ensure success. Typically, various departments within an organization have different goals and time orientations. A technical research department, for example, often sees its goals in scientific terms and has a long-term time perspective. A marketing department in the same company, on the other hand, focusing its goals on market considerations, would typically have a short-term time orientation. The production department, concerned with technical goals, would probably attempt to maintain a moderate time orientation in order to take advantage of the economies of scale associated with longer production runs.

A successful organization finds ways to integrate groups so they coordinate their efforts on behalf of corporate objectives. The trick is to achieve some commonly acceptable coordinating mechanism—not a state in which all units have the same goals and time orientations. It would prove disastrous, for example, if the research unit looked for short-term results or the marketing department ignored short-term shifts in the marketplace. Through integration, various units can accommodate each other's needs while maintaining their individuality. In this way, the strengths of all groups are used in addressing organizational problems.

When we put these various requirements and their antecedents together, we can see why achieving intergroup coordination and performance is no easy task. Exhibit 8.13 shows the defining characteristics of four typical units of an organization: research, development, sales, and manufacturing. The interdependence, task uncertainty, and time and goal orientation of each unit are shown. Consider the complexities managers face in attempting to lead such an organization efficiently and effectively. Indeed, business magazines are filled with examples of corporate failures that can be traced to poor coordination of such units. These examples point to an endless array of potential sources of conflict that can reduce the capacity of a company to compete successfully in an ever-changing environment.

Managing Intergroup Behavior and Performance

When we analyze the challenge of managing intergroup behavior and performance, the key issue facing managers is the issue of coordination. That is, in most situations, various units or departments in the organization all have talent needed to ensure task accomplishment. Yet each unit has its own culture,

Exhibit 8.13
Intergroup Characteristics in Four Units of One Company

Group	Interdependence Examples	Task Uncertainty	Time and Goal Orientation
Research	*Reciprocal* with development *Sequential* with market research *Pooled* with shipping	High	*Time:* Long term *Goal:* Science
Development	*Reciprocal* with market research *Sequential* with manufacturing *Pooled* with shipping	Moderate to high	*Time:* Long term *Goal:* Science and technoeconomic
Sales	*Reciprocal* with market research *Sequential* with manufacturing *Pooled* with personnel	Moderate	*Time:* Moderate term *Goal:* Market
Manufacturing	*Reciprocal* with accounting *Sequential* with shipping *Pooled* with research	Low	*Time:* Short term *Goal:* Technoeconomic

Source: A. Szilagyi and M. Wallace, *Organizational Behavior and Performance,* 3rd ed. (Glenview, Ill.: Scott, Foresman and Company, 1987), p. 262. Reprinted by permission.

goals, norms, and so forth. Hence, the challenge for managers is harnessing and coordinating this talent in such a way that group harmony is maintained while organizational objectives are achieved.

There are several techniques for managing intergroup relations and performance. These techniques include using rules and procedures, member exchange, linking roles, task forces, and decoupling. Let us briefly consider each as it relates to intergroup coordination and performance.

Rules and Procedures.   A common way to manage intergroup relations is for senior management to establish rules and procedures governing the interactions of two or more departments or units. For example, if units consistently fail to communicate with one another, which leads to poor coordination, the company may institute a new policy requiring all groups to post certain types of information at regular time intervals or to inform other department heads of proposed new activities or changes. By simply increasing communication flow, group coordination should be increased.

Member Exchange.   In some circumstances, it is desirable for the organization to temporarily transfer a member from one group to another. Such exchanges offer the employee an opportunity to better understand the problems and procedures of the other group. Upon returning to his or her original group, the employee can share information about the other group. In addition, the transferred employee often develops better interpersonal contacts with the other department, thereby enhancing communication and coordination. An example of this can be seen when a company transfers a production engineer into the quality assurance department. As a result, the employee sees firsthand the problems of the quality control group and can take the knowledge back to production engineering.

Linking Roles.   A *linking role* is a position or unit within the organization that is charged with overseeing and coordinating the activities of two or more groups. A good example here would be a product manager who is responsible for coordinating manufacturing, sales, quality control, and product research for a certain product line (see Exhibit 8.14). In essence,

Exhibit 8.14
The Product Manager as a Linking Role

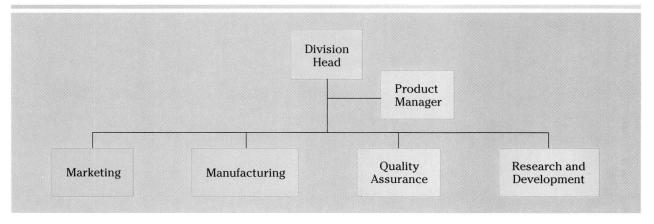

these linking role positions are designed to enhance communication among the various functional units and ensure that the right products are designed, manufactured, and marketed. We will say more about the product manager's role in Chapter 10.

Task Forces.　A *task force* serves much the same purpose as a linking role except that the role is temporary instead of permanent. In a task force, individuals from several units are brought together to solve a specific problem, usually in a short period of time. It is felt that each unit has expertise to contribute and that by coordinating these efforts a better solution can be achieved. A typical task force arrangement can be seen in Exhibit 8.15. For instance, a company facing a major financial cutback may create a task force consisting of members from across the company to identify ways to resolve the crisis. Or a company may create a task force to consider a joint venture offer from a foreign company. In both cases, the problem is immediate and diverse skills are required to reach an optimal solution.

Decoupling.　Finally, there are situations in which two or more closely related groups simply don't work together effectively. In such cases, *decoupling* may be the answer.[32] Decoupling involves separating two groups—physically or administratively—in such a way that the required tasks of the organization are fulfilled while the interaction between the two groups is minimized. For instance, ideally, hardware and software engineers should work closely together on the design of a new computing system. Yet sometimes these people see problems and solutions quite differently, which may lead to overt hostility and uncooperative behavior. One solution would be to

Exhibit 8.15
An Example of a
Typical Task Force

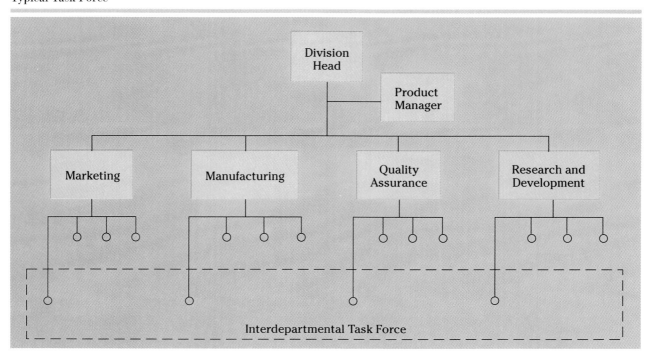

separate the two groups physically and then have one group (e.g., the hardware engineers) outline product specifications. Software engineers then could work more on their own to design software to meet these specifications. Obviously, some coordination would be required. Even so, such an approach could retain the services of two valued groups of engineers who see problems quite differently, and might be a wise compromise strategy for the high-tech company.

In essence, several strategies are available to assist managers in coordinating the diverse talents of interdependent groups in ways that help achieve organizational goals. The choice of an appropriate technique depends upon the unique situation facing the manager. One such approach to managing intergroup coordination was practiced at General Motors Company as it approached the design and manufacture of the Saturn.

IN PRACTICE
New Team Concepts at Saturn

Why is Karen Tibus upset that customers at her Saturn dealership are paying full price for their cars while customers at other rivals are enjoying deep discounts? It's simple. Ms. Tibus can't keep her showroom stocked. She estimates that she could be selling several times as many cars as she is, if she had them to sell. General Motor's new Saturn division couldn't keep up with demand. Saturn has become the highest-quality American-made brand with as few defects as Hondas and Nissans. It trails only Lexus and Infiniti in customer satisfaction, and these cars cost over twice as much as the Saturn models. What accounts for this amazing success?

One of the factors contributing to the high quality of the cars is the revolutionary (at least for GM) team structures at Saturn. At Saturn, blue-collar and white-collar workers are joined together in quality teams. Everyone is given authority to solve quality problems. For example, line workers who encounter quality problems can directly call suppliers to make them aware of the problems and even suggest how the problems might be corrected. Recently, a 14-member door team rearranged machinery to improve quality and productivity. Although the changes removed the need for two people, these people were redeployed within Saturn to other places where they were needed. This type of concern for quality and people fosters trust and commitment from employees. "You can trust the people you're working with. So if I come up with an idea, I won't be worked out of a job," says team member Gregory Arthur, a 20-year GM veteran. This new team approach at Saturn represented a radical departure in automobile manufacturing in this country. And the sales results for the cars support this effort.[33]

Even recalls are handled differently at Saturn. When it was discovered in late 1993 that a small part might present problems on some of the cars, the company immediately issued a recall of the affected cars. However, the recall was quite different from the myriad of other automobile recalls in recent years. First, the recall was voluntary; the company was not required to issue it but Saturn managers went ahead with it anyway to assure customers that everything possible was being done to ensure long-term product quality and reliability. And, second, when customers showed up to have the recall work done, many dealerships served them hamburger lunches and soft drinks while they waited for the two-hour job. As a result, customer commitment following the recall actually increased, and Saturn enhanced its reputation as a high-quality, customer-oriented car company.

PULLING IT ALL TOGETHER

Well-functioning teams or groups in complex tasks can be more productive and leave workers more satisfied than traditional arrangements. To function well, workers need the ability to effectively manage both the task requirements and the process or maintenance aspects of the group.

SUMMARY OF KEY POINTS

- A group is a collection of individuals who share a common set of norms, who generally have differentiated roles among themselves, and who interact with one another in the joint pursuit of common goals.

- Groups may be divided into permanent and temporary groups and formal and informal groups. Formal groups include command and task groups, whereas informal groups include friendship and interest groups.

- People join groups because they offer security, meet social needs, enhance self-esteem, fulfill economic interests, introduce them to people with mutual interests, and, sometimes, because they are in close physical proximity.

- Groups typically develop through several distinct stages, including forming, storming, norming, and performing.

- A role may be defined as an expected behavior pattern assigned or attributed to a particular position in the organization. Roles may be oriented toward the task, social relations, or the self.

- Interaction process analysis focuses on measuring who says what to whom within a group setting.

- Social loafing is a tendency for individual members of a group to reduce their task effort in the belief that other members will "cover" for them.

- A norm is a standard that is shared by group members and that regulates member behavior within an organization. Norms facilitate group survival, simplify expected behaviors, help members avoid embarrassing situations, and help identify group members.

- Asch's experiment in group pressure and individual judgment demonstrated that individuals will discount their own perceptions of a situation and follow the will of a group.

- Status systems serve to differentiate individuals on the basis of some criterion or set of criteria. Status incongruence occurs when one individual holds a position in the status hierarchy that is inconsistent with the conventional criteria for that position.

- Group cohesiveness is the extent to which individual members of a group are motivated to remain in the group.

▓ Work group effectiveness is defined by three criteria: group productivity, personal need satisfaction of the members, and the group's capacity for future cooperation.

▓ Intergroup performance is influenced by three interaction requirements. These include the requirements for interdependence, information, and integration.

▓ A linking role is a position or unit within the organization that is charged with overseeing and coordinating the activities of two or more groups.

▓ A task force consists of members from several departments or units who are brought together on a temporary basis to solve a specific and immediate problem.

▓ Decoupling refers to the practice of physically or administratively separating groups that are not able to work together effectively.

KEY WORDS

command group	role ambiguity
decoupling	role conflict
formal group	role episode
friendship group	role overload
group	role set
group cohesiveness	sequential interdependence
informal group	social loafing
information flow	status incongruence
interaction process analysis	status system
interest group	task force
linking role	task group
norms	task uncertainty
pooled interdependence	work role
reciprocal interdependence	work technology
return potential model	

QUESTIONS FOR DISCUSSION

1. What are the various types of groups often found in work situations?
2. Why do people join groups?
3. Describe the stages of group development.
4. How does work group size influence individual and group behavior?
5. Discuss the role of work group norms in the work situation.
6. Consider how groups influence conformity and deviance in work situations.
7. What is the major conclusion of Asch's experiment on group pressure and individual judgment?
8. Define a *role episode.*
9. Why is a knowledge of role relationships important for managers?
10. What purposes are served by status differentiations in work organizations? What problems emerge from these differentiations?

11. What determines group cohesiveness, and what impact does it have on group behavior?

12. Discuss how managers can improve intergroup relations and performance. Provide examples from your own experience to defend your arguments.

NOTES

1. J. Hoerr. "Sharpening Minds for a Competitive Edge" *Business Week,* December 17, 1990, pp. 72–78.
2. J. Hackman and C. Morris, "Group Tasks, Group Interaction Process, and Group Performance Effectiveness," in L. Berkowitz, ed., *Advances in Experimental Social Psychology,* vol. 8 (New York: Academic Press, 1975), p. 49.
3. J. McDavid and M. Harari, *Social Psychology: Individuals, Groups, and Societies* (New York: Harper & Row, 1968), p. 237.
4. B. Bass. *Leadership, Psychology, and Organizational Behavior* (New York: Harper & Row, 1960), p. 39.
5. G. Homans, *Social Behavior* (New York: Harcourt, Brace and World, 1950).
6. B. Tuckman and M. Jensen, "Stages of Small Group Development Revisited," *Groups and Organizational Studies,* 1977, *2,* pp. 419–442.
7. L. Hoffman, "Applying Experimental Research on Group Problem Solving to Organizations," *Journal of Applied Behavioral Science,* 1979, 15, pp. 375–391.
8. A. Hare, "Group Size," *American Behavioral Scientist,* 1981, *24,* pp. 695–708.
9. R. Bales and E. Borgatta, "Size of Group as a Factor in the Interaction Profile," In A. Hare, E. Borgatta, and R. Bales, eds., *Small Groups* (New York: Knopf, 1956).
10. L. Cummings and C. Berger, "Organization Structure: How Does It Influence Attitudes and Performance?" *Organizational Dynamics,* 1976, *5,* pp. 34–49.
11. S. Rhodes and R. Steers, *Managing Employee Absenteeism* (Reading, Mass.: Addison-Wesley, 1990).
12. L. Porter and R. Steers, "Organizational, Work, and Personal Factors in Employee Turnover and Absenteeism," *Psychological Bulletin,* 1973, *80,* pp. 151–176.
13. Cummings and Berger, op. cit.
14. T. Mitchell, *People in Organizations* (New York: McGraw-Hill, 1978), p. 188.
15. B. Latane, K. Williams, and S. Harkins, "Many Hands Make Light the Work: The Causes and Consequences of Social Loafing," *Journal of Personality and Social Psychology,* June 1979, pp. 822–832; J. Jackson and S. Harkins, "Equity in Effort: An Explanation of the Social Loafing Effect," *Journal of Personality and Social Psychology,* November 1985, pp. 1199–1206.
16. J. Hackman, "Group Influences on Individuals," in M. D. Dunnette, ed., *Handbook of Industrial and Organizational Psychology* (Chicago: Rand McNally, 1976).
17. D. Feldman, "The Development and Enforcement of Group Norms," *Academy of Management Review,* January 1984, pp. 47–53.
18. S. Asch, "Studies of Independence and Conformity: A Minority of One Against a Unanimous Majority," *Psychological Monographs,* 1955, *20,* Whole No. 416.
19. H. Reitman and M. Shaw, "Group Membership, Sex Composition of the Group, and Conformity Behavior," *Journal of Social Psychology,* 1964, 64, pp. 45–51.
20. S. Schachter, "Deviation, Rejection, and Communication," *Journal of Abnormal and Social Psychology,* 1951, *46,* pp. 190–207.
21. I. Janis, *Victims of Groupthink* (Boston: Houghton Mifflin, 1972), p. 32.
22. W. Scott, *Organization Theory* (Homewood, Ill.: Irwin, 1967).
23. J. Dean, *Blind Ambition* (New York: Simon & Schuster, 1976).

24. A. Harmetz, "Hollywood Office Politics Demands Marble and Natural Fabrics," *International Herald Tribune,* November 5, 1987, p. 1.

25. M. Yazinuma and R. Kennedy, "Life Is So Simple When You Know Your Place," *Intersect,* May 1986, pp. 35–39.

26. M. Shaw, *Group Dynamics* (New York: McGraw-Hill, 1981), p. 197.

27. D. Cartwright and A. Zander, *Group Dynamics: Research and Theory* (New York: Harper & Row, 1968); M. Shaw, op. cit.

28. J. Hoerr, "Benefits for the Back Office, Too," *Business Week,* July 10, 1989, p. 59.

29. J. R. Hackman, "The Design of Work Teams," in J. Lorsch, ed., *Handbook of Organizational Behavior* (Englewood Cliffs, N.J.: Prentice-Hall, 1987), pp. 300–345.

30. B. Dumaine, "Who Needs a Boss?" *Fortune,* May 7, 1990, pp. 52–60.

31. A. Szalagyi and M. Wallace, *Organizational Behavior and Performance* (Glenview, Ill.: Scott, Foresman, 1987).

32. J. Pfeffer, *Organizations and Organization Theory* (Boston: Pittman, 1982).

33. D. Woodruff, "Saturn," *Business Week,* August 17, 1992.

EXPERIENTIAL EXERCISE 8

The Paper Tower

This exercise focuses on understanding how task-oriented groups operate under specific time limits. In preparation for this exercise, the class should be divided into groups of five to eight persons. Each team should be provided with one 12-inch stack of newspapers and a roll of masking tape.

The Assignment   Each group is to design and build a paper tower that will be judged on the basis of one criteria: height.

> *Planning phase:* To begin, each group should spend 20 minutes planning its construction project. No actual construction or physical work can take place during this phase.
>
> *Construction phase:* Next, each group should actually construct its tower. The time limit here is 5 minutes.

Evaluation   After the group exercise, the instructor will determine which tower is the tallest. Next, as a class, you should answer the following questions:

1. During your group exercise, did all group members participate equally? Why, or why not?
2. Did you have a group leader? How was this leader selected?
3. Did different members serve different roles within the group? In what way?
4. Would you describe your group as effective or ineffective? Why?
5. What could your group have done to work more efficiently?
6. Was time utilized effectively? How did time constraints affect the group?

Source: This exercise is based on earlier work reported in Phillip Hunsaker and Johanna Hunsaker, "The Paper Tower Exercise: Experiencing Leadership and Group Dynamics," unpublished manuscript, 1979, and in Judith Gordon, *A Diagnostic Approach to Organizational Behavior,* 2nd ed. (Boston: Allyn and Bacon, 1983), pp. 321-322.

MANAGEMENT DILEMMA 8

Group Productivity at TCA Microelectronics

Warren Johnson is the general manager of TCA Microelectronics, a small nonunion Massachusetts-based electronics assembly company that is part of a larger conglomerate. Reporting directly to Mr. Johnson are his key staff officers, the office manager, the personnel and safety manager, and the production manager. The assembly units have unit supervisors, who report directly to the production manager.

Within the assembly groups, the workers have clear expectations concerning their own rights and privileges. Some of these "privileges" are obvious, whereas others are rather subtle. One of the more widely held values on the part of the workers is what they call "team autonomy." The workers know they have a job to do and expect that management will leave them alone to do it. The group members feel that their main obligation to the company is that of producing. Obedience to supervisors is displayed so long as it is directly related to a job to be done. Hostility often occurs when managers use discipline or forced obedience as means of asserting the will of management. By the same token, the workers appreciate management when they are given certain privileges or when flexibility is shown in discipline.

A second traditional right at TCA is "job bidding." Workers often use this as a way to circumvent formal supervisory authority. Job bidding is done by "bidding" for a vacant job in the plant; it can be prompted by a desire for either a job with higher status or a means of escaping an unpleasant foreman. The supervisors resent this practice, because they feel that they should have the prerogative of choosing their own subordinates, not the other way around.

A third benefit of working at TCA is the right to use company material for home repairs. The workers expect that they should have access to the company's finished product, either without charge or at a very large discount, and that company equipment should be made available for use in repairing broken-down machinery or household furnishings.

Recently, Mr. Johnson received word from the home office that he could expect about $15 million worth of new equipment to be added to his plant's assembly facility. Along with the equipment, the home office notified Johnson that they were transferring Ralph Moxon from the home office to replace TCA's retiring production manager. Moxon had served as an officer in the U.S. Marines and had an outstanding industrial record, too. It was hoped by the board of directors that the change of leadership and the addition of equipment would add considerably to TCA's productivity and profit margin.

Among Moxon's first moves upon arrival were stopping the practice of allowing workers to have access to company equipment and reducing the discount given on the purchase of company-made equipment. He was able to do this after showing Johnson that several thousands of dollars in sales had been lost from abuse of this particular privilege in the last year alone; some workers had resold company equipment at considerable profits. Another move by Moxon was to eliminate the job-bidding policy and to replace it with a new seniority system. The new system was roundly applauded by the supervisors, but workers became noticeably irritable and frustrated. However, Moxon maintained that once an order was given, it was to be followed without question.

Moxon made rounds every hour to check on the progress of the work flow. During the course of his first four months, he instituted many technical changes designed to speed up production and reduce labor costs. During this period, however, tensions with the workers mounted. Dissatisfaction over the installment of new machinery became a focal point of the disruption. If the company could afford to spend so much for machinery, workers complained, why couldn't it afford higher wages for the employees?

After six months on the job, Moxon received a notice from the home office inviting him to attend a month-long managerial training seminar in New York. Mr. Johnson decided to leave Moxon's position vacant in his absence and to ask each shift supervisor to be responsible for his or her particular shift with no further supervision. Shortly after Moxon left, Johnson learned from a supervisor that the employees wanted the lunchroom painted; it had been years since it was last painted, and it looked dismal. Without hesitation Johnson instructed the maintenance crew to go to work on the job. In addition, he told the supervisors to feel free to handle such minor grievances and requests on their own authority until Moxon returned.

During the following week another complaint emerged from the employees. This time the problem concerned the company's policy of requiring mandatory overtime to get production out. Johnson considered the complaint and proposed that if production reached 3000 units per day (a 500-unit increase), he could then eliminate mandatory overtime. Within a few days production reached the level indicated. Unfortunately, this action backfired, because the head office then demanded that production be increased again to meet a new backlog of orders. Johnson went back to his employees and asked that they return to the overtime schedule until the back orders were filled. Although there was some grumbling, most of the workers continued to perform effectively. Within a week, the press for more production was reduced so that it was possible to drop the overtime requirement again.

A third problem the employees brought up concerned the plant whistle. This whistle traditionally blew at the beginning and end of the shift, as well as at five-minute rest periods and at lunch. One of the employees suggested that the company use the public address system instead. At first, employees ridiculed the new system, but in a few days they took announcements as a matter of course; in one instance, when the announcement was not made, the employees returned from lunch just the same. Later on in the month, announcements were dropped, yet the employees started and stopped work on time.

One month after Moxon had left for New York, Johnson surveyed the production record for the plant and discovered that it had actually increased by 20 percent. Johnson couldn't understand what had happened. Production had increased significantly without the presence of the production manager.

On the basis of the above information, answer the following:

1. Why do you think production was up by 20 percent with no production manager present?
2. How do you think Johnson's actions affected employees' "higher-order needs"?
3. Do you think Johnson handled the situation correctly?
4. What would you do now if you were Johnson?

9

Job Design and Productivity

The Management Challenge

- To design jobs in an efficient yet rewarding manner.
- To integrate the latest job technology with the human needs of the workplace.
- To understand how to schedule work so it meets both organizational and individual needs.
- To secure employee participation in workplace efficiency and effectiveness.
- To stay ahead of the competition in production technology.

CLOSE UP — Job Redesign at Citibank

Mildred Gorman worked in the stock and bond transfer department of Citibank. The department was responsible for the transfer of ownership of stocks and bonds from one person to another. This process involved 11 different functions from opening envelopes containing transfer requests to printing the new certificates. Each of the steps involved a separate job that was designed to be simple and easy to learn. Because of the volume of requests, literally dozens of people might be employed to do one job such as opening envelopes. Mildred's job was "the yellows" or taking the yellow verification sheets and stamping them and then putting them in a pile to move on to the next step. Mildred processed thousands of yellows each week, week in and week out.

Job redesign in the department was undertaken because costs for the department were high, service was slow, and mistakes were common, all of which resulted in dissatisfied customers and workers. The redesign involved combining all previous 11 steps and jobs into one job. Mildred received a new title of Work Station professional. In her new job, she examined the transfer request to make sure it was in order, entered the necessary information into the computer, verified the information, authorized the transfer, checked the transfer, made sure it was recorded in the central computer, and printed the new certificate.

The time it took to complete the entire transaction went from two days to just a few minutes. Costs also came down, in part because fewer supervisors were need but also because mistakes and the time and cost to correct them nearly disappeared. Both customers and employees were also much more satisfied.[1]

Whether we are talking about improving quality or improving productivity, companies around the globe are seeking ways to redesign the workplace so it is both more efficient and more rewarding for its workers. How to accomplish this in an effective and economical way is clearly a challenge to management. As we enter the 1990s, employees are demanding more and more from their jobs and companies, while companies are increasingly facing external threats if they do not become more efficient. One way that many companies have achieved a balance between these competing forces is through job redesign efforts. Through such means, employees can often be given "better" jobs while the company gets higher operating results. How companies achieve this balance is the topic of this chapter.

THE TEN WORST JOBS IN THE WORLD

People are often overhead saying things such as, "I hate my job" or "My job is one of the worst in the world." Sometimes when people say such things it simply means that they have had a bad day or week; other times, they are quite serious. Obviously, some jobs are less challenging or less rewarding than others. Some jobs carry higher status, and some jobs have greater long-term opportunities. In an effort to highlight these differences, one study went so far as to try to identify the ten worst jobs in contemporary industrial society.[2] Here, in no particular order, are the jobs identified:

Assembly line worker
Highway toll collector
Car watcher in tunnel
Typist in a typing pool
Bank guard
Copy machine operator
Bogus typesetter (typesetters who set type that is not to be used)
Computer tape librarian (a fancy title for a person whose job it is to roll up spools of tape all day)
Housewife (not to be confused with mother)
Automatic elevator operator

Although we may disagree with specific choices here—and many of us may wish to add our own jobs to this list—jobs such as these clearly lack the attributes or qualities we expect in decent jobs. Even so, someone has to do them. The challenge for managers is how to take boring or routine jobs and reshape them so they are both more rewarding and more productive. This may involve engineering or technical changes, or it may involve changing the social context in which such jobs are carried out. In both cases, managers bear a responsibility to consider job redesign efforts to the extent that they affect operations efficiency and employee well-being.

In this chapter, we will consider several aspects of job redesign and productivity enhancement techniques. We begin by reviewing early approaches to job design to provide a frame of reference for understanding the more contemporary approaches. Next, we will examine how job redesign works. Two specific models of the impact of job redesign will be presented. The importance of quality control in any manufacturing system is then considered. On the basis of this, we will review several specific techniques for redesigning jobs. Some of these will rely on engineering approaches, some on work rescheduling, and some on integrating the technical and the social systems. Finally, we will conclude with a brief look at the problems and prospects associated with job redesign in the workplace.

EARLY APPROACHES TO JOB REDESIGN

Serious efforts to efficiently structure the jobs that people perform date from the early 1800s and the rise of the Industrial Revolution. As factories grew in size and developed in sophistication, greater efforts were made to break down jobs so they could be performed more quickly and with less training cost and time. It was reasoned that because workers were mostly economically motivated, efforts at job fractionization would benefit both companies and workers. Companies would benefit because of increased efficiency and output. Workers would benefit, it was thought, because the piece-rate compensation system tied monetary rewards directly to output—the greater the production, the higher the wages.

Scientific Management

Prior to the Industrial Revolution, output of goods was primarily carried out by skilled craftworkers organized into various guilds. Everyone had a trade, and quality was reasonably good; but production was very slow and inefficient. The Industrial Revolution changed this by standardizing manufacturing techniques with the aim of increasing output and reducing costs. The resulting attempts to simplify work design reached their zenith, from a technological standpoint, in the assembly line production techniques that became popular in the early 1900s (see Exhibit 9.1). For example, a study of assembly line technology in automobile manufacturing identified six predominant characteristics of job fractionization:[3]

1. *Machine pacing.* The production rate is determined by the speed of the conveyor belt and not by the workers.
2. *Repetitiveness.* Tasks are performed over and over during a single work shift. On auto assembly lines, for example, typical work cycles (that is, the time allowed for an entire piece of work) range from 30 seconds to 1.5 minutes. This means the worker performs the same task up to 500 times per day.
3. *Low skill requirements.* Because of the simplified task requirements, jobs can be easily learned, and workers are easily replaced.
4. *Task specialization.* Each job consists of only a few operations. Final product assembly is often done elsewhere in the factory, so workers seldom see the complete product.

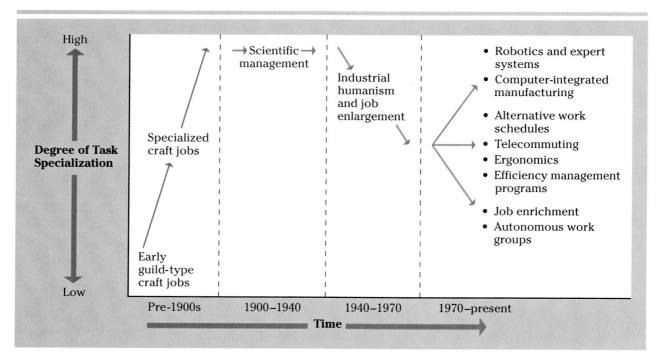

Exhibit 9.1
Evolution of Approaches
to Job Design

5. *Limited social interaction.* Because of the speed of the assembly line, noise, and physical separation, it is difficult to develop meaningful social relationships on the job.

6. *Tools and techniques specified.* Staff specialists (usually industrial engineers) select the tools and techniques to be used by the workers to maximize efficiency of operations.

These principles are typical of the techniques suggested by advocates of *scientific management* (such as Frederick Taylor). Although these techniques led to early successes on the shop floor in terms of increased productivity, drawbacks also began to appear that nullified many of the advances made. First, job fractionization or fragmentation ignored human needs for growth and development. Taylor, considered the father of scientific management, noted that "one of the very first requirements for a man who is fit to handle pig iron as a regular occupation is that he more nearly resembles in his mental makeup the ox than any other type."[4] This view of employees hardly encouraged efforts to improve working conditions.

Second, it became apparent in the early 1920s that job fractionization led to boredom and unauthorized breaks. People simply did not like their jobs, and they reacted by not cooperating with the wishes of management. Sabotage and unionization efforts also became prevalent during this period.

Industrial Humanism

Partly as a result of these problems, concern for improving job attitudes at work began in the 1930s. Behavioral scientists began seriously examining the plight of the worker, and, under the rubric of *industrial humanism* (also known as the Human Relations movement—see Chapter 6), efforts were made to make employees happier on their jobs. Human relations training came into vogue, as did company newspapers, employee awards, and company social events. However, the basic nature of the job itself remained unchanged, and the problems persisted. It was not until the 1960s that the concept of job enrichment emerged as a potential solution to problems of worker aberration and poor performance.

Herzberg's Contribution to Job Enrichment

One of the most significant early contributors to job design was Frederick Herzberg.[5] In fact, it was Herzberg who first called for *job enrichment*—that is, actually changing the nature of the tasks employees perform instead of simply giving employees more of the same kinds of tasks (called *job enlargement*). On the basis of a study of accountants and engineers, Herzberg discovered that employees tended to describe satisfying experiences in terms of factors that were intrinsic to the job itself. These factors were called *motivators* and included such variables as achievement, recognition, responsibility, advancement, and personal growth. On the other hand, these same employees described dissatisfying experiences in terms of non-job-related factors (called *hygiene* factors). Hygiene factors included salary, company policies, supervisory style, and co-worker relations; all of these were factors that surrounded but did not include the job activities themselves.

On the basis of these findings, Herzberg argued against the efforts toward industrial humanism that prevailed at the time. These efforts treated hygiene factors, although the roots of employee motivation lay in the job itself. The implication of this conclusion for managers is clear: employee motivation can be enhanced through changes in the nature of the job (job enrichment). Efforts to change or enrich the job could include the following:

> *Control over resources.* Employees should have maximum control over the mechanisms of task performance.
> *Accountability.* Employees should be held accountable for their performance.
> *Feedback.* Supervisors have a responsibility to provide direct, clear, and frequent feedback.
> *Work pace.* Within limits, employees should be able to set their own work pace.
> *Achievement opportunities.* Jobs should allow employees to experience a feeling of accomplishment.
> *Personal growth and development.* Employees should be able to learn new and different procedures on the job and should be able to experience some degree of personal growth.

Herzberg formulated a series of principles for vertically "loading" jobs so they would be more motivating. These principles are shown in Exhibit 9.2. A comparison of this list with the earlier list pertaining to attributes of scientific management will show a marked difference in management philosophies of the nature of tasks in the workplace. The philosophy underlying job enrichment takes a more optimistic view of the nature of workers and their needs, drives, and aspirations. It assumes that employees want to tackle problems

Exhibit 9.2
Herzberg's Principles of
Vertical Job Loading

- Remove job controls while retaining employee accountability.
- Increase accountability of employees for their own work.
- Provide employees with a complete unit of work.
- Provide employees with increased authority where possible.
- Provide employees with direct feedback on job performance.
- Give employees new and more difficult tasks than they have previously handled.
- Assign employees specific or specialized tasks, enabling them to become experts.

at work and want to use their creative abilities. In this sense, it assumes that money, although important, is clearly not the only important motivator of good performance.

As is the case with any new theory, Herzberg's model did not escape criticism. It has been sharply criticized on several points: (1) it ignores individual differences, assuming all employees want an enriched job; (2) the existence of two independent and unrelated factors (motivators and hygiene factors) has not been substantiated; (3) the theory itself is open to different interpretations, and Herzberg failed to present an unambiguous statement of the model; and (4) the model does not explain how factors such as achievement and recognition influence motivation; it does not describe the psychological processes underlying job design and motivation.[6] Despite his model's limitations, however, Herzberg deserves considerable credit for ushering in the concept of job enrichment as a central topic in the study of people at work. In fact, much of the current work on job design can be traced directly to his early formulations.

HOW JOB REDESIGN WORKS

Today there exist several contemporary and often overlapping approaches to changing the design of work. Moreover, there are innumerable specific techniques that have been used by companies in their efforts to improve the workplace. Instead of comparing the nuances or finer points of these models, we may make better progress by simply combining the various models into the study of work redesign. This is the approach taken here. Specifically, we will examine two divergent approaches to job design: the job characteristics model and the social-information-processing approach. First, however, we should pause to consider for a moment why managers should be interested in job redesign.

Why Redesign Work?

Redesigning jobs does not offer a panacea for organizational problems. Nor is it appropriate in all situations. Rather, job redesign is a systematic technique that has been found to be useful for improving life at work in a number of situations. Why has job redesign proved successful as a change strategy? Richard Hackman, a noted job redesign researcher, suggests four basic reasons.[7]

1. *Job redesign alters the basic relationship between people and their jobs.* It is based on the premise that the work itself can be a powerful influence on motivation, performance, and satisfaction. Changing the job can increase intrinsic motivation.

2. *Job redesign directly changes behavior.* Instead of attempting to change attitudes and hope that attitude change results in behavior change, work redesign focuses directly on what employees do—on their behavior. It is thought that as a result of experiencing more rewarding work, employees develop more favorable attitudes, which then reinforce behavior. Hence, the behavior change tends to be longer lasting.

3. *Job redesign opens numerous opportunities for initiating other changes.* Advocates of systems theory note that changes in one area often cause changes in other areas. So it is with work redesign. The very act of implementing this technique points to other areas within the organization where changes could be made (such as offering supervisory training, skills training, or a career development program). The initiation of one change in a work situation often makes it easier to initiate others.

4. *If done correctly, job redesign can ultimately result in organizations that rehumanize rather than dehumanize people at work.* In contrast to the effects of assembly line technology, work redesign can help individuals experience feelings of personal growth and development as a result of engaging in challenging work activities. People are rewarded for creative activities and for accepting responsibility for task accomplishment. As a result, they may find it easier to satisfy their higher-order needs at work.

In short, job redesign offers the promise that organizations can develop work environments that challenge employees and make better use of their human resources. If properly carried out, job redesign can help managers facilitate organizational effectiveness while at the same time improving the quality of working life.

The Job Characteristics Model

There have been several recent attempts to develop a model of how job redesign influences employees and their behavior. To date, the model that has received the widest attention is that proposed by Hackman and Oldham, known as the *job characteristics model.*[8] This model summarizes and integrates much of the earlier work in the area.

The job characteristics model, shown in Exhibit 9.3, consists of four parts. As shown, five core job dimensions influence three critical psychological states, which in turn influence several desired personal and work outcomes. The links between job dimensions and psychological states and between psychological states and outcomes are moderated by employee growth need strengths. We will briefly review this process.

Exhibit 9.3
The Job Characteristics
Model of Job Redesign

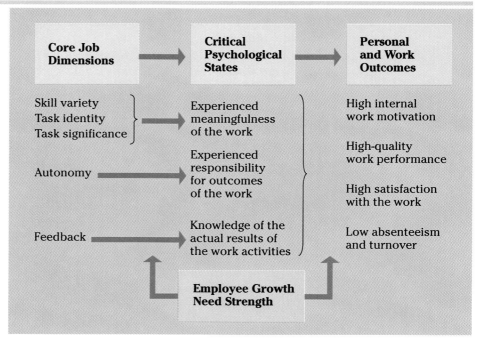

Source: J. R. Hackman and G. R. Oldham, "Motivation Through the Design of Work: Test of a Theory," *Organizational Behavior and Human Performance 16* (1976): 250–279. Reprinted by permission.

Critical Psychological States.   According to the model, an employee's motivation and satisfaction are influenced by three psychological states:

1. *Experienced meaningfulness of the work.* Employees must feel that the work is important, worthwhile, and valuable.
2. *Experienced responsibility for work outcomes.* Employees must feel personally responsible and accountable for the results of the work they perform.
3. *Knowledge of results.* Employees must receive regular feedback concerning the quality of their performance.

As Hackman explains, "The model postulates that internal rewards are obtained by an individual when he *learns* [knowledge of results] that he *personally* [experienced responsibility] has performed well on a task that he *cares about* [experienced meaningfulness]."[9] The more these three psychological states are present on a job, the more satisfied individuals will feel when they perform well. These internal rewards act as incentives for individuals to continue their efforts to perform; they hold forth the promise of additional intrinsic rewards. When individuals fail to perform well, positive reinforcement is not forthcoming, and they may be motivated to try harder on subsequent tasks in order to regain the intrinsic rewards.

It is worthwhile to point out some similarities between these three factors articulate by Hackman and Oldham and principles of motivation covered in Chapter 6. For example, experienced meaningfulness of the work is similar to valued outcomes in the expectancy theory of motivation in that both ideas require that workers care about what happens in order to be motivated. The notion of experienced responsibility for work outcomes in the job characteristic model is similar to the E→P and P→O relationships in expectancy theory in that both require that workers see a link between what they put in to the job and what results. Finally, the requirement of knowledge of results in the job characteristic model is also a critical component of goal-setting theory.

Core Job Dimensions.   What activates these psychological states? According to Exhibit 9.3, five core job dimensions combine to determine motivational level. *Skill variety* is the degree to which a job requires the use of a number of different skills and talents. *Task identity* is the degree to which the job requires completion of a whole and identifiable piece of work—that is, to which it permits doing a job from beginning to end with a visible outcome. *Task significance* is the degree to which a job has an impact on the lives or work of other people in the immediate organization or in the external environment. *Autonomy* is the degree to which a job provides substantial freedom, independence, and discretion to an individual for purposes of scheduling work and determining the procedures to be used in carrying it out. The fifth core job dimension is *feedback*—the degree to which carrying out work activities required by the job results in individuals obtaining direct and clear information about the effectiveness of their performance.

The first three job dimensions above are believed to influence the experienced meaningfulness of work, as shown in the exhibit. Autonomy influences experienced responsibility for work outcomes, whereas feedback influences knowledge of results. Any work redesign effort should, according to the model, attempt to develop jobs that are high in these core dimensions.

The job dimensions are often measured by a questionnaire developed by Hackman and Oldham. On the basis of this questionnaire, it is possible to calculate a *motivating potential score (MPS)* that reflects the extent to which employees see their jobs as motivating. According to the model, a high MPS is only possible if a job is high on at least one of the three dimensions that influence experienced meaningfulness and on both autonomy and feedback. The existence of these three dimensions creates the necessary work environment for all three critical psychological states. Mathematically, then, the MPS can be calculated as follows:

$$\text{Motivating potential score} = \frac{\left[\begin{array}{c}\text{Skill} \\ \text{variety}\end{array} + \begin{array}{c}\text{Task} \\ \text{identity}\end{array} + \begin{array}{c}\text{Task} \\ \text{significance}\end{array}\right]}{3} \times \text{Autonomy} \times \text{Feedback}$$

This formula shows that a near-zero score on any of the three critical psychological states will reduce the MPS score to near zero. Again, it is important to note that all three factors are imperative in redesigning work. Exhibit 9.4 illustrates how this works. This exhibit shows the hypothetical employee responses to two jobs—one enriched and one unenriched. As can be seen, the resulting motivating potential scores (MPSs) are quite different.

If you are interested in applying this MPS model to a job you currently hold or previously held, simply complete Self-Assessment 9.1. Follow the

Exhibit 9.4
Profiles of Enriched and
Unenriched Jobs

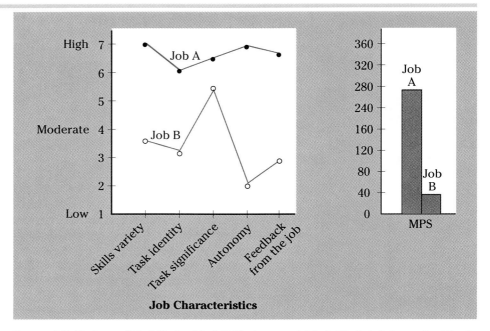

Job Characteristics

Source: J. R. Hackman, "Work Design," in J. R. Hackman and J. L. Suttle (eds.), *Improving Life at Work: Behavioral Science Approaches to Organizational Change* (Santa Monica, Calif.: Goodyear, 1977), p. 135. Reprinted by permission of J. R. Hackman.

instructions, and you will discover not only how your job compares on the core job dimensions, but also what your MPS score is. Refer to Appendix B for scoring procedures when you have finished.

Employee Growth Need Strength. Hackman and Oldham use *growth need strength* to refer to a collection of higher-order needs (achievement, affiliation, autonomy) that they believe moderate the way in which employees react to the work environment (see discussion in Chapter 5). This influence emerges at two points in the model (refer to Exhibit 9.3). First, employees with high growth need strength (GNS) are more likely to experience the desired psychological states when their objective job has been enriched than those with low GNS. This occurs because, on the basis of their needs, they are more sensitive to (have a greater demand for) these job characteristics.

Second, high GNS individuals tend to respond more favorably to the psychological states when they occur than do low GNS individuals, because these states are more likely to facilitate the satisfaction of these higher-order needs. For instance, a person who has a high need for achievement can satisfy that need by successfully performing challenging tasks (tasks with a high MPS). On the other hand, a person with a low need for achievement may experience frustration or anxiety by being placed on a job with such demands. The role of individual differences must be emphasized when designing work for people. It must be recognized that enriched jobs may have greater impact on some people (high GNS individuals) than on others.

SELF-ASSESSMENT 9.1
The Job Diagnostic Survey

Instructions (Part One): Please describe your present job (or a previous paid or unpaid job you have had) using the questionnaire below. For each question, circle the number (1 through 7) that best describes your own job. Be as objective as possible in describing this job on the various scales.

Name of the job to be described: _____

1. How much *variety* is there in your job? That is, to what extent does the job require you to do many different things at work, using a variety of your skills and talents?

    1_____2_____3_____4_____5_____6_____7

    | Very little; the job requires me to do the same routine things over and over again. | Moderate variety. | Very much; the job requires me to do many different things, using a number of different skills and talents. |

2. To what extent does your job involve doing a *"whole"* and *identifiable piece of work?* That is, is the job a complete piece of work that has an obvious beginning and end? Or is it only a small part of the overall piece of work, which is finished by other people or by automatic machines?

    1_____2_____3_____4_____5_____6_____7

    | My job is only a tiny part of the overall piece of work; the results of my activities cannot be seen in the final product or service. | My job is a moderate-sized "chunk" of the overall piece of work; my own contribution can be seen in the final outcome. | My job involves doing the whole piece of work from start to finish; the results of my activities are easily seen in the final product or service. |

3. In general, *how significant or important* is your job? That is, are the results of your work likely to significantly affect the lives or well-being of other people?

    1_____2_____3_____4_____5_____6_____7

    | Not very significant; the outcomes of my work are *not* likely to have important effects on other people. | Moderately significant. | Highly significant; the outcomes of my work can affect other people in very important ways. |

4. How much *autonomy* is there in your job? That is, to what extent does your job permit you to decide *on your own* how to go about doing the work?

    1_____2_____3_____4_____5_____6_____7

    | Very little; the job gives me almost no personal "say" about how and when the work is done. | Moderate autonomy; many things are standardized and not under my control, but I can make some decisions about the work. | Very much; the job gives me almost complete responsibility for deciding how and when the work is done. |

continued

continued from p. 289

5. To what extent does *doing the job* itself provide you with information about your work performance? That is, does the actual *work* itself provide clues about how well you are doing—aside from any "feedback" co-workers or supervisors may provide?

1_____2_____3_____4_____5_____6_____7

| Very little; the job itself is set up so I could work forever without finding out how well I am doing. | Moderately; sometimes doing the job provides "feedback" to me; sometimes it does not. | Very much; the job is set up so that I get almost constant "feedback" as I work about how well I am doing. |

Instructions (Part Two): On the basis of your answers to the Job Diagnostic Survey, you can now calculate your Motivating Potential Score (see text). the MPS represents a summary score indicating how motivating the job you have described is. Insert you scores on the Job Diagnostic Survey (the numbers 1 through 7) into the following formula to calculate your MPS.

$$\text{MPS} = \frac{\left[\begin{array}{c} \text{skill} \quad \text{task} \quad \text{task} \\ \text{variety} + \text{identity} + \text{significance} \end{array}\right]}{3} \times \text{autonomy} \times \text{feedback}.$$

Your MPS = _____

Source: Based on the work of J. R. Hackman and G. R. Oldham, in *Work Redesign,* pp. 277–279. © 1980, Addison-Wesley Publishing Company, Inc., Reading, Massachusetts. Reprinted with permission of the publisher.

This may also mean that jobs which have low potential for enrichment may be less frustrating to individuals with low GNS than individuals with high GNS, which in turn has implications for selection practices.

Personal and Work Outcomes.   Finally, the model indicates that several personal and work-related outcomes result from the interaction of psychological states and GNS. Specifically, when people experience the psychological states described in the model, one would expect them to exhibit high levels of internal work motivation, high quality of performance, high job satisfaction, and low turnover and absenteeism. Although the psychological states are clearly not the only variables to affect these outcomes, they are believed to be important influences.

Research on the Job Characteristics Model.   As is the case with any conceptual model of human behavior, providing for a thorough test is difficult. Although considerable research on the model has been published, most of it has taken the form of correlational designs rather than experimental designs (see Appendix A). Although caution is advised in evaluating the results, it is possible to summarize the research to date on the validity of the model.

On the positive side, several studies have found that people who work on jobs high in the core job dimensions are more motivated and satisfied than people who work on jobs low in these dimensions. Similar (though weaker) findings exist for absenteeism. Second, the MPS-outcome relationship has been found to be stronger for employees with a high GNS than for those with a low GNS. Third, some inferential evidence supports the claim that the core job dimensions work through psychological states to influence outcomes.[10]

On the negative side, however, several limitations should be noted. First, the forecasting powers of the model are far less significant in predicting performance than job satisfaction. In fact, the model is rather poor at predicting performance, although this may be caused by the difficulty of measuring the study variables. In addition, considerable trouble has been experienced in attempting to demonstrate conclusively that core job dimensions work through psychological states to influence outcomes. In view of the fact that we are dealing with psychological (and nonobservable) variables, this difficulty is understandable.[11]

In summary, the job characteristics model does appear to represent a useful conceptual framework for understanding how and why work redesign influences employee behavior and attitudes. Although more work on the topic is needed, the utility of the model for management practice should not be overlooked.

Principles for Redesigning Work

On the basis of the job characteristics model (and earlier work on the topic), Hackman has proposed five principles, or guidelines, for enriching jobs and redesigning work. These principles suggest ways in which managers can make substantive work changes as well as ways in which such changes will affect the core job dimensions (refer to Exhibit 9.3). Together, the principles illustrate very clearly how the model can be applied to work situations.

1. *Form mutual work units.* To the extent possible, work load should be divided into natural work units—pieces of work that logically fit together. For instance, an assembly line worker may be given the responsibility for both assembling and inspecting a particular part instead of just assembling it. Forming natural work units allows employees to increase their ownership of the work and to see its significance.
2. *Combine tasks.* Similarly, jobs can be enlarged by combining several of their related aspects. For instance, an assembler can be assigned responsibility for assembling several interrelated parts instead of just one. By combining tasks, skill variety and task identity are both increased.
3. *Establish client relationships.* Jobs that are traditionally designed (assembly line or fractionated jobs) provide little or no contact between the producer (employee) and the clients, whether these clients are inside or outside the organization. Establishing client relationships has several consequences. First, feedback increases, because the ultimate user is now in a position to respond to the quality of the product or service. Second, skill variety may increase, because the producer (employee) now needs to develop the interpersonal skills necessary to interact with clients. Third, autonomy may also increase, as the producer now has the responsibility of deciding how to manage the relationship with the clients.
4. *Vertical loading.* Hackman's fourth principle, the principle of vertical loading, aims at closing the gap between the doing and controlling

aspects of work. For example, employees are permitted to select their own work methods, inspect their own work, choose their hours of work, or participate in decisions affecting their jobs or the organization. By doing so, employee autonomy is increased.

5. *Open feedback channels.* A manager can make a fifth substantive work change, according to Hackman, by opening feedback channels. Most employees receive supervisor-provided feedback about their job performance. However, using work redesign, another kind of feedback emerges: job-provided feedback. When jobs are designed so they provide built-in feedback mechanisms (having employees check their own work), employees are continually reminded of their performance quality, and these reminders come from the job, without the interpersonal problems inherent in supervisor-provided feedback.

The principles suggested here are meant to illustrate the types of intervention that can be used in organizations. Through techniques such as these, it may be possible to build core job dimensions that sufficiently cue psychological states and lead to employee motivation and satisfaction. But as we will see in the examples below, this is easier said than done.

IN PRACTICE
Enriched Jobs at General Mills

General Mills Factory jobs in General Mills' plants were typical of those based on principles of scientific management; they were simple, limited, repetitive, and boring. Supervisors would tell workers what to do and they would do it, though not always enthusiastically. A worker simply focused on his or her own job. If you were in charge of punching a button every time a large container of cereal was full, you didn't worry if the cereal looked bad or if the machine broke down. Those were someone else's problems.

Although the continuous nature of the cereal-making process would not allow workers to be involved from the beginning to the end of the process, it was possible to redesign jobs so that they were more meaningful and involved some responsibility and autonomy. One of the first, simple, but dramatic changes was making workers responsible for the maintenance of the machines they operated. Thus, instead of waiting around for maintenance people to come and repair machines, workers could take care of their own preventive maintenance and repairs.

In plants where these changes have been made, production is up 40 percent over comparable traditional factories within General Mills. In general, workers like the added responsibility.[12]

The Social-Information-Processing Model

A second way to examine the effects of job redesign efforts is to analyze the process from the standpoint of social information processing. The basic assumptions of this approach were discussed in Chapter 3. It will be remembered that this approach argues that employees create their own perceptions concerning the nature of the job on the basis of socially constructed realities. It is these perceptions, and not the objective realities of the situation, that then govern employee responses. Thus, if an employee thinks he or she has a monotonous, routine job (regardless of how others would describe it), the employee will respond accordingly. Job satisfaction will probably decline and absenteeism increase as the employee tries to avoid a nonrewarding situation. This is the employee's socially constructed reality.

The *social-information-processing model* suggests four basic ways in which an employee's social environment (especially his or her co-workers) can affect the employee's views of a job:[13]

1. An employee's social environment often provides cues concerning which *dimensions* employees should use in describing a job. These dimensions may include the length of rest breaks, the rapidity of the work pace, the interpersonal skills of the supervisor, and so forth. Perhaps the new employee's co-workers will stress the difficulty of the job as the central dimension and ignore the compensation rate or company benefits. Whatever dimensions are selected, the social environment can influence the newcomer by highlighting those particular dimensions as being salient.

2. An employee's social environment can also provide cues concerning how the employee should evaluate or *weight* these various dimensions. For example, the group may emphasize job autonomy over job variety.

3. An employee's social environment often provides cues concerning *co-workers' previous evaluations* of these job dimensions. For instance, group members may warn a new employee to watch out for a certain supervisor or to avoid a certain job assignment on the basis of their own past experiences.

4. Finally, at times the social context provides *direct evaluations* of the work environment, leaving it to the employee to construct a rationale or explanation for the group's overall assessment. For instance, group members may tell new employees that the supervisor is "bad news" but may not explain why. Such definitive assessments often color the new employee's opinions, although the rationale behind such judgments often is not explained.

Social influences such as these combine with the new employee's own assessments to determine how the job is actually perceived. This process is shown in Exhibit 9.5. Here it can be seen that an employee's perceptions of the job are influenced by three factors: objective observations, input from other members of the work group, and personal opinions and expectations. The resulting perceptions largely determine the employee's attitudes toward and behavior on the job.

If there is a lesson for management here it is that managers cannot assume that because they have changed (enriched?) a job, the employee will share the perception that the new job is, indeed, better. In view of the fact that behavior is largely governed by perceptions, managers would be wise to consider how the employees themselves see the nature of work, not just how the manager sees it. Managers may also need to worry as much about communicating and establishing the perception that job enrichment and its specifics have been undertaken as they do about implementing the specific changes in the jobs.

Exhibit 9.5
The Social-Information-
Processing Model of
Job Redesign

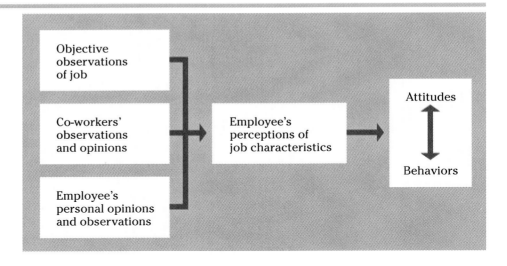

TOTAL QUALITY CONTROL

The new emphasis on quality in manufacturing and service represents an important shift for industry and must be recognized in any effort to redesign or modify production technologies in the workplace. That is, redesigning employees' jobs so they are more challenging and rewarding helps little if the basic product lacks quality and market acceptance. Hence, the notion of total quality control must be integrated into any job redesign effort. Productivity in any operation can be measured by two interrelated factors: how much you can produce efficiently and how good your product is. For many years, many Western countries focused on expanding the former, often at the expense of the latter. Now the emphasis has changed. That is, wherever we look in North American industries—from cars to computers to machinery to airplanes—we can find pace-setting examples of companies producing high-quality products for the marketplace and making a profit in the process.

Quality as a Way of Doing Business

This central role of quality in production and service is shown in Exhibit 9.6, which shows both the short- and long-term effects of producing quality products. This exhibit was suggested by C. Edwards Deming, considered by many to be the founder of modern-day quality control techniques. Deming argues that quality assurance efforts must be scientific, systematic, and comprehensive. From this, we get the term *total quality control.*

Recently, managers have come to realize that quality is not something that is measured at or near the end of the production process. Rather, quality is an essential ingredient of the production process itself.[14] It is an overall way of doing business and becomes the concern of all employees. When viewed in this way, the following conditions can be expected:

■   The number of product defects decreases, causing an increase in yield.

■   Making it right the first time reduces reject rates and rework time.

■   Making employees responsible for quality reduces the need for added inspectors.

It has been argued that if quality control is to be effective, management's commitment to quality must be absolute and systematic. As Tom Peters notes, effective quality control programs are characterized by the following:[15]

■   Management is obsessed with quality and places it on the top of every agenda.

■   Quality is measured. This is often done through *statistical quality control,* or the application of quantitative techniques to measure and guarantee high standards of excellence.

■   Quality is rewarded. Executive pay includes quality incentives, and subcontractors or suppliers are penalized if quality declines.

■   Every employee, from the CEO down, is trained in quality assessment.

■   Teams comprising members from different functions or departments in the organization cooperate to identify and solve quality problems.

Exhibit 9.6
The Deming Chain Reaction
of Quality

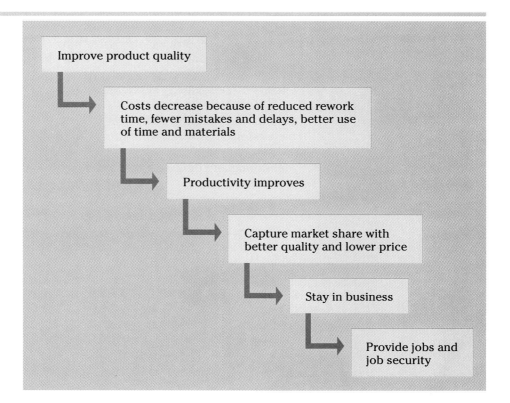

■ Small improvements are not overlooked. The Japanese call this *kaizen engineering,* or the process of making continual though small improvements in both the product and the production process.

■ There is a never-ending encouragement of ways to improve quality.

■ There is a parallel organization structure devoted to quality improvement. That is, each department and division has its respective quality unit, and these units are arranged hierarchically.

■ Everybody, including employees, suppliers, and customers, participates in the quality improvement effort.

■ Quality improvement is the primary source of cost reductions.

Quality Circles

In addition to statistical quality control, previously mentioned, the other principal method for ensuring product quality is the *quality circle* (or QC). Here, a small group of employees (usually between 10 and 12) from the same work area get together voluntarily on a weekly basis for about 90 minutes. At these meetings, any problems that affect production or production quality are identified and analyzed. Typically, the group will come up with solutions that save time, save money, or improve quality.

The underlying premise behind quality circles is simple: People on the shop floor should know more about operations than managers in the front office. The employees themselves are often best able to identify problems and suggest improvements, if we assume, of course, that they have the necessary problem-solving skills, data, time, and financial support. To help employees with this process, organizations offer training in problem-solving tactics, technical information, and data analysis techniques. Moreover, employees are typically given time off to conduct their enquiries.

Quality circles usually serve four objectives. These include[16]

1. Encouraging employees to accept responsibility for improving quality.
2. Increasing employees' awareness of production and production costs.
3. Enhancing employee motivation and involvement in the company.
4. Identifying and developing future supervisory talent.

Quality circles were invented in the United States about 40 years ago, but they were widely ignored here until the past few years, when U.S. firms realized how effective they have been in Japan. In Japan over 8 million workers participate in quality circles, whereas in the United States the number is only 300,000, although it is increasing rapidly.[17]

We can identify three primary requirements that are essential for the success of quality circles. First, workers must be adequately trained in problem-solving techniques so that they have the necessary skills to analyze the problem. Second, workers must be assured that suggested changes will not lead to their being penalized in any way (e.g., increased layoffs, increased job fractionization). And third, workers must believe that top management clearly and actively supports QC efforts. Without this support, it is difficult to imagine the QC being taken seriously by employees.

IN PRACTICE
Designing for Quality at Motorola

In the early 1990s, Motorola decided to do something it had not done in 40 years—start a business from scratch. On October 3, 1991, it announced the formation of Motorola Lighting Inc. The new company would enter the business of building electronic ballasts, the transformers that run fluorescent-lighting systems. Motorola estimated that in the U.S. market alone there were roughly 1.5 billion ballasts that would need to be replaced at a cost of about $40 each over the next decade. A $60 billion market is hard to ignore. However, giants such as Toshiba, Matsushita, and NV Philips were already well established in the market.

To compete, Motorola had to hire 100 employees and build a $10 million-plus factory. It also had to apply everything it knew about world-class manufacturing and quality. Motorola started by choosing suppliers based on their ability to deliver defect-free parts on time. In exchange for meeting these high quality demands, Motorola gave it suppliers long-term, sole-source contracts. It also had 22 employees from engineering, marketing, and manufacturing working together in one room on the design of the product. This facilitated fast simultaneous design and manufacturing of the product. Normal redesign work that would have taken three weeks in a traditional Motorola factory took two days. The lines were structured so that bells and lights will go off whenever a defect is detected. Whenever this happens, team members get together and try to solve the problem so that the goal of defect-free parts can be achieved.

The efforts at total quality seem to be paying off. Test customers are satisfied. The president of Amtech Lighting Services, Sam Duff, says Motorola's products outshine the competition. "Its energy savings were superior and we had zero failures."[18]

TECHNICAL APPROACHES TO JOB REDESIGN

We have seen above how changes in the nature of work can affect employee motivation, performance, and satisfaction, as well as product quality. Now, in light of this analysis, we will review several specific techniques used by companies to redesign jobs. These methods can be organized into three general approaches, as shown in Exhibit 9.7. These are (1) technical approaches, (2) work-scheduling approaches, and (3) sociotechnical systems approaches. As you read each section below, refer to the job redesign models described above to see how these various approaches affect employee motivation and performance.

Technical approaches to job redesign typically attempt to modify the way in which people actually perform their tasks. They focus on job technology and industrial engineering. Several such techniques can be readily identified in industry today, including ergonomics, efficiency management programs, suggestion programs, robotics and expert systems, and computer-integrated manufacturing (CIM).

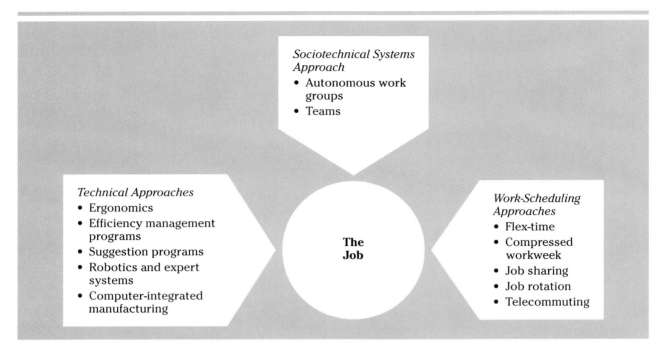

Exhibit 9.7
Three General Approaches
to Job Redesign

Ergonomics

Simply put, *ergonomics* is the science of adapting machines to people. It is believed that employees are less satisfied and less productive if they experience physical discomfort on the job. As a result, ergonomic techniques aim to redesign the machines people use and thereby reduce such conditions as eyestrain, back pain, fatigue, and stress.[19]

The job-design effects of ergonomics can be seen in many places, including the design of instruments, heavy machinery, and even automobiles. But perhaps the best place to see the potential effects of ergonomics is in the design and use of video display terminals (VDTs). Many employees complain bitterly about eye and back strain as results of sitting in front of a terminal for eight hours a day, and a large number of worker's compensation claims relate to such problems. As a result, ergonomic engineers at companies such as Digital Equipment and IBM are attempting to improve screen size, brightness, and resolution, as well as the chairs and desks people use while working at the terminals. The hope is that as a result of the redesign of this person-machine interface, employees can face a healthier work environment while companies benefit from the increased productivity of computer technology.

Efficiency Management Programs

A second area in which managers can make real changes in the workplace has to do with the use and misuse of the materials that go into manufacturing. A key issue here concerns the inefficient utilization of resources and its subsequent impact on the cost of operations. As industrial competition increases, any effort to reduce waste and inefficient operations can add up to substantial savings for a company.

Consider the case of Boeing Aircraft. In one year alone, Boeing lost $1.6 billion (yes, *billion!*) because of waste of materials. This represents a full 7 percent of their annual sales. At one point Boeing executives brought onto the shop floor three huge garbage trucks and dumped $15 million worth of bent metal and paper scrap in front of the 6000 shift workers. "These parts will never get into the air," said one executive. "We didn't get them from the back lot of McDonnell Douglas or Airbus. Every part here belongs to every one of us!"[20] Boeing has initiated a waste and materials management program designed to reduce such inefficiency. Its target is to cut the waste by 80 percent. Employees and managers are being asked to examine systematically possible ways to cut costs without jeopardizing product quality. Rewards are being offered for significant improvements. If successful, this will substantially increase operating efficiency and profitability in a very competitive market.

Other companies, such as Caterpillar, Xerox, and Ford, have taken similar approaches, with positive results. Although these techniques do not change the actual tasks people perform at work, they are nonetheless important to the overall approach to job design, because they involve a different way of thinking about manufacturing. As with total quality control, reducing waste and increasing efficiency has a direct impact on a company's ability to manufacture and sell quality products at competitive prices.

Suggestion Programs

Many of the key workplace changes that we discover in industry occurred because an employee on the shop floor had an idea concerning how to make something better and offered a suggestion. Indeed, employee suggestion programs represent a central aspect of many of the quality control efforts discussed above. The notion of *kaizen* engineering noted above (that is, making continual small improvements to a product or a manufacturing process) is closely tied to having a work force vigilantly looking for small ways to improve the manufacturing process. Although employee suggestions can relate to any aspect of organizational operations, the majority focus on the production process.

With many aspects of total quality control, comparisons with Japan yield disappointing results for Westerners. In the case of suggestion systems, the comparison is startling. At Matsushita Electric Industrial Company, for example, the 81,000 employees made over 6 million suggestions in one year, or 80 suggestions per employee per year. At Hitachi, each employee made 63 suggestions per year, and at Mazda, each employee made an average of 127 suggestions per year.[21] If we compare such results with the situation in the United States, the race is not even close, as shown in Exhibit 9.8. Although far more American employees are eligible for suggestion programs, the number of employees who actually participate, the per capita number of suggestions made, and the number of suggestions adopted by the companies is much smaller than in Japan.

What about the cost savings to industry? Japan's Canon estimated the annual cost savings at $430 million. For Japan as a whole, the estimated

Exhibit 9.8
Suggestion Programs in
Japan and the United States

	Japan	United States
Number of eligible employees	1.9 million	9.2 million
Total suggestions made	47.9 million	1.2 million
Suggestions per employee	24	0.14
Percent of employees participating	65%	13%
Percent of suggestions adopted	77%	26%
Average cost savings per suggestion	$384	$5,554

Source: Data from D. Kilburn, "The Power of Suggestion," *Business Tokyo,* April 1988, pp. 23–26.

annual cost saving is thought to be over $3 billion.[22] Suggestion programs involve employees in efforts to improve productivity and increase product quality, which results in improved profits and more secure jobs.

Robotics and Expert Systems

The advent of artificial intelligence and expert systems has created a renaissance in manufacturing technology and job design efforts, and nowhere is this more evident than in the increased use of robotics and related automation techniques in factories.

At General Motors' new Saginaw Vanguard facility, for example, front-wheel-drive axles are assembled by robots and lasers and very few people.[23] In fact, the entire factory has only 42 workers covering two shifts. Soon, Vanguard will add a third overnight shift with no workers at all. Manufacturing is controlled by computers overseen by a handful of technicians. As a result, the plant has a high degree of efficiency and flexibility. In fact, Vanguard can switch from one product to another in 10 minutes, compared to typical changeover times in the automotive industry ranging from 10 hours to 10 days.

Facilities such as these are based on the latest advances in computer technology. In particular, extensive use is made of *artificial intelligence* (AI), an attempt to give computers and their related software humanlike capabilities such as seeing, hearing, and thinking. More specifically, a subset of AI, known as *expert systems,* attempts to achieve expert-level results in problem solving through computer programs designed to imitate the behaviors of human experts. This is done by analyzing how a human expert—perhaps a quality control engineer—analyzes a problem and makes a decision. A simulation of this process is then programmed into a computer in a way that the computer mimics or imitates. When this is done properly, the computer assumes the decision-making role of the expert at considerably less cost and greater speed.

As noted in the GM-Vanguard case, these expert systems are then built into advanced *robotics* that can actually make quality control checks and self-corrective changes throughout the assembly process. A case in point is the newly opened Diamond-Star Motors Corporation.

IN PRACTICE
Automated Manufacturing at Diamond-Star Motors

Recently, Chrysler Motors and Mitsubishi Motors established a joint venture called Diamond-Star Motors Corporation to manufacture cars for the North American market. The facility, in Illinois, represents one of the most technologically advanced plants in the United States. From the beginning, it was decided that Diamond-Star would be a high-tech manufacturing plant. A horde of robots installs doors, hoods, front seats, engines, suspensions, wheels, dashboards, steering wheels, and so forth. In fact, Diamond-Star uses ten times the number of robots as most car plants. As a result, quality is designed right into the car.[24]

For this to be accomplished, the cars themselves had to be redesigned so they were compatible with robotic assembly. This meant giving body panels relatively simple shapes so they could be stamped out more easily and redesigning the instrument panels so they could be assembled and attached to the car's electrical system mechanically. The results are the new Plymouth Laser and the Mitsubishi Eclipse, and by the end of 1989 the plant was producing 240,000 cars annually.

In addition to the robots, computers track the mix of cars on the line and adjust carousels and indicator lights to tell workers which parts belong on what models. The same computer alerts outside suppliers when it is time to ship more parts to the plant so inventories can be kept to a minimum (called *just-in-time scheduling*). As a result, Diamond-Star is poised to go after a major market with efficiently produced quality products.

Computer-Integrated Manufacturing

When we carry expert systems and automated manufacturing to their ultimate conclusion, we come to *computer-integrated manufacturing* (CIM). The basic premise underlying CIM is that by totally automating and linking all of the functions of a factory as well as corporate headquarters, a manufacturer should be able to turn out a nearly perfect product at the lowest possible cost almost overnight. That is, by making use of computer technology (especially artificial intelligence and expert systems), the "factory of the future" could (1) conceive new products on a *computer-aided design* (CAD) system that would allow designers to optimize their ideas, (2) pass along the CAD data electronically to a *computer-aided engineering* (CAE) system to verify that the design will do the job intended and can be produced economically, (3) extract from the CAE data the information needed to make the product, using a *computer-aided manufacturing* (CAM) system to send electronic instructions for product assembly to computer-controlled machines and robots, and (4) coordinate the entire process with computerized *management information systems* (MISs).[25]

As a result, management has tight "real time" controls over every aspect of the design-to-manufacture-to-market process and can make changes or corrections on short notice. This CIM approach is shown in Exhibit 9.9. Computer-integrated manufacturing is flexible and cost-efficient. From a

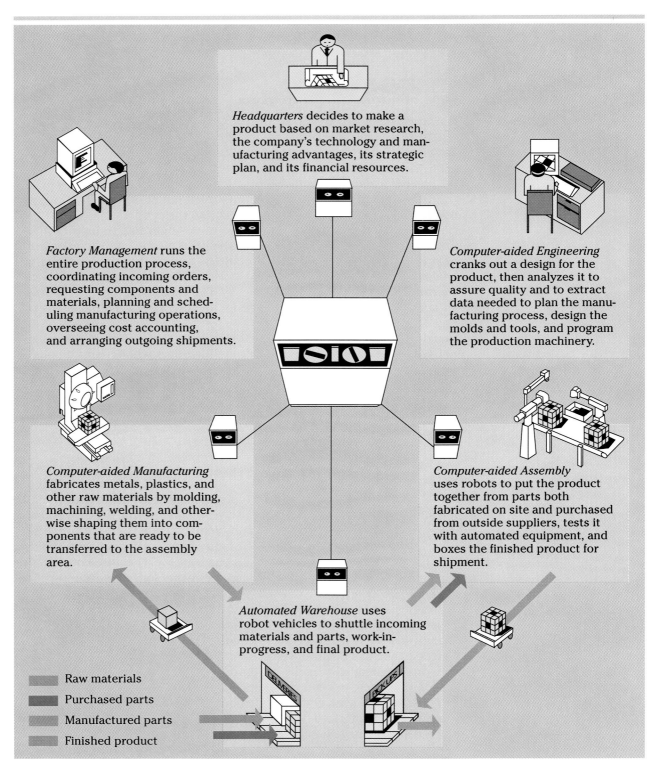

Headquarters decides to make a product based on market research, the company's technology and manufacturing advantages, its strategic plan, and its financial resources.

Factory Management runs the entire production process, coordinating incoming orders, requesting components and materials, planning and scheduling manufacturing operations, overseeing cost accounting, and arranging outgoing shipments.

Computer-aided Engineering cranks out a design for the product, then analyzes it to assure quality and to extract data needed to plan the manufacturing process, design the molds and tools, and program the production machinery.

Computer-aided Manufacturing fabricates metals, plastics, and other raw materials by molding, machining, welding, and otherwise shaping them into components that are ready to be transferred to the assembly area.

Computer-aided Assembly uses robots to put the product together from parts both fabricated on site and purchased from outside suppliers, tests it with automated equipment, and boxes the finished product for shipment.

Automated Warehouse uses robot vehicles to shuttle incoming materials and parts, work-in-progress, and final product.

Raw materials
Purchased parts
Manufactured parts
Finished product

Exhibit 9.9
The Factory of the Future

Source: "The Factory of the Future," reprinted from March 3, 1986, issue of *Business Week* by special permission. Copyright © 1986 by McGraw-Hill, Inc.

behavioral standpoint, however, questions remain concerning what role is played by the employees in such efforts. Although CIM systems are quite new, initial evidence suggests that fully integrated factories require fewer people. However, those who are employed require greater technical skills and abilities and have jobs that are considerably more challenging than the traditional work of the assembly line. In short, the world of tomorrow is made for technicians.

International Challenge

IN PRACTICE
Computer-Integrated Manufacturing at Benetton

In an industry not known for its technology, Italian sweater manufacturer Benetton has achieved remarkable success in its worldwide business by adopting the latest technological advances in production, telecommunications, and distribution systems and putting them together in a computer-integrated manufacturing system. Consider the following. The clothes are designed on computer screens by Benetton's 15 stylists, who have a choice of 250 colors to work with. The computers then translate the designs directly into data that can be fed into the knitting and cutting machines, which are also completely computerized. As a result, a new design can be created and moved into production within hours.[26]

Benetton has also developed a technique for dyeing finished items instead of yarn. As a result, over 20 percent of Benetton's woolen production is in the natural color and is dyed only when the season's fashion preferences are established.

To handle its 60 million units of output per year, the company built a fully computerized warehouse. With a staff of only seven employees, the warehouse processes 36,000 boxes per day. Arriving delivery trucks simply insert a card in a slot at the loading bay, and the right shipment is automatically loaded onto the truck. Bar codes and lasers are used to ensure correct deliveries, which are untouched by human hands.

The crucial link between the company and its field representative and agents is provided by an advanced data communications system. Daily updates of sales and inventories are transmitted to the communications center in Ponzano, where they are analyzed and distributed to the relevant departments. If certain items or colors are selling especially well or poorly, production can be shifted immediately. As a result, concludes a Benetton executive, "This technology has brought us close to the customer, to eliminate all the filters between the factory and the person who buys our products."

WORK-SCHEDULING APPROACHES TO JOB REDESIGN

The second general approach to job redesign efforts (after the technical approaches discussed above) focuses on making changes in the work schedules of the employees themselves. These techniques usually go under the rubric of *alternative work schedules*. If we examine corporate experiences, we can find a wide array of possible work schedule configurations, all designed to make work more attractive and/or more efficient by offering work schedules that are compatible with employee life-styles. It is reasoned that if attendance is made easier through altered work schedules, valued employees will be more likely to join and remain with the organization. Many of these techniques have also found favor with employees (most notably female) who have either a dual career conflict or a work-family conflict. Here we examine several of the more commonly found approaches (refer to Exhibit 9.7).

Flex-Time

One work-scheduling approach to job redesign that has received increasing attention in recent years is *flex-time*. It is currently being used by over 4 million workers in firms of varying sizes. Flex-time is a technique that allows employees more latitude and freedom in determining their own work schedules. In essence, flex-time requires all employees to be on the job during certain "core hours," but beyond this employees are allowed to select their starting and finishing times.

For example, a New Jersey company, Sandoz-Wander, introduced a flex-time program that contained the following parameters:[27]

Earliest starting time:	7:30 a.m.
Latest starting time:	9:30 a.m.
Earliest leaving time:	4:00 p.m.
Latest leaving time:	6:00 p.m.
Lunch period:	12:00 noon–2:00 p.m.
Maximum lunch period:	2 hours
Minimum lunch period:	1 hour
Core hours (when everyone must be present):	9:30–12:00 noon and 2:00–4:00 p.m.
Average workweek:	37.5 hours
Maximum workweek:	40 hours
Minimum workweek:	22.5 hours
Average workday:	7.5 hours
Maximum workday:	9.5 hours
Minimum workday:	4.5 hours

Within these guidelines, employees are free to select the working hours that best fit their own needs and desires. The flexibility of this schedule is shown in Exhibit 9.10. Following this plan, then, does not alter the basic nature of the job but does provide employees with some discretion as to when to perform. And results of employee surveys indicate that most employees like the plan. Although such an approach does not necessarily enhance productivity, it does make it easier for employees with special needs (e.g., single parents) to attend work on a regular basis.

Compressed Workweek

In the early 1970s, companies began experimenting with the *compressed workweek* (also referred to by some as the "4/40," or 4 days/40 hours, plan). Under this plan, workers work 4 days for 10 hours per day (or some variation of this).

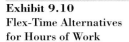

Exhibit 9.10
Flex-Time Alternatives
for Hours of Work

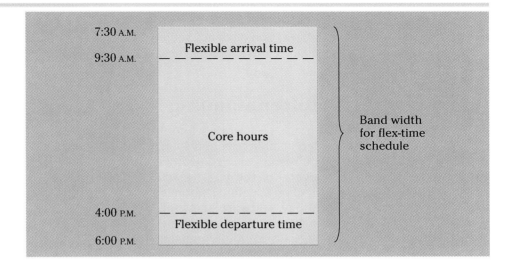

As a result, they still work 40 hours per week, but they are on the job only 4 days instead of 5. It is estimated that nearly 2000 companies employing over a million people now use the compressed workweek.[28] The major push behind the compressed workweek plan came from companies who hoped to gain greater productivity and efficiency and workers who wanted more leisure time. The plan aims at accomplishing both without changing the job technology.

Research into the effectiveness of such plans generally suggests that compressed workweeks can improve productivity and employee job attitudes for certain kinds of jobs (most notably in the manufacturing sector).[29] This technique has also proved successful in recruiting employees in professions where it is difficult to find sufficient personnel, such as nursing. Here, the compressed workweek offers prospective workers an attractive way to support themselves while retaining more usable free time.

Job Sharing

Another strategy to relieve many of the problems associated with routine jobs while at the same time accommodating the needs of part-time workers is *job sharing*.[30] In job sharing, two or more persons jointly cover one job over a normal 40-hour week. For instance, two computer operators may share a job, with one working in the morning and one in the afternoon. The work gets done, and both employees have ample time for outside activities. Although job sharing does not change the basic nature of the work, it does allow an organization to tap previously unavailable labor markets.

Job Rotation

When an organization has a series of routine jobs that cannot be combined or enriched, it is possible to rotate workers from one job to the next over time. The aim of this *job rotation* is to minimize the routine and boredom to the extent possible through a change in activities. The employee learns different jobs, and the company develops a more flexible work force. Even so, job rotation does not solve the basic problem of unenriched and unchallenging jobs and should be used only as a temporary or last-resort technique.

Telecommuting

The newest work-scheduling approach to job redesign is *telecommuting*. Here, employees remain at home, and they perform their work and transmit the results electronically to the office. Telecommuting takes advantage of several of the latest electronic media, including personal computers, fax machines, cellular phones, and electronic mail (or E-mail). With such technology, software engineers, for example, can devise their software in the comfort of their own homes—perhaps several hundred miles from the workplace—and simply transmit it to work using modems attached to their computers. When hard copy is required, a fax machine can be employed. In most cases, the employees arrange to come into work on certain days to attend meetings and make face-to-face contact with their associates.

It is believed that by 1995 over 3 million employees will be telecommuting. Most of these will be the so-called "knowledge workers" that have become highly valued by companies.[31] Telecommuting offers many benefits to both employee and employer. For the employee, this can mean less commuting to work on crowded freeways, more privacy for concentrated work, and more free time. For the employer, telecommuting often means access to talented workers who might not otherwise wish to work in crowded cities. Research suggests that such workers are also often highly productive, partly because of their uninterrupted work environments. Clearly, the future will see increased use of such technologies as corporations scramble to capitalize on the latest in efficiency-producing methods.

IN PRACTICE
Christopher Leinberger, Telecommuter

If you are tired of working in the big city, consider the life of Christopher Leinberger. Leinberger is a real estate consultant in Los Angeles. He works hard at his job and has been quite successful. What makes him somewhat unique, however, is that Leinberger lives in Tesuque, New Mexico—over 1000 miles from his job.[32]

Leinberger flies to Los Angeles and spends two days a week in the city making personal contacts, searching out new ventures, signing contracts, and so forth. The rest of the week he lives on his New Mexico ranch and sends his work back and forth to Los Angeles via computer and fax hookups. Although his business opportunities are in California, he simply does not want to put up with the congestion and expense. Lifestyle is important to him. Moreover, he estimates the rather considerable costs of commuting weekly by air are offset by the lower cost of living in New Mexico. And Leinberger is not alone. In fact, he will tell you that the flights to and from Los Angeles are fully booked. So are the flights in and out of Park City, Utah; Vail, Colorado; and so forth. For many people, telecommuting has provided a synthesis of desirable lifestyle and financial security. And the future will probably see more and more Leinbergers who are willing to search out unique solutions to the problems of the workplace.

SOCIOTECHNICAL SYSTEMS APPROACHES TO JOB REDESIGN

We have seen that some approaches to job redesign focus on technical or engineering solutions (e.g., the use of robotics or automation), whereas others focus on work schedules (e.g., telecommuting). Now we come to the third approach, generally known as the sociotechnical systems approach. Here, the principal change efforts are focused on the nature of the relationship between employees and the technologies they use. The word *systems* is used here to denote that this approach is comprehensive and systematic. In fact, this approach embodies many of the key features of the job characteristics model described above.

As shown in Exhibit 9.11, this approach identifies two aspects of the workplace: the technical subsystem, which includes how the work is done, and the social subsystem, which includes the people and work culture in which the work gets done. These two subsystems come together to determine the *person-job interface.* Thus, the sociotechnical approach deliberately designs work roles that integrate people with technology in ways that maximize the long-term performance results.

Perhaps the best way to see how this works is to look at *autonomous work groups* (also called *self-managing teams*). Here, jobs are designed around groups instead of individuals. The group is given considerable discretion concerning work scheduling, individual work assignments, and other issues that have traditionally been management prerogatives. Considerable autonomy is given to these teams in the belief that highly cohesive, committed work teams are better able to innovate and produce high-quality products than are workers in other production systems (e.g., assembly line workers).

A good example of a self-managing team is the Aid Association for Lutherans (AAL), a church-related organization that operates a substantial insurance program for members. Before the conversion to the team approach, it took an average of 20 days to process a policyholder's claim. The sequential process for each claim is shown in Exhibit 9.12. Each small task was done independently by one person, who then passed along the paperwork to the

Exhibit 9.11
The Sociotechnical
Systems Model

The Social Subsystem	Moderators	The Technical Subsystem
• Individual and group incentives • Corporate culture • Leadership and supervision	• Work roles • Goals • Skills and abilities	• Job technologies • Type of production processes • Physical work setting • Time pressures

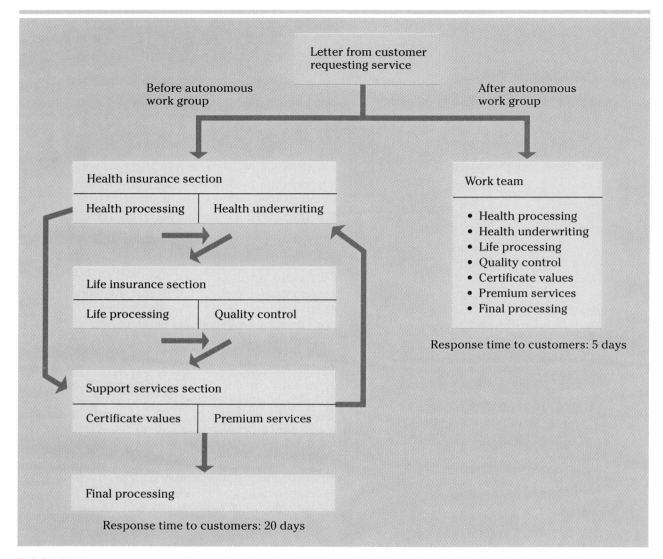

Exhibit 9.12
How Autonomous Work
Groups Speed Up Customer
Service at AAL

Source: Based on data in J. Hoerr, "Work Teams Can Rev Up Paper-Pushers, Too," *Business Week,* November 28, 1988, pp. 64–72.

next person, who did another small task. After the company reorganized, using a team approach, each team was assigned responsibility for the entire process. As a result, employee morale increased, and claim-processing time was reduced to only 5 days.[33]

Performance results from the establishment of work teams in other industries can also be dramatic. For example, at A. O. Smith, an automotive supplier, the implementation of work teams doubled the productivity growth rate within one year while simultaneously improving both product quality and employee attitudes.[34] Other studies found absolute productivity growth rates of over 30 percent, significant reductions in turnover, and improved employee attitudes.[35] In fact, in many ways, autonomous work groups represent the most sophisticated approach to redesigning work to take full advantage of an organization's human resources. This approach is not restricted to knowledge workers, as is telecommuting, and it does not require sophisticated and costly automation (although this may be included in the redesign, depending upon the jobs being performed). What are required, however, are a belief by management that the organization's workers are capable of assuming greater responsibility for the means of production and a willingness on the part of management to assist workers in this endeavor. Nowhere is such a commitment more evident than in the continuing effort by Sweden's Volvo to humanize the automobile assembly line.

International Challenge

IN PRACTICE
Volvo's Radical New Plant

Sweden's Volvo has been a leader in the area of job redesign for over 20 years. Whereas we have seen efforts to automate car assembly lines (such as Diamond-Star's) and efforts to enrich service workers' tasks (such as AAL), Volvo has determined to eliminate the assembly line altogether. In 1974 it opened its famous Kalmar facility, where major parts of a car were assembled by self-managing teams. And now Volvo is going one step farther. Beginning in 1988, Volvo established a new facility in Uddevalla, Sweden, where teams of seven to ten workers are responsible for the complete assembly of four cars per shift. Because work team members are trained to handle all assembly jobs, they work an average of 3 hours before repeating the same task, compared to 1.5 minutes in Detroit.[36]

The Uddevalla facility is divided into six assembly plants, each of which has eight teams. The teams largely manage themselves—handling scheduling, quality control, hiring, and other duties normally performed by first-line supervisors. In fact, Uddevalla has no first-line supervisors and only two levels of management. Each team has a spokesman/ombudsman who reports to one of six plant managers, who in turn reports to the director of the entire complex. Each work team is even assigned to specific car dealerships, so it knows where its cars are going and can discuss any problems directly with the dealers.

Product quality and employee morale are up, and absenteeism stands at 8 percent, compared to the 20 percent industry average in Sweden. Turnover is well below industry norms, and workers eagerly talk about wanting their sons and daughters to join Volvo when they grow up. And, finally, according to management, the facility is cost-efficient. Whereas Japan and the United States continue to take technological approaches to the problems of the assembly line, Sweden may be taking the ultimate in people-oriented approaches. Notes one Volvo executive, "This isn't just new production technology. It is the death of the assembly line. We've brought back craftsmanship to auto making."

WORK REDESIGN: PROBLEMS AND PROSPECTS

Before we close, we should consider for a moment what the future holds for job redesign efforts. Several constraints on many job redesign efforts should be recognized, as well as several potential means of overcoming these constraints.

Problems with Work Redesign

Although work redesign holds much promise for improving both employee performance and the quality of working life, it is by no means a panacea. In fact, several rather serious problems have been identified by various researchers that suggest caution in work redesign attempts.

Individual Differences.   Some employees may respond more positively to enriched jobs than others. For an employee with a high need for achievement, an enriched job may serve to cue the achievement motive, facilitating increased effort. However, putting an employee with a low need for achievement on an enriched job may heighten his or her anxiety, frustration, and dissatisfaction.

Technical Constraints.   Moreover, in some cases the nature of the job does not lend itself to enrichment or redesign. Such technical constraints are present in continuous-process jobs, where the jobs are paced by machines. In these circumstances, job rotation or flex-time may, perhaps, offer a partial solution.

Cost.   In many cases, the costs of work redesign efforts are simply very high. These increased costs include additional expenditures for training, tools, construction, start-up, and, sometimes, wages. The problem is whether the consumers are willing to pay the additional costs associated with work redesign that are passed along in the form of higher prices. Often, companies rush into innovation without careful study of the nature and costs of either the problems they are facing or the possible solutions.

No Commitment to Change.   Many attempts at job redesign have failed because no substantive changes were actually made in the job itself. Because the jobs were not changed, there were no changes in attitudes or behavior. Instead, lip service was paid by indifferent or hostile managers.

Fear of Change.   Managers may occasionally feel threatened by the increased autonomy given to workers under work redesign. They may fear loss of both power and status. This managerial resistance may be demonstrated by dragging feet and sabotaging efforts in numerous ways. Similarly, unions often resist work redesign efforts—surprisingly, for many of the same reasons as managers. Unions develop power bases as a result of their ability to represent workers to management. Work redesign often allows a more direct interchange between workers and management and bypasses the union. Unions frequently feel that these efforts are simply another attempt to increase productivity. One union official described work redesign as a "speed-up in sheep's clothing." Traditional unions tend to have traditional demands (wages, hours, job security) and as a result, they are often less innovative even than management when it comes to improving the quality of working life.

Overcoming Problems with Work Redesign

The seriousness of work redesign problems must not be overlooked, but, there are several steps that managers can take to help reduce the impact of these problems and enhance the chances for program success.

Prior Diagnosis.   Begin by diagnosing the work system prior to changing it. Know what the problems are (union resistance, individual differences, etc.) before beginning to consider specific changes. As much as possible, get the union involved in the diagnosis.

Focus on the Work Itself.   Next, keep the focus on the work itself. Keep personal differences outside the discussion. Suspend, at least for the moment, the "it can't be done" syndrome. Assume that it can be done, and prepare ahead of time for unexpected problems. Develop contingency plans ahead of time, and be ready for possible problems that could sidetrack redesign efforts.

Evaluate Continuously.   Another suggestion is to evaluate continuously. Whether evaluation is done by outside consultants or by union-management teams, continuous feedback can assist in pinpointing potential trouble spots so that remedial action can be taken. In addition, don't bury important issues or potential problems in the hope they will disappear. Confront potential problems early. If some levels of management are not committed to change, consider ways of increasing (not bypassing) their commitment.

Use Appropriate Change Technologies.   Finally, design change processes that are appropriate to the specific objectives. For instance, if you want to develop work teams that exhibit high levels of participation and autonomy, use a participative change strategy. Get workers involved in designing job changes. Use techniques in the design and planning phases that you wish continued in the actual program; in that way, employees can become familiar with those techniques gradually and have an opportunity to test management's sincerity and their commitment to the proposed changes.

By following these guidelines, managers can provide a work environment conducive to experimentation in redesigning work. Although these changes by themselves certainly do not guarantee that the quality of working life will be significantly improved, they will at least make a useful contribution in that direction.

PULLING IT ALL TOGETHER

The objectives of job redesign are to gain the maximum motivation from employees and maximum utilization of the abilities they have. It assumes that workers are capable of and are at least willing to learn how to utilize their actual and latent potential. This assumption, however, does not hold for all people, and consequently successful job redesign must involve not only the principles of perceived and experienced meaningfulness, responsibility, and knowledge of results but also the appropriate matching of redesigns and people.

SUMMARY OF KEY POINTS

■   Job fractionization exists when jobs are characterized by machine pacing, repetitiveness, low skill requirements, task specialization, limited social interaction, and the use of highly specified tools and techniques.

▨ Job enrichment consists of changing the nature of a job by increasing employee control over resources, accountability, feedback, and opportunities for achievement, personal growth, and development. This is done primarily through vertical loading.

▨ Job enrichment differs from job enlargement in that job enrichment attempts to alter the basic nature of production technology—the way the job is actually performed—whereas job enlargement consists simply of adding a larger number of equally routine tasks to an employee's job.

▨ The job characteristics model asserts that changes in core job dimensions alter critical psychological states, resulting in higher personal and work outcomes. This process is moderated by an employee's growth need strength.

▨ A motivating potential score represents the extent to which employees see their jobs as motivating.

▨ The fundamental principles for job redesign include (1) forming natural work units, (2) combining tasks, (3) establishing client relationships, (4) vertical loading, and (5) opening feedback channels.

▨ The social-information-processing model suggests that an employee's perceptions of a job are influenced by objective job characteristics, co-workers' observations, and the employee's own opinions.

▨ Statistical quality control is the application of quantitative techniques to measure and regulate standards of performance excellence.

▨ *Kaizen* engineering is the process of making continual small improvements in both the product and the production process.

▨ Quality circles consist of small groups of employees who meet to discover ways to improve production efficiency or the quality of a product.

▨ There are three general approaches to job redesign: technical approaches, work-scheduling approaches, and sociotechnical approaches.

▨ Technical approaches to job redesign focus on reengineering the job in a way that maximizes production efficiency. This approach includes ergonomics, efficiency management programs, suggestion plans, robotics and expert systems, and computer-integrated manufacturing.

▨ Work-scheduling approaches to job redesign focus on modifying work hours to meet employee needs. Included here are flex-time, the compressed workweek, job sharing, job rotation, and telecommuting.

▨ Sociotechnical approaches to job redesign view the person-job interaction from both the technical and the social perspectives and attempt to design jobs that are both productive and satisfying.

▨ The most common sociotechnical approach is the autonomous work group, or self-managing team, where work is divided into large units and assigned to groups (instead of individuals) for assembly. This approach allows employees considerably more job enrichment than traditional assembly line technology.

KEY WORDS

alternative work schedules
artificial intelligence
autonomous work groups
compressed workweek
computer-aided design
computer-aided engineering
computer-aided manufacturing
computer-integrated manufacturing
efficiency management programs
ergonomics
expert systems
flex-time
growth need strength
industrial humanism
job characteristics model
job enlargement
job enrichment
job rotation

job sharing
just-in-time scheduling
kaizen engineering
management information systems
motivating potential score
quality circles
robotics
scientific management
self-managing teams
social-information-processing model
sociotechnical systems
statistical quality control
suggestion programs
task identity
task significance
telecommuting
total quality control
vertical job loading

QUESTIONS FOR DISCUSSION

1. Describe the primary characteristics of scientific management. Why did this approach lose its appeal in organizations?
2. When should companies consider job redesign efforts? When should they not consider such changes?
3. Describe the job characteristics model of job redesign. Provide an example of a job that could be redesigned using this model.
4. Describe the social-information-processing approach to job design. What implications for management follow from this model?
5. Discuss some of the changes in corporate culture that will result from the increased use of robotics and expert systems.
6. Do you feel telecommuting will increase significantly in the near future? Why?
7. Which work-scheduling approaches to job design do you feel hold the most promise for both employees and managers? Why?
8. Describe how an autonomous work group differs from a conventional work group. What are the advantages and disadvantages of each?
9. In your opinion, what lies ahead in the area of job design?

NOTES

1. Personal communication.
2. P. Dickson, *The Future of the Workplace* (New York: Wybright and Talley, 1975).
3. C. Walker and R. Guest, *The Man on the Assemblyline* (Cambridge, Mass.: Harvard University Press, 1952).
4. F. Taylor, *The Principles of Scientific Management* (New York: Harper & Row, 1911), p. 59.

5. F. Herzberg, B. Mausner, and B. Snyderman, *The Motivation to Work* (New York: Wiley, 1959).

6. R. M. Steers and L. W. Porter, *Motivation and Work Behavior,* 5th ed. (New York: McGraw-Hill, 1991).

7. J. R. Hackman, "Work Design," in J. R. Hackman and J. L. Suttle, eds., *Improving Life at Work* (Santa Monica, Calif.: Goodyear, 1976).

8. J. R. Hackman and G. R. Oldham, "Motivation Through the Design of Work," *Organizational Behavior and Human Performance,* 1976, pp. 250–279.

9. Hackman, op. cit.

10. R. Aldag, S. Barr, and A. Brief, "Measurement of Perceived Task Characteristics," *Psychological Bulletin,* November 1981, pp. 415–431; J. Idazak and F. Drasgow, "A Revision of the Job Diagnostic Survey," *Journal of Applied Psychology,* February 1987, pp. 69–74.

11. Ibid.

12. B. Dumaine, "Who Needs a Boss?" *Fortune,* May 7, 1990, pp. 52–60.

13. J. Pfeffer, "Management as Symbolic Action: The Creation and Maintenance of Organizational Paradigms," in L. Cummings and B. Staw, eds., *Research in Organizational Behavior* (Greenwich, Conn.: JAI Press, 1981).

14. R. Johnson and W. Winchell, *Management and Quality* (Milwaukee: American Society for Quality Control, 1989).

15. T. Peters, *Thriving on Chaos* (New York: Knopf, 1987).

16. J. Bowditch and A. Buono, *A Primer on Organizational Behavior* (New York: Wiley, 1985).

17. M. Marks, "The Question of Quality Circles," *Psychology Today,* March 1986, pp. 36–38, 42–46.

18. K. Kelly. "Motorola Wants to Light Up Another Market." *Business Week,* October 4, 1991, p. 50.

19. W. McQuade, "Easing Tensions Between Man and Machine," *Fortune,* March 19, 1984, pp. 58–66.

20. R. McCluskey, "Boeing Develops a New Design to Cut Down on Corporate Drag," *International Management,* April 1987, p. 57.

21. D. Kilburn, "The Power of Suggestion," *Business Tokyo,* April 1988, pp. 23–25.

22. Ibid.

23. W. Hampton, "GM Bets an Arm and a Leg on a People-Free Plant," *Business Week,* September 12, 1988, pp. 66–67.

24. W. Hampton, "Can Steel-Collar Workers Build Better Cars?" *Business Week,* September 12, 1988, p. 67.

25. R. Brandt, "How Automation Could Save the Day," *Business Week,* March 3, 1986, pp. 72–74.

26. "Portable Patterns from High Tech Knitting," *International Management,* November 1987, p. 30.

27. Dickson, op. cit.

28. bid.

29. R. Dunham, J. Pierce, and M. Castenada, "Alternative Work Schedules: Two Field Quasi-Experiments," *Personnel Psychology,* Summer 1987, pp. 215–242.

30. C. English, "Job Sharing Gains Ground Across the U.S.," *U.S. News & World Report,* October 4, 1985, p. 76.

31. G. Lewis, "The Portable Executive," *Business Week,* October 10, 1988, pp. 102–112.

32. F. Clifford, "City Office, Home on the Range," *Los Angeles Times,* October 29, 1989, p. A-1.

33. J. Hoerr, "Work Teams Can Rev Up Paper-Pushers, Too," *Business Week,* November 28, 1988, pp. 64–67.

34. J. Hoerr, "The Cultural Revolution at A. O. Smith," *Business Week,* May 29, 1989, pp. 66–68.

35. T. Wall, N. Kemp, P. Jackson, and C. Clegg, "Outcomes of Autonomous Workgroups: A Long-Term Field Experiment," *Academy of Management Journal,* June 1986, pp. 280–304; J. Hoerr, "The Payoff from Teamwork," *Business Week,* July 10, 1989, pp. 56–62.
36. J. Kapstein, "Volvo's Radical New Plant," *Business Week,* August 28, 1989, pp. 92–93.

EXPERIENTIAL EXERCISE 9

Redesigning Your Job

This exercise will focus on redesigning a job using the principles outlined in this chapter.

Most students are at least familiar with the job of "flipping hamburgers" at a fast food restaurant such as McDonald's or Burger King; some may have actually worked in a fast food restaurant. Basically, the cook takes different weight frozen hamburger patties, cooks them, and then places them on buns after which someone else places the necessary additional items such as lettuce or tomatoes on the hamburger.

As a Group: On the basis of this knowledge, students should gather in groups of four to six and answer the following questions (20 minutes):

1. How would your group describe the current job using the dimensions outlined in the job characteristics model?
2. What do you think the motivating potential score of this job would be?
3. Develop a job redesign program to improve both productivity and job satisfaction on the bases of the materials covered in this chapter.
4. What obstacles do you envision in trying to implement your program?
5. What steps would you take in order to overcome these obstacles and successfully implement your proposed changes? Explain.

As a Class: When they have finished, the small groups should report back to the class on their proposed plans of action and see what similarities and differences exist among the groups.

MANAGEMENT DILEMMA 9

Job Redesign at National Insurance Company

Jerry Taylor has been involved with the administrative functions of the National Insurance Company for almost twenty years. About three months ago, Jerry was appointed group manager of the Policyholder Service and Accounting Departments at the home office. Before he actually assumed the job, Jerry was able to get away for a three-week management development program at the State University College of Business. One of the topics covered in the program was the concept of job enrichment, or job redesign. Jerry had read about job enrichment in several of his trade journals, but the program was his first opportunity to think about the concept in some detail.

In addition, several of the program participants had had some experience (both positive and negative) with job redesign projects.

Jerry was intrigued with the idea. He knew how boring routine administrative tasks could become, and he knew from his previous supervisory work that turnover of clerical personnel was a real problem. In addition, his conversations with the administrative vice-president and Joe Bellows, the personnel manager, led him to believe that some trials and redesigning the work would be supported and favorably regarded.

Description of the Work

Group Policyholder Service Department.   The principal activities undertaken in this department are the sorting and opening of incoming mail and then matching to accounting files; reviewing of group insurance bills from policyholders; and coding required changes to policies (e.g., new employees and terminations). These activities are carried out by 28 people; 54 percent of them are over age 35, 82 percent are female, 89 percent are high school graduates, and 54 percent have less than two years' experience in their current job.

Organizationally, the department is headed by a manager. The employees are grouped into the four functional categories of clerical support, senior technician, change coder, and special clerk. The general work flow and a more specific list of the tasks carried out within each functional category are shown in Exhibit 9A.

The Group Policyholder Service Department shares the same physical working area as the Accounting Department. The people within Policyholder Service who work in the different functional categories are in very close proximity to one another, frequently at adjacent desks. The files for the department are located at one corner of the work area and the supervisors have offices along one side (see Exhibit 9B).

In the last few months, Jerry has observed that the functional specialization and the accompanying physical arrangement of people and files lead to a number of problems. Since work is assigned or selected on a random basis, there is no personal accountability for it. Files are at one corner of the work area where they can be retrieved by the clerical group and distributed to a senior technician who randomly distributes them to be processed. After a file is coded, it is placed in a holding area for processing by the Accounting Department. Here, assignment of work is also done on a random basis. It is difficult to respond to phone calls or written requests for information promptly, because it is frequently difficult to find a file. In fact, several people are kept busy doing nothing but looking for files.

The typical employee performs a job which consists of two tasks on approximately an eleven-minute cycle. All work is cross-checked. The training for the job is minimal, and there are a number of individuals performing the same set of tasks on files randomly issued. A clerk occasionally corresponds with a policyholder, but all correspondence goes out with the manager's signature on it. The manager thus receives all phone calls and correspondence from policyholders.

Because of the random distribution of work, individual performance is difficult to measure. There are spot checks on some completed work by

Exhibit 9A
Policyholder Service
Department Work Flow
and Tasks

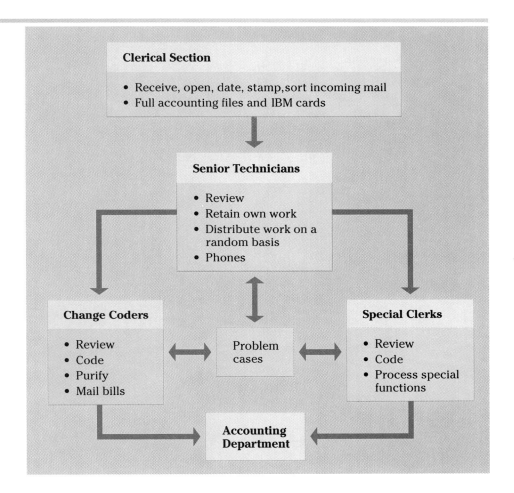

someone other than the doer, but it is difficult or impossible to determine the individual responsible for a specific piece of work. Consequently, it is not possible to provide specific information to individuals at regular intervals about their work performance.

Accounting Department.   The Accounting Department processes the files, bills, and checks received from the Group Policyholder Service. Premiums are posted on IBM cards and worksheets. Necessary adjustments are made to accounts and the checks, cards, and worksheets are balanced. Twenty-eight people are employed at any one time performing these tasks. Seventy-five percent of the work force are under 35 years of age. Everyone has at least a high school degree, and 54 percent have less than two years' experience on the job they are performing.

The department has both a manager and a supervisor. The employees are divided into senior technicians, premium posters, and special clerks. The general work flow and tasks carried out in each of these functional areas are shown in Exhibit 9C. As shown in Exhibit 9B, the Accounting Department shares its work and files with Policyholder Service.

Exhibit 9B
Policyholder Service
Department and Accounting
Department Physical Layout

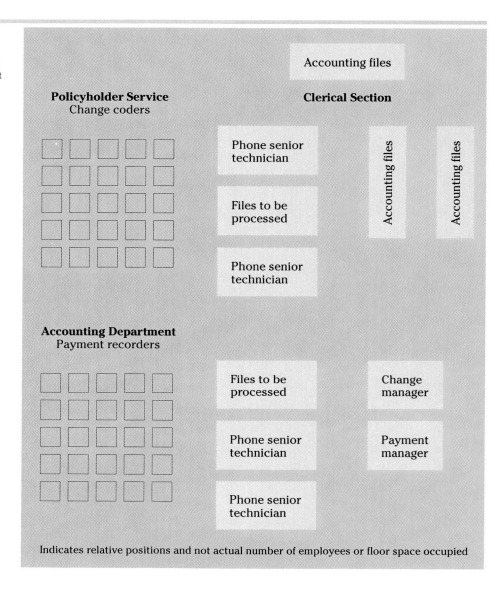

Indicates relative positions and not actual number of employees or floor space occupied

Work is selected on a random basis. Clerks go to a bookcase file and choose the cases they wish to do. Occasionally, correspondence with a policyholder is necessary and is signed by the manager.

The Problem of Change

Jerry believes that if the work in his department can be *properly* redesigned, then departmental effectiveness can be improved. In addition, he believes that substantial improvements can be made in terms of individual employee work satisfaction.

Exhibit 9C
Accounting Department
Work Flow and Tasks

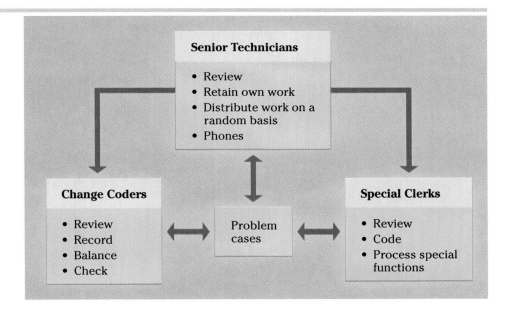

In thinking about redesigning the work, Jerry has separated the problem into two parts. First, he is concerned about the *process* of change. How can he best accomplish a job redesign project? Second, Jerry has been concerned with the arrangement of the tasks themselves. Before he begins such a project, Jerry hopes to have at least some preliminary ideas about the feasibility of such a change.

On the basis of this information, consider the following:

1. If you were Jerry, how would you approach the process of redesigning the jobs?
2. Exactly how would you redesign the jobs if you were Jerry?
3. In doing so, how would you employ the enriching variables incorporated in the job characteristics model?
4. In addition to work redesign, what else might Jerry do to improve employee attitudes and performance?

Source: From Randall S. Schuler and Dan R. Dalton, *Case Problems in Management,* 3rd ed. (St. Paul: West, 1986), pp. 175–179. The case and the analysis are adapted (with permission) from Antone F. Alber, *An Exploratory Study of the Benefits and Costs of Job Enrichment,* Ph.D. dissertation, Pennsylvania State University, 1977. Several figures are reproduced directly, and major portions of the text are quoted directly. The case was written in conjunction with Henry P. Sims, Jr., and Andrew D. Szilagyi, Jr.

10

Designing Effective Organizations

The Management Challenge

- ■ To identify the stakeholders in an organization and assess the various ways of meeting their divergent needs.

- ■ To create and maintain an efficient and effective department or work team.

- ■ To help develop an organization structure that fits individual talents as well as the goals and objectives of the organization as a whole.

- ■ To understand the advantages and disadvantages of various forms of organization and know when to modify an organization's design.

- ■ To understand the opportunities and limitations inherent in interorganizational linkages.

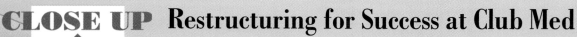 

CLOSE UP

Restructuring for Success at Club Med

Fun and sun have been the essence of Club Med since its formation in 1950. The growth of Club Med has been as successful as its ability to create a strong image. Originally a village of tents on a camping site in the Balearic Isles, over 40 years it has grown to a capacity of nearly 80,000 beds in settings ranging from spartan villages to luxury hotels. It boasts over $1 billion in sales in over 40 countries. At one point in the mid-1980s, this resulted in an organizational structure in which Serge Trigano, head of operations and the son of Chairman Gilbert Trigano, had 104 village chiefs, 16 country managers, and 8 product directors all reporting to him.[1]

Realizing that having 128 people report to one person was probably too centralized, Club Med reorganized. The restructuring was based primarily on an assessment of the environment. In its early days, Club Med customers were primarily French. Gradually, the customer base expanded to include a variety of Western Europeans. However, over the years the customer base also included North Americans and Asians as well. This diverse set of customers had different expectations in what they wanted in a vacation and what they expected in service—for example, "baby boomers" in America were increasingly interested in settings to which they could bring their children. However, a majority of the customers from each world region tended to visit Club Meds within their own region.

In response to these changes, Club Med reorganized itself into three regional divisions. Coordination mechanisms were established so that accounting, purchasing, and other functions could occur on a global and more centralized basis, while many aspects of product development, sales, and marketing were decentralized on a regional basis. One consequence of this reorganization was that "Baby Clubs" or resorts to which customers could bring their children and for whom day-care and organized children's activities were available were created and successfully marketed to American customers.

What happened at Club Med has been repeated over and over around the world as companies attempt to restructure themselves so they can be more competitive in an ever-changing business environment. To understand how organizations can meet this managerial challenge, it is necessary to have a thorough understanding of the topic of organization design—how organizations are put together. The topic of organization design is the subject of this and the next chapter. In this chapter, we will examine the basic nature of organization design and structure as well as the issue of organizational effectiveness. In Chapter 11, we will consider several contingencies that impact on organization design and effectiveness—most notably, the external environment and technology. Taken together, these two chapters build upon our analysis of group processes and job design and set the stage for our exploration of organizational processes in Part Four.

ORGANIZATIONS: BASIC CONSIDERATIONS

We begin with some basics concerning organizations, starting with a definition of organizations and the basic subsystems of organizations.

What Is an Organization?

In the literature on business management, a wide variety of definitions can be found for *organization*. One of the earliest definitions was advanced by Barnard, who viewed an organization as "a system of consciously coordinated activities of two or more persons."[2] According to this definition, organizations are considered to have stated purposes, communications systems and other coordinating processes, and a network of individuals who willingly cooperate on tasks necessary for organizational goal attainment. Similarly, Etzioni describes organizations as "planned units, deliberately structured for the purpose of attaining specific goals."[3] Finally, Porter, Lawler, and Hackman argue that organizations are typically characterized by five basic factors: (1) social composition, (2) goal orientation, (3) differentiated functions, (4) intended rational coordination, and (5) continuity through time.[4]

Common themes run through these definitions of organizations. First, organizations are seen as groups of people working together for common goals. The members of an organization may differ as to the relative values they attach to the various objectives, but individuals might pursue goals valued by the organization in exchange for the organization pursuing goals that are more highly valued by the individuals. Through coalition and cooperation, individual members of an organization try to satisfy their own diverse needs and goals commensurate with available resources.

Organizations come in many sizes and shapes. Consider, for example, a local chapter of Mothers Against Drunk Driving (MADD), depicted in Exhibit 10.1. As you can see, the structure (lines of authority, communication channels, decision-making mechanisms, etc.) of this organization is quite simple. Now compare this structure to that of the Hewlett-Packard Corporation, one of America's largest high-tech firms (Exhibit 10.2). Hewlett-Packard is involved in a wide range of technology-based industries and businesses. The organization's

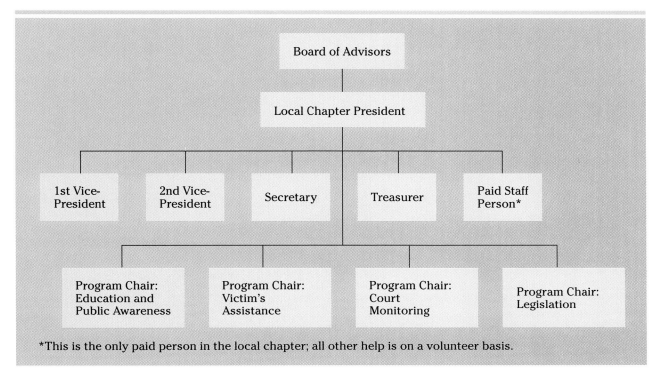

*This is the only paid person in the local chapter; all other help is on a volunteer basis.

Exhibit 10.1
Organization Chart for a
Local Chapter of Mothers
Against Drunk Driving
(MADD)

structure is complex, and the potential organizational problems are tremendous. Moreover, in Exhibit 10.2 each box represents hundreds and sometimes thousands of employees, whereas each box in Exhibit 10.1 represents a single person. Still, both the local chapter of MADD and Hewlett-Packard represent organizations, and both face the myriad problems and challenges facing contemporary organizations.

A Systems View of Organizations

Perhaps the best way to understand the intricacies of organizational dynamics is to view organizations as *open systems*. By doing so, we recognize that all organizations receive *inputs* from the external environment (for example, new employees, raw materials for manufacturing, capital investment, etc.) and also return *outputs* to the environment (for example, finished goods and services, return on shareholders' equity, etc.). This systems approach emphasizes the dynamic nature of organizations; they exist in a constant state of flux (see Exhibit 10.3). Moreover, this approach emphasizes the symbiotic relationship between an organization and its external environment. An organization simply cannot survive without the support and resources available from outside the organization.

Organizations also carry out a variety of *transformation processes*. That is, they bring in inputs from outside the organization and transform them into outputs before returning them to the outside environment. For instance, raw materials are brought in and transformed into new products, which are then sold to

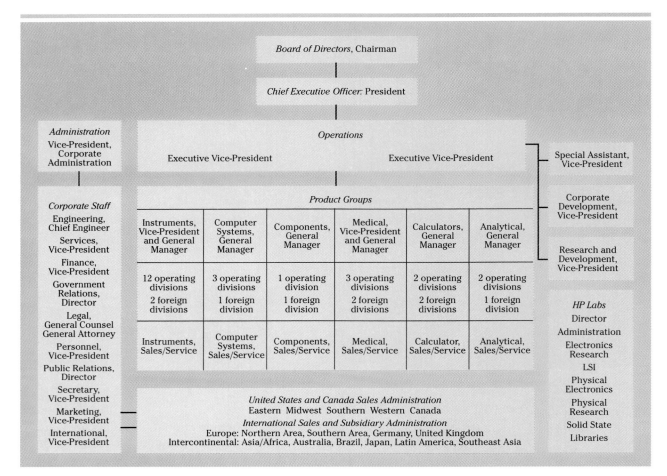

Exhibit 10.2
Organization Chart for
Hewlett-Packard Corporation

Source: A. Szalagyi and M. Wallace, *Organizational Behavior and Performance* (Glenview, Ill.: Scott, Foresman, 1987), p. 552. Courtesy of Hewlett-Packard Company.

the marketplace as outputs. Or, capital is invested, and shareholders receive a profit for their investment. Most often, the transformation process involves some form of "value-added" change. That is, the organization attempts to produce a product that has more value than the sum of the raw materials required to produce it; without this added value, efficiency and competitiveness are reduced, and the long-term survivability of the organization is in doubt.

In order to accomplish this transformation process and realize organizational goals and objectives, organizations must obviously divide and distribute tasks and engage in some form of specialization. When we view organizations as open systems, these various areas of specialization can be categorized into five subsystems (refer to Exhibit 10.3). These are:

1. The *productive* subsystem, where concern is focused on the major functions or work of the system (e.g., a manufacturing department).
2. The *supportive* subsystem, which acquires necessary raw materials for the productive subsystem or distributes the system's finished products (e.g., a purchasing or marketing department).

3. The *maintenance* subsystem, which maintains and protects the organization's structural integrity and character (e.g., training programs, compensation plans, company newspapers).
4. The *adaptive* subsystem, which focuses on the adaptation and long-range survival of the organization in a changing environment (e.g., an R&D [research and development] department; long-range planning functions).
5. The *managerial* subsystem, which coordinates, controls, and directs the other four subsystems so that maximum effort can be directed toward goal attainment.[5]

All five subsystems, when taken together, constitute the organization. As should be evident throughout this book, virtually all aspects of managing people at work are influenced by the nature of these subsystems.

It is important to note that the characteristics of each of these subsystems can vary considerably across organizations. In fact, a major problem that continues to complicate the study of organizational behavior is the heterogeneity of organizations. Organizations differ not only in their size and shape (tall versus flat) but also in the technologies they employ, the external environments in which they function, the corporate cultures they create, and the types of goals and objectives they pursue. It is this property of uniqueness that complicates attempts to draw meaningful generalizations about what managers can do to improve their operations. Such a fact cautions against the search for hard and fast principles of management and instead suggests a contingency approach to the study of organizations and the people who work within them.

Exhibit 10.3
A Systems View
of Organizations

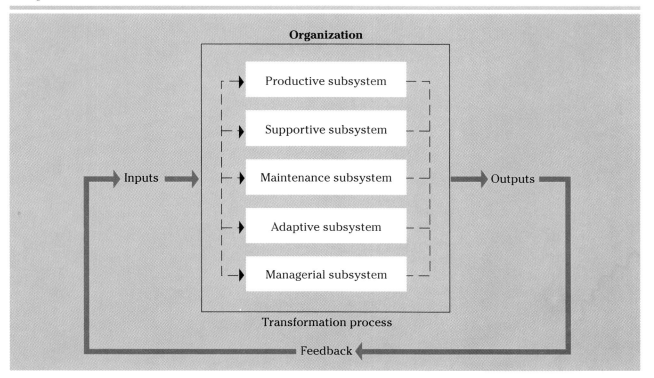

ORGANIZATIONAL EFFECTIVENESS

In today's competitive world, an organization must exert considerable effort to survive and prosper. Otherwise, it runs the risk of being taken over or simply run out of business. This is the challenge of industrial competitiveness. Organizations have to compete, and, typically, only the best survive. In order to survive, an organization must be effective; it must meet certain requirements of the external environment.

What Is Organizational Effectiveness?

The term *organizational effectiveness* has been used and misused in a variety of ways in the literature on organizations. Some people equate the term with profit or productivity; others view it with regard to job satisfaction; and still others see it in light of societal good. However, such simplistic definitions tend to be far too narrow to be useful; they are situation-specific and value-laden. Instead, as noted earlier, organizations are quite diverse in their natures and missions. As such, a more comprehensive approach to defining the terms is to follow Talcott Parsons and Amitai Etzioni and define *organizational effectiveness* in terms of an organization's ability to acquire and efficiently use available resources to achieve specific goals.[6]

The definition requires elaboration. To begin, we are focusing on *operative goals,* not *official goals.* That is, our concern here is with what the organization is really trying to do, not with public relations statements concerning what it says it is doing. For many years, for example, a major electronics firm used to say "progress is our most important product"; obviously, this was not the case. Profit was their most important product (goal), and their products were simply a means to that goal. Second, inherent in this definition is the realization that effectiveness is best judged by an organization's ability to compete in a turbulent environment and successfully acquire and utilize resources. This emphasizes the fact that managers must deal effectively with their external environments to secure needed resources (see Chapter 11). Finally, this approach clearly recognizes that the concept of efficiency is a necessary yet insufficient ingredient of effectiveness (see below).

To be effective, an organization must obtain and efficiently use resources to achieve operative goals. However, as stated previously, members of an organization may not completely agree on the importance of a particular goal. The value that the board of directors attaches to a goal is likely to differ from that of employees or society as a whole. In short, it seems logical to conclude that organizational effectiveness is best assessed by those whose goals are involved. That is, it is necessary to take a "multiple constituency" or stakeholder approach and recognize that various groups have a stake in the organization's success. As Friedlander and Pickle argue:

> Clearly, effectiveness criteria must take into account the profitability of the organization, the degree to which it satisfies its members, and the degree to which it is of value to the larger society of which it is a part. These three perspectives include systems maintenance and growth, subsystem fulfillment and environment fulfillment.[7]

In other words, when we assess effectiveness, clear recognition must be given to simultaneously satisfying diverse and often opposing interest groups. This balancing act represents a real challenge to managers.

IN PRACTICE

Multiple Stakeholders and Organizational Restructuring at San Diego State

San Diego State University (SDSU) was the crown jewel of "tier two universities" in the three-tiered higher education system of California, but in 1992 drastic changes in the environment seemed about to shatter this diamond. In 1960, California designed a higher education system that virtually guaranteed that all California high school graduates could go on to college. The University of California was the highest tier and included research-oriented campuses (Berkeley, UCLA, Irvine, etc.). The California State University system (Cal State Long Beach, Fullerton, etc.) constituted the tier two schools and were designed for the top third of graduating high school students. The community college system was open to virtually anyone who had a high school diploma.

In 1992, tough economic conditions led to dramatic budget cuts in higher education funding. At SDSU, state funding, which represented over 80 percent of the university's revenue, was cut 16.2 percent over two years. Several restructuring steps had already been taken to try to cope with the situation, including cutting 600 faculty members from the payroll and increasing tuition by 40 percent. Thomas Day, the president of SDSU, had to consider organizational restructuring options. In considering his alternatives he also had to consider a diverse set of stakeholders including taxpayers, students, faculty, alumni, and employers.

He was considering cutting a total of nine departments, including aerospace engineering and industrial studies. This would also require cutting more faculty, including tenured faculty. Obviously the faculty, especially tenured faculty, affected by the potential cuts vigorously opposed them. But so did many local employers. "Cutting things like the chemistry department is just stupid, "said Howard Greene, chairman of a San Diego biotechnology firm. Students who had plans to work in areas related to the proposed departmental cuts were also opposed.

Day was also considering another 40 percent increase in annual tuition above its $1,308 level in 1992. Some taxpayers were in favor of the increase and felt that those who could pay more should do so and that California schools must not be so heavily subsidized by taxes. Students argued that for many of them, the low tuitions and high-quality education were vital to their moving out of lower socioeconomic conditions. The previous tuition increase was one reason why student enrollment had dropped 17 percent in 1991.

Day was also considering increasing teaching loads and class sizes. Students protested because already it was difficult to get into classes needed for graduation. In fact, it now took 20 percent longer to graduate, and in one semester, 1,200 students were unable to get a single class for which they registered. Furthermore, even when desired classes were obtained, there was often standing-room-only in the classes. Teachers complained that with such a workload, they had to use multiple-choice tests that were graded by computers.

In considering how to restructure SDSU, president Day was confronted with issues of efficiency, effectiveness, and conflicting demands among various stakeholders. What was his responsibility to students, faculty, the San Diego community, and taxpayers of California?[8]

Requirements of Organizations

To understand organizational effectiveness, it is necessary to first understand what most organizations need just in order to survive. In order to maintain a certain amount of stability and predictability within the surrounding external environment, organizations must meet a series of *organizational requirements* to stay in business. The extent to which organizations can successfully satisfy these requirements will largely determine their ability to persist in the pursuit of their goals and objectives. If an organization cannot fulfill these requirements, severe threats to its stability can jeopardize its chances for survival. These threats may take the forms of loss of resources, loss of legitimation from the supporting environment, or organizational stagnation. Such losses have obvious implications for the people who work for the organization.

Organizational requirements include the following:

Resource acquisition. Organizations must be able to compete successfully for scarce resources for organizational activities.

Efficiency. Organizations must strive to secure the most advantageous ratio of inputs to outputs in the transformation process.

Production or output. Organizations must produce and deliver their goods and services in a steady and predictable fashion.

Rational coordination. The activities of the organization must be integrated and coordinated in a logical, predictable fashion consistent with the ultimate goals of the organization.

Organizational renewal and adaptation. Most organizations must invest some resources in activities that will enhance the net worth of the organization in the future (e.g., research and development). Without renewal efforts, organizational survival is often threatened by short-term shifts in market demands, resources, and so forth.

Conformity. Because of the close interrelationship between an organization and its external environment, organizations (and their members) must often follow the dictates and norms of the environment. Wide deviation from social norms, laws, regulations, and shifts in moral standards can result in a variety of sanctions being levied against the organization. This can reduce its sources of legitimacy and threaten its survival.

Constituency satisfaction. Finally, organizations are composed of a variety of constituencies, including employees, investors, and consumers. For system effectiveness, organizations must satisfy—or at least partially satisfy—their various constituencies to gain necessary support and cooperation. In view of the often conflicting demands made by these various constituents (e.g., employees want more money, investors want more profits, and consumers want lower prices), a major function of managers is to achieve a workable balance so that all parties are at least marginally satisfied and willing to continue participating in the venture.

Criteria for Evaluating Effectiveness

In view of these requirements, how do we assess the degree of effectiveness of an organization? Following the multiple constituency approach described above, we need criteria that recognize that most organizations must satisfy different—and often competing—constituencies. Such an approach has been proposed by Kim Cameron[9] and is shown in Exhibit 10.4. On the basis of this work, we can identify four primary criteria for evaluating the extent to which an organization is effective. These are as follows:

1. *Goal accomplishment.* To what extent has the organization met or exceeded its operative goals? Is the organization doing what it set out to do?
2. *Resource acquisition.* To what extent is the organization successful in acquiring the resources it needs to accomplish its mission?
3. *Healthy internal processes.* Is the organization running smoothly? Is information flow efficient? Are employee trust and loyalty high? Is intergroup conflict low? In short, is this a healthy organization?
4. *Strategic constituency satisfaction.* Are the demands and interests of the key constituencies, or stakeholders, in the organization being met? These constituencies include customers, stockholders, employees, and so forth. To what extent are these various stakeholders satisfied with their relationship with the company?

One way to gauge the effectiveness of an organization is to ask how well these four criteria are met. Although this is an imprecise analytic technique, it nonetheless offers a comprehensive way to evaluate the extent to which the organization is doing what it set out to do as well as its ability to survive in the long term.

Exhibit 10.4
Four Interrelated Approaches
to Organizational Effectiveness

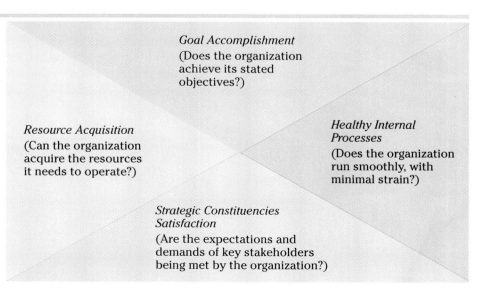

Goal Accomplishment
(Does the organization achieve its stated objectives?)

Resource Acquisition
(Can the organization acquire the resources it needs to operate?)

Healthy Internal Processes
(Does the organization run smoothly, with minimal strain?)

Strategic Constituencies Satisfaction
(Are the expectations and demands of key stakeholders being met by the organization?)

Source: Based on research by K. Cameron, "Effectiveness as Paradox: Consensus and Conflict in Conceptions of Organizational Effectiveness," *Management Science,* May 1986, pp. 539–553.

Effectiveness and Efficiency

Many managers equate the terms *effectiveness* and *efficiency*. However, treating these two related but distinct concepts as interchangeable only serves to confuse the assessment process. Whereas effectiveness is the extent to which operative goals can be attained, *efficiency* is the cost/benefit ratio incurred in the pursuit of those goals. It is possible to have one without the other. An example of efficiency without effectiveness might be a firm that makes thousands of buggy whips with virtually no scrap and very few employees. The firm is efficient but not effective because the market for buggy whips these days is virtually nonexistent. Efficiency relates to the issue of how much input of raw materials, money, and people is necessary to attain a given level of output or a particular goal. If two companies making the same product finish the fiscal year with equal production levels, but the first invested fewer resources than the second, then the first company would be described as more efficient—it achieved the same level of output with fewer inputs. A crude example of this can be seen in Exhibit 10.5, which summarizes a study of the number of employees required to make automobiles in various companies in the United States, Europe, and Japan. (Note that Japan makes more extensive use of robots to replace humans and increase production efficiency.)

It is easy to see how decreased efficiency could be detrimental to organizational effectiveness. The more costly it becomes to achieve a goal, the less likely the organization will be able to survive. For instance, while many managers and employees believe in the merits of job enrichment, what happens if the costs of such efforts make the company's products too expensive in the marketplace? The resulting inefficiency could force the organization out of business.

Another example of how inefficiency, however well-intentioned, can affect effectiveness can be seen in the recent flight of a British Airways Boeing 747 from Tokyo to London. Because of mechanical difficulty, the plane was delayed 24 hours. As a result, all but one of the 191 passengers transferred to other flights. But not Mrs. Yamamoto. She remained with the plane and in the end became BA's sole passenger on the 8000-mile flight. During the flight, she had her choice of six inflight movies, a wide variety of food and beverages, and the undivided attention of 15 flight attendants. Afterward, Mrs. Yamamoto observed that the service had been good. Besides, the airline upgraded her to business class! But the 13-hour flight cost British Airways roughly $100,000, including $25,000 for fuel.[10]

Exhibit 10.5
Employee Efficiency
Ratios for Various
Automobile Companies

Company	Number of Cars Produced	Number of Employees	Efficiency Ratio
Austin-Rover	500,000	130,000	4:1
General Motors	4,000,000	517,000	8:1
Volkswagen	1,600,000	150,000	11:1
Renault	1,700,000	100,000	17:1
Toyota	2,000,000	45,000	44:1

Source: R. Daft and R. Steers, *Organizations: A Micro/Macro Approach.* (Glenview, Ill.: Scott, Foresman, 1986), p. 335. Copyright © 1986 Scott, Foresman and Company.

Relative labor costs, productivity per man-hour, costs of raw materials, and technological advances are just a few of the many factors used to determine the efficiency of a given organization. In the last decade, for example, many business enterprises have moved their factories from one country to another because of lower taxes or labor costs or to have better access to sources of raw materials and reduced transportation costs. Such moves may be seen as attempts at improving efficiency, if not effectiveness.

The concept of efficiency may be viewed as being closely related to effectiveness. Whether or not efficiency is a determinant of effectiveness depends upon several additional factors, such as the availability or scarcity of resources. In general, efficiency is defined here as the extent to which resources are rationally utilized in the pursuit of organizational goals. In this sense, factors such as employee turnover and absenteeism (that is, the wasting of human resources) may represent more a statement of organizational inefficiency than ineffectiveness.

International Challenge

IN PRACTICE
Flying the Friendly Skies of Aeroflot

It has often been observed both in the United States and abroad that a key contributor to inefficiency and poor quality is a bureaucratic monopoly. In most countries, people point to the postal service and other government bureaucracies as classic examples of how not to organize. In socialist countries such as the Soviet Union, numerous examples of the inefficient consequences of government bureaucracies can be found. One such example is Aeroflot, the airline of the former USSR.

By any standard of comparison, Aeroflot is the largest airline in the world. For instance, Aeroflot has a total of 2300 aircraft and flies 116 million passengers per year on a total of 4000 daily flights to 3500 domestic cities and 99 countries. United Airlines, by contrast, has 373 aircraft and flies 56 million passengers per year on 1804 daily flights to 146 domestic cities and 13 countries. Yet if we look at effectiveness or efficiency, Aeroflot is consistently found at the bottom of any world ranking.

Why? Several reasons can be found. First, in a country whose constitution guarantees full employment, considerable pressure is placed on the airline to hire far more employees than it needs. In fact, the largest single airline office staff in the world can be found in Moscow. At a Russian ticket counter, for example, it often takes four agents to issue a single airline ticket. One punches the reservation into the computer, a second verifies the entry, a third writes out the ticket by hand, while a fourth takes the money.

The organization is highly centralized—all 46 divisions of the enterprise are run from Moscow—and has been a source of political patronage for decades. There are no competitors, and ticket prices are unrelated to costs. For instance, of the 116 million tickets sold in one year, 110 million were sold inside the Soviet Union at heavily discounted rates. As a result, you can fly from Moscow to St. Petersberg (formerly Leningrad) for $61 or from Moscow to Khabarovsk—almost halfway around the world—for a mere $207. Moreover, the airplanes it flies are gas guzzlers with dubious safety records. (Hungary recently purchased the West European Airbus at three times the price of the Russian equivalent because it calculated the Airbus's greater fuel economy and lower repair time and cost would easily save money in the long run.) Add to this a reputation for daredevil pilots and surly cabin crews (who are often described as having a "take it or take the train" attitude), and you begin to understand the problem.

Efforts under the new *perestroika* to improve efficiency have met with no success. In fact, a recent Pravda editorial called Aeroflot the "Ministry of Closed Doors" and noted that "attempts to change the style of management have come up against a stone wall." A new director attempted to reorganize the airline and introduce cost-cutting measures and better service. To date, no measurable results can be seen. The bureaucracy continues along its merry way.[11]

ORGANIZATION DESIGN: THE BUREAUCRATIC MODEL

At about the same time that industrial engineers such as Frederick Taylor and Henri Fayol were formulating the basic principles of scientific management (see previous chapter), Max Weber was developing a model of organization later to be known as *bureaucracy*. Weber, a German sociologist of the late 1800s, examined the work organizations of his day and found that organizations were run primarily on the basis of customs and politics, not merit or efficiency. People secured administrative jobs principally through contacts, not expertise. Moreover, lines of authority and accountability were often scattered. In response to this, Weber sought to define an ideal organization—one governed by rationality rather than politics.[12]

Characteristics of Bureaucracy

According to Weber, the ideal organization is characterized by the following (see Exhibit 10.6):

Exhibit 10.6
Characteristics of
Bureaucracy

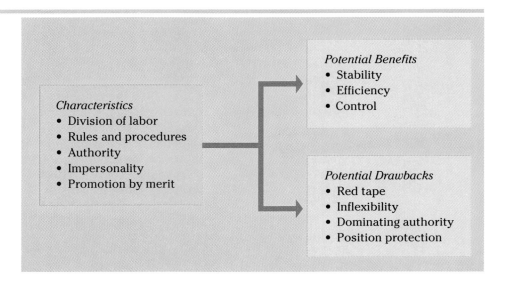

Characteristics
• Division of labor
• Rules and procedures
• Authority
• Impersonality
• Promotion by merit

Potential Benefits
• Stability
• Efficiency
• Control

Potential Drawbacks
• Red tape
• Inflexibility
• Dominating authority
• Position protection

Specialization and division of labor. Tasks required to accomplish the organization's goals are broken down into highly specialized jobs so that everyone can become an expert in his or her area.

Rules and procedures. Weber believed it was important that each task be performed according to a consistent system of abstract rules—thus, the beginning of "standard operating procedures." Such rules and procedures were to lead to a standardized high quality of output, because everyone would know precisely what was expected.

Authority. All positions in an organization are to be arranged in hierarchical form with domains of authority clearly established.

Impersonality of office. Position holders are required to assume an impersonal attitude in dealing with others. Authority is vested in the office, not in the individual; the individual simply acts impersonally as a trustee of the office.

Employment and promotion by merit. Whereas the previous practice had been to make political appointments to office, Weber argued that office holders at all levels should be selected on the bases of merit and qualifications. Here we have an impetus for civil service examinations in Western Europe (although, curiously, such examinations were used in China since the time of Confucius).

It has been argued that some individuals tend to have a "bureaucratic orientation." That is, some people have a greater tendency than others to behave in a bureaucratic fashion. To see if you have such an orientation, you may wish to complete Self-Assessment 10.1. Simply answer "mostly agree" or "mostly disagree" to the 20 questions. When you have finished, score your questionnaire as described in Appendix B.

Problems with Bureaucracy

These ideal characteristics of bureaucracy were meant to result in organizations that were both more productive and more equitable to employees. Stability, efficiency, and control of the organization were all theoretically enhanced. Unfortunately, however, the gulf between theory and actual practice can be great, and the bureaucratic model has been criticized on several grounds (see Exhibit 10.6).

For example, many people feel that the bureaucratic approach creates excessive *red tape.* When a bureaucracy is faced with a new problem, however small, it typically responds with new rules or procedures. The ever-increasing multitude of rules serves to constrain creative behavior. Instead of finding solutions to problems, people often spend their time following rules. This may contribute to another criticism—that bureaucracies have *reduced flexibility* of operations. The nature of a highly structured organization makes adaptation and innovation difficult. Instead, the organization continues on its preordained path.

In some situations, bureaucracies create conditions in which there is a *dominance of authority.* That is, having more authority—and exercising that authority—becomes almost an end in itself. Likewise, people with less authority tend to blindly follow the dictates of those with more authority, regardless of whether such dictates are wise, prudent, or ethical.

SELF-ASSESSMENT 10.1
What Is Your Bureaucratic Orientation?

Instructions: For each statement, check the response (either mostly agree or mostly disagree) that better represents your feelings.

	Mostly Agree	Mostly Disagree
1. I value stability in my job.	_____	_____
2. I like a predictable organization.	_____	_____
3. The best job for me would be one in which the future is uncertain.	_____	_____
4. The U.S. Army would be a nice place to work.	_____	_____
5. Rules, policies, and procedures tend to frustrate me.	_____	_____
6. I would enjoy working for a company that employed 85,000 people worldwide.	_____	_____
7. Being self-employed would involve more risk than I'm willing to take.	_____	_____
8. Before accepting a job, I would like to see an exact job description.	_____	_____
9. I would prefer a job as a freelance house painter to one as a clerk for the Department of Motor Vehicles.	_____	_____
10. Seniority should be as important as performance in determining pay increases and promotion.	_____	_____
11. It would give me a feeling of pride to work for the largest and most successful company in its field.	_____	_____
12. Given a choice, I would prefer to make $30,000 per year as a vice-president in a small company to $35,000 as a staff specialist in a large company.	_____	_____
13. I would regard wearing an employee badge with a number on it as a degrading experience.	_____	_____
14. Parking spaces in a company lot should be assigned on the basis of job level.	_____	_____
15. If an accountant works for a large organization, he or she cannot be a true professional.	_____	_____
16. Before accepting a job (given a choice), I would want to make sure that the company had a very fine program of employee benefits.	_____	_____
17. A company will probably not be successful unless it establishes a clear set of rules and procedures.	_____	_____
18. Regular working hours and vacations are more important to me than finding thrills on the job.	_____	_____
19. You should respect people according to their rank.	_____	_____
20. Rules are meant to be broken.	_____	_____

Source: A. J. DuBrin, *Human Relations: A Job Oriented Approach,* Fourth Edition, © 1988, pp. 386–387. Reprinted by permission of Prentice Hall, Inc., Englewood Cliffs, N.J.

Finally, the hierarchical progression of careers proposed by bureaucratic theory is supposed to create a condition where people rise in rank as a result of merit. In actual fact, however, people often rise by seniority. Hence, a *psychology of position protection* is created, in which employees exert energy to maintain and protect their positions (and the perquisites that go with such positions) instead of exerting energy on organizational goals or effectiveness. Although other shortcomings could be mentioned here, the point is that bureaucracy in practice is very different from bureaucracy in theory. Although bureaucracy was designed to reduce inefficiencies and incompetence in organizations, modern bureaucracies often contribute to such ills; recent efforts in organization design have attempted to develop new approaches that minimize these negative influences on organizational life. We turn now to an examination of these approaches.

International Challenge

IN PRACTICE
Life Inside Egypt's Mugamma

The Mugamma (Arabic for "central complex") is a massive grey stone building in the center of Cairo that houses several of Egypt's ministries. It is a place where citizens come for a variety of government-related services and approvals. The Mugamma was designed and built in the early 1960s as a symbol of what the government could do for its people. Instead, to many Egyptians, it has come to represent the inefficiency of governmental bureaucracy.

On any given day, tens of thousands of people wander through the grim corridors in search of a government stamp or an official document. Oftentimes, they discover that to get a stamp from one ministry one must have a stamp from another ministry elsewhere in the building or across Cairo. And all the time, things go very slowly. In fact, one young Egyptian observed that "unless you know somebody in the Mugamma, unless you have a connection, you could be in there for a week before you got your stamp." The only way to deal with bureaucracy is to circumvent it, either with *wasta* (influence) or *baksheesh* (bribes).

No one knows how many employees work in the Mugamma. What is known is that they actually work very little. As people wander the halls in search of government stamps, employees sit idly by in side offices drinking endless cups of tea or coffee and gossiping quietly. Much of the time, the employees are not even present. Many hold down second jobs (during ministry hours) and simply check in during the morning, only to leave again to get to their second jobs. In fact, one government study found that a typical government employee worked only 27 minutes a day! To make up for this, the government hires more employees, now estimated to be as many as 3 million, or one-third of the entire country's work force. And all the while, Egypt's population continues to receive less than desired service from its government, and Egypt as a country continues to lose ground in the battle for economic development.[13]

DIMENSIONS OF ORGANIZATION STRUCTURE

Before moving on to organizational structure, it is useful to briefly reiterate several key issues. First, organizations are open systems, existing within and influenced by the larger environment. In general, organizations must be both efficient and effective in order to survive and in being effective must satisfy multiple stakeholders. Consequently, in the last 200 years, most efforts at organizational design have focused on a rational approach in which division of labor, procedures, and established levels and lines of authority have been in focus as means of achieving organizational efficiency and effectiveness. In the context of this backdrop, we can now more productively examine the topic of organizational structure. Simply put, *organization structure* refers to the way in which an organization puts together its human resources for goal-directed activities. The way the various human parts of an organization fit together into relatively fixed relationships defines patterns of social interaction, coordination, and task-oriented behavior. The role of structure in the success and functioning of an enterprise has long been a topic of concern among both organizational analysts and managers.

The concept of organization structure can, in turn, be broken down into various *dimensions*. At least four such dimensions have relevance for the study of organizational behavior: (1) decentralization versus centralization, (2) tall versus flat, (3) division of labor, and (4) departmentalization.

Decentralization

Decentralization refers to the extent to which various types of power and authority are extended down through the organizational hierarchy. The more decentralized an organization, the greater the extent to which the rank-and-file employees can participate in and accept responsibility for decisions concerning their jobs and the future activities of the organization.

Historically, an increase in organization size has typically brought with it an increase in centralization of authority and power in the upper echelons of management. As organizations grew, the distance between the relevant sources of information for decision making (often located near the bottom of the hierarchy) and the decision makers themselves became greater, resulting in poor communications, unfortunate decisions, and reduced effectiveness. Although it is not possible to pinpoint precisely when this trend toward increased centralization plateaued, business historian Alfred Chandler has suggested that it may have been during the 1920s, when Alfred P. Sloan, Jr., then president of General Motors, introduced the concept of the *central office*.[14] The central office was to concentrate the most important organization-wide *policy* decisions in the hands of major corporate executives while decentralizing responsibility for *operating* decisions to the lowest level possible in the various operating divisions. In theory, most decisions would be made closer to their information sources, which would lead to increased flexibility of operation and increased divisional autonomy while maintaining corporate control over major policy matters (see Chapter 14).

Decentralization in organizations often leads to improvements in several facets of organizational effectiveness, including managerial efficiency, open communications and feedback, job satisfaction, and employee retention. Decentralization has led to improved performance and greater innovation and creativity in organizations such as the 3M Company and others, although the findings here are not entirely consistent.[15] These findings suggest that decentralized organizations allow for greater autonomy and responsibility among employees at lower levels in the hierarchy, and therefore that they allow for more effective utilization of an organization's human resources. This is consistent with recent findings that among individual employees, increased autonomy and responsibility often lead to increased job involvement, satisfaction, and performance.

It should be pointed out, however, that a close relationship between decentralization and improved effectiveness is not always found. For example, one study discovered that decentralized control led to improved performance in research laboratories but caused poorer performance in production departments.[16] Such findings will be examined more closely in the next chapter, when we consider environment and its impact on organization design and effectiveness. Moreover, it is possible that differing job technologies, work environments, or goals may call for varying degrees of decentralization in order to be successful. Thus, although we must clearly recognize the benefits of decentralization in work organizations, several potential weaknesses should also be recognized.[17] These include the following:

- Innovation and growth may tend to be restricted to existing projects or functional areas, because fewer means of coordinating and integrating the various decentralized units exist.

- In some cases, it may be difficult to allocate pooled resources such as laboratory space.

- Decentralization makes it more difficult for certain functions (e.g., personnel, purchasing) to be shared.

- Decentralization can lead to jurisdictional disputes and/or conflicts over priorities because each unit essentially becomes an independent entrepreneurial area.

- Decentralization may create conditions in which competence and expertise deteriorate because of inbreeding and isolation. It may increase the difficulty of attracting technical specialists.

- In the extreme, decentralization may lead to ultimate ineffectiveness of operations because of a lack of high-level coordination and integration.

Managers of effective organizations must seek the optimal balance of decentralization and centralization. The decentralization concept should not be seen as good or bad in itself. The organization must decentralize enough power and authority to allow for the full use of the knowledge and expertise of lower-level participants; but it must simultaneously maintain the degree of centralization necessary to ensure coordination and control.

Tall Versus Flat Organizations

A second dimension of organization structure focuses on the vertical structural arrangements of the organization—that is, the extent to which an organization is tall or flat. As shown in Exhibit 10.7, a tall organization typically has more levels of management than a flat one. Both the tall and flat organizations shown in the exhibit have the same number of employees; they are simply arranged differently.

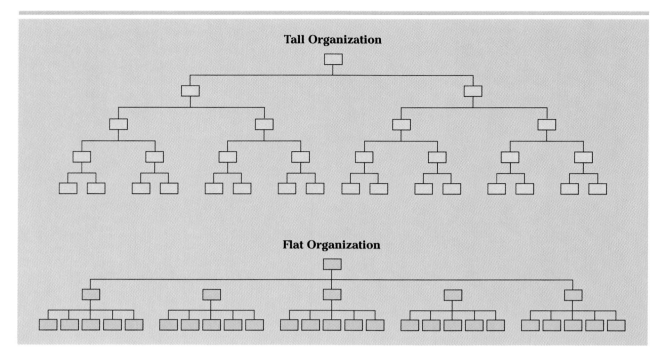

Tall Organization

Flat Organization

Exhibit 10.7
Examples of Tall and Flat
Organization Structures

What difference does such variation in organization structure make? To begin, tall organizations allow for closer control over subordinates. Because a manager has fewer subordinates, he or she has more time to focus on the activities of those few people. Managers in flat organizations, on the other hand, must oversee the activities of more people; this places greater responsibility for task accomplishment on subordinates. In a very definitive manner, flat organizations facilitate increased decentralization of power and authority.

Second, tall organizations allow for greater personal contact between manager and subordinate, again because the manager has fewer people to oversee. The risk, however, is that the manager comes to know two or three subordinates very well but fails to become acquainted with those further down the hierarchy. In contrast, a flat organization forces a manager to get to know more people, albeit on a somewhat more superficial level.

Finally, tall organizations often serve to inhibit interpersonal communication. This occurs because the greater number of levels through which a message must be transmitted allows for more distortion of the message (see Chapter 13). In contrast, managers in flat organizations come into direct contact with a greater number of subordinates; this allows for increased direct communication and accuracy of message transmission. Furthermore, it is often the case that in flat organizations, decision-making authority is pushed down, so managers can concentrate on activities such as coordination rather on directly monitoring subordinate behavior. Thus in turn a manager in a flat organization can supervise twice as many subordinates than in tall organizations without having to work twice as hard or having to spend twice as much time at work.

In summary, it would be inappropriate to conclude that one type of organization (tall or flat) is superior to the other. The appropriate number of levels in an organization depends upon many factors, including the purpose of the organization, the people, the technology involved, and the resources available. For instance, one can make an argument that an R&D organization (which requires an open exchange of ideas and has rather long time horizons for planning) requires a flatter organization structure than a military organization (which requires quick and unquestioning response in times of crisis). One form is not "better" than the other. Instead, each organization utilizes the form that is more suitable for its purpose and environment.

Division of Labor

Even though Weber formulated the concept of *division of labor* (or functional specialization) in the late 1800s in Germany, it traces its American origins to the scientific management movement around the turn of this century. Frederick Taylor and his associates argued that a major determinant of success was the ability of an organization to divide its work functions into highly specialized activities (see discussion on early approaches to job design in previous chapter). As support for specialization, these writers (looking at effectiveness from the standpoint of industrial engineering) cited Adam Smith's example of the manufacture of straight pins in England. Smith had noted that in the late eighteenth century (before the advent of the Industrial Revolution), 1 worker by himself could make 20 straight pins per day. However, when the tasks required to make such pins were divided into 10 separate operations and each worker carried out only 1 such operation, 10 workers could make 48,000 pins per day (4,800 pins per worker). Thus, specialization brought about a 240-fold increase in productivity. Examples such as this represented major sources of support for Taylor and other advocates of increased specialization.

The major hypothesis underlying the concept of increased division of labor is that it leads to increased effectiveness because it allows each employee to develop expertise in one particular area, which maximizes his or her contribution to production. This hypothesis formed the basis for Henry Ford's introduction of the assembly line and the mass production of cars.

Unfortunately, few rigorous attempts have been made to examine this hypothesis in organizational settings. The evidence that does exist seems to indicate that increased specialization is often associated with reduced labor costs and increased innovation and creativity—both enhancers of organizational effectiveness. However, specialization has also been shown to be related to increased friction and conflict within organizations. Apparently, increased specialization causes frustration among some employees because it limits their behavior and their attempts to satisfy their personal goals. The employees may express their dissatisfaction in various forms of industrial conflict.

In other words, although division of labor is frequently beneficial in terms of employee performance, it may simultaneously be detrimental to employees' job attitudes, mental health, and willingness to remain with the organization. Thus, the benefit of increased productivity derived from a high degree of specialization may be more than offset by such negative consequences as strikes, sabotage, turnover, absenteeism, and so forth. Again, management must decide how best to balance costs and benefits in its attempts to discover the optimal organizational design.

Perhaps the concept of division of labor is best seen in the many experiments with job redesign. For instance, Exhibit 10.8 compares a traditional automobile assembly line with the autonomous work group approach taken by Swedish automobile makers Volvo and Saab (see Chapter 9). With this new technique, the traditional assembly line, with its high degree of specialization,

Exhibit 10.8
Two Different Approaches
to Division of Labor at
Saab-Scania

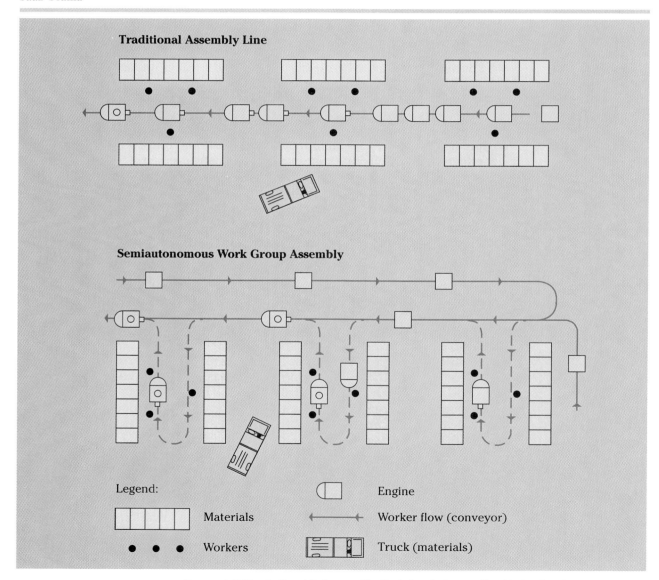

Source: J. P. Norstedt and S. Aguren, The Saab-Scania Report (Stockholm: Swedish Employers' Confederation, 1973), pp. 35 and 37. Reprinted by permission.

is virtually eliminated. Instead, workers return to the "craftsperson" approach in which each employee is trained in multiple functions and supposedly has a better idea about how the whole product fits together. Employees form work teams to jointly build subunits.

Departmentalization

The final dimension of organization structure to be discussed here is departmentalization. In brief, *departmentalization* focuses on how the various primary tasks of an organization are grouped and can be thought of as a means of division of labor and specialization. Although many approaches to departmentalization have been taken, three of the most common can be identified: departmentalization by function, product, and matrix.

Functional Departmentalization.   We often hear managers refer to the various "functions" of an organization. By function we mean a particular specialized activity that is central to an organization's continued survival. Such functions for a typical business organization include marketing, finance, manufacturing, research and development, personnel, and so forth. *Functional* departmentalization, then, organizes the work force according to specialized activities. A simplified example of functional departmentalization can be seen in Exhibit 10.9.

Specialization is one of the primary advantages of departmentalization based on function. Many believe that functional departmentalization leads to increased efficiency and economic utilization of the employees. On the other hand, functional specialization may also lead to situations of goal suboptimization as each department focuses on its own specialty or function at the expense of others. This problem can be clearly seen in the study of selective perception by Dearborn and Simon that was described in Chapter 3.

When a company uses a functional organization design in an international context, we get an organization chart that looks something like Exhibit 10.10. Here we can see the functional design that is typical of multinational

Exhibit 10.9
Simplified Functional
Departmentalization

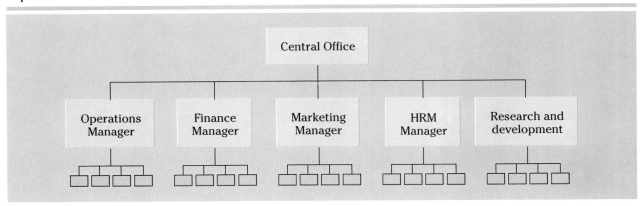

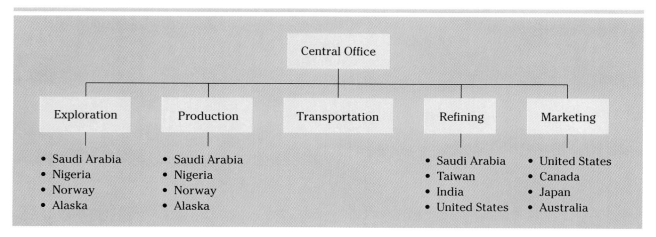

Exhibit 10.10
Functional Organization
Design for Multinational
Oil Firm

oil companies, where certain functions (e.g., exploration and production) are done in one region of the world, and other functions (e.g., refining and marketing) are done in other regions.

Product Departmentalization.   A second approach to departmentalization, often favored by larger organizations, is *product* departmentalization. Under this approach, work units are organized on the basis of products rather than functions. This can be seen in Exhibit 10.11, which provides a simplified diagram of a company that makes two product lines—one for consumers and one for industry. Within each product group, most, if not all, of the various functional areas are represented.

With product departmentalization, each product grouping (consumer products or industrial products, for example) becomes essentially a "company" of its own or, more accurately, a cost center of its own. General Motors, for example, has different divisions to manufacture cars and trucks, locomotives, refrigerators, automobile accessories, and so on. In this way, each division manager focuses all of his or her attention on one business. This makes it easier to control the division and reduces conflict among functional areas.

Exhibit 10.11
Simplified Product
Departmentalization

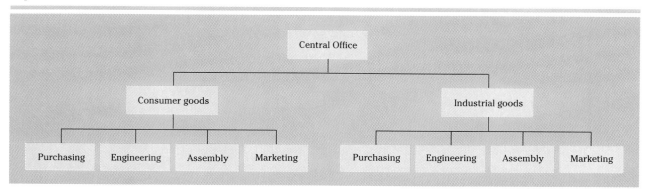

International Challenge

IN PRACTICE
Product Organization and the Japanese Luxury Cars

In 1987, Honda introduced the first Japanese "luxury car" to the American market. It was called the Acura, and it was designed to compete with the upscale European cars that held a solid market share among upper-middle-class American managers and professionals. In 1989, Toyota followed with its Lexus and Nissan with its Infiniti models. All three were instant successes.

What makes these cars distinctive (aside from their attractive styling, high performance, and high quality) is that in each case, the manufacturer decided to establish an entirely separate dealer network to sell the cars. All three, in essence, set up product-based organization structures, with their cheaper cars in one division and their luxury cars in another. This can be seen in Exhibit 10.12, which shows a partial organization chart for Honda. Note the separation between American Honda and Acura. Companies such as Honda felt that the typical Japanese dealership in North America symbolized efficiency and practicality, not luxury. Moreover, having only one integrated dealership might make its less-expensive cars look bad by comparison.

To go after the luxury market, it was reasoned, the manufacturers had to create a separate line of dealers with an up-scale image. As a result, when you enter a Lexus dealership, for example, you will likely find that champagne and hors d'oeuvres are being served and that sales representatives are dressed semiformally. This is just what you would expect to find if you were shopping for image and you were choosing between BMW, Mercedes, or a

Exhibit 10.12
Product Organization for
Honda-U.S.A.

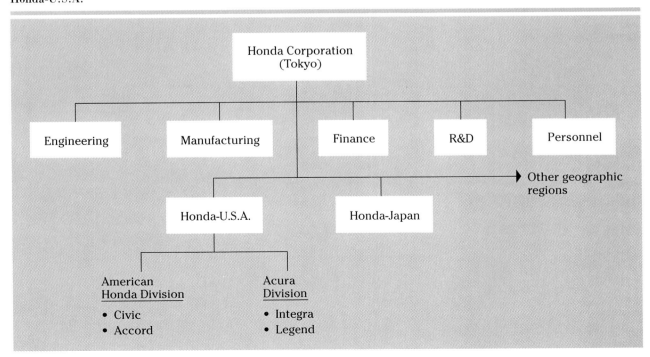

new Lexus or Infiniti. To date, the decision to organize on the basis of product lines appears to have been a sound one. Market share among BMW and Mercedes has fallen significantly, and both companies have mounted aggressive advertising campaigns highlighting the Teutonic traditions of their cars. As the chairman of Mercedes-Benz recently observed, "It's not a BMW but cars like Lexus and Infiniti scare me."[18]

Matrix Organization.   A third approach to departmentalization is the *matrix organization*. In essence, a matrix design represents nothing more than a product departmentalization superimposed on a functional departmentalization. Although authority patterns under matrix vary considerably and are often muddled or ambiguous, a typical pattern would be for the functional managers (e.g., marketing, engineering) to be given some authority and control over the specialists in their own departments (i.e., all marketing representatives would ultimately be accountable to the corporate head of marketing). In this way, clear lines of authority are present to ensure the integrity and viability of the functions. This is referred to as "functional professionalism."

In addition, however, under the matrix design each functional specialist would be assigned to a project group as part of a focused team with specific responsibilities (see Exhibit 10.13). As such, the marketing representative would be responsible both to the corporate marketing department and to the project director. In other words, almost everyone has *two* bosses instead of one.

Exhibit 10.13
Matrix Organization Design at Dow Corning

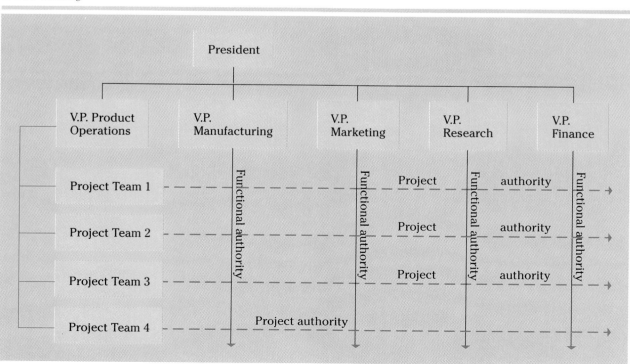

Companies using the matrix design identify several advantages. These include the following:

▪ Each product or project is given special attention, in that a product manager is appointed specifically to look after that product.

▪ Employee utilization is flexible, in that a reservoir of specialists is kept in the various functional organizations.

▪ Specialized knowledge is available to all product or project areas, and this knowledge can be transferred from one project to another.

▪ Project people have a functional home to return to when they are no longer required on a given project.

▪ Response to market fluctuations or customer needs is typically faster, because decision making is centralized within a project group and because each group has the needed functional expertise to act quickly.

▪ A system of checks and balances is established between concerns for product and concerns for function in which both areas of responsibility can receive necessary consideration.

In addition, however, several drawbacks should be noted, as summarized in Exhibit 10.14.

Exhibit 10.14
Comparison of Three
Approaches To
Departmentalization

Functional Departmentalization

Advantages	*Disadvantages*
Encourages specialization	Emphasizes routine tasks
Reduces duplication of scarce resources	Fosters parochial perspectives by managers
Encourages career advancement for specialists	Reduces communication among departments
Facilitates communication within one department	Increases interdepartmental dependencies
	Obscures accountability for overall outcome

Product Departmentalization

Advantages	*Disadvantages*
Fosters orientation toward overall outcome	Limits career advancement by specialists outside their departments
Fosters skill diversification and straining	Increases multiple role demands on employees
Fosters accountability by department managers	Skills and resources may be used inefficiently
Increases department cohesion	

Matrix Departmentalization

Advantages	*Disadvantages*
Brings specialized knowledge to each project	Difficult to introduce without broad-based support
Encourages flexible use of employees	Increases role ambiguity and stress
Increases interdepartmental communication	May reward political skills instead of technical skills
Increases adaptability of products to changing demands	Allows for conflict between functional and product subgroups

IN PRACTICE

Matrix Design at Dow Corning

A long-standing example of a successful matrix design can be seen in the case of Dow Corning. In order to facilitate better communication, planning, and control, Dow Corning implemented a matrix organization design early in its existence. For each of its ten businesses, it set up project groups called "business boards" consisting of a business manager (primarily responsible for the profitability of the business) and representatives from marketing, manufacturing, human research, and technical services and development. (The latter is a troubleshooter who ensures that the customer is satisfied with the technical workings of the product.) (Refer to Exhibit 10.13.)

At Dow Corning, each functional representative reports directly to his or her functional department but also contributes to the design, implementation, and success of the particular business to which he or she is assigned. Thus, each person essentially has two bosses. As a result, care must be taken to ensure that both the functional and business board managers are given sufficient authority and accountability to attain their respective objectives. Coordination and trust are essential ingredients if such a system is to work.

After long experience with the matrix design, the company concluded that the system had both advantages and drawbacks. On the positive side, the matrix design led to higher profit generation, even in industries squeezed by competition; increased competitive ability, based on technical innovation and product quality; sound, prompt decision making, facilitated by open communications; resource allocations proportionate to expected results; more stimulating tasks and on-the-job training; visible and measurable results; more time for top management to focus on long-range planning instead of day-to-day operations; and accountability that is more closely related to responsibility and authority.

But the matrix design was not without its costs, including the need to cope with resistance to change; the need for strong top management support for extended periods; the need for an intelligent and highly motivated middle management anxious to see the whole organization progress; a determination to minimize internal politics; and the need for board members, top management, and middle management to exercise abundant patience. Overall, however, the matrix design at Dow Corning has proved to be an effective organizational tool that facilitates both individual managerial self-development and increased corporate profitability.[19]

INTERORGANIZATIONAL DESIGNS

Before closing our discussion of organization design, we should recognize the existence of a somewhat more complicated approach to organization design. At times, it is necessary for a company to work closely with another company to produce and market a product jointly. Similarly, it is not uncommon to see a group of relatively independent companies joined together in a loosely coupled group bound together primarily by common ownership. In such cases, an organization design is needed to coordinate the activities of the diverse concerns. Such designs may be referred to as *interorganizational designs.* Two general approaches to interorganizational design that are commonly found in today's business world are conglomerates and joint ventures.

Conglomerates

A *conglomerate* is essentially a group of several reasonably autonomous companies that are melded together to form a megacorporation. Several features make conglomerates unique. The first feature is their size; conglomerates are typically quite large. A second feature is the breadth and diversity of goods and services typically produced by the various companies comprising the organization. And a third feature is that despite their diversity and size, conglomerates are typically highly centrally controlled from the central office.

Conglomerates can be found in many parts of the world. In Korea, for instance, this type of organization is called a *chaebol,* or financial clique.[20] Companies such as Samsung and Hyundai produce everything from supertankers to cars to home electronics to textiles to chemicals—all in one conglomerate. The largest Korean *chaebols* consist of over 40 diverse companies that are bonded together by the strong central leadership of the chairman of the group. In Japan, such an organization is called a *keiretsu.* Like the *chaebol,* a *keiretsu* normally consists of a host of diverse business organizations, large and small, all clustered together in a network of reciprocal relationships and all under the direction (formally or informally) of a central office.

A good example of a *keiretsu* can be seen in the case of Mitsubishi (see Exhibit 10.15). As will be noted in the exhibit, the Mitsubishi Group seems to make everything. Moreover, as is typical in *keiretsus* and *chaebols,* Mitsubishi has its own access to financing (Mitsubishi Bank) and its own access to world markets through its own trading company. Consider the simple example of making beer. When Kirin Brewery (a Mitsubishi company) needs glass bottles for its beer, it turns to Asahi Glass, another group company. Paper labels for the bottles comes from Mitsubishi Paper Mills, and shipping is done through Nippon Yusen. World marketing is handled through the group's general trading company and financed through the group's bank. This network of companies provides a reliable source of inputs and raw materials for each company in the group. It also often provides a ready market for its products or services.

The six largest *keiretsu* in Japan account for approximately 15 percent of the Japanese economy, 4 percent of the labor force, and 13 percent of all corporate assets. Generally, firms within a *keiretsu* hold stock in each of the other group companies. Typically, no more than 25 percent of a given firm's stock is held by other *keiretsu* members and any given firm would generally hold less than 5 percent of any other given firm within the *keiretsu.* However, beyond these cross-share holdings, the CEOs of the firms within a *keiretsu* meet on a regular basis. For example, the approximate 29 presidents of firms within the Mitsubishi keiretsu have a meeting called *kinyokai,* which is held every second Tuesday of each month. In these meetings they exchange new ideas, problems, and solutions. In addition, they often exchange executives; practice that is called *amakudari* or gift from heaven. Actually, the practice is less of an exchange and more a movement of executives from the central

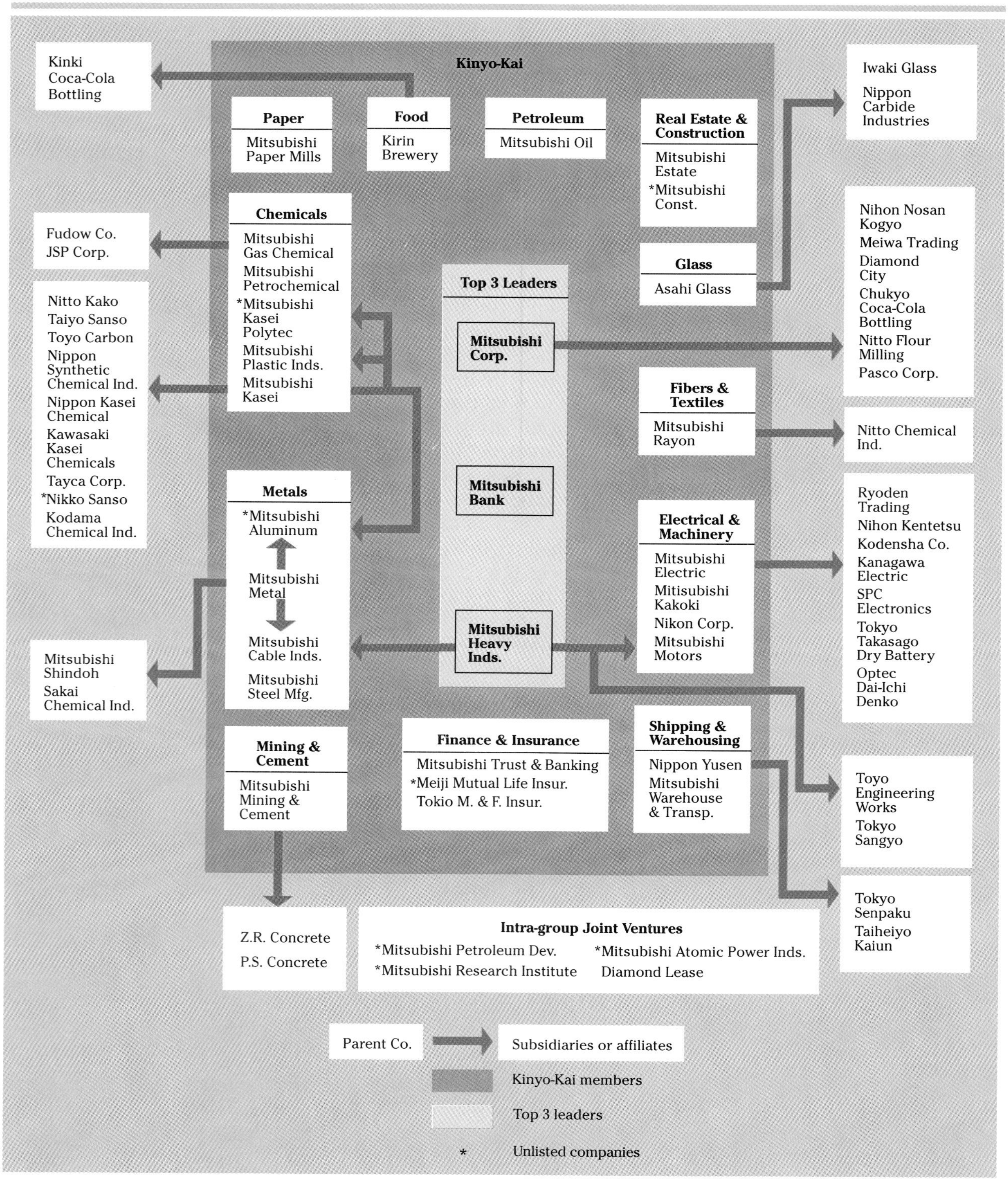

Exhibit 10.15
The Mitsubishi *Keiretsu*

Source: Reprinted with permission from Dodwell Marketing Consultants, *Industrial Groupings in Japan,* Ninth Edition (Tokyo, 1990), p. 52

firms within the *keiretsu,* such as the bank, to less key companies. For example between 1960 and 1982, Mitsubishi Bank placed 27 directors in 21 firms within its group.

Although this system works well for the Japanese business groups, consider what happens to an outsider. In fact, the existence of the *keiretsu* is often at the heart of Western claims concerning "structural impediments" to international trade. As an example, take the case of IBM.[21] IBM used to be the largest computer seller in Japan. They had the right technology, and Japanese companies sought out IBM for the best products. However, as Japanese companies such as NEC and Fujitsu improved their own products, IBM slipped to number three in sales. Why? Part of the answer lies in the fact that when NEC makes a product, all the companies in its *keiretsu* are expected to purchase this product over its non-*keiretsu* rivals (such as IBM). As a result, IBM sales dropped, and charges of structural impediments to trade emerged.

In any case, conglomerates such as Japan's Mitsubishi, Korea's Samsung, or America's ITT all represent powerful business forces on the international scene. And all have the same type of managerial problems as smaller companies, although such problems are often magnified many times over because of the conglomerate's size. This problem will become evident when we turn to an analysis of organizational environments in the following chapter.

Joint Ventures

The second interorganizational structure is the *joint venture.* Here, two legally independent corporations join together to produce a specific product. Typically, such alliances are formed because each partner has something to contribute to the marriage (for example, a new technology, financing, market access, management know-how, and so forth.) Both parties to the agreement hope to gain as a result of the exchange. In the heavy construction equipment industry, for example, Caterpillar held a virtual monopoly until challenged by Komatsu. In order to keep its competitive edge in world markets, Caterpillar responded by forming a joint venture with Mitsubishi in 1984. This gave Caterpillar better access to Japanese markets and product know-how. Then, in 1988, Komatsu formed a joint venture with Dressler Industries to expand its manufacturing presence and market access in the United States. So today we see two major players in the heavy construction equipment field, both Japanese-American joint ventures.[22]

Joint ventures are often used in developing countries where economic development is critical and the local government agrees to the venture in order to gain needed technology or expertise. Through such efforts, it is hoped that the local industry will grow and develop. Many of Korea's initial industrial efforts after the Korean War were joint ventures with Japan or the United States. After Koreans learned the appropriate technologies, they were able to begin developing their own products and technologies. This can be seen in the example of the manufacture of microchips in Korea, a country that now ranks third in the world in microchip production.[23] In the case of cars, Korea's Hyundai first signed a joint venture with Ford and then turned to Mitsubishi to help it design and manufacture its first cars. Once it mastered the technology, it went on to design its own Excel and Sonata models, using partial licensing arrangements from Mitsubishi where needed.

In fact, as business competition becomes more global, many feel that the joint venture form of organization holds considerable promise for ensuring the competitiveness of many nations—including the United States and Canada. However, to be successful, such partnerships require informed managers who understand the intricacies of cross-cultural business transactions. We will examine this issue in Chapter 16.

PULLING IT ALL TOGETHER

Organizations are designed to obtain necessary resources (raw materials, capital, technology, and people) and to efficiently transform them into outputs that effectively satisfy multiple stakeholders. Organizations take different structures and forms to achieve these objectives. This chapter has provided the foundation for moving toward, in Chapter 11, an understanding of how to determine what the most appropriate structure is for a particular organization.

SUMMARY OF KEY POINTS

■ An organization may be described as "a system of consciously coordinated activities of two or more persons." Organizations are typically characterized by (1) social composition, (2) a goal orientation, (3) differentiated functions, (4) intended rational coordination, and (5) continuity through time.

■ Organizations may be viewed from a systems perspective as consisting of inputs, throughputs (the transformation process), and outputs. In this regard, five subsystems can be identified that comprise the transformation process. These subsystems are the productive, supportive, maintenance, adaptive, and managerial subsystems.

■ Organizational effectiveness can be defined as an organization's ability to acquire and efficiently use available resources to achieve specific goals. In this definition, official goals must be differentiated from operative goals. Efficiency is the cost/benefit ratio incurred in the pursuit of effectiveness.

■ Seven organizational requirements can be identified: (1) resource acquisition, (2) efficiency, (3) production or output, (4) rational coordination, (5) organizational renewal and adaptation, (6) conformity, and (7) constituency satisfaction. We may assess organizational effectiveness in terms of four factors: (1) goal accomplishment, (2) resource acquisition, (3) health of internal processes, and (4) strategic constituencies' satisfaction.

■ Bureaucracy refers to organizations characterized by high division of labor, rigid authority patterns, impersonality of office, and employment and promotion by merit. Although bureaucratic organizations provide for stability, efficiency, and control, they also often lead to excessive red tape, inflexibility, authority, and position protection.

■ Organizations can be differentiated along four dimensions. These are (1) decentralization, (2) tall versus flat hierarchies, (3) division of labor, and

(4) departmentalization. These dimensions help define the working relationships of employees and facilitate or inhibit the effective operations of a business.

■ There are three basic ways to structure an organization: (1) by function, (2) by product, and (3) by matrix. In matrix design, most employees report to more than one manager (i.e., one employee may report to both a functional and a product manager). Advantages and disadvantages of each approach were reviewed.

■ Two types of interorganizational design are the conglomerate and the joint venture. A conglomerate is a loosely coupled network of companies under the same ownership, whereas a joint venture is a corporate entity formed by two or more companies that join forces to fulfill a certain goal.

KEY WORDS

bureaucracy
central office
chaebol
conglomerate
decentralization
division of labor
efficiency
functional departmentalization
inputs
joint venture
keiretsu

matrix organization
official goals
open systems
operative goals
organization
organizational effectiveness
organization structure
outputs
product departmentalization
transformation processes

QUESTIONS FOR DISCUSSION

1. Discuss the various approaches to defining organizations.
2. Describe some of the requirements of organizations. Which ones do you feel are most important for organizational survival?
3. Identify the five subsystems of organizations.
4. What is meant by organizational effectiveness?
5. Compare and contrast organizational effectiveness and efficiency.
6. Identify the major influences on organizational effectiveness.
7. What are the defining characteristics of an ideal bureaucracy? Identify several problems with the bureaucratic model.
8. What is meant by organization structure? Identify the various dimensions of structure.
9. What are the advantages and disadvantages of tall and flat organizations?
10. Compare and contrast functional, product, and matrix departmentalization.
11. What are some unique problems faced by companies using matrix organizations? Given these problems, why are matrix organizations so popular today?
12. Discuss some special problems faced by managers in the new interorganizational designs. What can managers do to overcome these problems?

NOTES

1. J. Levine, "I am sorry, we have changed." *Forbes,* September 4, 1989.
2. C. Barnard, *The Functions of the Executive* (Cambridge, Mass.: Harvard University Press, 1938), p. 73.
3. A. Etzioni, *Modern Organizations* (Englewood Cliffs, N.J.: Prentice-Hall, 1964), p. 4.
4. L. Porter, E. Lawler, and J. Hackman, *Behavior in Organizations* (New York: McGraw-Hill, 1975).
5. D. Katz and R. Kahn, *The Social Psychology of Organizations* (New York: Wiley, 1978).
6. A. Etzioni, op. cit.; R. Steers, *Organizational Effectiveness: A Behavioral View.* (Santa Monica, Calif.: Goodyear, 1977).
7. F. Friedlander and H. Pickle, "Components of Effectiveness in Small Organizations," *Administrative Science Quarterly,* 1967, 13, p. 293.
8. S. Nazario, "Funding Cuts Take a Toll at University," *Wall Street Journal,* October 5, 1992, pp. B1, B11.
9. K. Cameron, "Effectiveness as Paradox: Consensus and Conflict in Conceptions of Organizational Effectiveness," *Management Science,* May 1986, pp. 539–553.
10. "Them's the Breaks," *Frequent Flyer Magazine,* February 1989, p. 18.
11. J. Trimble, "A Bumpy Ride for Perestroika," *Business Week,* January 18, 1988, pp. 46–47.
12. M. Weber, *The Theory of Economic and Social Organization* (New York: Free Press, 1947).
13. J. Kifner, "Next Queue, Next Stamp, Next Day: Welcome to Egyptian Bureaucracy," *International Herald Tribune,* July 21, 1987, p. 2.
14. A. Chandler, *Strategy and Structure* (Cambridge, Mass.: MIT Press, 1962).
15. Cited in *Wall Street Journal,* February 5, 1982, p. 1.
16. P. Lawrence and J. Lorsch, *Organization and Environment* (Boston: Division of Research, Graduate School of Business Administration, Harvard University, 1967).
17. R. Duncan, "The Characteristics of Organizational Environments and Perceived Environmental Uncertainty," *Administrative Science Quarterly,* 1972, 17, pp. 313–327.
18. S. Toy, "The Americanization of Honda," Business Week, April 25, 1988, pp. 90–96; J. Templeman, "Infiniti and Lexus: Characters in a German Nightmare," *Business Week,* October 9, 1989, p. 64.
19. W. Goggin, "How the Multidimensional Structure Works at Dow Corning," *Harvard Business Review,* January–February 1974, pp. 33–52.
20. R. Steers, Y. Shin, and G. Ungson, *The Chaebol: Korea's New Industrial Might* (New York: Harper & Row, 1989).
21. J. Dreyfuss, "IBM's Vexing Slide in Japan," *Fortune,* March 28, 1988, pp. 73–77.
22. K. Kelly, "A Weakened Komatsu Tries to Come Back Swinging," *Business Week,* February 22, 1988, p. 48.
23. Steers et al., op. cit.

EXPERIENTIAL EXERCISE 10

Designing a Small Firm (Part One)*

This exercise focuses on the structure and design of small firms. It requires some field research prior to class.

---

*Note: Part Two of this exercise can be found in the next chapter. It will make use of the same observations and interview data that you collected here, so you may wish to save your field notes in preparation for Experiential Exercise 11.

As a Group

To begin, the class should be divided into small groups of between three and five. Each group should select one small company. This could be a local fast food outlet, a dry cleaners, a restaurant, a camera shop, and so on. As a group, visit the firm, and do the following:

1. Identify the firm, what they sell or produce, and the number of employees. Interview several of the employees of the firm, including the manager, if possible.
2. On the basis of the information you gather, draw an organization chart including all employees on the premises. What is the basic organization design? What is the chain of command? Is this a tall or flat organization?
3. What are the qualifications for the position of manager in this firm? What are the qualifications to be hired here as an employee? Are these sets of criteria realistic in view of the job requirements of both the manager and the employee?
4. Is the organization effective? Why, or why not?
5. Are the employees satisfied with their jobs?
6. If you were the manager of this small firm, what would you do differently in terms of organization design and management practice? Why?

As a Class

After collecting this information, each group should return to class and report its findings. As a class, you should look for similarities and differences across the various small firms you have studied. Why do these similarities or differences occur? What have you learned about the organization and management of small companies?

MANAGEMENT DILEMMA 10

C & C Grocery Stores

The first C & C grocery store was started in 1947 by Doug Cummins and his brother Bob. Both were veterans who wanted to run their own business, so they used their savings to start the small grocery store in Charlotte, North Carolina. The store was immediately successful. The location was good, and Doug Cummins had a winning personality. Store employees adopted Doug's informal style and "serve the customer" attitude. C & C's increasing circle of customers enjoyed an abundance of good meats and produce.

As business grew, Doug used the store's profits to open two additional stores in the Charlotte area. Over a period of twenty years the C & C chain expanded up the East Coast and through the southeastern United States. Growth was at a moderate rate, because Doug did not want to overextend the chain's resources or take chances. Giving customers good service and value were more important than rapid growth. During the 1970s new stores were opened in the South and reached as far west as Texas.

By 1993, C & C had over 200 stores. A standard physical layout was used for new stores. Company headquarters moved from Charlotte to Atlanta in 1975. The organization chart for C & C is shown in Exhibit 10A. The central offices in Atlanta handled personnel, merchandising, financial, purchasing, real estate, and legal affairs for the entire chain. For management of individual stores, the organization was divided by regions. The southern, southeastern, and northeastern regions each had about seventy stores. Each region was divided into five districts of ten to fifteen stores each. A district director was responsible for supervision and coordination of activities for the ten to fifteen district stores.

Each district was divided into four lines of authority based upon functional specialty. Three of these lines reached into the stores. The produce department manager within each store reported directly to the produce specialist for the division, and the same was true for the meat department manager, who reported directly to the district meat specialist. The meat and produce managers were responsible for all activities associated with the acquisition and sale of perishable products. The store manager's responsibility included the grocery line, front-end departments, and store operations. The store manager was responsible for appearance of personnel, cleanliness,

Exhibit 10A
Organization Structure of
C & C Grocery Stores, Inc.

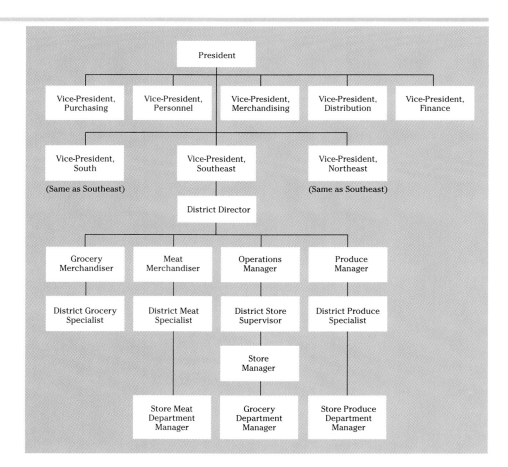

adequate check-out service, and price accuracy. A grocery manager reported to the store manager and maintained inventories and restocked shelves for grocery items. The district merchandising office was responsible for promotional campaigns, advertising circulars, district advertising, and for attracting customers into the stores. The grocery merchandisers were expected to coordinate their activities with each store in the district.

During the recession in 1990–91, business for the C & C chain dropped off in all regions and did not increase with improved economic times in 1993–94. This caused concern among senior executives. They also were aware that other supermarket chains were adopting a trend toward one-stop shopping, which meant the emergence of super stores that included a pharmacy, dry goods, and groceries—almost like a department store. Executives wondered whether C & C should move in this direction and how such changes could be assimilated into the current store organization. However, the most pressing problem was how to improve business with the grocery stores they now had. A consulting team from a major university was hired to investigate store structure and operations.

The consultants visited several stores in each region, talking to about fifty managers and employees. The consultants wrote a report that pinpointed four problem areas to be addressed by store executives.

1. The chain is slow to adapt to change. Store layout and structure were the same as had been designed fifteen years ago. Each store did things the same way even though some stores were in low-income areas and other stores in suburban areas. A new grocery management system for ordering and stocking had been developed, but after two years was only partially implemented in the stores.

2. Roles of the district store supervisor and the store manager were causing dissatisfaction. The store managers wanted to learn general management skills for potential promotion into district or regional management positions. However, their jobs restricted them to operational activities and they learned little about merchandising, meat, and produce. Moreover, district store supervisors used store visits to inspect for cleanliness and adherence to operating standards rather than to train the store manager and help coordinate operations with perishable departments. Close supervision on the operational details had become the focus of operations management rather than development, training, and coordination.

3. Cooperation within stores was low and morale was poor. The informal, friendly atmosphere originally created by Doug Cummins was gone. One example of this problem occurred when the grocery merchandiser and store manager in a Louisiana store decided to promote Coke and Diet Coke as a loss leader. Thousands of cartons of Coke were brought in for the sale, but the stockroom was not prepared and did not have room. The store manager wanted to use floor area in the meat and produce sections to display Coke cartons, but those managers refused. The produce department manager said that Diet Coke did not help his sales and it was okay with him if there was no promotion at all.

4. Long-term growth and development of the stores chain would probably require reevaluation of long-term strategy. The percent of market share going to traditional grocery stores was declining nationwide due to

competition from large super stores and convenience stores. In the future, C & C might need to introduce non-food items into the stores for one-stop shopping, and add specialty sections within stores. Some stores could be limited to grocery items, but store location and marketing techniques should take advantage of the grocery emphasis.

To solve the first three problems, the consultants recommended reorganizing the district and the store structure as illustrated in Exhibit 10B. Under this reorganization, the meat, grocery, and produce department managers would all report to the store manager. The store manager would have complete store control and would be responsible for coordination of all store activities. The district supervisor's role would be changed from supervision to training and development. The district supervisor would head a team that included himself and several meat, produce, and merchandise specialists who would visit area stores as a team to provide advice and help for the store managers and other employees. The team would act in a liaison capacity between district specialists and the stores.

Exhibit 10B
Proposed Reorganization of
C & C Grocery Stores, Inc.

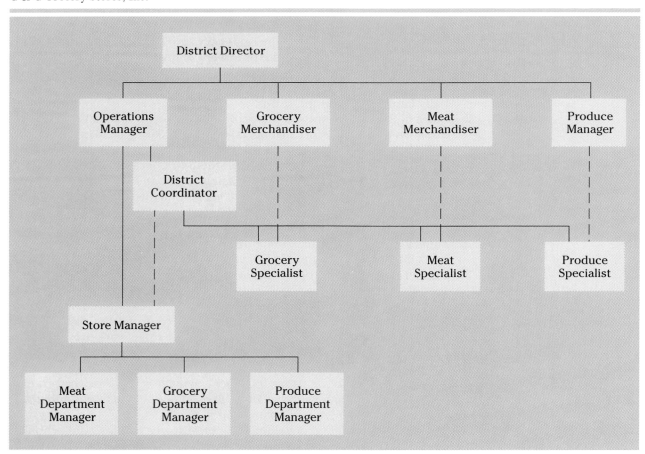

The consultants were enthusiastic about the proposed structure. By removing one level of district operational supervision, store managers would have more freedom and responsibility. The district liaison team would establish a cooperative team approach to management that could be adopted within stores. The focus of store responsibility on a single manager would encourage coordination within stores, adaptation to local conditions, and provide a focus of responsibility for store-wide administrative changes.

The consultants also believe that the proposed structure could be expanded to accommodate non-grocery lines if enlarged stores were to be developed in the future. Within each store, a new department manager could be added for pharmacy, dry goods, or other major departments. The district team could be expanded to include specialists in these departments who would act as liaison for stores in the district.

As you look at this company, consider the following:

1. Use the materials discussed in this chapter to describe the organization design of C & C Grocery Stores for both the current and the proposed structures.
2. What mechanisms are currently used to integrate or coordinate across units of the company? How will these mechanisms be changed under the new structure?
3. Evaluate the proposed new structure. Does it meet the needs for both departmentalization and coordination for the company? Do you foresee any problems? Would you recommend any modifications to the proposed structure?

Source: Reprinted with permission from R. Daft and R. Steers, *Organizations: A Micro/Macro Approach* (Glenview, Ill.: Scott, Foresman, 1986), pp. 395–398. This case is based on Robert A. Luke, Jr., Peter Block, Jack M. Davey, and Vernon R. Averch, "A Structural Approach to Organizational Change," *Journal of Applied Behavioral Science,* 1973, 9, pp. 611–635; Ross A. Webber, "Sherman and Jackson Stores, Inc.," *Management* (Homewood, Ill.: Richard D. Irwin, 1979); and John Merwin, "A Piece of the Action," *Forbes,* September 24, 1984, pp. 146–156.

Chapter 11

Environment, Technology, and Organization Design

The Management Challenge

■ To understand the environment in which a particular organization operates.

■ To accurately assess environmental changes and respond accordingly.

■ To create an organizational structure that facilitates corporate strategy in a turbulent environment.

■ To make use of appropriate work technologies.

■ To integrate work technologies with organization design in an effective, efficient manner.

CLOSE UP — The Changing Environment at Big Blue

The year 1991 was a difficult one for IBM. It was the first year since 1946 that "Big Blue" did not get any bigger. It also was the first year in the history of the firm that it lost money—nearly $3 billion![1]

In response to what Chairman John Akers called a "crisis," IBM was reorganized into 13 "Baby Blues." However, each of these "babies" weighed in at a hefty $2 to $26 billion in annual revenue. The reorganization was designed to give business groups, such as personal computers, a chance to be more autonomous and be closer to their customers. Whether the reorganization was "too little, too late" or was "just in the nick of time" will not be known for years. What was clear at the time of the reorganization was that the environment had changed radically on IBM.

IBM had built is reputation, gigantic size, and successful financial performance on its ability to produce mainframe computers. It built an organizational structure and a marketing focus around this primary product. Unfortunately, environmental changes in technology left Big Blue too big. Technological advances that led to ever increasing memory and computing capacity, as well advances in software, such as network software, meant that customers could buy much less expensive personal computers or slightly larger work stations and connect them rather than buying large and expensive mainframe computers. Also, environmental changes that demanded more timely and customized analysis of data meant the replacement of the information specialist, to whom data analysis requests went and from whom reams of printout came, by an environment in which the manipulator of the data and the user of the analysis were one and the same.

Although many in IBM saw these changes coming, just as it is impossible to turn a giant aircraft carrier as quickly as a small speedboat, so too was it difficult for IBM executives to initiate and implement organizational changes within Big Blue in order to weather the environmental storms without suffering any damage to the ship. Unfortunately for many lifetime IBMers, the load was lightened and the ship downsized by lowering them into lifeboats and setting them off to find new jobs at other organizations. Included in these departures was John Akers, who stepped down as chairman in January 1993. Whether IBM will be successful at adjusting to an environment that changed so quickly and dramatically will take some time to determine.

What happened to IBM illustrates why it is important for managers to understand environmental change. At any given time, organizations are likely to face various and often conflicting pressures from the external environment. These pressures come from the government, the marketplace, competitors, and the economy. For example, job security and salary levels are influenced by competitors and the economy. Strict regulations for disposal of industrial waste have been imposed and enforced by the government. And the increase in the price of gasoline has had a tremendous effect on organizations and people. It is essential that managers anticipate change and adapt to the external environment. They must be able to take actions that buffer the organization from adverse environmental effects and sometimes even to turn external environmental pressure into opportunity.

In addition to the external environment, managers, such as those at IBM, must understand the changing nature of technology and how it affects their business. In our world of increasing innovation and sophistication, technology plays a pivotal role. Management must plan for the influence of technology through long-range forecasts, product innovation, and research and development. Because technological change is continuous, organizations must keep pace if they are to survive.

Both the environment and technology represent *contingencies* in organizational design. That is, variations in these variables can have a profound impact on the survival of an organization, so informed managers structure their organizations to accommodate these outside forces. As such, we shall examine both the environment and technology in this chapter as they affect organizational structure and subsequent effectiveness. As was discovered at IBM, such an understanding is essential.

ORGANIZATIONS AND THEIR ENVIRONMENTS

Organizations obviously do not exist in a vacuum. They must interact with the outside world. The *external environment* is made up of all entities and forces that impinge upon organizational activities and with which the organization must deal with if it is to be effective. Let us look at a typical external environment, shown in Exhibit 11.1. The first thing to note is that we can differentiate this environment into a general environment and a task environment.

The *general environment* refers to those aspects of the external world that affect organizations. This environment includes such factors as the economy, governmental and political affairs, financial resources, natural resources and geography, technology, and culture and demography. Although organizations may face similar aspects of the environment, they can be differentially affected by them. For example, Hurricane Andrew devastated much of South Florida in 1992. Most retailers were hurt financially by the storm. However, camp trailer manufacturers significantly benefited from the storm because people bought them for temporary housing.

In contrast, the *task environment* refers to those aspects of an organization's environment that directly affect its goal and the degree of goal attainment. This is the more specific environment in which the organization operates and thus is somewhat different for each organization. The task environment usually

Exhibit 11.1
The External Environment
of an Organization

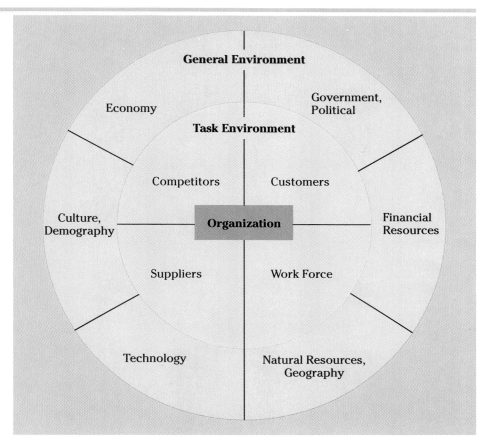

Source: Adapted from R. Daft and R. Steers, *Organization: A Micro/Macro Approach* (Glenview, Ill.: Scott, Foresman, 1986), p. 288. Copyright © 1986 Scott, Foresman and Company.

includes four factors: competitors, customers, work force, and suppliers. These are the key factors that affect day-to-day life within an organization.

For a specific example of a company's external environment, consider a typical airline company operating both in the U.S. and abroad. Examples of such companies include United Airlines, American Airlines, SAS, Lufthansa, and so forth. As shown in Exhibit 11.2, a typical airline has both a general and a task environment. The general environment is the environment that faces all air carriers in the commercial airline industry. This environment includes the general economic environment (e.g., inflation or recession, interest rates, the need for operating efficiency); culture and demography (e.g., the values and beliefs of the flying public; mobility patterns of the public, importance of leisure travel); technology (e.g., the need for fuel-efficient planes, computerized reservation systems); government and political issues (e.g., federal regulations of various countries, landing rights, lawsuits); financial resources (e.g., stock prices, bond ratings, money supply); and natural resources and geography (e.g., fuel availability, weather conditions over flying routes, route structures).

In addition to the general environment, every airline has a more immediate task environment that is tailored to its specific problems and challenges. That is, while United Airlines and American Airlines both share the same general

Exhibit 11.2
The Environment of an
Airline Company

General Environment

Economy
- Inflation or recession
- National interest rates
- Need for operating efficiency

Culture and Demography
- Values and beliefs of the flying public
- Mobility patterns of the public
- Leisure travel

Technology
- Need for fuel-efficient planes
- Computerized reservation systems

Government and Politics
- Federal regulations of various countries
- Landing rights
- Lawsuits

Financial Resources
- Stock prices
- Bond ratings
- Money supply

Natural Resources and Geography
- Fuel availability
- Weather conditions
- Route structures

Task Environment

Competitors
- Other airlines
- Buses, trains, cars

Customers
- Business versus leisure travelers
- Frequent flyers
- Freight companies
- Postal services

Labor Force
- Pilots
- Flight attendants
- Machinists
- Unions

Suppliers
- Aircraft manufacturers
- Fuel companies
- Airline caterers
- In-flight movies
- Uniform suppliers
- Tool and equipment companies

environment (that is, the commercial aviation environment), each company has its own niche in the marketplace and its own problems that make its task environment somewhat unique. For example, one company may have a new fleet of aircraft, while the other is in need of major aircraft replacement. Similarly, one company may have considerable capital at its disposal for expansion or price competition, while another may be in need of cash. The nature and quality of these factors help establish the company's particular task environment. Within this task environment are four considerations. These are (1) competitors (e.g., other airlines, alternative modes of transportation); (2) customers (e.g., business versus leisure travelers, frequent flyers, freight companies, postal services); (3) labor force (e.g., pilots, flight attendants, machinists and their unions); and (4) suppliers (e.g., aircraft manufacturers, fuel companies, airline caterers, in-flight movies, uniforms, suppliers, tool and equipment companies, etc.).

Other examples could be cited. The point here in this simplified example is to demonstrate how complex and diverse the environment of just one airline company can be. The challenge for management is somehow to coordinate and satisfy these often conflicting parts of the environment in a way that furthers the survival and prosperity of the company.[2]

ENVIRONMENTAL UNCERTAINTY

Why does the external environment have such a profound effect on the shape and nature of organizations? First, all inputs used by the organization ultimately come from the environment. For example, the supply of raw materials and financing must come from somewhere. Moreover, outputs must find a market in the environment. Finally, many aspects of the transformation process are limited by environmental factors such as legal or governmental regulations. Because each of these factors can affect the lives of people at work, it is important for managers to know something about differences in environments.

From a managerial standpoint, the key defining characteristic of the external environment is its degree of certainty or predictability. The more uncertain the environment, the more care and attention must be devoted to it for the organization to be successful. If we compare the U.S. Postal Service with a high-tech firm such as Hewlett-Packard, we see significant differences in their environments. The postal service faces a reasonably stable, predictable environment that requires few organizational changes, whereas Hewlett-Packard exists in a turbulent, ever-changing environment that requires managerial vigilance and adaptability. Hence, *environmental uncertainty* emerges as a central variable of concern for any management team and is perhaps the best way to get a general description of the external environment.

The most commonly accepted approach to assessing environmental uncertainty is to examine it using a two-dimensional model (Exhibit 11.3) suggested by Robert Duncan.[3] These dimensions are (1) the extent of environmental complexity and (2) the rate of environmental change or stability. We turn first to environmental complexity.

Environmental Complexity

Environmental complexity refers to the intricacy and qualitative nature of the environment. It is described along a continuum ranging from simple to complex. A simple or placid environment is one in which the external factors with which an organization must deal are few in number and relatively homogeneous. For example, consider a company that exclusively manufactures spark plugs for the major automotive companies. Its product line is restricted, its technology is fairly stable, and its market is relatively constant. Moreover, its customers are few in number. In short, it exists in a fairly simple environment.

Contrast this example with a company that builds commercial aircraft, such as Boeing, McDonnell-Douglas, or Airbus. The manufacture of various components of the aircraft is subcontracted to hundreds of other firms, which significantly increases the coordination problems among major production units. Moreover, the jet engines themselves must be purchased from still other companies, which themselves have hundreds of subcontractors. The technological aspects of manufacture are tremendously complex and varied, and the final product must meet not only the specifications of the domestic and foreign airline companies who purchase the aircraft, but a series of U.S. government regulations as well. Certainly, this environment is a more complex one than that of the company manufacturing spark plugs.

Just as the manufacture and sale of spark plugs differs from that of a Boeing 747 or MD-11 aircraft in terms of complexity and cost (approximately $1 versus $100 million), so too are there differences in the manner in which organizations must manage themselves in response to such divergent environments. The degree of environmental complexity can have a significant impact both on organizational behavior and on organizational effectiveness, as we will see presently.

Environmental Stability

In addition to environmental complexity, we must also consider the relative degree of stability in organization-environment relations. Here, we can envision a continuum ranging from stable to unstable. For example, compare the stability of our automotive parts company, which will make spark plugs year after year, to that of an aerospace firm, which may receive a contract to build a satellite one year and modular houses the next. One environment is fairly stable, the other is quite dynamic. Environments that are in a constant state of flux often require different organizational structures and approaches to management than do more static, predictable environments.

To complicate the picture further, the static-dynamic dimension is, in reality, a multifaceted phenomenon. Certain portions of the environment may remain static, while others change radically over time. Automobile companies provide a good example of this. Although the production technology of automotive manufacturing has remained relatively stable with few new technological breakthroughs, the *marketing* component of the environment has changed dramatically as people have shifted from large cars to small cars to no cars and back again. In part, this volatile marketing environment is a function of environmental complexity. Oil prices, general economic conditions, and governmental regulations are all considerations. Even so, such environmental turbulence has little effect on the stability of the *technological* environment (as we will see later in this chapter).

Major Causes of Environmental Uncertainty

Let us see how the simple-complex and static-dynamic dimensions of the external environment influence the degree of environmental certainty or uncertainty in which organizational decisions are made. According to Duncan, environmental uncertainty is a result of three conditions: a lack of information concerning the environmental factors associated with a particular organizational decision-making situation; an inability to assign probabilities accurately with regard to how environmental factors will affect the success or failure of a decision unit in performing its functions; and a lack of information regarding the costs associated with an incorrect decision or action.[4]

In an effort to integrate the stability and complexity dimensions discussed above with the issue of uncertainty in organizational decision making, the model outlined in Exhibit 11.3 describes the environmental states resulting from the interrelationships between these two factors. Note that the "static-simple" environments contain the least amount of uncertainty for organizational planners and decision makers, whereas the "dynamic-complex"

Environmental Complexity

	Simple	*Complex*
Static	**Cell 1:** **Low Perceived Uncertainty** 1. Small number of factors and components in the environment 2. Factors and components are somewhat similar to one another 3. Factors and components remain basically the same *Example:* Cardboard container industry	**Cell 2:** **Moderately Low Perceived Uncertainty** 1. Large number of factors and components in the environment 2. Factors and components are not similar to one another 3. Factors and components remain basically the same *Example:* State universities
Dynamic	**Cell 3:** **Moderately High Perceived Uncertainty** 1. Small number of factors and components in the environment 2. Factors and components are somewhat similar to one another 3. Factors and components of the environment continually change *Example:* Fashion industry	**Cell 4:** **High Perceived Uncertainty** 1. Large number of factors and components in the environment 2. Factors and components are not similar to one another 3. Factors and components of the environment continually change *Example:* Banking industry

Rate of Environmental Change (row label, left side)

Exhibit 11.3
Influences on
Environmental Uncertainty

Source: Reprinted from "Characteristics of Organizational Environments and Perceived Uncertainty" by Robert B. Duncan, in *Administrative Science Quarterly,* Vol. 17, No. 3, by permission of *Administrative Science Quarterly.*

environments contain the greatest amount of uncertainty. Examples are shown for each of the four cells of the diagram.

An empirical investigation provided general support for the model. In this study, not only was the dynamic-complex environment found to be associated with the greatest perceived environmental uncertainty, but the static-dynamic dimension was found to be a more important contributor to perceived uncertainty than was the simple-complex dimension. Commenting on his findings, Duncan concluded:

> Decision units with dynamic environments always experience significantly more uncertainty in decision making, regardless of whether their environment is simple or complex. The difference in perceived uncertainty between decision units with simple and complex environments is not significant, unless the decision unit's environment is also dynamic.[5]

To see a vivid example of how environments can change and create considerable uncertainty, consider the emerging business environment of Thailand.

IN PRACTICE
Thailand's New Business Environment

When we look at the economic power and development in the Pacific basin, we typically refer to Japan or possibly Taiwan or Korea as examples. However, it is important to recognize that several other economies are changing very rapidly, which is causing considerable uncertainty—and opportunity—for managers on both sides of the ocean. One such country is Thailand. According to economists, Thailand's environment has changed radically in recent years because of four interrelated factors:

1. The rise in the Japanese yen forced many Japanese companies to look to other countries (including Thailand) for lower-cost manufacturing.
2. Political turmoil in many areas of Southeast Asia led many investors to see Thailand as a relatively stable place in which to do business.
3. A dramatic decline in oil prices sharply reduced energy costs in Thailand.
4. Wage rates in many other Asian countries (e.g., Korea, Taiwan) escalated considerably in the late 1980s while they remained relatively stable in Thailand. As a result, wage rates are now only one-fourth of those in Hong Kong, Singapore, and Korea.

As a result of these four changes—none of which Thailand controlled—the country has changed almost overnight from a sleepy underdeveloped nation into a highly coveted place in which to do business. Over the past several years, companies from Japan, Europe, and North America have rushed in to establish factories, thereby increasing economic development. As a result, gross domestic product has increased at a rate of over 10 percent per year, and exports have risen by over 30 percent per year.

Although economic growth has brought substantial business opportunities to the region, it has also brought problems. The country's only metropolitan area (Bangkok) is virtually gridlocked by increased traffic. The country's only seaport is similarly backlogged. And the country's universities can only turn out 3,000 engineers per year, when there is a need for 10,000. Thailand's business environment is turbulent, complex, and highly uncertain—thereby presenting special challenges to companies attempting to do business there. Such is the nature of international competition.[6]

MANAGING THE ORGANIZATION'S ENVIRONMENT

Given the kinds of variations in environmental uncertainty discussed above, it is useful to consider how organizations attempt to cope with such uncertainty. That is, how do organizations adapt to the environment? Three perspectives on organizational adaptation can be identified. These perspectives are not mutually exclusive; rather, they simply focus on different aspects of the adaptation process. The three approaches are (1) the structural contingencies approach, (2) the resource dependence approach, and (3) the population ecology approach. The principal variables associated with each are summarized in Exhibit 11.4. We will consider each of these in turn.

Redesigning the Organization to Fit the Environment

The first approach to meeting the challenges of the external environment is to redesign the organization to fit the new environmental realities. This is called the *structural contingencies approach*. For example, how does a company organize itself to cope with a dynamic and unstable environment? The premise underlying this perspective is that one key to organizational effectiveness is the degree to which a company can design organizational forms suited to environmental needs. In other words, is there a congruence between environment and structure? Several important studies have focused on this topic, and we will summarize their findings here.

Organic Versus Mechanistic Structures.   One of the earliest studies of organization-environment relations was carried out by Burns and Stalker.[7] They surveyed 20 British industrial firms, most with interests in electronics, in an effort to identify relationships between certain environmental characteristics and resulting managerial practices. The researchers focused on the rate of change in both the relevant technology and the market—that is, environmental instability—as it related to managerial behavior and organization structure.

They concluded that there existed two relatively distinct approaches to the management of organizations and that these approaches were largely a function of the relative degree of stability in the external environment. They called these two approaches mechanistic and organic. As indicated in Exhibit 11.5, these two approaches are quite different. *Mechanistic systems* are characterized by centralization of control and authority, a high degree of task specialization, and primarily vertical (particularly downward) lines of communication. *Organic systems,* on the other hand, generally exhibit a higher degree of task

Exhibit 11.4
Three Approaches to
Organizational Adaptation

Approach	Focus	Examples
Structural contingency model	How organizations develop structures in response to environment	Organic versus mechanistic structures Strategy-structure contingencies Differentiation versus integration
Resource dependence model	How organizations attempt to manage environmental dependencies	Joint ventures Contractual relations Mergers and acquisitions Co-optation
Population ecology model	How environment influences growth, development, and survival of organizations	How a company finds a unique niche in the marketplace; why one company survives while another fails

Mechanistic	Organic
1. Tasks are highly fractionated and specialized; little regard paid to clarifying relationships between tasks and organizational objectives.	1. Tasks are more interdependent; emphasis on relevance of tasks and organizational objectives.
2. Tasks tend to remain rigidly defined unless altered formally by top management.	2. Tasks are continually adjusted and redefined through interaction of organizational members.
3. Specific role definition (rights, obligations, and technical methods prescribed for each member).	3. Generalized role definition (members accept general responsibility for task accomplishment beyond individual role definition).
4. Hierarchical structure of control, authority, and communication. Sanctions derive from employment contract between employee and organization.	4. Network structure of control, authority, and communication. Sanctions derive more from community of interest than from contractual relationship.
5. Information relevant to situation and operations of the organization formally assumed to rest with chief executive.	5. Leader not assumed to be omniscient; knowledge centers identified where located throughout organization.
6. Communication is primarily vertical between superior and subordinate.	6. Communication is both vertical and horizontal, depending upon where needed information resides.
7. Communications primarily take form of instructions and decisions issued by superiors, of information and requests for decisions supplied by inferiors.	7. Communications primarily take form of information and advice.
8. Insistence on loyalty to organization and obedience to superiors.	8. Commitment to organization's tasks and goals more highly valued than loyalty or obedience.
9. Importance and prestige attached to identification with organization and its members.	9. Importance and prestige attached to affiliations and expertise in external environment.

Exhibit 11.5
Comparison of Mechanistic and Organic Systems of Organization

interdependence, greater decentralization of control and authority, and more horizontal (that is, department-to-department) communication. Moreover, mechanistic systems are seen as relatively fixed and inflexible entities, whereas organic systems are viewed as being more flexible and adaptable.

Burns and Stalker argued that each system of management can be effective under certain circumstances. In highly stable and predictable environments where market and technological conditions remain largely unchanged over time (for example, the automotive industry), the mechanistic system may be more appropriate. Because the environment is highly predictable under such conditions, it is possible to routinize tasks and centralize directions in order to maximize efficiency and effectiveness in operation. (Note that Burns and Stalker do not suggest that such a system of management is personally satisfying to employees—only that it is efficient.) On the other hand, where the environment is in a constant state of flux and where an organization has to change direction constantly to adapt to its environment (such as in the aerospace industry), organic systems appear to be more appropriate because of their added flexibility and adaptability.

Thus, consistent with the structural contingency approach, Burns and Stalker argue for what might be termed *environmental determinism,* where the organization design and resulting management style are largely determined by external factors in the environment. The role of management thus becomes one of properly understanding environmental conditions and adapting organizational structure and practices to meet and accommodate those conditions.

To see how this model works, you might wish to complete Self-Assessment 11.1. Here you are asked to identify an organization you are familiar with and use the questionnaire to determine whether it is organic or mechanistic in management style. You are also asked to assess the organization's external environment in relative stability or uncertainty. Finally, you can put the two scores together to determine whether the management system in use is appropriate for the environment. When you have completed the questionnaire, refer to Appendix B for details.

IN PRACTICE
McDonald's Mechanistic Approach to Management

A good example of the mechanistic approach to management can be seen in many fast food outlets. In one such case, *Business Week* correspondent Kathleen Deveny filed the following report:

> On my way down Chicago's Magnificent Mile, past Tiffany's and Gucci, to the McDonald's restaurant, I keep thinking back to the Tastee Treat in Minneapolis. That was my first job, making ice cream cones and flipping burgers for the high school students who swarmed into the converted gas station during the short summers.
>
> McDonald's is nothing like Tastee Treat. Here every job is broken down into the smallest of steps, and the whole process is automated. The videotape that introduces new employees to French fries, for example, starts with boxes of frozen fries rolling off a delivery truck. Stack them in the freezer six boxes high. Leave one inch between the stacks, two inches between the stacks and the wall. Cooking and bagging the fries is explained in even greater detail: 19 steps.
>
> Anyone could do this, I think. But McDonald's restaurants operate like Swiss watches, and the minute I step behind the counter I am a loose part in the works. By noon the place is mobbed. I keep thinking of the McDonald's commercial that shows former Raiders coach John Madden diagramming the precision moves of a McDonald's crew in action. I imagine a diagram of my own jerky movements, zigzagging wildly behind the counter because I keep forgetting the order.
>
> I bag French fries for a few minutes, but I'm much too slow. Worse, I can't seem to keep my station clean enough. Failing at French fries is a fluke, I tell myself.
>
> Condiment detail sounds made to order. First comes the mustard, one shot of the gun, five perfect drops centered on the bun. Next, the ketchup: One big shot. Quite a difference from Tastee Treat, where I used to measure out the ketchup by writing my boyfriend's initials on each hamburger bun.
>
> I try to speed up. Now a quarter ounce of onions and two pickles— three, if they're small. Cover them with a slice of cheese, slap on the burger. Another slice of cheese.
>
> I am happy with the tidy piles I am making, but the grillman is not as pleased. I move too slowly, and he could cook the patties and dress the buns a lot faster without my help.
>
> Disheartened, I move on to Filet-O-Fish. I put six frozen fish patties into the fryer basket and drop them into the hot grease. When the red

SELF-ASSESSMENT 11.1
Do You Work in a Mechanistic or an Organic Environment?

Instructions: Think of an organization for which you have worked, and answer the following questions about it. Circle the number that best answers each item. When you have completed Part 1, add up your score and complete Part 2.

Part 1: Describe the company:

1. What is the amount of task definition and knowledge required by the average employee?

    | Narrow;
technical | 1 | 2 | 3 | 4 | 5 | 6 | 7 | Broad;
general |

2. How clearly specified are the work procedures and policies for employees?

    | Specific | 1 | 2 | 3 | 4 | 5 | 6 | 7 | General |

3. What is the extent of task flexibility for employees?

    | Rigid;
routine | 1 | 2 | 3 | 4 | 5 | 6 | 7 | Flexible;
varied |

4. How closely related are individual employees' contributions to the goals of the organization?

    | Vague;
indirect | 1 | 2 | 3 | 4 | 5 | 6 | 7 | Clear;
direct |

5. How much emphasis is there on following superiors and being loyal to the organization?

    | High | 1 | 2 | 3 | 4 | 5 | 6 | 7 | Low |

6. What is the primary pattern of communication?

    | Top-down | 1 | 2 | 3 | 4 | 5 | 6 | 7 | Horizontal |

7. What is the primary decision-making style in the organization?

    | Authoritarian | 1 | 2 | 3 | 4 | 5 | 6 | 7 | Participative |

8. How much control is exerted over employees from superiors?

    | High
control | 1 | 2 | 3 | 4 | 5 | 6 | 7 | Low (or self-)
control |

Your total score on Part 1 is: _____

Part 2: Describe the environment:

1. Does the organization exist in a stable, predictable environment or an unstable, turbulent one?

    | Stable,
predictable | 1 | 2 | 3 | 4 | 5 | 6 | 7 | Unstable,
turbulent |

light flashes, I put the buns in to steam. After a few minutes, the square patties are done. I line them up in neat rows and center the cheese on each. I try to move faster, but my co-workers are playing at 45 RPM, and I'm stuck at 33.

Debbie, the crew member who rescued my French fries earlier, comes back to see how I'm doing. It's my last chance to shine. I pull out more cooked fish, slap on the cheese, burn my hands on the buns, and pinch my finger in the tartar sauce gun. "You're doing O.K.," she somehow says. That's all I wanted to hear. The regimented work is wearing on my nerves. The strict rules, which go so far as to prescribe what color nail polish to wear, are bringing out the rebel in me. I can't wait to get back to my cluttered office, where it smells like paper and stale coffee and the only noise is the gentle hum of my personal computer.[8]

Matching Organization Design with Corporate Strategy.   Taking an historical and evolutionary approach to the study of organizational effectiveness, Alfred Chandler traced the growth and development of nearly 100 major U.S. business concerns. On the basis of these case studies, he concluded, in his classic book entitled *Strategy and Structure,* that each major change in the design or structure of these organizations has been necessitated by environmental shifts. More specifically, changes in the external environment required an organization to modify its strategies for dealing with the environment. These strategic changes in turn necessitated modifications in organizational structure so that it would be consistent with the revised strategy. In other words, "structure followed strategy." A schematic representation of this is shown in Exhibit 11.6. As Chandler describes this relationship:

> Strategic growth resulted from an awareness of the opportunities and needs—created by changing population, income, and technology—to employ existing or expanding resources more profitably. A new strategy required a new or at least refashioned structure if the . . . enterprise was to be operated efficiently. The failure to develop a new internal structure, like the failure to respond to new external opportunities and needs, was a consequence of over-concentration on operational activities by the executives responsible for the destiny of their enterprise, or from their inability, because of past training and education and present position, to develop an entrepreneurial outlook.[9]

Chandler sums up his point by adding that growth or change "without structural adjustment can lead only to economic inefficiency."[10] By way of example, he cites Henry Ford's venture into farm tractors in the late 1930s. In an effort to expand his base of operations and find substitutes for the declining automobile market of the time, Ford and his engineering staff designed and built an inexpensive tractor that had the potential of competing effectively against the tractors then on the market. The design was appropriate, and the quality was high. However, Ford attempted to sell his tractors through his car dealerships, which were inexperienced in farm needs and which were principally located in cities. The new tractor failed commercially until a new structure (particularly, a new marketing structure) was designed

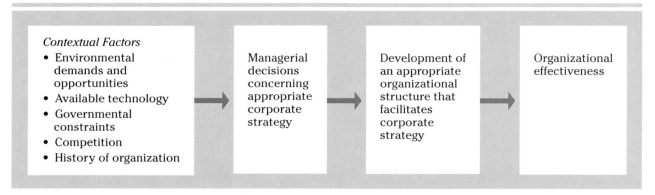

Exhibit 11.6
Chandler's Strategy-
Structure Hypothesis

that was consistent with Ford's marketing goals and strategy. Chandler concludes: "The incredibly bad management of his enormous industrial empire, which was so clearly reflected by the lack of any systematic organizational structure, not only prevented the Ford Motor Company from carrying out a strategy of diversification, but also helped cause the rapid drop in Ford's profits and share of the market."[11]

The point here is not to single out one company for criticism. On the contrary, many examples could be cited in which organizations showed an inability to adapt structure to corporate strategies and goals. We must recognize that a key factor in effectiveness and efficiency is the ability of managers to properly understand their environments, make strategic decisions on the basis of their understanding, and then organize their human resources around these strategic decisions.

Working together, working separately.   Following the lead of these earlier studies, Lawrence and Lorsch carried out an intensive study of environmental influences on organization design and effectiveness among a small sample of American firms. They began by posing four specific research questions:

1. How are the environmental demands facing various organizations different, and how do environmental demands relate to the internal functioning of effective organizations?
2. Is it true that organizations in stable environments make more exclusive use of the formal hierarchy to attain integration? If so, why—because less integration is required, or because in a certain environment these decisions can be made more effectively at higher organization levels or by fewer people?
3. Is the same degree of differentiation in orientation and departmental structure found among different industrial environments?
4. If greater differentiation among functional departments is required in some industries, does this influence the problems of integrating the organization's parts? Does it influence the organization's means of achieving integration?[12]

To find suitable answers to these questions, Lawrence and Lorsch studied organization-environment relations in three widely divergent industries: plastics, packaged foods, and standardized containers. The external environment for firms in the plastics industry was typically characterized by a high degree of uncertainty and unpredictability. The rate of technological innovation and shift in market demands in this industry were quite high, requiring fairly rapid change in products, procedures, and sometimes structures. The container industry, on the other hand, was characterized by a highly stable and predictable environment. Competition in this industry centered around the quality of the product or service instead of on product innovation, as was the case in the plastics industry. In between the plastics and container industries, in terms of environmental stability, came the packaged-foods companies, which were characterized by a moderate amount of predictability and stability in environmental relations.

Lawrence and Lorsch investigated how corporations adapted to diverse external environments and which adaptation processes were generally most successful. Structural variations within organizations were defined in terms of differentiation and integration. *Differentiation,* as defined by Lawrence and Lorsch, refers to "the difference in cognitive and emotional orientation among managers in different functional departments."[13] It refers not only to the degree of specialization of labor or departmentalization, but also to what might be termed "psychological" departmentalization, that is, the extent to which managers in different departments are characterized by different attitudinal and behavioral orientations. The greater the psychological distance between managers in different departments, the greater the differentiation.

Integration refers to "the quality of the state of collaboration that exists among departments that are required to achieve unity of effort by the demands of the environment"[14]—in short, to the nature and quality of interdepartmental relations and processes. Integration can be brought about by several means, including rules and standard operating procedures that govern behavior, plans and objectives, and mutual adjustment and agreement.

Several important findings emerged from the investigation. To begin, as indicated in Exhibit 11.7, organizations operating in more complex environments tended to exhibit a greater degree of differentiation among functional departments than did firms operating in less turbulent environments. The more effective plastics firm had a score of 10.7 on the differentiation measure,

Exhibit 11.7
Average Differentiation and Integration across Three Environments

Industry	Organization	Average Differentiation*	Average Integration
Plastics	High Performer	10.7	5.6
	Low Performer	9.0	5.1
Foods	High Performer	8.0	5.3
	Low Performer	6.5	5.0
Containers	High Performer	5.7	5.7
	Low Performer	5.7	4.8

*Higher differentiation scores mean greater differences between functional units; higher integration scores mean higher degrees of integration.

Source: From Paul H. Lawrence and Jay W. Lorsch, *Organization and Environment.* Boston: Division of Research, Harvard Business School, 1967, p. 103. Republished as a Harvard Business School Classic. Boston: Harvard Business School Press, 1986. Reprinted by permission.

compared to 5.7 for both container firms. The packaged-foods firms, which operated in a moderately dynamic environment, exhibited a moderate degree of differentiation. In other words, the greater the instability in the external environment, the more psychological distance was needed between departments.

Second, it was noted that, with one exception, more successful firms within each industry had higher scores on both differentiation and integration. Thus, it would appear that one component of organizational effectiveness is the capacity of an organization to achieve an optimal balance of differentiation and integration consistent with environmental demands. A hallmark of less effective organizations is an inability to grant departments sufficient latitude and autonomy to increase their efficiency through specialization; another is an inability to integrate and coordinate diverse departments for the common good.

Lawrence and Lorsch concluded that different environments call for different structural approaches to integration. In the dynamic plastics industry, the more effective organization employed a formal integrating department whose purpose was to ensure that the various functional areas worked together. In the moderately dynamic food-packaging industry, the more effective organization used individual integrators—that is, individuals whose primary responsibility was to ensure mutuality of purpose. In the more stable, effective containers industry, integration was facilitated by direct managerial contact through the chain of command. Thus, each of the organizations in the study is characterized by an ability to achieve integration commensurate with its respective environment. The more complex the environment, the more elaborate the integrative mechanisms.

In summary, an organization must understand its environment and structure itself accordingly. Although the findings of Lawrence and Lorsch are more comprehensive than those of Burns and Stalker and of Chandler, the basic conclusion is the same: environment does play an important role in the relationship between structuring activities and organizational success. This finding is at the heart of the structural contingencies approach to organizational adaptation.

Reducing an Organization's Dependence on the Environment

A perspective significantly different from the structural contingency approach described above is the *resource dependence approach*. This perspective examines organization-environment relations by focusing on the extent to which the organization is dependent upon the external environment for its resources, and how the organization responds to such dependency.[15] The resource dependence model suggests that the effectiveness of a company depends on the extent to which it can successfully manage environmental relations.

The model begins by defining organizational effectiveness as the extent to which an organization can satisfy the demands of those in the environment whose support is necessary to ensure continued existence. A company is said to be dependent on another group to the extent that the input or output of the company is controlled by that group. And the more outside groups controlling the input or output, the more vulnerable the organization is. For example, a mining company that can corner the titanium market would exert considerable influence over aircraft manufacturers who require titanium for new airplane designs. The manufacturers would be dependent on the mining company for an essential resource.

Assessing Environmental Dependence.   The resource dependence model focuses on situations in which organizations are dependent in some way on outside forces. An essential part of the model deals with the extent to which organizations accurately assess their true degree of dependence on the environment. Misreading the environment can result in major corporate failure. Pfeffer and Salancik note four possible reasons why organizations fail to properly assess the extent of their dependence on outsiders or fail to adapt to such dependencies.[16] These include the following:

1. *Misreading interdependence.* An organization may simply fail to identify all of the external groups on which it depends or the relative power of each group. At least one major personal computer company lost a significant share of its market when it underestimated the power of its distributors and ran roughshod over them. The angry distributors responded by showcasing competing personal computers with the predictable result on sales.
2. *Misreading demands.* A second problem emerges when the importance of an outside force is recognized, but the organization misreads what demands the outsiders are making. For example, as budget problems in many states lead to a reduction in state funds for higher education, many colleges and universities have responded by re-emphasizing the quality of their product (that is, their students and their research). However, what many of these schools failed to grasp was that the states were not questioning the effectiveness of the output; rather, they were questioning the efficiency of it. The states were saying that there was simply no more money and schools would have to find cheaper ways to serve students.
3. *Commitment to the past.* Often, organizations feel threatened by change and rely on past practices to get them through modern crises. In a changing market, Henry Ford's commitment to the old Model T, produced in one style and one color only, almost ruined the company. Finally, when it was almost too late and Ford had lost significant market share to Chevrolet, Henry Ford relented and decided to introduce a new product.
4. *Conflicting demands.* Organizations sometimes face situations where response to one outside pressure aggravates another outside pressure. Consider, for example, the plight of many municipal and state agencies who have to decide whether to strengthen pollution rules. More stringent rules may help the environment but will in many cases lead to sizable job reductions (and tax bases) in the area. What do you do?

Meeting Environmental Demands: Making Friends and Changing Behaviors

How does an organization respond when confronted by external demands from a source on which it is dependent? Two general strategies can be identified—developing interorganizational linkages and attempting to modify the environment (see Exhibit 11.8).

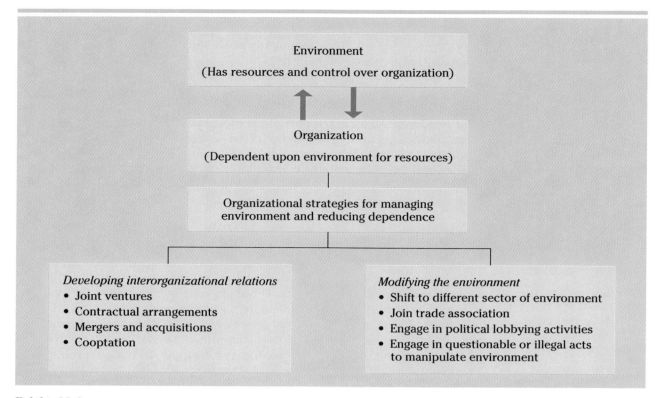

Exhibit 11.8
The Resource Dependence
Model of Organizational
Adaptation

In the first strategy, organizations attempt to develop exchange relationships with outsiders in such a way that a mutually beneficial partnership is established. By doing so, it is hoped that a continued source of vital resources can be established. This can be done in several ways, including joint ventures, contractual relationships, mergers and acquisitions, and co-optation of outsiders. *Co-optation* involves bringing a potentially hostile individual or group inside the organization and essentially "buying it off" in such a way that the potential opponent becomes a supporter of the organization. For example, a company might appoint an important bank director to its own board of directors, hoping to ensure a continued source of financing.

The second approach to managing the environment and continuing the flow of vital resources involves efforts to change or modify the environment itself. In this way, the new environment may be more supportive of the organization and continue to meet its needs. Several strategies can be identified here: (1) move to a different environment that is more hospitable, as many tobacco firms have done by shifting their resources to recreation and food industries; (2) join trade associations to further the goals of the entire industry; (3) engage in individual lobbying efforts with regulators and government officials to create a more supportive environment; and (4) engage in questionable or illegal activities to reshape the environment in a favorable way.

Clearly, the more an organization depends on others in the environment for scarce and valued resources, the more likely it is that it will engage in some form of behavior aimed at reducing the dependence. By doing so, organizations increase their flexibility and degrees of freedom in managerial action. If an organization is to be effective, it must gain control over its own destiny. Whether this is done by winning more independence from others or by establishing long-term coalitions, it is necessary that dependence on hostile or threatening forces for resources be reduced. As noted by Pfeffer and Salancik, the central thesis of this model is this:

> To understand the behavior of an organization you must understand the context of that behavior—that is, the ecology of the organization. This point of view is important for those who seek to understand operations as well as for those who seek to manage and control them. Organizations are inescapably bound up with the conditions of their environment. Indeed, it has been said that all organizations engage in activities which have as their logical conclusion adjustment to the environment.[17]

Ethical Challenge

IN PRACTICE
Insider Information in Pentagon Contracts

For a huge defense contractor, dealing with the Pentagon bureaucracy cannot be easy. The stakes are extremely high, and the competition can be fierce. In many instances, the very survival of the company depends upon winning a certain number of defense contracts. These companies are clearly resource dependent upon the largesse of the Defense Department. As a result, it is not surprising that we often hear accusations of collusion or of inside information being illegally acquired and used in an effort to secure a desired contract. A case in point is Boeing.

In November 1989, Boeing pleaded guilty in federal court to criminal conspiracy and was fined $5 million for illegally using classified Pentagon planning documents to help it secure defense contracts. According to the indictment, three former Boeing executives participated in the criminal activity, and a number of supervisors probably were aware of what was happening but did nothing. As a result, Boeing received inside information that made it easier for it to win certain contracts. Apparently, some individuals inside the company felt that this information was necessary to ensure the continued funding for their defense contracts. It was a convenient way to modify the environment.

As a result of the conviction, Boeing was not only fined but also may be barred from bidding on future government contracts (although this is usually an idle threat, seldom made good). For its part, Boeing claims it has taken steps to ensure that such collusion does not happen again. These actions include trebling the number of corporate security supervisors and administrators and having them carry out a self-inspection and monitoring program for Defense Department documents; implementing a new system to track and identify Pentagon papers; and revising ethics policies and employee training about procedures and handling of classified materials. Meanwhile, the government continues to investigate several other defense contractors on similar charges.[18]

Economic Darwinism: Survival of the Fittest

The third approach to understanding organization-environment relations is the *population ecology model*. Perhaps a better name here is "economic Darwinism." This model draws upon the biological concept of natural selection; it attempts to describe the growth and survival of organizations in a hostile environment. In essence, it argues that the environment selects organizations that will survive on the basis of the degree of fit between the organization form and environmental characteristics. Organizations that have a close fit survive and often prosper; organizations that do not simply go out of existence.[19]

For example, when there is an overabundance of a particular product (for instance, personal computers), companies either find a unique and defensible niche in that market or they fail. This niche may be in offering the most inexpensive PC (as many "IBM clones" do) or in finding a special market (as Apple Macintosh has done). Niches may be found in offering higher quality products, more accessories (e.g., larger data storage capacities), or faster processing speeds (e.g., 486 as opposed to 386 chips). In any case, the company must secure environmental support—that is, people to buy its computers—or become extinct.

The population ecology model is interesting for understanding how companies grow and die. However, its lack of specificity means that it offers little beyond rather obvious lessons for the manager. Telling managers that they must find a market niche or die is fine; telling them how to do this is critical, and the model says little about that. Hence, we suggest that this approach to understanding organization-environment relations be seen simply as a recognition of the importance of strategic planning in organizations facing turbulent environments.

ORGANIZATION-ENVIRONMENT RELATIONS: A SUMMARY

In any discussion of the impact of organization-environment relations on organization effectiveness, several critical variables appear to be consistently interrelated. They are (1) the degree of predictability, (2) the accuracy of perception of environmental states, and (3) the notion of rationality in organizational actions. On the basis of the available evidence, these variables—predictability, perception, and rationality—are important factors in managing environmental relations. Because an optimal response to environmental conditions contributes to organizational effectiveness, managers must fully understand each of these variables.

Increasing Predictability and Control of the Environment

First, consider the issue of predictability and control. In discussing the degree of complexity and stability in the environment, we are in effect raising questions about the degree of uncertainty in organization-environment relations.

The greater the uncertainty, the less the predictability and control. The capacity of an organization to successfully adapt to its environment is a function of its ability to predict the course of the external environment. The more certain managers are about future environmental states, the more opportunity they have to respond appropriately. For example, managers in the plastics firms studied by Lawrence and Lorsch were not unduly hampered by the instability of their market so long as their organization was structured to accommodate market changes with relative ease; that is, they had the appropriate amount of differentiation and integration.

Environmental instability is not necessarily detrimental to effectiveness. Its impact on organizations is more a function of the extent to which the instability and the direction of changes can be predicted in advance and the ability of the organization to appropriately adapt. Research indicates that if the environment is highly unpredictable, a more organic structure may be more effective. A mechanistic structure may be more appropriate for predictable environments. In conclusion, then, it would appear that the greater the predictability concerning environmental states, the greater the potential for appropriate organizational response (see Exhibit 11.9).

Increasing Understanding of the Environment

At least two *filters* may affect the ultimate response of an organization to the existing environment. First, there is the problem of the *accuracy* with which management perceives the environment. As pointed out by Karl Weick, managers respond to what they perceive, and such perceptions may or may not correspond to objective reality. Weick calls this the *enacted environment.*[20] In essence, people create their own environments on the basis of what they see and then act according to these perceptions (see Chapter 3). Thus, if

Exhibit 11.9
Managing Environmental
Contingencies for
Organizational Effectiveness

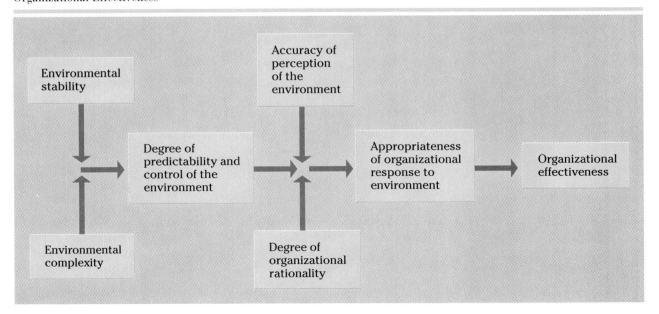

management accurately perceives the degrees of complexity, stability, and uncertainty existing in the external environment, the probability of appropriate organizational response and adaptation is enhanced. If, on the other hand, an organization "enacts" an unrealistic environment, through managerial myopia, lack of expertise, insufficient time, or whatever, the negative effects on organizational success could be substantial.

Second, there is the question concerning which cues are picked up by organizational decision makers. As individuals and in groups, managers often exhibit certain biases about what they see or how they see it. This phenomenon has been referred to as the "organization man" syndrome, the "corporate mentality," "groupthink," and so on. Executive managers work together, socialize together, and often think along similar lines. Thus, it is not surprising that their perceptions of the environment may be filtered by similar work experiences and professional associations. When these perceptions are in error, or when only some of the relevant cues are received from the environment, decisions concerning appropriate responses are made on the basis of distorted or incomplete information. Inaccurate perception can severely constrain organizational response to the environment.

Increasing Rational Behavior by Organizations

A third problem that can affect managerial reaction to environmental events deals with the extent to which managers behave rationally in making environmentally relevant decisions. Although organizations may strive for rational behavior, it has long been recognized that, because of insufficient information or because of a decision maker's inability to adequately process all the relevant information, managers likely engage in some form of *bounded rationality* (see Chapter 14). That is, they seek a solution that is acceptable, but not ideal. The concept of rationality is important because no matter how predictable the environment and no matter how accurate the perceptions concerning environmental states, organizations and managers still have to determine a course of action to respond to changes in the environment. The more rational the choice processes are for selecting viable alternatives, the greater the probability that the chosen response will be appropriate to meet environmental demands.

A classic case in point is the Women's Christian Temperance Union. During the era of prohibition, the WCTU was an active and powerful foe of the legalization of any type of alcoholic beverage. However, as environmental demands changed and popular support shifted in favor of the legalization of liquor, the WCTU remained firm in its opposition. Even though the environment in which this organization operated had changed, and even though the group clearly recognized the change, it made a decision to continue its support for prohibition. As a result, the organization lost most of its popular support and virtually all of its power. One might argue that, under the circumstances, a more "rational" decision for the WCTU would have been to compromise on the issue while it could still bargain from a position of strength. Instead, the organization chose to remain firm in spite of environmental changes, with dire consequences to the organization's effectiveness.

In conclusion, predictability, perception, and rationality are all important factors in environmental relations. Moreover, there is a pattern to this relationship, where the actual degree of predictability of the environment is "filtered" by decision makers through the accuracy of their perception and through their rationality. The resulting selection of a particular course of action can be seen as leading to organizational effectiveness to the extent that it is appropriate for a given environment. If the environment is, in fact, highly unpredictable, and management perceives it to be stable, one would not expect a high degree of organizational success over the long term. Similarly, if management perceives that the environment is unpredictable but chooses to ignore the fact, again one would not expect a high degree of success. Thus, only when accurate perception and high rationality are both present can we predict that an organization's response to environmental conditions will be optimal in contributing to effectiveness.

TECHNOLOGICAL CHANGE IN ORGANIZATIONS

In addition to the external environment, technology affects nearly everyone who works. Consider the example of Paul Laincz, who has worked for a local telephone company for many years. As are most telephone installers and repairpersons, Laincz is now known as a "systems technician" instead of a telephone repairman. He used to go to work wearing jeans, with a tool belt around his waist. Now he makes his calls wearing a suit and tie and carrying his tools in a briefcase. Instead of a van, he drives a company sedan. Instead of receiving his job assignments from a supervisor and having each job closely timed, Laincz now works with only five corporate clients. He decides himself what needs doing, and when. Paul Laincz's experience is similar to that of thousands of employees across North America. Laincz has not experienced a job change, he has experienced a *technological* change in the same job.[21]

Technological changes are evident in most every aspect of work. For example, the number of industrial robots in use in the United States has grown dramatically in recent years, causing a profound change on the shop floor. Moreover, the number of desk-top computers or terminals has similarly increased dramatically, changing the nature of work inside the office. The advent of computer-based technology leads to fundamental changes both in the way work is done and in the kind of jobs available. Thus, it is important for managers to examine how technological changes affect organizational behavior and effectiveness if they are to successfully adapt to a changing work environment.

What Is Technology?

The word *technology* refers to anything that involves either the mechanical or intellectual processes by which an organization transforms inputs (raw materials) into outputs (finished products) in the pursuit of organizational goals. In discussing the role of technology in organizations, we are, in essence, focusing our attention on "who does what with whom, when, where, and how often."[22] An example of technology at work can be seen in such processes as the way a computer transforms data into a usable report, or the way an assembly line transforms steel, rubber, and glass into an automobile. In both cases, we see examples of transformation processes in organizations in which mechanical, electronic, and intellectual energies are exercised in the efficient utilization of scarce and valued resources.

IN PRACTICE
Zenith and HDTV

High-definition television (HDTV) promises to be the television of the future and, as such, represents a potential multi-billion dollar market for companies who can successfully enter. Until recently, however, most American companies had ceded this market to the Japanese and West Europeans, who are ahead of the United States in technology. But recently, several small and medium-sized American firms have begun attempting to catch up in the race to produce and sell a viable HDTV system. At issue are several things, including the development of relevant technologies and the ability to put together an organization capable of manufacturing the technology. Many of the technological advances are already coming from the United States, and in digital HDTV, the United States is ahead of Japan.

What is needed beyond this technology is the means to organize in a way that increases the chances of success. One company responding to this challenge is Zenith. Zenith had been a leader in the manufacture of personal computers, including a best-selling laptop model. It was also the sole remaining American manufacturer of televisions. In 1989, Zenith announced that it would sell off its highly profitable computer division so it could concentrate its resources on television development. The chairman noted that for a company of Zenith's size, it did not make sense to compete in both turbulent environments.

As a result, the company will reorganize and focus its research efforts on developing the television technology of the future and on capturing a larger market share in a sector of this emerging industry. For Zenith, the effort will initially focus on developing signal-processing and broadcast equipment, because it currently lacks the capability to produce large display panels. Even so, this foot-in-the-door approach allows Zenith to continue in the field. As a result, Zenith is well positioned technologically and structurally to grow with the market.[23]

INFLUENCE OF TECHNOLOGY ON DEPARTMENTS

One of the first challenges Zenith faces as it shifts its strategy is how to organize to manage the new technology. Is its current organization design appropriate, or are structural changes necessary? To understand this challenge, it is necessary to consider how technology affects organizations. As we examine the role of technology and its managerial implications in organizations, we will make several distinctions. First, it is necessary to differentiate between *departmental technology* (the various processes associated with a given department within an organization, such as the finance department) and *organizational technology* (the transformation processes that take place within the technological core of the organization). In addition, within organizational technology, it is necessary to differentiate between technologies in the manufacturing sector and in the service sector. We shall examine each of these in turn.

If we look at departmental units across organizations (e.g., a hospital, a small business, or a government agency), it is easy to note differences in their use of technology. Moreover, if we look at different departments within the same company (e.g., the accounting, engineering, and personnel departments), it is again easy to note technological differences. In order to better understand these differences and their impact on organization design, a model has been proposed by Charles Perrow.[24] Perrow argues that technology in departments can be examined using two dimensions: variety and analyzability (see Exhibit 11.10).

Exhibit 11.10
Four Types of
Departmental Technology

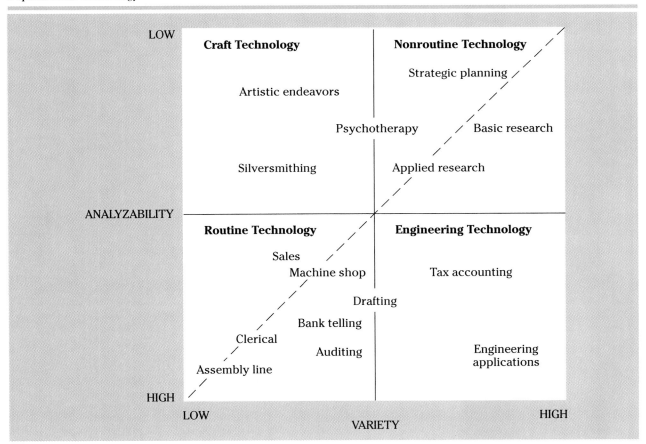

Source: Adapted from Charles Perrow, "A Framework for the Comparative Analysis of Organizations," *American Sociological Review* 32 (1967): 194–208; and Richard L. Daft and Norman Macintosh, "A New Approach to Design and Use of Management Information," *California Management Review* 21 (1978): 82–92. Reprinted from R. Daft and R. Steers, *Organizations: A Micro/Macro Approach* (Glenview, Ill.: Scott, Foresman, 1986), p. 254.

Variety refers to the amount of variation and diversity on the job, and *analyzability* refers to the degree to which the job can be analyzed and reduced to a number of explicit steps. Low-variety jobs would include assembly line work and clerical positions, and high-variety jobs would include most managerial positions. People with low-analyzability jobs would include strategic planners and artists, and those with high-analyzability jobs would include bank tellers and auditors. As can be seen in Exhibit 11.10, it is possible to plot these jobs on a two-dimensional chart to see how various jobs are categorized technologically. As a result, we can identify four cells on the exhibit that correspond to Perrow's four types of departmental technology. These are (1) routine, (2) craft, (3) engineering, and (4) nonroutine.

In business organizations, most departments fall into the routine-nonroutine dichotomy. This is represented in Exhibit 11.10 by a broken line. In another study, 2600 managers in 14 manufacturing firms were surveyed about their jobs.[25] The results, shown in Exhibit 11.11, clearly indicate the variability in technology across the departments. We can see marked differences in departmental approaches to organization structure. For example, departments that emphasize routine technology tend to be highly formalized and to have centralized decision making; infrequent communication, which is in writing only; and a production or efficiency goal. (See previous chapter for a discussion of these terms.) The manufacturing unit within a corporation is an example, as is a typical finance department. On the other hand, departments that emphasize nonroutine technologies (such as a company's research and development unit) tend to exhibit low formalization, decentralized decision making, frequent verbal communication, and quality and outputs for goals. Clearly, the nature of the departmental technology affects departmental structure and effectiveness.

Exhibit 11.11
Percentage of Functional
Groups with Routine and
Nonroutine Technologies

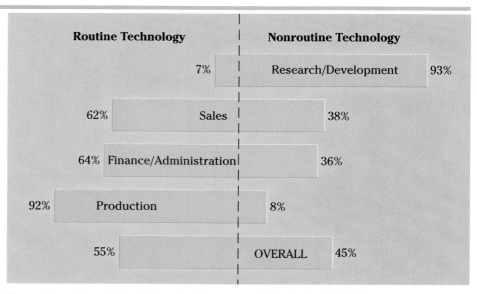

Source: From *Organization Design, Development and Behavior* by Karl O. Magnusen, p. 19. Copyright © 1977 Scott, Foresman and Company. Reprinted by permission.

MANUFACTURING VS. SERVICE: THE TECHNICAL CORE OF ORGANIZATIONS

As was noted above, *organizational technology* refers to transformation processes that transcend departmental boundaries and represent the core technologies of the corporation. These core technologies contribute to the primary output of the organization. First, we will consider organizational technology for the manufacturing sector, and then we will expand our assessment to include the service sector.

Manufacturing Technology

The earliest detailed examination of the relationships between technology, structure, and organizational success in the manufacturing sector was carried out by Joan Woodward and her colleagues.[26] Woodward, a British sociologist, began her research in the early 1950s by addressing the question of whether "the principles of organization laid down by an expanding body of management theory correlate with business success when put into practice."[27] She and her associates surveyed about 100 British manufacturing firms, which varied in size from 100 to over 1000 employees, and collected information on a variety of structural variables. She examined span of control, organization size, levels of authority, degree of formalization, and the relative success or effectiveness of the various enterprises.

Technical Complexity.   Initially, Woodward focused her attention on the relation of organization size to structure; however, no consistent pattern emerged. This absence of relationship may be accounted for by the relatively restricted range in the sizes of the firms surveyed. Moreover, no association was found between size or other structural variables and organizational success. These findings led Woodward to question the validity of the early "principles" of management; indeed, they did not appear to have universal applicability in all types of organizations.

In an effort to account for the variations in managerial practices and the absence of a clear structure-effectiveness association, Woodward decided to classify the organizations in the survey by technology. Focusing specifically on manufacturing firms, Woodward suggested three categories of technology *based on the level of technical complexity* of the production process. These three categories are as follows:

1. *Small-batch, or unit, production.* The product is custom-made to individual customer specifications (for example, airplanes, locomotives, and printing jobs). Operations performed on each unit are typically nonrepetitive in nature.
2. *Mass production.* The product is manufactured in assembly line fashion (for example, automobiles). Operations performed are repetitious, routine, and predictable.
3. *Continuous-process production.* The product is transformed from raw material to a finished good using a series of machine or process transformations (for example, chemicals and oil refining).

Woodward argued that the technical complexity of an organization increases as it moves from unit production through mass production to continuous-process production. Although such a trend may occur in many cases, it is easy to envision exceptions. For example, one could argue that the development and production of an MD-11 or a Boeing 767 (small-batch technology) is far more complex technologically than either mass production or continuous-process production. Thus, it may be necessary to differentiate standard or routinized from nonstandard forms of small-batch production technologies when discussing technical complexity. Although the printing process may employ fairly routine production techniques, designing and manufacturing an airplane certainly do not.

On the basis of this classification of manufacturing technology, Woodward assigned the various firms to each category and reanalyzed the data. Her results demonstrated the following (see Exhibit 11.12):

■ There was no significant relationship between technological complexity and organizational size.

■ The span of control of first-level supervision (e.g., foremen) increased from unit to mass production technology, but then it decreased markedly from mass production to continuous-process technology.

■ The span of control of the chief executive increased with increasing technological complexity (from unit to mass to continuous process).

■ The number of levels of authority in an organization increased somewhat with increases in technological complexity.

■ The ratio of administrators to workers increased with increases in technological complexity.

■ The ratio of supporting staff and specialists to workers increased with increases in technological complexity.

■ Relative labor costs decreased with increases in technological complexity.

■ Formalization (clear definitions of duties, rules, amount of paperwork) was greatest under mass production technology, tapering off considerably under unit and continuous process technologies.

Technological Determinism.   Next, Woodward asked what impact these findings had for the study of organizational effectiveness. Firms were classified according to relative degree of success, and structure and technology were again compared. The surprising conclusion resulting from this analysis was that "the organizational characteristics of the successful firms in each production (that is, technology) category tended to cluster around the medians for that category as a whole, while the figures of the firms classified below average in success were found at the extremes of the range."[28] In other words, there appeared to be an optimal level for several structural characteristics (such as span of control) for successful firms in each of the three technological categories. Less successful firms in each category exhibited structural ratios that were either too large or too small. It is important to stress here that the optimal level for success was different for each technological category.

Exhibit 11.12
Relationships Between
Technological Variables and
Organizational Structure

Structural Variables*	Small-Batch Production	Mass Production	Continuous-Process Production
Supervisory span of control	23	48	15
Executive span of control	4	7	10
Number of levels of authority	3	4	6
Ratio of administrators to workers	9:1	4:1	1:1
Ratio of staff/specialists to workers	8:1	5:1	2:1
Relative labor costs	High	Medium	Low
Degree of formalization	Low	High	Low

*Data reported are median scores.

Source: Developed from Woodward, *Industrial Organization: Theory and Practice* (London: Oxford University Press, 1965).

From these findings, Woodward concluded that "the fact that organizational characteristics, technology, and success were linked together in this way suggested that not only was the system of production (that is, technology) an important variable in the determination of organizational structure, but also that one particular form of organization was most appropriate to each system of production."[29] In short, Woodward was arguing in favor of a contingency approach to management, whereby different technologies require different structures and interpersonal styles. This technological determinism concept essentially proposes that under mass production technology, a highly structured, formalized, bureaucratic managerial style may be more appropriate for organizational success. However, at the two opposite ends of the technological continuum, small batch and continuous-process, more successful firms employed less structured, less formalized managerial styles with fewer rules, fewer controls, and a greater degree of interpersonal interaction (see Exhibit 11.13).

Service Technology

The service sector of the economy is substantially different from the manufacturing sector. Differences can be noted in at least two areas:

1. *Intangibility of outputs.* First, the output of a service is intangible. Banks and department stores, for example, offer customers services that cannot be stored in inventories and that cannot be seen.
2. *Closeness to customer.* Second, service industries are typically closer to their customers than are typical manufacturing firms. In fact, if you do not like the service you are receiving from one firm, you will often try another. For a service industry to succeed, the customer must be accommodated.

In view of these differences, a comprehensive look at technology and its impact would have to broaden its classification scheme to include both manufacturing and service industries. This has been done in a series of studies

Exhibit 11.13
Structural Characteristics
of Effective Organizations
Grouped According
to Technology

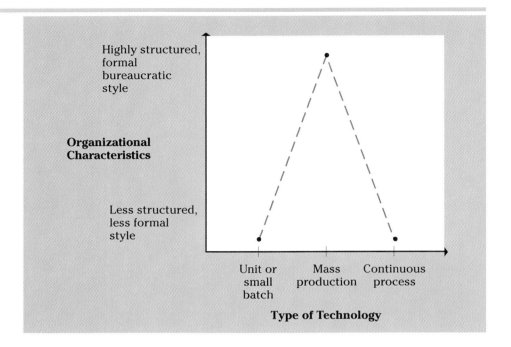

carried out by a group of British social scientists led by Pugh and Hickson.[30] Collectively, this research team has become known as the "Aston Group," because much of their early research was carried out at the University of Aston. Although a good deal of this research focused on relationships among structural variables, our primary focus here is on the findings pertaining to the structure-technology relationship and organizational performance.

Work Flow Integration.   Using this broader approach, we can consider technology in terms of a general factor called work flow integration. Included in this concept are such variables as the degree of task interdependence, the rigidity of work flow sequences, the automation of equipment, and the specificity of evaluation of operations. The greater the automation, task specificity, and so forth, the greater the extent of work flow integration. Using this concept, Hickson and his associates surveyed 46 firms and calculated a numerical index of work flow integration for each organization. Partial results are shown in Exhibit 11.14. As can be seen, manufacturing firms consistently have greater work flow integration scores than service firms, meaning that service firms may also have different structural configurations from manufacturing firms.

To test this assertion, the index of work flow integration was compared to a variety of structural variables with several interesting results. To begin with, no general relationship was found between technological complexity and structural characteristics (specialization and standardization). This finding was in direct contradiction to the earlier findings by Woodward. "In general, our studies have confirmed that the relationship of technology to the main structural dimensions in manufacturing organizations is always very small and plays a secondary role relative to other contextual features such as size and interdependence with other organizations."[31]

Work Flow Integration Score	Organization	Organization Type	
		Service	Manufacturing
17	Vehicle manufacturer		✓
16	Brewery		✓
15	Packaging manufacturer		✓
14	Metal components manufacturer		✓
13	Vehicle tire manufacturer		✓
12	Glass components manufacturer		✓
11	Printer		✓
10	Local authority water department	✓	
9	Nonferrous metal processor		✓
8	Toy manufacturer		✓
7	Local authority civil engineering department	✓	
6	Insurance company	✓	
5	Research division	✓	
4	Savings bank	✓	
3	Chain of shoe repair stores	✓	
2	Department stores	✓	
1	Chain of retail stores	✓	

Exhibit 11.14
Examples of Work Flow Integration Scores for Manufacturing and Service Firms

Source: Based on David J. Hickson, D. S. Pugh, and D. C. Pheysey, "Operations Technology and Organization Structure: An Empirical Reappraisal," *Administrative Science Quarterly* 14 (1969):385. Reprinted from R. Daft and R. Steers, *Organizations: A Micro/Macro Approach* (Glenview, Ill.: Scott, Foresman, 1986), p. 265. Copyright © 1986 Scott, Foresman and Company.

Under closer analysis, however, technology was found to be related to various aspects of structure in a number of highly specific ways. For example, Woodward's curvilinear relationship between span of control of first-line supervisors and technological complexity was confirmed. Moreover, the ratio of quality inspectors and maintenance personnel to workers was also greatest in mass production and tapered off for both unit and continuous-process technologies.

Limitations on Technological Determinism

When the Aston Group findings concerning technology are considered as a whole, though, there appear to be two related conclusions. First, the evidence indicates that "only those [structural characteristics] directly centered on the production work flow itself show any connection with technology. Away from the shop floor, technology appears to have little influence on organization structure."[32] In other words, technology appears to affect organization structure only in those departments actually using the technology (e.g., a production unit). Other departments, such as accounting or marketing, appear to be unaffected, according to these data; this reinforces Perrow's arguments discussed earlier.

Second, and almost a corollary of the first point, the evidence appears to support the position that "the smaller the organization the more its structure will be pervaded by such technological effects, the larger the organization the more these effects will be confined to variables such as job counts of employees on activities linked to the work flow itself, and will not be detectable in variations of the more remote administrative and hierarchical structure."[33] In other words, variations in technology have a more pronounced effect on organization structure for small organizations than for large ones.

Thus, Pugh, Hickson, and their associates interpret their findings within a contingency framework, whereby technology can affect the structural design of an organization only as moderated by additional intervening variables, such as organization size or department function. In small organizations, technology largely dictates structure; in large organizations, technology dictates structure only in production-related units. Such findings raise questions concerning the validity of the technological determinism point of view advanced by Woodward and others. The Aston Group would argue that determinism is contingent upon several mediating variables, such as size of organization and departmental function, which may serve to intervene in the technology-structure relationship. Moreover, it is possible that technological determinism may be operative only for specific aspects of structure, such as formalization and span of control, and not for others, such as complexity of department and levels of authority. In any event, although some disagreement exists concerning the exact role of technology, both studies clearly point to the relevance of this variable in consideration of the determinants of organizational effectiveness.

What can we conclude about the way in which technology and structure *jointly* relate to organizational effectiveness? Although it has been demonstrated that neither technology nor structure by itself shows any appreciable relationship to effectiveness, several investigations have suggested the existence of an interactive relationship between these two variables as they affect ultimate organizational success. This contention may be called the *consonance hypothesis.* Specifically, it can be argued that the effectiveness of an organization is largely a result of the extent to which an organization can successfully match its technology with an appropriate structure. Thus, an organization that employs very routine, repetitive technology, for example, may perform best when it relies on a highly formalized structure. Evidence in support of the consonance hypothesis can be found in the studies reviewed in this and the previous chapter.

However, it can also be argued that social and historical factors may affect structure more than does technology. Although the data from these latter studies clearly do not reject the hypothesis in its entirety, they do suggest the existence of a series of individual and social factors (which have been ignored in earlier studies on technology) that might influence effectiveness. Therefore, it may be necessary to expand the consonance hypothesis to include a recognition of the role of human behavior. Thus, effectiveness may be seen as a function of an organization's ability to successfully integrate technology, structure, and personal characteristics and social factors into a congruent, goal-oriented entity. For instance, not only would the use of assembly line technology call for a structured approach to organizing human resources, it would also suggest the need for individuals with the willingness and the capacity to work in such an environment. It appears that the inclusion of this human variable in any consideration of the technology-structure relationship would considerably increase our understanding of organizational dynamics and success.

International Challenge

IN PRACTICE
Motorola's Challenge in Semiconductors

MOTOROLA

Ask around in Japan, and many business executives will tell you that American chips make a poor showing because U.S. engineers have forgotten how to design for consumer products. Others will say that American companies cannot match the Japanese in terms of quality and customer service standards. However, that is not what executives at Canon would say. At the heart of Canon's best-selling EOS 35mm camera is a Motorola microprocessor. It is there, Canon executives say, because Motorola provides superior design expertise and service, along with equal quality.

At first, Canon sought out Japanese manufacturers to help them design the microcircuitry for the new EOS camera. When these companies seemed uninterested in the special needs facing Canon, it approached Motorola. From the first, Canon found that the American company responded to the technical challenge with netsui (passion). "From the first time we talked, they let us know how much we mattered to them," commented a Canon executive. In fact, Motorola did more than simply tailor a chip for Canon. Its engineers also invented two other key components for the camera that set the new product apart from the competition.

How can a company such as Motorola compete in Japan's high-tech business environment? It does so by a combination of strong R&D efforts, built-in quality control, and zealous service to customers. From the CEO on down, Motorola employees know that being on the cutting edge is the only thing that keeps the company competitive in world markets. Continual efforts are made to reduce costs, streamline operations, and capture market share. (Motorola ranks first in the United States and fourth in the world in semiconductor sales.) Above all, however, Motorola is committed to product innovation. It has shown itself to be a successful innovator.

To accomplish this, close collaboration is required between the company's R&D efforts and marketing and manufacturing. As a result, new products are allowed to enter the market sooner and keep ahead of the competition. And close interdepartmental cooperation has also boosted quality control efforts. For example, by working together, the defect rate on new products has been cut from 3000 per million products to fewer than 200, saving the company over $250 million during the past three years. By developing an organizational structure and corporate culture appropriate for its intended market, and by ensuring interdepartmental cooperation, Motorola continues to prosper in the high-tech marketplace.[34]

PULLING IT ALL TOGETHER

What is the right organizational structure? It's hard to say. It depends on the complexity and dynamism of the external and task environment—the more the environment is complex and dynamic, the more the structure of the organization should be organic and facilitate integration and coordination. However, organizational effectiveness is a function of not only an appropriate fit between the organizational structure and the environment, but between the structure and other organizational systems (human resources, communication, management, etc.) as well as among these systems. These organizational systems and processes are covered in the next section (Part 4) of this text.

SUMMARY OF KEY POINTS

▓ Variations in the external environment and technology have a marked impact on both the structure and effectiveness of an organization.

▓ The external environment consists of all those organizations and forces with which a company must deal. The external environment can be divided into the general environment, consisting of factors that affect a company in an indirect or tangential way, and the task environment, consisting of those factors that directly affect a company.

▓ Environmental uncertainty affects many aspects of managerial decision making and action. Uncertainty can be assessed using a model proposed by Duncan. The model consists of three major variables: (1) the simple-complex dimension, (2) the static-dynamic dimension, and (3) environmental uncertainty. Using these three dimensions, we can fairly readily categorize a particular organization and thereby understand its relationship with the external environment.

▓ There are three ways to examine organizational adaptation: (1) the structural contingency model, (2) the resource dependence model, and (3) the population ecology model. The structural contingency approach focuses on how the organization attempts to structure itself in response to environmental demands. Examples of this approach include the organic-mechanistic, strategy-structure contingencies, and differentiation-integration models.

▓ The resource dependence model of organization adaptation focuses on how organizations attempt to manage their environmental dependencies. Examples of this approach can be seen in joint ventures, contractual relations, mergers and acquisitions, and cooptation.

▓ The population ecology model of organizational adaptation emphasizes how the external environment influences the growth, development, and survival of organizations.

▓ Organizational effectiveness is a function of the extent to which an organization appropriately responds to the external environment. The appropriateness of the response is influenced by at least three variables: (1) the accuracy of perception of the environment, (2) the degree of predictability of the environment, and (3) the extent of organizational rationality. The manner in which an organization responds to changes in the external environment greatly influences the capacity of that organization to become effective.

▓ Technology refers to any mechanical or intellectual process by which inputs are transformed into outputs.

▓ Departmental technology refers to the various processes associated with a given department (e.g., finance or accounting). Four types of departmental technology are (1) craft, (2) engineering, (3) routine, and (4) nonroutine.

■ Organizational technology refers to transformation processes that transcend departmental boundaries and represent the technological core of the organization. In the manufacturing sector, such technologies can be divided into small-batch or unit production, mass production, and continuous-process production.

■ Work flow integration refers to the extent to which the various subprocesses involved in technological transformations are interrelated or independent. Included in this concept are the degree of task interdependence, the rigidity of work flow sequences, the automation of equipment, task specificity, and so forth.

KEY WORDS

consonance hypothesis
continuous-process production
cooptation
departmental technology
differentiation
enacted environment
environmental complexity
environmental determinism
environmental stability
environmental uncertainty
external environment
general environment
integration
mass production

mechanistic systems
organic systems
organizational technology
population ecology
resource dependence
small-batch production
strategy-structure contingency
structural contingencies
task environment
technical complexity
technological determinism
technology
work flow integration

QUESTIONS FOR DISCUSSION

1. What is meant by the external environment of an organization? What are the dimensions of such an environment?
2. Describe Duncan's model of environmental states.
3. What are the major conclusions of the Burns and Stalker study?
4. Discuss Chandler's basic hypothesis concerning the relationship between strategy and structure.
5. Define and discuss the relationship between integration and differentiation according to the Lawrence and Lorsch model.
6. Describe the resource dependence model of organization-environment relations. How does this model differ from the structural contingency model? How does it differ from the population ecology model? Which of the three models makes most sense to you in understanding organization-environment relations?
7. Discuss the practical significance of the enacted environment concept.
8. Compare and contrast the three approaches to classifying technology. Which approach do you prefer? Why?
9. Differentiate between technology in the manufacturing sector and in the service sector.

10. What was the major finding of the classic Woodward study? Is this conclusion still valid today?
11. What is technological determinism? How valid is the concept?
12. Describe the consonance hypothesis as it relates to organization design.

NOTES

1. D. Kirkpatrick, "Breaking Up IBM," Fortune, July 27, 1992, pp. 44–58.
2. *1989 Annual Report—United Airlines* (Chicago, Ill.); *American Airlines: 1988 Annual Report* (Dallas, Tex.); *Scandinavian Airline System (SAS): 1989 Annual Report* (Copenhagen, Denmark).
3. R. Duncan, "Characteristics of Perceived Environments and Perceived Environmental Uncertainty," *Administrative Science Quarterly,* 1972, *17,* 313–327.
4. Ibid.
5. Ibid., p. 325.
6. C. Wallace, "How Thailand Has Become Asia's Fifth Tiger," *Los Angeles Times,* November 20, 1989, p. D3.
7. T. Burns and G. Stalker, *The Management of Innovation* (London: Tavistock, 1962).
8. Reprinted from Kathleen Deveny, "Bag Those Fries, Squirt That Ketchup, Fry That Fish," *Business Week,* October 13, 1986.
9. A. Chandler, *Strategy and Structure* (Cambridge, Mass.: MIT Press, 1962), pp. 18–19.
10. Ibid., p. 19.
11. Ibid., p. 462.
12. P. Lawrence and J. Lorsch, *Organization and Environment* (Boston: Harvard Business School, 1967), p. 16.
13. Ibid., p. 11.
14. Ibid.
15. J. Pfeffer and G. Salancik, *The External Control of Organizations* (New York: Harper & Row, 1978).
16. Ibid.
17. Ibid., p. 1.
18. A. Pasztor and R. Wartzman, "Boeing Pleads Guilty in Use of Documents," *Wall Street Journal,* November 14, 1989, p. A4.
19. M. Hannan and J. Freeman, "The Population Ecology of Organizations," *American Journal of Sociology,* 1977, *82,* pp. 929–964.
20. K. Weick, *The Social Psychology of Organizing* (Reading, Mass.: Addison-Wesley, 1972).
21. Cited in *Fortune,* June 28, 1982, p. 59.
22. E. Chapple and L. Sayles, *The Measure of Management* (New York: Macmillan, 1961), p. 34.
23. E. Lachica, "Small U.S. Firms Challenge Japanese Grip on HDTV," *Wall Street Journal,* October 23, 1989, pp. B1–B2; C. Lazzareschi, "Zenith to Get Out of Computers, Focus on Electronics," *Los Angeles Times,* October 3, 1989, p. IV–1.
24. C. Perrow, *Organizational Analysis: A Sociological Approach* (Belmont, Calif.: Wadsworth, 1970).
25. K. Magnusen, *Organization Design, Development and Behavior* (Glenview, Ill.: Scott, Foresman, 1977).
26. J. Woodward, *Industrial Organization: The Theory and Practice* (Oxford: Oxford University Press, 1965); J. Woodward, *Management and Technology* (London: H.M. Stationery Office, 1958).

27. Woodward, *Management and Technology,* op. cit., p. 23.
28. Woodward, *Industrial Organization,* op. cit., p. 69.
29. Ibid., pp. 69–70.
30. D. Hickson, D. Pugh, and D. Pheysey, "Operations Technology and Organization Structure: An Empirical Reappraisal," *Administrative Science Quarterly,* 1969, 14, pp. 378–397.
31. D. Pugh, D. Hickson, and C. R. Hinings, *Organizations* (Middlesex, England, 1973), p. 32.
32. Ibid., p. 33.
33. Hickson et al., op. cit., pp. 394–395.
34. L. Therrien, "The Rival Japan Respects," *Business Week,* November 13, 1989, pp. 108–118.

EXPERIENTIAL EXERCISE 11

Designing a Small Firm (Part Two)

This exercise focuses on developing a better understanding of environmental and technological contingencies in the management of a small enterprise. This exercise builds upon Experiential Exercise 10 and requires some field research prior to class.

As a Group

To begin this exercise, you should group yourselves as you did in Experiential Exercise 10. As a group, you should answer the following questions on the basis of your investigation of a small firm:

1. Using the framework outlined in this chapter, how would you describe the external environment of this firm?
2. How would you characterize this firm's environmental uncertainty? Why?
3. How does the firm's organizational structure reflect its external environment? Is this a good match between structure and environment? Why, or why not?
4. Using the materials in this chapter, how would you describe this firm's core technologies? How do these technological constraints influence organization structure?
5. If you were in charge of this firm, what managerial changes would you make to accommodate these environmental and technological forces?

As a Class

When your group is finished, you should reconvene as a class and report and compare your findings on these questions. Again, look for similarities and differences across the small firms studied.

MANAGEMENT DILEMMA 11

First National City Bank

The First National City Bank was founded in 1965 by William Jacks, who owned a controlling interest in the bank. His family had been in banking for many years, and he saw this as an opportunity to apply his banking and management experience to his own bank. The bank was located in a rapidly growing urban area in Arizona. During the initial years, First National City Bank concentrated on two goals: attracting and retaining depositors through personal service, and establishing a reputation as a safe and solid financial institution. The goals were successful, and the bank grew to $475 million in assets by 1984.

During the late 1980s, the bank's growth slowed, and Bill Jacks and the bank experienced some reversals. Two new branch locations were closed because they could not show a profit. One of the branches was located in a nearby city that had a large population of ethnic and minority people. The other branch had been located near a major university where most of the residents were college students. In both cases, the First National City branches seemed unable to attract depositors and borrowers from their local areas. The Bank did not have a positive reputation with those population segments, and did not seem to have the flexibility or types of service desired by potential customers.

By 1988, Bill Jacks began to replace some middle managers, hoping to bring in new energy and fresh ideas. Bill Jacks still believed that a bank succeeded because of its safety as a financial institution, and because it established personal relationships with middle class customers. He passed this philosophy and other management ideas on to the new managers. He stressed a traditional management structure, including centralized decision making and standardized procedures. All branch banks were encouraged to offer the same services, and many decisions were passed up the hierarchy to the top. Vertical communication and "following the rules" were deemed a safe and responsible management approach for a community bank.

As the new managers gained experience in the bank, they began to propose changes. One branch manager suggested that each of the branch locations establish an advisory board. The purpose of the advisory board would be to select people from the surrounding community to serve on a committee that would serve as a liaison between the community and First National City Bank and make recommendations to management. The advisory boards would be composed of the bank manager, Bill Jacks, and important people from the local area, including women, minority group members, and college students. The manager who proposed the idea argued that advisory board members could counsel prospective customers about bank services and in general provide good information to the bank manager and promote good will for the bank.

Another new manager proposed that the bank engage in more advertising and public relations. She argued that bank employees should become more involved in community groups, such as the Chamber of Commerce and United Way. She also argued that the bank should make a contribution to the State Association of Bankers to support lobbyists working at the state capitol to increase the interest rate ceilings, and to support lobbyists working in Washington to influence bank regulation.

As Bill Jacks considered these and other proposals, he thought of the recent bank deregulation policies passed by Congress. New powers had been given to thrift institutions—credit unions, savings and loan associations—to compete directly with banks in business and consumer lending, retirement annuities, and other services. Deregulation had also given banks the freedom to become financial supermarkets and provide services such as the sale of stocks and bonds, to offer high interest rates, and to charge for services. The new regulations seemed to favor large banks because interstate banking and bank holding companies were possible.

Bill Jacks and the other managers were very uncertain about the long-term impact of deregulation on First National City Bank. A bank consultant was hired to assess the impact of deregulation on First National City's strategy. The consultant said that as deregulation continued, the bank would need "a strong commitment to the development and delivery of new products. Moreover, customer loyalty will fade and price competition combined with technological advances and internal efficiencies will be essential for maintaining and increasing a customer base."

A university professor conducted a survey of successful community banks to learn how they were coping with deregulation. The survey found that successful banks were making changes in four areas: (1) asset-liability management, (2) cost control, (3) marketing, (4) pricing and non-interest income. Better asset-liability management in many banks was accomplished through a new asset-liability committee that helped the bank make a transition to variable-rate loans, make loans according to profit margin, and explore new investment opportunities. Cost control was accomplished through technology and data processing, such as automated tellers and the automatic transfer of funds. New marketing techniques included market segmentation and the packaging of new products for each segment. Money market accounts, discount brokerage services, increased advertising, retirement accounts, and other marketing ideas were being adopted. Important new income was also being derived from non-interest sources for successful community banks. Seventy-five percent of the banks increased fees for returned checks, overdrafts and checking account services. Fees were also increased for routine balance inquiries and saving accounts.

In January of 1993, Bill Jacks felt overwhelmed, and wondered whether he was up to managing the bank. The bank had grown little over five years, and was losing market share to other, often recently established banks. Two of the newer managers quit out of frustration over not having impact on bank policy. The impact of bank deregulation was difficult to anticipate, and he was not sure how the bank should respond. Two of the brightest young managers in the bank had been to see him about a change in management structure and approach. They encouraged the creation of several internal committees to study the problem and to coordinate the needs of each department and branch. They also suggested the bank begin planning for the addition of new departments that would be responsible for new electronic technology, new services, and stronger advertising. "The banking industry is becoming more complex and its changing rapidly," one manager argued, "and if we don't adapt to it we will be left behind." Bill Jacks also thought back to earlier proposals, such as for advisory boards, on which he had not acted. Could the bank afford to invest in advertising, lobbying, new technology, and new departments? Would customers pay fees for services that had been provided free? Should the bank provide non-banking services? Could all of these activities be coordinated when things change so quickly? If he was unable to resolve these problems, Bill Jacks thought the best thing might be to retire and perhaps sell his interest in the bank to someone else.

As you look over this case, consider how you would answer the following:

1. Evaluate the complexity and rate of change in the environment of this bank. What domains seem most important? Where would you place this bank on the environmental uncertainty exhibit shown in Exhibit 11.3?
2. Should the bank try to adapt to the external environment or try to exert greater control over the environment? Which of the proposals would you recommend that the bank adopt?
3. How should the bank change its structure in response to these proposals so it is more congruent with its environment?

Source: Reprinted with permission from R. Daft and R. Steers, *Organizations: A Micro/Macro Approach* (Glenview, Ill.: Scott, Foresman, 1986), pp. 314–318. This case was inspired by and adapted from John F. Veiga and John N. Yanouzas, "The Constitution National Bank," *The Dynamics of Organization Theory: Gaining a Macroperspective* (St. Paul, Minn.: West, 1979), pp. 139–140; Peter S. Rose, "What, How, Why and Whither of U.S. Bank Deregulation," *Canadian Banker 91,* (1) (February 1984), pp. 36–41; Judy Brown, "How High Performance Community Banks Cope with the Effects of Deregulation," *Journal of Retail Banking 5* (3) (Fall 1983), pp. 17–24; and Richard C. Aspinwall, "Anticipating Banking Deregulation," *The Journal of Business Strategy,* Spring 1983, pp. 84–86.

Part Four

Organizational Processes

Chapter 12

Leadership and Group Performance

The Management Challenge

- To provide effective leadership for subordinates.
- To understand how the nature and quality of leadership vary, depending on one's position in the managerial hierarchy.
- To recognize the transactional, symbolic, and charismatic aspects of leadership in organization.
- To select the right leaders and managers for a given situation.
- To recognize the impact leaders and managers have on corporate culture.

CLOSE UP   New Leadership at Xerox

In 1990 Xerox appointed a new CEO, Paul Allaire. In the past Xerox had invented a number of technologies that other companies commercialized, including the "mouse" and the software that helped make Apple Computers (especially the Macintosh) famous. Allaire was determined that in the future Xerox would capitalize on its own inventions.

Allaire's vision for Xerox had two major components. First, he saw Xerox as the "Document Company," a company focused on helping office workers create, use, and share reports, memos, and databases and not just make copies of these documents. Second, he was determined to make Xerox more market driven by being closer to its customers. "I have to change the company substantially to be more market driven. If we do what's right for the customer, our market share and our return on assets will take care of themselves." Allaire spends time on the road reinforcing these two messages to executives and factory workers alike. He often tells the story of how, when he was a young boy working with his father in a quarry outside of Worcester, Massachusetts, his father would have him put a few extra shovelfuls of gravel into every order to make sure that the customer was pleased.

Allaire is an unusual leader at a time when CEO perks have escalated because he drives himself to work and flies coach. He also reads widely, including books such as *One of Us* by Tom Wicker in which he studies the administration and leadership of Nixon. Although Allaire's day typically runs from 7 A.M. to 7 P.M., he rarely works on Sunday and never on Saturday.

While Allaire is considered a tough-minded leader, his style is one of a listener. But a senior VP at Xerox pointed out that "A mild rebuke from Paul is like a tongue-lashing from other people. You immediately get the point."

It will take years to determine the total impact that Allaire will have on the performance of a giant such as Xerox. However, not long after Allaire was installed as CEO, Wall Street had a very positive response and the stock price of Xerox nearly doubled within his first year as its new leader.[1]

In many ways Paul Allaire exemplifies the successful corporate leader. He has a vision, is knowledgeable, goal-directed, charismatic, and driven. He makes timely decisions, communicates these decisions in an effective manner, and handles interpersonal conflict when it emerges. Perhaps most important, he sets an example others will follow.

In previous sections of this book, we discussed many of the challenges facing contemporary organizations and the nature of individual factors as they relate to work behavior and performance. Following this, we discussed the nature of work groups and organizations, with a particular focus on how such units are structured and managed. Beginning with this chapter, we begin Part Four and shift our focus to an examination of what are called *organizational processes*. Organizational processes represent the interpersonal and intergroup dynamics within organizations that make the organization function. Without such processes as leadership, communication, and decision making, there would be little behavior in organizations, and certainly no performance. These processes represent the glue that holds the organization together and makes it work. We begin here with a discussion of these processes. The first process we shall examine is leadership.

THE NATURE OF LEADERSHIP

What exactly does it mean to say that Paul Allaire is a leader? Leadership has been viewed as an attribute of *position* (e.g., the president of a corporation), a characteristic of a *person* ("she's a natural-born leader"), and a category of *behavior*. From the standpoint of understanding the nature of people at work, perhaps the most useful approach is to consider leadership as a category of behavior—as something one person does to influence others.

Following this approach we will employ Katz and Kahn's definition of *leadership* as "the influential increment over and above mechanical compliance with routine directives of the organization."[2] In other words, leadership occurs when one person can influence others to do something of their own volition instead of doing something because it is required or because they fear the consequences of noncompliance. It is this voluntary aspect of the response to leadership that sets it apart from other influence processes, such as power or authority. This characteristic will be seen as we examine various approaches to understanding leadership throughout this chapter.

Why Is Leadership Necessary?

One may well ask why managers need leadership skills. Most organizations are highly structured, with relatively clear lines of authority, stated objectives, and the momentum to carry them forward. Why, then, do organizations need leadership? Four reasons, or functions, of leadership can be identified that serve to facilitate organizational operations.[3]

To begin, there is the incompleteness of organization design. That is, because it is not possible to design the perfect organization and account for every member's activities at all times, something must ensure that human behavior is coordinated and directed toward task accomplishment. This something is leadership. In addition, we must consider changing environmental conditions. Leadership helps maintain the stability of an organization in a turbulent environment by allowing for rapid adjustment and adaptation to changing environmental conditions. Third, there are internal dynamics of organizations. Leadership can assist in the internal coordination of diverse organization units, particularly during periods of growth and change. It can act as a buffer between conflicting parties. Finally, the nature of human membership in organizations must be recognized. Organizations consist of individuals who pursue various needs and make difficult demands. Leadership can play a major role in maintaining a stable work force by facilitating personal need satisfaction and personal goal attainment.

Leadership thus plays a crucial role in organizational dynamics. It fills many of the voids left in conventional organization design, allows for greater organizational flexibility and responsiveness to environmental changes, provides a way to coordinate the efforts of diverse groups within the organization, and facilitates organizational membership and personal needs satisfaction. It is the quality of managerial leadership that often differentiates effective from ineffective organizations.

Leadership and the Managerial Hierarchy

It is useful to understand basic differences in *leadership patterns* across different levels in the managerial hierarchy. Here, *pattern* refers to the primary focus or responsibility of managers according to level. That is, how does the leadership role of top administrators and executives differ from the role of middle-level or lower-level managers and supervisors? A careful look at these different levels in the organizational hierarchy suggests that each level requires a different leadership pattern (see Exhibit 12.1). The three basic types of leadership patterns are:

1. *Origination,* or the introduction of structural change or policy formulation.
2. *Interpolation,* or piecing out the incompleteness of existing formal structure and attempting to supplement or develop structure.
3. *Administration,* or the use of the structure that is formally provided to keep the organization in motion and in effective operation.

The exercise of each of these three patterns of leadership calls for different cognitive styles (see Chapter 2) as well as different affective (or attitudinal) characteristics. *Top-level executives* concerned with origination need a systemwide perspective when making policy decisions. They are primarily concerned with goal formulation, strategic decision making, and buffering the effects of the external environment; their concern must be almost exclusively "macro." The type of leadership they exhibit, as seen by the rank-and-file employee, is charismatic; they symbolize the organization and what it stands for.

On the other hand, *mid-level managers* are concerned with what has been called subsystem decisions. They are responsible for a department or

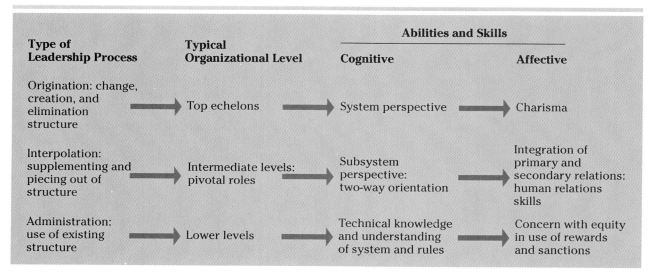

Type of Leadership Process	Typical Organizational Level	Abilities and Skills	
		Cognitive	**Affective**
Origination: change, creation, and elimination structure	Top echelons	System perspective	Charisma
Interpolation: supplementing and piecing out of structure	Intermediate levels: pivotal roles	Subsystem perspective: two-way orientation	Integration of primary and secondary relations: human relations skills
Administration: use of existing structure	Lower levels	Technical knowledge and understanding of system and rules	Concern with equity in use of rewards and sanctions

Exhibit 12.1
Leadership Patterns According to Level in Managerial Hierarchy

Source: D. Katz and R. Kahn, *The Social Psychology of Organizations,* Second Edition (New York: Wiley, 1978), p. 539. Copyright © 1978 by John Wiley & Sons. Inc. Reprinted by permission of John Wiley & Sons, Inc.

a division and the people and activities within it. Their focus is along a shorter term than that of executives, although typically not directed at routine activities on the shop floor. Although human relations skills are clearly necessary, many interpersonal relations are impersonal and distant.

Finally, the *low-level managers* or supervisors are primarily responsible for day-to-day operations in a single work group. Their technical knowledge of operations is important, as is their understanding of rules and policies made higher up in the hierarchy. These managers deal continually with the rewards and punishments that accrue to individual employees, and they are responsible for ensuring that work is accomplished in a timely fashion.

Although this distinction among three levels of managers is somewhat arbitrary (and exceptions no doubt exist), the framework is useful in emphasizing the fact that all leaders do not have the same responsibilities. Some leaders are almost the embodiment of the organization (Bill Gates of Microsoft, for example), whereas others are simply people trying to work through people to accomplish their group's performance goals. This distinction should be kept in mind as we examine the various contemporary models of leadership effectiveness.

A Transactional Framework for Understanding Leadership

It has been suggested that a solid understanding of the basic nature of leadership processes can be achieved by examining the *transactions* among leaders and followers.[4] According to this approach, effective leaders are those individuals who "give" something and who "get" something in return. In other words, leadership is viewed as a social exchange process.

This transactional approach involves three basic variables: the leader, the followers, and the situation (see Exhibit 12.2). Leaders bring to a situation their personalities, motivations, competencies, and legitimacy; followers bring their personalities, motivations, competencies, and expectations. Each situation has its own unique characteristics, including the availability of resources and nature of the tasks, social structure and rules, physical setting, and history. Where these three areas overlap, there exists what has been called the *locus of leadership,* or that realm where leader and followers are bound together in a relationship within a specific situation. Leader and followers all contribute something to the relationship, and each receives something in return. Neither is self-sufficient.

In view of this model, it becomes clear that in a systematic study of leadership processes in organizations, we must examine all three variables (leaders, followers, and situations) as well as the interactions among them. Much of the current work on the topic attempts to do this. In examining this material, we will first review some of the basics—specifically, research that has been done on leader attributes and leader behavior. After this, we will focus on several contemporary theories of leadership that attempt to account for the variables involved in the locus of leadership.

Exhibit 12.2
Three Elements
of Leadership

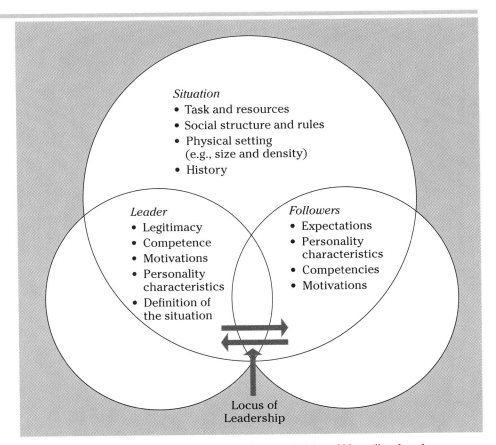

Source: Reprinted with permission of The Free Press, a division of Macmillan, Inc., from *Leadership Dynamics* by Edwin P. Hollander, p. 8. Copyright © 1978 by The Free Press.

International Challenge

IN PRACTICE
Symbolic Leadership in Japan

Observers of international management note a key difference between Japanese executives and their North American counterparts. This difference concerns what happens when something within the company goes very wrong. In Japan, there is a tradition called *inseki jishoku* (literally translated, "to take full responsibility and resign one's position"). When a Japan Airlines 747 crashed into a hillside killing all 500 passengers on board, the president of JAL personally visited the relatives of all the victims to express his sorrow and then resigned his position, even though the crash was caused by an aircraft design flaw and not the company. (The Japanese mechanic who was in charge of service for the plane committed suicide.)

Similarly, when a division of Toshiba was accused of selling classified (American) technology that had applications in submarine manufacture to the Soviet Union, the Americans protested, and the president resigned. In both cases, it was seen as the president's responsibility to resign—to show symbolic leadership on behalf of the company.

In contrast, when disaster strikes a Western firm, CEOs typically call their lawyers and press agents. Unless found legally culpable, no American executive would think of resigning as a symbolic gesture to preserve harmony. That is not their job. Their job is to convince the public—especially the stockholders—that the company is sound and will continue. Witness Exxon's behavior after it caused the worst oil spill in Alaska history. The president remained and hired more lawyers. A major cleanup effort was initiated with considerable publicity, but it was soon abandoned. Nor did the U.S. Secretary of Defense resign when the guided missile frigate *Vincennes* accidentally shot down an Iranian airliner, killing 290 people. Symbolic leadership of this magnitude is culture-specific and seldom found in the West.[5]

LEADER ATTRIBUTES AND BEHAVIOR

The earliest work on leadership, dating from ancient Greece, assumed that great leaders were born to their greatness. This view, later termed the *great man* theory of leadership, took a historical approach and concluded that in most instances leaders were destined for positions of influence as a result of birth. This position was popular throughout the nineteenth century. In 1869, for example, Sir Francis Galton wrote a widely read book entitled *Hereditary Genius* in which he argued that leadership qualities were based on heredity. In the early twentieth century, however, belief in inherited leader traits diminished, although belief in the importance of the traits themselves remained popular.

Leader Attributes

Much of the research in the first half of the twentieth century focused on attempts to identify the traits common to great leaders throughout history.

Ignoring the situation and followers, this research assumed that a person who exhibited these traits would be successful in leading any group. The conclusion of this work is often referred to as the *trait theory* of leadership. This research on leader attributes was brought together in a classic work by Ralph Stogdill in 1948.[6]

Stogdill reviewed 124 empirical studies of leader attributes covering 27 recurring characteristics. Among these studies, he discovered some consistencies. Successful leaders generally exhibited the following characteristics: *height*—leaders tended to be taller than the followers; *intelligence*—leaders tended to be rated higher on IQ tests, verbal fluency, overall knowledge, originality, and insight; and *initiative*—leaders tended to show high levels of energy, ambition, and persistence. Interestingly, no clear relationship was found between leader success and characteristics such as emotional stability or extroversion.

Stogdill's review also came to a conclusion that led the way to subsequent more comprehensive research. That is, he found that in many instances the profile of a successful leader varied with the situation! Different groups and different group activities required different types of leaders. As a result of this finding, emphasis shifted in the early 1950s toward looking into how leaders interacted with groups under various conditions and how these interactions succeeded or failed. Much of this research focused on leader behavior as the basic unit of analysis.

Leader Behavior

On the basis of this early work, studies were begun in the 1950s to discover what leaders did that caused others to follow. Two major research projects are noteworthy. The first was conducted at the University of Michigan under the direction of Rensis Likert and his associates, and the second was done at Ohio State University under the direction of Ralph Stogdill, Edwin Fleishman, John Hemphill, and others.

The findings of both projects led to similar conclusions. Essentially, effective leader behavior was found to be multidimensional; effective leaders exhibit different behavior in different situations. This multidimensional nature of leadership is clearly shown in the case of the Ohio State Leadership Studies, which began by identifying nine leader behaviors. However, when these nine behaviors were examined more closely, two relatively distinct clusters emerged:

1. *Consideration,* including such leader behaviors as helping subordinates (i.e., doing favors for them, looking out for their welfare, and explaining things).
2. *Initiating structure,* including such behaviors as getting subordinates to follow rules and procedures, maintaining performance standards, and making the leader and subordinate roles explicit.

Consideration has also been called socioemotional orientation and employee-centeredness; initiating structure has been referred to as promoting instrumental activity and as production-centeredness and task orientation.

In summarizing research on consideration (socioemotional orientation) and initiating structure (task orientation), House and Baetz concluded:

- ▨ Task-oriented leadership is necessary for effective performance in all working groups.

- ▨ Acceptance of task-oriented leadership requires that the task-oriented leader allow others to respond by giving feedback, making objections, and questioning the task-oriented leader.

- ▨ Socioemotionally oriented leadership is required in addition to task-oriented leadership when groups are not engaged in satisfying or ego-involving tasks.

- ▨ Groups requiring both kinds of leadership behavior will be more effective when these leader behaviors are performed by one person rather than divided among two or more persons.

- ▨ When the leadership roles are differentiated, groups will be most effective if those assuming the roles are mutually supportive and least effective when they are in conflict with each other.

- ▨ When formally appointed leaders fail to perform the leader behaviors for group success, an informal leader will emerge and will perform the necessary leader behaviors, provided the group members desire success.[7]

In other words, research on leader behaviors has demonstrated rather conclusively that *both* consideration and initiating structure are necessary (albeit at different times) for group effectiveness. If the manager cannot provide leadership in both these areas, the group will often find someone else who can; it will develop a surrogate leader to accommodate group needs.

The major drawback to these findings was the limited attention given to situations. Although leader-follower interactions were rather carefully considered, little effort was made to examine how situational differences might influence leader effectiveness. In other words, the important role of *contingencies* in organizational dynamics was largely ignored. These contingencies, or situational differences, were considered in leadership research commencing in the 1960s that culminated with the publication of several contemporary theories of leadership. In contrast to earlier work on leader attributes or behaviors, these theories attempt to explain leadership dynamics within the context of the larger work situation.

Several contemporary approaches to leadership can be identified. We will focus on four: (1) Fiedler's contingency theory, (2) House's path-goal theory, (3) Graen's vertical dyad linkage model, and (4) charismatic, or transformational, leadership theory. We now turn our attention to an examination of each of these models.

CONTINGENCY THEORY OF LEADERSHIP

Certainly one of the most popular contemporary theories is the *contingency theory of leadership* advanced by Fred Fiedler.[8] Fiedler's model argues that group performance or effectiveness is dependent upon the interaction of leadership style and the amount of control the supervisor has over the situation. We will examine each of these two factors separately and then put them together to consider how the theory works.

Situational Control

First, Fiedler's model suggests that the situation in which a leader operates can be characterized by three factors:

1. *Leader-member relations.* This refers to the degree of confidence, trust, and respect followers have for the leader. Is the leader accepted? Do leader and members get along well, or poorly?
2. *Task structure.* How clear are the task goals and role assignments? Does everyone know precisely what to do (e.g., assembly line workers), or is the job more ambiguous (e.g., research scientists)? The more structured the task, the easier it is for the leader to tell group members what to do.
3. *Position power.* Finally, who holds the power—the leader or the group? The more rewards and punishments leaders can use, the more influence they will have.

These three factors are believed to determine who—the supervisor or the subordinates—has more control over the current work situation. By differentiating these three dimensions, it is possible to develop a list of eight leadership situations (called octants). These eight situations are shown in Exhibit 12.3. In other words, leader-member relations can be either good (octants 1–4) or bad (octants 5–8); task structure can be high (octants 1, 2, 5, and 6) or low (octants 3, 4, 7, and 8); and leader position power can be strong (octants 1, 3, 5, and 7) or weak (octants 2, 4, 6, and 8). These octants contain all possible permutations or combinations of the three major situational variables.

Once the situation is defined according to these three major situational variables, questions are raised about which octant or situation represents the most desirable from the leader's situation. Fiedler proposes that *situation favorableness* is highest (from the leader's viewpoint) in octant 1 and lowest in octant 8. That is, a leader is in a far superior position when leader-member relations are good, when task structure is high, and when position power is strong (as in octant 1) than when the reverse is true (as in octant 8).

Exhibit 12.3
Fiedler's Classification of
Situation Favorableness

Leader/member relations	Good				Poor			
Task structure	High		Low		High		Low	
Position power	Strong	Weak	Strong	Weak	Strong	Weak	Strong	Weak
Situation	I	II	III	IV	V	VI	VII	VIII

Very favorable ←———————————————→ Very unfavorable

Source: Fred E. Fiedler, *A Theory of Leadership Effectiveness* (New York, McGraw-Hill, 1967). Reprinted by permission of the author.

Leadership Orientation

The second key variable in this model is the leader. Fiedler suggests that two basic leader orientations are useful, following earlier leadership research. These are relationship-oriented (a more lenient, people-oriented style) and task-oriented (where task accomplishment is a prominent concern). These orientations are measured by the *Least Preferred Co-worker* (LPC) scale. On this scale, the individual is asked to think of the person with whom he or she has worked who was least preferred as a co-worker and to describe this person on several bipolar scales (gloomy-cheerful, tense-relaxed, trustworthy-untrustworthy). A favorable description of the least preferred co-worker (high LPC) suggests a relationship-oriented leader, whereas an unfavorable description (low LPC) suggests a task-oriented leader.

You might want to see what your own LPC score is. To do this, simply complete Self-Assessment 12.1. Once you have completed the scale, refer to Appendix B for details concerning scoring.

Finally, combining leader LPC scores with situation favorableness, Fiedler examined the statistical correlations between LPC scores and group performance for each situational octant. As shown in Exhibit 12.4, negative correlations emerged at both ends of the situational continuum, and positive correlations were found toward the middle of the continuum. In other words, it was found that *high LPC* (relationship-oriented) leaders were more effective in facilitating group performance when the situation was moderately favorable or

Exhibit 12.4
Results From Contingency
Theory Research

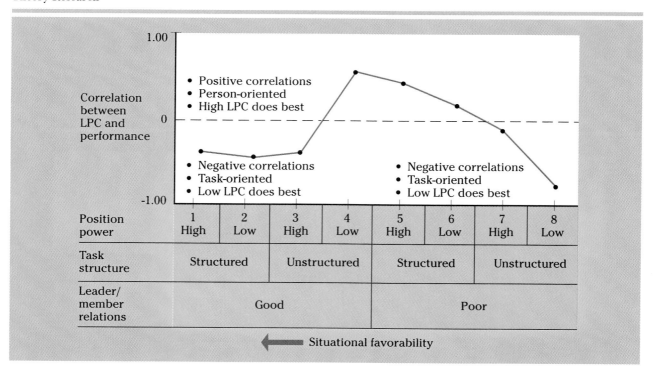

Source: Fred E. Fiedler, *Leadership* (Morristown, N.J.: General Learning Press, 1971). Reprinted by permission of the author.

SELF-ASSESSMENT 12.1
What Is Your LPC?

Instructions: Throughout your life you have worked in many groups with a wide variety of different people—on your job, in social clubs, in church organizations, in volunteer groups, on athletic teams, and in many others. You probably found working with most of your co-workers quite easy, but working with others may have been very difficult or all but impossible.

Now, think of all the people with whom you have ever worked. Next, think of the one person in your life with whom you could work least well. This individual may or may not be the person you also disliked most. It must be the one person with whom you had the most difficulty getting a job done, the one single individual with whom you would least want to work—a boss, a subordinate, or a peer. This person is called your "least preferred co-worker" (LPC).

On the scale below, describe this person by placing an "X" in the appropriate space.

Scoring

	8	7	6	5	4	3	2	1		
Pleasant	8	7	6	5	4	3	2	1	Unpleasant	_____
Friendly	8	7	6	5	4	3	2	1	Unfriendly	_____
Rejecting	1	2	3	4	5	6	7	8	Accepting	_____
Tense	1	2	3	4	5	6	7	8	Relaxed	_____
Distant	1	2	3	4	5	6	7	8	Close	_____
Cold	1	2	3	4	5	6	7	8	Warm	_____
Supportive	8	7	6	5	4	3	2	1	Hostile	_____
Boring	1	2	3	4	5	6	7	8	Interesting	_____
Quarrelsome	1	2	3	4	5	6	7	8	Harmonious	_____
Gloomy	1	2	3	4	5	6	7	8	Cheerful	_____
Open	8	7	6	5	4	3	2	1	Guarded	_____
Backbiting	1	2	3	4	5	6	7	8	Loyal	_____
Untrustworthy	1	2	3	4	5	6	7	8	Trustworthy	_____
Considerate	8	7	6	5	4	3	2	1	Inconsiderate	_____
Nasty	1	2	3	4	5	6	7	8	Nice	_____
Agreeable	8	7	6	5	4	3	2	1	Disagreeable	_____
Insincere	1	2	3	4	5	6	7	8	Sincere	_____
Kind	8	7	6	5	4	3	2	1	Unkind	_____

Total _____

Source: From *Improving Leadership Effectiveness: The Leader Match Concept,* Revised Edition, by Fred E. Fiedler and Martin M. Chemers with Linda Mahar. Copyright © 1977 by John Wiley & Sons, Inc. Reprinted by permission.

moderately unfavorable (that is, toward the middle of the continuum). Here, the leader is moderately liked, has some power, and supervises jobs that are somewhat vague. A leader with high interpersonal skills can exert the necessary leadership in such situations to clarify task ambiguity through discussion and participation.

On the other hand, when the situation is either highly unfavorable or highly favorable (that is, at either end of the continuum), Fiedler argues that a low LPC (task-oriented) leader is more effective in securing group performance (if not satisfaction). The logic of this argument is simple. If the situation is highly favorable (everyone gets along, the task is clear, and the leader has power), all that is needed is for someone to take charge and show direction (that is, a low LPC person). Similarly, if the situation is highly unfavorable (exhibiting the opposite characteristics), the leader is placed in a battle of wills with the group members. In this situation, Fiedler contends that a strong leader (low LPC) is necessary to counterbalance the power of the group and show direction in an ambiguous task environment. Being task-oriented in this situation will not make the leader unpopular, because leader-member relations are already poor.

Improving Leader Effectiveness with Leader Match

Fiedler and his colleagues stress that changing one's personality or leadership style (that is, LPC) is quite difficult, if not impossible. Therefore, efforts to improve leadership effectiveness must focus on *changing the situation, not the person.* Fiedler proposes that this be done by discovering ways to change the degree of situational control so that it matches the leader's LPC. Specifically, efforts can be made to alter leader-member relations, task structuring, and/or position power. Possible ways to accomplish this are shown in Exhibit 12.5. Hence, a manager who has a high LPC (is relationship-oriented) may not be comfortable in a high-control situation and may make efforts to allow his or her subordinates greater participation in decisions affecting their own jobs. As a result, by changing the situation—not the supervisor or manager—the appropriate degree of situational control and a balanced work environment can be achieved.

During the past 25 years, Fiedler and his colleagues have used this model to examine leader behavior and effectiveness among diverse samples of leaders and organizations. In general, consistent support has emerged for his hypothesis concerning the relationship between LPC and group performance for the various degrees of situation favorableness (see Exhibit 12.4). The results suggest that the model has some utility in helping managers understand leadership processes in organizations.

Even so, the model has also been criticized on several grounds.[9] In particular, critics have questioned the use of the LPC scale to measure leader orientation. It is argued that better and more reliable measures of leader orientation are needed. In addition, critics have suggested that Fiedler's system of classifying situations is overly simplistic and that additional factors should be included in a more comprehensive description of situation favorability.

Exhibit 12.5
Strategies for Changing
Situational Control

Modifying Leader-Member Relations

- Leader can spend more (or less) time with subordinates (e.g., lunch, leisure time, etc.).
- Leader can request certain people for work group.
- Leader can volunteer to supervise troublesome subordinates.
- Leader can transfer certain subordinates in or out of group.
- Leader can improve morale by getting additional rewards for subordinates.

Modifying Task Structure

If leader wants to create *less*-structured tasks, he/she may
- Ask the boss to give the group new or unusual problems to tackle.
- Ask the group's help in solving these new problems.

If leader wants to create *more*-structured tasks, he/she may
- Ask the boss to give the group more structured or standardized assignments.
- Divide these tasks into smaller, more routine subtasks for the group members to complete.

Modifying Position Power

If leader wishes to *raise* position power, he/she may
- Show the subordinates who's boss by using available powers to the fullest.
- Ensure that all information to the group is channelled through the leader.

If leader wishes to *reduce* position power, he/she may
- Invite group members to participate in planning and decision making.
- Delegate increased power and authority to group members.

Source: Based on F. E. Fiedler and J. E. Garcia, *New Approaches to Effective Leadership* (New York: Wiley, 1987), pp. 49–93.

Although these criticisms may be justified, they do not diminish the utility of the basic model as a tool to help understand some of the variables that combine to influence leadership effectiveness in work organizations.

IN PRACTICE
Leona Helmsley, Former Queen of the Palace

A key principle of Fiedler's contingency theory is that leader style must fit the situation. If you are the director of a research laboratory, for example, a relationship-oriented style will likely be more desirable than a task-oriented one. But what if you run a chain of hotels? Hotels are clearly low-tech, employing low-skilled but heavily unionized workers. Strikes are frequent, competition is keen, costs are important, and service is critical.

One such chain is Helmsley Hotels, whose owner and former president is Leona Helmsley, known unaffectionately as the "Queen of the Palace." Before her conviction and prison sentence in 1991 for tax evasion, Helmsley had been known as a no-nonsense boss. She demanded complete adherence to her standards, fired employees frequently, and was often described as being rude and condescending. She was not charismatic or participative; instead, she was highly autocratic. *Newsweek* even ran an article about her entitled, "Rhymes with Rich." Everyone seemed critical of Helmsley.

The irony here is twofold. First, she managed a very successful and profitable hotel chain. And second, as Fiedler might note, her seemingly autocratic style may have been suitable—even desirable—given the situation. Can you imagine running a hotel chain using participative decision making? The techniques that work in the research lab might prove disastrous in a hotel chain. Thus, despite her detractors (and legal problems), Leona Helmsley may just have been the right leader for the competitive, service-oriented hotel business. Besides, as someone once remarked, if Leona were a man, some people would probably hold her up as an example of a tough, results-oriented high achiever, instead of a rhyme for "rich."[10]

PATH-GOAL THEORY OF LEADERSHIP

In the second leadership model to be discussed, we approach the topic from quite a different perspective. Fiedler's contingency theory focuses on how performance can be affected by the manipulation of power, leader-member relations, task clarity or structuring, and attempting to engineer the job to fit the manager. In contrast, the *path-goal theory* emphasizes how leaders can facilitate task performance by showing subordinates how performance can be instrumental in achieving desired rewards. The path-goal model builds heavily on the expectancy/valence theory of work motivation (see Chapter 6).

Although many people have contributed to this model, the most fully developed path-goal approach can be found in the work of Martin Evans and Robert House.[11] Essentially, the model focuses on how managers influence subordinates' perceptions of work, personal goals, and various paths to goal attainment. The basic emphasis is on the extent to which managerial behavior is motivating or satisfying for subordinates. It is argued that managerial behavior is motivating or satisfying to the extent that it increases goal attainment by subordinates and clarifies the paths to these goals.

Basic Propositions of Path-Goal Theory

The path-goal theory of leadership rests on two primary propositions:

1. Leader behavior will be acceptable and satisfying when subordinates perceive it as an immediate source of satisfaction or as instrumental in obtaining future satisfaction.
2. Leader behavior will be motivating to the extent that it makes subordinate satisfaction contingent upon effective performance and to the extent that it complements subordinates' work environment by providing necessary guidance, clarity of direction, and rewards for effective performance.

Leaders have at their disposal a variety of mechanisms to facilitate increased subordinate motivation. Among these mechanisms are (1) recognizing and arousing subordinates' needs for outcomes over which leaders have some control; (2) increasing personal payoffs to subordinates for effective performance or goal attainment; (3) clarifying the path to those payoffs, through either coaching or additional direction; (4) helping subordinates clarify expectancies; (5) reducing obstacles or frustrations that inhibit goal attainment; and (6) increasing opportunities for personal satisfaction from effective performance. Thus, leaders and managers have several available strategies for facilitating goal attainment by integrating employees' personal goals with organizational goals. When these two sets of goals are congruent, conflict is reduced, and employees can pursue what they desire most by simultaneously pursuing managerial directives.

A representation of the path-goal model is shown in Exhibit 12.6. As can be seen, four parts of the model stand out: (1) leader behaviors, (2) subordinate characteristics, (3) environmental factors, and (4) employee attitudes and behavior. Let us consider each of these separately.

Path-Goal Leader Behaviors

In the original formulation, it was argued that leadership serves two important functions.[12] The first is called *path clarification.* This deals with the extent to which the leader helps subordinates understand the kind of behavior necessary to accomplish goals and obtain valued rewards. The second function of the leader is to increase the *number of rewards* available to subordinates by being supportive and paying attention to their welfare, status, and comfort.

In expanding on this original formulation, House argued that a comprehensive theory of leadership must recognize at least four distinctive types of leader behavior:

Exhibit 12.6
The Path-Goal
Theory of Leadership

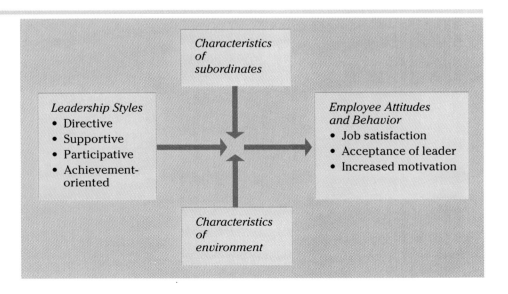

1. *Directive leadership.* Leader provides specific guidance, standards, and schedules of work, as well as rules and regulations; lets subordinates know what is expected of them.
2. *Supportive leadership.* Leader shows concern for the status, well-being, and personal needs of subordinates; focuses on developing satisfactory interpersonal relations among group members.
3. *Achievement-oriented leadership.* Leader sets challenging goals, emphasizes improvement in performance, and establishes high expectations of subordinates' ability to meet standards of excellence.
4. *Participative leadership.* Leader consults with subordinates, solicits suggestions and advice in decision making.[13]

In contrast to Fiedler's, this theory asserts that these four styles can be practiced by the same manager at varying times and in varying situations. Fiedler, we remember, argues that managers can have considerable difficulty changing styles.

Contingency Factors

As does Fiedler's theory, the path-goal theory presents a situational model. Hence, it holds that effective leadership is a function of the interaction between leader behaviors and situational or contingency variables. In particular, House identifies two basic contingency factors. These are seen in Exhibit 12.6.

Subordinate Characteristics. The personal characteristics of subordinates determine how they will react to leader behavior. Several personality characteristics have been found to be related to the way in which subordinates respond to influence attempts. The first of these is *authoritarianism* (see Chapter 2). High authoritarian subordinates tend to be less receptive to a participative style of leadership and more responsive to directive leadership.

In addition, it has been shown that an individual's *locus of control* also affects responses. Individuals who have an internal locus of control (who believe rewards are contingent upon their own efforts) are generally more satisfied with a participative leadership style, whereas individuals who have an external locus of control (who believe rewards are beyond their own control) are generally more satisfied with a directive style.

Finally, individuals' own *personal abilities* can influence how they respond to different leadership styles. Individuals who feel they have high levels of task-related abilities are not likely to be receptive to a close or directive leadership style. Instead, these individuals may prefer a more challenging achievement-oriented style.

Environmental Factors. In addition to subordinate characteristics, the path-goal model suggests that at least three environmental factors moderate the impact of leader style on outcomes (see Exhibit 12.6)—(1) the nature of the *task* performed by subordinates, (2) the *formal authority* of the organization, and (3) the *primary work group.*

These factors can influence an individual's response to leader behavior in a variety of ways. They may *motivate* individuals, such as when a person performs an intrinsically satisfying job. Or, they may *constrain* variability on the job, such as on an assembly line, where behavior is prescribed by technology. Finally, they may clarify and provide *rewards* for satisfactory performance. For instance, group members may praise individuals who did most to help the group achieve its performance objectives. As House and Dessler point out, "When goals, and paths to desired goals, are apparent because of the routine nature of the task, clear group norms, or objective controls of the formal authority system, attempts by the leader to clarify paths and goals would be redundant and would be seen by subordinates as an imposition of unnecessarily close control."[14]

Employee Attitudes and Behavior

These contingency factors interact with leader behaviors (discussed above) to determine employee attitudes and behavior. As shown in Exhibit 12.7, different leadership styles are more effective in some situations than in others. That is, a directive style will facilitate satisfaction or task effort for employees with an external locus of control, whereas a participative style will prove more effective for employees with an internal locus of control.

According to the model, three possible outcomes emerge from this interaction. First, individual perceptions, which are influenced by subordinate characteristics, can lead an employee to determine that the job itself can indeed lead to the receipt of rewards; hence, *job satisfaction* may be increased. Personal perceptions can also lead employees to conclude that the leader does, in fact, control many of the desired rewards; hence, *leader acceptance* may be increased. Finally, the motivational stimuli, constraints, and potential

Exhibit 12.7
Contingencies in
Path-Goal Leadership

Leader Style	Situation in Which Style Is Most Effective
Directive	Positively influences satisfaction among people with external locus of control or low task ability and people working on ambiguous tasks.
	Negatively influences satisfaction of people with high task ability.
Supportive	Positively influences people working on stressful, frustrating, or dissatisfying tasks.
Participative	Positively influences people with internal locus of control and people who are ego-involved in ambiguous tasks.
Achievement-oriented	Positively influences motivation of people working on ambiguous, nonrepetitive tasks.

Source: Based on R. J. House and T. R. Mitchell, "Path-Goal Theory of Leadership," *Journal of Contemporary Business,* Autumn 1974, pp. 81–97.

rewards can serve to heighten *motivation and job effort*. They can increase an employee's expectations that effort will lead to rewards. The model leads to very specific outcomes that are useful, if not imperative, in the pursuit of organizational effectiveness.

IN PRACTICE
Path-Goal Leadership at Corning

James Houghton, CEO of Corning Glass Works, believes in path-goal leadership. After he became head of Corning, he spent considerable time developing and then communicating his vision for the company. He formulated a clear set of goals for his company along with action plans for accomplishing these goals. As a result, managers at Corning have a better understanding of where they are going and how to get there.

One example of how this works can be seen in the company's commitment to quality. To achieve consistently good quality, Corning set quality assurance targets and implemented an employee suggestion system. Managers were held accountable for meeting these targets. Each manager was asked to help his or her subordinates learn how to achieve good results through targeting.

Each year, Houghton makes 40 or 50 trips to various factories to restate his goals and objectives for the company. Employees are provided with extra training in support of these objectives and are shown how to make products right the first time. Houghton estimates that improved quality can have direct economic benefits; it can save the company up to 30 percent of sales. So far, results have been encouraging, in part because every employee knows that Houghton himself believes in and rewards quality. He sets the example of an executive who knows where he is going.[15]

VERTICAL DYAD LINKAGE MODEL OF LEADERSHIP

Where are we so far? Fiedler's contingency theory asserts that each leader has a relatively stable leader style and that effective leaders modify the situation to match their style. House's path-goal theory is characterized by the belief that effective leaders focus their attention on showing subordinates how they can attain their own goals by working with—rather than against—the supervisor. Neither model pays a great deal of attention to the potential interpersonal differences between a supervisor and his or her various subordinates. Both seem to assume that the subordinates of a given leader are relatively similar to each other, and therefore while Fiedler suggests that leader be matched to the appropriate situation and House indicates that leaders should change their behavior to that which is appropriate for the situation, neither examine the possibility of different situational demands within a given set of subordinates. This is the focus of our third leadership model: the *vertical dyad linkage model* (or VDL model), developed by George Graen and his associates.[16]

In fact, a distinguishing feature of the VDL model of leadership is the assertion that supervisors or leaders do not treat all subordinates in the same way. Instead, over time, supervisors come to develop closer interpersonal relationships with some subordinates (called the "in-group"), while keeping their distance from other subordinates (called the "out-group"). Thus, the focus of this model is on the dyadic (or one-on-one) relationships between a leader and his or her group members. (The term vertical comes from the fact that we are focusing on relationships up and down the hierarchy.) This model is shown in Exhibit 12.8.

As can be seen, instead of treating everyone equally, the leader develops closer ties with some of the members of the group. These in-group members develop a relationship with the supervisor characterized by mutual trust, affection, reciprocal influence, shared goals, and a sense of common fate. Members of the out-group do not share these characteristics with the leader and, as such, are largely excluded from important decisions and activities.

It is not clear why these different relationships occur, but they may be based on personal compatibility or subordinate competence. Whatever the reason, research clearly shows that groups tend to have in-group/out-group relations with their supervisors and that in-group members tend to be more satisfied and to have more influence with their supervisors.[17] Moreover, the larger the in-group—that is, the larger the percentage of employees that feels close to the supervisor—the greater overall group productivity we would expect. Hence, the task for the leader is to recognize the existence of such dyadic relationships and to minimize the negative impact of out-group relationships. However, you will recall our discussion of the equity theory of motivation (see Chapter 6), which suggests that if leaders vary their behavior relative to a set of subordinates that if those subordinates view the situation (including the leader's behavior) as inequitable, motivational problems are likely to result. Therefore, while leaders might be wise to appropriately match to specific subordinates, they must do so in a way that is perceived by subordinates as equitable.

Exhibit 12.8
The Vertical Dyad
Linkage Model

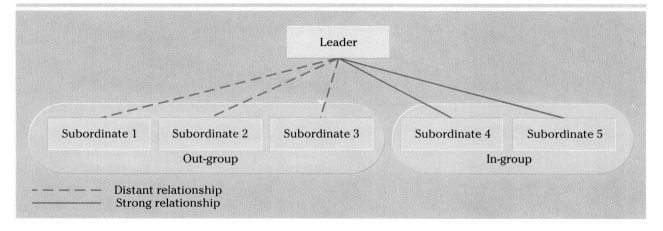

TRANSFORMATIONAL/CHARISMATIC LEADERSHIP

The fourth and final leadership model we will examine is the *transformational, or charismatic, model.* This approach to the study of leadership is quite new and is based on the assertion that effective leaders (referred to as either charismatic or transformational leaders) are those who can influence major changes in the attitudes and assumptions of subordinates and build commitment to the organization's goals and overall mission. Although several variations on this model can be identified, we will restrict our analysis to the general process.

Barnard Bass, one of the proponents of this approach, argues that there are essentially two types of leader: transactional and transformational.[18] *Transactional* leaders motivate employees by appealing to self-interest. That is, transactional leaders treat leadership as an exchange-relationship between themselves and their employees. In essence, they are saying, "I will look after your interests if you will look after mine (and the company's)." In some respects this is similar to the path-goal theory in which the leader motivates subordinates by showing that by following the leader's directives or requests the subordinates will achieve outcomes they desire. Although nothing may be wrong with the transactional approach, Bass and others argued that it fails to lead to the kind of employee commitment and dedication necessary for greatness. To achieve this, the leader must exhibit charismatic, or transformational, characteristics.

A *transformational* leader is one who inspires trust, confidence, admiration, and loyalty from his or her followers. As a result, followers are motivated to exert high levels of effort out of a sense of personal loyalty to the leader, if not the organization. In the past, President John F. Kennedy exhibited this charismatic nature in his inaugural address to the nation when he said, "Ask not what your country can do for you; ask what you can do for your country." More recently, in industry, we can see examples in people such as Steven Jobs or Bill Gates.

The transformational approach to the study of leadership relies heavily on the trait approach discussed earlier. That is, it is believed that effective leaders exhibit several unique characteristics that give them influence over their followers. According to one study, these characteristics include:

High self-confidence. Charismatic leaders exhibit strong confidence in their own judgments and actions.

Ability to articulate a vision. Such leaders have a unique ability to put into words an idealized vision of what the future could hold. In fact, the greater the disparity between the status quo and the idealized vision, the greater the likelihood that followers will attribute extraordinary vision to the leader. (Note: This has a positive and a negative side. Witness, for example the popular reaction to Adolf Hitler's vision.)

Willingness to assume high personal risks to pursue the vision. Charismatic leaders are often seen as being willing to assume great risks to pursue their vision. This commitment to the future and self-sacrifice often entices others to follow.

Use of unconventional strategies. These leaders often use unconventional behavior or break accepted norms as a sign of their confidence in their course of action. Such attention-getting behavior often attracts the admiration of the followers.

Perception of leader as change agent. Finally, charismatic leaders are often seen by followers as a change agent, especially when followers are disaffected or unhappy with current events.[19]

Through mechanisms such as these, the transformational leader establishes a clear and often undisputed position within the group or organization. With a clear vision of a better future—either for a company or a country—and with a highly visible power position, such leaders find it relatively easy to inspire extraordinary efforts on the part of their followers. Witness, for example, the case of Steven Jobs.

IN PRACTICE
Steven Jobs at NeXT

When Steven Jobs was abruptly forced out of Apple Computer (a company he had founded) in 1985, many thought it was the end of the young, articulate computer visionary. But they were quite wrong. Within months, Jobs rebounded by starting a new computer company called NeXT. NeXT was to build the next generation of desk-top supercomputers. They would have the latest technology and would be sought after by university researchers and businesspeople alike. Features would include a more efficient machine architecture, more storage capacity, high-quality sound, sharper images, cheaper printing, and easier programming compared to existing models of microcomputers. But perhaps most of all, NeXT would show Apple that Steven Jobs was still in charge.

When he left Apple, many of his close associates followed him. They wanted to work with the charismatic leader who was on the cutting edge of technology. For over two years, this small group of highly skilled engineers and technicians labored over the new machine, and all the while they were led, cajoled, pushed, and encouraged by Jobs. They even joked about following the "Quotations of Chairman Jobs." When money became a problem, financiers such as H. Ross Perot stepped in with multi-million-dollar investments.

Throughout, Jobs was in charge, using his messianic zeal to capture the attention and imagination of his followers. In 1988, the new machine was ready and was introduced to an excited marketplace. But without Jobs's leadership—and his ability to create a vision of the future in high technology—the small company would probably have never gotten off the ground.[20] In 1993, Jobs refocused his vision for NeXT on its unique software and away from hardware. As a result, many experts in the field are more excited about Jobs's vision for the future of NeXT than ever before.

LEADERSHIP AND CORPORATE CULTURE

Before leaving the topic of leadership, we should recognize that variations of leadership behavior can have profound effects on corporate culture. *Corporate culture* may be defined as the basic assumptions and beliefs that are shared by the members of a group or organization and considered important and valid enough to pass on to new members.[21] These assumptions and beliefs involve the group's view of the world, of the group's place in it, of the nature of time and space, of human nature, and of human relationships. Thus, one organization may have a culture that is characterized by open communication, trust, and egalitarianism, whereas another organization may be characterized by limited communications, distrust, and entrenched status systems. Whatever the prevailing culture, employees attempt to respond and behave in a manner consistent with group forces.

In view of this, it is interesting to recognize the powerful influence leaders have on existing corporate culture. According to Edgar Schein, a noted social psychologist, leaders—including managers—influence corporate culture in at least five ways. These are as follows:

1. *What they talk about.* Leaders communicate their values, priorities, expectations, and concerns by the topics they choose to talk about, the praise they give, the things they ask about, and the things they measure. Through planning sessions, departmental meetings, "management by walking around," and even their emotional outbursts, managers express their opinions concerning which values and goals the group or organization should highlight and which should be ignored or given "lip service."
2. *How they respond to crises.* Leaders and managers also influence culture by the signals they send during a crisis. For instance, a manager who refuses to lay off low-level employees during an economic downturn sends a clear signal that preserving employee jobs is important. Compare this to the manager who claims to endorse the "group spirit" but who lays off employees at the first sign of financial problems.
3. *How they behave.* Through role modeling, managers also send clear signals concerning what is important. A manager who wants all employees to arrive for work on time can set the example for them. On the other hand, a "do as I say, not as I do" attitude tells employees that the behavior in question is not that important.
4. *How they allocate rewards.* Managers send signals in the way they reward employee behavior. If a company wants to encourage a culture of entrepreneurship, for example, employees must be encouraged to try on projects until they find the right innovation. If the price of failure is high—if employees are fearful of failure—they will more than likely not "stick their necks out." On the other hand, if innovative efforts are praised, even when they do not work out, employees will come to learn that it is all right to try and fail; hence, they will try again.
5. *How they hire and fire people.* Finally, leaders and managers can influence culture by the kinds of people they recruit and hire and the people they

dismiss. Do all people look the same or come from similar backgrounds, or does the manager value diversity among the work force? Claiming that women or minorities are "welcome" carries little credibility in a group where the manager never seems to find a "qualified applicant."

Through mechanisms such as these, managers can have considerable influence on how corporate culture develops and grows. This point has not been lost on James Houghton, CEO of Corning Glass Works or Steven Jobs of NeXT. Both of these leaders focused attention on developing a culture suitable to the goals and aspirations of the company.

LEADERSHIP IN PRACTICE: KEYS TO SUCCESS

We have examined four contemporary theories of effective leadership and have discussed the role of leadership in the development and maintenance of corporate culture. Each of the four theories focuses on a different aspect of the work environment, and each defines leader effectiveness differently. For example, Fiedler defines effectiveness in terms of group performance and focuses his attention on the interaction of personality and situational control as they relate to performance. The path-goal model defines effectiveness as the extent to which members of a group are motivated and are satisfied. The vertical dyad linkage model focuses more narrowly on the interpersonal relationships that develop between the leader and the led. Finally, the charismatic or transformational leadership approach emphasizes the personal appeal of the leader in getting his or her subordinates to commit themselves to a common vision and goal.

Taken together, these models should help us better understand leadership dynamics in work organizations. Indeed, they may tell us something about our own future management potential. How would you behave as a leader? What model makes the most sense to you in explaining leader behavior? Although no model is comprehensive, they all should make us think about influence processes in organizations.

Constraints on Leadership

Up to this point, we have assumed that leaders are relatively free to act on their environment and that they behave according to theory, with few constraints. Obviously, this is not always the case. There are many factors that inhibit leader behavior. We now turn our attention to these problems in the leadership process as well as to what managers can do to minimize them.

An important part of evaluating leadership processes work is recognizing occasions when they may have a diminished impact on employee behavior. If we view leadership as a central process in facilitating group performance and effectiveness, then constraints on the process must be clearly recognized. At least six constraints on leadership effectiveness have been suggested:

1. The extent to which managerial decisions and behavior are prepro- grammed because of precedent, structure, technological specificity, or lack of familiarity with available alternative solutions.

2. The traits and skills (particularly leadership skills) of the manager. Research has indicated, for instance, that effective leaders tend to exhib- it specific personal attributes. Good leaders demonstrate expertise in their own areas of endeavor (such as the foreman who can perform any departmental job). A lack of skills may preclude effective leader behavior to some extent.

3. The inability of leaders to vary their behavior to suit the particular situa- tion. Rigid patterns of leadership behavior may be inappropriate for many situations.

4. The extent to which a leader controls rewards desired by subordinates, such as pay raises and promotions.

5. The characteristics of the situation, such as how much power a leader has, the importance of a given decision or action, and the quality of inter- personal relations between leader and subordinate.

6. The nature of the corporate culture; specifically, the openness of the organization to variations in leader behavior (e.g., a participative leader- ship style may be discouraged or prohibited in a military organization).[22]

These constraints to a large extent set the stage for which influence attempts occur. The greater the skills and abilities of the leader or manager, the more easily constraints can be handled. To the extent that these con- straints are recognized and accounted for, the leader can use available lati- tude to best advantage in securing the support of subordinates for task accomplishment.

Improving Leadership Effectiveness

Although good leadership may not be a panacea for all performance ills of organizations, there are many instances in which leaders can make a real dif- ference. Unfortunately there may be cultural aspects of American business in general that keep potentially good leaders from reaching leadership posi- tions. For example, in the United States, women have had difficulty gaining access to top leadership positions. Interestingly, a recent study found that women tend to describe themselves in terms that are more in line with what we termed earlier in this chapter as "transformational leadership," while men tended to describe themselves in terms that would be characterized as "transactional leadership." The women leaders in this study tended to try to convince subordinates to transform their own self-interest into the interest of the group through participation and sharing power and information with sub- ordinates.[23] Thus, one way of improving leadership effectiveness may be by ensuring that all people who have the potential to become leaders are given equal opportunities to realize that potential.

It is important to consider other ways in which managers can develop leadership talents that will facilitate organizational effectiveness. Many tech- niques could be suggested here. In one Fortune magazine study of corporate leadership, seven suggestions for improving leadership effectiveness were identified (see Exhibit 12.9). On the basis of the above discussions, however, we can offer some additional strategies concerning how to improve leader success.[24] These five additional strategies are (1) managerial selection and placement, (2) leadership training, (3) rewarding leader behavior, (4) rewarding subordinate behavior, and (5) organizational engineering. As we will see, many of these suggestions have their roots in the leadership theories discussed above.

Managerial Selection and Placement.   Improved leadership effectiveness can be facilitated by increasing the likelihood that those in command possess the necessary skills to influence their subordinates on task-related activities. Following Fiedler's model, for example, we might wish to select a task-oriented (low LPC) person to supervise a work group characterized by high task structuring, centralized power, and distant leader-member relations. On the other hand, a relationship-oriented (high LPC) leader may be more appropriate when the task structuring is less concrete, power is diffused, and leader-member relations are cordial but not overly warm. The notion of matching people to leadership roles contradicts the current practice in many organizations of promoting employees to supervisory positions on the basis of seniority or even good job performance. Although good job performance may be a desirable trait for supervisors to possess, it does not by itself ensure good supervisory skills.

Leadership Training.   Attempts can also be made to develop individuals already in leadership positions to their fullest potential as managers through

---

Exhibit 12.9
Seven Keys to
Effective Leadership

1. *Trust your subordinates.* A leader cannot expect subordinates to maximize their efforts if they do not believe the leader trusts them.
2. *Develop a vision.* People want to follow someone who knows where they are going. Plan for the long term. Translation: "Lead, follow, or get out of the way!"
3. *Keep your cool.* The best leaders show their mettle under fire. Translation: "Don't get mad; get even!"
4. *Encourage risk.* Nothing can demoralize followers more than the belief that the slightest failure could ruin their career. Translation: "Nothing ventured, nothing gained."
5. *Be an expert.* Followers must be confident that the leader knows what he or she is talking about.
6. *Invite dissent.* Subordinates must not be afraid to speak up if the leader really wants to get the best advice from them. Translation: "Don't tolerate yes-men."
7. *Simplify.* When communicating with subordinates, present the "big picture" in simple, direct—and honest—language. Let the details come later, after agreement is reached on a general course of action.

Source: Based on K. Labich, "The Seven Keys to Business Leadership," *Fortune,* October 24, 1988, pp. 58–66.

a variety of training techniques. Training can take many forms, including general management skills programs, human relations training, problem-solving and decision-making programs, and a variety of specialized programs. It may also take the form of strategic assignments, such as a temporary assignment overseas, or job rotations, such as moving from marketing to human resource management.

Reward Leader Behavior. A third method of improving leadership effectiveness involves designing reward systems so that desired leader behavior is amply rewarded. If pay and promotions are based on a manager's ability to elicit successful subordinate efforts on goal-directed activities, then managers will see effective leader behavior as instrumental in obtaining desired rewards. A performance-reward contingency should serve to make managers more aware of the role of leadership in task accomplishment, making them more likely to attempt to improve their capacity for leadership activity.

Rewarding Subordinate Behavior. It is also possible to structure reward systems so that they stimulate desired subordinate behavior. Where managers have greater discretion in rewarding subordinates, the probability that subordinates will follow managerial directives is increased, because this behavior will be instrumental to their own personal goal attainment. House's path-goal theory is essentially based on this relationship; to the extent that subordinates see following a manager's directives as instrumental to the accomplishment of their own goals, they will be more likely to follow them.

Organizational Engineering. Finally, in some instances it is more suitable to adopt a structural (as opposed to behavioral) approach to improving leader effectiveness. Here, one attempts to modify either the manager's job or the way jobs are clustered (reporting procedures, lines of authority, decentralization) and allow the structure itself to facilitate task accomplishment. In other words, as Fiedler might say, organizations may wish to "engineer the job to fit the manager." This approach is particularly useful when a specific individual (e.g., an R&D scientist) is necessary to the organization yet does not possess the requisite interpersonal skills for leadership. In these cases, the job can be engineered around the individual so that many necessary leadership roles are fulfilled by other means.

PULLING IT ALL TOGETHER

Leadership has remained one of the most difficult topics in organizational behavior to research and to which clear, consistent prescriptions can be attached. Its essence is providing a compelling vision of direction and then motivating people to move in that direction. However, the exact behaviors or style that are effective in achieving this depend on the situation. Although many questions still remain unanswered, factors such as the nature of the task and the dispositions of the subordinates are important when trying to determine situationally appropriate leadership behaviors.

SUMMARY OF KEY POINTS

■ Leadership is the process of securing voluntary compliance from others on tasks that facilitate organizational goal attainment.

■ Leadership patterns vary by level in the managerial hierarchy. Leadership among top executives focuses on attaining long-term systemwide goals, whereas leadership among mid-level managers focuses on attaining the more immediate goals of a subsection of the organization (e.g., department or division). Supervisory leadership emphasizes achieving the day-to-day tasks of the department or group.

■ Leadership involves three elements: the leader, the follower, and the situation. The intersection of these three factors is usually referred to as the locus of leadership.

■ Leader behaviors are divided into consideration (relationship-oriented) and initiating structure (task-oriented).

■ Fiedler's contingency theory of leadership suggests that leadership effectiveness is determined by a good match of leadership style with situation favorableness. Leadership style may be measured by the Least Preferred Co-worker scale, with some managers being described as relationship-oriented and some task-oriented. Situation favorableness is a function of leader-member relations, task structure, and position power. When situation favorableness is extremely high or low, a task-oriented (or low LPC) leader tends to be more effective, whereas a relationship-oriented (or high LPC) leader tends to be more effective under moderate situation favorableness. Overall, Fiedler argues that in order to be effective, organizations should change the situation to match the leader, because it is difficult or impossible to change the person.

■ The path-goal theory emphasizes that leaders can facilitate task performance by showing workers how performance can be instrumental in helping them achieve desired rewards. Leaders can use one of four leadership styles (directive, supportive, participative, or achievement-oriented) according to subordinate and environmental characteristics. The end result should be a more motivated work force that has a clear understanding of the required tasks and potential rewards for task accomplishment.

■ The vertical dyad linkage model assumes that leadership operates through a process in which the leader develops one-to-one (dyadic) relationships with each of his or her subordinates. Some of these relationships may be closer than others, and this affects the nature of the interpersonal leadership style.

■ Transformational, or charismatic, leadership involves the ability of a leader to elicit trust, confidence, loyalty, and admiration from his or her followers. The leader creates a vision concerning some future state of affairs and inspires followers to work to achieve the vision.

■ Corporate culture represents the basic assumptions and beliefs that are shared by the members of an organization or group. Leaders influence corporate culture through their behaviors, reward allocations, hiring decisions, and verbal and nonverbal communications.

■ Leadership effectiveness is often constrained by several factors. These include the amount of management discretion in decision making, the traits and skills of the leader, the flexibility of the leader, control over desired rewards, situational factors, and the organization's corporate culture.

■ Leadership effectiveness can often be improved through better managerial selection and placement, leadership training, rewarding appropriate leader behavior, rewarding appropriate subordinate behavior, and organizational engineering.

KEY WORDS

achievement-oriented leadership
charismatic leadership
consideration
contingency theory
corporate culture
directive leadership
great man approach
high LPC
initiating structure
leader match
leadership
least preferred co-worker
locus of leadership

low LPC
organizational engineering
organizational processes
participative leadership
path-goal theory
situation favorableness
supportive leadership
task structure
trait theory
transactional leaders
transformational leadership
vertical dyad linkage model

QUESTIONS FOR DISCUSSION

1. What is meant by the term *leadership?* How does a leader differ from a manager?
2. What functions do leaders serve?
3. Describe the leader-follower transactional process. What role does the locus of leadership play in this process?
4. What are some rather generalizable leader traits?
5. What major conclusion can be drawn from the research on consideration and initiating structure?
6. What is the basic thesis of Fiedler's contingency theory of leadership? How does it differ from the other two theories of leadership discussed in this chapter?
7. What is the significance of the term "least preferred co-worker"?
8. Describe the vertical dyad linkage model of leadership. What implications for management follow from this model?
9. Discuss the path-goal theory of leadership and its implications for management. How do these implications differ from those of the VDL model above?

10. Describe several constraints on leader behavior.
11. How can managers improve their leadership effectiveness?

NOTES

1. B. Dumaine, "The Bureaucracy Busters." *Fortune,* June 17, 1991, p. 38.
2. D. Katz and R. Kahn, *The Social Psychology of Organizations* (New York: Wiley, 1978), p. 528.
3. Katz and Kahn, op. cit.; G. Yukl, *Leadership in Organizations* (Englewood Cliffs, N.J.: Prentice-Hall, 1988).
4. E. P. Hollander, *Leadership Dynamics* (New York: The Free Press, 1978).
5. S. Chira, "After Toshiba, A Low Bow Seems Wise in Japan," *International Herald Tribune,* July 20, 1987, p. 11; "When Japan Says Sorry," *The Economist,* July 30, 1988, p. 30.
6. R. Stogdill, "Personal Factors Associated with Leadership," *Journal of Psychology,* 1948, *25,* pp. 35–71.
7. R. House and M. Baetz, "Leadership: Some Generalizations and New Research Directions," in B. M. Staw, ed., *Research in Organizational Behavior* (Greenwich, Conn.: JAI Press, 1979), p. 359.
8. F. Fiedler and J. Garcia, *New Approaches to Effective Leadership* (New York: Wiley, 1987).
9. House and Baetz, Yukl, op. cit.
10. "Queen of the Palace," *60 Minutes,* videotape (New York: CBS, 1986).
11. M. Evans, "The Effects of Supervisor Behavior on the Path-Goal Relationship," *Organizational Behavior and Human Performance,* 1970, *5,* pp. 277–298; R. House, "A Path-Goal Theory of Leadership," *Administrative Science Quarterly,* 1970, *16,* pp. 321–338.
12. Evans, op. cit.
13. House, op. cit.
14. R. House and G. Dessler, "The Path-Goal Theory of Leadership," in J. G. Hunt and L. L. Larson, eds., *Contingency Approaches to Leadership* (Carbondale, Ill.: Southern Illinois University Press, 1974), p. 40.
15. K. Ballen, "At Corning, A Vision of Quality," *Fortune,* October 24, 1988, p. 64.
16. F. Dansereau, G. Graen, and W. Hage, "A Vertical Dyad Linkage Approach to Leadership in Formal Organizations," *Organizational Behavior and Human Performance,* February 1975, pp. 46–78; D. Duchon, S. Green, and T. Taber, "Vertical Dyad Linkage: A Longitudinal Assessment of Antecedents, Measures, and Consequences," *Journal of Applied Psychology,* February 1986, pp. 56–60.
17. Ibid.
18. B. Bass, *Leadership and Performance Beyond Expectations* (New York: The Free Press, 1985).
19. J. Conger and R. Kanungo, "Toward a Behavioral Theory of Charismatic Leadership in Organizational Settings," *Academy of Management Review,* October 1987, pp. 637–647. See also Yukl, op. cit.
20. B. Schlender, "How Steve Jobs Linked Up with IBM," *Fortune,* October 9, 1989, pp. 48–61; R. Brandt, "Steve Jobs: Can He Do It Again?" *Business Week,* October 24, 1988, pp. 74–80.
21. E. H. Schein, *Organizational Culture and Leadership* (San Francisco: Jossey-Bass, 1985).
22. R. M. Steers, *Organizational Effectiveness: A Behavioral View* (Santa Monica, Calif.: Goodyear, 1977).

23. J. Rosener, "Ways Women Lead," *Harvard Business Review,* 68 (6), pp. 119–125.
24. R. M. Steers, *Organizational Effectiveness: A Behavioral View* (Santa Monica, Calif.: Goodyear, 1977).

EXPERIENTIAL EXERCISE 12

My Favorite Supervisor

This exercise focuses on identifying the qualities that characterize successful leaders.

As an Individual

You should begin by thinking about your favorite supervisor. This supervisor could be from any present or previous organized activity (e.g., a current or past job, a volunteer group, a social group, etc.). (Students without sufficent work experience may simply want to think of their ideal supervisor.) Once you have identified the person, think about why this particular person is your favorite boss. List the behavioral traits that characterize this boss.

As a Group

Next, the class should be divided into small groups of between four and six. Group members should share their information concerning the traits of outstanding supervisors. Each group should then make a list of the various traits identified by the students and count the number of students who used each of the various traits to describe his or her favorite boss. (This part should take approximately 30 minutes.)

As a Class

Finally, the class should reconvene as a whole, and each group should identify those characteristics of superior bosses that were most frequently cited in the group. On the basis of this information, the class should look for similarities and differences across the groups. For instance, are there certain traits that recur across most of the groups in identifying favorite bosses? If so, why? What lessons can be learned from this exercise about the behavioral traits of good supervisors?

MANAGEMENT DILEMMA 12

Budget Motors

Plant *Y* was the largest and oldest of six assembly plants of Econocar division, a subsidiary of Budget Motors, Inc. It had close to 10,000 employees and was managed by Mr. Wickstrom. During the last few years, it fell behind all the others in performance. Not unexpectedly, headquarter management (HQM) started showing some uneasiness, as there were signs that things would not improve in the foreseeable future. In its attempt to straighten things out, HQM has exerted steady pressure and issued specific directions for local plant management to follow.

Wickstrom was a respected and competent manager. He was not new to the responsibility of running a large plant. After all, he came up the hard way through the ranks, and was well known for his ambition, technical competence, human-relations skills, and hard work. Moreover, he was a no-nonsense manager, well liked by his subordinates. Under his leadership, plant *Y* had performed adequately until the energy and environmental crises teamed up to hit the auto industry hard in the early 1970s. At that time, in all six plants, there was a hysteria to fill the demand for little compacts that are economically cheap to run and environmentally safe to use. The speed of the lines was stepped up, three-shift operations were begun, workers (mostly immigrants) were hired, and a large number of managers had to be placed in new jobs.

Although all the plants of the Econocars division had their share of the stress and strain inherent in the sudden changeover from bigger to smaller cars, the managers of these plants adapted themselves differently to this new development in the market situation. Instead of comparing Wickstrom's adaptive behavior with that of his counterparts in other plants, we would rather concentrate on contrasting his style with that of Mr. Rhenman, his successor in the same plant. Following are some examples that illustrate how Wickstrom tried to cope with this crisis atmosphere:

One day, while doing his regular plant tour, he personally ordered the foreman of a given section to change the sequence of assembling the instrument panels. He thought this change would speed up the operation. When his production manager, Mr. Aberg, found out about the new system, he was uneasy because the change disturbed the schedule. He went to see Wickstrom in his office and to make a new suggestion about the sequencing—one that coordinated Wickstrom's plan with his own. Much to Aberg's surprise, Wickstrom reacted in a rude manner and told Aberg that things would remain the way he had ordered.

When Wickstrom read the weekly performance record of the body assembly line, he flew into a terrific temper and called in the foreman of this line, Jorgen, to his office and threatened to fire him if the production was not speeded up. This tactic shook up Jorgen who instantly thought of the incident two weeks before when his colleague, Ulf, had indeed been fired. He tried to justify the slowness of production by complaining that he was operating against overwhelming handicaps: antiquated and rundown equipment, inexperienced workforce, and uninteresting and noninvolving job structure. Unfortunately, nobody cared to listen to him.

One day the supply of electric power for the plant was reduced and the next day it was shut off completely. This was due to a breakdown in the power station outside the plant. It was not Wickstrom's policy to run the plant by committee meetings, but faced with this crisis at hand, he summoned a meeting of the production managers and the foremen. It was clear the electric company would need at least a week to repair its network. The upshot of the meeting was a decision to shut down production and to seek union's support for half pay for the workers in exchange for two days of paid holidays. Upon submitting the minutes of this meeting to the HQM, his decisions were vetoed immediately. The HQM argued that since economical compacts sell almost as fast as they can be rolled off lines, production should not stop and that a mobile auxiliary power unit be brought in, no matter what its cost would be. This proved to be a very expensive proposition and also meant a lot of trouble for workers and managers alike. For no sooner had Wickstrom called his second meeting to give his top aides the feedback he received from the HQM, when some of his managers angrily protested this high-handed interference in their "domestic affairs." Here again, they said, is one more example of "the HQ boys telling us how to run our show." Other plant managers, equally concerned, blamed their boss, Wickstrom, for his inability to stand by his guns, fight with the HQM and challenge its excessive domination, as other plant managers did. They felt they were put at the order-receiving side, which had no real feeling for what was going on in the plant.

Some plant managers further complained that carrying out daily instructions from HQM had become Wickstrom's chief preoccupation. Managers in such staff services as accounting, quality control, material control, and personnel also complained that they themselves were receiving too many specific orders from HQM. Like their line counterparts, they generally resented this controlling behavior on the part of the HQM. They complained that they were no longer allowed to run their own departments or stations, or to manage within their sphere of competence. This, in turn, left them no choice but to withdraw legitimate authority from their immediate subordinates and interfere in the handling of the subordinates' affairs, thereby compounding the problem through the hierarchy.

In responding to the voices from below, HQM argued that the trouble with plant *Y* lay in Wickstrom's lack of control rather than in bad equipment, boring jobs, and inexperienced personnel.

With the intensification of the energy crisis caused by the sudden outbreak of the Mideast War of October 1973, the demand for little cars far outstripped the available supply. Being dissatisfied with plant *Y*'s performance, HQM decided to replace Wickstrom with Rhenman. The latter accepted the job on conditions that he should have "carte blanche" in running his own show for a reasonable period of time. This he got from HQM, which also assured him that there would be no interference and that he was free to proceed in any manner he saw fit.

At the outset, Rhenman indicated that although HQM thought the dead wood should be removed from the staff, he disagreed and would give everyone ample opportunity to prove their worth. (It developed, in fact, that only a handful of people in an organization of 10,000 were dismissed during his regime). He asked for money from HQM to modernize the plant, starting first with the cafeteria and washrooms used by blue-collar workers. Rhenman also went to the cafeteria during lunch hours, mingled with workers, foremen, and the lower-level managers. He not only listened to their complaints, he also secured their cooperation and suggestions. He encouraged groups to meet regularly to solve common problems and, more importantly, to engage his long-range planning and consultation to prevent daily crises. His foremen often met informally, thereby increasing lateral communication. He structured an ongoing problem-solving dialogue between his staff and line personnel. Through this dialogue, staff personnel had learned how irrelevant or self-defensive their services had been in the line. He inspired confidence and loyalty and erased the fear-and-crisis syndrome that had prevailed. He did not change the formal organization structure of the plant. He expected his managers to set goals for their units and be responsible for their achievements. He delegated to them the requisite authority and left them alone to perform their jobs.

Now, after about six months in his job, plant *Y* has started heading toward a rebound. Its performance record shows marked improvements. Rhenman was promoted to a top executive job at the HQ. Interestingly enough, plant *Y* is performing well without him. On the other hand, Wickstrom was given an early retirement.

On the basis of the above, consider the following:

1. Using the material from the book dealing with Fiedler's description of leadership, describe Wickstrom's situation and leadership style.
2. How would the path-goal model describe the situation and what leadership style would be predicted to be effective? What style did Rhenman use?
3. Describe the organization culture under Wickstrom. How did Rhenman change it?

Source: Reprinted by permission of Sami Kassem, University of Toledo, Toledo, Ohio.

13

Communication and Information Processing

The Management Challenge

■ To be able to communicate effectively with superiors, subordinates, co-workers, suppliers, and customers.

■ To recognize barriers to effective communication and to overcome such impediments where possible.

■ To understand the richness of various communications media and be able to select among such media based upon the circumstances.

■ To know how to use personal and electronic networks.

■ To recognize special communications roles within organizations that serve to enhance overall communications effectiveness.

CLOSE UP   Internal Communication at Union Pacific

Mike Walsh, CEO of Union Pacific Railroad, is new to the railroad industry but is an old hand at effective internal communications. His belief is that "It's the free flow of information inside the company that enables you to identify and attack problems, say, when a customer service representative first get an earful about some quality glitch, or salesmen in the field encounter a new competitor. Recently, Mr. Walsh, without a script or rehearsal, talked with employees at 24 sites across the country via satellite for 5 1/2 hours.[1]

Walsh has opened up internal communication channels in an effort to transform Union Pacific from a fat, bureaucratic organization to a lean and agile one. Before Mr. Walsh, employees addressed each other by title or by Mr. or Ms. Now, first names are the norm. In addition to satellite conversations, Mr. Walsh has crisscrossed the country holding "town meetings" with 300 to 1,000 employees per session. During these sessions, Mr. Walsh not only listens to employee concerns, complaints, and suggestions, but he explains the new strategy of the firm and recent changes in the industry to employees first hand. Says Mr. Walsh, "A CEO must be visible, vulnerable, and willing to put himself on the line. It is essential to tell the truth and demonstrate that you share employees concerns, even when you can't do much about them."

His efforts to improve the internal communications at Union Pacific seem to be paying off. In the early 1990s, profits have surged and customer satisfaction is way up.

As we can see in the Union Pacific example, effective managers recognize that communication is one of the vital processes that make organizations run. The quality of the decisions that managers make rests on the accuracy and amount of information they receive from other employees and from the external environment and on the manner in which they process that information. The more timely and precise the information, the greater the likelihood that appropriate decisions will result. In fact, as Chester Barnard noted many years ago, "In any exhaustive theory of organization, communication would occupy a central place, because the structure, extensiveness, and scope of the organization are almost entirely determined by communication techniques."[2]

There are several distinct types of communication used in organizational settings. The manager who is familiar with the various types has a greater array of techniques to apply on the job. In addition, a variety of strategies exist for improving accuracy and receptivity of communication in the workplace. Managers can learn both to clarify their own messages and to receive messages accurately. Finally, it is useful to understand how communication breakdowns occur. When managers are aware of barriers to effective communication and information processing, they can take action to reduce or eliminate them.

INTERPERSONAL COMMUNICATION

In this chapter, we shall distinguish between communication primarily between two individuals—*interpersonal communication*—and communication among several individuals or groups—*organizational communication*. We begin by turning our attention to interpersonal communication. In a classic study of management practices, Henry Mintzberg found that managers tend to spend between 50 and 80 percent of their time in communication with others.[3] Moreover, these managers were found not only to prefer face-to-face communication, but to devote a good deal of their time to such activity.

Because of the central role played by interpersonal communication processes, we shall examine four aspects of the topic here: (1) the reasons for interpersonal communication, (2) a basic model of interpersonal communication, (3) types of interpersonal communication, and (4) major influences on the interpersonal communication process.

Reasons for Interpersonal Communication

At least four reasons can be identified for the importance of interpersonal communication to effective management. These include the following:

1. It influences the opinions, attitudes, and behaviors of those around us.
2. It expresses our feelings and emotions to others.
3. It is the vehicle for providing, receiving, or exchanging information concerning some event or activity that concerns us.
4. It reinforces the formal structure of the organization by such means as making use of formal channels of communication.

In other words, interpersonal communication allows employees at all levels of an organization to attempt to interact with others, to secure desired ends, to request or extend support, and to make use of and reinforce the formal design of the organization. These purposes serve not only the individuals involved, but the larger aim of improving the quality of working life and organizational effectiveness as well.

A Basic Model of Interpersonal Communication

Any attempt to diagram communication between two individuals, or the way information is processed by individuals, must necessarily be an oversimplification of what really happens. Even so, it is possible to outline the basic process involved in a dyadic communication exchange. This is done in Exhibit 13.1. A simple communication episode consists of a communicator who encodes and sends a message to a receiver who decodes it and responds in some way, either verbally or behaviorally.[4]

Encoding and Decoding.   Two important aspects of this model are encoding and decoding. *Encoding* is simply the process by which individuals initiating the communication translate ideas into a systematic set of symbols (language). Encoding is influenced by the sender's previous experiences with the topic and people involved, his or her emotional state at the time, and the importance attached to the message. *Decoding,* on the other hand, is the process by which the recipient of the message interprets it. The receiver attaches meaning to the message and tries to uncover its underlying intent. Decoding is influenced by factors such as the receiver's previous experiences and frame of reference at the time of receiving the message.

Feedback.   Several types of feedback can result from the intended transmission of a message from the sender to the receiver. Feedback can be seen as the final step in completing the communication episode and may take the

Exhibit 13.1
A Basic Model
of Communication

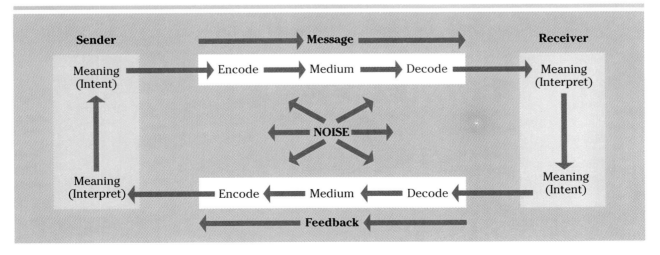

form of a verbal response, a nod of the head, a question seeking further information, or no response at all. As with the original message transmission, feedback also involves encoding, medium, and decoding.

It has been suggested that there are three basic types of feedback.[5] In *informational* feedback, the receiver simply provides nonevaluative information to the communicator. For instance, how many sales were made last month, or how many people are working on this problem? In *corrective* feedback, the receiver responds by challenging or correcting the original message. For instance, the receiver may point out that it is not his or her responsibility to monitor sales. Finally, feedback may be *reinforcing* when the receiver acknowledges clear receipt of the intended message. In this sense, a professor's grade on a term paper or examination is reinforcing feedback (positive or negative) to the student's original communication (the paper or exam).

Noise.   Finally, there are a variety of ways in which the intended message can get distorted. Factors that distort message clarity are referred to as *noise*. Noise can occur at any point along the process shown in Exhibit 13.1. For example, a manager may be under considerable time pressure and issue a succinct message that lacks the needed clarity for employees to carry out a task correctly. The manager may tell his or her foreman, "I want this job done today, regardless of how much it costs," when in fact the manager does care how much it costs. Noise can also occur in the decoding process. As shown in Exhibit 13.2, there are many ways in which message transmission can be distorted.

Types of Interpersonal Communication

In the communication episode discussed above, three types of communication can be used by either the sender in the transmission phase or the receiver in the feedback phase. These three types are:

Exhibit 13.2
Examples of Noise and Distortion in the Communication Process

What the Manager Said	What the Manager Meant	What the Subordinate Heard
I'll look into hiring another person for your department as soon as I complete my budget review.	We'll start interviewing for that job in about three weeks.	I'm tied up with more important things. Let's forget about hiring for the indefinite future.
Your performance was below par last quarter. I really expected more out of you.	You're going to have to try harder, but I know you can do it.	If you screw up one more time, you're out.
I'd like that report as soon as you can get to it.	I need that report within the week.	Drop that rush order you're working on and fill out that report today.
I talked to the boss, but at the present time, due to budget problems, we'll be unable to fully match your competitive salary offer.	We can give you 95 percent of that offer and I know we'll be able to do even more for you next year.	If I were you, I'd take that competitive offer. We're certainly not going to pay that kind of salary to a person with your credentials.

Source: Adapted table from *Organizational Behavior: Theory and Practice* by S. Altman, E. Valenzi, and R. Hodgetts. Copyright © 1985 by Harcourt Brace Jovanovich. Reprinted by permission of the publisher.

Oral Communication.   This consists of all messages or exchanges of information that are spoken, and it represents by far the most prevalent type of communication.

Written Communication.   This includes letters, reports, manuals, scribbled notes, and so forth. Although most managers prefer oral communication for its efficiency and immediacy, some managers prefer written communications for important messages (e.g., contracts), where precision of language and documentation of message content is important.

Nonverbal Communication.   A growing area of interest in managerial communication focuses on the transmission of messages without use of the spoken or written word. Two forms of nonverbal communication can be identified. *Physical or symbolic language,* such as traffic lights, sirens, and status symbols (e.g., office size), relates a message concerning something or someone important. *Body language,* such as facial expression, posture, or eye movements, relays conscious or unconscious messages to others. For example, some research has shown that people show tension by clenching their fists or crossing their arms. Boredom is conveyed by yawning or looking markedly disinterested.

In a classic book entitled *The Silent Language,* anthropologist Edward T. Hall points out that although most of us attain considerable proficiency in the use of the spoken word, we learn very little about the equally important area of nonverbal language—what Hall calls the "language of behavior."[6] This silent language represents a significant influence on us and our success in organizations, yet we seem to be almost unaware of its existence. The silent language, or nonverbal communication, in organizations can be seen in a multitude of ways, though these ways often differ across cultures. Consider the following examples:

> *Time.* Most Western cultures have a linear perspective of time. Consequently, time lost today is lost forever. Therefore, one way to determine someone's importance is to see how long he or she has to wait to meet someone else. If one is kept waiting a long time, one is probably not considered very important. Other cultures have a circular perspective of time. Consequently, time lost today can be recovered tomorrow. In such cultures, being kept waiting is neither rude nor an indication of one's importance or status.
>
> *Space.* When we enter someone's work space, we receive signals concerning who and how important that person is. Private offices, large desks, wood paneling, scenic views, and a private secretary all indicate relative importance. But private space is not interpreted the same across cultures. For example, in America the normal distance between two people during an interpersonal conversation is about the length of one's arm. However, in cultures in the Middle East, the distance is a matter of a few inches so that when speaking the breath of one person can be felt by the other.
>
> *Dress.* Simply looking at someone helps us "classify" the individual. Do the clothes indicate a manager or a worker? A military officer or enlisted person? For example, in the United States, the whole "dress for success" phenomenon is based on the premise that strong attributions are made about you just on the type of tie, scarf, shoes, or suit you wear.

Physical appearance. Such factors as hair length, posture, and attractiveness send us signals (rightly or wrongly) about the person's personality, status, and even political philosophy. However, physical features are not interpreted the same across cultures. For example, in the United States people who have large and protruding ears sometimes have them surgically "pinned back." In cultures such as the Chinese, large ears are a sign of sensitivity and spiritual depth.

Titles. Our reactions to others can be influenced by the titles they possess. Examples include "attorney-at-law," "senator," and "janitor." While titles make a differences in most cultures, in some they can make all the difference. For example, in both Japan and Russia, some argue that titles are more important than actual responsibilities or position.

Interpersonal interaction. The way people behave toward us also sends signals concerning their status and intent. For example, in Japan it is customary to bow when meeting someone, and the depth of the bow is determined by the relative status of both parties. Similarly, most of us have seen "glad-hander" politicians and salespersons who raise questions in our minds about their sincerity or honesty.

In short, as Hall has suggested, there is a very pervasive silent language of behavior that significantly affects how we see others, how they see us, and how we interact with each other. To paraphrase Marshall McLuhan, the medium is the message. In many instances, how a message is conveyed may be far more important than what is said.

Major Influences on Interpersonal Communication

Regardless of the type of communication involved, the nature, direction, and quality of interpersonal communication processes can be influenced by several factors.[7]

Social Influences. Communication is a social process; obviously, it takes at least two participants to complete a communication episode. A variety of *social influences* can affect the accuracy of the intended message. For example, status barriers between employees on different levels of the organizational hierarchy influence modes of address (e.g., "Sir" as opposed to "Joe"). Prevailing norms and roles may dictate who initiates which kinds of messages, who speaks to whom, and how one responds. The social processes at work in a group or organization determine what is said, to whom it is said, and how it is said.

Perception. In addition, the communication process is heavily influenced by employees' *perceptual processes.* The extent to which employees accurately receive job instructions from supervisors may be influenced by their opinions of the supervisors, the extent to which the instructions are controversial or conflicting, or their interest in the job. If an employee has stereotyped the boss as an incompetent manager, chances are that little the boss says will be regarded seriously. On the other hand, if the boss is seen as influential in the company, everything he or she says may be interpreted as important, even when it is not.

Interaction Involvement.   Communication effectiveness can be influenced by the extent to which one or both parties are actually involved in the conversation. This attentiveness is called *interaction involvement*.[8] If the intended receiver of the message is preoccupied with the personal problem, for example, the effectiveness of the message may be diminished. Interaction involvement consists of three interrelated dimensions: *responsiveness,* the extent to which individuals are clear about how to respond in social situations; *perceptiveness,* the extent to which individuals understand the meaning attached to their words and behaviors; and *attentiveness,* the degree to which individuals heed cues emerging from their immediate social environment.

If you are interested in determining your own interaction involvement, simply complete Self-Assessment 13.1 on page 442. When you are finished, refer to Appendix B for scoring details.

Organization Design.   Finally, the communication process is influenced by the *design of the organization.* For instance, it has often been argued that a major reason to decentralize an organization is that decentralized structures are more participative and lead to improved communications among parties. When messages must travel through several levels in the hierarchy, opportunities for message distortion are greatly increased, which leads to problems that possibly would not occur if face-to-face communication were possible.

Other factors that influence communication processes in organizations could be mentioned. However, these four should be recognized as principal influences on the communication processes. They play a role regardless of the type of communication involved.

INFORMATION RICHNESS

Effectiveness of communication is affected by the quality of the information. This factor is called *information richness* (or media richness).[9] Information richness concerns the amount of learning that can be achieved in a communication episode. Rich information facilitates understanding better than information that lacks richness. As shown in Exhibit 13.3, oral and written messages can be divided into four types of media: face-to-face, telephone, addressed documents (letters, memos), and unaddressed documents (flyers, bulletins). These four types of media differ with respect to feedback and the number of channels, or cues, they use during a communication episode. The better the feedback and the more channels used, the richer the information sent through the medium.

For example, face-to-face and telephone communication provide immediate feedback; memos and letters provide delayed feedback; and unaddressed flyers or bulletins provide no feedback. With respect to channels and cues, face-to-face communication uses several channels simultaneously (including voice, facial expression, and body language), whereas telephone

SELF-ASSESSMENT 13.1
What Is Your Interaction Involvement?

Instructions: This statement focuses on people's patterns of interaction with others. For each of the items, circle the number that best describes your agreement or disagreement with the item. Remember: there are no right or wrong answers.

		Strongly Disagree				Strongly Agree
1.	Often in conversations I'm not sure what the other is really saying.	1	2	3	4	5
2.	Often I feel sort of "unplugged" from the social situation of which I am a part; that is, I'm uncertain of my role, others' motives, and what's happening.	1	2	3	4	5
3.	Often in conversations, I'm not sure how I'm expected to relate to others.	1	2	3	4	5
4.	I am very observant in my conversations with others.	1	2	3	4	5
5.	During conversations I am sensitive to others' subtle or hidden meanings.	1	2	3	4	5
6.	I am keenly aware of how others perceive me durng my conversations.	1	2	3	4	5
7.	Often, I pretend to be listening to someone when in fact I'm thinking about something else.	1	2	3	4	5
8.	Often, I am preoccupied in my conversations and do not pay complete attention to others.	1	2	3	4	5
9.	My mind wanders during conversations and I often miss parts of what is going on.	1	2	3	4	5

Source: Excerpted from Donald J. Cegala, "Affective and Cognitive Manifestations of Interaction Involvement During Unstructured and Competitive Interactions." *Communication Monographs,* December 1984, p. 322. Reprinted by permission of the Speech Communication Association and the author.

conversations provide no nonverbal cues other than voice inflection. Letters, memos, and unaddressed communications are limited to the words written on the piece of paper.

Available research suggests that managers select the medium for their intended message depending upon the message they wish to communicate. That is, when a message is difficult or ambiguous, or when differences in backgrounds or opinions exist between the sender and receiver, managers prefer face-to-face communication, because greater learning is needed.[10] Multiple channels combined with immediate feedback enable managers to exchange information and ideas rapidly until disagreements are overcome

	Media		Characteristics		Media Richness	Best for Communications That Are:
			Feedback	**Cues and Channels**		
Face-to-face	Oral		Immediate	Audio and visual	High	Ambiguous, emotional, divergent in background
Telephone			Rapid	Audio	↕	↕
Addressed documents	Written		Slow	Limited visual		
Unaddressed documents			Slowest	Limited visual	Low	Clear, rational, official, similar in background

Exhibit 13.3
Hierarchy of Media
Richness for Managerial
Communication

Source: Adapted from Richard L. Daft and Robert H. Lengel, "Information Richness: A New Approach to Managerial Information Processing and Organization Design," in Barry Staw and Larry L. Cummings, eds., *Research in Organizational Behavior,* vol. 6 (Greenwich, Ct.: JAI Press, 1984), pp. 191–233. Reprinted from R. Daft and R. Steers, *Organizations: A Micro/Macro Approach* (Glenview, Ill.: Scott, Foresman, 1986), p. 532.

and a common understanding is reached. On the other hand, managers prefer written memos when the message is clear and well defined and when everyone involved has similar backgrounds and understanding about the issue. Thus, a reminder of an upcoming meeting or information concerning cost figures for last month would more than likely be transmitted through memos.

At times, managers make use of multiple media in order to develop a more complete portrait of the organization. For example, it is easy for senior managers to become isolated from lower-level employees in the field or in a different part of the building if they rely solely on written communications. Written reports fail to provide sufficient richness concerning possible problems people encounter, how employees feel about things, or about job attitudes throughout the organization. To learn this, managers must leave the office and talk face-to-face with employees. One executive who does this is the president of Hyatt Hotels.

IN PRACTICE
Face-to-Face at Hyatt Hotels

The image customers have of a hotel comes not from the managers and executives who run the operation, but rather from the lower-level service personnel (clerks, receptionists, waitresses) that customers actually see and deal with. Here is where the quality of service is defined and measured, and here is where profitability is ultimately determined. As a result, at hotels like Hyatt, it is common practice for high-level executive to meet face-to-face with lower-echelon employees on a regular basis to assess employee morale and to identify any problems that affect customer service that are bypassed or ignored by written communications.

In fact, the president of Hyatt Hotels makes it a practice to have lunch with small groups of employees at least twice a month. During these "gripe sessions," any topic may be discussed, from the items on the restaurant menu to supervisory problems to company uniforms. Moreover, because their immediate supervisors are not present, employees have come to develop trust in the executive and feel that the company values both them and their input.

Hyatt has found such sessions helpful in identifying problems and possible solutions that would more than likely never be included in weekly or monthly written reports. As a result, the company feels that customer service, as well as employee morale, has improved. And for the president, better information—that is, information of higher richness—is achieved for purposes of decision making and planning.[11]

ORGANIZATIONAL COMMUNICATION

We come now to an examination of communication processes in the larger organizational context. In other words, what happens when individuals are put into groups? What happens when we impose structure on the patterns of interpersonal relationships? To consider these questions, we examine three related topics: how managers communicate within organizations, the direction of organizational communication, and special communication roles in organizations.

How Do Managers Communicate?

Let us briefly consider communication patterns among typical managers. Which forms of communication do managers prefer, and with whom do they most frequently communicate? In a recent study of managerial communication, it was found that managers tended to emphasize face-to-face communication in their daily activities.[12] This accounted for 81 percent of all reported communication (see Exhibit 13.4). This was followed by 39 percent for scheduled meetings (another form of face-to-face communication). The fact that both of these types of communication emphasize information richness highlights the importance of securing complete and timely information for managerial action. Forms of communication requiring written information (and less richness) are used far less frequently by the managers.

It is also instructive to note whom managers actually talk with in the course of the workday. Again, as shown in Exhibit 13.4, managers spend most of their time (45 percent) talking with subordinates. This is followed by 24 percent talking with people outside the organization, 18 percent with others within the organization, and 15 percent with one's boss. Thus, according to these findings, the most common form of managerial communication is face-to-face discussions with one's subordinates. Such a finding is not surprising considering the importance of keeping close interpersonal relations with members of the work group (see, for example, the discussion in Chapter 12 on leadership).

Exhibit 13.4
Patterns of Managerial
Communication

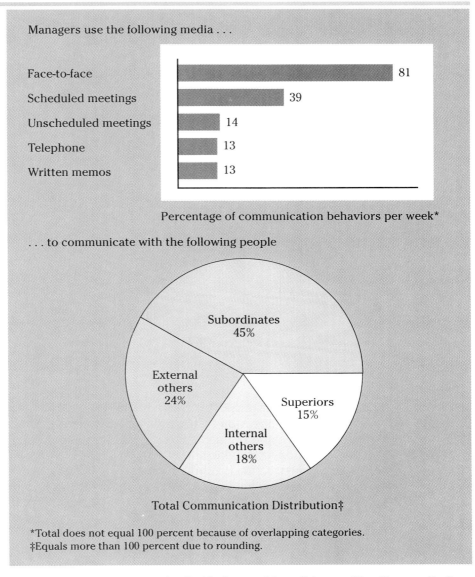

Managers use the following media . . .

Face-to-face	81
Scheduled meetings	39
Unscheduled meetings	14
Telephone	13
Written memos	13

Percentage of communication behaviors per week*

. . . to communicate with the following people

Subordinates
45%

External
others
24%

Superiors
15%

Internal
others
18%

Total Communication Distribution‡

*Total does not equal 100 percent because of overlapping categories.
‡Equals more than 100 percent due to rounding.

Source: Based on data presented in Fred Luthans and Janet K. Larsen, "How Managers Really
Communicate," *Human Relations,* February 1986, pp. 167–168.

Direction of Organizational Communication

In the study of organizational communication, we typically identify three general directions in which a message can flow: upward, downward, and horizontally. Not surprisingly, the purposes of communication can vary considerably depending upon its direction. This is shown in Exhibit 13.5.

Downward Communication.   Downward communication is primarily used by managers to direct and influence the activities of those below them in the organizational hierarchy. As shown in Exhibit 13.5, such communication has

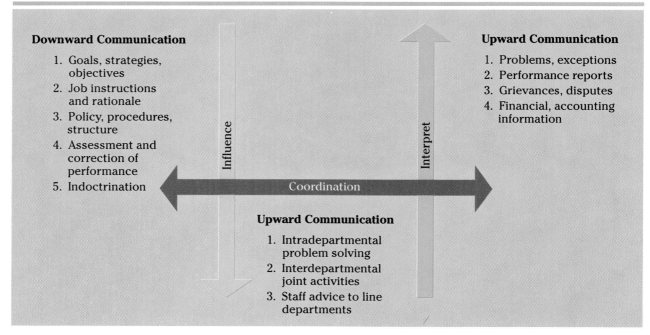

Exhibit 13.5
Downward, Upward, and
Horizontal Communication
in Organizations

Source: R. Daft and R. Steers, *Organizations: A Micro/Macro Approach* (Glenview, Ill.: Scott, Foresman, 1986), p. 538. Copyright © 1986 Scott, Foresman and Company.

several purposes. These include providing employees with a sense of purpose and direction by providing clear goals and objectives both for the organization and the department. In addition, managers use downward communication to provide specific job instructions as well as the rationale behind the instructions. Third, such efforts establish policies, procedures, and structural arrangements for the organization. Through policy manuals, organization charts, and so forth, managers tell people how the organization is put together and how it runs.

Downward communication is also used to assess and correct employee performance, as, for example, in the performance appraisal process (see Chapter 7). And finally, downward communication is often used for purposes of indoctrination and socialization. It tells employees what the organization thinks is important and what it does not. For example, serious company efforts (and time) on behalf of the United Way campaign tell employees that the company thinks this is an important community effort.

Efforts at downward communication are not always successful. As the intended message moves down the hierarchy, it often becomes misinterpreted and distorted. In fact, in one study of 100 companies, it was found that only 20 percent of top management's intended message ever reached production line workers.[13] And only 63 percent of top management's message ever reached the vice-presidential levels. This loss of message accuracy is shown in Exhibit 13.6. Consider, as you read the remainder of this chapter, what you could do to improve the accuracy of messages as they move down the organization.

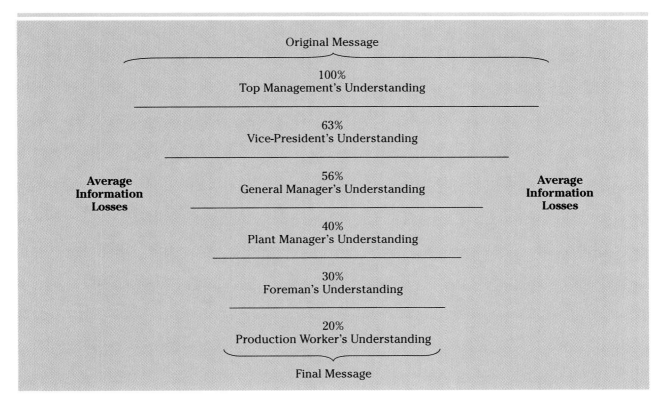

Original Message

100%
Top Management's Understanding

63%
Vice-President's Understanding

Average Information Losses

56%
General Manager's Understanding

Average Information Losses

40%
Plant Manager's Understanding

30%
Foreman's Understanding

20%
Production Worker's Understanding

Final Message

Exhibit 13.6
Percentage of Information Filtered Out During Downward Communication

Source: Adapted from Ralph G. Nichols, "Listening Is Good Business," *Management of Personnel Quarterly* 1, 2 (1962): 4; and E. Scannell, *Communication for Leadership* (New York: McGraw-Hill, 1970). Reprinted from R. Daft and R. Steers, *Organizations: A Micro/Macro Approach* (Glenview, Ill.: Scott, Foresman, 1986), p. 539.

Upward Communication.   As noted above, the type of information that usually works its way up the organizational hierarchy can be quite different from the type that goes down. Here, we typically see attention being drawn to problems or exceptions to normal operating policies that require management attention. In fact, one approach to management suggests "management by exception," in which only unusual events or problems are brought to the attention of management. Beyond this, management receives only standard weekly or monthly reports concerning productivity or sales. In addition, upward communication is used for performance reports, grievances and disputes, and financial and accounting information.

When upward communication does occur, it is likely to be influenced to a considerable degree by what the subordinate thinks his or her superior wants to hear. One study found, for example, that junior managers with strong aspirations of upward mobility and promotion tended to filter their upward communication in such a way that positive messages were highlighted or exaggerated and negative messages were downplayed or omitted altogether.[14] This study also revealed that the accuracy of upward communication was enhanced to the extent that the subordinates trusted their superiors, and also to the extent that they perceived that their superiors had little influence over their own career advancement. When trust was lacking or where an employee felt his or her superior had considerable influence over promotion decisions, however, upward messages became highly distorted.

Horizontal Communication.   Finally, horizontal communication is typically used as a means of coordinating activities or projects between departments or units. Organization design may serve to discourage horizontal communication, in that it may identify proper chains of command through which messages are supposed to flow. Naturally, if this procedure is followed, the speed and accuracy of the message will be decreased. Hence, most organizations acknowledge the right of individuals to cross departmental boundaries to secure or provide information that is germane to their own particular jobs. This process of circumventing formal organization structure was first recognized by the noted French industrialist Henri Fayol, who noted, "There are many operations where success depends on rapid execution; we must find some means of reconciling respect for the hierarchic channel with the need for quick action."[15] Thus, interdepartmental communication that departs from the formal chain of command but is necessary to task accomplishment is often referred to as *Fayol's bridge.*

On the basis of a review of relevant literature, Szilagyi attempted to rank various methods of upward and downward communication in terms of their effectiveness. These rankings are shown in Exhibit 13.7.[16] As can be seen, effective downward techniques (such as small-group meetings or direct organizational publications) differ from effective upward communication methods (such as informal discussions or supervisory meetings). Even so, the approaches that have proved successful make use of information richness. In view of the need for both forms of communication, it seems important for managers to understand these various techniques, as well as when and where they are most likely to be successful.

Exhibit 13.7
Rankings of the Effectiveness of Various Upward and Downward Communication Techniques

Rank	Upward Communication Techniques	Rank	Downward Communication Techniques
1	Informal discussion	1	Small group meeting
2	Meeting with supervisors	2	Direct organizational publications
3	Attitude surveys	3	Supervisory meetings
4	Grievance procedures	4	Mass meetings
5	Counseling	5	Letters to employees' homes
6	Exit interviews	6	Bulletin boards
7	Union representatives	7	Pay envelope inserts
8	Formal meetings	8	Public address system
9	Suggestion boxes	9	Posters
10	Employee newsletter	10	Annual reports, manuals, media advertising

Source: A. Szilagyi, *Management and Performance* (Glenview, Ill.: Scott, Foresman and Company, 1981). p. 384. Reprinted by permission.

Special Communication Roles in Organizations

The final aspect of organizational communication to be addressed in this section concerns the roles played by various individuals in facilitating communication effectiveness. Obviously, all individuals do not play the same role, nor are they equally important, in communication within the organization. In fact, communication researchers Rogers and Rogers have identified four individual roles in such communication.[17] These are the gatekeeper, the liaison, the opinion leader, and the cosmopolite (see Exhibit 13.8).

Gatekeeper.   A *gatekeeper* is an employee who is located in such a position in the flow of information as to control certain messages into or away from a given channel. For example, secretaries have long been known to serve an

Exhibit 13.8
Individual Communication
Roles in Organizations

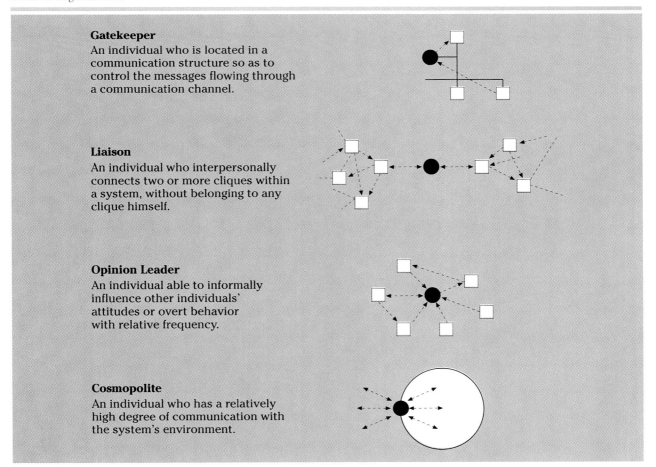

Gatekeeper
An individual who is located in a communication structure so as to control the messages flowing through a communication channel.

Liaison
An individual who interpersonally connects two or more cliques within a system, without belonging to any clique himself.

Opinion Leader
An individual able to informally influence other individuals' attitudes or overt behavior with relative frequency.

Cosmopolite
An individual who has a relatively high degree of communication with the system's environment.

Source: Reprinted with permission of The Free Press, a division of Macmillan, Inc., from *Communication in Organizations* by Everett M. Rogers and Rekha Agarwala Rogers, p. 133. Copyright © 1978 by The Free Press.

important gatekeeper function by making screening decisions concerning which mail, telephone calls, and visitors are allowed to reach their bosses. Other gatekeepers are those who have strong contacts outside the organization and serve as primary sources of information from the outside world. In using their contacts, such individuals decide what information is conveyed and to whom it is sent.

Liaison.　A *liaison* interpersonally connects two or more groups or departments within a system. The liaison is usually not a member of either group; rather he or she is a go-between who builds the bridges necessary to exchange needed information. In commenting on the role of liaisons in organizations, Rogers and Rogers note, "The liaison role has important practical implications for organizational communication, as liaisons are undoubtedly crucial for the effective operation of an organization's interpersonal network. Liaisons occupy strategic positions within the organizations; they can be either expeditors of information flow or bottlenecks in communication channels."[18]

Opinion Leaders.　*Opinion leaders* have the ability to informally influence the attitudes or behaviors of others in a desired way and with relative frequency. They generally have considerable access to external sources of information and tend to hold respected positions within the organization, so their opinions are heard and valued. In comparison to their peers, opinion leaders are often characterized by a wide range of exposure to external and technically competent sources of information, greater accessibility to their followers, and higher conformity to the norms of the group they lead.

Cosmopolite.　Finally, a *cosmopolite* is a person who has a high degree of interaction and communication with the organization's external environment. In a sense, cosmopolites represent a special type of gatekeeper, in that they control communication flow by which new ideas enter the organization. In general, such individuals are characterized "by their wide travel, readership of nonlocal publications, national and international group affiliations, and membership in professional occupations with a high rate of migration."[19]

It has been suggested that cosmopolites are concentrated at the very top and very bottom of an organization. At the top, executives travel widely and typically have memberships in a wide variety of external organizations. At the bottom, many employees come into daily contact with the "outside world" through their work with customers, suppliers, and so forth. In both cases, cosmopolites represent an important resource to the organization in helping it to learn more about and cope with the external environment.

In summary, each role has its place in facilitating organizational effectiveness. The gatekeeper helps prevent information overload by filtering and screening messages. The liaison integrates and interconnects the various groups or cliques in the network, and the opinion leader facilitates informal decision making in the network. Finally, the cosmopolite generally relates the organization to its external environment by providing an openness of ideas and an exchange of information. In all, then, each of the four functions plays an important role in facilitating organizational effectiveness by helping members of the organization collect, analyze, and act upon relevant information.

COMMUNICATION NETWORKS

In Chapters 10 and 11, we examined the nature of organization design, and it was pointed out that variations in design have important ramifications for several aspects of behavior. One of these concerns communication practices. Specifically, what is the impact of organization design on the way in which information is exchanged in organizational settings? To answer this question, we will employ the concept of communication networks. A *communication network* represents the pattern of interpersonal communication among the members of a group or organization. That is, it shows who talks to whom and who is "connected" to whom. Clearly, patterns of communication—who is able or allowed to speak with whom—are quite varied in organizational situations, and this diversity in large part is determined by the structure of the organization itself.

We shall discuss two forms of communication networks, those that largely person-to-person and those that are largely electronic in nature.

Person-to-Person Networks

In the literature on person-to-person communication networks, four different types of network are usually identified. These are (1) the chain, (2) the wheel, (3) the circle, and (4) the all-channel, or "star," as shown in Exhibit 13.9. This exhibit depicts the possible interaction patterns for a group of five people in a communication episode. The first two types (the chain and the wheel) represent centralized networks, whereas the second two (the circle and the all-channel) represent decentralized networks.

Exhibit 13.9
Characteristics of Group Communication Networks

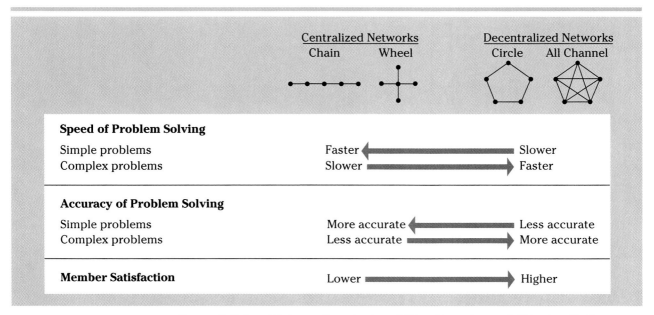

	Centralized Networks		Decentralized Networks	
	Chain	Wheel	Circle	All Channel
Speed of Problem Solving				
Simple problems	Faster ⟵			Slower
Complex problems	Slower		⟶	Faster
Accuracy of Problem Solving				
Simple problems	More accurate ⟵			Less accurate
Complex problems	Less accurate		⟶	More accurate
Member Satisfaction	Lower		⟶	Higher

Source: R. Daft and R. Steers, *Organizations: A Micro/Macro Approach* (Glenview, Ill.: Scott, Foresman, 1986), p. 534. Copyright © 1986 Scott, Foresman and Company.

The *chain* represents a communication pattern most frequently found in "tall" organization structures, where most communication flows up or down a formally defined chain of command. The chain shown in the exhibit can be thought of as five levels in the organization hierarchy, perhaps from the president of a company down through a first-line supervisor. In contrast, a *wheel* network shows the communication patterns most typically found in a work group where shop floor employees report to one supervisor or in a "flat" organization structure, where decision making is more decentralized.

Among the more decentralized networks, the *circle* network shows the interaction pattern among individuals such as shift supervisors. Supervisors from the day shift pass on information to the swing supervisor as the former leaves and the later begins works, and then the swing shift supervisor passes information on to the night shift supervisor at the next shift change. Finally, an *all-channel,* or star, network represents such situations as members of a task force or committee or situations that exist outside the formal organization structure (for instance, a grapevine). The star also represents interaction patterns typically found in the autonomous work groups that characterize many work redesign efforts. Although the task force may have a formal leader or chairperson, interaction patterns are clearly more diffuse among the members; that is, far more lateral, or horizontal, communication is possible. In situations such as a grapevine, there is typically no leader (formal or informal), and communication can be initiated by anyone in the network to anyone else in the network.

A good deal has been learned about the manner in which and the effectiveness with which different networks handle information.[20] In problem-solving situations, communication and actual problem solving are fastest in chain and wheel networks so long as the tasks are relatively simple. However, communication would be much slower in chains and wheels where the tasks are complex, because the leader may become overloaded with information and feedback. In such circumstances, the circle and the all-channel would generally lead to faster results.

In terms of accuracy of problem solving, we see similar results. On simple problems, chains and wheels tend to emerge with high-quality answers, whereas circles and all-channels do better on complex or difficult tasks. Presumably, this is because more complex problems require greater interaction (more decentralization) which characterizes these latter approaches.

Finally, what can we say about the satisfaction levels among group members working under these four communication networks? In general, chain and wheel networks do not lead to positive attitudes by employees, largely because of a lack of participation in decisions. The employee role is more often that of a message recipient, not an active participant in a dialogue. In contrast, members of a circle or all-channel network, such as many committees or autonomous work groups, tend to report more positive attitudes toward their role in communication episodes.

In summary, communication networks play a significant role in several aspects of organizational behavior, including problem solving and the determination of job attitudes. It must be remembered that trends are being discussed here; exceptions or variations can easily be identified. Even so, an understanding of communication networks can help students of organizational behavior to comprehend the communication process in work organizations.

Electronic Networks

The second kind of network involves the use of computer-based technologies to distribute and collect information across different parts of the organization. Increasingly, companies are being faced with voluminous amounts of data, and making use of this information in a timely way is becoming an increasingly difficult task. To facilitate the sharing of useful information among those who need it, companies are taking advantage of a variety of electronic hardware and software applications now available. Among these computer-based technologies are included the use of large-scale data bases, electronic mail, local area networks (LAN), Bitnet-type electronic communication networks, and so forth. Moreover, the advent of fax machines has furthered visual communications by allowing managers to transmit actual "hard copy" over phone lines. As the volume of information required for decision making increases, such applications will become more common.

From a managerial standpoint, a question arises concerning how such changes will affect managerial communication and decision-making practices in the 1990s. In one interview, Kenneth Olsen, former president of Digital Equipment Corporation, provides some insight.

IN PRACTICE
The Future of Electronic Networking

Interviewer: What single thing do organizations need most from computer makers right now?

Olsen: I am filled with prejudices and enthusiasm for the answer to that question. Not everyone sees it this way, but from my prejudiced point of view—prejudiced because it's been our strategy for 10 years—the greatest need is to tie together all parts of an organization to allow them to work together. This means that work groups, as we call them, can be expanded and contracted spontaneously, as the need develops. They can share computing software and transmit pictures, documents, and data. It's just common sense. If you can get the whole organization to work together, it's so much more effective.

A few years ago we were ridiculed because we said that personal computers working alone weren't good enough. But people thought miracles would happen when they used personal computers. Miracles didn't happen because they weren't tied together to work on a common problem. When everybody in an organization has a different personal computer, different software, different spreadsheet, different word processing, they obviously do not work together. Networking can force them to work together.

Interviewer: What will the fully networked organization look like?

Olsen: It's like the telephone. Any time you want to hook up a telephone, you plug it into the wall and it's on. People are free to communicate. I think the same is true with a networked organization. Take the way we used to introduce a product. I'd have a drawing. If the engineering group had a problem, it would contact manufacturing or outside suppliers. They'd make suggestions, mark up the drawing, and send it back to engineering. The engineer would finally get it, finally mark it up and send it back to manufacturing. They'd go through the whole thing a few times. Each argued a point of view, but it took forever to introduce a product.

In networked organizations, the group that is introducing the product has a database and can spontaneously absorb these changes on a CAD (computer-aided design) system. People in engineering, in other departments, and at the supplier can all make the same part together, even if they are miles apart. They can bring on a change; push the button and that's it.

I have four secretaries here. They all work on one database, one computer. They have complete access to each other's files and records. Anybody can start a job and anybody else can pick it up. If somebody calls up and wants to know what happened to a letter, anyone can find out. Before the caller finishes telling his or her name and address, a secretary knows what was done with the letter. They work as a team.[21]

BARRIERS TO EFFECTIVE COMMUNICATION

If, as Chester Barnard said, communication forms the basis of organizations, then it is logical to consider several common problems associated with communication processes in organizations. Indeed, a lengthy list of such problems could be generated with ease. However, for the sake of brevity, we can summarize much of the available information on impediments to effective communication into a list of five barriers: distortion, omission, overload, timeliness, and acceptance.

Distortion

Communication *distortion* occurs when an intended message becomes altered as it passes through the information channel from sender to receiver. There are several reasons why distortion can occur, including differing frames of reference of the sender and receiver, imprecision of language, interpretation errors in the receipt of the message, the necessity to condense information for purposes of transmission, and the social distance or status barriers between sender and receiver.

A tragic example from history, the episode of the Black Hole of Calcutta, serves to demonstrate what can happen when an intended message is distorted because of interpretation errors and status barriers between sender and receiver. In 1756, the Nawab of Calcutta led a successful uprising against the British East India Company in Calcutta. The British outpost surrendered, and the Nawab ordered his lieutenants to place the 146 captives in prison for the night. He then went to bed. The only facility available for the prisoners was a small cell measuring 20 feet by 20 feet. It was referred to locally as the Black Hole and was used to hold occasional thieves. The soldiers interpreted the Nawab's orders strictly, and all 146 captives were forced into the tiny cell. Without ample air and under claustrophobic conditions, panic broke out among the captives. Appeals to guards, who dared not wake the Nawab, went unanswered. By morning, 123 of the captives were dead. As a result, the Black

Hole of Calcutta became a rallying cry in England symbolizing Indian hostility toward foreigners. Shortly thereafter, the British sent forces against the Nawab and won, and they went on to colonize the remainder of India. As Watney concluded of the incident, the tragedy began with a "not very bright subordinate who . . . obeyed [orders] in too literal a fashion. Later, no one dared to take the responsibility of releasing the prisoners on their own initiative."[22]

Distortion also occurs because of language barriers. This form of distortion is especially important when working internationally (for example, selling a product or negotiating a contract overseas) or nationally with employees from diverse cultural backgrounds (for example, an Anglo manager supervising primarily Spanish-speaking workers). In both cases, what we say often gets distorted. Examples of such distortion caused by translation errors are shown in Exhibit 13.10.

Message distortion occurs regularly in organizations. Some of it is unintentional, occurring either because the sender is not clear or because the receiver fails to understand the intended message. On the other hand, considerable distortion occurs by design. That is, we often don't want to hear the message or are afraid to be the bearer of bad news. As a result, we have a tendency to filter out or distort important bits of information that we do not want conveyed. For example, a supervisor intending to fire an employee who has consistently failed on the job may tell the employee that there is not a good "career match" between him and the company, or he may claim to be "overstaffed." This allows the supervisor to avoid the real issue of poor performance.

However, before being too critical of people who engage in this type of behavior, why not see how you do on information distortion. Please complete Self-Assessment 13.2, using your current or previous job as a frame of reference. Answer each question as accurately as possible. When you have finished, refer to Appendix B for results.

Exhibit 13.10
Examples of Distortion in
International Communication

Nonverbal Communication

- Shaking your head up and down means "no" in Greece, and shaking it from side to side means "yes."
- The American sign for "OK" is an obscene gesture in Spain.

Verbal Communication

- When Coca-Cola entered the Chinese market, they discovered that their product name translated as "Bite the head of a dead tadpole."
- When Chevrolet introduced its Nova car into Latin America, it discovered that the word translates into Spanish as "doesn't go."
- To "table a motion" in the United States means to remove a motion or proposal from consideration, but in England it means to put the motion on the table for discussion.
- The word *yes* is often translated into Japanese as "hai." But in Japan, this means "Yes, I understand you" not "Yes, I agree."
- When a Japanese executive says he will "positively consider your offer," it means no, not yes.
- When an American asks "How are you doing?" or "How is it going?" he or she probably isn't very interested in knowing the answer.

SELF-ASSESSMENT 13.2
How Effective Is Your Organizational Communication?

Instructions: Using a current or previous job as a frame of reference, answer each of the following items by circling the appropriate number.

		Strongly Disagree				Strongly Agree
1.	I feel free to discuss my problems with my boss without feeling that it could jeopardize my job.	1	2	3	4	5
2.	I typically keep job-related information from my boss.	5	4	3	2	1
3.	When speaking with my boss, I try to emphasize information that makes me look good.	5	4	3	2	1
4.	In general, I think my boss and I have fairly open communications.	1	2	3	4	5
5.	My boss is candid and honest with me concerning what happens in the workplace.	1	2	3	4	5
6.	I often feel that no one tells me anything on my job.	5	4	3	2	1

Omission

The second barrier to effective communication is omission. *Omission* occurs when only one part of an intended message is conveyed to the receiver. For example, a machine operator in a factory may tell his supervisor that his machine has broken down but fail to point out that he failed to properly maintain the machine and caused the breakdown. Omission results either when the sender intentionally filters the intended message (perhaps because of fear of retribution) or when the sender is unable to grasp the entire message and therefore transmits incomplete information.

A rather interesting example of omission in message transmission can be seen in an episode from Richard M. Nixon's presidency, as described by Dan Rather and Gary Gates in *The Palace Guard:*

The president was working alone, very late at night in a hotel room while on a trip. He opened the door, beckoned to a waiting aide and ordered, "Get me coffee." The aide immediately responded to the request. Most of the activities of the hotel including the kitchen were not operating at such a late hour. Hotel personnel had to be called in and a fresh pot of coffee brewed. All this took time and the president kept asking about coffee while waiting. Finally, a tray was made up with a carafe of coffee, cream, sugar and some sweet rolls and was rushed to the president's suite. It was only at this point that the aide learned that the president did not want coffee to drink, but rather wanted to talk to an assistant whose name was Coffee.[23]

Overload

Often we see the opposite problem—a receiver is buried in an abundance of information, and rational decision making and management suffer. This condition is called communication *overload.* Managers often face this problem when their subordinates fail to adequately screen information presented to the manager. As a result, managers are forced to spend so much time sorting through the information that they may fail to identify the major issues in time to take appropriate steps.

A good example of this problem is provided by Graham Allison in his analysis of the events leading up to the Cuban missile crisis of 1962.[24] Allison found that the Central Intelligence Agency had sufficient information to assess accurately the deployment of missiles in Cuba and to take quiet diplomatic steps to solve the problem long before events reached crisis proportions. Unfortunately, however, the CIA possessed so much information that it was months behind in its intelligence processing. By the time the information was properly analyzed, opportunities for quiet, diplomatic conflict resolution had long passed.

Critics have noted similar characteristics in the *Challenger* space shuttle disaster, where sufficient information was supposedly available before launch to predict failure (e.g., weather conditions were inappropriate). Even so, the various management staffs—of which there were many—were unable to coordinate and evaluate all of the pertinent data in sufficient time to avert the disaster.

Timeliness

A major factor in the effectiveness of communication is *timing.* Because messages are intended to stimulate action, it is important that their transmissions be timed so that they receive the necessary attention. Providing detailed instructions to employees on a task one month prior to the time the task is to be done, for example, may lead to problems of performance failure because of the lengthy time interval between task instruction and task performance. Conversely, we often see situations in which important memos are distributed to employees requesting actions but giving unrealistically short deadlines. If information is to be properly acted upon, it must arrive in a timely fashion.

Acceptance

Even if all four of the above barriers could be overcome, it is necessary that there be acceptance of the message by the receiver if it is to be acted upon. If employees refuse to accept a message, perhaps because they feel it is inappropriate or comes from a noncredible source (e.g., a supervisor asks the secretary of another supervisor to type a letter), there is little reason to believe the message will be acted upon.

Recognition by managers of the existence of these barriers represents a first and useful step toward surmounting them. Once they have been recognized, concrete actions can be initiated to improve speaking and writing abilities, as well as listening abilities. Managers and employees will learn not only *how* to communicate, but also *when* to communicate and with *whom* to communicate. In this way, considerable progress can be made in overcoming these barriers to effective communication.

Ethical Challenge

IN PRACTICE
The Art of Communicating with Stockholders

We can see examples of many of these barriers to the communication process simply by reading a variety of corporate annual reports. Annual reports have always been a game for companies; how do you provide the stockholders with enough accurate information about what is happening in the company without revealing any disturbing information? In fact, distortion and omission errors have become an art form for some companies.

When we read annual reports, we expect that corporations have emphasized the positive in reviewing the year's activities. We even expect such reports to contain editorial comments, such as the phone company's arguments against regulation or steelmakers' complaints about foreign imports. However, there is an increasing trend in these reports toward hiding information.

For example, a recent Apple Computer annual report carried pictures of such celebrities as Lee Iacocca and David Rockefeller even though these celebrities are not regular users of Apple products. And Mattel, Inc., buried in its accounting explanations the fact that it had to sell off its electronics business because of heavy losses. United Technologies noted that it elected a new president but neglected to say what happened to the old one.[25]

Other examples can be cited. In fact, you may want to look for your own examples as you read either company annual reports or other news releases from various corporations. How much accurate information is provided, and what has been hidden? As a consumer of business information—and a prospective stockholder yourself—how can you get enough accurate information from these companies to really know what is happening?

IMPROVING COMMUNICATION EFFECTIVENESS

None of the above barriers to communication effectiveness is insurmountable. The problem for managers is how to improve the accuracy, flow, and acceptance of relevant communication so that uncertainty and distortion are reduced and acceptance is enhanced. The remedies for achieving this goal can be grouped for convenience according to the direction of the intended communication: downward, upward, or horizontal.

Improving Downward Communication

There are a variety of ways in which managers can facilitate improved communication with their subordinates. Most of these techniques involve clarifying the nature of the job or task. The more employees understand about the nature of the job, including what they are to do and why, the less search behavior is required, and the more time for goal-directed effort is available, assuming the employees accept the task and are motivated to perform.

In addition to clarifying job instructions and the rationale behind the instructions, managers can provide more feedback to keep employees on target. Managers can also use multiple communication channels (written and verbal messages simultaneously) and repeat messages to reinforce the impact of the intended message. Such efforts will increase the likelihood that the message will be received and understood. Finally, it is desirable at times to bypass formal communication channels and to go directly to the intended receiver with the message; this way, one can avoid considerable noise and distortion in transmission.

Improving Upward Communication

One of the most important problems in upward communication is information overload. One popular way to reduce overload is *screening,* or transmitting only the important aspects of a message through the hierarchy and omitting the peripheral aspects. Screening has several formats. One consists of a *management-by-exception* procedure, in which routine decisions and actions are handled through policy guidelines. Only exceptions, deviations, and emergencies are reported upward. A second approach is the *principle of sufficiency,* where organizations intentionally regulate both the quantity and quality of upward information (e.g., where managers at each level in the hierarchy write summary reports for their superiors, or where managers intentionally schedule meetings for less time than is thought to be needed so they can "get right to the point"). Finally, a third screening technique is *queuing,* where messages are handled sequentially by managers, usually in order of importance.

Another way to improve upward communication involves attempting to improve the organizational climate so subordinates have less fear about reporting negative outcomes to their superiors. A major problem in upward communication is that bad news often gets filtered out as it moves up the hierarchy, and quick remedial action is inhibited. If employees had less fear of negative consequences for admitting mistakes, superiors would be more likely to receive rapid and accurate information on trouble spots for which they could then seek remedy.

Other strategies can be employed as well, including the use of *distortion-proof messages,* where employees' messages are structured (perhaps through the use of a standard form); the reduction of social and status barriers; and an increased awareness by managers of potential sources of bias in reporting. An alternative strategy is to recognize different individual communication roles in organizations, as discussed earlier in this chapter. As a result, managers should receive more accurate and timely information from employees who feel secure about reporting information upward.

Improving Horizontal Communication

If managers are to be successful in coordinating and integrating the efforts of individuals and groups in all areas of an organization, it is crucial that a concerted effort be made to develop accurate, rapid lines of horizontal communication. Work groups and departments must pool their efforts to achieve organizational effectiveness. But how can managers facilitate horizontal communication among groups?

Several mechanisms exist. One is to foster high levels of interpersonal trust and openness among work groups. To the extent that these efforts are successful, more spontaneous efforts can emerge, and less energy will be devoted to promoting group or departmental territoriality. Reward systems can be implemented to reward cooperation among departments instead of competition. One example would be to include in a manager's performance appraisal a question about the extent to which the manager helped *other* departments reach their goals. Such techniques might reduce the propensity to conceal information that could be helpful to other groups and departments.

Another technique involves having interdepartmental meetings (instead of or in addition to departmental meetings), where members of two or more departments or groups come together and share information, problems, and possible solutions. In this way, members of one department can gain a better understanding of the problems of others and learn how to be of assistance. Using a matrix organization design is another way to accomplish the same end. There are many ways managers can facilitate communications at work so less effort is wasted and more energies are devoted toward goal attainment. However, managers must make it happen; they must take an active part in developing a climate best suited for open and accurate interchange among employees at various levels.

Or, as communication specialist Jay Jackson puts it:

What we call communication problems are often only symptoms of other difficulties which exist among persons and groups in an organization. To summarize . . . I should like to point to four problems which people in organizations must solve in order to overcome barriers to communication:

1. *The problem of trust or lack of trust.* Communication flows among friendship channels. When trust exists, content is more freely communicated, and the recipient is more accurate in perceiving the sender's opinion.
2. *The problem of creating interdependence among persons: common goals and agreement about means for achieving them.* When persons have different goals and value systems, then it is especially important to create mutual understanding about needs and motives.
3. *The problem of distributing rewards fairly,* so that people's needs are being met and so that they are motivated to contribute to the overall objectives of the organization. Nothing can be so restrictive of the free flow of ideas and information, for example, as the feeling that you may not obtain credit for your contribution.
4. *The exceedingly important problem of understanding and coming to common agreement about the social structure of the organization.* I can think of nothing which would facilitate more the free and accurate

SELF-ASSESSMENT 13.3
How Are Your Listening Skills?

Instructions: For each of the items listed below, circle the answer that most closely describes your behavior when you are talking with another person.

	Strongly Agree				Strongly Disagree
1. While listening to others, I think about what I am going to say next.	1	2	3	4	5
2. I always try to maintain good eye contact with the speaker.	5	4	3	2	1
3. I always try to have the last word in a conversation.	1	2	3	4	5
4. I withhold judgment of what the speaker is saying until he or she is finished.	5	4	3	2	1
5. I frequently ask speakers questions to clarify what they are saying.	5	4	3	2	1
6. I listen for both factual content and the emotion behind the words.	5	4	3	2	1
7. A speaker's appearance and delivery say a lot about the merits of his or her message.	1	2	3	4	5
8. I try to understand the specific facts or details in a speaker's message, not just the basic message.	5	4	3	2	1
9. I try to put myself in the speaker's position to better understand his or her views.	5	4	3	2	1
10. I always try to evaluate the logic and consistency of what is being said.	5	4	3	2	1

flow of communication in an organization than consensus about questions of work, authority, prestige, and status relationships.[26]

Finally, success in these efforts also depends upon the ability of all people involved to *listen actively* to what is being said. The role of listening in communication effectiveness cannot be underestimated. In fact, a recent survey of CEOs found that listening to subordinates ranked high as a key ingredient in managerial effectiveness.[27] As the chairman of Pitney Bowes notes, ignoring the wishes and advice of subordinates "won't work here. The employees would throw you out."[28] Subordinates and colleagues often have good ideas and input worthy of notice, and ignoring such input jeopardizes both the corporation and the effectiveness of interpersonal communications within the organization. One way to see this in action is to examine your own listening skills, as shown in Self-Assessment 13.3. See Appendix B for scoring procedures.

PULLING IT ALL TOGETHER

Managers spend a large majority of their time communicating. A skilled manager will be proficient at both sending and receiving messages, though the typical manager is less skilled at effectively receiving. Although the basic model of communication is generalizable across cultures, many differences exist between countries and cultures that affect who, how, when, where, and by what means messages are sent and how they are interpreted. Effective managers must understand this as well as the factors that influence both interpersonal and organizational communication.

SUMMARY OF KEY POINTS

- A basic model of interpersonal communication consists of an encoded message, a decoded message, feedback, and noise. Noise refers to distortions that inhibit message clarity.
- Interpersonal communication can be oral, written, or nonverbal.
- Body language refers to conveying messages to others through such techniques as facial expressions, posture, or eye movements.
- Interpersonal communication is influenced by social situations, perception, interaction involvement, and organization design.
- Information richness is the quality of information transmitted or received. The value of information can vary depending upon the message and the media. Ways to improve information richness were discussed.
- Organizational communication can travel upward, downward or horizontally. Each direction has its own special problems.
- Four special communication roles can be identified. Individuals may serve as gatekeepers, liaisons, opinion leaders, or cosmopolites. They may also assume some combination of these roles. It is important to recognize that communication processes involve different people in different functions and that all of these functions are necessary in order to fulfill the organization's key objectives.
- There are at least four widely recognized person-to-person communication networks, each with different implications for power and authority, speed and accuracy of communication, and group satisfaction. We must also recognize electronic networks in organizational settings.
- Five barriers to effective communication are distortion, omission, overload, timeliness, and acceptance of the message. Specific strategies for improving communication effectiveness exist according to which direction the message is traveling in.

KEY WORDS

active listening
body language

communication network
communication overload

cosmopolite
decoding
distortion
distortion-proof messages
encoding
Fayol's bridge
gatekeeper
information richness
interaction involvement
interpersonal communication

liaison
management by exception
noise
nonverbal communication
omission
opinion leader
organizational communication
principle of sufficiency
screening
symbolic language

QUESTIONS FOR DISCUSSION

1. What is the importance of communication in organizations?
2. Distinguish between interpersonal and organizational communication.
3. Identify several commonplace sources of noise in a communication episode.
4. Why is it important for managers to understand the concept of information richness?
5. Compare and contrast the three primary forms of interpersonal communication.
6. Why is it important to understand variations in communication networks? What experience have you had personally with such networks?
7. Describe various individual communication roles in organizations. Which role is more important in facilitating managerial effectiveness?
8. Identify several barriers to effective communication. How can these barriers be overcome by managers?

NOTES

1. F. Rice, "Champions of Communication," *Fortune,* June 3, 1991, pp. 111–120.
2. C. Barnard, *The Functions of the Executive* (Cambridge, Mass.: Harvard University Press, 1938).
3. H. Mintzberg, *The Nature of Managerial Work* (New York: Harper & Row, 1973).
4. C. Shannon and W. Weaver, *The Mathematical Theory of Communications* (Urbana: University of Illinois Press, 1948). See also R. Huseman, J. Lahiff, and J. Penrose, *Business Communications: Strategies and Skills* (New York: Dryden, 1988).
5. R. Kreitner and A. Kiniki, *Organizational Behavior* (Homewood, Ill.: Irwin, 1989).
6. E. Hall, *The Silent Language* (New York: Doubleday, 1959).
7. F. M. Jabin, L. L. Putnam, K. H. Roberts, and L. W. Porter, eds., *Handbook of Organizational Communication* (Newbury Park, Calif.: Sage, 1987).
8. D. J. Cegals, "Affective and Cognitive Manifestations of Interaction Involvement During Unstructured and Competitive Interactions," *Communication Monographs,* 1984, pp. 320–334.
9. R. Daft and R. Lengel, "Information Richness: A New Approach to Managerial Behavior and Organization Design," in B. Staw and L. Cummings, eds., *Research in Organizational Behavior* (Greenwich, Conn.: JAI Press, 1984), pp. 191–233.
10. Ibid.

11. R. Daft and R. Steers, *Organizations: A Micro/Macro Approach* (Glenview, Ill.: Scott, Foresman, 1986).

12. F. Luthans and J. Larsen, "How Managers Really Communicate," *Human Relations,* February 1986, pp. 167–168.

13. R. Nichols, "Listening Is Good Business," *Management of Personnel Quarterly,* 1962, *2,* pp. 2–10. See also W. Kiechel, "Learn How to Listen," *Fortune,* August 17, 1987, pp. 107–108.

14. W. Read, "Upward Communications in Industrial Hierarchies," *Human Relations,* 1962, *15,* pp. 3-16. See also M. Sinetar, "Building Trust into Corporate Relationships," *Organizational Dynamics,* Winter 1988, pp. 73–79.

15. H. Fayol, *General and Industrial Management* (London: Pitman, 1949).

16. A. Szalagyi, *Management and Performance* (Glenview, Ill.: Scott, Foresman, 1981).

17. E. Rogers and R. Rogers, *Communication in Organizations* (New York: The Free Press, 1976).

18. Ibid., p. 138.

19. Ibid., p. 140.

20. Ibid. See also W. Gudykunst, S. Ting-Toomey, and E. Chua, *Culture and Interpersonal Communication* (Newbury Park, Calif.: Sage, 1988).

21. "DEC President Ken Olsen: On Computer Needs in the 1990s," *High Technology Business,* January 1988, pp. 46–49.

22. J. Watney, *Clive in India* (London: Saxon, 1974), p. 96.

23. D. Rather and G. Gates, *The Palace Guard* (New York: Harper & Row, 1974), p. 109.

24. G. Allison, *Essence of Decision* (Boston: Little, Brown, 1971). See also C. Downs, *Communication Audits in Organizations* (Glenview, Ill.: Scott, Foresman, 1988).

25. S. Prokesch, "The Creative Writing in This Year's Annual Reports," *Business Week,* April 15, 1985, p. 48.

26. J. Jackson, "The Organization and Its Communication Problems," *Journal of Communication,* 1959, *9,* p. 165.

27. M. Barlow, "A Whole New Breed of CEO Running the Big Businesses," *Los Angeles Times,* October 29, 1989, p. D 11.

28. Ibid.

EXPERIENTIAL EXERCISE 13

One-Way Versus Two-Way Communication

This exercise examines the differences between one-way and two-way communication and how they relate to barriers to effective interpersonal communication.

Select one member of the class to serve as the "leader," based on his or her recognized communication skills. All other students should have paper and pen ready and prepare to follow the leader's instructions.

In Stage One, the leader will stand with his or her back to the class and describe a picture (to be called Figure 1) that has been given to the leader. The leader will not answer any questions and will not use any gestures in giving instructions. Without consulting with one another, students will then be asked to draw the figure.

In Stage Two, the same leader faces the class and describes Figure 2. In this case, students can ask as many questions as they wish concerning the figure (although the leader still may not use any gestures). Again without consultation, students will be asked to draw the figure.

Next, the leader will draw both figures on the blackboard. The number of correct student drawings for both Figure 1 and Figure 2 should then be counted. Following this, the class should discuss the meaning of the results in terms of how both the leader and the class felt and performed under conditions of one-way and two-way communication.

Source: Based upon an exercise proposed in H. Leavitt and R. Mueller, "Some Effects of Feedback on Communication," *Human Relations,* 1951, *4,* 401–410.

MANAGEMENT DILEMMA 13

Southern Bank

Southern Bank, established shortly after the Civil War, had developed a distinguished record for prudent, conservative financial service. An independent single-location bank situated in a medium-sized city, it now employs some 750 persons and is one of the largest institutions of its kind in the area.

The bank is organized into eight divisions: General Administrative; Banking; Investment; Trust Administration; Business Development; Management Consulting; Marketing; and Legal. In addition, there are three service groups: Planning and Personnel, Building and Office Services, and the Controller's Group. There are six levels of management in the bank: President; Division; Group; Department; Section; and Unit.

About a hundred of the bank's employees are officers, of whom six are women; another hundred employees are men in various stages of professional banking careers. The remaining 350 employees are women, about fifty of whom are highly trained career specialists. Approximately one half of the female employees are young, unmarried high-school graduates. These women typically work for the bank for two or three years.

Since the inauguration of a new president in 1990 and the subsequent employment of a number of "bright young men," the bank has aggressively been exploring new ways of rendering financial services to its customers. This combination of aggressiveness and innovation has proved to be highly successful in promoting the growth and profitability of the bank. The Management Consulting Division, for example, has become a profitable new service and has also served to bring valued new accounts to the bank.

The top management people in Southern Bank believe that if the institution is to continue to grow through aggressiveness and innovation, the ideas and cooperation of all employees at all levels should be solicited and encouraged. Excellent communication is considered by top management to be vital to the successful operation of this dynamic organization. To this end, Mr. Harold Walsh of the personnel office has been designated as the coordinator of communication and training. Also to this end, a variety of communication techniques, channels, and devices, described on the following pages, have been adopted.

Officers' Meetings

The president meets formally with the board of directors once each month. A day or two after this meeting, the president holds his regular monthly meeting for the bank officers. In this meeting, the president reports on selected topics from the board meeting and reviews the monthly financial statements. At the end of this presentation, which usually lasts about fifteen minutes, the president asks for and responds to questions from the officers in attendance.

Each officer is free to decide which of the nonconfidential topics covered in the officers' meetings, if any, will be reported back to his subordinates. Officers typically do not hold group meetings for this purpose.

The officers' meetings are the only regularly scheduled meetings in the bank designed for the purpose of routinely disseminating information.

Comcom

Comcom (a popular abbreviation for "Communications Committee") was the brainchild of Alice Davey, an officer in the bank, who suggested her idea to President Libbert at a cocktail party one evening two years ago. Mrs. Davey felt that something was needed to bolster communication to and from the lower levels of the organization. The stated objective of comcom was to "promote internal understanding of all matters of common concern at all levels throughout the organization."

President Libbert accepted Mrs. Davey's suggestion and announced the establishment of comcom in a memo dated October 2, 1991:

ALL-BANK MEMO, OCTOBER 2, 1991

For an extended period of time, I have personally felt that a committee should be established to serve as an organized pipeline for the flow of information throughout the organization. We all like to know "what's going on when it's going on," and I believe that the Communications Committee can provide this type of information for all of us. I have appointed the following to serve on this committee:

George Storm—Co-Chairman
Alice Davey—Co-Chairman
Ronald Brooks
John Cassidy
Norman Euler
Ruth Hobgood
Roy Munford
Elmer Nagel
Jack Phillips
Ed Ralston
George Robinson

The committee is currently in the organizational stage, and when its program for effective internal communication has been established, it will be announced.

Frederick E. Libbert

Each of the eleven members of comcom is an officer in the bank; all eight divisions are represented on the committee. George Storm and Alice Davey are the co-chairmen. Each comcom member is expected to solicit questions from employees at all levels in his division for submission to President Libbert for discussion at the monthly officers' meetings. Questions on any topic except grievances and personalities are welcomed.

Comcom members report that they devote perhaps two hours each month to the task of gathering questions. These questions are reviewed at a regular monthly comcom meeting held one week prior to the officers' meeting. Suitable questions are agreed upon and an average of four questions per month are forwarded to the President in advance of the officers' meeting. Most of these questions originate with the comcom members themselves or from persons in the top three levels of the organization.

The President feels that comcom is working well; the comcom co-chairmen feel that the committee is reasonably successful in reaching its objectives; the Personnel Manager feels that comcom is failing to attain its objectives and wonders how it might be made more effective.

Southern Messenger

The *Southern Messenger,* the bank's unusual house organ, originated in 1966 through spontaneous employee interest. A few employees volunteered to produce the publication on their own time if the bank would provide the necessary supplies and equipment.

The *Southern Messenger* is now published bi-monthly entirely on company time and entirely at company expense. The present editor spends about 40 percent of her time at the editor's job; the remainder of her time is spent at a clerical job in the bank. Nine hundred fifty copies of each issue are printed.

The editor has twenty people (including three officers) scattered throughout the bank who serve as informal reporters. These reporters serve on a voluntary basis and tend to obtain and report news items on an opportunistic, rather than a systematic, basis. According to the editor, *Southern Messenger* space allocations run about as follows:

1/3	News about company plans and activities
1/6	Information regarding company policy
1/6	"Profiles of New Employees"
1/12	Gossip and personal items
Rest	Crossword and scientific puzzles

The puzzles have proved to be highly popular with the employees, partly because of their intrinsic appeal and partly because of the prizes offered for the best solutions. The winner for each puzzle receives a pair of theater tickets. The crossword puzzles often contain words related to business and banking.

Task Force

The Communications Task Force was established in February, 1990, at the suggestion of John Templeton, vice-president and personnel manager for the bank. Templeton felt that the task force might be more successful than comcom had been in improving communication to and from personnel in the lower echelons of the bank. The task force consists of five nonofficer employees nominated for the part-time assignment by their respective division heads. Task force members are notified of their appointments by interoffice memorandum from Mr. Templeton.

The task force's basic assignment, as seen by the chairman, Stuart Seaton, is to circulate among and talk with lower-level employees to discover questions, problems, and suggestions from the ranks. These items are then cleared by comcom, which may modify but not block them, after which they are passed on to the Management Committee, which consists of the president and four vice presidents. The personnel manager's memo directing the establishment of the task force is below.

INTEROFFICE MEMORANDUM,

FEBRUARY 1, 1993

To: Stuart Seaton
cc: June Hugger
    Louis Newton
    Benjamin Allen
    Byron Edwards

The Management Committee of Southern Bank is interested in the effectiveness of communications within the company, especially as it affects the ability of supervisors and officers to apply and to interpret to others the policies and procedures of the Company, and to supply information about new developments that should be of interest to all employees.

The Committee requested nominations from Division Heads and selected you to organize and direct the project. You will be assisted in this task force study by the persons listed above as recipients of copies of this memo.

For purposes of this project, "communications" refers to formal and informal exchange and diffusion of information about such matters as:

a. Responsibilities and authorities.
b. Policies governing personnel administration.

   c. Applications of various procedures, such as performance review, purchase requisitions, expense approvals, etc.

   d. Information about significant new developments, new personnel, changes in benefit programs.

   e. Problems in supervision and administration which require the attention of higher levels of management.

To carry out this project, the task force will be expected to:

   a. Determine the best way to assess communications; e.g., by interviews, questionnaires to supervisors, etc.

   b. Consult with the Chairmen of the Communications Committee, with personnel officers, and with the Supervisory Development Groups to establish the kinds of possible communications problems that may exist.

   c. With the Chairmen of the Communications Committee, meet with the Management Committee to discuss findings.

I shall be available to assist in whatever way seems appropriate to the task force.

John Templeton

The task force, which has now been in existence for five months, had a flurry of meetings immediately following its establishment but has had only one meeting during the past two months because of vacations and the demands of other work. To date, the task force has made six suggestions to the Management Committee via comcom.

The Communications Task Force is only one of several task forces presently operating in the bank. Others include the Training, New Services (Marketing), and Trust Administration task forces. Conceptually, each task force is assembled to accomplish a specific, well-defined job, and upon completion of that job the task force is to be disbanded.

Chairman Seaton indicated that Communications Task Force members spend perhaps one hour per week on this assignment, and that most of the group's suggestions to date have originated from among its members.

When asked what caused him to believe there was a need for a Communications Task Force, the personnel manager replied, "There's no feedback around here, particularly from the lower levels. An order, report, or policy change is sent down the line and we wait for questions, or complaints, or some kind of response. What we get back is silence. Absolutely nothing. We find it very difficult to measure the impact of, say, a policy change. It's like shouting down a well and getting no echo. It's eerie."

Asked whether employees complain about poor communication in the bank, the personnel manager replied, "No. Oh, there is an occasional comment in the lunch room, but these are not specific and are mentioned in a very casual way. No one appears to be disturbed about it." The chairman of the Communications Task Force, when asked about the condition of the bank's grapevine, replied, "Healthy."

Performance Review

Top management at Southern Bank believes that the bank's system of regular performance review provides an excellent opportunity to foster communication between each supervisor, at whatever level, and his subordinates. The private performance review sessions, which deal primarily with the employee's job performance, also provide an opportunity for the employee to talk and for superior and subordinate to plan together the employee's future growth and progress.

Performance reviews are held after 90 days for new employees, then annually on the employee's anniversary date. The reviews, which are keyed to the employee's job description, average perhaps thirty minutes in length. The same basic system is used for all employees—for clerks to vice presidents.

Supervisors use a checklist form in rating their subordinates and use this form as a basis for the performance review discussion. Items on the checklist include such things as job knowledge, quality of work, effort, dependability, teamwork, communication, and profit-mindedness. The applicability of each item on the form with respect to the employee's particular job is recorded. The supervisor then checks whether the employee's performance "exceeds," "meets," or "falls short" of standard on each item. The resulting profile provides the core of the review discussion.

The supervisor retains the checklist rating form and notifies the personnel office regarding the result of the review in a separate summary report. Most employees receive a pay increase following their annual performance review. The amount of this increase, which usually ranges between 5 percent and 10 percent of present rate, depends upon the supervisor's evaluation of the employee's performance. The typical supervisor in the bank has from eight to ten subordinates to review during the course of a year.

The personnel manager believes that many of the performance reviews are too superficial, but wonders how much time and effort a supervisor should spend in reviewing a young clerk who may leave the bank next month. He also is concerned about what he believes to be inadequate training in interviewing techniques on the part of some supervisors in the bank. (Supervisors receive nine hours of in-bank training on the performance review system, of which one hour is devoted to interviewing techniques.)

When asked how the nonmanagement people feel about the performance review system, the personnel manager said, "We really don't know. There is very little feedback. Occasionally, in an exit interview, a terminating employee will say that his supervisor had not kept him informed as to the adequacy of his performance or about his future potential with the bank."

All-Bank Memo

When information on matters of bank-wide interest is to be disseminated, an "All-Bank Memo" is used. Each employee receives a personal copy. An average of two All-Bank Memos per month are issued. All-Bank Memos may deal with such matters as holiday announcements, changing hours of work, etc. Occasionally an All-Bank Memo deals with a policy change. In such cases, supervisors sometimes call their subordinates together to discuss the change and to answer pertinent questions.

On the basis of this case, how would you respond to the following?

1. What are the methods of communication used within Southern Bank? What are the objectives of each method?
2. Why do people disagree on the effectiveness of the media?
3. What problems do you see in the methods currently being used? How could these media be used differently?

Source: Reprinted by permission of Jack Rettig, School of Business Administration, Oregon State University, Corvallis, Oregon.

Individual and Group Decision Making

The Management Challenge

- To understand the role of risk and uncertainty in decision making.
- To recognize and account for the limits of rationality in the decision process and to seek the highest-quality decisions possible.
- To know when decisions are best made individually and when they are best made collectively.
- To facilitate group participation in decision making where appropriate.
- To recognize barriers to decision making and know how to overcome them.

CLOSE UP   A Tale of Two Decision Makers

Increased complaints by foreign customers about mistakes and misunderstandings made by salespeople led Lonnie Combs to believe that his sales force needed some cross-cultural training in order to be more effective with the growing international customer base. His first step in finding a trainer was to ask his assistant to gather general information on cross-cultural training as well as specific information on cross-cultural sales training. Once this information was put together, Lonnie called some professional associates and asked for their recommendations of firms for cross-cultural training. He also called a professor at the local university for suggestions. Based on these recommendations, he selected three firms and invited them to make proposals for a cross-cultural training seminar for his 30 salespeople. He invited his assistant and the three district sales managers to be present at the presentations by each of the three firms. After the presentations, he asked each of the others what they thought of the presentation and proposal. Within a week after the last presentation, Lonnie decided to award the contract for a three-day seminar and a one-day follow-up to the second firm that presented.

Increased complaints by foreign customers about mistakes and misunderstanding made by salespeople led Jiro Kurokawa to believe that his sales force needed some cross-cultural training in order to be more effective with a growing international customer base. His first step in finding a trainer was to ask his district sales managers if they thought their salespeople were having any special problems with foreign customers. The sales managers in turn spoke with their salespeople to get their view on the question. In general both the salespeople themselves and the sales managers felt that there were some cases of misunderstandings or mistakes committed by salespeople because of a lack of knowledge about specific norms and practices of etiquette for certain foreign customers. Once all were in agreement that this lack of cross-cultural knowledge was a major factor of customers complaints and that some training might be an effective means of solving this problem, Jiro asked his subordinates as well as peers in other departments for suggestions of firms that might be able to effectively conduct the desired training. Jiro also met with the head of the marketing department to talk about the proposed training to make sure that the marketing manager supported the idea and to provide the manager with a chance to provide input into the content of the training and how the content related to marketing activities. Jiro repeated this process with the three manufacturing managers and the general administration manager.

After he had secured the cooperation and endorsement and input of these other managers, Jiro had one of his district sales managers write up a short formal proposal (called *ringisho* in Japanese) and circulate it among the relevant department heads. Once all the department heads had signed the *ringisho,* Jiro passed it on to his boss, who in turn signed it. In the process of all the hall conversations, Jiro had come to the conclusion that two firms were respected by the strong majority of people. He had each of the firms present their proposal for the training. He as well as several of the district sales managers attended at least part of each presentation.

After the presentations, Jiro discussed both proposals at length with the district managers. He also had several conversations after work at a local restaurant with the other department heads. Three months after the last firm had made their presentation, the second firm was informed that they had been selected to provide a three-day seminar and a one-day follow-up cross-cultural training seminar.[1]

This true but disguised case illustrates that while making decisions is clearly one of management's primary responsibilities, there are different ways in which they can be made. Management decisions may involve allocating scarce resources, hiring employees, investing capital, or introducing new products. If resources were abundant, few difficult decisions would be necessary; however, that is not usually the case. As a result, managers need to be aware of the basic processes by which decisions are made in organizations. Several frameworks are available to help explain how decisions are made. Each framework is based on different assumptions about the nature of people at work. An informed manager should understand the models and the different assumptions underlying each.

Another concern of management is the extent to which subordinates should be included in decisions affecting their jobs. When are group decisions superior (or inferior) to individual ones? How much participation can be accommodated in work organizations where managers still assume responsibility for group actions? The phenomena of groupthink and escalating commitment have emerged as important considerations in decision making. How do these phenomena affect decision quality? Finally, what are some strategies that can be used by managers to improve decisions in organizations? A knowledge of these strategies can help managers make the most efficient use of their limited time and resources in their efforts to facilitate goal attainment.

Because of the importance of decision making for managerial effectiveness, we will consider this topic in some detail. First, decision making will be defined, and the general process will be outlined. Next, four major models of decision-making processes will be compared, along with the assumptions underlying each model. Following this, individual and group decision making will be compared, and a normative model of participation in decision making will be presented. Next, the issue of decision speed and quality is addressed. Following this, several constraints on the decision process will be considered, including groupthink and escalating commitment to a course of action. In closing, six strategies for improving the quality and acceptability of decisions will be presented. Throughout, emphasis will be on major lessons for management that will ease the responsibility of decision making.

DECISION MAKING: BASIC CONCEPTS

A common characteristic of effective leaders and effective work groups is their ability to make decisions that are appropriate, timely, and acceptable. If organizational effectiveness is the ability to secure and utilize resources in the pursuit of organizational goals, the decision-making processes that determine how these resources are acquired and used emerge as a central topic in organizational analysis. For our purposes here, we define *decision making* as a process of specifying the nature of a particular problem and selecting among available alternatives in order to solve it.[2] We look at how individuals and groups attempt to identify problem areas, examine various potential solutions to problems, and select the most suitable solution (or solutions) in light of the particular situation.

In this process, people generally go through two distinct stages—problem formulation and problem solution (see Exhibit 14.1). *Problem formulation* involves the acquisition of information, the development of desired performance expectations, and the diagnosis of causal relationships affecting the problem. A problem exists when a manager detects a gap between existing and desired performance. The manager then analyzes the nature and causes of the problem. On the basis of this analysis, the manager then moves to the *problem solution* phase, where efforts are made to consider alternative solutions and to select and implement that course of action most appropriate for the problem. Following the implementation of the chosen solution, the manager monitors the situation to determine the extent to which that solution was successful.

Types of Decisions

The decision-making process is affected to a large extent by whether the decision is programmed or nonprogrammed. A *programmed decision* represents a standardized response to a simple or routine problem. The nature of the problem is well defined and clearly understood by the decision maker, as is the array of possible solutions. For example, programmed decisions can be seen in college admission decisions, reimbursement for managers' travel expenses, and promotion decisions with many unionized personnel. In all of these decisions, specific criteria can be identified (e.g., grade-point and test scores for college admission, per diem allowances for expense account reimbursements, or seniority for union promotions). The programmed decision process is characterized by high levels of certainty for both the problem formulation and the problem solution phases, and rules and procedures typically spell out exactly how one is to respond.

On the other hand, *nonprogrammed decisions* occur in response to problems that are either poorly defined or novel. For example, should a university president with limited funds expand the size of the business school to

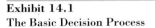

Exhibit 14.1
The Basic Decision Process

Problem Formulation

Monitor information, compare data to performance expectations, diagnose reasons and causes for shortcomings

Problem Solution

Search for alternative answers, appraise alternatives, select and implement best alternative

Source: R. Daft and R. Steers, *Organizations: A Micro/Macro Approach* (Glenview, Ill.: Scott, Foresman, 1986), p. 439. Copyright © 1986 Scott, Foresman and Company.

meet growing student demand, or should the university's science facilities be expanded in order to bring in more federal research contracts? No alternative is clearly correct; instead, he or she must weigh the alternatives and their consequences carefully to make a *unique* —nonprogrammed—decision. Preceding decisions will be of little help.

Although managers at all levels in the organizational hierarchy make decisions, there is a distinct relationship between one's level in the hierarchy and the type of decisions one typically faces. As shown in Exhibit 14.2, top managers usually face nonprogrammed decisions, such as in the case of the university president above. College deans or department heads—let alone faculty or students—seldom get to make such decisions. On the other hand, lower-level managers (such as first-line supervisors) typically focus on programmed, or routine, decisions. Their options and resources—and risks—are usually far fewer than those of top managers. And, as we might expect, middle managers fall somewhere in between.

One final point should be made here concerning the relationship between programmed and nonprogrammed decisions. Whereas programmed decisions are usually made through structured bureaucratic techniques (such as standard operating procedures), nonprogrammed decisions must be made by managers using available information and their own judgment. Often, such decisions must be made under considerable time pressure. As a result, there is a tendency among managers to let programmed activities overshadow nonprogrammed activities. Thus, if a manager has a series of decisions to make, those that are routine and repetitive in nature will tend to be made before those that are unique and require considerable thought. Presumably, this happens because managers wish to clear their desks so they can concentrate on the

Exhibit 14.2
Relationship of Decision
Type to Management Level
in Organizations

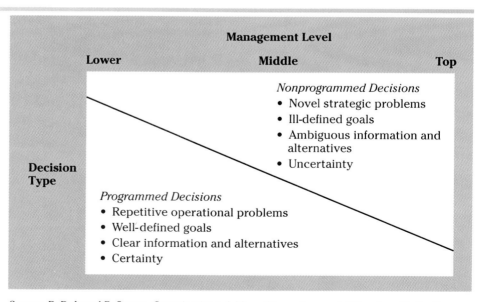

Source: R. Daft and R. Steers, *Organizations: A Micro/Macro Approach* (Glenview, Ill.: Scott, Foresman, 1986), p. 442. Copyright © 1986 Scott, Foresman and Company.

really serious problems. Unfortunately, however, because of time pressures, managers often never actually get to the more difficult—and perhaps more important—decisions. This tendency is called *Gresham's Law of Planning.*[3]

The implications of Gresham's Law for managerial decision making are clear. Provisions must be made to ensure that decisions are made in a timely fashion. This can be done in several ways, including having special organizational units assume this responsibility. Staff units in major companies serve this purpose. Where this is not possible, time management programs may be helpful in training managers to better allocate their limited time. In any event, it is important for managers to ensure that nonprogrammed decisions receive the time and attention they deserve.

Risk, Uncertainty, and Environmental Scanning

Especially in nonprogrammed decisions (compared to programmed decisions), managers often face problems and challenges that are characterized by higher levels of risk and *uncertainty.* For the university president, for example, making the wrong decision could be costly, both financially and politically. In fact, the president's job may depend on making the "right" decision. If you expand the science facility, there is no guarantee that the added faculty will indeed bring in more contracts and grants; besides, by doing so, you may be denying admission to a large number of qualified business students. You will also alienate the business students and faculty. On the other hand, building the business programs will almost certainly alienate the science students and faculty, may allow a rival university to get ahead, and may prompt many of your best scientists to go elsewhere. Risks and uncertainty permeate such decisions.

As a result, decision makers usually engage in considerable *environmental scanning* prior to making the decision. That is, they will seek out as much useful information as they can from outside the organization. In this case, if our university president discovers that a rival school is about to expand its own science complex and wants to hire away your best scientists, he may wish to defend what he has, especially if he views the business school as expendable. On the other hand, if his state's governor and the legislature have made it clear that they want more business education to make the state more competitive, this too is helpful information. In other words, through environmental scanning, managers attempt to gain useful information that can lead to a higher quality decision.

By way of summary, then, at least three components to a decision episode can be identified (see Exhibit 14.3).[4] First, there are the characteristics of the decision maker. These include such factors as his or her knowledge of the problem, ability to analyze and solve it, and motivation to solve it. Second are the characteristics of the problem itself. These factors include the extent to which the nature of the problem is familiar to the managers, the ambiguity and complexity of the problem, and the extent to which the problem is stable or volatile. Third, the decision episode includes the environment in which the decision is to be made. Included here are the degree to which the decision is

Exhibit 14.3
Major Influences on the
Decision Process

Decision-Maker Characteristics

- Knowledge
- Ability
- Motivation

Problem Characteristics

- Unfamiliarity
- Ambiguity
- Complexity
- Instability

Decision Environment Characteristics

- Irreversibility
- Significance
- Accountability
- Time and/or monetary constraints

irreversible, its significance, who is accountable for the decision and its consequences, and any time or money constraints involved in the decision process. Taken together, these sets of factors represent the major ingredients involved in the decision.

INDIVIDUAL DECISION MAKING

It is no easy task to outline or diagram the details of the decision-making process. We actually know very little about how individuals and groups make decisions.[5] Even so, at least four attempts have been made that are worthy of note. While reading these models, note the different assumptions they make about the nature of decision makers; also note the differences in focus. These three models are (1) the rational/classic model; (2) the administrative, or bounded rationality, model; and (3) the retrospective decision-making model. Each model is useful for understanding the nature of decision processes in organizations.

The Rational/Classical Model

The *rational model* (also known as the *classical model*) represents the earliest attempt to model decision processes.[6] It is viewed by some as the original classical approach to understanding decision processes. Briefly, this model rests on two assumptions: (1) people are economically rational, and (2) people attempt to maximize outcomes in an orderly and sequential process.

Economic rationality, a basic concept in many early models of decision making, exists when people attempt to objectively *maximize* measured advantage, such as money or units of goods produced. That is, it is assumed that people will select the decision or course of action that has the greatest advantage or payoff from among the many alternatives; and furthermore, they go about this search in a planned, orderly, and logical fashion. This model has also been referred to as the *economic man model.*[7]

A basic rational, or classical, decision model is shown in Exhibit 14.4. As can be seen, the model suggests the following orderly steps in the decision process; they are based on the above two assumptions about the nature of people:

▓ Continually monitor the decision environment.

▓ Identify any problems as they emerge.

▓ Diagnose each problem to discover its underlying characteristics.

▓ Develop alternative solutions to the problem.

▓ Consider the consequences of each alternative as well as the likelihood of success of each.

▓ Choose the best alternative by comparing the consequences of each alternative with the decision objectives.

▓ Implement the chosen alternative.

The simplicity of the rational model is disarming. In fact, however, the model rests on two rather questionable foundations.[8] First, the model portrays individuals or groups capable of gathering all necessary information for a decision. It assumes having complete information, which is rarely achieved. As a result, rationality itself is rarely achieved. As Nobel laureate Herbert Simon notes:

Exhibit 14.4
Steps in the Rational
Decision Process

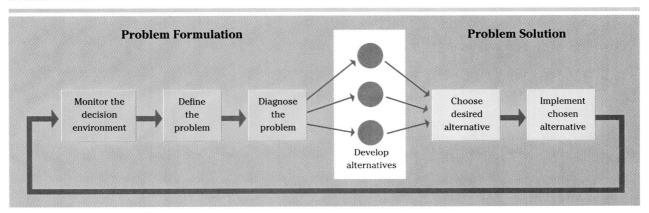

Source: R. Daft and R. Steers, *Organizations: A Micro/Macro Approach* (Glenview, Ill.: Scott, Foresman, 1986), p. 442. Copyright © 1986 Scott, Foresman and Company.

(1) Rationality requires a complete knowledge and anticipation of the consequences that will follow on each choice. In fact, knowledge of consequences is always fragmentary. (2) Since these consequences lie in the future, imagination must supply the lack of experienced feeling in attaching value to them. But values can be only imperfectly anticipated. (3) Rationality requires a choice among all possible alternative behaviors. In actual behavior, only a very few of all these possible alternatives ever come to mind.[9]

In addition, the rational model is based on the assumption that people can process the tremendous amounts of information generated for one decision. It assumes that people can (1) mentally store the information in some stable form, (2) manipulate the information in a series of complex calculations designed to provide expected values, and (3) rank all the consequences in a consistent fashion for purposes of identifying the preferred alternative. Unfortunately, a large body of research has shown that the human mind is incapable of executing such transactions at the level and magnitude that would be required for complex decisions. In fact, we can identify a series of factors that inhibit people's ability to accurately identify and analyze problems, as shown in Exhibit 14.5.

Thus, while the rational model is a useful representation of how decisions should be made (that is, a prescriptive model), it seems to fall somewhat short concerning how decisions actually *are* made.

The Bounded Rationality Model

An alternative model, one not based on the above assumptions, has been presented by Simon.[10] This model is called the *bounded rationality model* (or the *administrative man model*). As the name implies, this model does not assume individual rationality in the decision process. Instead, it assumes that people, while they may seek the best solution, usually settle for much less because the decisions they confront typically demand greater information processing capabilities than they possess. They seek a kind of bounded (or limited) rationality in decisions.

The concept of bounded rationality attempts to describe decision processes in terms of three mechanisms. First, using *sequential attention to alternative solutions,* people examine possible solutions to a problem one at a time. Instead of identifying all possible solutions and selecting the best (as suggested in the rational model), people identify and evaluate various alternatives individually. If the first solution fails to work or is evaluated as unworkable, it is discarded, and another solution is considered. When an acceptable (though not necessarily the best) solution is found, search behavior is discontinued.

The second mechanism is the use of heuristics. A *heuristic* is a rule that guides the search for alternatives into areas that have a high probability for yielding satisfactory solutions. For instance, some companies continually hire MBAs from certain schools because in the past such graduates have performed well for the company. According to the bounded rationality model,

Exhibit 14.5
Factors that Inhibit Accurate
Problem Identification
and Analysis

Factor	Characteristics
Informational bias	A reluctance to communicate negative information.
Uncertainty absorption	A tendency for information to lose its uncertainty as it is passed along, resulting in information that is seen as more precise than it really is.
Selective perception	A tendency to ignore or avoid certain information, especially ambiguous information.
Stereotyping	Making a decision about someone on the basis of characteristics ascribed by others.
Cognitive complexity	The amount of information people can process at one time.
Stress	Can reduce people's ability to cope with informational demands.

Source: Adapted from R. N. Taylor, *Behavioral Decision Making* (Glenview, Ill.: Scott, Foresman, 1984), pp. 16–23.

decision makers use heuristics to reduce large problems to manageable propositions so decisions can be made rapidly. They look for obvious solutions or previous solutions that worked in similar situations.

The third mechanism is the concept of *satisficing* (not to be confused with "satisfying"). Whereas the rational model focused on the decision maker as an optimizer, this model sees him or her as a satisficer. As explained by March and Simon:

> An alternative is *optimal* if (1) there exists a set of criteria that permits all alternatives to be compared and (2) the alternative in question is preferred, by these criteria, to all other alternatives. An alternative is satisfactory if (1) there exists a set of criteria that describes minimally satisfactory alternatives, and (2) the alternative in question meets or exceeds all these criteria . . . Finding that optimal alternative is a radically different problem from finding a satisfactory alternative . . . To optimize requires processing several orders of magnitude more complex than those required to satisfice.[11]

On the basis of these three assumptions about decision makers, it is possible to outline the decision process as seen from the standpoint of the bounded rationality model. As shown in Exhibit 14.6, the model consists of eight steps:

1. Set the goal to be pursued, or define the problem to be solved.
2. Establish an appropriate level of aspiration, or criterion level (that is, when do you know that a solution is sufficiently positive to be acceptable, even if it is not perfect?).

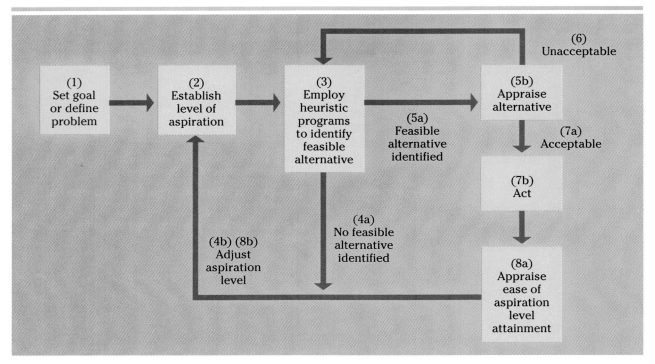

Exhibit 14.6
The Bounded Rationality
Model of Decision Making

Source: From Orlando Behling and Chester Schriesheim, *Organizational Behavior: Theory, Research, and Application.* Copyright © 1976 by Allyn and Bacon. Reprinted by permission.

3. Employ heuristics to narrow problem space to a *single* promising alternative.
4. If no feasible alternative is identified (4a), lower the aspiration level, and (4b) begin the search for a new alternative solution (repeat steps 2 and 3).
5. After identifying a feasible alternative (5a), evaluate it to determine its acceptability (5b).
6. If the individual alternative is unacceptable, initiate search for a new alternative solution (repeat steps 3–5).
7. If the identified alternative is acceptable (7a), implement the solution (7b).
8. Following implementation, evaluate the ease with which the goal was (or was not) attained (8a), and raise or lower the level of aspiration accordingly on future decisions of this type (8b).

Certainly, this decision process is quite different from the rational model. In it we do not seek the *best* solution; instead, we look for a solution that is acceptable. The search behavior is sequential, involving the evaluation of one or two solutions at once. Finally, in contrast to the prescriptive rational model, it is claimed that the bounded rationality model is *descriptive;* that is, it describes how decision makers actually arrive at the identification of solutions to organizational problems.

IN PRACTICE
The President's New Plane

Shortly after Ronald Reagan became president of the United States in 1981, discussions arose concerning the deteriorating state of Air Force One, the president's plane. At a time when most airlines were replacing their Boeing 707s because of their noise and expense, the nation's president was still "stuck" with his. Several parties began pushing for a new plane (or, more accurately, several new planes) for the president. It was argued that the existing plane was old and unsafe, was too small for the president's entourage, and did not carry sufficient status for the nation's leader. A decision was therefore made in 1981 to replace the 707.

No sooner had the decision been made when a major problem emerged. The decision makers were seeking an optimal solution, and none was available. The new plane had to meet two primary criteria. First, it had to be made in the United States, for political reasons. It simply wouldn't look right for the American president to be flying around in an Ilyushin-62. And second, the Secret Service insisted that the plane have four engines, for safety reasons. (Presumably, three engines made in the United States might be insufficient to keep the plane aloft.) This created a real dilemma. The wide-bodied DC-10 and L-1011 were large enough and were American-made but had only three engines. The more recent Boeing 757 and 767 had only two engines.

This left only the Boeing 747. But here, too, were problems. Many airport runways were not long enough to allow a 747 to land. Moreover, the massive 747 might send a signal of governmental extravagance in a time of financial exigency. As a result, a decision was made to make no decision. "It was a null set," noted one observer. There was no acceptable solution.

However, over time it was realized that something had to be done. Repairs and upkeep on the old 707 were mounting, and the president's entourage was increasing in size. Finally, in 1988, the decision makers tried again. This time, without changing the decision rules, they decided to satisfice—that is, to seek a decision that was acceptable, if not perfect. They chose the 747 (actually, two of them). This met both criteria (it was American-made and had four engines). At the same time, Congress was asked to increase funding for airport expansions around the country. And because economic conditions in the late 1980s had improved, it was thought that the massive expenditure would probably be acceptable to the American public. The first of two planes was delivered in September 1990.[12]

The Retrospective Decision Model

A third model deals primarily with nonprogrammed decisions and focuses on how decision makers attempt to rationalize their choices on a retrospective basis. It relies heavily on the theory of cognitive dissonance discussed in Chapter 3. It has been variously referred to as the *retrospective decision model* or the *implicit favorite model*.[13]

This model emerged when MIT professor Per Soelberg observed the job choice processes of graduating business students and noted that, in many cases, the students identified implicit favorites (that is, the alternative they wanted to win) very early in the recruiting and choice process. For example, one student might identify a manufacturer in Arizona as a favorite. However, they continued their search for additional alternatives and quickly selected the best alternate (or second) candidate, known as the "confirmation candidate." To continue our example, the student might select a high tech firm in California as an alternate firm. Next, the students attempted to develop decision rules that demonstrated unequivocally that the implicit favorite was superior to the confirmation candidate. This was done through the perceptual distortion of information about the two alternatives and through weighting systems designed to highlight the positive features of the implicit favorite. For example, the student might leave out vacation time as a criterion because the favorite firm (i.e., the one in Arizona) has a very poor vacation policy compared to the alternate firm in California. However, the student might heavily weight a criterion of housing costs because housing is cheaper in the location of the student's favored choice. Finally, after a decision rule was derived that clearly favored the implicit favorite, the decision was announced. The student would accept the job in Arizona.

Ironically, Soelberg noted, the implicit favorite was typically superior to the confirmation candidate on only one or two dimensions. Even so, the decision makers generally characterized their decision rules as being multidimensional in nature. For example, in the case of the two firms in Arizona and California, the jobs offered were quite similar and the salary, travel, benefits, and promotion prospects were also nearly identical.

The process is shown in Exhibit 14.7. As noted, the entire process is designed to justify to the individual, through the guise of scientific rigor, a nonprogrammed decision that has already been made in an intuitive fashion.

Exhibit 14.7
The Retrospective
Decision Model

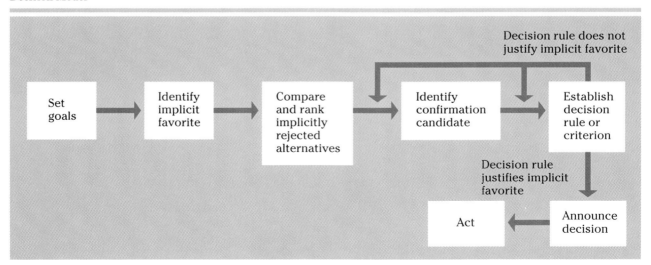

Source: From Orlando Behling and Chester Schriesheim, *Organizational Behavior: Theory, Research, and Application.* Copyright © 1976 by Allyn and Bacon. Reprinted by permission.

By this means, the individual becomes convinced that he or she is acting in a rational fashion and making a logical decision on an important topic. Before dismissing this approach as naive or simplistic, consider how many times you have made a decision in such a way when looking for clothes, cars, stereo systems, and so on. You start with an item that catches your eye and then spend considerable time convincing yourself and your friends that this is the "best" choice. If your implicit favorite is the cheapest among the competition, you emphasize price; if it is not, you emphasize quality or styling. Ultimately, you end up buying the item you saw in the first place, feeling comfortable that you made the right choice.

GROUP DECISION MAKING

The three models described above attempt to explain certain aspects of individual decision making. However, these same models can help us understand some aspects of group decision making also. Many of the basic processes remain the same. For instance, using the rational model, we can observe that both individuals and groups often identify money as an objective to be sought. Both individuals and groups in some cases attempt to identify all possible outcomes before selecting one, and, more than likely, both will fail in such attempts. Both individuals and groups are often observed engaging in satisficing behavior or using heuristics in the decision process. And both individuals and groups develop implicit favorites and attempt to justify those favorites by procedures that appear to others to be rationalization.

Role of Groups in Decision Making

What makes group decision making different is the social interaction patterns implicit in the decision process. A new social dimension has been added, thereby complicating decision dynamics. As we will see, the major difference here is with respect to the role played by *group participation* in the decision-making process. There are situations where group decision making can be an asset and other times when it can be a liability, and the trick for the manager is to discover how and when to allow participation.

Clearly, the nature of the decision-making process changes noticeably when groups enter the picture. Some assets and liabilities of group decision making are shown in Exhibit 14.8. Going one step further, let us look at what we know about the impact of groups in the decision process itself, especially for nonprogrammed decisions.[14]

> In *establishing objectives,* groups are typically superior to individuals in that they possess greater cumulative knowledge to bring to bear on problems.
>
> In *identifying alternatives,* individual efforts are important to ensure that different and perhaps unique solutions are identified from various functional areas that later can be considered by the group.

Exhibit 14.8
Assets and Liabilities of
Group Decision Making

Assets	Liabilities
• Groups can accumulate more knowledge and facts.	• Groups often work more slowly than individuals.
• Groups have a broader perspective and consider more alternative solutions.	• Group decisions involve considerable compromise that may lead to less than optimal decisions.
• Individuals who participate in decisions are more satisfied with the decision and are more likely to support it.	• Groups are often dominated by one individual or a small clique, thereby negating many of the virtues of group processes.
• Group decision processes serve an important communication function as well as a useful political function.	• Overreliance on group decision making can inhibit management's ability to act quickly and decisively when necessary.

In *evaluating alternatives,* group judgment is often superior to individual judgment, because it brings into play a wider range of viewpoints.

In *choosing alternatives,* involving group members often leads to greater acceptance of the final outcome.

In *implementing the choice,* individual responsibility is generally superior to group responsibility. Regardless of whether decisions are made individually or collectively, individuals perform better in carrying out the decision than groups do.

Hence, it is not possible to conclude that either individual or group decision making is superior. Rather, the specific situations and the individuals involved must be considered before choosing a decision technique.

One question about the effects of participation remains to be asked: Why does participation seem to work in many instances? A partial answer to this question has been offered by Ebert and Mitchell.[15] First, they suggest that participation clarifies organizational contingencies so employees understand more fully what is expected of them. Second, it increases the likelihood that employees will work for rewards and outcomes they value. Third, it heightens the effects of social influence on behavior. Finally, it enlarges the amount of control employees have over their own behavior. In many cases, participation in decision making can represent a useful vehicle for facilitating both organizational goal attainment and personal need satisfaction.

If you are interested in seeing how much participation you have or had on your own current or previous job, complete Self-Assessment 14.1. This instrument asks you about how much participation you feel you are given by your supervisor. When you have answered all ten items, follow the scoring procedures outlined in Appendix B.

The Garbage Can Model

One model that recognizes the role of group processes in decision making is known by the rather strange title of the *garbage can model.* This is a recent model and was advanced by James March and his colleagues.[16] In essence,

SELF-ASSESSMENT 14.1
How Participative Is Your Boss?

Instructions: Think of a supervisor you have had on a paid or unpaid job (or project), and answer the following items with this person in mind. Circle the number that best approximates your answers.

		Strongly Disagree				Strongly Agree
1.	My boss actively encourages everyone to participate.	1	2	3	4	5
2.	My boss creates an atmosphere of trust and openness.	1	2	3	4	5
3.	My boss shares information with us.	1	2	3	4	5
4.	My boss calls group meetings often.	1	2	3	4	5
5.	My boss tries to develop teamwork among the group.	1	2	3	4	5
6.	My boss asks for our views on important matters.	1	2	3	4	5
7.	My boss reinforces members who participate.	1	2	3	4	5
8.	My boss tries to facilitate group consensus.	1	2	3	4	5
9.	My boss actively listens to our opinions.	1	2	3	4	5
10.	My boss makes sure we have the resources to make a good decision.	1	2	3	4	5

the garbage can model begins by focusing on those situations in which decisions are being made under conditions of high uncertainty. In particular, March and his associates coined the term *organized anarchies* to describe an organization or decision episode characterized by three general factors: (1) *problematic preferences,* where problems, alternatives, preferences, and solutions are unclear, ambiguous, or in dispute among the decision makers; (2) *unclear technology,* where trial and error are necessary to find the appropriate solution; and (3) *fluid participation,* where members of the decision group come and go in accordance with the time they have to invest in the problem. In short, organized anarchies exist when the people involved are unclear about what the problem and possible range of solutions are, where little is known about how to solve the problem because of its uniqueness, and where the decision makers themselves have varying amounts of time to spend on the problem because of other commitments.

In such situations, considerable uncertainty is created for the decision makers, causing the process to become disorganized and chaotic. Examples of organized anarchies are frequent in organizational settings. For example, consider the decision to launch a new product line (e.g., when Toyota decided to produce Lexus to compete head-on with Mercedes and BMW), a new defense system (e.g., the B-2 bomber), or a new organizational form (e.g., the new organization emerging from a merger, such as RJR). In each case, uncertainty (about markets, about safety and effectiveness, about how to reorganize efficiently and effectively) rules.

Under such circumstances, the garbage can model argues, decisions are made as a result of the almost random interaction of four factors: (1) the problems, (2) the solutions, (3) the participants, and (4) the choice opportunities. In other words the model says, in essence, that all of the ingredients of a good or bad decision are "floating around" in organizational space—called, for lack of a better phrase, a garbage can. In the garbage can we have problems in search of solutions, solutions in search of problems, people entering and leaving the organization, and choice opportunities (or unique windows of opportunity). Thus, decisions are made when the right people identify the right problem and attach to it the right solution at the right time. At other times, things simply do not come together, and decisions (or at least good decisions) are not made. As a result, decision quality depends heavily on timing (i.e., when these four variables come together at a fortuitous time). This process can be seen in the decision by Mazda to build a new sports car for the North American market.

International Challenge

IN PRACTICE
The Mazda Miata

An interesting application of the garbage can model can be seen in the developments that led up to the introduction by Mazda of the new sports car called Miata. The original idea for a sports car was proposed by Mazda's American design team in Irvine, California. However, in Tokyo, the Japanese executives failed to see either the market or the need for such a car. After all, Mazda already had the RX-7; why should it build a second sports car?

Despite resistance, the American design team persisted and continued to push Mazda to accept the new car. In short, the car had advocates who were committed to a positive decision. Moreover, as it turned out, Mazda was looking for ways to enhance market share in the United States and came to realize that a car such as the Miata, if successful, would help Mazda reach its goal. Opportunity was present; Pontiac had just dropped its popular Fiero car, leaving a hole in the market.

Finally, after several years of persistence, The Senior Managing Director for Advanced Technology approved of the idea and several teams began their design and prototype programs. The American design team had visions of the old MG and other sports cars and came up with a design that had rear-wheel drive, styling that made dramatic use of lights and shadows, a shifter with a throw of only 1.8 inches and an exhaust sound (selected from over 100) that was strong but not overbearing. When executives in Japan drove the prototype in southern California, the public reaction they got from onlookers was so strong that they decided to go ahead with the American design team's proposal without any focus groups or survey research studies. The Miata was born—and proved to be an overnight success. As it turned out, all four factors discussed above were present and ultimately matched up in a way that spelled success both for the design team and for Mazda.[17]

A NORMATIVE MODEL OF DECISION MAKING

A central issue facing managers is the extent to which they should allow their subordinates in the work group to participate in decisions affecting their own jobs. Participation represents one method of decentralizing authority and influence throughout an organization. It is believed that this action will in many cases lead to improved decision quality, increased commitment of members to decision outcomes, and the satisfaction resulting from involvement. These results are often associated with effective organizations.

On the basis of a long-term research project, Victor Vroom and his colleagues Phillip Yetton and Arthur Jago have developed a theory of participation in decision making that has clear managerial implications.[18] The model is called the *normative theory of leadership and decision making.* It is difficult to determine whether this model is really a model of leadership or a model of decision making. In essence, the model focuses on the extent to which subordinates should be allowed to participate in decisions affecting their jobs. In addition, it also considers how managers should behave in decision-making situations. Suffice it to say that the Vroom-Yetton-Jago model is a theory of how leaders should approach group-related decisions.

What makes the normative model unique is its attempt to prescribe correct leader behavior regarding the degree of allowed participation. The model rests on several assumptions, one being (like Fiedler's contingency theory of leadership; see Chapter 12) that there is no single leadership style that is appropriate for all situations. Instead, leaders must develop a repertoire of responses ranging from autocratic to consultative and employ the style that is most appropriate to the particular situation. Unlike Fiedler's model, however, this model assumes that leaders must adapt their style to the situation. Fiedler, it will be remembered, argues that situations should be altered to match what he considers a fairly unalterable leader style.

Two primary factors form the basis of the model: (1) influences on decision effectiveness and (2) variations in leader style with respect to the amount of subordinate participation.

Decision Effectiveness: Quality, Acceptance, and Timeliness

Whereas Fiedler uses group performance as the evaluation criterion for whether or not a leader is effective, the normative model uses *decision effectiveness.* Decision effectiveness is evaluated on the basis of three factors:

1. *Decision quality. Decision quality* refers to the extent to which decisions under consideration are important for facilitating group performance. For instance, a decision on where to place a water cooler in a plant requires low decision quality, because it has little impact on group performance, whereas a decision of where to place a new machine in the work flow could significantly affect performance and requires high decision quality.

2. *Decision acceptance. Decision acceptance* refers to how important it is for group members to accept decisions in order for them to be successfully

implemented. Some decisions do not require group acceptance to be successfully executed (what color to paint the walls in an office), whereas others must be accepted by group members in order to be successful (setting sales objectives).

3. *Timeliness. Time required to reach a decision* is the third factor. Decisions must be made in a timely fashion. Some decisions can be made slowly (choice of color when repainting an office), whereas others may require immediate action (whether or not to invest in a particular stock).

Leader Decision-Making Styles

On the basis of the above definition of what constitutes an effective decision, the normative model next turns its attention to how leaders might behave relative to group members in order to arrive at these decisions. The model suggests that leaders have five decision-making styles available to them and that these five styles can be placed on a continuum from highly autocratic (called *A I* to highly participative (called *G II*). The five styles are shown in Exhibit 14.9. As shown, *A* represents a more autocratic style of leadership; *C* represents a more consultative style; and *G* represents a highly consultative, or group, decision.

Again, remember that one manager should be able to exhibit all five different styles, depending upon particular situations. The manager may be called upon to make an *A I* decision at one time, followed by a *G II* decision a short time later. Needless to say, this presumes the manager has the intuition to recognize the appropriate style for a given problem and the flexibility to implement that style.

Exhibit 14.9
Five Decision Styles

Decision Style	Definition
A I	Manager makes the decision alone.
A II	Manager asks for information from subordinates but makes the decision alone. Subordinates may or may not be informed about what the problem is.
C I	Manager shares the problems with subordinates and asks for information and evaluations. Meetings take place as dyads, not as a group, and the manager then goes off alone and makes the decision.
C II	Manager and subordinates meet as a group to discuss the problem, but the manager makes the decision.
G II	Manager and subordinates meet as a group to discuss the problem, and the group makes the decision.

Note: *A* = autocratic; *C* = consultative; *G* = group

Source: Reprinted from *Leadership and Decision-Making* by Victor H. Vroom and Philip W. Yetton by permission of the University of Pittsburgh Press. © 1973 by University of Pittsburgh Press.

Using the Normative Model

With these two aspects of the models in mind, we are now in a position to see how the model works. In essence, the normative model provides a decision tree to facilitate arriving at an effective decision (that is, one characterized by high quality, acceptance by subordinates, and timeliness). This decision tree is shown in Exhibit 14.10. The leader is supposed to work through the decision process by answering a series of questions that shows the proper amount of participation that will maximize decision effectiveness.

Exhibit 14.10
The Normative Model of
Decision Making

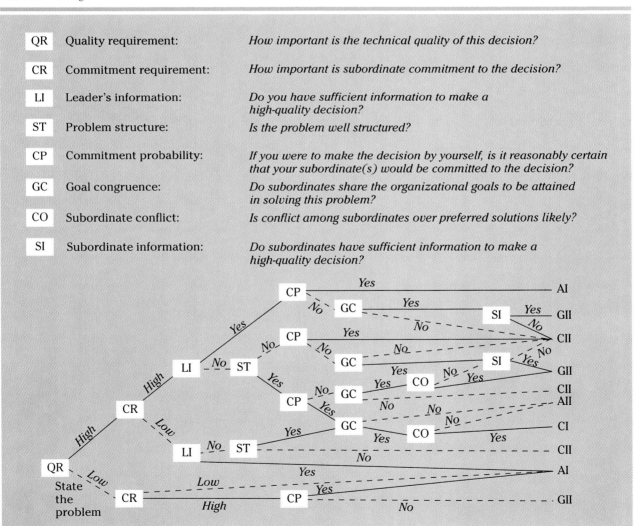

QR	Quality requirement:	*How important is the technical quality of this decision?*
CR	Commitment requirement:	*How important is subordinate commitment to the decision?*
LI	Leader's information:	*Do you have sufficient information to make a high-quality decision?*
ST	Problem structure:	*Is the problem well structured?*
CP	Commitment probability:	*If you were to make the decision by yourself, is it reasonably certain that your subordinate(s) would be committed to the decision?*
GC	Goal congruence:	*Do subordinates share the organizational goals to be attained in solving this problem?*
CO	Subordinate conflict:	*Is conflict among subordinates over preferred solutions likely?*
SI	Subordinate information:	*Do subordinates have sufficient information to make a high-quality decision?*

Source: From *The New Leadership: Managing Participation in Organizations* by Victor H. Vroom and Arthur G. Jago (Englewood Cliffs, N.J.: Prentice-Hall, 1988). Copyright 1987 by V. H. Vroom and A. G. Jago. Used with permission of the authors.

SELF-ASSESSMENT 14.2
How Would You Make This Decision?

Instructions: The following example demonstrates how the normative decision-making model works. Use the decision tree (Exhibit 14.10) to decide how much participation you should allow in the decision process.

Suppose you are the supervisor of a group of 12 engineers. Their formal training and work experience are very similar, permitting you to use them interchangeably on projects. Today you received a fax from your Saudi Arabian office requesting that four of your engineers be sent there immediately for a six-month period to help out on a project. Your boss agrees with this request and has asked you to select the personnel.

All of your people are capable of doing the job, and there are no extenuating circumstances requiring anyone to remain behind. However, none of your people are particularly interested in going.

Your job is to select the people to be sent. How would you do it?

Source: Based on V. Vroom and P. Yetton, *Leadership and Decision Making* (Pittsburgh: University of Pittsburgh Press, 1973); V. Vroom and A. Jago, *The New Leadership* (Englewood Cliffs, N.J.: Prentice-Hall, 1988).

The first question leaders are asked concern the importance of the technical quality of the decision. (This is called the "QR" requirement, as shown in the exhibit.) Next, leaders are asked how important subordinate commitment is to the effective implementation of the resulting decision. (This is called the "CR" requirement.) And so on across the decision tree. Ultimately, the decision maker arrives at the right side of the diagram, which will show whether the decision should be made alone by the leader (*A I*), the group (*G II*), or somewhere in between.

You may wish to try this procedure to see how it works. To do so, you can either use a real-life organizational decision from your own experience, or you can complete Self-Assessment 14.2. Simply take your problem, and use the decision tree to work through a solution. According to the model, this will tell you not what decision to make, but rather how to make it (that is, whether to be more or less participative). See Appendix B for details after you have made your selection.

It is not the intent of the model to have a manager work through the decision tree for each decision he or she has to make. This could well lead to chaos. Instead, the model is meant as a training device to show managers how they should approach and analyze a decision. After practice, the manager would become better able to quickly analyze situations and realize when to make an autocratic decision and when to make a participative one.

DECISION SPEED AND QUALITY

In the early 1980s, Gavilan Computer was at the forefront of computer technology and had a virtual monopoly on the developing—and lucrative—laptop computer market. By 1984, however, Gavilan had filed for bankruptcy. In spite of a $31 million stake from venture capitalists, the company experienced long delays and indecision that cost it its early technological and market advantage. Competitors entered the market niche, and Gavilan failed to exploit its advantage. As one executive observed, "We missed the window."[19] What happened to Gavilan has occurred with alarming frequency in corporations—especially those involved in high-technology industries—as the indecisive fall by the wayside.

In a recent series of studies of decision making in industries characterized by frequent change and turbulence—the so-called *high-velocity environments*—researchers Kathleen Eisenhardt and L. J. Bourgeois have attempted to discover what distinguishes successful decision makers and managers from unsuccessful ones.[20] Clearly, in such industries (e.g., microelectronics, medical technology, genetic engineering), rapid, high-quality decision making by executives and their companies is closely related to good corporate performance. In these industries, mistakes are costly; information is often ambiguous, obsolete, or simply incorrect; and recovery from missed opportunities is extremely difficult. In view of the importance of speed for organizational innovation, performance, and survival, it is important to understand how successful decision makers make rapid decisions of high quality.

If rapid action is important for effectiveness, how do we get it? Eisenstadt found that five factors influenced a manager's ability to make fast decisions in high-velocity environments (see Exhibit 14.11):

1. *Real-time information.* First, fast decision makers must have access to and be able to process real-time information—that is, information that describes what is happening right now, not yesterday.
2. *Multiple simultaneous alternatives.* Second, decision makers examine several possible alternative courses of action simultaneously, not sequentially (e.g., "Let's look at alternatives *X, Y,* and *Z* together and see how each stacks up."). This adds complexity and richness to the analysis and reduces the time involved in information processing.
3. *Two-tiered advice process.* Third, fast decision makers use a two-tiered advisory system, whereby all team members are allowed input, but greater weight is given to more experienced co-workers.
4. *Consensus with qualification.* Fourth, fast decision makers attempt to gain widespread consensus on the decision as it is being made, not after it is made (e.g., "Can everyone support decision *X* if we go this way?").
5. *Decision integration.* And, finally, fast decision makers integrate tactical planning and issues of implementation within the decision process itself (e.g., "If we are going to do *X,* how might we do it?").

These five characteristics are moderated or affected by three "mediating processes" that determine the ability of the manager and group to effectively

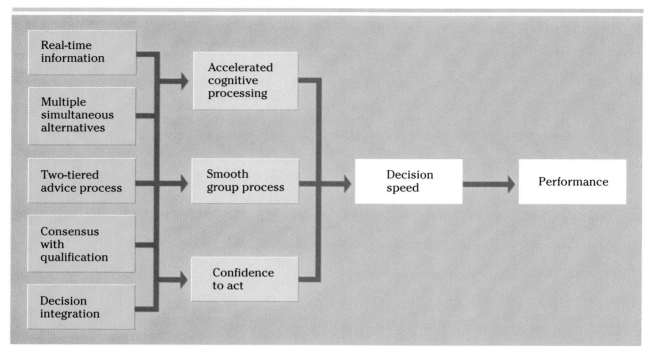

Exhibit 14.11
Major Influence On Decision
Speed and Performance

Source: Adapted from K. M. Eisenhardt, "Making Fast Strategic Decisions in High-Velocity Environments," *Academy of Management Journal,* 1989, *32,* p. 571. Reprinted by permission of the Academy of Management and the author.

deal with the quantity and quality of information generated by the above five factors. These three mediating processes are:

1. *Accelerated cognitive processing.* The decision maker must have the ability to process and analyze great amounts of information quickly and efficiently. Cognitive complexity was discussed in Chapter 2, where it was noted that some people—and some groups—can simply process information faster and better than others. Obviously, the faster a manager can process what is presented, the quicker the decision.
2. *Smooth group processes.* To be effective, the manager must be working with a group that is characterized by smooth, harmonious relations. This is not to say that everyone always agrees. Quite the contrary—members of effective groups often disagree. However, it is the way in which they disagree and resolve their disagreements that counts. Fast decisions are aided by group members and subordinates who share a common vision and who are mutually supportive and cohesive.
3. *Confidence to act.* Finally, fast decision makers must not be afraid to act. Some managers are reluctant to make concrete decisions in the face of uncertainty, and there is a tendency to wait until the manager can reduce the uncertainty. Unfortunately, in high-velocity environments, this uncertainty is never reduced. Thus, to be effective, fast decision makers must be willing to make the choice when the appropriate time comes.

It must be remembered that this research is focused on high-velocity environments, not all organizational environments. That is, in businesses that are characterized by relative stability (e.g., the banking industry), rapid decisions may prove disastrous. Because there is time for more complete data collection and processing (within reason), there is less need for immediate action. Thus, one decision a manager must make is to assess the time horizons that characterize his or her industry. Once this is completed, the manager is in a better position to use an appropriate decision timeline for managerial action.

PROBLEMS IN GROUP DECISION MAKING

In the realm of group decision making, at least two problems can be identified that can have significant negative repercussions for decision effectiveness. These are the phenomena of groupthink and escalating commitment to a course of action.

Groupthink

Increased attention has been focused in recent years on a phenomenon known as *groupthink*. This phenomenon, first discussed by Irving Janis, refers to a mode of thinking in which the pursuit of agreement or consensus among members becomes so dominant that it overrides any realistic appraisal of alternative courses of action.[21] The concept emerged from Janis's studies of high-level policy decisions by government leaders. These included decisions by the U.S. government about Vietnam, the Bay of Pigs, and the Korean War. In analyzing the decision process leading up to each action, Janis found numerous indications pointing to the development of group norms that improved morale at the expense of critical thinking. A model of this process is shown in Exhibit 14.12.

Symptoms of Groupthink.   In studies of both government and business leaders, Janis identified eight primary symptoms of groupthink. The first is the *illusion of invulnerability*. Group members often reassure themselves about obvious dangers and become overly optimistic and willing to take extraordinary risks. Members fail to respond to clear warning signals. For instance, in the disastrous Bay of Pigs invasion, the United States operated on the false assumption that it could keep the fact that it had invaded Cuba a secret. Even after news of the plan had leaked out, government leaders remained convinced of their ability to keep it a secret.

Victims of groupthink also tend to collectively engage in *rationalization* aimed at discounting warning signs and other types of negative feedback that could lead to reconsideration of the course of action if taken seriously. For example, many American firms have discounted the new economic potential of a united Europe in the 1990s by saying that because Europeans have never been able to cooperate in the past, the likelihood of it happening in 1992 is slim.

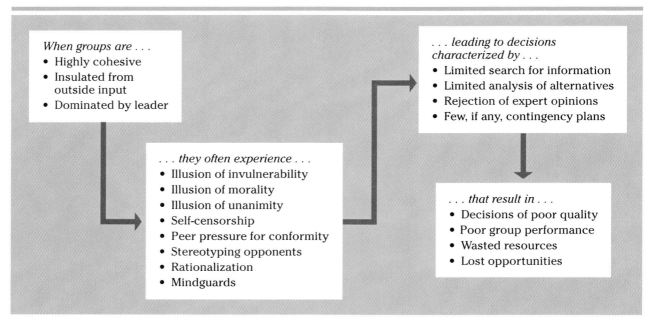

Exhibit 14.12
The Groupthink Process

Source: Adapted from Gregory Moorhead, "Groupthink: Hypothesis in Need of Testing," *Group and Organization Studies,* Vol. 7, No. 4 (December 1982), pp. 429–444. Copyright © 1982 by Sage Publications, Inc. Reprinted by permission of Sage Publications, Inc.

Group members often believe in the inherent morality of the group. Because of this *illusion of morality,* they ignore the ethical or moral consequences of their decisions. Leading tobacco companies continue to run advertisements about free choice in decision making about smoking, completely ignoring all the medical evidence on the hazards involved.

Stereotyping the enemy is another symptom of groupthink. In-group members often stereotype leaders of opposition groups in so harsh a fashion as to rule out any need to negotiate with them on differences of opinion. Often they also place tremendous *pressure to conform* on members who temporarily express doubts about the group's shared illusions or who raise questions about the validity of the arguments supporting the decisions of the group.

Moreover, group members often use *self-censorship* to avoid deviating from what appears to be a group consensus. They often minimize to themselves the seriousness of their doubts. Partly because of self-censorship by group members, another symptom of groupthink, the *illusion of unanimity,* is often created. Members assume everyone holds the same opinion. It is assumed that individuals who remain silent are in agreement with the spoken opinions of others.

Finally, victims of groupthink often appoint themselves as *mindguards* to protect the leader and other members of the group from adverse information that may cause conflict in the group over the correctness of a course of action. The mindguard may tell the dissident that he or she is being disruptive or nonsupportive, or may simply isolate the dissident from other group members. For many years, FBI agents in the Washington headquarters who expressed views contrary to the party line found themselves transferred to less desirable locations.

In order to see how this works, consider a group or organization to which you belong (or used to belong, if this is easier). This group could be a fraternity or sorority, a sports club or team, a work group or company, and so forth. Think about this group and its competitor (perhaps another fraternity or sorority, team, etc.) Now, on the basis of your assessment, complete Self-Assessment 14.3. After you have finished, add up the total number of points to see the extent to which your group experiences groupthink. Refer to Appendix B for scoring procedures.

Consequences of Groupthink.   Groupthink can have several deleterious consequences for the quality of decision making. First, groups often limit their search for possible solutions and avoid a comprehensive analysis of all possible alternatives. Second, groups frequently fail to reexamine their chosen course of action after new information or events suggest a change in course. Third, group members spend little time considering whether there are any nonobvious advantages to alternative courses of action that make those alternatives preferable to the chosen course of action. Fourth, groups often make little or no attempt to seek out the advice of experts either inside or outside their own organization. Fifth, members show positive interest in facts that support their preferred decision alternative and either ignore or show negative interest in facts that fail to support it. Finally, groups often ignore any consideration of possible roadblocks to their chosen decision and, as a result, fail to develop contingency plans for potential setbacks.

Overcoming Groupthink.   In view of the potentially serious consequences of the emergence of a groupthink mentality in organizations, questions are logically raised about what can be done to minimize its effects. Janis suggests several strategies. To begin, group leaders can reduce groupthink by encouraging each member to evaluate proposals critically. Also, by not stating their own positions but instead promoting open inquiry, leaders can ensure that the group considers a range of alternatives.

Other strategies for preventing groupthink involve getting more suggestions for viable solutions. This can be done by assigning the same problem to two independent groups. Or, at intervals before the group reaches a decision, members can take a respite and seek advice from other parts of the organization. Another technique is to invite experts from outside the group to challenge members' views at group meetings.

Groupthink may also be prevented with strategies that directly involve the group members themselves. For example, for each group meeting, a member can be appointed to serve as a devil's advocate to challenge the majority position. Another means of stopping groupthink is to split the group into two sections for independent discussions. They can then compare results. An additional tactic is, after reaching a preliminary consensus on a course of action, to schedule a second-chance meeting. This allows group members an opportunity to express doubts and rethink the issue.

In other words, if groups are aware of the problems of groupthink, several specific and relatively simple steps can be taken to minimize the likelihood

SELF-ASSESSMENT 14.3
Are You a Victim of Groupthink?

Instructions: Think of a group of which you are (or were) a member (e.g., a fraternity or sorority, a sports team, political club, a company or business, etc.). Next, think about who your competitor is (e.g., another fraternity or sorority, sports team, company, etc.). With this in mind, complete the following items to describe the attitudes and behaviors of your fellow group members. Mark a "5" to indicate your strong agreement, a "1" to indicate your strong disagreement, a "3" to indicate a neutral response, and so on. When you have finished, add up your scores.

	Strongly Disagree		Neutral		Strongly Agree
1. Group members usually feel their actions or opinions on various issues are inherently correct compared to the opposition group.	1	2	3	4	5
2. Group members often view members of the other group as the "enemy; they are not as good as we are."	1	2	3	4	5
3. Group members tend to be overly optimistic when they begin a new project and often underestimate the risks of failure.	1	2	3	4	5
4. Group members tend to ignore warning signs or negative feedback once they have decided to begin a new project.	1	2	3	4	5
5. Group members actively voice support for the group; even if they have doubts about what the group is doing, they will keep these doubts to themselves.	1	2	3	4	5
6. Group members will often conceal bad news or negative information for fear of hurting group cohesiveness.	1	2	3	4	5
7. Group members often feel that expressing dissenting views shows disloyalty to the group; there is pressure to support the "party line."	1	2	3	4	5
8. My group tends to feel that everyone is in agreement with the opinions and actions of the group.	1	2	3	4	5

of falling victim to this problem. These steps, summarized in Exhibit 14.13, offer advice for leaders, organizations, individuals, and the process itself. As is usually the case, however, recognizing the problem represents half the battle in the effort to make more effective decisions in organizational settings.

Ethical Challenge

IN PRACTICE
Groupthink at Citibank

To understand the negative repercussions of groupthink, consider the example of Davis Edwards, a senior manager of Citibank. For over two years, Edwards had gone to his boss and his boss's boss with a story of tax evasion and currency-trading violations in his department. Edwards was in charge of foreign exchange traders in the Paris branch, and he warned that major problems were coming if the bank did not take immediate action. He had discovered that his bank was "parking"—that is, making bogus transfers of foreign deposits to shift bank profits to countries with low tax rates. This practice led to lower worldwide taxes. Edwards also discovered kickback schemes associated with the illegal monetary transfers.

From the company's standpoint, the banking regulations surrounding parking were ambiguous. Bank officers involved in the scheme failed to see either the ethical, legal, or public relations consequences of the practice, and they resisted any changes that might curtail bank profitability. Groupthink

Exhibit 14.13
Guidelines for
Overcoming Groupthink

For the company:

- Establish several independent groups to examine the same problem.
- Train managers in groupthink prevention techniques.

For the leader:

- Assign everyone the role of critical evaluator.
- Use outside experts to challenge the group.
- Assign the devil's advocate role to a member of the group.
- Try to be impartial and refrain from stating your own views.

For group members:

- Try to retain your objectivity and be a critical thinker.
- Discuss group deliberations with a trusted outsider, and report back to the group.

For the deliberation process:

- At times, break the group into subgroups to discuss the problem.
- Take time to study what other companies or groups have done in similar situations.
- Schedule "second chance" meetings to provide an opportunity to rethink the issues before making a final decision.

was rampant. The bank was right, the group was right, and anyone who disagreed must be the enemy. But Edwards persisted, because, as he noted, "It's bad for business. We risk being tossed out of some of these countries."

By the time word of Citibank's parking practices leaked out and bank regulators became involved, the reality of the shady practice finally hit bank officials. Citibank received heavy fines for back taxes in several European countries, and the U.S. controller of the currency determined that the bank's practices had violated banking ethics. The SEC recommended civil action but did not prosecute. Eventually, the bank changed its ways. In the meantime, what happened to Edwards? The bank fired him.[22]

Escalating Commitment to a Decision

Whereas groupthink helps to explain how policy-making groups put blinders on and stifle dissenting opinions when making major decisions, the concept of *escalating commitment* to decisions offers an explanation of why decision makers adhere to a course of action after they know it is incorrect (that is, why managers "throw good money after bad"). To understand the problem of escalating commitment, consider the following true examples:[23]

■ At an early stage in the U.S. involvement in the Vietnam War, George Ball, then Undersecretary of State, wrote the following in a memo to President Johnson: "The decision you face now is crucial. Once large numbers of U.S. troops are committed to direct combat, they will begin to take heavy casualties in a war they are ill equipped to fight in a noncooperative if not downright hostile countryside. Once we suffer large casualties, we will have started a well-nigh irreversible process. Our involvement will be so great that we cannot without national humiliation stop short of achieving our complete objectives. Of the two possibilities, I think humiliation would be more likely than the achievement of our objectives—even after we have paid terrible costs.

■ A company overestimates its capability to build an airplane brake that will meet certain technical specifications at a given cost. Because it wins the government contract, the company is forced to invest greater and greater effort into meeting the contract terms. As a result of increasing pressure to meet specifications and deadlines, records and tests of the brake are misrepresented to government officials. Corporate careers and company credibility are increasingly staked on the airbrake contract, although many in the firm know the brake will not work effectively. At the conclusion of the construction period, the government test pilot flies the plane; it skids off the runway and narrowly misses injuring the pilot.

■ An individual purchased a stock at $50 a share, but the price has gone down to $20. Still convinced about the merit of the stock, he buys more shares at this lower price. Soon the price declines further and the individual is again faced with the decision to buy more, hold what he already has, or sell out entirely.

How do we account for such commitment by individuals and groups to obvious mistakes? At least three explanations are possible. First, we can point to individual limitations in information processing and suggest that people are limited in both their desire and ability to handle all of the information necessary for such complex decisions. As a result, errors in judgment are possible. A second approach is to explain decisional errors by suggesting that a breakdown in rationality occurred because of interpersonal elements such as group dynamics. For example, power considerations may outweigh the more rational aspects of organizational decision making. Although both of these explanations may contribute to a better understanding of decisional error, Staw suggests that they do not go far enough. "A salient feature of the preceding case examples is that a series of decisions is associated with a course of action rather than an isolated choice."[24]

In order to help explain such behavior, Staw turned to the social psychological literature on *forced compliance.* In studies of forced compliance, individuals are typically induced to perform an unpleasant or dissatisfying act (e.g., eating grasshoppers) when no compensating external rewards are present. In general, after compliance, individuals will bias their own attitudes in a positive direction so as to justify their previous behavior. This biasing of attitudes is most likely to occur when the individuals feel personally responsible for the negative consequences and when the consequences are difficult to undo.

On the basis of these findings, Staw and his colleagues carried out a series of experiments focusing on how willing people would be to continue to commit valued resources to a course of action after it was clear that the original decision had been in error. It was found in these experiments that decision makers actually allocated more money to company divisions that were showing poor results than to those that were showing good results. Also, decision makers allocated more money to a division when they themselves (instead of another party) had been responsible for the original decision to back the division. In short, decision makers were most likely to spend money on projects that had negative consequences for which they were responsible.

To find out why, Staw suggested a model of escalating commitment, as shown in Exhibit 14.14. In this abbreviated model, we can see that four basic determinants of commitment to a course of action can be identified. First, people are likely to remain committed to a course of action (even when it is clearly incorrect) because of a desire or need to justify previous decisions. When people feel a responsibility for negative consequences and at the same time feel a need to demonstrate their own competence, they will often stick to a decision in hopes of "turning the situation around" or "pulling a victory out of defeat." This is referred to as *retrospective rationality;* that is, the individual seeks to appear competent in previous as opposed to future actions. This process can be seen in the example from the Vietnam War cited above.

In addition, commitment to a previous decision is influenced by a *norm for consistency.* That is, in most contemporary societies, managers who are consistent in their actions are often considered better leaders than those who switch around from one course of action to another. For instance, in a Gallup poll on President Carter's popularity, respondents who were dissatisfied with his performance consistently described him as "inconsistent."

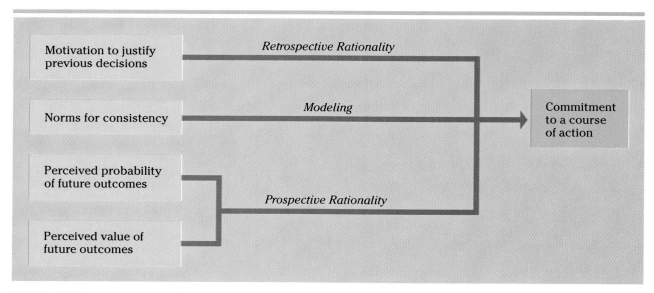

Exhibit 14.14
Influences on
Behavioral Commitment

Source: Based on B. M. Staw, "The Escalation of Commitment to a Course of Action," *Academy of Management Review,* 1981, *6,* p. 582. Used by permission.

Hence, we often see a "we'll make it work" syndrome, caused by an unwillingness on the part of a manager (or government leader) to change course in the midst of turmoil or threat. Often, these norms for consistency results from managers who model their behavior after people they see as successful, either within the organization or in society.

Finally, two additional factors—the perceived probability of future outcomes and the perceived value of future outcomes—jointly influence what is called *prospective rationality.* Prospective rationality is simply one's belief that future courses of action are rational and correct. When people feel they can "turn the situation around" or that "prosperity is just around the corner," and when the goal is highly prized, we would expect strong commitment to a continued course of action, influenced in part by the feeling that it is the proper thing to do at that point in time.

In summarizing the model, Staw argues:

> Thus, commitment decisions to a course of action may be determined as much by a desire to rectify past outcomes as to attain future ones. In addition, because the decisions are associated with each other, norms for consistency in action may override SEU [subjective expected utility] or economic considerations.[25]

Staw suggests when this "escalation hypothesis" is expected to be most common:

> Prime candidates for escalation therefore include resource allocation or investment decisions that are identified by an entering and exit value, life

choices that are linked together with the label of a career, and policy decisions for which administrators are held accountable by others in the organization or by the general public.[26]

In summary, when we consider effective decision-making processes in organizations, special attention must be given to the two related threats of groupthink and escalating commitments. Each process has the potential to constrain or subvert even the most carefully considered decisions. Therefore, managers need to be alert to the existence of both and to initiate positive actions to reduce their impact in organizations.

IN PRACTICE
A Sinkhole Called Hibernia

International Challenge

In 1973–74, North America was hit with the most severe oil crisis in its history. Long lines at the gas pump were commonplace, and both the U.S. and Canadian governments launched massive oil projects to promote oil self-sufficiency. The crisis (if not the concern over energy conservation) has long since disappeared in the intervening twenty years. Market stability has returned and consumers have learned to live with somewhat higher energy costs. So the crisis is over, right? Not according to the Canadian government. In January 1993, the Canadian Parliament approved spending another $15 billion to continue the development of the Hibernia oil fields off the shores of Newfoundland.[27]

For over a decade, scientists have described Hibernia as financial sinkhole and an environmental crisis just waiting to happen. Producing oil in waters near where the Titanic sank will be one of the most costly and perilous oil projects ever. The huge platform that must be built will have to be anchored in 240 feet of water on a 60,000 ton steel-and-concrete base surrounded by an iceberg-deflecting concrete wall 90 feet thick. The estimated recovery costs for Hibernian oil are five times current recovery costs, making it potentially the most expensive oil in the market by far.

In addition, environmentalists warn that the Hibernia area contains some of Canada's most vulnerable marine life. The constant traffic of oil tankers to and from the oil platform through iceberg-infested areas increases the chances of oil spills dramatically, the environmentalists claim.

In view of these problems, why is the Canadian government still spending lavishly for an oil crisis that ended twenty years ago? The answer, according to analysts, lies in the politics of bureaucratic action. To begin with, after spending $800 million on the project, the government is concerned that it will look "wasteful" if it admits the project is ill-advised. Moreover, the Newfoundland economy has become dependent upon the government support for the area; curtailing such spending would further aggravate the unemployment situation there. Finally, despite expert's assessments that at best the venture will yield "the smallest of profits," the oil companies that are working with the Canadian government continue to contend that Hibernia is a "good project that will provide a positive return." Apparently, no one wants to acknowledge to their stockholders that past decisions may have been in error.

STRATEGIES FOR IMPROVING DECISION MAKING

Up to now, we have focused on the problems and processes involved in decision making. We have examined several decision models, differences between individual and group decisions, participation in decision making, and constraints on effective decision making. Throughout, various limitations to the process were noted. On the basis of this discussion, we are now in a position to consider ways of improving the decision-making process beyond those discussed above.

It was noted at the beginning of the chapter that decisions can be divided into two phases: problem formulation and problem solution. Strategies to improve decision making can be divided into the same two categories.[28]

Improving Problem Formulation

Problem formulation focuses on identifying the causes for unsatisfactory behavior and performance or the emergence of new opportunities and challenges. This process is often inhibited by the failure of group members to look beyond the familiar. Forces resulting from groupthink and escalating commitment constrain critical analysis or comprehensive searches for information and possible solutions.

As a result, efforts to improve problem formulation require the use of structured debate. As shown in Exhibit 14.15, improvements can be made by using three related techniques.

Devil's Advocate.   This is where one member of the group is assigned the role of disagreeing with the group and taking an opposing position. For example, if you asked a group of American automobile company executives why their sales are down, they might blame Japanese imports. In this case, a devil's advocate would argue that the problem lies not with the Japanese, but rather with the Americans themselves and their poor product quality. Through this process, the group is forced to justify its position, and, it is hoped, a more precise and accurate portrait of the problem and its underlying causes will result.

Multiple Advocacy.   This process is like the devil's advocate approach, except that more than one opposing view is presented. Each group involved

Exhibit 14.15
Techniques for Improving
Decision Making

Problem Formulation (Structured Debate)	Problem Solution (Creativity Stimulants)
Devil's advocate	Brainstorming
Multiple advocacy	Nominal group technique
Dialectical inquiry	Delphi technique

in a decision is assigned the responsibility to represent the opinions of its constituents. Thus, if a university is concerned with accommodating racial and cultural diversity on campus, it might establish a commission including blacks, Hispanics, Asians, women's groups, and so forth. The resulting dialogue should lead to the identification of a useful agenda for discussion.

Dialectical Inquiry.   This process occurs when a group or individual is assigned the role of questioning the underlying assumptions associated with problem formulation. It begins by identifying the prevailing view of the problem and its associated assumptions. Next, an individual is asked to develop an alternative problem that is credible but rests on different assumptions. By doing so, the accuracy or generalizability of the original assumptions is examined and possibly altered. As a result, group members are forced to look at new ways to analyze the problem. These efforts are particularly helpful in overcoming groupthink and escalating commitment, because they question the underlying assumptions of group behavior.

Improving Problem Solution

Problem solution involves the development and evaluation of alternative courses of action plus the selection and implementation of the preferred alternatives. In this process, it is important that group members be as thorough and creative as practicable, given the circumstances. To do this, they need *creativity stimulants,* or mechanisms to economically expand the search for and analysis of possible alternatives. Three such mechanisms can be identified.

Brainstorming.   This process is a frequently used mechanism to provide the maximum number of ideas in a short period of time. A group comes together and is given a specific problem. It is told to propose any ideas that come to mind that may represent a solution to the problem. In such sessions—at least at the early stages—criticism is minimized so as not to inhibit expression. Once all the ideas are on the table, the group turns its attention to considering the positive and negative aspects of each proposal. Through a process of continual refinement, the best possible solution under the circumstances should emerge.

Nominal Group Technique.   This technique, typically referred to as NGT, consists of four phases in the group decision-making process.[29] First, individual members meet as a group (as in the interacting technique), but they begin by sitting silently and independently generating their ideas on a problem in writing. This silent period is followed by a round-robin procedure in which each group member presents an idea to the group. No discussion of the idea is allowed at this time. The ideas are summarized and recorded (perhaps on a blackboard). After all individuals have had an opportunity to present their ideas, each idea is discussed for the purpose of clarification and evaluation. Finally, the group members conclude the meeting by silently and independently recording their rank-ordering of the various ideas or solutions to the problem. The final decision is determined by the pooled outcome of the members' votes on the issue.

The NGT allows the group to meet formally, but it does not allow members to engage in much discussion or interpersonal communication; hence, the term nominal group technique. A chief advantage of this procedure, then, is that everyone independently considers the problem without influence from other group members. As we found, this influence represents one of the chief obstacles to open-minded discussion and decision making.

Delphi Technique.   In contrast to NGT, the delphi technique never allows decision participants to meet face-to-face. Instead, a problem is identified, and members are asked through a series of carefully designed questionnaires to provide potential solutions. These questionnaires are completed independently. Results of the first questionnaire are then circulated to other group members (who are still physically separated). After viewing the feedback, members are again asked their opinions (to see if the opinions of others on the first questionnaire caused them to change their own minds). This process may continue through several iterations until group members' opinions begin to show a consensus on a prospective solution to the problem.

The existence of such decision-making techniques demonstrates that poor decisions do not have to be tolerated in organizations. Clearly, there are a variety of problems in decision-making processes. Individuals and groups have various biases and personal goals that may lead to suboptimal decisions. Groups often censor themselves, as noted earlier in the discussion on groupthink. Even so, techniques such as those discussed here aim to minimize many of these problems by insulating individual participants from the undue influences of others. This allows individuals greater freedom of expression, and the group receives far less filtered or slanted information with which to make its decision. Thus, although not perfect, these techniques can assist managers in need of mechanisms to improve both the quality and the timeliness of decisions made in work organizations.

PULLING IT ALL TOGETHER

The decision-making process typically has two aspects: problem formation and problem solution. Individually, people often select solutions that meet their minimum objectives rather than spend extra time and energy trying to find the solution that maximizes their objectives. However, in order to appear totally rational to themselves or others, they often construct objectives and criteria after the fact in order to justify the decision they have already made or the solution they have already selected. Groups add a social dynamic to the decision-making process that depending on the dynamics can either result in better or worse decisions than individuals might make on their own. Finally, the decision of how involved to make others in the process is a function of several factors relative to the potential participants in the decision, the nature of the problem and decision themselves, and the context in which the problem exits and the decision needs to be made.

SUMMARY OF KEY POINTS

■ Decision making is a process of specifying the nature of a particular problem and selecting among available alternatives in order to solve it.

■ Decision making typically goes through two phases: problem formulation and problem solution.

■ Decisions can be categorized into programmed decisions, which require standardized responses to simple problems, and nonprogrammed decisions, which require unique solutions to more complex problems.

■ Environmental scanning is the process of attempting to gather useful information from the outside environment that can enhance the quality or timeliness of a decision.

■ Three individual decision-making models can be identified: (1) the rational/classical model, which assumes people are rational and attempt to maximize their potential outcomes from a decision; (2) the bounded rationality model, which assumes that people typically are unable to make perfect decisions and instead attempt to make acceptable decisions on the basis of imperfect information; and (3) the retrospective model, which assumes people first make a decision by intuition and then attempt to justify or rationalize the decision with postdecision analyses.

■ Satisficing represents an attempt to discover a solution to a problem that is acceptable but not necessarily optimal.

■ Group decision making differs in many respects from individual decision making, although both approaches have merit.

■ The garbage can model of group decision making asserts that many decisions are made by the chance encounter of several unrelated factors that happen to come together at an appropriate moment.

■ The normative model of decision making suggests that there is no best decision-making style. Instead, a manager must use either participative or nonparticipative methods depending upon the nature of the specific decision being made. In this endeavor, decision effectiveness is evaluated on the basis of three factors: decision quality, decision acceptance by subordinates, and timeliness of the decision.

■ In industries characterized by frequent change and turbulence (high-velocity environments), successful decision making requires accelerated cognitive processing, smooth group processes, and managerial confidence to take action.

■ Groupthink is the process by which the pursuit of consensus among group members becomes so dominant that it overrides any realistic appraisal of alternative courses of action. Symptoms of groupthink include an illusion of invulnerability, rationalization, the illusion of morality, stereotyping of the opposition, self-censorship, the illusion of unanimity, and the presence of mindguards.

■ Escalating commitment to a course of action results when decision makers refuse to reassess the basic assumptions upon which a decision was originally made and instead continue to invest more resources in a poor solution.

■ Decision-making processes can be improved either by improving problem formulation through structured debates (such as devil's advocacy, multiple advocacy, or dialectical inquiry) or improving problem solution through the use of creativity stimulants (such as brainstorming, nominal group technique, or the delphi technique).

KEY WORDS

administrative man model
bounded rationality model
brainstorming
cognitive complexity
creativity stimulants
decision making
delphi technique
devil's advocate
dialectical inquiry
economic man model
economic rationality
environmental scanning
escalating commitment
forced compliance
garbage can model
Gresham's Law of Planning
groupthink
heuristics
high-velocity environments
informational bias
mindguards

multiple advocacy
nominal group technique
nonprogrammed decision
normative theory
organized anarchies
problem formulation
problem solution
programmed decision
prospective rationality
rational/classical model
retrospective decision model
retrospective rationality
risk
satisficing
selective perception
self-censorship
stereotyping
structured debate
uncertainty
uncertainty absorption

QUESTIONS FOR DISCUSSION

1. What are the two stages in decision making?
2. What is the basic premise of the rational/classical model of decision making? How does it differ from the bounded rationality model?
3. What are the primary advantages of the bounded rationality model of decision making?
4. What is satisficing?
5. How does the retrospective decision model work?
6. Describe Gresham's Law of Planning.

7. Describe the normative model of decision making and leadership. What implications for management follow from this model?
8. Discuss the advantages and disadvantages of group decision making compared to individual decision making.
9. When is it more appropriate for a manager to be more participative in decision making?
10. Describe the phenomenon of groupthink. What are its symptoms? Its outcomes?
11. How can we overcome groupthink?
12. Can you identify examples in your own life of escalating commitment to past decisions?
13. How can managers work to overcome the effects of escalating commitment to past decisions?
14. Compare and contrast the nominal group technique and the delphi technique of decision making.
15. What are some of the more prominent roadblocks to effective managerial decision making?

NOTES

1. Personal conversations with the second author. (Names have been disguised).
2. K. MacKrimmon and R. Taylor, "Decision Making and Problem Solving," in M. D. Dunnette, ed., *Handbook of Industrial and Organizational Psychology* (Chicago: Rand McNally, 1976), pp. 1397–1453.
3. H. A. Simon, *The New Science of Management Decisions* (Englewood Cliffs, N.J.: Prentice-Hall, 1977.)
4. T. R. Mitchell and J. R. Larson, *People in Organizations* (New York: McGraw-Hill, 1987).
5. G. R. Ungson and D. N. Braunstein, *Decision Making* (Boston: Kent, 1982).
6. D. Miller and M. Star, *The Structure of Human Decisions* (Englewood Cliffs, N.J.: Prentice-Hall, 1967).
7. Simon, op. cit.
8. H. A. Simon, *Administrative Behavior* (New York: The Free Press, 1957).
9. Ibid., p. 81.
10. Ibid.
11. J. G. March and H. A. Simon, *Organizations* (New York: Wiley, 1958), pp. 140–141.
12. "A Replacement for the President's Plane Is Missing," Frequent Flyer, September 1982, pp. 28–30.
13. P. Soelberg, "Unprogrammed Decision Making," *Industrial Management,* 1967, *8,* pp. 19–29.
14. E. Harrison, *The Managerial Decision Making Process* (Boston: Houghton-Mifflin, 1975.)
15. R. Ebert and T. Mitchell, *Organizational Decision Processes: Concepts and Analysis* (New York: Crane, Russak, 1975).
16. J. G. March and J. P. Olsen, "A Garbage Can Model of Organizational Choice," *Administrative Science Quarterly,* March 1972, pp. 1–25; J. G. March and R. Weissinger-Baylon, *Ambiguity and Command* (Marshfield, Mass.: Pitman, 1986).
17. "When I Was a Lad," *The Economist,* December 23, 1989, p. 70.
18. V. Vroom and P. Yetton, *Leadership and Decision Making* (Pittsburgh: University of Pittsburgh Press, 1973); V. Vroom and A. Jago, *The New Leadership: Managing Participation in Organizations* (Englewood Cliffs, N.J.: Prentice-Hall, 1988).

19. R. Hof, "Why Once-Ambitious Computer Firm Quit," *Peninsula Times Tribune,* September 29, 1984, p. B1.

20. K. Eisenhardt, "Making Fast Strategic Decisions in High-Velocity Environments," *Academy of Management Journal,* 1989, *32,* pp. 543–576.

21. I. Janis, *Victims of Groupthink* (Boston: Houghton Mifflin, 1972).

22. R. Rowan, "The Maverick Who Yelled Foul at Citibank,"*Fortune,* January 10, 1983, pp. 46–56.

23. B. M. Staw, "The Escalation of Commitment to a Course of Action,"*Academy of Management Review,* 1981, *6,* pp. 577–587.

24. Ibid., p. 578.

25. Ibid., p. 584.

26. Ibid., p. 585.

27. W. Symonds, "A Sinkhole Called Hibernia," *Business Week,* February 1, 1993, pp. 74–75.

28. C. Schwenk and H. Thomas, "Formulating the Mess: The Role of Decision Aids in Problem Formulation," *Omega,* 1983, *11,* pp. 239–252.

29. A. VanDeVen and A. Delbecq, "The Effectiveness of Nominal, Delphi, and Interacting Group Decision-Making Processes," *Academy of Management Journal,* 1974, *17,* pp. 607–626; Schwenk and Thomas, op. cit.

EXPERIENTIAL EXERCISE 14

Midwest Manufacturing Corporation

Midwest Manufacturing Corporation (MMC) is a medium-sized firm located in Cleveland, Ohio. Its primary products are components for automobile assembly, and the firm serves as a subcontractor for one of the major automobile companies in Detroit. With recent cutbacks in the industry, Midwest has lost business and now has too many employees. As personnel officer for the company, you have been ordered to lay off one-third of the workforce immediately. When you complained to top management about the possible shortsightedness of such an action, your complaints were ignored.

As you begin to consider who has to go, you start with the company's small engineering group. The group consists of nine employees, and, following the procedures set down by your boss to make across-the-board cuts, three of them must be laid off immediately. You examine brief resumes on each employee.

Robert Johnson, age 27, married, two children. Johnson has been with Midwest for almost two years. He is a solid engineer with a degree from the University of Michigan. He has held two prior jobs and lost both of them because of cutbacks in the automotive industry. He moved to Ohio from Michigan to take this job. Johnson is well liked by his co-workers.

Patricia Wong, age 38, single parent, two children. Wong has a B.S. in engineering from the Chinese University of Hong Kong. She is very active in community affairs, including Girl Scouts and the United Fund. She is a friend of the vice-president through her church work. Her ratings have been average, although some recent ones indicate that she may be somewhat behind the times. She is well liked, but some feel she is too quiet and reserved at work. Wong has been employed at Midwest for 13 years.

Donald Rice, age 54, married, three children. Rice is a graduate of "the school of hard knocks." After getting out of the service following the Korean War, he started to go to school. But his family expenses were too much, so he dropped out. Rice has worked at the company for 20 years. His ratings were excellent for 15 years. For the last 5 years they have been average. Rice feels his supervisor grades him down because he doesn't "have sheepskins covering my office walls." He would like to stay with the company until retirement.

Kareem Abduhl Jones, age 25, single. Jones is black, and the company worked hard to recruit him because of affirmative action pressure. He is not very popular with most of his co-workers. Because he has been employed less than a year, little is known about his performance or potential. On his one performance evaluation, he received a "satisfactory." Jones has openly criticized his supervisor for bias against minorities. He is a graduate of Ohio State University.

Alan Trump, age 34, married, no children. Trump holds a B.S. and an M.S. from the University of Minnesota and has been with the company for five years. He is well liked by his co-workers. Trump's performance ratings have been mixed—some supervisors rated him high, some average. Trump's wife is an M.D., and he claims to be related to important people in New York. He drives a BMW to work.

Carter Johnson, age 28, single. Johnson is a hard worker but is seen by many as a loner. He has a B.S. in engineering from the University of California, Berkeley. He is working on his M.S. at night at Case Western, always trying to improve his technical skills. His performance ratings have been above average for the four years he has been employed at Midwest.

Kathleen Mitchell, age 22, single. Mitchell has a B.S. in engineering from Illinois Institute of Technology and has been employed less than a year. She is enthusiastic, a very good worker, and is well liked by her co-workers. She is also a close friend of one of your vice-presidents. The company feels she has a bright future with the firm, and you know how difficult it is to recruit well-trained female engineers.

William Garcia, age 45, married, five children. Garcia grew up in East Los Angeles and was educated at Cal State–L.A. He joined Midwest 15 years ago and at one time served as the group's supervisor. He worked so hard that he had a heart attack. Under doctor's orders, he resigned from the supervisory position. Since then he has done good work, though because of his health, he is a bit slower than the others. Now and then, he must spend extra time on a project because he got somewhat out-of-date during the eight years he headed the section. His performance evaluations for the last two years have been above average.

Terrence Hitt, age 44, single. Hitt began an engineering degree at Cal Tech but had to drop out for financial reasons. He came to work at Midwest 15 years ago. He has tried to compensate for the lack of a degree by reading engineering journals on a regular basis and taking short courses at Case Western. His performance evaluations have varied, but they tend to be average to slightly above average. He is a loner, and many people feel that this has negatively affected his performance evaluations.

As you review the files, several things come to mind. Each employee has good points, and most have been good employees. They all can pretty much do each other's work. No one has special training. You are fearful that the section will hear about this and morale and productivity will suffer. You have until tomorrow morning to make your selection of the three who must go. In doing so, you must be cognizant of legal and moral guidelines and must follow acceptable personnel practices. After all, what you do here will serve as a guide for the layoffs affecting other sections in the company.

1. What guidelines would you develop to serve in your decision process? Remember, these guidelines will be applied to all other sections within the company.
2. Which three people would you lay off? Why?
3. What might the company do, within reason, to make the transition as smooth as possible for the three people who must leave?
4. What might be done among those remaining to maintain the best possible morale during a difficult time?

MANAGEMENT DILEMMA 14

American Pharmaceutical Company

American Pharmaceutical Company is a 75-year-old firm whose corporate headquarters and research laboratories are in New Caledonia. A pioneer in the ethical drug industry, American Pharmaceutical has been a highly profitable company, primarily by achieving "lead time" in bringing new prescription drugs to market ahead of competitors.

The engine for such competitive success is American Pharmaceutical's Advanced Research Facility in the Corporate Research Park complex outside Metropolis. American Pharmaceutical has attracted an outstanding group of biomedical researchers to this facility, which has been called the Bell Labs of the drug industry. Top scientists from universities, government health institutes, and health regulatory agencies have been attracted by the frontier research, tradition of scientific inquiry, and high prestige afforded to research scientists at American Pharmaceutical.

This attraction was symbolized by two events in 1988. Philip Macready, Chief Executive Officer of American Pharmaceutical, received the National Medical Association's Industry Excellence Award for advancing public health in the United States through the company's research and development achievements in combating disease. Also in 1988, American Pharmaceutical created an annual prize of $100,000 to be awarded to the research scientist in academia who has made the most important discovery in the field of geriatrics, thereby advancing the health of senior citizens.

However, a major problem has arisen at American Pharmaceutical, involving the development of a new drug that the company expects to market shortly. You are Michael Armstrong, Senior Vice President for Operations, and have just received three memos.

Key Persons Involved

Michael Armstrong, *Senior Vice President for Operations*
Harry T. Jennings, M.D., *Executive Director of Laboratory Research*
Marie Pawling, M.D., *Director of Medical Research/Therapeutics*
Ingrid J. Scalise, *Director, Public Affairs*
Jacob Lindt, M.D., *Director, Prolidamine Project Team*
McKinley Knight, Ph.D., *Chief Toxicologist*
T. Grayson Hurd, Jr., M.D., *Director of Clinical Studies*
Charles Rouse, *Assistant Director, Marketing*

Memorandum #1

Date: April 3
To: Michael Armstrong, Senior Vice President for Operations
From: Harry T. Jennings, M.D., Executive Director of Laboratory Research
Re: Clinical Trials of Prolidamine

I regret that I must bring to your attention a potentially serious obstacle in our development of prolidamine for introduction into the American market. Although progress up to this point has been rapid and the product is ready for clinical testing, we now find ourselves faced with an unprecedented problem. A key member of the development team feels that we should not move ahead with clinical trials, and has carried her opposition to the point of insubordination.

Prolidamine was originally developed by our Danish affiliate, Maarten, for treatment of acute and chronic diarrhea. Under the name Prolidam, it has been successfully marketed as a prescription medication in several European countries for the past two years, and no medical or legal problems have arisen in connection with its use. There is at present in this country no formulation that offers comparable effectiveness and ease of administration. Thus, it seems reasonable to expect that prolidamine could eventually command a substantial share of the market for antidiarrheal medications, estimated by Marketing at more than $150 million per annum. Accordingly, it is our aim to introduce prolidamine, under the trade name Damolid, to the domestic market as quickly as possible. Current plans call for initiation of clinical trials by May 1; conclusion of clinical trials by June 1; FDA approval by December 1; and test marketing next spring.

Our present difficulties with prolidamine stem, paradoxically, from one of its most advantageous characteristics. The wide acceptance of prolidamine can be attributed in large part to the fact that it is administered in liquid form, making it especially well suited to the needs of infants, children, the elderly, and any other patients who cannot conveniently take solid medication. As the active ingredients have a markedly bitter taste, the new artificial sweetener dematril is used to improve palatability. The

American Pharmaceutical project team that has been working on proli-damine since May of last year initially questioned the advisability of using large doses of dematril in prolidamine, in view of recent (but highly controversial) allegations that this substance may have carcinogenic effects on laboratory animals. (Background memos are available from Dr. Jacob Lindt, director of the prolidamine project team, and subsequent memos from Dr. McKinley Knight, the team's chief toxicologist, and Dr. Marie Pawling, its clinician). It was suggested that, as there are unresolved questions about dematril, an alternative formula containing sugar and/or smaller amounts of dematril should be developed.

On February 15, a number of members of the prolidamine team, including Dr. Lindt, Dr. Pawling, and Dr. Knight, met with management representatives, including myself; Charles Rouse, Assistant Director of Marketing (Prescription Medications Division); and Dr. T. Grayson Hurd, Jr., Director of Clinical Studies. The concerns of the prolidamine team over the dematril level in the original Maarten version of prolidamine were discussed at some length. Dr. Knight submitted a written summary of the objections to the Maarten formula, including a review of the clinical literature relating to dematril as a possible carcinogen. At this meeting, Dr. Pawling, who as the team's chief clinician would be in charge of clinical trials of prolidamine, asserted that she could not in good conscience administer prolidamine to human subjects in its present formulation. She suggested that an alternative means of sweetening the product be developed—a process that, according to Dr. Lindt, would probably take no more than six months.

Dr. Hurd then made the following points:

▮ That to date there is no incontrovertible evidence that dematril is a carcinogen in humans

▮ That, while the quantity of dematril in a *bottle* of prolidamine is large (about 44 times the amount currently allowed by the FDA in a 12-ounce can of diet soda), the prescribed dosage of prolidamine is quite small, so that the amount of dematril actually consumed by a patient using the medication during a 24-hour period would be less than that found in a single can of diet soda

▮ That the Maarten formula has encountered neither clinical complications nor regulatory problems during its two years of use in Europe

Thus, a change in the formula of prolidamine for the American market did not seem warranted. Rouse added that the six months required for such a change, though it might seem negligible to the research personnel, was by no means insignificant. A delay of this length might allow competitors to establish themselves in what is currently a wide-open market, as well as adversely affecting the profitability of the company for the fourth quarter of the fiscal year.

It was agreed that Dr. Lindt should inform the rest of the team as to the points raised by management, and initiate further discussions of the dematril issue. As a result of these discussions, and a number of follow-up meetings, the prolidamine project team decided on March 12 to approve the original Maarten formula and begin field trials at once. At this point, however, Dr. Pawling indicated that she refused to be bound by the team's decision. She stated to me personally, and in a memo dated March 16, that as a physician she considered it unethical to undertake clinical trials with a product when there were serious doubts—in her mind at least—about its safety. Accordingly, she will not be a party to human testing of prolidamine. She views the matter as one involving professional responsibility, and thus transcending any consideration of loyalty to American Pharmaceutical.

In nearly thirty years of research work—the past seventeen of them with this company—I cannot recall a comparable issue having arisen. While I have no firm evidence to support this view, I have received the sense from various discussions that Dr. Pawling is working on an alternative to dematril, which, if successful, would obviously enhance her scientific status in the company and beyond. I suspect that her high moral stance on this issue may simply be a tactic to increase the likelihood of recognition for her own work. In any case, I cannot see how we can allow her purely personal beliefs or motives in this matter to prevail over the considered judgment of the entire team, which includes many highly competent scientists. I therefore see no alternative but to remove her from the prolidamine project. I would appreciate it, however, if you would review the facts in the case and let me know whether you concur, before we embark on an action that could have consequences that are difficult to foresee.

Memorandum #2

Date: April 14
To: Michael Armstrong, Senior Vice President for Operations
From: Marie Pawling, M.D., Director of Medical Researching/Therapeutics
Re: Unwarranted Personnel Actions

I am writing to protest, in the most vehement terms, the recent actions taken against me by my superior, Dr. Harry Jennings, Executive Director of Laboratory Research. Dr. Jennings has informed me that I am to be demoted; that I will no longer be permitted to work on therapeutic drug development, which has been the focus of my activities with American Pharmaceutical up to the present; and that management considers me "unpromotable." I feel that these actions are completely unfair and unjustified. Moreover, I am convinced that the motivation underlying them is not that which Dr. Jennings has alleged in his conversations with me. Although Dr. Jennings has made broad and unsubstantiated accusations of irresponsibility against me, I feel that in reality I am being punished for being *too* responsible. I refer to my refusal to take part in clinical trials of prolidamine, a decision that I feel is at the root of these attacks.

Although Dr. Jennings has questioned my loyalty as well as impugned my judgment, I consider myself to be a loyal—indeed, dedicated—employee of American Pharmaceutical. I have been working at the New Caledonia labs for nearly four years now, and I have always attempted to perform my assignments in a conscientious and professional manner. I have had no reason to think that Dr. Jennings or anyone else was dissatisfied with my work, for I have received no complaints. On the contrary, my evaluations have always been excellent, to which my promotion two years ago attests. It is certainly *not* my habit to arbitrarily defy the wishes of management or the directives of my supervisors. Nor am I accustomed to imposing my will on my colleagues and peers. Thus my stand on the prolidamine matter was not taken without long reflection and soul-searching. Since I believe this to be the heart of the matter, let me restate—and try to explain—my position:

- Dematril has not been *proved* to be deleterious to humans. However, neither has it been proved safe. Since the issue is unresolved, it is inappropriate to market a medication containing dematril in high concentrations.

- The amount of dematril in the recommended 24-hour dosage of prolidamine is not excessive by current FDA standards. However, this medication is intended to be used by children and the elderly. How can we be sure that a user will not exceed the recommended dosage? What is to stop a child or an ill or senile adult from drinking an entire bottle? Moreover, the cumulative effects of substances such as dematril are not yet well understood. What might be the consequences of prolonged use of prolidamine? We do not know.

- The tumors with which dematril is thought to be associated have a latency period of some seventeen years. Thus, it would be many years before dematril-induced damage became apparent. In the meantime, countless people might be put at risk.

- Alternatives to the current, high-dematril formulation could easily be developed.

I should add that as a physician, I feel a special responsibility in this matter. It is true that the other members of the project team eventually approved prolidamine for clinical trials (after being subjected to heavy pressure from management, I should add). However, no one else on the team is a physician; no one else has taken the Hippocratic oath; no one else would have the responsibility of actually dispensing the drug to test subjects. I do not feel that I can be absolved of this responsibility by considerations of corporate loyalty, "team play," or any of the other notions that have been advanced to justify ignoring one's conscience.

I hope that the actions taken against me will be reconsidered. I have no desire for further conflict with the company, and I hope that this unpleasant episode can be put behind us as quickly as possible. However, I must state that if management continues to treat me in this way, I will have to consider legal recourse—not so much to protect my own livelihood and professional standing (although these are important to me) as to defend the principle that the first obligation of a physician is to his or her professional conscience.

Memorandum #3

Date: April 26
To: Michael Armstrong, Senior Vice President for Operations
From: Ingrid J. Scalise, Director, Public Affairs
Re: Dr. Marie Pawling

In response to your request for an analysis of the issues in the Pawling case, here is my evaluation of what is at stake for American Pharmaceutical.

Pawling has threatened to resign if she is not reinstated to her former position, and her memo of April 14 makes it clear that she is likely to undertake legal action against the company if her request is denied. Thus, a great deal of trouble would be saved if Pawling were to be reinstated. However, it is difficult to see how we could proceed with clinical trials of prolidamine with Pawling as Director of Medical Research/Therapeutics. Even if we went ahead under the supervision of another physician, there is no assurance that Pawling would not then make her objections public and/or take legal steps to block testing of prolidamine. While this is speculation, my feeling—based on my contacts with Pawling and the tone of her communications on this subject—is that she would do just that. It therefore seems that there is no way to avoid publicity in this case, unfortunate as that may be for AP.

It is my understanding that management is committed to the speedy introduction of prolidamine, and that this decision is based on three considerations:

▧ Since most of the development costs have already been borne by Maarten, the drug can be introduced at little additional expense to AP.

▧ Marketing assures us that sales in excess of $110 million a year are highly likely.

▧ Owing to the expiration of our patents in the tranquilizer field, and to the general erosion of profits in the area of contraceptive products as a result of competition and shifts in public practices, the company badly needs profitable new products—preferably sometime within the next two years.

Accordingly, our efforts should be directed to anticipating the problems that might arise if we move forward with prolidamine and Dr. Pawling resigns as expected. Three problems are potentially serious and should not be minimized.

1. It is the contention of our legal department that the demotion of Pawling—or even her firing, should that become necessary—probably cannot be successfully challenged in court. As Pawling is not a contract employee, she has no tenure and serves on an "at will" basis. The courts in New Caledonia have long held that management can fire a noncontract employee at its discretion, in the absence of a union collective-bargaining agreement or a violation of any employee protection statute (such as Equal Employment Opportunity or Occupational Safety and Health). However, we should note that in the past decade, almost half the states have established various exceptions to the employment-at-will doctrine. Some of these are based on implied contract (such as promises made at hiring or written in an employee handbook), and others are based on wrongful-conduct (tort) grounds (such as intentional infliction of emotional distress or invasion of privacy). One area of such new judicial doctrines involves protection of an employee who refuses to follow directions of the employer for reasons that the law recognizes as a legitimate "public policy," such as protecting public health or safety, and where the employee is then fired or punished by the employer for having done so.

In our state, New Caledonia, the courts have not in recent years considered revision of the traditional employment-at-will doctrine, and have not yet endorsed the public policy doctrine. We do not know how they might rule. Nor does our state have a whistle-blower protection law, as Pennsylvania, Michigan, New York, and half a dozen other states do. Even if these conditions were otherwise, Dr. Pawling, as I understand the facts, cannot cite any law or regulation that AP has broken, and she has not reported—and could not report—the company for a legal violation. Her basic claim would have to be that her physician's oath and her "professional code" of ethics allow her to take the actions she has, and that it is wrong for the company to remove her from her post or give her an adverse performance evaluation or undesirable assignment.

2. From a public relations viewpoint, however, our situation is less attractive.

a. With respect to the product, any hint of controversy concerning its safety is likely to prove damaging. This is true even if the FDA and other regulatory bodies ultimately back us completely. In today's climate of alarm about the safety of the environment generally, and drugs in particular, a new product must be considered "above suspicion" if it is to succeed.

b. With respect to the public image of AP, we would certainly want to avoid being seen as a company that would take chances with the safety of a new product, would bring pressure to bear on an employee who had raised concerns over safety, or would take retaliatory action against a "whistle-blower." Our reputation has always been that of a company committed to sound and thorough clinical research, with the greatest regard for public safety. We naturally do not wish to jeopardize this reputation, or our reputation as a fair employer.

c. Bad publicity could also impair our ability to recruit top younger scientists. If various medical or scientific groups were to take up Dr. Pawling's case as a cause célèbre, we could be made to look like the classic "blackhat" company, and experience a significant drop in the quality of our research staff.

3. At the same time, we do not want to encourage disgruntled or eccentric employees to feel that they can single-handedly veto or sabotage legitimate projects and activities of the company. If we back down in this case, we run the risk of compromising discipline and losing control of our own operations. We will be sending the "wrong message" to our personnel, leading them to think that their personal judgments and values must take precedence over the policies of the company and the objective, scientific weighing of evidence on which all research is based. Ultimately, it is hard to see how corporate management could continue to run responsible enterprises, especially when new scientific and technological developments are involved, if self-appointed "whistle-blowers" can set themselves up as independent decision makers.

Taking all these considerations into account, I feel that we should make one more attempt to work out some kind of modus vivendi with Dr. Pawling. We might agree to submit this case to an outside confidential review by a panel of top industry research scientists not in the drug field.

Failing to work out a resolution, however, I think we should hold to our position, and prepare as well as we can for whatever legal or public relations steps Dr. Pawling may decide to take.

On the basis of the above case, answer the following:

1. As Armstrong, would you approve Jennings's recommendation to remove Pawling from the prolidamine project? What factors would you want to take into consideration before making your decision?
2. How should Armstrong deal with Jennings's speculation that Pawling was seeking to advance her own career by blocking the use of dematril as a sweetener for prolidamine?
3. As Armstrong, what would be your response to Pawling's memo dated April 14?
4. Explain Pawling's rationale for acting on the basis of professional ethics. What other professions or occupations might have members who are inclined to claim ethical responsibilities in today's corporations, and what are the implications of this situation for managers?
5. What procedures for receiving and resolving employee complaints do you believe the firm might have used to handle the Pawling problem? Why might the chances of handling the issue be improved with other procedures?
6. Assume that Dr. Pawling is forced to leave American Pharmaceutical and that she sues the firm for wrongful discharge. What values or interests would need to be balanced in arriving at a decision on the merits of her claim? If you were the presiding judge, would you award damages to Pawling or uphold the company? If you found for Pawling, and she had asked for reinstatement as well as damages, how would you rule on that request?

Source: From Alan F. Westin and John D. Aram, *Managerial Dilemmas* (Cambridge, Mass.: Ballinger, 1988), pp. 27–34. Copyright 1988 by Ballinger Publishing Company. Reprinted by permission of HarperBusiness, a division of HarperCollins Publishers.

15

Organizational Power and Politics

The Management Challenge

- To understand how power bases work in organizational life.
- To recognize and account for the exercise of counterpower.
- To make appropriate use of strategic contingencies in interunit or interorganizational relations.
- To cope effectively with organizational politics.
- To know how to limit inappropriate or unethical political behavior where it occurs.

CLOSE UP ## Power Play in the GM Boardroom

The year 1992 produced a major power play in the boardroom of General Motors (GM) that had not been seen since 1920, when a group of financiers led by Pierre DuPont and J.P. Morgan & Co. bought out and shoved aside the founder of GM, William Crapo Durant. By the time the power struggle was over in late 1992, GM had lost over $7 billion.[1]

Like many U.S. board of directors, the board at GM was composed of both GM executives and outside directors. Roger Smith, who became CEO and chairman in 1981, remained on the board but helped select Robert Stempel, age 57, as the first engineer to become CEO and chairman in 30 years. Mr. Stempel had been with GM for 32 years when he took over the helm. Unfortunately, he took over at a time when GM was losing money at over $5 million a day.

In April of 1992, a group of outside directors, including John Smale (former chairman of P&G), J. Willard Marriott Jr. (CEO of Marriott Hotels), Ann McLaughlin (former U.S. labor secretary), Thomas Wyman (former CBS chairman, and Dennis Weatherstone (co-chairman of J. P. Morgan), pressured Mr. Stempel to make drastic changes in the top management of GM and were successful in the demotion of Mr. Reuss (56, and then president of GM) and Mr. O'Connel (CFO). The board then promoted John F. Smith (age 54 and no relation to Roger Smith) to the position of president. Mr. Smith had built a reputation as a turnaround artist because of his role in taking the European operations from red ink to over $9 billion in profits in the space of a few years.

Despite the frustration of outside directors with the pace of the changes under Stempel, he had considerable support within GM. As an engineer, Stempel was thought of as a true "car guy." Most of the executives and union officials inside GM thought that he simply inherited a mess from his predecessor, Roger Smith. "To give Stempel only two years to patch up the hole in the bottom of this ship, I don't think is fair," said Steve Featherston, president of United Auto Workers Local 1999. President of another UAW local, Dick Long, commented, "They give him just two years to fix what Roger took 10 years to screw up."

However, by October 1992, the red ink was still flowing at a pace that would have done in all but the very largest of firms, and the outside directors grew more impatient. The outside directors sent intermediaries to Stempel suggesting that he resign. They also put pressure on Roger Smith to give up his seat on the board. Despite denials the day before, Robert Stempel resigned as CEO and chairman of GM on October 26, 1992. Along with Mr. Stempel, Lloyd Reuss, 56 and GM's former president, vice-chairman Robert Schultz, 62, and executive vice-president F. Alan Smith, 61, all announced they were taking early retirement.

In November of 1992, John Smith was named CEO. At age 54, Mr. Smith was the youngest CEO at GM since 1923 when Alfred P. Sloan took over at age 48. In addition to Mr. Smith, G. Richard Wagoner Jr., 39, leaped past several positions and more senior executives to become the CFO. Louis R. Hughes, 43, became the head of all international operations. Harry J. Pearce, 50, was named as executive vice-president. All of these positions had been traditionally reserved for executives in their 50s and 60s. Finally, for the first time in 30 years, the duties of CEO and chairman were split, and Mr. Smale, who led the revolt by the outside directors, was named as chairman of the board.

Though the impact of this power struggle on GM's bottom line, as well as on the boardrooms of other firms in trouble, will take time to fully emerge, it remains one of the more dramatic and public boardroom power plays in modern times.

Although the circumstances of Stempel's departure from GM may be unique, the exercise of power and political behavior in organizations is certainly not. Power and politics are the lifeblood of most organizations, and, as a result, informed managers need to understand power dynamics. In fact, organizations are composed of coalitions and alliances of different parties that continually compete for available resources. As such, a major influence on how decisions are made is the distribution of power among the decision makers. Unequal distribution of power in organizations can have a critical impact on many aspects of work life, including employee motivation, job satisfaction, absenteeism and turnover, and stress. Hence, an awareness of the nature and pervasiveness of power and politics is essential for a better understanding of these other behavioral processes.

The concept of power is closely related to the concepts of authority and leadership. It is important to understand when one method of influence ceases and another begins. For example, when does a manager stop using legitimate authority in a work situation and start using unauthorized power?

Finally, on an individual level, many people attempt to exercise influence in organizations by using power tactics. An awareness of such tactics helps managers to recognize them and to take appropriate actions. Keep in mind that attempts by others to exercise power do not have to be successful. A number of mechanisms are available to countermand or neutralize influence attempts. Knowledge of these strategies gives a manager greater latitude in his or her response to power plays by others.

In short, power and political processes in organizations represent a topic of central importance to students of organizational behavior. Along with other group processes, such as communication and decision making, power and politics can considerably influence both the behavior and the attitudes of employees at various levels of the organization. In addition, they can further influence the extent to which various units within the organization secure the necessary resources for task accomplishment and ultimate organizational success. In short, General Motors is not alone.

POWER IN INTERPERSONAL RELATIONS

In this chapter, we will examine various aspects of power and politics in organizations, beginning with the topic of power in interpersonal relations. Here power is defined and distinguished from the related concepts of authority and leadership, and several bases of power and aspects of power dependency are discussed. Although these aspects of power also relate to group situations, they are more germane to interpersonal relations.

What Is Power?

Numerous definitions of power abound in the literature on organizations. One of the earliest was suggested by Max Weber, the noted German sociologist, who defined power as "the probability that one actor within a social relationship will be in a position to carry out his own will despite resistance."[2]

Similarly, Emerson wrote, "The power of actor A over actor B is the amount of resistance on the part of B which can be potentially overcome by A."[3] Following these and other definitions, we will define *power* for our purposes as an interpersonal relationship in which one individual (or group) has the ability to cause another individual (or group) to take an action that would not be taken otherwise.

In other words, power involves one person changing the behavior of another. It is important to note that in most organizational situations, we are talking about *implied* force to comply, not necessarily actual force. That is, person *A* has power over person *B* if person *B* believes that person *A* can, in fact, force person *B* to comply.

Power, Authority, and Leadership

Clearly, the concept of power is closely related to the concepts of authority and leadership (see Exhibit 15.1). In fact, power has been referred to by some as "informal authority," whereas authority has been called "legitimate power." However, these three concepts are not the same, and important differences among the three should be noted.[4]

As stated previously, power represents the capacity of one person or group to secure compliance from another person or group. Nothing is said here about the *right* to secure compliance—only the ability. In contrast, *authority* represents the right to seek compliance by others; the exercise of authority is backed by legitimacy. If a manager instructs a secretary to type certain letters, he or she presumably has the authority to make such a request. However, if the same manager asked the secretary to run personal errands, this would be outside the bounds of the legitimate exercise of authority. Although the secretary may still act on this request, the secretary's compliance would be based on power or influence considerations, not authority.

Hence, the exercise of authority is based on group acceptance of someone's right to exercise legitimate control. As Grimes notes, "What legitimates authority is the promotion or pursuit of collective goals that are associated with group consensus. The polar opposite, power, is the pursuit of individual or particularistic goals associated with group compliance."[5]

Finally, as we saw in Chapter 12, *leadership* is the ability of one individual to elicit responses from another person that go beyond required or mechanical compliance. It is this voluntary aspect of leadership that sets it apart from

Exhibit 15.1
Three Major Types
of Influence

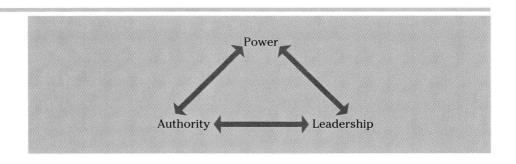

power and authority. Hence, we often differentiate between headship and leadership. A department head may have the right to require certain actions, whereas a leader has the ability to inspire certain actions. Although both functions may be served by the same individual, such is clearly not always the case.

TYPES OF POWER

If power is the ability to secure compliance by others, how is such power exercised? On what is it based? At least two efforts have been made to identify the bases of power. One model has been proposed by Etzioni, identifying three types of power.[6] In fact, it is argued that organizations can be classified according to which of the three types of power is most prevalent. *Coercive* power involves forcing someone to comply with one's wishes. A prison organization is an example of a coercive organization. *Utilitarian* power is power based on performance-reward contingencies; for example, a person will comply with a supervisor in order to receive a pay raise or promotion. Business organizations are thought to be essentially utilitarian organizations. Finally, *normative* power rests on the beliefs of the members in the right of the organization to govern their behavior. An example here would be a religious organization.

Bases of Power

Although useful for comparative analysis of divergent organizations, this model may have limited applicability, because most business and public organizations rest largely on utilitarian power. Instead, a second model, developed by French and Raven, of the *bases of power* may be more helpful.[7] French and Raven identified five primary ways in which power can be exerted in social situations.

Referent Power.   In some cases, person *B* looks up to or admires person *A,* and, as a result, *B* follows *A* largely because of *A*'s personal qualities, characteristics, or reputation. In this case, *A* can use *referent power* to influence *B*. Referent power has also been called *charismatic power,* because allegiance is based on interpersonal attraction of one individual for another. Examples of referent power can be seen in advertising, where companies use celebrities to recommend their products; it is hoped that the star appeal of the person will rub off on the products. In work environments, junior managers often emulate senior managers and assume unnecessarily subservient roles more because of personal admiration than because of respect for authority.

Expert Power.   *Expert power* is demonstrated when person *A* gains power because *A* has knowledge or expertise relevant to *B*. For instance, professors presumably have power in the classroom because of their mastery of a particular subject matter. Other examples of expert power can be seen in staff specialists in organizations (e.g., accountants, labor relations managers, management consultants, and corporate attorneys). In each case, the individual has credibility in a particular—and narrow—area as a result of experience and expertise, and this gives the individual power in that domain.

Legitimate Power.   *Legitimate power* exists when person *B* submits to person *A* because *B* feels that *A* has a right to exert power in a certain domain.[8] Legitimate power is really another name for authority, as explained earlier. A supervisor has a right, for instance, to assign work. Legitimate power differs from reward and coercive power in that it depends on the official position a person holds, and not on his or her relationship with others.

Legitimate power derives from three sources. First, prevailing cultural values can assign power to some group. In Japan and Korea, for instance, older employees derive power simply because of their age. Second, legitimate power can be attained as a result of the accepted social structure. For example, many Western European countries, as well as Japan, have royal families that serve as a cornerstone to their societies. Third, legitimate power may be designated, as in the case of a board of directors choosing a new company president, or a person being promoted into a managerial position. Whatever the reason, people exercise legitimate power because subordinates assume they have a right to exercise it. A principal reason given for the downfall of the Shah of Iran is that the people came to first question and then denounce his right to legitimate power.

Reward Power.   *Reward power* exists when person *A* has power over person *B* because *A* controls rewards that *B* wants. These rewards can cover a wide array of possibilities, including pay raises, promotions, desirable job assignments, more responsibility, new equipment, and so forth. Research has indicated that reward power often leads to increased job performance as employees see a strong performance-reward contingency.[9] However, in many organizations, supervisors and managers really do not control very many rewards. For example, salary and promotion among most blue-collar workers is based on a labor contract, not a performance appraisal.

Coercive Power.   *Coercive power* is based primarily on fear. Here, person *A* has power over person *B* because *A* can administer some form of punishment to *B*. Thus, this kind of power is also referred to as punishment power. As Kipnis points out, coercive power does not have to rest on the threat of violence. "Individuals exercise coercive power through a reliance upon physical strength, verbal facility, or the ability to grant or withhold emotional support from others. These bases provide the individual with the means to physically harm, bully, humiliate, or deny love to others."[10] Examples of coercive power in organizations include the ability (actual or implied) to fire or demote people, transfer them to undesirable jobs or locations, or strip them of valued perquisites. Indeed, it has been suggested that a good deal of organizational behavior (such as prompt attendance, looking busy, avoiding whistle-blowing) can be attributed to coercive, not reward, power. As Kipnis explains, "Of all the bases of power available to man, the power to hurt others is possibly the most often used, most often condemned and most difficult to control."[11]

It is interesting to note how executives see their bases of power. In a recent survey, over 200 CEOs were asked to rank the importance of a series of sources of power. Results, shown in Exhibit 15.2, indicate a wide array of sources. They also indicate that effective CEOs maintain solid lines of support in many quarters that can be drawn upon when needed. Asked if today's CEOs had more or less power than they did 10 years ago, 42 percent said they had less, 36 percent said the same, and 19 percent said more.[12]

Exhibit 15.2
Bases of Power for
American CEOs

Source of Power	Percent*
Personality and leadership skills	83
Support of the board of directors	70
Support of senior colleagues	64
Expertise and knowledge	43
Management control (power to hire, fire, allocate resources)	28
Support of the financial community	9

*Percent of CEOs who identified this factor as one of the top three sources of power in their job.

Source: Based on a survey of 216 Chief Executive Officers reported in T. Stewart, "CEOs See Clout Shifting," *Fortune,* November 6, 1989, p. 66.

Before moving on, you might find it interesting to look at your own bases of power in an organization you have worked with. To do this, simply think of your present or past job and complete Self-Assessment 15.1. When you have finished, refer to Appendix B for scoring procedures.

Behavioral Consequences of Power

We have seen, then, that at least five bases of power can be identified. In each case, the power of the individual rests on a particular attribute of the power holder, the follower, or their relationship. In some cases (e.g., reward power), power rests in the superior; in others (e.g., referent power), power is given to the superior by the subordinate. In all cases, the exercise of power involves subtle and sometimes threatening interpersonal consequences for the parties involved. In fact, when power is exercised, employees have several ways in which to respond. These are shown in Exhibit 15.3.

Exhibit 15.3
Employee Reactions to
Bases of Power

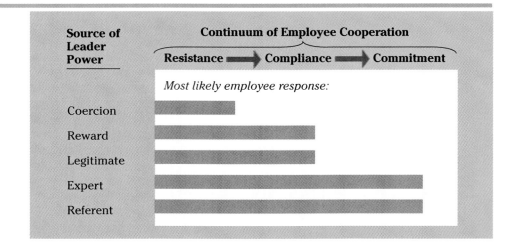

SELF-ASSESSMENT 15.1
What Are Your Bases of Power?

Instructions: Using a current or former job, answer each of the following items by circling the response that most suits your answer.

		Strongly Disagree				Strongly Agree
1.	I always try to set a good example for other employees.	1	2	3	4	5
2.	My co-workers seem to respect me on the job.	1	2	3	4	5
3.	Many employees view me as their informal leader at work.	1	2	3	4	5
4.	I know my job very well.	1	2	3	4	5
5.	My skills and abilities help me a lot on this job.	1	2	3	4	5
6.	I continually try to improve the way I do my job.	1	2	3	4	5
7.	I have considerable authority in my job.	1	2	3	4	5
8.	Decisions made at my level are critical to organizational success.	1	2	3	4	5
9.	Employees frequently ask me for guidance.	1	2	3	4	5
10.	I am able to reward people at lower levels in the organization.	1	2	3	4	5
11.	I am responsible for evaluating those below me.	1	2	3	4	5
12.	I have a say in who gets a bonus or pay raise.	1	2	3	4	5
13.	I can punish employees at lower levels.	1	2	3	4	5
14.	I check the work of lower-level employees.	1	2	3	4	5
15.	My diligence helps to reduce the errors of others on the job.	1	2	3	4	5

If the subordinate accepts and identifies with the leader, his or her behavioral response will probably be one of *commitment.* That is, the subordinate will be motivated to follow the wishes of the leader. This is most likely to happen when the person in charge uses referent or expert power. Under these circumstances, the follower believes in the leader's cause and will exert considerable energies to help the leader succeed.

A second possible response is *compliance.* This occurs most frequently when the subordinate feels the leader has either legitimate power or reward power. Under such circumstances, the follower will comply, either because it is perceived as a duty or because a reward is expected; but commitment or enthusiasm for the project is lacking. Finally, under conditions of coercive power, subordinates will more than likely use *resistance*. Here, the subordinate sees little reason—either altruistic or material—for cooperating and will often engage in a series of tactics to defeat the leader's efforts.

Power Dependencies

In any situation involving power, at least two persons (or groups) can be identified: the person attempting to influence others and the target or targets of that influence. Until recently, attention focused almost exclusively on how people tried to influence others. Only recently has attention been given to how people try to nullify or moderate such influence attempts. In particular, we now recognize that the extent to which influence attempts are successful is determined in large part by the *power dependencies* of those on the receiving end of the influence attempts. In other words, all people are not subject to (or dependent upon) the same bases of power. What causes some people to be more submissive or vulnerable to power attempts? At least three factors have been identified.[13]

Subordinate's Values.   To begin, person B's values can influence his or her susceptibility to influence. For example, if the outcomes that A can influence are important to B, then B is more likely to be open to influence than if the outcomes were unimportant. Hence, if an employee places a high value on money and believes the supervisor actually controls pay raises, we would expect the employee to be highly susceptible to the supervisor's influence. We hear comments about how young people don't really want to work hard anymore. Perhaps a reason for this phenomenon is that some young people don't place a high value on those things (for example, money) that traditionally have been used to influence behavior. In other words, such complaints may really be saying that young people are more difficult to influence than they used to be.

Nature of Relationship Between A and B.   In addition, the nature of the relationship between A and B can be a factor in power dependence. Are A and B peers or superior and subordinate? Is the job permanent or temporary? A person on a temporary job, for example, may feel less need to acquiesce, because he or she won't be holding the position for long. Moreover, if A and B are peers or good friends, the influence process is likely to be more delicate than if they are superior and subordinate.

Counterpower.   Finally, a third factor to consider in power dependencies is counterpower. The concept of counterpower focuses on the extent to which B has other sources of power to buffer the effects of A's power. For example, if B is unionized, the union's power may serve to negate A's influence attempts. The use of counterpower can be clearly seen in a variety of situations where various coalitions attempt to bargain with each other and check the power of their opponents.

Exhibit 15.4 presents a rudimentary model that combines the concepts of bases of power with the notion of power dependencies. As can be seen, A's bases of power interact with B's extent of power dependency to determine

Exhibit 15.4
Typical Response Patterns in
Dyadic Power Relationships

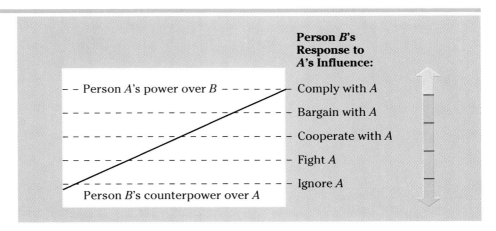

B's response to *A*'s influence attempt. If A has significant power and *B* is highly dependent, we would expect *B* to comply with *A*'s wishes.

If *A* has more modest power over *B*, but *B* is still largely power dependent, *B* may try to bargain with *A*. Despite the fact that *B* would be bargaining from a point of weakness, this strategy may serve to protect *B*'s interests better than outright compliance. For instance, if your boss asked you to work overtime, you might attempt to strike a deal whereby you would get compensatory time off at a later date. If successful, although you would not have decreased your working hours, at least you would not have increased them. Where power distribution is more evenly divided, *B* may attempt to develop a cooperative working relationship with *A* in which both parties gain from the exchange. An example of this position is a labor contract negotiation where labor-management relations are characterized by a balance of power and a good working relationship.

If *B* has more power than *A*, *B* will more than likely reject *A*'s influence attempt. *B* may even become the aggressor and attempt to influence *A*. Finally, when *B* is not certain of the power relationships, he or she may simply try to ignore *A*'s efforts. In doing so, *B* will discover either that *A* does indeed have more power, or that *A* cannot muster the power to be successful. A good illustration of this last strategy can be seen in some companies' responses to early governmental efforts to secure equal opportunities for minorities and women. These companies simply ignored governmental efforts until new regulations forced compliance.

IN PRACTICE:
Secretaries: The Power Behind the Throne

It is relatively easy to see the power of managers. They often have the ability to hire and fire, make important decisions, sign contracts, spend money, and so forth. They are, in fact, powerful entities within a corporation. What may be less apparent, however, is the power that managers' secretaries often have. In fact, if you want to discover just how powerful secretaries are, think of what would happen if they were not there. Most paperwork would not get done; many important decisions would not be made; and the organization would eventually grind to a halt.

And as highly skilled secretaries become increasingly hard to recruit and retain, their power only increases. Secretaries represent a true example of counterpower within the organization. Yes, their bosses have power over them; but at the same time, they have considerable power over their bosses. Secretaries—the word is derived from the Latin word meaning "keeper of secrets"—are often privy to considerable confidential information. They routinely handle private calls, correspondence, and reports. They often serve as the manager's sounding board for new ideas, and they more than likely know how the boss feels about co-workers and superiors. In many cases, they even decide who gets to see their boss and who does not. This knowledge, along with their increasing scarcity, gives high-quality secretaries considerable leverage in dealing with their bosses and their organizations.[14]

USES OF POWER

As we look around organizations, it is easy to see the manifestations of power almost anywhere. In fact, there are a wide variety of power-based methods used to influence others. Here we will examine three aspects of the use of power: commonly used power tactics in organizations, symbols of managerial power, and the ethical use of power.

Common Power Tactics in Organizations

As noted above, many power tactics are available for use by managers. However, as we will see, some are more ethical than others. Here, we look at some of the more commonly used power tactics found in both business and public organizations.[15]

Controlling Access to Information.   Most decisions rest on the availability of relevant information, so persons *controlling access to information* play a major role in decisions made. A good example of this is the common corporate practice of pay secrecy. Only the personnel department and senior managers typically have salary information—and power—for personnel decisions.

Controlling Access to Persons.   Another related power tactic is the practice of *controlling access to persons*. A well-known factor contributing to President Nixon's downfall was his isolation from others. His two senior advisors had complete control over who saw the president. Similar criticisms were leveled against President Reagan.

Selective Use of Objective Criteria.   Very few organizational questions have one correct answer; instead, decisions must be made concerning the most appropriate criteria for evaluating results. As such, significant power can be exercised by those who can practice *selective use of objective criteria* that will lead to a decision favorable to themselves. According to Herbert Simon, if an individual is permitted to select decision criteria, he or she needn't care who actually makes the decision. Attempts to control objective decision criteria can be seen in faculty debates in a university or college over who gets hired or promoted. One group tends to emphasize teaching and will attempt to set criteria for employment dealing with teacher competence, subject area, interpersonal relations, and so on. Another group may emphasize research and will try to set criteria related to number of publications, reputation in the field, and so on.

Controlling the Agenda.   One of the simplest ways to influence a decision is to ensure that it never comes up for consideration in the first place. There are a variety of strategies used for *controlling the agenda.* Efforts may be made to order the topics at a meeting in such a way that the undesired topic is last on the list. Failing this, opponents may raise a number of objections or points of information concerning the topic that cannot be easily answered, thereby tabling the topic until another day.

Using Outside Experts.   Still another means to gain an advantage is by *using outside experts.* The unit wishing to exercise power may take the initiative and bring in experts from the field or experts known to be in sympathy with their cause. Hence, when a dispute arises over spending more money on research versus actual production, we would expect differing answers from outside research consultants and outside production consultants. Most consultants have experienced situations in which their clients fed them information and biases they hoped the consultant would repeat in a meeting.

Bureaucratic Gamesmanship.   In some situations, the organization's own policies and procedures provide ammunition for power plays, or *bureaucratic gamesmanship.* For instance, a group may drag its feet on making changes in the workplace by creating red tape, work slowdowns, or "working to rule." (Working to rule occurs when employees diligently follow every work rule and policy statement to the letter; this typically results in the organization's grinding to a halt as a result of the many and often conflicting rules and policy statements.) In this way, they let it be known that the work flow will continue to slow down until they get their way.

Coalitions and Alliances.   The final power tactic to be discussed here is that of *coalitions and alliances.* One unit can effectively increase its power by forming an alliance with other groups that share similar interests. This technique is often used when multiple labor unions in the same corporation join forces to gain contract concessions for their workers. It can also be seen in the tendency of corporations within one industry to form trade associations to lobby for their position. Although the various members of a coalition need not agree on everything—indeed, they may be competitors—sufficient agreement on the problem under consideration is necessary as a basis for action.

Although other power tactics could be discussed, these examples serve to illustrate the diversity of techniques available to those interested in acquiring and exercising power in organizational situations. In reviewing the major research carried out on the topic of power, Pfeffer states:

> If there is one concluding message, it is that it is probably effective and it is certainly normal that these managers do behave as politicians. It is even better that some of them are quite effective at it. In situations in

which technologies are uncertain, preferences are conflicting, perceptions are selective and biased, and information processing capacities are constrained, the model of an effective politician may be an appropriate one for both the individual and for the organization in the long run.[16]

Symbols of Managerial Power

How do we know when a manager has power in an organizational setting? Harvard professor Rosabeth Kanter has identified several of the more common symbols of managerial power.[17] For example, managers have power to the extent that they can intercede favorably on behalf of someone in trouble with the organization. Have you ever noticed that when several people commit the same mistake, some don't get punished? Perhaps someone is watching over them.

Moreover, managers have power when they can get a desirable placement for a talented subordinate (this can be seen in the mentoring process, discussed in Chapter 18) or get approval for expenditures beyond their budget. Other manifestations of power include the ability to secure above-average salary increases for subordinates and the ability to get items on the agenda at policy meetings.

And we can see the extent of managerial power when someone can gain quick access to top decision makers or can get early information about decisions and policy shifts. In other words, who can get through to the boss, and who can't? Who is "connected," and who is not?

Finally, power is evident when top decision makers seek out the opinions of a particular manager on important questions. Who gets invited to important meetings, and who does not? Who does the boss say "hello" to when he or she enters the room? Through such actions, the organization sends clear signals concerning who has power and who does not. In this way, the organization reinforces or at least condones the power structure in existence.

The Ethical Use of Power

People are often uncomfortable discussing the topic of power, which implies that somehow they see the exercise of power as unseemly. On the contrary, the question is not whether power tactics are or are not ethical; rather, the question is *which* tactics are appropriate and which are not. The use of power in groups and companies is a fact of organizational life that all employees must accept. In doing so, however, all employees have a right to know that the exercise of power within the organization will be governed by ethical standards that prevent abuse or exploitation.

Several guidelines for the ethical use of power can be identified. These can be arranged according to our previous discussion of the five bases of power, as shown in Exhibit 15.5. As will be noted, several techniques are available that accomplish their aims without compromising ethical standards. For example, a manager using reward power can verify subordinate compliance with work directives, ensure that all requests are both feasible and reasonable, make only ethical or proper requests, offer rewards that are valued by employees, and ensure that all rewards for good performance are credible and reasonably attainable.

Exhibit 15.5
The Ethical Use of Power

Basis of Power	Guidelines for Use
Referent power	• Treat subordinates fairly • Defend subordinates' interests • Be sensitive to subordinates' needs, feelings • Select subordinates similar to oneself • Engage in role modeling
Expert power	• Promote image of expertise • Maintain credibility • Act confident and decisive • Keep informed • Recognize employee concerns • Avoid threatening subordinates' self-esteem
Legitimate power	• Be cordial and polite • Be confident • Be clear and follow up to verify understanding • Make sure request is appropriate • Explain reasons for request • Follow proper channels • Exercise power regularly • Enforce compliance • Be sensitive to subordinates' concerns
Reward power	• Verify compliance • Make feasible, reasonable requests • Make only ethical, proper requests • Offer rewards desired by subordinates • Offer only credible rewards
Coercive power	• Inform subordinates of rules and penalties • Warn before punishing • Administer punishment consistently and uniformly • Understand the situation before acting • Maintain credibility • Fit punishment to the infraction • Punish in private

Source: From Gary A. Yukl, *Leadership in Organizations,* © 1981, pp. 44–58. Adapted by permission of Prentice-Hall, Inc., Englewood Cliffs, N.J.

Even coercive power can be used without jeopardizing personal integrity. For example, a manager can make sure that all employees know the rules and penalties for rule infractions, provide warnings before punishing, administer punishments fairly and uniformly, and so forth. The point here is that managers have at their disposal numerous tactics that they can employ without crossing over into questionable managerial behavior. In view of the increasing number of lawsuits filed by employees for harmful practices, it seems wise for a manager to consider his or her behaviors before acting; this will help ensure the highest ethical standards.

IN PRACTICE:
Investigating the Challenger Disaster

The January 1986 explosion of the space shuttle *Challenger,* at a cost of seven lives, has been analyzed from several managerial standpoints: poor decision making, poor management control, and poor leadership have all been blamed. We can also see in this tragedy an example of the unethical use of organizational power.

It has been determined that the explosion that doomed the space shuttle was caused by poorly designed seals on the booster rockets. The boosters were manufactured by Morton Thiokol, a major defense contractor. When the U.S. Congress initiated its investigation of the causes of the disaster, it found several disturbing facts. To begin with, several Morton Thiokol engineers had warned that the boosters were unsafe early in the design stage, but no one listened. Once the boosters were in production, engineers again warned of possible problems, but to no avail. The company kept the information quiet.

Equally disturbing was the fact that after two company engineers testified in the congressional hearing, they were abruptly transferred to undesirable assignments elsewhere in the company. When asked by Congress whether they thought their transfers were in retaliation for their "whistle-blowing," both engineers responded yes. One noted, "I feel I was set aside so I would not have contact with the people from NASA." The company had, in effect, used its power to try to isolate those who talked freely with the congressional investigators. In its defense, Morton Thiokol responded that it had *demoted* no one as a result of the investigation. "We've changed a lot of duties . . . because we're reorganizing," a management representative said.[18]

POLITICAL BEHAVIOR IN ORGANIZATIONS

Closely related to the concept of power is the equally important topic of politics. In any discussion of the exercise of power—particularly in intergroup situations—a knowledge of basic political processes is essential. We will begin our discussion with this in mind. Next, on the basis of this analysis, we will consider political strategies for acquiring, maintaining, and using power in intergroup relations. Finally, we look at ways to limit the impact of political behavior in organizations.

What Is Politics?

Perhaps the earliest definition of politics was offered by Lasswell, who described it as who gets what, when, and how.[19] Even from this simple definition, one can see that politics involves the resolution of differing preferences in conflicts over the allocation of scarce and valued resources. Politics represents one mechanism to solve allocation problems when other mechanisms, such as the introduction of new information or the use of a simple majority rule, fail to apply. For our purposes here, we will adopt Pfeffer's definition of politics as involving "those activities taken within organizations to acquire, develop, and use power and other resources to obtain one's preferred outcomes in a situation in which there is uncertainty or dissensus about choices."[20]

In comparing the concept of politics with the related concept of power, Pfeffer notes:

> If power is a force, a store of potential influence through which events can be affected, politics involves those activities or behaviors through which power is developed and used in organizational settings. Power is a property of the system at rest; politics is the study of power in action. An individual, subunit or department may have power within an organizational context at some period of time; politics involves the exercise of power to get something accomplished, as well as those activities which are undertaken to expand the power already possessed or the scope over which it can be exercised.[21]

In other words, from this definition it is clear that political behavior is activity that is initiated for the purpose of overcoming opposition or resistance. In the absence of opposition, there is no need for political activity. Moreover, it should be remembered that political activity need not necessarily be dysfunctional for organization-wide effectiveness. In fact, many managers often believe that their political actions on behalf of their own departments are actually in the best interests of the organization as a whole. Finally, we should note that politics, like power, is not inherently bad. In many instances, the survival of the organization depends on the success of a department or coalition of departments challenging a traditional but outdated policy or objective. That is why an understanding of organizational politics, as well as power, is so essential for managers.

Intensity of Political Behavior

Contemporary organizations are highly political entities. Indeed, much of the goal-related effort produced by an organization is directly attributable to political processes. However, the intensity of political behavior varies, depending upon many factors. For example, in one study, managers were asked to rank several organizational decisions on the basis of the extent to which politics were involved.[22] Results showed that the most political decisions (in rank order) were those involving interdepartmental coordination, promotions and transfers, and the delegation of authority. Such decisions are typically characterized by an absence of established rules and procedures and a reliance on ambiguous and subjective criteria.

On the other hand, the managers in the study ranked as least political such decisions as personnel policies, hiring, and disciplinary procedures. These decisions are typically characterized by clearly established policies, procedures, and objective criteria.

On the basis of findings such as these, it is possible to develop a typology of when political behavior would generally be greatest and least. This model is shown in Exhibit 15.6. As can be seen, we would expect the greatest amount of political activity in situations characterized by high uncertainty and complexity and high competition among employees or groups

Exhibit 15.6
Probability of Political
Behavior in an Organization

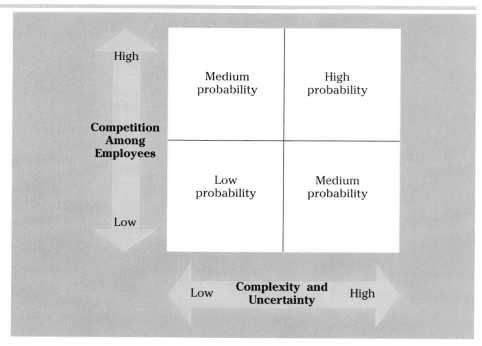

Source: From "The Use and Abuse of Corporate Politics" by Don R. Beeman and Thomas W. Sharkey. Reprinted from *Business Horizons,* March–April 1987. Copyright 1987 by the Foundation for the School of Business at Indiana University. Used with permission.

for scarce resources. The least politics would be expected under conditions of low uncertainty and complexity and little competition among employees over resources.

Reasons for Political Behavior

Following from the above model, we can identify at least six conditions conducive to political behavior in organizations.[23] These are shown in Exhibit 15.7, along with possible resulting behaviors. The conditions include the following:

1. *Ambiguous goals.* When the goals of a department or organization are ambiguous, more room is available for politics. As a result, members may pursue personal gain under the guise of pursuing organizational goals.
2. *Limited resources.* Politics surfaces when resources are scarce and allocation decisions must be made. If resources were ample, there would be no need to use politics to claim one's "share."
3. *Changing technology and environment.* In general, political behavior is increased when the nature of the internal technology is nonroutine and when the external environment is dynamic and complex. Under these conditions, ambiguity and uncertainty are increased, thereby triggering political behavior by groups interested in pursuing certain courses of action.

4. *Nonprogrammed decisions.* A distinction was made in the previous chapter between programmed and nonprogrammed decisions. When decisions are not programmed, conditions surrounding the decision problem and the decision process are usually more ambiguous, which leaves room for political maneuvering. Programmed decisions, on the other hand, are typically specified in such detail that little room for maneuvering exists. Hence, we are likely to see more political behavior on major questions, such as long-range strategic planning decisions.

5. *Organizational change.* Periods of organizational change also present opportunities for political rather than rational behavior. Efforts to restructure a particular department, open a new division, introduce a new product line, and so forth, are invitations to all to join the political process as different factions and coalitions fight over territory (see Chapter 19).

Because most organizations today have scarce resources, ambiguous goals, complex technologies, and sophisticated and unstable external environments, it seems reasonable to conclude that a large proportion of contemporary organizations are highly political in nature.[24] As a result, contemporary managers must be sensitive to political processes as they relate to the acquisition and maintenance of power in organizations. This brings up the question of why we have policies and standard operating procedures (SOPs) in organizations. Actually, such policies are frequently aimed at reducing the extent to which politics influences a particular decision. This effort to encourage more "rational" decisions in organizations was a primary reason behind Max Weber's development of the bureaucratic model (see Chapter 10). That is, increases in the specification of policy statements often are inversely related to political efforts, as shown in Exhibit 15.8. This is true primarily because such actions reduce the uncertainties surrounding a decision and hence the opportunity for political efforts.

Before leaving this topic, it might be interesting for you to evaluate your own level of political behavior. To do this, complete Self-Assessment 15.2. When you have finished, score your questionnaire according to the procedure outlined in Appendix B.

Exhibit 15.7
Conditions Conducive to
Political Behavior

Prevailing Conditions	Resulting Political Behaviors
Ambiguous goals	Attempts to define goals to one's advantage
Limited resources	Fight to maximize one's share of resources
Dynamic technology and environment	Attempts to exploit uncertainty for personal gain
Nonprogrammed decisions	Attempts to make suboptimal decisions that favor personal ends
Organizational change	Attempts to use reorganization as a chance to pursue own interests and goals

Exhibit 15.8
Relationship Between
Company Standard
Operating Procedures and
Political Behavior

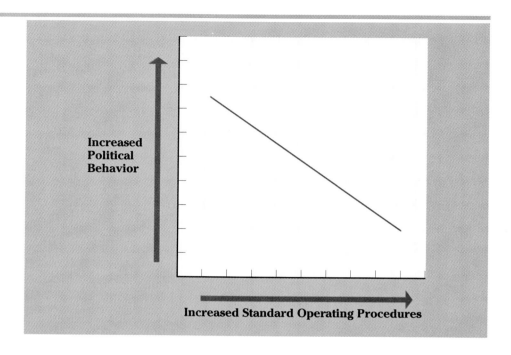

**Increased
Political
Behavior**

Increased Standard Operating Procedures

IN PRACTICE
Politics in Performance Appraisals

> There is really no getting around the fact that whenever I evaluate one of my people, I stop and think about the impact—the ramifications of my decisions on my relationship with the guy and his future here. I'd be stupid not to. Call it being politically minded, or using managerial discretion, or fine-tuning the guy's ratings, but in the end I've got to live with him, and I'm not going to rate a guy without thinking about the fallout. There are a lot of games played in the rating process and whether we (managers) admit it or not we are all guilty of playing them at our discretion.

The above statement comes from one of 60 executives that participated in in-depth interviews concerning their performance appraisal processes. These 60 executives—from seven large corporations—had performance appraisal experience in a total of 197 different companies. An analysis of over 100 hours of tape-recorded interviews resulted in the following conclusions:

■ Political considerations were nearly always part of the performance evaluation process.

■ Politics played a role in the performance appraisal process because (1) executives took into consideration the daily interpersonal dynamics between them and their subordinates; (2) the formal appraisal process results in a permanent written document; and (3) the formal appraisal can have considerable impact on the subordinate's career and advancement.

SELF-ASSESSMENT 15.2
How Political Are You?

Instructions: To determine your political appreciation and tendencies, please answer the following questions. Select the answer that better represents your behavior or belief, even if that particular behavior or belief is not present all the time.

1. You should make others feel important through an open appreciation of their ideas and work. _____ True _____ False

2. Because people tend to judge you when they first meet you, always try to make a good first impression. _____ True _____ False

3. Try to let others do most of the talking, be sympathetic to their problems, and resist telling people that they are totally wrong. _____ True _____ False

4. Praise the good traits of the people you meet and always give people an opportunity to save face if they are wrong or make a mistake. _____ True _____ False

5. Spreading false rumors, planting misleading information, and backstabbing are necessary, if somewhat unpleasant, methods to deal with your enemies. _____ True _____ False

6. Sometimes it is necessary to make promises that you know you will not or cannot keep. _____ True _____ False

7. It is important to get along with everybody, even with those who are generally recognized as windbags, abrasive, or constant complainers. _____ True _____ False

8. It is vital to do favors for others so that you can call in these IOUs at times when they will do you the most good. _____ True _____ False

9. Be willing to compromise, particularly on issues that are minor to you but important to others. _____ True _____ False

10. On controversial issues, it is important to delay or avoid your involvement if possible. _____ True _____ False

Source: Joseph F. Byrnes, "Connecting Organizational Politics and Conflict Resolution," *Personnel Administrator,* June 1986, p. 49. Reprinted by permission of the Society for Human Resource Management.

■ In addition, the research clearly showed that executives believed there was usually a justifiable reason for generating appraisal ratings that were less than accurate. Overall, they felt it was within their managerial discretion to do so. Thus the findings suggest that the formal appraisal process is indeed a political process, and that few ratings are determined without some political consideration.

■ Perhaps the most interesting finding from the study (because it debunks a popular mythology) is that accuracy is *not* the primary concern of these practicing executives when appraising subordinates. Their main concern is how best to use the appraisal process to motivate and reward subordinates. Hence, managerial discretion and effectiveness, not accuracy, are the real goals. Managers made it clear that they would not allow excessively accurate ratings to cause problems for themselves, and that they attempted to use the appraisal process to their own advantage.[25]

POLITICAL STRATEGIES IN INTERGROUP RELATIONS

Up to this point, we have explained the related concepts of power and politics primarily as they relate to interpersonal behavior. When we shift our focus from the individual or interpersonal to the *intergroup* level of analysis, the picture becomes somewhat more complicated. In developing a portrait of how political strategies are used to attain and maintain power in intergroup relations, we will highlight two major aspects of the topic. The first is the relationship between power and the control of critical resources. The second is the relationship between power and the control of strategic activities. Both will illustrate how subunit control leads to the acquisition of power in organizational settings.

Power and the Control of Critical Resources

On the basis of what has been called the *resource dependence model,* we can analyze intergroup political behavior by examining how critical resources are controlled and shared.[26] That is, when one subunit of an organization (perhaps the purchasing department) controls a scarce resource that is needed by another subunit (for example, the power to decide what to buy and what not to buy), that subunit acquires power. This power may be over other subunits within the same organization or over subunits in other organizations (for example, the marketing units of other companies who are trying to sell to the first company). As such, this unit is in a better position to bargain for the critical resources it needs from its own or other organizations. Hence, although all subunits may contribute something to the organization as a whole, power allocation within the organization will be influenced by the relative importance of the resources contributed by each unit. To quote Salancik and Pfeffer,

> Subunit power accrues to those departments that are most instrumental in bringing or in providing resources which are highly valued by the total organization. In turn, this power enables these subunits to obtain more of those scarce and critical resources allocated within the organization.

Stated succinctly, power derived from acquiring resources is used to obtain more resources, which in turn can be employed to produce more power—"the rich get richer."[27]

To document their case, Salancik and Pfeffer carried out a major study of university budget decisions. The results were clear. The more clout a department had (measured in terms of the department's ability to secure outside grants and first-rate graduate students, plus its national standing among comparable departments), the easier it was for the department to secure additional university resources. In other words, resources were acquired through political processes, not rational ones.[28]

International Challenge

IN PRACTICE
Purchasing Power in International Trade

Back home in New Jersey, Joseph Antonini wouldn't rate more than a glance and a smile of greeting while on a factory tour. So Mr. Antonini is clearly embarrassed by what is happening here.

As he rides up to the Hanil Synthetic Fiber Industrial Co. plant, security guards straighten and bark a word that sounds like "choof." Workers spring to open Mr. Antonini's door, and dozens of applauding Hanil office workers crowd around, hailing the startled visitor. Mr. Antonini and his associate, Ronald L. Buch, are handed large floral displays.

"Can you beat that?" asks Mr. Antonini, the president of K-Mart Apparel Corp.

Lots of people are trying. A few days earlier, Mr. Antonini survived a 21-course banquet in his honor at a Chinese clothing factory. Then there was the *mao-tai* party, an affair of fortitude at which toasts were continually exchanged in gulped servings of the potent Chinese liquor. "I tasted that for days," Mr. Antonini says.

This is an Asian buying trip. It sounds like great fun, but it is serious business for the 30 or so buyers of K-Mart Apparel, the clothing arm of the U.S. discount chain. The buyers, often with their bosses in tow, scour a dozen Asian nations for . . . fall merchandise worth hundreds of millions of dollars. They look for bargains, but they also use the trip to make contacts for new sources of supply and to learn what the competition is doing.

It is a demanding, ritualized process of negotiating to the third decimal point by day, cementing deals, and then renewing good will at night in an atmosphere of luxury, power, and privilege.

"It can go to your head," notes Mr. Antonini, a 20-year K-Mart veteran who remembers living in one-room apartments as a young store manager. Now he and his buyers fly first-class, stay only in luxury hotels, and drive around Hong Kong in Mercedes-Benz limousines. In Hong Kong a merchandise source treats Mr. Antonini to a $400 bottle of wine at dinner. And in Japan, a source serves him rich meals of Kobe beef at $200 a plate.

Indeed, those with "the pencil"—the buyers' term for the authority to order merchandise—are treated royally. "But once you lose the pencil, it's over," says the wife of one K-Mart executive. "You've got to understand it's for the pencil, not you."[29]

Power and the Control of Strategic Activities

In addition to the control of critical resources, subunits can also attain power by gaining control over activities that are needed by others to complete their tasks. These critical activities have been called *strategic contingencies;* they were discussed in Chapter 11. A "contingency" is defined by Miles as "a requirement of the activities of one subunit that is affected by the activities of other subunits."[30] For example, the business office of most universities represents a strategic contingency for the various colleges within the university because it has veto or approval power over financial expenditures of the schools. Its approval of a request to spend money is far from certain. Thus, a contingency represents a source of uncertainty in the decision-making process. A contingency becomes *strategic* when it has the potential to alter the balance of interunit or interdepartmental power in such a way that interdependencies among the various units are changed.

Perhaps the best way to illustrate this is to consider the example of power distribution in various organizations attempting to deal with a major source of uncertainty—the external environment. In a classic study by Lawrence and Lorsch (see Chapter 11), influence patterns were examined for companies in three divergent industries: container manufacturing, food processing, and plastics. It was found that in *successful* firms, power distribution conformed to the firm's strategic contingencies. For example, in the container-manufacturing companies, where the critical contingencies were customer delivery and product quality, the major share of power in decision making resided in the sales and production staffs. In contrast, in the food-processing firms, where the strategic contingencies focused on expertise in marketing and food sciences, major power rested in the sales and research units. In other words, those who held power in the successful organizations were in areas that were of central concern to the firm and its survival at a particular time. The functional areas that were most important for organizational success were under the control of the decision makers. For less-successful firms, this congruence was not found.

The changing nature of strategic contingencies can be seen in the evolution of power distribution in major public utilities. Many years ago, when electric companies were developing and growing, most of the senior officers of the companies were engineers. Technical development was the central issue. More recently, however, as utilities face greater litigation, government regulation, and controversy over nuclear power, lawyers are predominating in the leadership of most companies. This example serves to emphasize that "subunits could inherit and lose power, not necessarily by their own actions, but by the shifting contingencies in the environment confronting the organization."[31]

To better understand how this process works, consider the model shown in Exhibit 15.9. This diagram suggests that three factors influence the ability of one subunit (called *A*) over another (called *B*). Basically, it is argued that subunit power is influenced by (1) *A*'s ability to help *B* cope with uncertainty, (2) the degree to which *A* offers the only source of the required resource for *B,* and (3) the extent to which *A*'s contributions are central to organizational success. Let us consider each of these separately.

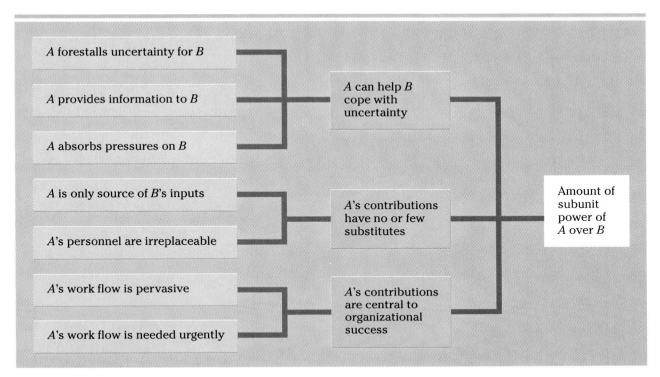

Exhibit 15.9
A Strategic Contingencies
Model of Subunit Power

Ability to Cope with Uncertainty.   According to advocates of the strategic contingencies model of power, the primary source of subunit power is the unit's ability to help other units cope with uncertainty. In other words, if our group can help your group reduce the uncertainties associated with *your* job, then our group has power over your group. As Hickson and his colleagues put it:

> Uncertainty itself does not give power; coping gives power. If organizations allocate to their various subunits task areas that vary in uncertainty, then those subunits that cope most effectively with the most uncertainty should have most power within the organization, since coping by a subunit reduces the impact of uncertainty on other activities in the organization, a shock absorber function.[32]

As shown in Exhibit 15.8 above, three primary types of coping activity relating to uncertainty reduction can be identified. To begin, some uncertainty can be reduced through steps by one subunit to *prevent or forestall uncertainty* for the other subunit. For example, if the purchasing group can guarantee a continued source of parts for the manufacturing group, it gains some power over manufacturing by forestalling possible uncertainty surrounding production schedules. Second, a subunit's ability to cope with uncertainty is influenced by its capacity to *provide or collect information*. Such information can forewarn of probable disruptions or problems, so corrective action can be taken promptly. Many business firms use various forecasting techniques to predict sales, economic conditions, and so forth. The third mechanism for coping with uncertainty is the unit's *ability to absorb pressures* that actually impact on the organization. For instance, if one manufacturing facility runs low on raw materials and a second facility can supply it with needed materials, this second facility effectively reduces some of the uncertainty of the first facility—and in the process gains influence over it.

In short, subunit A gains power over B subunit if it can help B cope with the contingencies and uncertainties facing it. The more dependent B is upon A to ensure the smooth functioning of the unit, the more power A has over B.

Nonsubstitutability of Coping Activities.　Substitutability is the capacity for one subunit to seek needed resources from alternate sources. Two factors influence the extent to which substitutability is available to a subunit. First, the *availability of alternatives* must be considered. If a subunit can get the job done using different products or processes, it is less susceptible to influence. In the IBM-compatible personal computer market, for example, there are so many vendors that no one can control the market. On the other hand, if a company is committed to a Macintosh computing environment, only one vendor (Apple Computer) is available, which increases Apple's control over the marketplace.

Second, the *replaceability of personnel* is important. A major reason for the power of staff specialists (personnel managers, purchasing agents, etc.) is that they possess expertise in a specialized area of value to the organization. Consider also a reason for closed-shop union contracts: they effectively reduce the replaceability of workers.

Thus, a second influence on the extent of subunit power is the extent to which subunit A provides goods or services to B for which there are no (or only a few) substitutes. In this way, B needs A in order to accomplish subunit objectives.

Centrality of Coping Activities.　Finally, one must consider the extent to which a subunit is of central importance to the operations of the enterprise. This is called the subunit's *centrality.* The more interconnected subunit A is with other subunits in the organization, the more "central" it is. This centrality, in turn, is influenced by two factors. The first is *work flow pervasiveness*—the degree to which the actual work of one subunit is connected with the work of other subunits. If subunit B cannot complete its own tasks without the help of the work activities of subunit A, then A has power over B. An example of this is an assembly line, where units toward the end of the line are highly dependent upon units at the beginning of the line for inputs.

The second factor, *work flow immediacy,* relates to the speed and severity with which the work of one subunit affects the final outputs of the organization. For instance, companies that prefer to keep low inventories of raw materials (perhaps for tax purposes) are, in effect, giving their outside suppliers greater power than those companies that keep large reserves of raw materials.

When taken as a whole, then, the strategic contingency model of intergroup power suggests that subunit power is influenced when one subunit can help another unit reduce or cope with its uncertainty, when the subunit is difficult to replace, and when the subunit is central to continued operations. The more these three conditions prevail, the more power will become vested in the subunit. Even so, it should be recognized that the power of one sub-unit or group can shift over time. As noted by Hickson and his colleagues, "As the goals, outputs, technologies, and markets of organizations change, so, for each subunit, the values of the independent variables [such as coping with uncertainty, nonsubstitutability, and centrality] change, and the patterns of power change."[33] In other words, the strategic contingency model suggested here is a dynamic one that is subject to change over time as various subunits and groups negotiate, bargain, and compromise with one another in an effort to secure a more favorable position in the organizational power structure.

IN PRACTICE
The Politics of Innovation

A good example of the strategic contingencies approach to the study of power and politics can be seen in a consideration of organizational innovation. It has long been recognized that it is easier to invent something new from outside an organization than to innovate within an existing company. As a result, a disproportionate share of new products originates from small businesses and entrepreneurs, not the major corporations with all the resources to innovate. Why? Much of the answer can be found in politics.

When a person or group has a new idea for a product or service, it is often met with a barrage of resistance from different sectors of the company. These efforts are motivated by the famous "not-invented-here syndrome," the tendency of competing groups to fight over turf, and the inclination to criticize and destroy any new proposal that threatens to change the status quo. Other groups within the company simply see little reason to be supportive of the idea.

This lack of support—indeed, hostility—occurs largely because within every company there is competition for resources. These resources can include money, power, and opportunities for promotion. As one consultant noted, "One person's innovation is another person's failure." As a result, there is often considerable fear and little incentive for one strategic group within a company to cooperate with another. Because both groups usually need each other for success, nothing happens. To the extent that politics could be removed from such issues, far more energy would be available to capitalize on an innovative idea and get it to market before the competition.[34]

LIMITING THE INFLUENCE OF POLITICAL BEHAVIOR

The final topic we will examine concerns ways in which people and groups can attempt to lessen the impact of political behavior. Clearly, politics in organizations cannot be eliminated. Yet to some extent, the negative aspects of it can be neutralized if managers carefully monitor the work environment and take remedial action where necessary. Part of this issue was discussed above, in the section on counterpower. Beyond this, however, several strategies can be identified that can help manage organizational politics. As shown in Exhibit 15.10, four basic strategies can be used.[35]

First, efforts can be made to reduce the uncertainty in the organization through clarifying job responsibilities, bases for evaluations and rewards, and so forth. The less ambiguity in the system, the less room for dysfunctional political behavior. Second, managers can try to reduce interpersonal or intergroup competition by using impartial standards for resource allocation and by emphasizing the superordinate goals of the entire organization—toward which all members of the organization should be working. Third, managers can attempt to break up existing political fiefdoms through personnel reassignment or transfer or by changing the reward system to encourage interunit cooperation. Finally, managers can work to prevent the development of future fiefdoms through training programs, selection and promotion, and reward distribution.

To the extent that employees see the organization as a fair place to work, and to the extent that clear goals and resource allocation procedures are present, office politics should subside, though not disappear. In organizations where politics prosper, in fact, you are likely to find a reward system that encourages and promotes such behavior. The choice is up to the organization.

Exhibit 15.10
Limiting the Effects of
Political Behavior

To Reduce System Uncertainty

- Make clear what are the bases and processes for evaluation.
- Differentiate rewards among high and low performers.
- Make sure the rewards are as immediately and directly related to performance as possible.

To Reduce Competition

- Try to minimize resource competition among managers.
- Replace resource competition with externally oriented goals and objectives.

To Break Existing Political Fiefdoms

- Where highly cohesive political empires exist, break them apart by removing or splitting the most dysfunctional subgroups.
- If you are an executive, be keenly sensitive to managers whose mode of operation is the personalization of political patronage. First, approach these persons with a directive to "stop the political maneuvering." If it continues, remove them from the positions and preferably from the company.

To Prevent Future Fiefdoms

- Make one of the most important criteria for promotion an apolitical attitude that puts organizational ends ahead of personal power ends.

Source: From "The Use and Abuse of Corporate Politics," by Don R. Beeman and Thomas W. Sharkey. Reprinted from *Business Horizons,* March–April 1987. Copyright 1987 by the Foundation for the School of Business at Indiana University. Used with permission.

PULLING IT ALL TOGETHER

We might think of power like a car battery and influence as the current that actually gets the starter motor to turn over. There are many potential sources of power such as knowledge, information, and money. But just as the car battery unconnected cannot start an engine, these sources of power do not by themselves cause others to do anything. Actually influencing others is achieved by possessing, or having others believe you possess, resources that they desire and depend upon and for which substitutes are not easily obtained and then establishing behavioral contingencies in the direction of the behaviors you desire to evoke.

SUMMARY OF KEY POINTS

- Power is an interpersonal relationship in which one person or group has the ability to cause another person or group to take an action that it would not have taken otherwise.

- There are five basic kinds of power: (1) referent, (2) expert, (3) legitimate, (4) reward, and (5) coercive.

- Depending upon which kind of power is employed, the recipient of a power effort can respond with commitment, compliance, or resistance.

- Power dependency is the extent to which a person or group is susceptible to an influence attempt. Included here is the notion of counterpower, or the ability of the subordinate to exercise some power and buffer the influence attempt of another.

- Common power tactics include controlling access to information, controlling access to persons, the selective use of objective criteria, controlling the agenda, using outside experts, bureaucratic gamesmanship, and forming coalitions and alliances.

- Politics involves those activities taken within an organization to acquire, develop, and use power and other resources to attain preferred outcomes in a situation in which there is uncertainty and disagreement over choices.

- Political behavior is more likely to occur when (1) there are ambiguous goals; (2) there is a scarcity of resources; (3) nonroutine technology and a complex external environment are involved; (4) nonprogrammed decisions are being considered; and (5) organizational change is occurring.

- The resource dependence model suggests that one unit within an organization has power over another unit when the first unit controls scarce and valued resources needed by the second unit.

- The strategic contingencies model asserts that one unit has power over another when the first group has the ability to block the second group's goal attainment—that is, when it controls some "strategic contingency" needed by the second group to complete its task.

- Political behavior can be reduced or minimized in organizations through four techniques: (1) reducing organization uncertainty, (2) reducing interunit competition, (3) breaking up political fiefdoms, and (4) preventing the development of future fiefdoms.

KEY WORDS

authority	power
bases of power	power dependencies
bureaucratic gamesmanship	referent power
coalition	resource dependence
coercive power	reward power
counterpower	strategic contingencies
expert power	utilitarian power
leadership	work centrality
legitimate power	work flow immediacy
normative power	work flow pervasiveness
politics	work to rule

QUESTIONS FOR DISCUSSION

1. Compare and contrast power, authority, and leadership.
2. Identify five bases of power, and provide an example of each. Which base (or bases) of power do you feel would be most commonly found in organizations?
3. Discuss the concept of power dependencies. What is the relationship between power dependencies and bases of power?
4. What is counterpower? Provide an example of counterpower from your own experience.
5. Why is it important to understand political behavior in organizations?
6. Define politics. How does politics differ from power?
7. Compare and contrast the resource dependence model of power and politics with the strategic contingency model.
8. Identify several specific power tactics in organizations, and provide an example of each.
9. Why is it important that the exercise of power and politics be handled in an ethical fashion? What might happen if employees felt that managers were using power in an unethical fashion?

NOTES

1. P. Ingrassia and J. B. White, "Stempel Quits as Head of GM," *Wall Street Journal,* October 27, 1992, p. A3. J. B. White and P. Ingrassia, "Major Restyling," *Wall Street Journal,* November 3, 1992, p. A1.
2. Cited in A. Henderson and T. Parsons, *Max Weber: The Theory of Social and Economic Organization.* (New York: The Free Press, 1947), p. 152.
3. R. Emerson, "Power Dependence Relations," *American Sociological Review,* 1962, *27,* p. 32.
4. H. Mintzberg, *Power In and Around Organizations* (Englewood Cliffs, N.J.: Prentice-Hall, 1983); R. J. House, "Power and Personality in Complex Organizations," in B. M. Staw and L. L. Cummings, eds., *Research in Organizational Behavior* (Greenwich, Conn.: JAI Press, 1988), pp. 307–357.
5. A. Grimes, "Authority, Power, Influence, and Social Control: A Theoretical Synthesis," *Academy of Management Review,* October 1978, p. 726.

6. A. Etzioni, *Modern Organizations* (Englewood Cliffs, N.J.: Prentice-Hall, 1964).
7. J. French and B. Raven, "The Bases of Social Power," in D. Cartwright and A. Zander, eds., *Group Dynamics* (New York: Harper & Row, 1968); P. Podsakoff and C. Schriesheim, "Field Studies of French and Raven's Bases of Power: Critique, Reanalysis, and Suggestions for Future Research," *Psychological Bulletin,* May 1985, pp. 376–398.
8. D. Tjosvold, "Power and Social Context in the Superior-Subordinate Interaction," *Organizational Behavior and Human Decision Processes,* June 1985, pp. 281–293.
9. Y. Shetty, "Managerial Power and Organizational Effectiveness: A Contingency Analysis," *Journal of Management Studies,* 1978, *15,* pp. 178–181.
10. D. Kipnis, *The Powerholders* (Chicago: University of Chicago Press, 1976), p. 77.
11. Ibid.
12. T. Stewart, "CEOs See Clout Shifting," *Fortune,* November 6, 1989, p. 66.
13. T. R. Mitchell and J. Larson, *People in Organizations* (New York: McGraw-Hill, 1988).
14. G. White, "Secretaries Are in the Driver's Seat," *Los Angeles Times,* July 17, 1989, p. IV–5.
15. J. Pfeffer, *Power in Organizations* (Marshfield, Mass.: Pittman, 1981).
16. Ibid., p. 370.
17. R. Kanter, "Power Failure in Management Circuits," *Harvard Business Review,* July–August 1979, pp. 31–54.
18. "Two Critics of Shuttle Perished," *Register-Guard,* May 11, 1986, pp. 1 and 4.
19. H. D. Lasswell, *Politics: Who Gets What, When, How* (New York: McGraw-Hill, 1936).
20. Pfeffer, op. cit., p. 7.
21. Ibid.
22. J. Gandz and V. Murray, "The Experience of Workplace Politics," *Academy of Management Journal,* 1980, *23,* pp. 237–251.
23. R. Miles, *Macro Organizational Behavior* (Glenview, Ill.: Scott, Foresman, 1980); C. Leana, "Power Relinquishment versus Power Sharing: Theoretical Clarification and Empirical Comparison of Delegation and Participation," *Journal of Applied Psychology,* 1987, *72,* pp. 228–233.
24. D. Madison, R. Allen, L. Porter, P. Renwick, and B. Mays, "Organizational Politics: An Exploration of Managers' Perceptions," *Human Relations,* February 1980, pp. 79–100.
25. C. Longnecker, H. Sims, and D. Gioia, "Behind the Mask: The Politics of Employee Appraisal," *Academy of Management Executive,* 1987, *1,* pp. 183–193.
26. J. Pfeffer and G. Salancik, *The External Control of Organizations* (New York: Harper & Row, 1978).
27. Ibid., p. 470.
28. Ibid.
29. S. Weiner, "K-Mart Apparel Buyers Hopscotch the Orient to Find Quality Goods," *Wall Street Journal,* March 19, 1985.
30. Miles, op. cit., p. 170.
31. Ibid., p. 169.
32. D. Hickson, C. Hinings, C. Lee, R. Schneck, and J. Pennings, "A Strategic Contingencies Theory of Intraorganizational Power," *Administrative Science Quarterly,* 1971, *14,* pp. 219–220.
33. Ibid., p. 227.
34. W. Kiechel, "The Politics of Innovation," *Fortune,* April 11, 1988, p. 131.
35. D. Beeman and T. Sharkey, "The Uses and Abuses of Corporate Politics," *Business Horizons,* March–April 1987, pp. 25–35.

EXPERIENTIAL EXERCISE 15

Power in a University Classroom

This exercise examines bases of power and power dependencies in a university classroom setting and considers how power and politics can facilitate personal and organizational goal attainment.

In groups of five or six, discuss the following situation and issues. Be prepared to present your group's discussion to the entire class.

Suppose that in the middle of a lecture your instructor asked everyone to close their books and to pull out a clean sheet of paper and something to write with. Other than groans and sighs, what would you expect the members of the class to do? With this very simple example as a springboard, discuss the following questions:

1. What are the sources of a professor's power?
2. Are some professors more powerful than others? If so, why?
3. Do professors have more influence over some students than others? If so, why?
4. What are the various sources of students' power in a classroom?
5. Do these sources of power for the professor or students differ or change within a short-term vs. long-term perspective?
6. In what ways do issues of substitution affect the balance of power between students and professors?
7. In what way does the larger context of the university in which a particular class exists affect the balance of power between students and professors?

MANAGEMENT DILEMMA

The New CEO

After nearly a year of rumors, it was finally announced that the president of ABC Corporation had been elected chairman of the board and that Jim Franklin, the vice president of finance, would replace him as president. While everyone at ABC was aware that a shift would take place soon, it was not at all clear before the announcement who would be the next president. Most people had guessed it would be Phil Cook, the marketing vice-president.

Nine months into his job as chief executive officer, Franklin found that Phil Cook (still the marketing vice-president) seemed to be fighting him in small and subtle ways. There was never anything blatant, but Cook just did not cooperate with Franklin as the other vice-presidents did. Shortly after being elected, Franklin had tried to bypass what he saw as a potential conflict with Cook by telling him that he would understand if Cook would prefer to move somewhere else where he could be a CEO also. Franklin said that it would be a big loss to the company but that he would be willing to help Cook in a number of ways if he wanted to look for a presidential opportunity elsewhere. Cook had thanked him but said that family and community commitments would prevent him from relocating and all CEO opportunities were bound to be in a different city.

Since the situation did not improve after the tenth and eleventh months, Franklin seriously considered forcing Cook out. When he thought about the consequences of such a move, Franklin became more and more aware of just how dependent he was on Cook. Marketing and sales were generally the keys to success in their industry, and the company's sales force was one of the best, if not the best, in the industry. Cook had been with the company for 25 years. He had built a strong personal relationship with many of the people in the sales force and was universally popular. A mass exodus just might occur if Cook were fired. The loss of a large number of salesmen, or even a lot of turmoil in the department, could have a serious effect on the company's performance.

After one year as chief executive officer, Franklin found that the situation between Cook and himself had not improved and had become a constant source of frustration.

1. What should Franklin do?
2. If confronted, is Cook likely to admit to going against Franklin?
3. What are the sources of power for both Cook and Franklin?
4. What countermeasures would you anticipate from Cook for each of several options Franklin might pursue to influence Cook?
5. If the power struggle between Cook and Franklin continues, how do you think it will affect the larger organization? Why? (Isn't this just an interpersonal struggle between two individuals?)

Source: John Kotter, "Acquiring and using power." *Harvard Business Review,* 1977, *55*, 4, p. 127.

16

Conflict and Negotiation

The Management Challenge

■ To recognize and resolve short- and long-term conflicts among group members and among groups.

■ To resolve employee grievances in a way that is acceptable to all parties.

■ To know when and how to negotiate and how to achieve a mutually advantageous agreement.

■ To recognize and respond to cultural differences in negotiation and bargaining strategies.

CLOSE UP

Conflict at Cat

Caterpillar Inc. is the world's leading maker of earth-moving equipment. Many employees have served the corporation for most of their adult lives. However, in 1992, problems arose. The United Automobile Workers at Caterpillar embarked on a strike demanding better wages, benefits and job security. Workers at John Deere & Co. had recently reached an agreement, and the union was pushing the old process of pattern bargaining.

The UAW certainly didn't know what they were up against at Caterpillar. CEO Donald V. Fites, didn't blink. Instead, he threatened to replace Cat's 11,000 striking workers with replacement workers. Most companies facing a strike do not threaten to use replacement workers — it diminishes trust in the company and tells the workers that management sees them as mere commodities. "We never thought he'd actually go that far," said UAW Local 145 President John Paul Yarbrough. "I didn't begin negotiations intending to hire replacements, but I felt I had no choice," responded Fites.

Since becoming CEO, Fites has restructured Cat's organization and changed its culture. His passion for efficiency is a result of his career overseas, especially in Japan. He is weary of labor relations that make America's manufacturers inefficient. Hence, while the union and Cat argued on about wages and benefits, the real clash is over power. Fites is adamant on reasserting the company's 'right to manage.' He wants flexibility in setting wages, benefits and working conditions in order to protect Cat from Japanese and European competition.

Half a century ago, under the leadership of Walter Reuther, the union transformed the blue-collar work force into the American middle class. The bosses in Detroit were forced to treat workers as humans, not as mere bundles of sweat and muscle. However, Fites' threat was able to bring this proud and powerful organization to its knees.

Caterpillar was vague on when the workers would be allowed to return to their old jobs, and whether they would all be invited back. This created tremendous animosity and a widespread sense of anguish and insecurity among workers. Hence, Fites victory may be Pyrrhic. The workers believe that Cat management attaches little value to the 25-year veteran workers (the average tenure at Cat). Workers feel that Fites does not perceive his labor force as an asset to be nurtured and respected. "This strike's going to be a tough one to recover from," said Bob Ferguson, a tool maker. "People won't forget." Since 1986, a teamwork style with labor has boosted Cat's productivity by 30 percent. Now that friendly and committed approach may be lost in rancor. In these times of global competition, Fites may have lost much more than he has won.[1]

In all organizations, including Cat, some conflict is inevitable. Simply making a decision to do *A* instead of *B* often alienates the supporters of *B,* despite the soundness of the reasons behind the decision. Moreover, the consequences of conflict (and failed negotiations) can be costly to an organization, whether it is between labor and management, groups, individuals, or nations. In an era of increasing business competition both from abroad and at home, reducing conflict is important. For these reasons, contemporary managers need a firm grasp of the dynamics of intergroup and interorganizational conflict and of negotiation processes.

We begin with a discussion of the conflict process, followed by a look at negotiations both within and between organizations.

CONFLICT IN ORGANIZATIONS: BASIC CONSIDERATIONS

By any standard of comparison, conflict in organizations represents an important topic for managers. Just how important can be seen in the results of a study of how managers spend their time. It was found that approximately 20 percent of top and middle managers' time was spent in dealing with some form of conflict.[2] In another study, it was found that managerial skill in handling conflict was a major predictor of managerial success and effectiveness.[3]

A good example of the magnitude of the problems that conflict can cause in an organization is the case of General Concrete, Inc., of Coventry, Rhode Island.[4] Operations at this concrete plant came to a halt for more than three weeks because the plant's one truck driver and sole member of the Teamsters Union began picketing after he was laid off by the company. The company intended to use other drivers from another of their plants. In response to the picketing, not a single employee of General Concrete crossed the picket line, thereby closing the plant and costing the company a considerable amount in lost production and profit. Could this problem have been handled better? We shall see.

In the sections that follow, several aspects of conflict in organizations are considered. First, conflict is defined, and variations of conflict are considered by type and by level. Next, constructive and destructive aspects of conflict are discussed. A basic model of the conflict process is then examined, followed by a look at several of the more prominent antecedents of conflict. Finally, effective and ineffective strategies for conflict resolution are contrasted. Throughout, emphasis is placed on problem identification and problem resolution.

There are many ways to determine conflict as it relates to the workplace. For our purposes here, we will define *conflict* as the process by which individuals or groups react to other entities that have frustrated, or are about to frustrate, their plans, goals, beliefs, or activities. In other words, conflict involves situations in which the expectations or actual goal-directed behaviors of one person or group are blocked—or about to be blocked—by another person or group. Hence, if a sales representative cannot secure enough funds to mount what he or she considers to be an effective sales campaign, conflict can ensue. Similarly, if *A* gets promoted and *B* doesn't, conflict can emerge. Finally, if a company finds it necessary to lay off valued employees because of difficult financial conditions, conflict can occur. Many such examples can be identified; in each, a situation emerges in which someone or some group cannot do what it wants to do (for whatever reason) and responds by experiencing an inner frustration.

Types of Conflict

If we are to try to understand the roots of conflict, we need to know what type of conflict is present. At least four *types of conflict* can be identified:

1. *Goal conflict.* Goal conflict can occur when one person or group desires a different outcome than others do. This is simply a clash over whose goals are going to be pursued.
2. *Cognitive conflict.* Cognitive conflict can result when one person or group holds ideas or opinions that are inconsistent with those of others. This type of conflict is evident in political debates.
3. *Affective conflict.* This type of conflict emerges when one person's or group's feelings or emotions (attitudes) are incompatible with those of others. Affective conflict is seen in situations where two individuals simply don't get along with one another.
4. *Behavioral conflict.* Behavioral conflict exists when one person or group does something (i.e., behaves in a certain way) that is unacceptable to others. Dressing for work in a way that "offends" others and using profane language are examples of behavioral conflict.

Each of these types of conflict is usually triggered by different factors, and each can lead to very different responses by the individual or group.

Levels of Conflict

In addition to different types of conflict, there exist several different *levels* of conflict. *Level* refers to the number of individuals involved in the conflict. That is, is the conflict within just one person, between two people, between two or more groups, or between two or more organizations? Both the causes of a conflict and the most effective means to resolve it can be affected by level. Four such levels can be identified:

1. *Intrapersonal conflict.* Intrapersonal conflict is conflict within one person. We often hear about someone who has an approach-avoidance conflict; that is, he or she is both attracted to and repelled by the same object. Similarly, a person can be attracted to two equally appealing alternatives, such as two good job offers (approach-approach conflict), or repelled by two equally unpleasant alternatives, such as the threat of being fired if one fails to identify a co-worker guilty of breaking plant rules (avoidance-avoidance conflict). In any case, the conflict is within the individual.

2. *Interpersonal conflict.* Conflict can also take an interpersonal form, where two individuals disagree on some matter. For example, you can have an argument with a co-worker over an issue of mutual concern. Such conflicts often tend to get highly personal, because only two parties are involved and each person embodies the opposing position in the conflict. Hence, it is sometimes difficult to distinguish between the opponent's position and his or her person.

3. *Intergroup conflict.* Third, conflict can be found between groups. Intergroup conflict usually involves disagreements between two opposing forces over goals or the sharing of resources. For example, we often see conflict between the marketing and production units within a corporation as each vies for more resources to accomplish its subgoals. Intergroup conflict is typically the most complicated form of conflict because of the number of individuals involved. Coalitions form within and between groups, and an "us-against-them" mentality develops. Here, too, is an opportunity for groupthink to develop and thrive (see Chapter 14).

4. *Interorganizational conflict.* Finally, we can see interorganizational conflict in disputes between two companies in the same industry (for example, a disagreement between computer manufacturers over computer standards); between two companies in different industries or economic sectors (for example, a conflict between real estate interests and environmentalists over land use planning); and even between two or more countries (for example, a trade dispute between the United States and Japan or France). In each case, both parties inevitably feel the pursuit of their goals is being frustrated by the other party.

IN PRACTICE
Labor Conflict at Greyhound

In 1987, Greyhound Lines Inc. chairman Fred G. Currey led a leveraged buyout of the company. He was welcomed by the drivers as Greyhound's savior. Curry merged the bus line with Continental Trailways and spent heavily to improve terminals, and marketing and training programs. He increased passenger traffic by 20 percent in the years 1987–89. In 1989, for the first time in several years, the bus line actually made money. Then, in 1990, 6,000 Greyhound drivers staged a walkout that raised havoc for passengers. Thousands of people who could not afford to own a car or travel by air were stranded in Greyhound terminals across the country. Many more were forced to cancel trips to distant weddings, funerals, new jobs, and new homes.

The National Labor Board charged that management precipitated the strike by imposing a new contract without sufficient bargaining. Drivers had demanded substantial pay increases. They wanted a share of Greyhound's profits. "Our impression is their profits are very, very understated," said Nick Nichols, a spokesman for the union. "In our view, they've been cooking the numbers all along."

As negotiations continued, the strike went into its ninth month. The profitable company began to fail once again. March, April and May of 1990 saw $87 million in losses. But the company tried to rebuild somewhat. Seven hundred non-union drivers hired and trained by Greyhound were offered permanent jobs. Another 1,200 new drivers were recruited through newspaper advertisements in 36 cities across the country for permanent jobs.

By the end of the nine-month dispute, parent company GLI Holding wished the bitter walkout could be forgotten. Greyhound filed a reorganization plan in the bankruptcy court that could severely limit the union's immense potential claims for back pay. But NLRB officials felt that this legal maneuver would be difficult. And union lawyers questioned if the judge had the legal right to disregard the NLRB's estimate.

Creditors doubted if Greyhound could emerge from Chapter 11 without making labor peace. If the bitter differences between Greyhound management and the union could have been handled better, the profitable company would probably not have been driven into bankruptcy, Curry could have continued to enjoy employee goodwill, and thousands of people could have continued to depend on Greyhound to reach their destinations.[5]

The Positive and Negative Sides of Conflict

People often assume that all conflict is necessarily bad and should be eliminated. On the contrary, there are some circumstances in which a moderate amount of conflict can be helpful. For instance, conflict can lead to the search for new ideas and new mechanisms as solutions to organizational problems. Conflict can stimulate innovation and change. It can also facilitate employee motivation in cases where employees feel a need to excel and, as a result, push themselves in order to meet performance objectives.

Conflict can at times help individuals and group members grow and develop self-identities. As noted by Coser:

> Conflict, which aims at a resolution of tension between antagonists, is likely to have stabilizing and integrative functions for the relationship. By permitting immediate and direct expression of rival claims, such social systems are able to readjust their structures by eliminating their sources of dissatisfaction. The multiple conflicts which they experience may serve to eliminate the causes for dissociation and to reestablish unity. These systems avail themselves, through the toleration and institutionalization of conflict, of an important stabilizing mechanism.[6]

Conflict can, on the other hand, have negative consequences for both individuals and organizations when people divert energies away from performance and goal attainment and direct them toward resolving the conflict. Continued conflict can take a heavy toll in terms of psychological well-being. As we will see in the next chapter, conflict has a major influence on stress and the psychophysical consequences of stress. Finally, continued conflict can also affect the social climate of the group and inhibit group cohesiveness.

Thus, conflict can be either functional or dysfunctional in work situations depending upon the nature of the conflict, its intensity, and its duration. Indeed, both too much and too little conflict can lead to a variety of negative

Exhibit 16.1
The Relationship
Between Conflict Intensity
and Outcomes

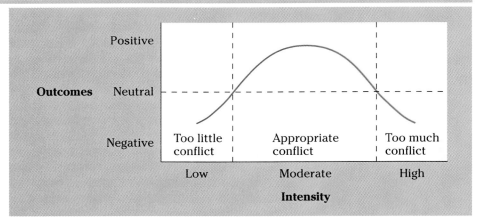

Source: L. David Brown, *Managing Conflict at Organizational Interfaces,* © 1986 by Addison-Wesley Publishing Co., Inc., Reading, Massachusetts, Figure 1.1, p. 8. Reprinted with permission of the publisher.

outcomes, as discussed above. This is shown in Exhibit 16.1. In such circumstances, a moderate amount of conflict may be the best course of action. The issue for management, therefore, is not how to eliminate conflict, but rather how to manage and resolve it when it occurs.

IN PRACTICE
Executive Conflict Resolution Strategies

A good way to see how conflict can be functional or dysfunctional is to observe the behaviors of many of America's CEOs. Consider the cases of Jack Welch, chairman of General Electric, and Fred Ackman, chairman of Superior Oil. Welch enjoys a good fight and takes pleasure in the give-and-take of discussions and negotiations. On one occasion, he engaged a senior vice-president in a prolonged and emotional shouting match over the merits of a certain proposal. Several managers who were present were embarrassed by the confrontation. Yet after the argument, Welch thanked the vice-president for standing up to him and defending his views. This is what Welch calls "constructive conflict."

On the other hand, according to one account, Fred Ackman approaches conflict quite differently. Ackman has been accused of being autocratic—refusing even to discuss suggestions or modifications to proposals he presents. Disagreement is seen as disloyalty and is often met with an abusive temper. As one former subordinate said, "He couldn't stand it when someone disagreed with him, even in private. He'd eat you up alive, calling you a dumb S.O.B. . . . It happened all the time."[7]

Which of these reactions to conflict do you feel would lead to more productive results? How do you feel you respond to such conflict? Would your friends agree with your assessment?

CAUSES OF CONFLICT IN ORGANIZATIONS

Here we will examine two aspects of the conflict process. First, several factors that have been found to contribute to conflict will be identified. After this, a model of conflict processes in organizations will be reviewed.

Why Organizations Have So Much Conflict

A number of factors are known to facilitate organizational conflict under certain circumstances. In summarizing the literature, Robert Miles points to several specific examples.[8] These are as follows:

Task Interdependencies.   The first antecedent can be found in the nature of *task interdependencies.* In essence, the greater the extent of task interdependence among individuals or groups (that is, the more they have to work together or collaborate to accomplish a goal), the greater is the likelihood of conflict if different expectations or goals exist among entities, in part because the interdependence makes avoiding the conflict more difficult. This occurs in part because high task interdependency heightens the intensity of relationships. Hence, a small disagreement can very quickly get blown up into a major issue.

Status Inconsistencies.   A second factor is *status inconsistencies* among the parties involved. For example, managers in many organizations have the prerogative to take personal time off during workdays to run errands, and so forth, whereas nonmanagerial personnel do not. Consider the effects this can have on the nonmanagers' view of organizational policies and fairness.

Jurisdictional Ambiguities.   Conflict can also emerge from *jurisdictional ambiguities*—situations where it is unclear exactly where responsibility for something lies. For example, many organizations use an employee selection procedure in which applicants are evaluated both by the personnel department and by the department in which the applicant would actually work. Because both departments are involved in the hiring process, what happens when one department wants to hire an individual, but the other department does not?

Communication Problems.   The topic of communication was discussed thoroughly in Chapter 13. Suffice it to say that the various *communication problems* or ambiguities in the communication process can facilitate conflict. When one misunderstands a message or when information is withheld, someone often responds with frustration and anger.

Dependence on Common Resource Pool.   Another previously discussed factor that contributes to conflict is *dependence on common resource pools.* Whenever several departments must compete for scarce resources, conflict is almost inevitable. When resources are limited, a zero-sum game exists in which someone wins and, invariably, someone loses.

Lack of Common Performance Standards.   Differences in performance criteria and reward systems provide more potential for organizational conflict. This often occurs because of a *lack of common performance standards* among differing groups within the same organization. For example, production personnel are often rewarded for their efficiency, and this efficiency is facilitated by the long-term production of a few products. Sales departments, on the other hand, are rewarded for their short-term response to market changes—often at the expense of long-term production efficiency. In such situations, conflict arises as each unit attempts to meet its own performance criteria.

Individual Differences.   Finally, as discussed in Chapter 2, a variety of *individual differences,* such as personal abilities, traits, and skills, can influence in no small way the nature of interpersonal relations. Individual dominance, aggressiveness, authoritarianism, and tolerance for ambiguity all seem to influence how an individual deals with potential conflict. Indeed, such characteristics may determine whether or not conflict is created at all.

A Model of the Conflict Process

Having examined specific factors that are known to facilitate conflict, we can ask how conflict comes about in organizations. The most commonly accepted model of the conflict process was developed by Kenneth Thomas.[9] This model, shown in Exhibit 16.2, consists of four stages: (1) frustration, (2) conceptualization, (3) behavior, and (4) outcome.

Stage 1: Frustration.   As we have seen, conflict situations originate when an individual or group feels *frustration* in the pursuit of important goals. This frustration may be caused by a wide variety of factors, including disagreement over performance goals, failure to get a promotion or pay raise, a fight over scarce economic resources, new rules or policies, and so forth. In fact, conflict can be traced to frustration over almost anything a group or individual cares about.

Stage 2: Conceptualization.   In Stage 2, the conceptualization stage of the model, parties to the conflict attempt to understand the nature of the problem, what they themselves want as a resolution, what they think their opponents want as a resolution, and various strategies they feel each side may employ in resolving the conflict. This stage is really the problem-solving and strategy phase. For instance, when management and union negotiate a labor contract, both sides attempt to decide what is most important and what can be bargained away in exchange for these priority needs.

Stage 3: Behavior.   The third stage in Thomas's model is actual *behavior.* As a result of the conceptualization process, parties to a conflict attempt

Exhibit 16.2
A Model of the
Conflict Process

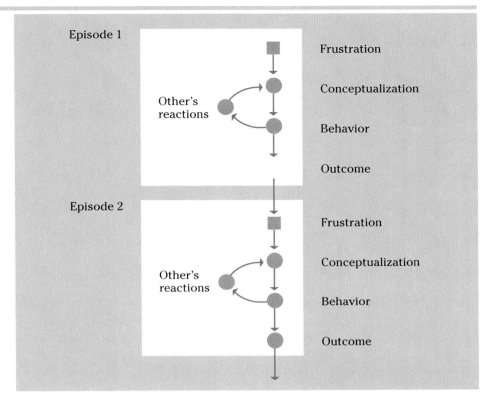

Source: Kenneth Thomas, "Conflict and Conflict Management," in M. D. Dunnette (ed.), *Handbook of Industrial and Organizational Behavior* (New York: Wiley, 1976), p. 895. Copyright © 1976 by John Wiley and Sons, Inc. Reprinted by permission.

to implement their resolution mode by competing or accommodating in the hope of resolving problems. A major task here is determining how best to proceed strategically. That is, what tactics will the party use to attempt to resolve the conflict? Thomas has identified five modes for conflict resolution, as shown in Exhibit 16.3. These are (1) competing, (2) collaborating, (3) compromising, (4) avoiding, and (5) accommodating. Also shown in the exhibit are situations that seem most appropriate for each strategy.

The choice of an appropriate conflict resolution mode depends to a great extent on the situation and the goals of the party. This is shown graphically in Exhibit 16.4. According to this model, each party must decide the extent to which it is interested in satisfying its own concerns—called *assertiveness*—and the extent to which it is interested in helping satisfy the opponent's concerns—called *cooperativeness*. Assertiveness can range from assertive to unassertive on one continuum, and cooperativeness can range from uncooperative to cooperative on the other continuum.

Once the parties have determined their desired balance between the two competing concerns—either consciously or unconsciously—the resolution

Conflict-handling Modes	Appropriate Situations
Competing	1. When quick, decisive action is vital—e.g., emergencies.
	2. On important issues where unpopular actions need implementing—e.g., cost cutting, enforcing unpopular rules, discipline.
	3. On issues vital to company welfare when you know you're right.
	4. Against people who take advantage of noncompetitive behavior.
Collaborating	1. To find an integrative solution when both sets of concerns are too important to be compromised.
	2. When your objective is to learn.
	3. To merge insights from people with different perspectives.
	4. To gain commitment by incorporating concerns into a consensus.
	5. To work through feelings which have interfered with a relationship.
Compromising	1. When goals are important, but not worth the effort or potential disruption of more assertive modes.
	2. When opponents with equal power are committed to mutually exclusive goals.
	3. To achieve temporary settlements to complex issues.
	4. To arrive at expedient solutions under time pressure.
	5. As a backup when collaboration or competition is unsuccessful.
Avoiding	1. When an issue is trivial, or more important issues are pressing.
	2. When you perceive no chance of satisfying your concerns.
	3. When potential disruption outweighs the benefits of resolution.
	4. To let people cool down and regain perspective.
	5. When gathering information supersedes immediate decision.
	6. When others can resolve the conflict more effectively.
	7. When issues seem tangential or symptomatic of other issues.
Accommodating	1. When you find you are wrong—to allow a better position to be heard, to learn, and to show your reasonableness.
	2. When issues are more important to others than yourself—to satisfy others and maintain cooperation.
	3. To build social credits for later issues.
	4. To minimize loss when you are outmatched and losing.
	5. When harmony and stability are especially important.
	6. To allow subordinates to develop by learning from mistakes.

Exhibit 16.3
Five Modes of
Resolving Conflict

Source: K. W. Thomas, "Toward Multidimensional Values in Teaching: The Example of Conflict Behaviors," *Academy of Management Review 2* (1977), Table 1, p. 487. Reprinted by permission.

strategy emerges. For example, if a union negotiator feels confident he or she can win on an issue that is of primary concern to union members (e.g., wages), a direct competition mode may be chosen (see upper left-hand corner of Exhibit 16.4). On the other hand, when the union is indifferent to an issue or when it actually supports management's concerns (e.g., plant safety), we would expect an accommodating or collaborating mode (on the right-hand side of the exhibit).

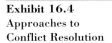

Exhibit 16.4
Approaches to
Conflict Resolution

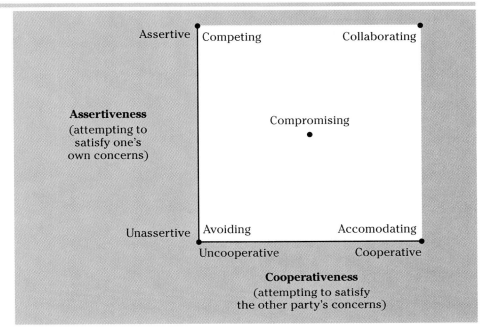

Source: Adapted from Kenneth Thomas, "Conflict and Conflict Management," in M. D. Dunnette (ed.), *Handbook of Industrial and Organizational Behavior* (New York: Wiley, 1976), p. 900. Copyright © 1976 by John Wiley and Sons, Inc. Reprinted by permission of John Wiley & Sons, Inc.

What is interesting in this process is the assumptions people make about their own modes compared to their opponents'. For example, in one study of executives, it was found that the executives typically described themselves as using collaboration or compromise to resolve conflict, whereas these same executives typically described their opponents as using a competitive mode almost exclusively.[10] In other words, the executives underestimated their opponents' concern as uncompromising. Simultaneously, the executives had flattering portraits of their own willingness to satisfy both sides in a dispute.

Before going farther, you might find it interesting to see how you approach conflict resolution. To do this, simply complete Self-Assessment 16.1. When you are done, refer to Appendix B for scoring details.

Stage 4: Outcome. Finally, as a result of efforts to resolve the conflict, both sides determine the extent to which a satisfactory resolution or outcome has been achieved. Where one party to the conflict does not feel satisfied or feels only partially satisfied, the seeds of discontent are sown for a later conflict, as shown in the preceding Exhibit 16.2. One unresolved conflict episode can easily set the stage for a second episode. Managerial action aimed at achieving quick and satisfactory resolution is vital; failure to initiate such action leaves the possibility (more accurately, the probability) that new conflicts will soon emerge.

SELF-ASSESSMENT 16.1
What Is Your Approach to Conflict Resolution?

Instructions: Think of a typical situation in which you have a disagreement with someone. Then, answer the following items concerning how you would respond to the conflict. Circle the number that you feel is most appropriate.

		Highly Unlikely				Highly Likely
1.	I firmly push for my goals.	1	2	3	4	5
2.	I always try to win an argument.	1	2	3	4	5
3.	I try to show my opponent the logic of my position.	1	2	3	4	5
4.	I like to discuss disagreements openly.	1	2	3	4	5
5.	I try to work through our differences.	1	2	3	4	5
6.	I try to get all concerns on the table for discussion.	1	2	3	4	5
7.	I try to work for a mutually beneficial solution.	1	2	3	4	5
8.	I try to compromise with the other person.	1	2	3	4	5
9.	I seek a balance of gains and losses on each side.	1	2	3	4	5
10.	I don't like talking about disagreements.	1	2	3	4	5
11.	I try to avoid unpleasantness for myself.	1	2	3	4	5
12.	I avoid taking positions that may incite disagreement.	1	2	3	4	5
13.	I try to think of the other person in any disagreement.	1	2	3	4	5
14.	I try to preserve relationships in any conflict.	1	2	3	4	5
15.	I try not to hurt the other person's feelings.	1	2	3	4	5

RESOLVING CONFLICT IN ORGANIZATIONS

We have discovered that conflict is pervasive throughout organizations and that some conflict can be good for organizations. People often grow and learn from conflict, as long as the conflict is not dysfunctional. The challenge for managers is to select a resolution strategy appropriate to the situation and individuals involved. A review of past management practice in this regard reveals that managers often make poor strategy choices. That is, as often as not, managers select repressive or ineffective conflict resolution strategies.

Common Strategies That Seldom Work

At leave five conflict resolution techniques commonly found in organizations fairly consistently prove to be ineffective.[11] In fact, not only do such techniques seldom work—in many cases, they actually serve to increase the problem. Nonetheless, they are found with alarming frequency in a wide array of business and public organizations. These five ineffective strategies are often associated with an avoidance approach and are described below.

Nonaction.   Perhaps the most common managerial response when conflict emerges is *nonaction*—doing nothing and ignoring the problem. It may be felt that if the problem is ignored, it will go away. Unfortunately, that is not often the case. In fact, ignoring the problem may serve only to increase the frustration and anger of the parties involved.

Administrative Orbiting.   In some cases, managers will acknowledge that a problem exists but then take little serious action. Instead, they continually report that a problem is "under study" or that "more information is needed." Telling a person who is experiencing a serious conflict that "these things take time" hardly relieves anyone's anxiety or solves any problems. This ineffective strategy for resolving conflict is aptly named *administrative orbiting*.

Due Process Nonaction.   A third ineffective approach to resolving conflict is to set up a recognized procedure for redressing grievances but at the same time to ensure that the procedure is long, complicated, costly, and perhaps even risky. The *due process nonaction* strategy is to wear down the dissatisfied employee while at the same time claiming that resolution procedures are open and available. This technique has been used repeatedly in conflicts involving race and sex discrimination.

Secrecy.   Oftentimes, managers will attempt to reduce conflict through *secrecy*. Some feel that by taking secretive actions, controversial decisions can be carried out with a minimum of resistance. One argument for pay secrecy (that is, keeping employee salaries secret) is that such a policy makes it more difficult for employees to feel inequitably treated. Essentially, this is a "what they don't know won't hurt them" strategy. A major problem of this approach is that it leads to distrust of management. When managerial credibility is needed for other issues, it may be found lacking.

Character Assassination.   The final ineffective resolution technique to be discussed here is *character assassination*. The person with a conflict, perhaps a woman claiming sex discrimination, is labeled a "troublemaker." Attempts are made to discredit her and distance her from the others in the group. The implicit strategy here is that if the person can be isolated and stigmatized, he or she will either be silenced by negative group pressures or else will leave. In either case, the problem is "solved."

Strategies for Preventing Conflict

On the more positive side, there are many things managers can do to reduce or actually solve dysfunctional conflict when it occurs. These fall into two categories: actions directed at conflict *prevention* and actions directed at conflict *reduction.* We shall start by examining conflict prevention techniques, because preventing conflict is often easier than reducing it once it begins. These include:

1. *Emphasizing organization-wide goals and effectiveness.* Focusing on organization-wide goals and objectives should prevent goal conflict. If larger goals are emphasized, employees are more likely to see the big picture and work together to achieve corporate goals.
2. *Providing stable, well-structured tasks.* When work activities are clearly defined, understood, and accepted by employees, conflict should be less likely to occur. Conflict is most likely to occur when task uncertainty is high; specifying or structuring jobs minimizes ambiguity.
3. *Facilitating intergroup communication.* Misperception of the abilities, goals, and motivations of others often leads to conflict, so efforts to increase the dialogue among groups and to share information should help eliminate conflict. As groups come to know more about one another, suspicions often diminish, and greater intergroup teamwork becomes possible.
4. *Avoiding win-lose situations.* If win-lose situations are avoided, less potential for conflict exists. When resources are scarce, management can seek some form of resource sharing to achieve organizational effectiveness. Moreover, rewards can be given for contributions to overall corporate objectives; this will foster a climate in which groups seek solutions acceptable to all.

These points bear a close resemblance to descriptions of the so-called Japanese management style. In Japanese firms, considerable effort is invested in preventing conflict. In this way, more energy is available for constructive efforts toward task accomplishment and competition in the marketplace. Another place where considerable destructive conflict is prevented is at Intel.

IN PRACTICE
Constructive Conflict at Intel

Dealing with conflict lies at the heart of managing any business. Confrontation—facing issues about which there is disagreement—is avoided only at a manager's peril. Many issues can be postponed, allowed to fester, or smoothed over; but eventually they must be solved. They are not going to disappear. Such is the philosophy of Intel president Andrew Grove.

At Intel, they believe that *constructive confrontation* accelerates problem solving. It requires that participants be direct, that they deal face-to-face. It pushes employees to deal with a problem as soon as it surfaces, keeping it from festering. It encourages all concerned to concentrate on the problem and not the people caught up in it. According to Grove, constructive confrontation does not mean being loud, unpleasant, or rude. It is not designed to affix blame. Instead, the essence of it is speaking up for your views in a forthright, businesslike way. If you disagree with something, you say you disagree with it. You don't wait until your opponent is out of the room and then criticize. You do it face-to-face.

To reinforce such behavior, Grove and his associates have gone to considerable lengths to create a corporate culture that is supportive of speaking out. The organization is highly decentralized; power is diffused throughout the organization; and status differences are minimized. The result is an atmosphere that is conducive to open and honest confrontation and problem solving. At Intel, the system works.[12]

Strategies for Reducing Conflict

Where dysfunctional conflict already exists, something must be done, and managers may pursue one of at least two general approaches: they can try to change employee *attitudes,* or they can try to change employee *behaviors.* If they change behavior, open conflict is often reduced, but groups may still dislike one another; the conflict simply becomes less visible as the groups are separated from one another. Changing attitudes, on the other hand, often leads to fundamental changes in the ways that groups get along. However, it also takes considerably longer to accomplish than behavior change, because it requires a fundamental change in social perceptions, as described in Chapter 3.

Nine conflict reduction strategies are shown in Exhibit 16.5. The techniques should be viewed as a continuum, ranging from strategies that focus on changing behaviors near the top of the scale to strategies that focus on changing attitudes near the bottom of the scale.

1. *Physical separation.* The quickest and easiest solution to conflict is physical separation. Separation is useful when conflicting groups are not working on a joint task or do not need a high degree of interaction. Though this approach does not encourage members to change their attitudes, it does provide time to seek a better accommodation.
2. *Use of rules and regulations.* Conflict can also be reduced through the increasing specification of rules, regulations, and procedures. This approach, also known as the bureaucratic method, imposes solutions on groups from above. Again, however, basic attitudes are not modified.
3. *Limiting intergroup interaction.* Another approach to reducing conflict is to limit intergroup interaction to issues involving common goals. Where groups agree on a goal, cooperation becomes easier. An example of this can be seen in recent efforts by firms in the United States and Canada to work together to "meet the Japanese challenge."
4. *Use of integrators.* Integrators are individuals who are assigned a boundary-spanning role between two groups or departments. To be trusted, integrators must be perceived by both groups as legitimate and knowledgeable. The integrator often takes the "shuttle diplomacy" approach, moving from one group to another, identifying areas of agreement, and attempting to find areas of future cooperation.
5. *Confrontation and negotiation.* In this approach, competing parties are brought together face-to-face to discuss their basic areas of disagreement. The hope is that through open discussion and negotiation, means can be found to work out problems. Contract negotiations between union

Exhibit 16.5
Conflict Reduction Strategies

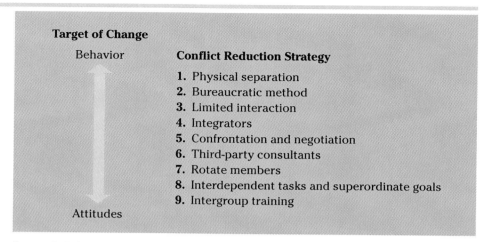

Target of Change

Behavior

Conflict Reduction Strategy

1. Physical separation
2. Bureaucratic method
3. Limited interaction
4. Integrators
5. Confrontation and negotiation
6. Third-party consultants
7. Rotate members
8. Interdependent tasks and superordinate goals
9. Intergroup training

Attitudes

Source: R. Daft and R. Steers, *Organizations: A Micro/Macro Approach* (Glenview, Ill.: Scott, Foresman and Company, 1986). Adapted from concepts in E. H. Neilsen, "Understanding and Managing Conflict," in J. Lorsch and P. Lawrence, eds., *Managing Group and Intergroup Relations* (Homewood, Ill.: Irwin, 1972).

and management represent one such example. If a "win-win" solution can be identified through these negotiations, the chances of an acceptable resolution of the conflict increase. (More will be said about this in the next section of this chapter.)

6. *Third-party consultation.* In some cases, it is helpful to bring in outside consultants who understand human behavior and can facilitate a resolution. An outside consultant not only serves as a go-between but can speak more directly to the issues, because he or she is not a member of either group.

7. *Rotation of members.* By rotating from one group to another, individuals come to understand the frames of reference, values, and attitudes of other members; communication is thus increased. When those rotated are accepted by the receiving groups, change in attitude as well as behavior becomes possible. This is clearly a long-term technique, as it takes time to develop good interpersonal relations and understanding among group members.

8. *Identification of interdependent tasks and superordinate goals.* A further strategy for management is to establish goals that require groups to work together to achieve overall success—for example, when company survival is threatened. The threat of a shutdown often causes long-standing opponents to come together to achieve the common objective of keeping the company going.

9. *Use of intergroup training.* The final technique on the continuum is intergroup training. Outside training experts are retained on a long-term basis to help groups develop relatively permanent mechanisms for working together. Structured workshops and training programs can help forge more favorable intergroup attitudes and, as a result, more constructive intergroup behavior.

IN PRACTICE
Grievance Panels at General Electric

General Electric has taken what many feel is a constructive step toward reducing conflict when it occurs. The effort began in an appliance assembly plant long characterized by poor labor relations. Although the employees were not unionized, they generally did not trust management, and, as a result, hostilities permeated the facility. In an effort to reduce the conflict level—and keep the union out—plant officials initiated employee-based grievance panels to evaluate all worker complaints.

A grievance panel consists of three hourly workers selected from a pool of volunteers by the aggrieved employee and two managers appointed by the company. All volunteers receive 12 hours of training in basic labor law and peer review procedures. When an employee files a grievance, the five-person panel hears the case and issues its judgment. Company management cannot overrule this decision. In their first nine years of operation, such panels heard about 80 grievances, ranging from protests over disciplinary actions to challenges of performance appraisals. The panel found in favor of the company in 80 percent of the cases.

As a result of the grievance panels, employee support for and trust in the company has improved markedly. As one employee notes, "If you have another peer listening to you, you think you can get a fair shot." By the same token, supervisors and managers have learned to take employee gripes more seriously. As one manager observed, "Your supervisors do a better job because they don't want their people going up before a panel—it's embarrassing." Other companies have followed General Electric's example with equally positive results. Although grievance panels certainly do not eliminate labor-management problems, they can at least help reduce their magnitude.[13]

NEGOTIATION BEHAVIOR

We have seen the central role played by conflict in organizational processes. Clearly, there are some areas where managers would prefer to solve a problem between two parties before it results in high levels of conflict. This is usually accomplished through negotiation. *Negotiation* is the process by which individuals or groups attempt to realize their goals by bargaining with another party who has at least some control over goal attainment. Throughout the negotiation process, considerable skill in communication, decision making, and the use of power and politics is required in order to succeed.

We will consider several aspects of negotiation, including stages of negotiation, types of negotiation behavior, and the negotiation process itself. We begin with the reasons why people engage in negotiation and bargaining in the first place.

Stages of Negotiation

In general, negotiation or bargaining is likely to have four stages. Although the length or importance of each stage can vary from situation to situation or from one culture to another, the presence and sequence of these stages are quite common across situations and cultures.[14]

1. *Non-task time.* During the first stage, the participants focus on getting to know and become comfortable with each other and do not focus directly on the task or issue of the negotiation. In cultures such as ours, this stage is often filled with small talk. However, it is usually not very long and is not seen as important as other stages. North Americans use phrases such as "Let's get down to business," "I know you're busy, so let's get right to it," "Let's not beat around the bush." However, in other cultures such as Mexico or Korea, the non-task stage is often longer and of more importance because it is during this stage the relationship is established. In these cultures, it is the relationship more than the contract that determines the extent to which each party can trust the other to fulfill its obligations.

2. *Information exchange.* The second stage of negotiations involves the exchange of background and general information. During this stage, participants may, for example, provide overviews of their company and its history. In Japan, this is an important stage because specific proposals or agreements must be considered and decided in the larger context. The information exchanged during the second stage provides this larger context.

3. *Influence and persuasion.* The third stage involves efforts to influence and persuade the other side. Generally, these efforts are designed to get the other party to reduce their demands or desires and to increase their acceptance of your demands or desires. There are a wide variety of influence tactics including promises, threats, questions, and so on. The use of these tactics as well as their effectiveness are a function of several factors. First, as was discussed in Chapter 15, the perceived or real power of one party relative to another is an important factor. For example, if one party is the only available supplier of a critical component, then threatening to go to a new supplier of that components unless the price is reduced is unlikely to be an effective influence tactic. Second, the effectiveness of a a particular influence tactics is also a function of accepted industry and cultural norms. For example, if threats are an unacceptable form of influence, then their use could lead to consequences opposite those desired by the initiator of such tactics.

4. *Closing.* The final stage of any negotiation is the closing. The closing may result in an acceptable agreement between the parties involved or it may result in failure to reach an agreement. The symbols that represent the close of a negotiation vary across cultures. For example, in the US, a signed contract is the symbol of a closed negotiation. At that point "a deal is a deal" and failure to abide by the contents of the document is considered a breach of contract. In China, however, there is not the strong legal history or perspective that exists in the US and a signed document is not necessarily a symbol of the close of the negotiations. In fact,

to some extent it symbolizes the beginning of the final points of negotiation. That is the signed document identifies the key issues that still need to be negotiated despite the fact that the document may contain specific obligations for the involved parties concerning these issues. Quite simply, even though the document may obligate one party to deliver a product on a certain day and obligate the other party to pay a certain price for delivery, the document itself does not symbolize that the negotiation concerning these specifics is closed.

Each of these four stages and the sequence described above is common across most situations and cultures. However, the length of time devoted to each stage, the importance of each stage, and the specific behaviors associated with each stage can vary by situation and certainly do vary by culture.

Bargaining Strategies

Within the context of these four stages, both parties must select an appropriate strategy that they believe will assist them in the attainment of their objectives. In general, two rather distinct approaches to negotiation can be identified. These are *distributive bargaining* and *integrative bargaining*. A comparison of these two approaches is shown in Exhibit 16.6.

Distributive Bargaining. In essence, distributive bargaining is "win-lose" bargaining. That is, the goals of one party are in fundamental and direct conflict with those of the other party. Resources are fixed and limited, and each party wants to maximize his or her share of these resources. Finally, in most cases, this situation represents a short-term relationship between the two parties. In fact, such parties may not see one another ever again.

A good example of this can be seen in the relationship between the buyer and seller of a house. If the buyer gets the house for less money (that is, he "wins"), the seller also gets less (that is, he "loses"). This win-lose situation can also be seen in classes where the professor insists on grading on a specified curve. If your friends get an A, there are fewer As to go around, and your chances are diminished.

Exhibit 16.6
Two Approaches
to Bargaining

Bargaining Characteristic	Distributive Bargaining	Integrative Bargaining
Payoff structure	Fixed amount of resources to be divided	Variable amount of resources to be divided
Primary motivation	I win, you lose	Mutual benefit
Primary interests	Opposed to each other	Convergent with each other
Focus of relationships	Short-term	Long-term

Under such circumstances, each side will probably adopt a course of action as follows. First, each side to a dispute will attempt to discover just how far the other side is willing to go to reach an accord. This can be done by offering outrageously low (or high) proposals simply to feel out the opponent. For example, in selling a house, the seller will typically ask a higher price than he or she actually hopes to get (see Exhibit 16.7). The buyer, in turn, typically offers far less than he or she is willing to pay. These two prices are put forth to discover the opponent's resistance price. The *resistance price* is the point beyond which the opponent will not go to reach a settlement. Once the resistance point has been estimated, each party tries to convince the opponent that the offer on the table is the best one the opponent is likely to receive and that thus, the opponent should accept it. As both sides engage in similar tactics, the winner is often determined by who has the best strategic and political skills to convince the other party that this is the best he or she can get.

Integrative Bargaining. Integrative bargaining is often described as the "win-win" approach. That is, with this technique, both parties try to reach a settlement that benefits both parties. Such an approach is often predicated on the belief that if people mutually try to solve the problem, they can identify some creative solutions that help everyone. A good example can be seen in bilateral trade negotiations between two nations. In such negotiations, participants usually agree that a trade war would hurt both sides; therefore, both sides attempt to achieve a balance of outcomes that are preferable to a

Exhibit 16.7
Distributive Bargaining in Buying a Home

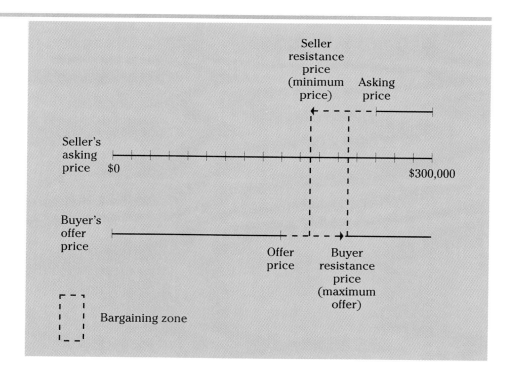

trade war for both sides. In doing so, however, the trick is to give away as little as possible to achieve the balance.[15]

As shown previously in Exhibit 16.6, this approach is characterized by the existence of variable resources to be divided, efforts to maximize joint outcomes, and the desire to establish or maintain a long-term relationship. The interests of the two parties may be convergent (that is, noncompetitive, such as preventing a trade war between two countries) or congruent (that is, mutually supportive, as when two countries reach a mutual defense pact).

In both cases, bargaining tactics are quite different from those typically found in distributive bargaining. Here, both sides must be able and willing to understand the viewpoints of the other party. Otherwise, they will not know where possible consensus lies. Moreover, the free flow of information is required. Obviously, some degree of trust is required here, too. In discussions, emphasis is placed on identifying communalities between the two parties; the differences are played down. And, finally, the search for solution focuses on selecting those courses of action that meet the goals and objectives of both sides. This approach requires considerably more time and energy than distributive bargaining, yet, under certain circumstances, it has the potential to lead to far more creative and long-lasting solution.

The Negotiation Process

The negotiation process consists of identifying one's desired goals—that is, what you are trying to get out of the exchange—and then developing suitable strategies aimed at reaching those goals. A key feature of one's strategy is knowing one's relative position in the bargaining process. That is, depending upon your relative position or strength, you may want to negotiate seriously or you may want to tell your opponent to "take it or leave it." The dynamics of bargaining power can be extrapolated directly from our discussion of power in Chapter 15. Exhibit 16.8 indicates several conditions

Exhibit 16.8
When To Negotiate

	Bargaining Strategies	
Characteristics of the Situation	**Negotiate**	**"Take It or Leave It"**
Value of exchange	High	Low
Commitment to a decision	High	Low
Trust Level	High	Low
Time	Ample	Pressing
Power distribution*	Low or balanced	High
Relationship between two parties	Important	Unimportant

*Indicates relative power distribution between the two parties. "Low" indicated that one has little power in the situation, whereas "high" indicates that one has considerable power.

affecting this choice. For example, you may wish to negotiate when you value the exchange, when you value the relationship, and when commitment to the issue is high. In the opposite situation, you may be indifferent to serious bargaining.

Once goals and objectives have been clearly established and bargaining strategy set, time is required to develop a suitable plan of action. Planning for negotiation requires a clear assessment of your own strengths and weaknesses as well as those of your opponents. Roy Lewicki and Joseph Litterer have suggested a format for preparation for negotiation.[16] According to this format, planning for negotiation should proceed through the following phases:

1. Understand the basic nature of the conflict. What are the primary areas of agreement and disagreement?
2. What exactly do you want out of this negotiation? What are your goals?
3. How will you manage the negotiation process? Here, several issues should be recognized:
    a. Identify the primary issues to negotiate.
    b. Prioritize these issues.
    c. Develop a desirable package including these important issues.
    d. Establish an agenda.
4. Do you understand your opponent?
    a. What are your opponent's current resources and needs?
    b. What is the history of your opponent's bargaining behavior? What patterns can you see that can help you predict his or her moves?

Research indicates that following such procedures does, in fact, lead to more successful bargaining. In Exhibit 16.9, for example, we can see differences in both the planning approaches and the actual behaviors of successful and average negotiators. Preparation clearly makes a difference, as does interpersonal style during the actual negotiation.

Exhibit 16.9
Differences Between Successful and Average Negotiations

Negotiation Behavior	Skilled Negotiators	Average Negotiators
Before the Negotiation		
Number of options considered per issue	5.1	2.6
Portion of time spent focusing on anticipated areas of agreement instead of conflict	39%	11%
During Negotiation		
Portion of time spent asking questions of opponent	21%	10%
Portion of time spent in active listening	10%	4%
Portion of time spent attacking opponent	1%	6%

Source: Based on data reported in N. Rackham, "The Behavior of Successful Negotiators" (Reston, Va.: Huthwaite Research Group, 1976), and N. Adler, *International Dimensions of Organizational Behavior* (Boston: PWS/Kent, 1986), pp. 165–181.

Cultural Differences in International Negotiations

In view of the increased emphasis on international industrial competitiveness, it is important to understand what happens when the two parties to a negotiation come from different cultures or countries. A knowledge of cultural differences can assist the manager both in understanding the other party's position and in striking the best possible deal given the circumstances.

A good place to start this analysis is to recognize how different cultures approach the art of persuasion; that is, how do people in different countries try to win you over to their side in a dispute? Although we cannot possibly examine all cultures, consider the results of a study of differences in *persuasion techniques* for North America, the Middle East, and the former Soviet Union.[17] As can be seen in Exhibit 16.10, Americans, Arabs, and Russians have significantly different approaches to persuasion. Americans tend to enter into a discussion emphasizing facts and figures, whereas Arabs may focus on emotions. The Russian may talk about ideals.

Moreover, in a negotiation situation, the American is ever-conscious of deadlines, whereas the Arab takes a more casual approach, and the Russian is often unconcerned about time. Americans make small concessions early in the bargaining process to establish a relationship. Arabs, on the other hand,

Exhibit 16.10
National Styles of Persuasion

	North Americans	Arabs	Russians
Primary negotiating style and process	Factual: appeals made to logic	Affective: appeals made to emotions	Axiomatic: appeals made to ideals
Conflict: opponent's arguments countered with . . .	Objective facts	Subjective feelings	Asserted ideals
Making concessions	Small concessions made early to establish a relationship	Concessions made throughout as a part of the bargaining process	Few, if any, small concessions made
Response to opponent's concessions	Usually reciprocate opponent's concessions	Almost always reciprocate opponent's concessions	Opponent's concessions viewed as weakness and almost never reciprocated
Relationship	Short-term	Long-term	No continuing relationship
Authority	Broad	Broad	Limited
Initial position	Moderate	Extreme	Extreme
Deadline	Very important	Casual	Ignored

Source: Reprinted with permission from *International Journal of Intercultural Relations,* Vol. 1; E. S. Glenn, D. Witmeyer, and K. A. Stevenson, "Cultural Styles of Persuasion," Fall 1977, p. 64. Copyright © 1977 Pergamon Press plc.

make concessions throughout the bargaining process, and the Russians try not to make any concessions at all. Clearly, this study has only highlighted trends, and exceptions can be easily found. Even so, a knowledge of such differences, however general, can greatly facilitate improved interpersonal relations and bargaining success for both parties.

We can also examine the personal characteristics of negotiators from different countries. A study by John Graham focused on the key characteristics of negotiators from different countries, in this case the United States, Japan, Taiwan, and Brazil. Results of the study are shown in Exhibit 16.11, which shows the rank order of the defining characteristics.[18] Again, we can see major differences in negotiators from around the world. Each has certain strengths, yet these strengths vary considerably from country to country. Americans are seen as prepared and organized, thinking well under pressure, whereas Japanese are seen as more dedicated and shrewd. Taiwanese negotiators were found in the study to be highly persistent and determined, working hard to win the opponent's respect, and the Brazilians were amazingly similar to the Americans.

Finally, we should note that negotiators from different countries differ markedly in their verbal and nonverbal *communication patterns.* In one study (again among Americans, representing North America; Japanese, representing East Asia; and Brazilians, representing South America), observers counted the number of times each negotiator did certain things within a given time limit.[19] The results are shown in Exhibit 16.12. As can be seen, these negotiators use both verbal and nonverbal communication in very different ways. Note, for example, that Brazilians on average said "no" 83 times within a 30-minute segment, compared to 5 times for Japanese and 9 times for Americans. On the

Exhibit 16.11
Key Individual Characteristics
of Negotiators (Rank Order)

American Managers	Japanese Managers	Chinese Mangers (Taiwan)	Brazilian Managers
Preparation and planning skill	Dedication to job	Persistence and determination	Preparation and planning skill
Thinking under pressure	Perceive and exploit power	Win respect and confidence	Thinking under pressure
Judgment and intelligence	Win respect and confidence	Preparation and planning skill	Judgment and intelligence
Verbal expressiveness	Integrity	Product knowlege	Verbal expressiveness
Product knowlege	Listening skill	Interesting	Product knowledge
Perceive and exploit power	Broad perspective	Judgment and intelligence	Perceive and exploit power
Integrity	Verbal expressiveness		Competition

Source: "Key Individual Characteristics of Negotiators" by John Graham, Graduate School of Management, University of California, Irvine. Reprinted by permission of the author.

Exhibit 16.12
Communication Patterns
during Negotiations for
Three Cultures

Tactic	Average Number of Times Tactic Was Used in a 30-minute Bargaining Session		
	Japan	**United States**	**Brazil**
Verbal Communication			
Making promises	7	8	3
Making threats	4	4	2
Making recommendations	7	4	5
Appealing to ideals and norms	4	2	1
Giving a command	8	6	14
Saying "no"	5	9	83
Making initial concessions	6	7	9
Nonverbal Communication			
Periods of silence	6	3	0
Interrupting opponent	12	10	29
Looking directly into opponent's eyes	1	3	5
Touching opponent	0	0	5

Source: Based on data reported in J. Graham, "The Influence of Culture on Business Negotiations," *Journal of International Business Studies,* Spring 1985, pp. 81–96.

other hand, Japanese appealed to ideals and societal norms and simply sat in silence more than the others. Such differences affect not only the negotiation process but also, in many cases, the outcomes. That is, if a negotiator from one culture has annoyed or insulted the opponent (intentionally or unintentionally), the opponent may resist doing business with that person or may fail to offer attractive terms. Hence, again we see the value of better understanding cultural variations in negotiations, as in other matters.

International Challenge

IN PRACTICE
Negotiating Styles in Malaysia and America

One of the emerging countries of Southeast Asia is Malaysia, whose natural resources are allowing it to develop as an important manufacturing center in the region along with Singapore, Indonesia, and Thailand. What happens when American businesspeople visit Malaysia to do business? In the following example, cross-cultural researcher George Renwick describes major differences between the two cultures as they approach a negotiation.

Americans' patterns of negotiation, like all of their patterns, differ somewhat depending upon their context. The negotiating patterns of government officials working out a treaty, for example, are somewhat different from those of a business executive "hammering out" a contract. The pattern portrayed here will be that of the business executive.

The American businessperson usually begins a series of negotiating sessions in a cordial manner, but he is intent upon "getting things under way." He is very clear as to what he and his company want, when it is wanted, and how he will go about getting it; he has planned his strategy carefully. And he has done what he could to "psyche out" his counterpart with whom he will be negotiating. From the outset, the American negotiator urges everyone to "dispense with the formalities" and get on with the business at hand. As soon as possible he expresses his determination, saying something like, "O.K., let's get down to brass tacks."

The American usually states his position (at least his first position) early and definitely. He plans before long to "really get down to the nitty gritty." He wants to "zero in" on the knotty problems and get to the points where "the rubber meets the road" (the point, that is, where "the action" begins). Once the negotiations are "really rolling," the American usually deals directly with obstacles as they come up, tries to clear them away in quick order, and becomes impatient and frustrated if he cannot.

Most of what the American wants to convey, of course, he puts into words—often many of them. His approach is highly verbal and quite visible—and thoroughly planned. He has outlined his alternative ahead of time and prepared his counterproposals, contingencies, backup positions, bluffs, guarantees, and tests of compliance, all carefully calculated, and including, of course, lots of numbers. Toward the end, he sees that some bailout provisions are included, but he usually doesn't worry too much about them; making and meeting business commitments "on schedule" is what his life is all about—he is not too concerned about getting out. If he has to get out, then he has to, and he will find a way when the time comes.

The American experiences real satisfaction when all the problems have been "worked out," especially if he has been able to get provisions very favorable to his company—and to his own reputation as a "tough negotiator." He rests securely when everything is "down in black and white" and the contract is initialled or signed.

Afterwards, the American enjoys himself; he relaxes "over some drinks" and carries on some "small talk" and "jokes around" with his team and their counterparts.

Malay patterns of negotiation, as might be expected, differ considerably. When they are buying something, Malays bargain with the merchant, and when they are working, they socialize with their boss and co-workers. Their purpose is to develop some sense of relationship with the other person. The relationship then provides the basis, or context, for the exchange. Malays take the same patterns and preferences into their negotiating sessions. When all is said and done, it is not the piece of paper they trust, it is the person—and their relationship with the person.

A Malay negotiator begins to develop the context for negotiations through the interaction routines appropriate to this and similar occasions. These routines are as complicated and subtle as customary American routines; they are cordial but quite formal. Like Americans and their own routines, Malays understand the Malay routines but are seldom consciously aware of them. Neither Malays nor Americans understand very clearly the routines of the other.

As the preliminary context is formed, it is important to the Malay that the proper forms of address be known beforehand and used, and that a variety of topics be talked about that are unrelated to the business to be transacted. This may continue for quite a while. A Malay negotiator wants his counterpart to participate comfortably, patiently, and with interest. As in other interaction, it is not the particular words spoken which are of most importance to the Malay; rather he listens primarily to the attitudes which the words convey—attitudes toward the Malay himself and toward the matter being negotiated. Attitudes are important to the relationship. At this point and throughout the negotiations, the Malay is as much concerned about the quality of the relationship as the quantity of the work accomplished. Motivation is more important to the Malay than momentum.

The Malay negotiator, as in other situations, is also aware of feelings—his own and those of his counterpart, and the effects of the exchanges upon both. He is also aware of, and concerned about, how he looks in the eyes of his team, how his counterpart looks in the eyes of the other team, and how both he and his counterpart will look after the negotiations in the eyes of their respective superiors.

The Malay is alert to style, both his own and that of his counterpart. Displaying manners is more important than scoring points. The way one negotiates is as important as what one negotiates. Grace and finesse show respect for the other and for the matter under consideration. Negotiating, like other interaction, is something of an art form. Balance and restraint are therefore essential.

The agenda which the Malay works through in the course of the negotiation is usually quite flexible. His strategy is usually rather simple. His positions are expressed in more general terms than the American's, but no less strongly held. His proposals are more offered than argued: they are offered to the other party rather than argued with him. Malays do not enjoy sparring. They deeply dislike combat.

In response to a strong assertion, the Malay negotiator usually expresses his respect directly by replying indirectly. The stronger the assertion and the more direct the demands, the more indirect the reply—at least the verbal reply.

The Malay and his team usually formulate their positions gradually and carefully. By the time they present their position, they usually have quite a lot of themselves invested in it. Direct rejection of the position, therefore, is sometimes felt to be a rejection of the person. Negotiating for the Malay is not quite the game that it is for some Americans.

If the Malay and his team have arrived at a position from which they and those whom they represent cannot move, they will not move. If this requires a concession from the counterpart, the Malays will not try to force the concession. If the counterpart sees that a concession from him is necessary, and makes it, the Malays, as gentlemen, recognize the move and respect the man who made it. A concession, therefore, is not usually considered by the Malay team to be a sign that they can press harder and extract further concessions. Instead, a concession by either side is considered as evidence of strength and a basis for subsequent reconciliation and cooperation.

What about getting out a contract? Making and meeting business commitments is *not* what a Malay's life is all about. He has other, often prior, commitments. He therefore enters into contracts cautiously and prefers to have an exit provided.

In addition, Malays are certain of their control over the future (even their control of their own country) than are Americans. Therefore, promising specific kinds of performance in the future by specific dates in a contract, especially in a long-term contract where the stakes are high, is often difficult for Malays. It is even more difficult, of course, if they are not certain whether they can trust the persons to whom they are making the commitment and from whom they are accepting commitments. Malays therefore give a great deal of thought to a contract and to the contracting party before signing it. And they are uneasy if provisions have not been made for a respectable withdrawal should future circumstances make their compliance impossible.[20]

PULLING IT ALL TOGETHER

Conflict is most likely to occur when the goals, expectations, and/or behaviors of at least two parties differ and when those differences are difficult to avoid (such as when interdependence between or among the parties involved is high). Conflict itself is neither good nor bad, productive nor destructive. The key to the outcome of conflict is the manner in which it is managed. Negotiation, as a key means of managing conflict, has four distinct stages. However, the length, importance, and norms for each stage can vary be situation and especially by culture.

SUMMARY OF KEY POINTS

- Conflict is the process by which a person or group feels frustrated in the pursuit of certain goals, plans, or objectives.
- Conflict may take one of four forms: (1) goal, (2) cognitive, (3) affective, or (4) behavioral.
- Conflict may occur on several levels, including intrapersonal, interpersonal, intergroup, and interorganizational.
- Conflict in organizations can be caused by task interdependencies, status inconsistencies, jurisdictional ambiguities, communication problems, dependence on common resource pools, lack of common performance standards, and individual differences.
- A model of the conflict process follows four stages. Conflict originates (Stage 1) when an individual or group experiences frustration in the pursuit of important goals. In Stage 2, the individual or group attempts to understand the nature of the problem and its causes. In Stage 3, efforts are made to change behavioral patterns in such a way that the desired outcome, or Stage 4, is achieved.
- Ineffective conflict resolution strategies include nonaction, administrative orbiting, due process nonaction, secrecy, and character assassination.
- Strategies for preventing conflict include (1) emphasizing organization-wide goals, (2) providing stable, well-structured tasks, (3) facilitating intergroup communication, and (4) avoiding win-lose situations.
- Strategies for reducing conflict include (1) physical separation, (2) use of rules and regulations, (3) limiting intergroup interaction, (4) use of

integrators, (5) confrontation and negotiation, (6) third-party consultation, (7) rotation of members, (8) identification of interdependent tasks and superordinate goals, and (9) use of intergroup training.

■ Negotiation is the process by which individuals and groups attempt to reach their goals by bargaining with others who can help or hinder goal attainment.

■ Negotiation is helpful in three primary instances: (1) a conflict of interest, (2) the absence of clear rules or procedures, and (3) when there is a desire to avoid a fight.

■ Distributive bargaining attempts to resolve a win-lose conflict in which resources are limited and each party wishes to maximize its share of these resources.

■ Integrative bargaining occurs when both parties attempt to reach a settlement that benefits both sides in a dispute.

■ A resistance point is the point beyond which an opponent will not go to reach a settlement.

■ Planning for a negotiation session involves (1) understanding the basic nature of the conflict, (2) knowing what the group wants to achieve in the session, (3) selecting a chief negotiator, and (4) understanding one's opponent.

■ Cultural differences play a major role in the negotiation process and influence such factors as persuasion techniques, the key characteristics of the negotiators, and communication patterns.

KEY WORDS

administrative orbiting	grievance panel
affective conflict	information flow system
assertiveness	integrative bargaining
behavioral conflict	intergroup conflict
character assassination	interorganizational conflict
cognitive conflict	interpersonal conflict
conflict	intrapersonal conflict
constructive confrontation	jurisdictional ambiguities
cooperativeness	negotiation
distributive bargaining	resistance price
due process nonaction	status inconsistencies
frustration	task interdependencies
goal conflict	third-party consultation

QUESTIONS FOR DISCUSSION

1. Identify the types of conflict commonly found in organizations, and provide examples of each.
2. How can conflict be good for an organization?
3. Identify some reasons for the prevalence of intergroup conflict in organizations.

4. How does intergroup conflict affect behavior within a work group? Behavior between two or more groups?
5. Review the basic conflict model discussed in this chapter. What lessons for management follow from this model?
6. Of the various strategies for resolving and preventing conflicts that are presented in this chapter, which ones do you feel will generally be most effective? Least effective? Why?
7. What is the difference between distributive and integrative bargaining? When would each be most appropriate?
8. How can cultural differences affect bargaining behavior? If you were negotiating with a Japanese firm, what might you do differently than if you were facing an American firm? Explain.

NOTES

1. "Caterpillar's Don Fites: Why He Didn't Blink," *Business Week,* August 10, 1992, pp. 56–57. "Caterpillar's Trump Card." *New York Times,* April 15, 1992, p. A1.
2. K. Thomas and W. Schmidt, "A Survey of Managerial Interests with Respect to Conflict," *Academy of Management Journal,* 1976, pp. 315-318.
3. J. Graves, "Successful Management and Organizational Mugging," in J. Paap ed., *New Directions in Human Resource Management* (Englewood Cliffs, N.J.: Prentice-Hall, 1978); M. Rahim, "A Measure of Styles of Handling Interpersonal Conflict," *Academy of Management Journal,* 1983, pp. 368–376.
4. Cited in the *Register-Guard,* October 31, 1981, p. 23.
5. W. Zellner. "Labor May Still Have Greyhound Collared." *Business Week,* November 26, 1992, p. 60. "T. Hayes. "Strike Hobbling Greyhound and Thousands of its Riders." *New York Times,* March 2, 1990.
6. L. Coser, *The Functions of Social Conflict* (New York: Free Press, 1956). p. 154.
7. M. A. Harris, "Can Jack Welsh Reinvent GE?" *Business Week,* June 30, 1986; S. Flax, "The Ten Toughest Bosses in America," *Fortune,* August 6, 1984, p. 21.
8. R. Miles, *Macro Organizational Behavior* (Glenview, Ill.: Scott, Foresman, 1980).
9. K. Thomas, "Conflict and Conflict Management," In M. D. Dunnette, ed., *Handbook of Industrial and Organizational Psychology* (Chicago: Rand McNally, 1976).
10. K. Thomas and L. Pondy, "Toward an Intent Model of Conflict Management Among Principal Parties," *Human Relations,* 1967, *30,* pp. 1089–1102.
11. Miles, op. cit.
12. A. S. Grove, "How to Make Confrontation Work for You." Fortune, July 23, 1984, pp. 73–75.
13. J. Tasini, "Letting Workers Help Handle Workers' Gripes," *Business Week,* September 15, 1986, pp. 82–86.
14. J. Graham, "The Influence of Culture on Business Negotiations," *Journal of International Business Studies,* Spring 1985, pp. 81–96.
15. Ibid.
16. Ibid.; M. Baserman, "Why Negotiations Go Wrong," *Psychology Today,* June 1986, pp. 54–58; J. Graham and Y. Sano, Smart Bargaining (New York: Harper & Row, 1989).
17. E. Glenn, D. Witmeyer, and K. Stevenson, "Cultural Styles of Persuasion," *International Journal of Intercultural Relations,* Fall 1977, pp. 62–66.
18. Data supplied by John Graham, Graduate School of Management, University of California, Irvine. Cited in N. Adler, *International Dimensions of Organizational Behavior* (Boston: PWS/Kent, 1986), p. 157.
19. J. Graham, "The Influence of Culture on Business Negotiations," *Journal of International Business Studies,* Spring 1985, pp. 81–96.
20. G. Renwick, *Malays and Americans: Definite Differences, Unique Opportunities* (Yarmouth, Maine: Intercultural Press, 1985), pp. 51–54.

EXPERIENTIAL EXERCISE 16

Doing Business in South Africa

This exercise is designed to illustrate the complexity and conflict involved when a company tries to make a "socially responsible" decision within the confines of global competition. Students will recognize that two groups may take opposing views on the same issue and that each may justify its views as socially responsible. This exercise takes about 45 minutes of class time.

Your dilemma is this: A certain North American company has extensive and profitable operations in South Africa, a country frequently accused of violating the basic human rights of a large section of its population. The company is faced with the decision of whether it should continue its operations in South Africa or pull out.

The class should be divided into three groups of approximately equal size. The first group will represent the board of directors of the company; it is responsible for making the decision of whether to continue or discontinue operations in South Africa. It is also responsible for minimizing the negative effects of the conflict surrounding the decision. The second group will represent management in the South African subsidiary, a mix of North Americans and local people; it believes that the company should maintain operations in South Africa. The third group will represent an activist group in North America; it believes that all American companies should pull out of South Africa. Some individuals may be assigned to observe the decision process.

Each group has a specific assignment:

> *Group 1—Board of Directors:* Your group is to develop a set of criteria that will be used to make your decision. You will listen to the arguments presented by the other two groups, ask questions, and ultimately make a decision on the basis of the criteria you develop. Throughout, your efforts should be aimed at reaching a satisfactory decision with a minimum of conflict.
>
> *Group 2—Management of Subsidiary:* Your group is to develop arguments to present to the board of directors to persuade the board to continue its operations in South Africa. You have a variety of reasons for recommending that the firm remain in South Africa including that fact that your firm has hired and trained a large number of nonwhites and has provided them with significant promotion and development opportunities. The subsidiary in South Africa abides by many of the EEOC (Equal Employment Opportunity Commission) guidelines that the parent company follows in the Sates. You will also have the opportunity to respond to the activist group; therefore, you should consider your response to the arguments it is likely to present.
>
> *Group 3—Activist Group:* Your group is to develop arguments to present to the board of directors to persuade the board to pull its operations out of the country. Much of the evidence that you have concerning the general discriminatory treatment of nonwhites in south Africa is not disputed by knowledgeable experts. You will also have the opportunity to respond to the local management group; therefore, you should consider your response to arguments they are likely to present.

MANAGEMENT DILEMMA 16

The Psychology Department

Marion Albers recently accepted a faculty position in the Psychology Department of a large midwestern university and was assigned to teach the introductory psychology course. Albers had trouble from the beginning. She was insecure and easily dominated by the students, and she failed to bring in relevant classroom examples. She was not a good lecturer and was consistently rated "below average" by the students in their class evaluations. Moreover, Albers had trouble relating to colleagues as well as to students. Her colleagues saw her as aloof and argumentative.

During the spring term, Tom McGowan (also a professor in the Psychology Department) was assigned a section of a senior honors elective and developed a strong following among students. Because this was the first time he had taught the course, he did considerable extra preparation in addition to the time-consuming work for the introductory course he already taught. The honors elective was in his area of expertise, however, and he did an outstanding job. Student evaluations were consistently excellent, and McGowan thoroughly enjoyed teaching the class. As a result, he assumed that he would be assigned to teach only the elective course the following term. This would have the added benefit of giving him somewhat more prestige and status, because teaching honors electives was viewed as more challenging—a task for only the best professors.

Toward the end of the term, the department head called a meeting of the faculty to discuss course assignments for the following year. The coordinator for the introductory course tactfully suggested that Marion Albers be reassigned elsewhere. Albers readily acknowledged that the experience had been an unhappy one for her and that her performance was not up to the usual college standards. McGowan asked to teach the honors elective again, but he didn't push the matter, assuming it was a logical assignment for him given his experience and expertise. Besides, he was currently up for tenure and promotion, and he did not want to appear to be overly assertive or uncooperative.

The following day, course assignments were sent to all faculty. Most of the professors were surprised and angered to discover that Albers was assigned three sections of the special elective, whereas McGowan was assigned to teach only the introductory course. Several professors went to the department head to complain. They argued that Albers had no knowledge of the elective area and that she had admitted she was apprehensive about teaching it. McGowan, on the other hand, had worked hard to prepare for the elective and had achieved outstanding evaluations. Moreover, the reputation of the course and the number of students enrolling would be adversely affected by putting a "bad" teacher in three sections out of four. It was also pointed out that McGowan had seniority over Albers. And, finally, the faculty argued that such a decision made it appear to many that Albers was being rewarded for failing.

The department head listened to the complaints but responded by saying that her decision represented the lesser of two evils. McGowan was, indeed, the superior teacher, but Albers needed experience so she, too, could develop into a first-rate instructor. "We have to develop the junior faculty," she concluded, "That's one of our responsibilities." Moreover, she believed it was important to support women and help them develop their competencies. She was proud that she had recruited another woman for the department, and she didn't want to let Albers go.

Faced with this situation, what would you do?

1. Describe how each party in the dispute (Tom McGowan, Marion Albers, the other faculty, and the department head) sees the situation.
2. What is your analysis of the dynamics of the conflict?
3. What would you recommend be done to resolve this conflict?
4. What consequences would you except to occur as a result of your recommendations?

17

Stress and Well-Being

The Management Challenge

- To recognize the symptoms of stress in oneself and in others.
- To identify the underlying causes of stress in a particular situation.
- To minimize the dysfunctional consequences of stressful behavior.
- To seek appropriate remedies for job-related stress.
- To motivate employees to participate actively in health promotion efforts for the benefit of all concerned.

CLOSE UP

Performance Pressures and Stress at Food Lion

The CEO of Food Lion, Tom E. Smith, thought he had come up with a way to increase efficiency at the $4.7 billion and fastest-growing supermarket chain in the United States. A system called "effective scheduling" allocates the labor hours a store manager can use each week based on expected sales. If a manager runs out of allocated hours, he or she will have to pitch in where needed.[1]

Too meet the targeted limits, baggers learn to bag with both hands, and stockers must stock shelves at a rate of 50 cases per hour. Some employees note the increase in efficiency that this system creates. A 31-year-veteran meat cutter commented, "I had one store where I had 1.5 employees—me full-time and a part-time employee up to 30–32 hours—doing almost as much business as I did at a Kroger store where I had three employees."

Others feel more stress under the system. A former store manager commented, "I put in more and more and more time—a hundred hours a week—but no matter how many hours I worked or what I did, I could never satisfy the supervisors. I lived, ate, breathed, slept Food Lion. The hardest thing for me was to be a bitch. And I was a bitch. I had to be. They wanted 100% conditions, seven days a week, 24 hours a day. And there's no damn way you could do it."

Not surprisingly, the stress was too much for this particular store manager, and she quit. Other employees are supporting an effort by the United Food & Commercial Workers union to organize the hundreds of employees in the 730-store chain. Meanwhile, the U.S. government has begun investigations of allegations that Food Lion "recycles" meat and other perishables to meet their efficiency quotas.

The example of Food Lion illustrates how work-related stress can have a significant impact on vendors and their customers. And Food Lion is not alone. Work-related stress is emerging to be one of the most prominent—and costly—issues of the 1990s. One way to see this is in the recorded cases of worker's compensation claims filed throughout the United States and Canada. In one such example, an employee of the Raytheon Company with 22 years' seniority suffered a nervous breakdown when told she was being transferred to another department. The Massachusetts Supreme Judicial Court ruled that she was entitled to worker's compensation because her breakdown was a "personal injury arising out of and in the course of employment."[2]

In addition to the human cost, stress-related illness and injuries in the workplace place a tremendous financial burden on companies, which impairs not only their productivity but also their profitability. The U.S. Office of Technology Assessment estimates that such illness costs American business between $50 billion and $70 billion per year.[3] Thus, however we look at it, stress and stress-related problems have a direct impact on the effective management of organizations, and contemporary managers must be willing to commit the necessary energy and resources to minimize the dysfunctional consequences of such problems if they are to achieve an effective level of operations.

In this chapter, we will examine several aspects of job-related stress and consider several ways in which corporations can facilitate employee health and well-being. We begin by looking at problems of work adjustment as a general framework for the study of stress.

PROBLEMS OF WORK ADJUSTMENT

Failure to adjust to work represents a major problem in industry today. It has been estimated that between 80 and 90 percent of industrial accidents are caused by personal factors.[4] Turnover, absenteeism, drug abuse, alcoholism, and sabotage remain relatively permanent fixtures of most contemporary work organizations. To the extent that individuals are unable to adjust to work, we would expect them to persist in counterproductive behavior.

W. S. Neff has identified five types of people who have problems adjusting to work. He suggests that each of the five types represents a "clinical picture of different varieties of work psychopathology":[5]

■ *Type I:* People who lack motivation to work. These individuals have a negative conception of the work role and choose to avoid it.

■ *Type II:* People whose predominating response to the demand to be productive is fear or anxiety.

■ *Type III:* People who are characterized predominantly by open hostility and aggression.

■ *Type IV:* People who are characterized by marked dependency. These people often exhibit the characteristic of helplessness. They are constantly seeking advice from others and are unable to initiate any action on their own.

■ *Type V:* People who display a marked degree of social naïveté. These individuals lack perception when it comes to the needs and feelings of others and may not realize that their behavior elicits reactions from and has an effect on others. Typically, these individuals are socially inept and unaware of appropriate behavior in ordinary social situations.

Several important points follow from this analysis. First, note that failure to adjust to a normal job or work schedule does not automatically imply that an individual is lazy or stupid. Several deeply ingrained psychological problems keep people from making normal adjustments in many cases. Second, note that only one of the five types (Type I) exhibits a motivational problem. Managers must look beyond motivation for answers to the psychopathology of work. One type (Type V) exhibits a form of personality disorder, or at least social immaturity. But the remaining three types—those exhibiting anxiety, aggression, or dependency—all have problems relating not only to personality, but more important, to how the nature of the job affects that personality. In fact, anxiety, aggression, and dependency are major factors inherent in stressful jobs in organizations. Hence, it seems that at least three of the five reasons for failure to adjust to work relate to the extent to which the job is experienced as stressful and causes the individual to want to withdraw.

It has been wisely observed that "if, under stress, a man goes all to pieces, he will probably be told to pull himself together. It would be more effective to help him identify the pieces and to understand why they have come apart."[6] This is the role of the contemporary manager in dealing with stress. Managers cannot simply ignore the existence of stress on the job. Instead, they have a responsibility to understand stress and its causes.

We will explore the topic of work-related stress in several stages, first examining major organizational and personal influences on stress, then considering several outcomes of stress, and finally exploring methods for coping with stress on the job. Throughout, emphasis will be placed on how stress and its consequences affect people at work and what role managers can play in attempting to minimize the effects of stress on both the individual and the organization. We will make liberal use of practical examples, and, as usual, you will be given an opportunity to evaluate yourself on several aspects of stress and wellness in organizations.

WORK-RELATED STRESS

For our purposes here, *stress* will be defined as a physical and emotional reaction to potentially threatening aspects of the environment. This definition points to a poor fit between individuals and their environments. Either excessive demands are being made, or reasonable demands are being made that individuals are ill-equipped to handle. Under stress, individuals are unable to respond to environmental stimuli without undue psychological and/or physiological damage, such as chronic fatigue, tension, or high blood pressure. This damage resulting from experienced stress is usually referred to as *strain*.

Before we examine the concept of work-related stress in detail, several important points need to be made. First, stress is pervasive in the work environment.[7] Most of us experience stress at some time. For instance, a job may require too much or too little from us. In fact, almost any aspect of the work environment is capable of producing stress. Stress can result from excessive noise, light, or heat; too much or too little responsibility; too much or too little work to accomplish; or too much or too little supervision.

Second, it is important to note that all people do not react in the same way to stressful situations, even in the same occupation. One individual (a high-need achiever) may thrive on a certain amount of job-related tension; this tension may serve to activate the achievement motive. A second individual may respond to this tension by worrying about his or her inability to cope with the situation. Managers must recognize the central role of individual differences in the determination of experienced stress.

Often the key reason for the different reactions is a function of the different interpretations of a given event that different people make, especially concerning possible or probable consequences associated with the event. For example, The same report is required of student *A* and student *B* on the same day. Student *A* interprets the report in a very stressful way and imagines all the negative consequences of submitting a poor report. Student *B* interprets the report differently and sees it as an opportunity to demonstrate the things he or she has learned and imagines the positive consequences of turning in a high quality report. Although both students face essentially the same event, they interpret and react to it differently.

Third, all stress is not necessarily bad. Although highly stressful situations invariably have dysfunctional consequences, moderate levels of stress often serve useful purposes. A moderate amount of job-related tension not only keeps us alert to environmental stimuli (possible dangers and opportunities) but in addition often provides a useful motivational function. Some experts argue that the best and most satisfying work that employees do is work performed under moderate stress. Some stress may be necessary for psychological growth, creative activities, and the acquisition of new skills. Learning to drive a car or play a piano or run a particular machine typically creates tension that is instrumental in skill development. It is only when the level of stress increases or when stress is prolonged that physical or psychological problems emerge.

Before we go into detail on the subject of stress and wellness, you may wish to see if you have experienced stress on your present (or previous) part- or full-time job. To do so, simply complete Self-Assessment 17.1. When you have finished, refer to the scoring procedures in Appendix B.

General Adaptation Syndrome

The general physiological response to stressful events is believed to follow a fairly consistent pattern known as the *general adaptation syndrome.*[8] This syndrome consists of three stages (see Exhibit 17.1). The first stage, *alarm,* occurs at the first sign of stress. Here the body prepares to fight stress by releasing hormones from the endocrine glands. During this initial stage, heartbeat and respiration increase, blood sugar level rises, muscles tense up, pupils dilate, and digestion slows. At this stage the body prepares basically

SELF-ASSESSMENT 17.1
How Stressful Is Your Job?

Instructions: This instrument focuses on the stress level of your current (or previous) job. Think of your job and answer the following items as frankly and honestly as possible.

		Strongly Disagree			Strongly Agree	
1.	I am often irritable with my co-workers.	1	2	3	4	5
2.	At work, I constantly feel rushed or behind schedule.	1	2	3	4	5
3.	I often dread going to work.	1	2	3	4	5
4.	I often experience headaches, stomachaches, or backaches at work.	1	2	3	4	5
5.	I often lose my temper over minor problems.	1	2	3	4	5
6.	Everything I do seems to drain my energy level.	1	2	3	4	5
7.	I often interpret questions or comments from others as a criticism of my work.	1	2	3	4	5
8.	Time is my enemy.	1	2	3	4	5
9.	I often have time for only a quick lunch (or no lunch) at work.	1	2	3	4	5
10.	I spend considerable time at home worrying about problems at work.	1	2	3	4	5

for a "fight or flight" response. That is, the body prepares to either get away from the threat or to combat it. Following this initial shock, the body moves into the second stage, *resistance.* The body attempts to repair any damage and return to a condition of stability and equilibrium. If successful, physical signs of stress will disappear. If the stress continues long enough, however, the body's capacity for adaptation becomes exhausted. In this third stage, *exhaustion,* defenses wear away, and the individual experiences a variety of stress-related illnesses, including headaches, ulcers, and high blood pressure. This third stage is the most severe and presents the greatest threat both to individuals and to organizations.

Exhibit 17.1
The General
Adaptation Syndrome

| Alarm | Resistance | Exhaustion |

Types of Stress: Frustration and Anxiety

There are several different ways to categorize stress. However, from a managerial perspective, it is useful to focus on only two forms: frustration and anxiety. *Frustration* refers to a psychological reaction to an obstruction or impediment to goal-oriented behavior. Frustration occurs when an individual wishes to pursue a certain course of action but is prevented from doing so. This obstruction may be externally or internally caused. Examples of people experiencing obstacles that lead to frustration include a salesperson who continually fails to make a sale, a machine operator who cannot keep pace with the machine, or even a person ordering coffee from a machine that fails to return the correct change. The prevalence of frustration in work organizations should be obvious from this and other examples.

Whereas frustration is a reaction to an obstruction in instrumental activities or behavior, *anxiety* is a feeling of inability to deal with anticipated harm. Anxiety occurs when people do not have appropriate responses or plans for coping with anticipated problems. It is characterized by a sense of dread, a foreboding, and a persistent apprehension of the future for reasons that are sometimes unknown to the individual.

What causes anxiety in work organizations? Hamner and Organ suggest several factors:

> Differences in power in organizations which leave people with a feeling of vulnerability to administrative decisions adversely affecting them; frequent changes in organizations, which make existing behavior plans obsolete; competition, which creates the inevitability that some persons lose "face," esteem, and status; and job ambiguity (especially when it is coupled with pressure). To these may be added some related factors, such as lack of job feedback, volatility in the organization's economic environment, job insecurity, and high visibility of one's performance (successes as well as failures). Obviously, personal, nonorganizational factors come into play as well, such as physical illness, problems at home, unrealistically high personal goals, and estrangement from one's colleagues or one's peer group.[9]

ORGANIZATIONAL INFLUENCES ON STRESS

We will now consider several factors that have been found to influence both frustration and anxiety; we will present a general model of stress, including its major causes and its outcomes. Following this, we will explore several mechanisms by which employees and their managers cope with or reduce experienced stress in organizations. The model presented here draws heavily on the work of several social psychologists at the Institute for Social Research of the University of Michigan, including John French, Robert Caplan, Robert Kahn, and Daniel Katz. In essence, the proposed model identifies two major sources of stress: organizational sources and individual sources. In addition, the moderating effects of social support and hardiness are considered. These influences are shown in Exhibit 17.2.

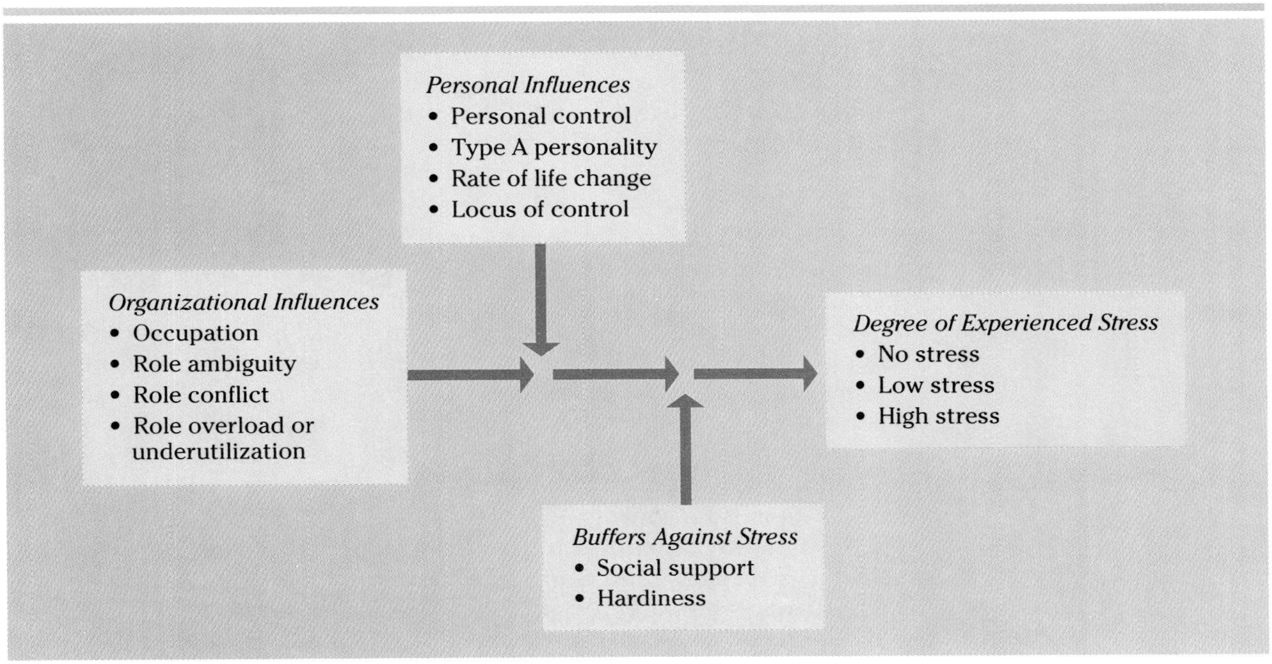

Personal Influences
- Personal control
- Type A personality
- Rate of life change
- Locus of control

Organizational Influences
- Occupation
- Role ambiguity
- Role conflict
- Role overload or underutilization

Degree of Experienced Stress
- No stress
- Low stress
- High stress

Buffers Against Stress
- Social support
- Hardiness

Exhibit 17.2
Major Influences on
Job-Related Stress

We begin with organizational influences on stress. Although many factors in the work environment have been found to influence the extent to which people experience stress on the job, four factors have been shown to be particularly strong. These are (1) occupational differences, (2) role ambiguity, (3) role conflict, and (4) role overload and underutilization. We will consider each of these factors in turn.

Occupational Differences

Tension and job stress are prevalent in our contemporary society and can be found in a wide variety of jobs. Consider, for example, the following quotes from interviews with working people. The first is from a bus driver:

> You have your tension. Sometimes you come close to having an accident, that upsets you. You just escape maybe by a hair or so. Sometimes maybe you get a disgruntled passenger on there who starts a big argument. Traffic. You have someone who cuts you off or stops in front of the bus. There's a lot of tension behind that. . . . Most of the time you have to drive for the other drivers, to avoid hitting them. So you take the tension home with you. Most of the drivers, they'll suffer from hemorrhoids, kidney trouble, and such as that. I had a case of ulcers behind it.[10]

Or consider the plight of a bank teller:

> Some days, when you're aggravated about something, you carry it after you leave the job. Certain people are bad days. (Laughs.) The type of person

who will walk in and says, "My car's double-parked outside. Would you hurry up, lady?" . . . you want to say, "Hey, why did you double-park your car? So now you're going to blame me if you get a ticket, 'cause you were dumb enough to leave it there?" But you can't. That's the one hassle. You can't say anything back. The customer's always right.[11]

Stress is experienced by workers in many jobs: secretaries, assembly line workers, foremen, waitresses, and managers. In fact, it is difficult to find jobs that are without some degree of stress. We seldom talk about jobs without stress; instead, we talk about the degree or magnitude of the stress.

The work roles that people fill have a substantial influence on the degree to which they experience stress.[12] These differences do *not* follow the traditional blue-collar/white-collar dichotomy, however. In general, available evidence suggests that high-stress occupations are those in which incumbents have little control over their jobs, work under relentless time pressures or threatening physical conditions, or have major responsibilities for either human or financial resources.

A recent study attempted to identify those occupations that were most (and least) stressful.[13] The results are presented in Exhibit 17.3. As shown, high-stress occupations (fire fighter, race car driver, and astronaut) are typified by the stress-producing characteristics noted above, whereas low-stress occupations (musical instrument repairperson, medical records technician, and librarian) are not. It can therefore be concluded that a major source of general stress emerges from the occupation at which one is working.

A second survey, focusing on secretaries, examined the specific causes of stress.[14] The results of the study showed that the most frequently cited reasons for stress among secretaries were interruptions (53 percent), lack of advancement opportunities (46 percent), lack of input into decision making (45 percent), and lack of communication from supervisor (41 percent).

Finally, a recent study among managers found that they, too, are subject to considerable stress arising out of the nature of managerial work.[15] Some of the more common work stressors for managers are shown in Exhibit 17.4.

Exhibit 17.3
The Most and Least Stressful Jobs

High-Stress Jobs	Low-Stress Jobs
1. Fire fighter	1. Musical instrument repairperson
2. Race car driver	2. Industrial machine repairperson
3. Astronaut	3. Medical records technician
4. Surgeon	4. Pharmacist
5. NFL football player	5. Medical assistant
6. City police officer	6. Typist/word processor
7. Osteopath	7. Librarian
8. State police officer	8. Janitor
9. Air traffic controller	9. Bookkeeper
10. Mayor	10. Forklift operator

Source: From *The Jobs Rated Almanac* by Les Krantz. Copyright © 1988 Les Krantz. Reprinted by permission of *The World Almanac.*

Exhibit 17.4
Typical Stressors Faced
by Managers

Stressor	Example
Role ambiguity	Unclear job duties
Role conflict	Manager is both a boss and a subordinate
Role overload	Too much work, too little time
Unrealistic expectations	Managers are often asked to do the impossible
Difficult decisions	Managers have to make decisions that adversely affect subordinates
Managerial failure	Manager fails to achieve expected results
Subordinate failure	Subordinates let boss down

Source: Based on D. Zauderer and J. Fox, "Resiliency in the Face of Stress," *Management Solutions,* November 1987, pp. 32–33.

These stressors range from task ambiguity and role conflict to overwork and the possibility of failure. Indeed, responsibility for others may be the greatest stressor of all for managers. Studies in the United States and abroad indicate that managers and supervisors consistently have more ulcers and experience more hypertension than the people they supervise. Responsibility for people was found to be a greater influence on stress than responsibility for nonpersonal factors such as budgets, projects, equipment, and other property. As noted by French and Caplan:

> If there is any truth to the adage that "man's greatest enemy is himself," it can be found in these data—it is the responsibility which organizational members have for other organizational members, rather than the responsibility for impersonal aspects of the organization, which constitutes the more significant organizational stress.[16]

Thus, a person's occupation or profession represents a major cause of stress-related problems at work. In addition to occupation, however, and indeed closely related to it, is the problem of one's role expectations in the organization. Three interrelated role processes will be examined as they relate to experienced stress: role ambiguity, role conflict, and role overload or underutilization.

Role Ambiguity

The first role process variable to be discussed here is *role ambiguity.* When individuals have inadequate information concerning their roles, they experience role ambiguity. Uncertainty over job definition takes many forms, including not knowing expectations for performance, not knowing how to meet those expectations, and not knowing the consequences of job behavior. Role ambiguity is particularly strong among managerial jobs, where role definitions and task specification lack clarity (refer to Exhibit 17.4). For example, the manager of accounts payable may not be sure of the quantity and quality standards for his or her department. The uncertainty of the absolute level of these two performance standards or their relative importance to each other makes predicting outcomes such as performance evaluation, salary increases or promotion opportunities equally difficult. All of this contributes to increased stress for the manager. Role ambiguity can also occur among nonmanagerial employees—for example, whose supervisors fail to make sufficient time to clarify role expectations, thus leaving them unsure of how best to contribute to departmental and organizational goals. (Note that a major benefit ascribed to management-by-objectives programs, as discussed in Chapter 7, is that they substantially reduce role ambiguity by specifying task goals.)

How prevalent is role ambiguity at work? In two independent surveys of employees, it was found that 35 percent of one sample (a national random sample of male employees) and 60 percent of the other sample (primarily scientists and engineers) reported some form of role ambiguity.[17] Hence, ambiguity of job role is not an isolated event.

Role ambiguity has been found to lead to several negative stress-related outcomes. French and Caplan summarized their study findings as follows:

> In summary, role ambiguity, which appears to be widespread, (1) produces psychological strain and dissatisfaction; (2) leads to underutilization of human resources; and (3) leads to feelings of futility on how to cope with the organizational environment.[18]

In other words, role ambiguity has far-reaching consequences beyond experienced stress, including employee turnover and absenteeism, poor coordination and utilization of human resources, and increased operating costs because of inefficiency.

It should be noted, however, that not everyone responds in the same way to role ambiguity. Studies have shown that some people have a higher *tolerance for ambiguity* and are less affected by role ambiguity (in terms of stress, reduced performance, or propensity to leave) than those with a low tolerance for ambiguity.[19] Thus, again we can see the role of individual differences in moderating the effects of environmental stimuli on individual behavior and performance.

Role Conflict

The second role-related factor in stress is *role conflict*. This may be defined as the simultaneous occurrence of two (or more) sets of pressures or expectations; compliance with one would make it difficult to comply with the other. In other words, role conflict occurs when an employee is placed in a situation where contradictory demands are placed upon him or her. For instance, a factory worker may find himself in a situation where the supervisor is demanding greater output, yet the work group is demanding a restriction of output. Similarly, a secretary who reports to several supervisors may face a conflict over whose work to do first.

One of the best known studies of role conflict and stress was carried out by Robert Kahn and his colleagues at the University of Michigan. Kahn studied 53 managers and their subordinates (a total of 381 people), examining the nature of each person's role and how it affected subsequent behavior. As a result of the investigation, the following conclusions emerged:

Contradictory role expectations give rise to opposing role pressures (role conflict), which generally have the following effects on the emotional experience of the focal person: intensified internal conflicts, increased tension associated with various aspects of the job, reduced satisfaction with the job and its various components, and decreased confidence in superiors and in the organization as a whole. The strain experienced by those in conflict situations leads to various coping responses, social and psychological withdrawal (reduction in communication and attributed influence) among them.

Finally, the presence of conflict in one's role tends to undermine his reactions with his role senders, to produce weaker bonds of trust, respect, and attraction. It is quite clear that role conflicts are costly for the person in emotional and interpersonal terms. They may be costly to the organization, which depends on effective coordination and collaboration within and among its parts.[20]

Other studies have found similar results concerning the serious side effects of role conflict both for individuals and organizations.[21] It should again be recognized, however, that personality differences may serve to moderate the impact of role conflict on stress. In particular, it has been found that introverts and people who lack flexibility respond more negatively to role conflict than do others.[22] In any event, managers must be aware of the problem of role conflict and look for ways to avert negative consequences. One way this can be accomplished is by ensuring that their subordinates are not placed in contradictory positions within the organization; that is, subordinates should have a clear idea of what the manager's job expectations are and should not be placed in "win-lose" situations.

Role Overload and Underutilization

Finally, in addition to role ambiguity and conflict, a third aspect of role processes has also been found to represent an important influence on experienced stress—namely, the extent to which employees feel either overloaded or underutilized in their job responsibilities. *Role overload* is a condition in which individuals feel they are being asked to do more than time or ability permits. Individuals often experience role overload as a conflict between quantity and quality of performance. *Quantitative* overload consists of having more work than can be done in a given time period, such as a clerk expected to process 1000 applications per day when only 850 are possible. Overload can be visualized as a continuum ranging from too little to do to too much to do. *Qualitative* role overload, on the other hand, consists of being taxed beyond one's skills, abilities, and knowledge. It can be seen as a continuum ranging from too-easy work to too-difficult work. For example, a manager who is expected to increase sales but has little idea of why sales are down or what to do to get sales up can experience qualitative role overload. It is important to note that *either* extreme represents a bad fit between the abilities of the employee and the demands of the work environment. A good fit occurs at that point on both scales of workload where the abilities of the individual are relatively consistent with the demands of the job.

There is evidence that both quantitative and qualitative role overload are prevalent in our society. A review of findings suggests that between 44 and 73 percent of white-collar workers experience a form of role overload.[23] What induces this overload? As a result of a series of studies, French and Caplan concluded that a major factor influencing overload is the high achievement needs of many managers. Need for achievement correlated very highly both with the number of hours worked per week and with a questionnaire measure of role overload.[24] In other words, much role overload is apparently self-induced.

Similarly, the concept of *role underutilization* should also be acknowledged as a source of experienced stress. Role underutilization occurs when employees are allowed to use only a few of their skills and abilities, even though they are required to make heavy use of them. The most prevalent characteristic of role underutilization is monotony, where the worker performs the same routine task (or set of tasks) over and over. Other situations that make for underutilization include total dependence on machines for determining work pace and sustained positional or postural constraint. Several studies have found that underutilization often leads to low self-esteem, low life satisfaction, and increased frequency of nervous complaints and symptoms.[25]

Both role overload and role underutilization have been shown to influence psychological and physiological reactions to the job. The inverted U-shaped relationship between the extent of role utilization and stress is shown in Exhibit 17.5. As shown, the least stress is experienced at that point where an employee's abilities and skills are in balance with the requirements of the job. This is where performance should be highest. Employees should be highly motivated, have high energy levels, sharp perception, and calmness. (Recall that many of the current efforts to redesign jobs and improve the quality of work are aimed at minimizing overload or underutilization in the workplace and achieving a more suitable balance between abilities possessed and skills used on the job.) When employees experience underutilization, boredom, decreased motivation, apathy, and absenteeism will be more likely. Role overload can lead to such symptoms as insomnia, irritability, increased errors, and indecisiveness.

Taken together, occupation and role processes represent a sizable influence on whether or not an employee experiences high stress levels. One job where the profession and its required roles almost guarantee significant stress is air traffic control. Consider for a moment whether you would want to have this job.

IN PRACTICE
Are the Japanese Working Themselves to Death?

Karoshi literally means death from overwork and unofficial estimates are that as many people die each year from *karoshi* as from traffic accidents in Japan—approximately 10,000. Half of those in a nationwide survey by a Japanese newspaper indicated that they were worried about *karoshi,* and about the same percentage feared it could kill a member of their family.

Shinji Masami worked as a design engineer at Hino Motors. He was responsible for making sure that all the auto parts fit together properly during final

Exhibit 17.5
The Underload-Overload
Continuum

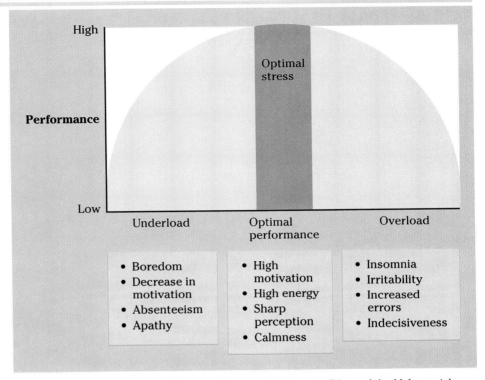

Source: Organizations: Behavior, Structure, Processes by James L. Gibson, John M. Ivanevich, and James H. Donnelly, Jr. Copyright © 1988 Business Publications, Inc. Reprinted by permission of Richard D. Irwin, Inc.

assembly of trucks produced by Toyota. The pressing deadlines caused Masami to work 2,600 hours a year for over six years which is 25% above the average hours worked in Japan and 42% above the hours in the United States. Typically, Masami would leave his home before 7 am and return home around midnight. Although he complained of severe headaches and stomach pains, he forced himself to go to work. At age 37, he died of a brain hemorrage at his office.

Jun Ishi was a manager in the Soviet division of Mitsui, one of the largest trading companies in Japan. During the 10 months before his death, he made numerous business trips totalling 103 days between Japan and the former Soviet Union. He died at age 47.

Judges in Japan are beginning to listen to the complaints of surviving family members. For example, recently a family won a settlement from a printer where a man put in 24-hour work days every other day for seven straight years.

The causes of *karoshi* are many but include low fines for companies that require excessive overtime work (approximately US $700), reluctance of workers to leave before their boss, long and extremely crowded commutes to and from work, and a high emphasis placed on interpersonal relationships that require significant "after hours" socializing and entertaining.[26]

PERSONAL INFLUENCES ON STRESS

The second major influence on job-related stress can be found in the employees themselves. As such, we will examine three individual-difference factors as they influence stress at work: (1) personal control, (2) Type A personality, and (3) rate of life change.

Personal Control

To begin with, we should acknowledge the importance of *personal control* as a factor in stress. Personal control represents the extent to which an employee actually has control over factors affecting effective job performance. If an employee is assigned a responsibility for something (landing an airplane, completing a report, meeting a deadline) but is not given an adequate opportunity to perform (because of too many planes, insufficient information, insufficient time), the employee loses personal control over the job and can experience increased stress. Personal control seems to work through the process of employee participation. That is, the more employees are allowed to participate in job-related matters, the more control they feel for project completion. On the other hand, if employees' opinions, knowledge, and wishes are excluded from organizational operations, the resulting lack of participation can lead not only to increased stress and strain, but also to reduced productivity.

The importance of employee participation in enhancing personal control and reducing stress is reflected in the French and Caplan study discussed earlier. After a major effort to uncover the antecedents of job-related stress, these investigators concluded:

> Since participation is also significantly correlated with low role ambiguity, good relations with others, and low overload, it is conceivable that its effects are widespread, and that all the relationships between these other stresses and psychological strain can be accounted for in terms of how much the person participates. This, in fact, appears to be the case. When we control or hold constant, through statistical analysis techniques, the amount of participation a person reports, then the correlations between all the above stresses and job satisfaction and job-related threat drop quite noticeably. This suggests that low participation generates these related stresses, and that increasing participation is an efficient way of reducing many other stresses which also lead to psychological strain.[27]

On the bases of this and related studies, we can conclude that increased participation and personal control over one's job is often associated with several positive outcomes, including lower psychological strain, increased skill utilization, improved working relations, and more positive attitudes. These factors, in turn, contribute toward higher productivity. These results are shown in Exhibit 17.6.[28]

Related to the issue of personal control—indeed, moderating its impact —is the concept of *locus of control.* Locus of control was discussed in some detail in Chapter 2. It will be remembered that some people have an *internal*

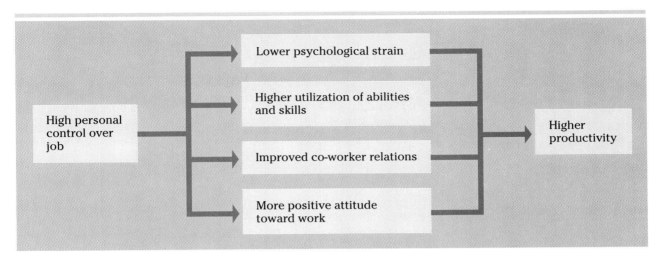

Exhibit 17.6
Consequences of High
Personal Control

locus of control, feeling that much of what happens in their life is under their own control. Others have an *external* locus of control, feeling that many of life's events are beyond their control. This concept has implications for how people respond to the amount of personal control in the work environment. That is, internals are more likely to be upset by threats to the personal control of surrounding events than are externals. Recent evidence indicates that internals react to situations over which they have little or no control with aggression—presumably in an attempt to reassert control over ongoing events.[29] On the other hand, externals tend to be more resigned to external control, are much less involved in or upset by a constrained work environment, and do not react as emotionally to organizational stress factors. Hence, locus of control must be recognized as a potential moderator of the effects of personal control as it relates to experienced stress.

Type A Personality

Research over the last 20 years has focused on what is perhaps the single most dangerous personal influence on experienced stress and subsequent physical harm. This characteristic was first introduced by Friedman and Rosenman and is called *Type A personality.*[30] Type A and Type B personalities are felt to be relatively stable personal characteristics exhibited by individuals. Type A personality is characterized by impatience, restlessness, aggressiveness, competitiveness, polyphasic activities (having many "irons in the fire" at one time), and being under considerable time pressure. Work activities are particularly important to Type A individuals, and they tend to freely invest long hours on the job to meet pressing (and recurring) deadlines. Type B people, on the other hand, experience fewer pressing deadlines or conflicts, are relatively free of any sense of time urgency or hostility, and are generally less competitive on the job. These differences are summarized in Exhibit 17.7.

Exhibit 17.7
Profiles of Type A and
Type B Personalities

Type A	Type B
Highly competitive	Lacks intense competitiveness
"Workaholic"	Work only one of many interests
Intense sense of urgency	More deliberate time orientation
Polyphasic behavior	Does one activity at a time
Strong goal-directedness	More moderate goal-directedness

Type A personality is frequently found in managers. Indeed, one study found that 60 percent of managers were clearly identified as Type A, whereas only 12 percent were clearly identified as Type B.[31] It has been suggested that Type A personality is most useful in helping someone rise through the ranks of an organization.

Are you interested in determining whether you are a Type A or Type B? If so, simply complete Self-Assessment 17.2. When you have finished, score your results as shown in Appendix B.

The role of Type A personality in producing stress is exemplified by the relationship between this behavior and heart disease. Rosenman and Friedman studied 3500 men over an $8\frac{1}{2}$-year period and found Type A individuals to be twice as prone to heart disease, five times as prone to a second heart attack, and twice as prone to fatal heart attacks when compared to Type B individuals.[32] Similarly, Jenkins studied over 3000 men and found that of 133 coronary heart disease sufferers, 94 were clearly identified as Type A in early test scores.[33] The rapid rise of women in managerial positions suggests that they, too, may be subject to this same problem. Hence, Type A behavior very clearly leads to one of the most severe outcomes of experienced stress.

One irony of Type A is that although this behavior is helpful in securing rapid promotion to the top of an organization, it may be detrimental once the individual has arrived. That is, although Type A employees make successful managers (and salespeople), the most successful *top* executives tend to be Type B. They exhibit patience and a broad concern for the ramifications of decisions. As Dr. Elmer Green, a Menninger Foundation psychologist who works with executives, notes, "This fellow—the driving A—can't relax enough to do a really first-rate job, at the office or at home. He gets to a level that dogged work can achieve, but not often to the pinnacle of his business or profession, which requires sober, quiet, balanced reasoning."[34] The key is to know how to shift from Type A behavior to Type B.

How does a manager accomplish this? The obvious answer is to slow down and relax. However, many Type A managers refuse to acknowledge either the problem or the need for change, because they feel it may be viewed as a sign of weakness. In these cases, several small steps can be taken, including scheduling specified times every day to exercise, delegating more significant work to subordinates, and eliminating optional activities from the daily calendar. Some companies have begun experimenting with retreats, where managers are removed from the work environment and engage in group psychotherapy over the problems associated with Type A

SELF-ASSESSMENT 17.2
Are You a Type A?

Instructions: Choose from the following responses to answer the questions below:

a.   Almost always true   c.   Seldom true
b.   Usually true   d.   Never true

Answer each question according to what is generally true for you:

_____   **1.**   I do not like to wait for other people to complete their work before I can proceed with my own.

_____   **2.**   I hate to wait in most lines.

_____   **3.**   People tell me that I tend to get irritated too easily.

_____   **4.**   Whenever possible I try to make activities competitive.

_____   **5.**   I have a tendency to rush into work that needs to be done before knowing the procedure I will use to complete the job.

_____   **6.**   Even when I go on vacation, I usually take some work along.

_____   **7.**   When I make a mistake, it is usually due to the fact that I have rushed into the job before completely planning it through.

_____   **8.**   I feel guilty for taking time off from work.

_____   **9.**   People tell me I have a bad temper when it comes to competitive situations.

_____   **10.**   I tend to lose my temper when I am under a lot of pressure at work.

_____   **11.**   Whenever possible, I will attempt to complete two or more tasks at once.

_____   **12.**   I tend to race against the clock.

_____   **13.**   I have no patience for lateness.

_____   **14.**   I catch myself rushing when there is no need.

Source: "Are You a Type A?" *The Stress Mess Solution: The Causes and Cures of Stress on the Job,* by G. S. Everly and D. A. Girdano. Copyright 1980. Reprinted by permission of the authors.

personality. Initial results from these programs appear promising.[35] Even so, more needs to be done if we are to reduce job-related stress and its serious health implications.

Rate of Life Change

A third personal influence on experienced stress is the degree to which lives are stable or turbulent. A long-term research project by Holmes and Rahe has attempted to document the extent to which *rate of life change* generates stress in individuals and leads to the onset of disease or illness.[36]

As a result of their research, a variety of life events were identified and assigned points based upon the extent to which each event is related to stress and illness.

The death of a spouse was seen as the most stressful change and was assigned 100 points. Other events were scaled proportionately in terms of their impact on stress and illness. It was found that the higher the point total of recent events, the more likely it is that the individual will become ill. Apparently, the influence of life changes on stress and illness is brought about by the endocrine system. This system provides the energy needed to cope with new or unusual situations. When the rate of change surpasses a given level, the system experiences overload and malfunctions. The result is a lowered defense against viruses and disease.

The Holmes and Rahe "Schedule of Recent Experiences" is shown here in Self-Assessment 17.3. You are encouraged to complete this scale by checking all those events that have occurred to you within the past year. Next, follow the scoring procedures described in Appendix B.

International Challenge

IN PRACTICE
Executive Stress Around The World

Before we leave the topic of organizational and personal influence on stress, it should be interesting to add an international dimension and see how the stress levels among American executives compare to those of executives in other parts of the world. This can be done by looking at the results of a recent study of 1100 senior executives in 10 countries that was conducted by noted stress researcher Cary Cooper.

In the study, stress was measured as a combination of depression, anxiety, and psychosomatic illness. Results were surprising. To begin with, American executives reported experiencing far less stress than executives in many other parts of the world. In fact, Cooper found that those exhibiting the best mental health were executives from Britain, Sweden, Germany, and the United States. The country whose executives suffered the least stress was Sweden. On the other hand, executives from Brazil, Nigeria, Egypt, Singapore, and Japan exhibited greater stress. In Japan, 32 percent of the executives studied had mental health scores that resembled those of psychiatric outpatients.

Moreover, the study found differences not only with regard to stress levels, but also with respect to the major causes of job-related stress. In the United States, for example, much of the stress was found to be related to pressures associated with business ethics, or doing what is right and just in a competitive world. In contrast, stress in Sweden was more than likely caused by the encroachment of work on private life. In Britain it was keeping up with technology that caused stress, and in West Germany and Brazil it was time pressures and deadlines. In South Africa it was long hours, and in Egypt it was work overload and taking work home. Finally, in Nigeria much executive stress was related to inadequately trained subordinates who increase the work burden on the executives themselves. Perhaps North American managers can take comfort in knowing that they are not alone in their plight; indeed, executive life in the United States and Canada looks pretty good compared to some other countries.[37]

SELF-ASSESSMENT 17.3
How Stable Is Your Life?

Instructions: Place a check mark next to each event you experienced within the past year. Then add the scores associated with the various events to derive your total life stress score.

Life Event	Scale Value	Life Event	Scale Value
Death of spouse	100	Trouble with in-laws	29
Divorce	73	Outstanding personal achievement	28
Marital separation	65	Wife begins or stops work	26
Jail term	63	Begin or end school	26
Death of a close family member	63	Change in living conditions	25
Major personal injury or illness	53	Revision of personal habits	24
Marriage	50	Trouble with boss	23
Fired from work	47	Change in work hours or conditions	20
Marital reconciliation	45	Change in residence	20
Retirement	45	Change in schools	20
Major change in health of family member	44	Change in recreation	19
Pregnancy	40	Change in church activities	19
Sex difficulties	39	Change in social activities	18
Gain of a new family member	39	Mortgage or loan for lesser purchase (car, etc.)	17
Business readjustment	39	Change in sleeping habits	16
Change in financial state	38	Change in number of family get-togethers	15
Death of a close friend	37	Change in eating habits	15
Change to a different line of work	36	Vacation	13
Change in number of arguments with spouse	35	Christmas	12
Mortgage or loan for major purchase (home, etc.)	31	Minor violations of the law	11
Foreclosure of mortgage or loan	30		
Change in responsibilities at work	29	Total Score = _____	
Son or daughter leaving home	29		

Source: "Scaling of Life Change: Comparison of Direct and Indirect Methods" by L. O. Ruch and T. H. Holmes, *Journal of Psychosomatic Research* 15 (1971):224. Copyright © 1971 by Pergamon Press, Inc. Reprinted by permission.

BUFFERING EFFECTS ON WORK-RELATED STRESS

We have seen in the previous discussion how a variety of organizational and personal factors influence the extent to which individuals experience stress on the job. Although many factors, or stressors, have been identified, their effect on psychological and behavioral outcomes is not always as strong as we might expect. This lack of a direct stressor-outcome relationship suggests the existence of potential moderator variables that buffer the effects of potential stressors on individuals. Recent research has identified two such buffers: the degree of social support the individual receives and the individual's general degree of what is called hardiness. Both are noted in Exhibit 17.2 above.

Social Support

First, let us consider social support. *Social support* is simply the extent to which organization members feel their peers can be trusted, are interested in one another's welfare, respect one another, and have a genuine positive regard for one another. When social support is present, individuals feel that they are not alone as they face the more prevalent stressors. The feeling that those around you really care about what happens to you and are willing to help blunts the severity of potential stressors and leads to less painful side effects. For example, family support can serve as a buffer for executives on assignment in a foreign country and can reduce the stress associated with cross-cultural adjustment.

Much of the more rigorous research on the buffering effects of social support on stress comes from the field of medicine, but it has relevance for organizational behavior. In a series of medical studies, it was consistently found that high peer support reduced negative outcomes of potentially stressful events (surgery, job loss, hospitalization) and increased positive outcomes.[38] These results clearly point to the importance of social support to individual well-being. These results also indicate that managers should be aware of the importance of building cohesive, supportive work groups—particularly among individuals who are most subject to stress.

IN PRACTICE
Stress Management in the Army

What was the Army's number one psychological discovery from World War II? According to Dr. David Marlowe, chief of the department of military psychiatry at Walter Reed Army Institute of Research, it was "the strength imparted by the small, primary work group." He further notes, "If a bond trader feels stress, he can go and meditate for 20 minutes. A soldier facing enemy fire can't."

The Army's research on stress shows that the primary issues are organizational.[39] Social support from the group is the most effective means of reducing the impact of naturally stressful situations. Notes Dr. Marlowe, "You want to build cohesion into a group, by making sure soldiers have good information, that they aren't faced with ambiguity, that they have solid relations with their leaders. If a man feels his squad is listening to him, if he can talk about his hopes, fears, anxieties, he's not likely to experience stress."

Dr. Marlowe also notes that keeping group cohesion after battle is important. By collectively reliving their experience and talking with trusted friends, soldiers are able to get emotions off their chests that otherwise may have stressed them for months or years to come. To facilitate this, squads use travel time to talk about what happened and how they felt. "It helps them detoxify," says Dr. Marlowe. "That's why we brought them back from in groups from Desert Storm. Epidemiologically, we know it works."

From a military perspective, a cohesive group can not only protect against stress, but it can also serve to reduce the negative effects after a stressful experience. An important question to consider is whether these findings by the Army are relevant only in a combat setting, or whether some or all of these insights apply to daily as well as work life settings.

Hardiness

The second moderator of stress is hardiness. *Hardiness* represents a collection of personality characteristics that involve one's ability to perceptually or behaviorally transform negative stressors into positive challenges. These characteristics include a sense of commitment to the importance of what one is doing, an internal locus of control (as noted above), and a sense of life challenge. In other words, people characterized by hardiness have a clear sense of where they are going and are not easily deterred by hurdles. The pressure of goal frustration does not deter them, because they invest themselves in the situation and push ahead. Simply put, these are people who refuse to give up.[40]

Several studies of hardiness support the importance of this variable as a stress moderator. One study among managers found that those characterized by hardiness were far less succeptible to illness following prolonged stress. And a study among undergraduates found hardiness to be positively related to perceptions that potential stressors were actually challenges to be met. Thus, factors such as individual hardiness and the degree of social support must be considered in any model of the stress process.

CONSEQUENCES OF WORK-RELATED STRESS

In exploring major influences on stress, it was pointed out that the intensity with which a person experiences stress is a function of organizational factors and personal factors, moderated by the degree of social support in the work environment and hardiness. We come now to an examination of major *consequences* of work-related stress. Here we will attempt to answer the "so what?" question. Why should managers be interested in stress and resulting strain?

As a guide for examining the topic, we recognize three intensity levels of stress—no stress, low stress, and high stress—and will study the outcomes of each level. These outcomes are shown schematically in Exhibit 17.8. Four major categories of outcome will be considered: (1) stress and health, (2) stress and counterproductive behavior, (3) stress and job performance, and (4) stress and burnout.

Exhibit 17.8
Major Consequences of
Work-Related Stress

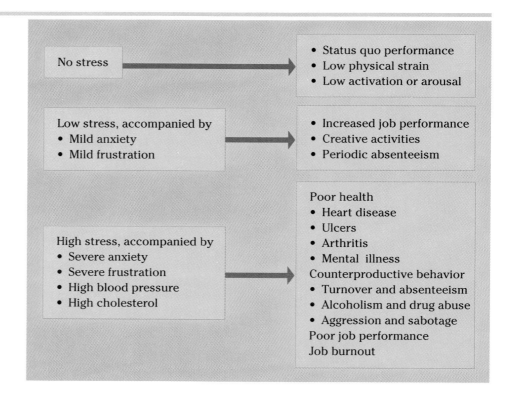

Stress and Health

High degrees of stress are typically accompanied by severe anxiety and/or frustration, high blood pressure, and high cholesterol levels. These psychological and physiological changes contribute to the impairment of health in several different ways. Most important, high stress contributes to heart disease.[41] The relationship between high job stress and heart disease is well established. In view of the fact that well over a half-million people die of heart disease every year, the impact of stress is important.[42]

High job stress also contributes to a variety of other ailments, including peptic ulcers, arthritis, and several forms of mental illness. In a study of Cobb and Kasl, for example, it was found that individuals with high educational achievement but low job status exhibited abnormally high levels of anger, irritation, anxiety, tiredness, depression, and low self-esteem.[43] In another study, Slote examined the effects of a plant closing in Detroit on stress and stress outcomes. Although factory closings are fairly common, the effects of these closings on individuals have seldom been examined. Slote found that the plant closing led to "an alarming rise in anxiety and illness," with at least half the employees suffering from ulcers, arthritis, serious hypertension, alcoholism, clinical depression, and even hair loss.[44] Clearly, this life change event took its toll on the mental and physical well-being of the work force.

Finally, in a classic study of mental health of industrial workers, Kornhauser studied a sample of automobile assembly line workers. Of the employees studied, he found that 40 percent had symptoms of mental health problems. His main findings may be summarized as follows:

◼ Job satisfaction varied consistently with employee skill levels. Blue-collar workers holding high-level jobs exhibited better mental health than those holding low-level jobs.

◼ Job dissatisfaction, stress, and absenteeism were all related directly to the characteristics of the job. Dull, repetitious, unchallenging jobs were associated with the poorest mental health.

◼ Feelings of helplessness, withdrawal, alienation, and pessimism were widespread throughout the plant. As an example, Kornhauser noted that 50 percent of the assembly line workers felt they had little influence over the future course of their lives; this compares to only 17 percent for non-factory workers.

◼ Employees with the lowest mental health also tended to be more passive in their nonwork activities; typically, they did not vote or take part in community activities.[45]

In conclusion, Kornhauser noted:

Poor mental health occurs whenever conditions of work and life lead to continuing frustration by failing to offer means for perceived progress toward attainment of strongly desired goals which have become indispensable elements of the individual's self-esteem and dissatisfaction with life, often accompanied by anxieties, social alienation and withdrawal, a narrowing of goals and curtailing of aspirations—in short . . . poor mental health.[46]

Managers need to be concerned about the problems of physical and mental health because of their severe consequences both for the individual and for the organization. Health is often related to performance, and to the extent that health suffers, so, too, do a variety of performance-related factors. Given the importance of performance for organizational effectiveness, we will now examine how it is affected by stress.

Stress and Counterproductive Behavior

It is useful from a managerial standpoint to consider several forms of counterproductive behavior that are known to result from prolonged stress. These counterproductive behaviors include turnover and absenteeism, alcoholism and drug abuse, and aggression and sabotage.

Turnover and Absenteeism.   Turnover and absenteeism represent convenient forms of withdrawal from a highly stressful job. Results of several studies have indicated a fairly consistent, if modest, relationship between stress and subsequent turnover and absenteeism.[47] In many ways, withdrawal represents one of the easiest ways employees have of handling a stressful work environment, at least in the short run. Indeed, turnover and absenteeism may represent two of the less undesirable consequences of stress, particularly when compared to alternative choices such as alcoholism, drug abuse, or aggression. Although high turnover and absenteeism may inhibit productivity, at least they do little physical harm to the individual or co-workers. Even so, there are many occasions when employees are not able to leave because of family or financial obligations, a lack of alternative employment, and so forth. In these situations, it is not unusual to see more dysfunctional behavior.

Alcoholism and Drug Abuse.   It has long been known that stress is linked to alcoholism and drug abuse among employees at all levels in the organizational hierarchy. These two forms of withdrawal offer a temporary respite from severe anxiety and severe frustration. One study by the Department of Health, Education, and Welfare reported, "Our interviews with blue-collar workers in heavy industry revealed a number who found it necessary to drink large quantities of alcohol during lunch to enable them to withstand the pressure or overwhelming boredom of their tasks."[48] A study in New York revealed a surprising amount of drug abuse by young employees on blue-collar jobs—especially among assembly line employees and long-haul truck drivers. A third study of a UAW local involving 3400 workers found 15 percent of the work force addicted to heroin. And, finally, there is an alarming increase of drug and substance abuse among managers.[49]

Both alcohol and drugs are used by a significant proportion of employees to escape from the rigors of a routine or stressful job. Although many companies have begun in-house programs aimed at rehabilitating chronic cases, these forms of withdrawal seem to continue to be on the increase, presenting another serious problem for modern managers. One answer to this dilemma involves reducing stress on the job that is creating the need for withdrawal from organizational activities.

Aggression and Sabotage.   Severe frustration can also lead to overt hostility in the form of aggression toward other people and toward inanimate objects. Aggression occurs when individuals feel frustrated and can find no acceptable, legitimate remedies for the frustration. For instance, a busy secretary may be asked to type a stack of letters, only to be told later that the boss changed his mind and no longer needs the letters typed. The frustrated secretary may react by covert verbal abuse or an intentional slowdown on subsequent work. A more extreme example of aggression can be seen in the periodic reports in newspapers about a worker who "goes berserk" (usually after a reprimand or punishment) and attacks fellow employees.

One common form of aggressive behavior on the job is sabotage. As one study found:

> The roots of sabotage, a frequent aspect of industrial violence, are illustrated by this comment of a steelworker. "Sometimes, out of pure meanness, when I make something, I put a little dent in it. I like to do something to make it really unique. Hit it with a hammer deliberately to see if it'll get by, just so I can say I did it." In a product world where everything is alike, sabotage may be a distortion of the guild craftsman's signature, a way of asserting individuality in a homogeneous world—the only way for a worker to say, "That's mine." It may also be a way of striking back against the hostile, inanimate objects that control

the worker's time, muscles, and brain. Breaking a machine in order to get some rest may be a sane thing to do.[50]

The extent to which frustration leads to aggressive behavior is influenced by several factors, often under the control of managers. Aggression tends to be subdued when employees anticipate that it will be punished, the peer group disapproves, or it has not been reinforced in the past (that is, when aggressive behavior failed to lead to positive outcomes). Thus, it is incumbent upon managers to avoid reinforcing undesired behavior and, at the same time, to provide constructive outlets for frustration. In this regard, some companies have provided official channels for the discharge of aggressive tendencies. For example, many companies have experimented with *ombudsmen,* whose task it is to be impartial mediators of employee disputes. Results have proved positive. These procedures or outlets are particularly important for nonunion personnel, who do not have contractual grievance procedures.

Stress and Job Performance

A major concern of management is the effects of stress on job performance. The relationship is not as simple as might be supposed. The stress-performance relationship resembles an inverted J-curve, as shown in Exhibit 17.9. At very low or *no-stress* levels, individuals maintain their current levels of performance. Under these conditions, individuals are not activated, do not experience any stress-related physical strain, and probably see no reason to change their performance levels. Note that this performance level may be high or low. In any event, an absence of stress probably would not cause any change.

On the other hand, studies indicate that under conditions of *low stress,* people are activated sufficiently to motivate them to increase performance.

Exhibit 17.9
The Relationship Between
Stress and Job Performance

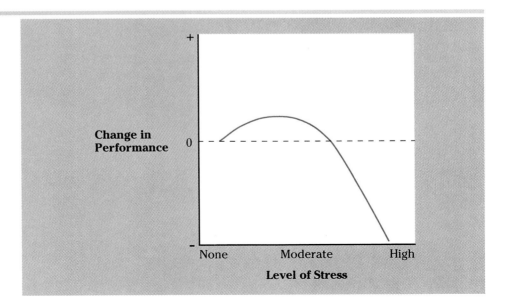

For instance, salespeople and many managers perform best when they are experiencing mild anxiety or frustration. Stress in modest amounts, as when a manager has a tough problem to solve, acts as a stimulus for the individual. The toughness of a problem often pushes managers to their performance limits. Similarly, mild stress can also be responsible for creative activities in individuals as they try to solve difficult (stressful) problems.

Finally, under conditions of *high stress,* individual performance drops markedly. Here, the severity of the stress consumes attention and energies, and individuals focus considerable effort on attempting to reduce the stress (often employing a variety of counterproductive behaviors as noted below). Little energy is left to devote to job performance, with obvious results.

Stress and Burnout

When job-related stress is prolonged, poor job performance such as that described above often moves into a more critical phase, known as burnout. *Burnout* is a general feeling of exhaustion that can develop when a person simultaneously experiences too much pressure to perform and too few sources of satisfaction.[51]

Candidates for job burnout seem to exhibit similar characteristics. That is, many such individuals are idealistic and self-motivated achievers, often seek unattainable goals, and have few buffers against stress. As a result, these people demand a great deal from themselves, and, because their goals are so high, they often fail to reach them. Because they do not have adequate buffers, stressors affect them rather directly. This is shown in Exhibit 17.10. As a result of experienced stress, burnout victims develop a variety of negative and often hostile attitudes toward the organization and themselves, including fatalism, boredom, discontent, cynicism, and feelings of personal inadequacy. As a result, the person decreases his or her aspiration levels, loses confidence, and attempts to withdraw from the situation.

Research indicates that burnout is widespread among employees, including managers, researchers, and engineers, that are often hardest to replace by organizations. As a result, it is estimated that 70 percent of the largest U.S. companies have some form of antiburnout/stress reduction training (see later discussion).[52]

If you are interested in your own potential for burnout, you may wish to complete Self-Assessment 17.4. Simply answer the ten questions as honestly as you can. When you have finished, follow the scoring instructions shown in Appendix B.

IN PRACTICE
Time Out at Tandem Computers

It was noted above that burnout and other stress-related reactions are most common among an organization's difficult-to-replace employees, namely its managers and engineers. In view of this, it is only natural that forward-thinking companies are exploring ways to slow down or eliminate the burnout process. One such way is through providing employees with sabbaticals.

SELF-ASSESSMENT 17.4
Are You Suffering from Burnout?

Instructions: Check whether each item is "mostly true" or "mostly untrue" for you. Answer as honestly as you can. When you have finished, add up the number of checks for "mostly true."

		Mostly True	Mostly Untrue
1.	I usually go around feeling tired.	____	____
2.	I think I am working harder but accomplishing less.	____	____
3.	My job depresses me.	____	____
4.	My temper is shorter than it used to be.	____	____
5.	I have little enthusiasm for life.	____	____
6.	I snap at people fairly often.	____	____
7.	My job is a dead end for me.	____	____
8.	Helping others seems like a losing battle.	____	____
9.	I don't like what I have become.	____	____
10.	I am very unhappy with my job.	____	____

Exhibit 17.10
Influences Leading to
Job Burnout

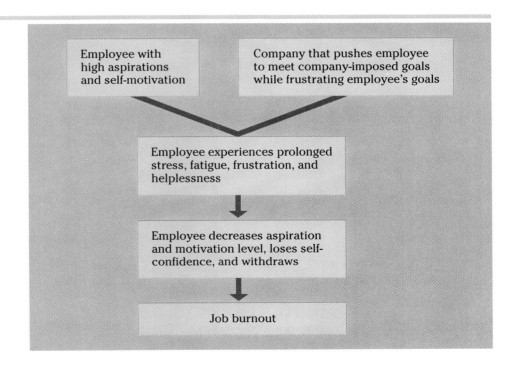

Currently, the U.S. Department of Labor estimates that 13 percent of American companies offer some form of long-term leave of absence to employees so they can pursue new ventures or simply recharge their intellectual batteries. One such company is Tandem Computers.

Begun in 1977, Tandem Computers' program allows employees with at least four years of service to take up to six weeks of paid leave. Explains a Tandem executive, "Like most high-tech companies, Tandem is very fast-paced. After working here four years, our employees often need to step back from their work and look at the personal side of their lives."

During their sabbatical, employees can do almost anything they wish. Some use the time to travel and reflect on their careers. Others take cooking classes, and one engineer even built an airplane. The returns to the company have been tremendous. Employees return to work with renewed energy and new ideas to pursue. And burnout rates have fallen dramatically compared to those of other companies in the industry.

To date, some 560 of the company's 5200 employees have taken advantage of this policy. In fact, notes the executive, "It's the most popular benefit we have."[53]

COPING WITH WORK-RELATED STRESS

We come now to the most important question from a managerial standpoint: What can be done to reduce job-related stress? Many suggestions for coping with stress are implicit in the previous discussions. However, it is possible to summarize several important actions employees and managers can take in order to provide a more desirable work environment and improve employee adjustment to work.

Individual Strategies

There are many things people can do to help eliminate the level of experienced stress or, at the very least, to help cope with continuing high stress. Consider the following:

Developing Self-Awareness.   Individuals can increase awareness of how they behave on the job. They can learn to know their own limits and recognize signs of potential trouble. Employees should know when to withdraw from a situation (known to some as a "mental health day" instead of absenteeism) and when to seek help from others on the job in an attempt to relieve the situation.

Developing Outside Interests.   In addition, individuals can develop outside interests to take their minds off work. This solution is particularly important for Type A people, whose physical health depends on toning down their drive for success. Employees can ensure that they get regular physical exercise to relieve pent-up stress. Many companies sponsor athletic activities, and some have built athletic facilities on company premises to encourage employee activity.

Leaving the Organization.   Sometimes an employee may be unable to improve his or her situation and, as a result, may find it necessary (i.e., healthful) simply to leave the organization and find alternative employment. Although this is clearly a difficult decision to make, there are times when turnover is the only answer.

Finding a Personal or Unique Solution.   Another means individuals can use to cope with stress is through a variety of personal or unique solutions. For instance, here is how one manager described his reaction to a stressful situation: "If someone finally bugs me, I politely hang up the phone and then pound the hell out of my typewriter, saying all the things on paper I wanted to say to that person on the phone. It works every time. Then, I rip up the paper and throw it into the trash can."[54] If an employee cannot leave a stressful situation, this may be a good temporary way out of it.

Physical Exercise.   Because part of the cause of the fatigue resulting from stress is the body's physical reaction, exercise can be an effective means of enabling the body to more effective deal with the physical components of stress. Regular exercise can be an important and effective individual strategy.

Cognitive Perspective.   Finally, because stress is in part a function of how events are perceived and interpreted, controlling one's cognitive perspective of events can also be an effective strategy. Although one would not want to go so far as framing a truck speeding toward you as an opportunity rather than a threat, positively framing situations as well as distinguishing factors that are within as well as outside your control and influence can be effective means of reducing stress.

Organizational Strategies

Because managers usually have more control over the working environment than do subordinates, it seems only natural that they have more opportunity to contribute to a reduction of work-related stress. Among their activities, managers may include the following eight strategies.

Personnel Selection and Placement.   First, managers can pay more attention in the selection and placement process to the fit between job applicants, the job, and the work environment. Current selection and placement procedures are devoted almost exclusively to preventing qualitative role overload by ensuring that people have the required education, ability, experience, and training for the job. Managers could extend these selection criteria to include a consideration of the extent to which job applicants have a tolerance for ambiguity and can handle role conflict. In other words, managers could be alert in the job interview and subsequent placement process to potential stress-related problems and the ability of the applicant to deal successfully with them.

Skills Training. Second, stress can be reduced in some cases through better job-related skills training procedures, where employees are taught how to do their jobs more effectively with less stress and strain. For instance, an employee might be taught how to reduce overload by taking shortcuts or by using new or expanded skills. These techniques would only be successful, however, if management did not follow this increased effectiveness by raising work quotas. Along with this could go a greater effort by managers to specify and clarify job duties to reduce ambiguity and conflict. Employees could also be trained in human relations skills in order to improve their interpersonal abilities so that they might encounter less interpersonal and intergroup conflict.

Job Redesign. Third, managers can change certain aspects of jobs or the ways people perform these jobs. Much has been written about the benefits of job redesign (see Chapter 9). Enriching a job may lead to improved task significance, autonomy, responsibility, and feedback. For many people, these jobs will present a welcome challenge, which will improve the job-person fit and reduce experienced stress. It should be noted, however, that all people do not necessarily want an enriched job. Enriching the job of a person with a very low need for achievement or external locus of control may only increase anxiety and fear of failure. Care must be taken in job enrichment to match these efforts to employee needs and desires.

In addition to job enrichment, a related technique aimed at reducing stress is *job rotation.* Job rotation is basically a way of spreading stress among employees and providing a respite—albeit temporary—from particularly stressful jobs. Job rotation is particularly popular in Japan as a means of allocating the more tedious or boring tasks among a large set of employees so prolonged stress is reduced. Japan is also finally working toward a reduced workweek as a means of reducing job-related stress.[55]

Company-Sponsored Counseling Programs. Several companies have begun experimenting with counseling programs, the fourth strategy suggested here. For instance, Stanford University's executive program includes a module on coping with stress, and the Menninger Foundation conducts a one-week antistress seminar in Topeka. In one experiment among police officers, the value of a stress management program was examined.[56] In the program, which consisted of six two-hour sessions, officers were told about the nature and causes of stress, were shown useful relaxation exercises, and were put through several simulated stressful situations—such as role playing the handling of an arrest. Throughout, emphasis was placed on reinforcing the officers' confidence that they could, in fact, successfully cope with on-the-job stress. The results of the program showed that those officers who went through the program performed better, exhibited greater self-control, and experienced less stress than officers in comparable positions who did not go through the program. Similar findings have emerged in a variety of business organizations. Once again, much work-related stress can be reduced simply by encouraging managers to be more supportive and to provide the necessary tools for people to cope with stress.

Increased Participation and Personal Control.   Fifth, managers can allow employees greater participation and personal control in decisions affecting their work. As noted above, participation increases job involvement and simultaneously reduces stress by relieving ambiguity and conflict. However, although the benefits of increased participation are many, it should be noted that being more participative is no easy task for some supervisors. One study, for example, found significant differences in the extent to which different supervisors would allow their subordinates to participate in decision making.[57] Females were found to allow more participation than males. Supervisors with high achievement needs, high levels of confidence in the abilities of their subordinates, and low feelings of being threatened by others allowed more subordinate participation. The issue of participation does not appear to be whether subordinates desire it; instead, it appears to be whether superiors will allow it.

Work Group Cohesiveness.   Sixth, managers can attempt to build work group cohesiveness. Team-building efforts are common in industry today (see Chapter 9). These efforts focus on developing groups that will be both more productive and mutually supportive. A critical ingredient in the extent to which stress is experienced is the amount of social support employees receive. Team building represents one way to achieve this support.

Improved Communication.   As discussed in Chapter 13, managers can open communication channels so employees are more informed about what is happening in the organization. With greater knowledge, role ambiguity and conflict are reduced. Managers must be aware, however, that communication is a two-way street; they should allow and be receptive to communication from subordinates. To the extent that subordinates feel their problems and complaints are being heard, they experience less stress and are less inclined to engage in counterproductive behavior.

Health Promotion Programs.   Finally, many companies have recently embarked on a more systematic and comprehensive approach to stress reduction and wellness in the workplace. These programs are usually referred to as health promotion programs, and they represent a combination of diagnostic, educational, and behavior modification activities that are aimed at attaining and preserving good health.[58] A typical program includes risk assessment, educational and instructional classes, and counseling and referrals. Health promotion programs tackle a wide array of health-related concerns, including physical fitness, weight control, dietary and nutritional counseling, smoking cessation, blood pressure monitoring, alcohol and substance abuse problems, and general lifestyle modification.

Companies involved in such programs usually feel that the costs invested to run them are more than returned through higher levels of productivity and reduced absenteeism and stress-related illness.[59] Moreover, many companies have found that providing such services serves as an attractive incentive when recruiting employees in a scarce job market.

IN PRACTICE
Health Promotion At Control Data

One of the earliest efforts to promote reduced stress and good health at work can be found at Control Data Corporation. Conceived in 1977, Control Data's "Staywell" program offers employees a private comprehensive screening, or risk analysis. On the basis of the results, each employee is provided with a specific proposed plan of action, consisting of a series of education and behavior change classes. The most common classes are offered in fitness, smoking cessation, stress management, nutrition, weight reduction, and back care.

In addition, the Staywell program has action teams in each facility that are responsible for such things as changing the food in the company cafeteria and vending machines, making safety glasses available for home use, and so forth. The company publishes a quarterly newsletter on staying well. And, finally, the Staywell program is offered to employees' family members free of charge.

Is the program successful? There are many ways to assess this. First, company records indicate that almost two-thirds of all employees have enrolled in at least one sponsored program. Moreover, what is particularly encouraging here is that among those who participated, a large percentage came from high-risk health groups, suggesting that the Staywell program is reaching its intended audience. Smoking rates declined among program participants. And, finally, the company itself estimates that the wellness efforts have resulted in an annual savings in health care claims of over $1.8 million. By any benchmark, the Staywell program at Control Data has been a success.[60]

Here, then, are eight specific techniques that have proved useful in work organizations in reducing the amount of experienced stress. None is particularly costly. However, all require an acknowledgment by management that stress is a significant problem on the job and a commitment by management to take positive actions to change the work environment. The alleviation of work-related stress is mostly in the hands of management, not employees, and solutions to the problem seem well within the reach of those who are concerned.

PULLING IT ALL TOGETHER

Stress is a function of the objective environment but also of individuals' subjective interpretation of events and their consequences. Both body and mind are involved the process. It is important for both firms and individuals to take preventive measures before the cumulative effects of stress manifest themselves in ways that cost both the individual and the company.

SUMMARY OF KEY POINTS

■ Stress is a physical and emotional reaction to potentially threatening aspects of the environment. The damage resulting from stress is called strain.

■ The general adaptation syndrome is the common pattern of events that characterizes someone who experiences stress. The three stages of the syndrome are alarm, resistance, and exhaustion.

■ Two primary types of stress can be identified: frustration and anxiety.

■ Four organization influences on stress can be identified: (1) occupational differences, (2) role ambiguity, (3) role conflict, and (4) role overload or underutilization.

■ Three personal influences on stress are (1) personal control, or the desire to have some degree of control over one's environment; (2) rate of life change; and (3) Type A personality. Type A personality refers to individuals characterized by impatience, restlessness, aggressiveness, competitiveness, and polyphasic activities (that is, attempting to do several activities at the same time).

■ The effects of potential stress can be buffered by two factors: (1) social support from one's co-workers or friends and (2) hardiness, or the ability to perceptually and behaviorally transform negative stressors into positive challenges.

■ Sustained stress can lead to (1) health problems; (2) counterproductive behavior, such as turnover, absenteeism, drug abuse, and sabotage; (3) poor job performance; and (4) burnout. Burnout is defined as a general feeling of exhaustion that can develop when a person simultaneously experiences too much pressure to perform and too few sources of satisfaction.

■ Individual strategies to reduce stress include (1) developing one's self-awareness about how to behave on the job, (2) developing outside interests, (3) leaving the organization, and (4) finding a unique solution.

■ Organizational strategies to reduce stress include (1) improved personnel selection and job placement, (2) skills training, (3) job redesign, (4) company-sponsored counseling programs, (5) increased employee participation and personal control, (6) enhanced work group cohesiveness, (7) improved communication, and (8) health promotion programs.

KEY WORDS

anxiety
burnout
frustration
general adaptation syndrome
hardiness
health promotion programs

locus of control
personal control
rate of life change
role ambiguity
role conflict
role overload

role underutilization
social support
strain

stress
tolerance for ambiguity
Type A personality

QUESTIONS FOR DISCUSSION

1. Discuss the five types of problem related to employee work adjustment.
2. Define stress. How does it differ from strain?
3. Describe the general adaptation syndrome.
4. Contrast frustration with anxiety.
5. Identify the major categories of variable that have been found to influence stress. What role does social support play in the process? What role does hardiness play?
6. In the chapter, the plight of assembly line workers was discussed. What realistic suggestions would you make to relieve the tension and stress of this job?
7. Compare and contrast role conflict and role ambiguity.
8. How does a manager achieve a useful balance in a person-job fit so neither role overload nor role underutilization occurs?
9. How should a manager deal with a subordinate who is clearly a Type A personality? How should a manager who is a Type A personality handle his or her own stress?
10. Of what utility is the rate-of-life-change concept?
11. In organizations with which you are familiar, which of the many suggestions for coping with stress would be most applicable? Are the strategies you selected individual or organizational strategies?

NOTES

1. T. Stewart, "Do You Push Your People Too Hard?" *Fortune,* October 22, 1990, pp. 121–128.
2. R. King, "Stress Claims Are Making Business Jumpy," *Business Week,* October 4, 1985, pp. 152–154.
3. "Health and Safety Review," *Monthly News on Human Resource Management,* November 1984, p. 3.
4. S. Yolles, "Mental Health at Work," in A. McLean, ed., *To Work Is Human* (New York: Macmillan, 1967); R. Poe, "Does Your Job Make You Sick?" *Across the Board,* January 1987, pp. 34–43.
5. W. S. Neff, *Work and Human Behavior* (New York: Atherton, 1968), p. 208.
6. R. Ruddock, *Six Approaches to the Person* (London: Routledge and Kegan Paul, 1972), p. 94.
7. J. McGrath, "Stress and Behavior in Organizations," in M. D. Dunnette, ed., *Handbook of Industrial and Organizational Psychology* (Chicago: Rand McNally, 1976).
8. H. Selye, *The Stress of Life* (New York: McGraw-Hill, 1956).
9. W. C. Hamner and D. Organ, *Organizational Behavior* (Dallas: BPI, 1978), p. 202.
10. S. Terkel, *Working* (New York: Avon, 1972), p. 275.
11. Ibid., p. 348.
12. C. Cooper and R. Payne, *Stress at Work* (London: Wiley, 1978); K. Hall and L. Savery, "Tight Rein, More Stress," *Harvard Business Review,* January–February 1986, pp. 160–162, 164.

13. L. Krantz, *The Jobs Rated Almanac* (New York: Pharos Books, 1988).
14. Panasonic Industrial Company, "Causes of Stress Among Secretaries," *Wall Street Journal,* March 18, 1986, p. 1.
15. D. Zauderer and J. Fox, "Resiliency in the Face of Stress," *Management Solutions,* November 1987, pp. 32–33.
16. J. French and R. Caplan, "Organizational Stress and Individual Strain," in A. Marrow, ed., *The Failure of Success* (New York: Amacom, 1972), p. 48.
17. Ibid.
18. Ibid., p. 36.
19. Cooper and Payne, op. cit.
20. R. Kahn, D. Wolfe, R. Quinn, J. Snoek, and R. Rosenthal, *Organizational Stress: Studies in Role Conflict and Ambiguity* (New York: Wiley, 1964), pp. 70–71.
21. J. Quick and J. Quick, *Organizational Stress and Preventive Management* (New York: McGraw-Hill, 1984); R. Sutton and A. Rafaeli, "Characteristics of Work Stations as Potential Occupational Stressors," *Academy of Management Journal,* June 1987, pp. 260–276.
22. French and Caplan, op. cit.
23. Ibid.
24. Ibid.
25. G. Gardell, *Arbetsinnehall och Livskvalitet* (Stockholm: Prisma, 1976).
26. L. do Rosario, "Salarymen Stalked by 'Unmentionable' Killer." *Far Eastern Economic Review,* April 25, 1991, pp. 25, 31.
27. French and Caplan, op. cit., p. 51.
28. R. Schuler and S. Jackson, "Managing Stress Through P/HRM Practices," in K. Rowland and G. Ferris, eds., *Research in Personnel and Human Resource Management* (Greenwich, Conn.: JAI Press, 1986), pp. 183–224.
29. C. Carver and D. Glass, "Coronary Prone Behavior Pattern and Interpersonal Aggression," *Journal of Personality and Social Psychology,* 1978, pp. 361–366; M. Fusilier, D. Ganster, and B. Mayes, "The Social Support and Health Relationship: Is There a Gender Difference?" *Journal of Occupational Psychology,* June 1986, pp. 145–153.
30. M. Friedman and R. Rosenman, *Type A Behavior and Your Heart* (New York: Knopf, 1974).
31. J. Howard, D. Cunningham, and P. Rechnitzer, "Health Patterns Associated with Type A Behavior: A Managerial Population," *Journal of Human Stress,* 1976, pp. 24–31.
32. Friedman and Rosenman, op. cit.
33. C. Jenkins, "Psychologic Disease and Social Prevention of Coronary Disease," *New England Journal of Medicine,* 1971, 284, pp. 244–255; T. Beehr and R. Bhagat, *Human Stress and Cognition in Organizations: An Integrated Perspective* (New York: Wiley, 1985).
34. *Business Week,* October 17, 1977, p. 137.
35. Ibid.
36. T. H. Holmes and R. H. Rahe, "The Social Readjustment Rating Scale," *Journal of Psychosomatic Research,* August 1967, pp. 213–218. See also O. Behling and A. Darrow, "Managing Work-Related Stress," in J. Rosenzweig and F. Kast, eds., Modules in Management (Chicago: SRA, 1984).
37. C. Kleinman, "U.S. Executives Less Stressed Than Those of Other Nations," *Chicago Tribune,* March 31, 1988, p. 1.
38. S. Cohen and T. Wills, "Stress, Social Support, and the Buffering Hypothesis," *Psychological Bulletin,* September 1985, pp. 310–357.
39. A. Farnham, "Who Beats Stress Best—and How?" *Fortune,* October 7, 1991, pp. 71–86.
40. S. Kobasa, S. Maddi, and S. Kahn, "Hardiness and Health: A Prospective Study," *Journal of Personality and Social Psychology,* January 1982, pp. 168-177; J. Hull, R.

VanTreuren, and S. Virnelli, "Hardiness and Health: A Critique and Alternative Approach," *Journal of Personality and Social Psychology,* September 1987, pp. 518–530.

41. Cooper and Payne, op. cit.
42. D. Glass, "Stress, Competition, and Heart Attacks," *Psychology Today,* July 1976, pp. 55–57.
43. S. Cobb and S. Kasl, "Blood Pressure Changes in Men Undergoing Job Loss: A Preliminary Report," *Psychosomatic Medicine,* January-February 1970.
44. A. Slote, *Termination: The Closing of Baker Plant* (Ann Arbor: Institute for Social Research, University of Michigan, 1977).
45. A. Kornhauser, *Mental Health and the Industrial Worker* (New York: Wiley, 1965).
46. Ibid., p. 342.
47. W. Mobley, *Managing Employee Turnover* (Reading, Mass.: Addison-Wesley, 1982); S. Rhodes and R. Steers, *Managing Employee Absenteeism* (Reading, Mass.: Addison-Wesley, 1990).
48. U.S. Department of Health, Education, and Welfare, *Work in America,* 1973. p. 85.
49. T. Rosen, "Identification of Substance Abuse in the Workplace," *Public Personnel Management,* Fall 1987, pp. 197–207; S. Flax, "The Executive Addict," *Fortune,* June 24, 1985, pp. 24–31.
50. U.S. Department of Health, Education, and Welfare, op. cit.
51. S. Jackson, R. Schwab, and R. Schuler, "Toward an Understanding of the Burnout Phenomenon," *Journal of Applied Psychology,* November 1986, pp. 630–640.
52. B. Dumaine, "Cool Cures for Burnout," *Fortune,* June 20, 1988, pp. 78–84.
53. D. Cody, "Time out," *Republic,* December 1985, p. 22. See also N. Frenkiel, "Sabbaticals: More Professionals Tune into Trend of Dropping Out," *Los Angeles Times,* February 6, 1989, pp. E1, E6.
54. Cited in *U.S. News & World Report,* March 13, 1978, p. 81.
55. C. Smith, "Labor: Working on a Change," *Far Eastern Economic Review,* April 14, 1988, pp. 62–63.
56. I. Sarason, J. Johnson, J. Berberich, and J. Siegel, *Helping Police Officers Cope with Stress: A Cognitive-Behavioral Approach,* Technical Report, University of Washington, February 1978.
57. R. M. Steers, "Individual Differences in Participative Decision Making," *Human Relations,* 1977, *30,* pp. 837–847.
58. M. Matteson and J. Ivancevich, "Health Promotion at Work," in C. Cooper and I. Robertson, eds., *International Review of Industrial and Organizational Psychology* (London: Wiley, pp. 279–306).
59. M. Roberts and T. Harris, "Wellness at Work," *Psychology Today,* May 1989, pp. 54–58.
60. J. R. Terborg, "The Organization as a Context for Health Promotion," in S. Oskamp and S. Spacapan, eds., *Social Psychology and Health: The Claremont Symposium on Applied Social Psychology* (Newbury Park, Calif.: Sage), 1988.

EXPERIENTIAL EXERCISE 17

Managing Stress in the Office

This exercise focuses on developing a better understanding of possible ways to manage stress in the workplace. To conduct the exercise, students should divide into groups of between four and six. Each group should focus on the same problem.

As a Group

Your group represents the management team of the office services division of a major company. Employees consist of about 100 clerical and secretarial personnel who perform various secretarial duties for other units of your company. Many of these duties include spending long hours sitting in front of microcomputers entering text and data. Employees often complain of headaches and backaches, and turnover and absenteeism are high. Moreover, the work atmosphere is often described as "tense" because of the time pressures associated with the work. The division works with a number of other design and production units within the company, and each unit feels it should have priority on work completion.

Your team has decided to get together to discuss the issue of stress and see if there are ways that dysfunctional stress can be reduced. However, no additional funds are available, and you cannot increase staff size. Moreover, it is important not to jeopardize current employee productivity. Read one of the following roles and follow the role guidelines during the group's discussion.

Roles

Supervisor: Over the last six months you have found that productivity overall is down about 15 percent, though it is up for certain individuals. In addition, absenteeism is overall is up about 17 percent and costs you a loss in productivity of slightly over the average productivity for one-worker-day because of the extra coordination costs. You are receiving pressure from your boss to increase productivity by nearly 20 percent.

Employee 1: You did not finish high school and find the quantity of work expected to be excessive. You are not sure exactly how to process certain forms and feel your boss has put you under the gun to produce more. Specifically, your boss has made you feel that you are holding down the productivity of the group. You know that you make about 10 percent more errors than the group average. Some days it is all too much and you stay home to get away from it all.

Employee 2: You have an associate's degree in business and feel the duties of a clerk are well beneath your current abilities and do nothing to develop your potential. You have worked at this job for nearly two years and hoped to have moved up by now. You need a higher salary to afford night classes so that you can get your B.A. degree. In short, you find this job boring and frustrating.

Employee 3: This job is literally a pain in the neck. You are fast at entering numbers on a 10-key pad, and so you always seem to get data to enter. Your wrist is sore and sometimes you have to stop entering data and massage your wrist before you can continue. Because you know your boss is under pressure, you feel as though you need to continue as the data specialist, but it's frustrating. Also, two divisions are constantly asking you to enter their data first. After all the stress of work, you can't wait to get home and watch TV or read a book so you can forget about the day.

Employee 4:   Generally, you enjoy your job. You work with people that you basically like and you enjoy talking with them at lunch. Although you are not always sure what work has first priority, you do not let yourself get too bothered by it. You make the best judgment you can and assume that if your judgment were consistently wrong that someone would let you know about it. Getting the volume of work done is a challenge and you are usually able to meet it. When you do meet your goals, it gives you a sense of satisfaction. You get the same sort of satisfaction from you daily jog down at the beach. In fact, your time for a three mile run has come down about 15 percent in the last four months. Your spouse encourages and supports your job, and the extra money is nice too. although there are aspects of the job that get to you, most of them are outside your control, so you don't worry about it.

As a team, your assignment is therefore the following (30 minutes):

1.   Making use of the materials presented in this chapter, design a program to reduce employee stress levels without adversely affecting productivity or spending additional resources.
2.   Why do you think this program will succeed?

As a Class

When your team is done, the class should reconvene as a whole and compare the various proposed solutions. Look for similarities and differences. How realistic are the proposed plans of action?

MANAGEMENT DILEMMA 17

Software Research, Inc.

On a late Friday afternoon, 24-year-old software genius David Grant entered Jim Rogers's office. "Jim, you're going to have to do something about Sellers, or my people are going to walk out on the Micro-Tech project." Rogers, principal stockholder and CEO of Software Research, Inc. (SRI), was dumbfounded. "He knows nothing about what we're doing, and he's upsetting my team with his constant interference," Grant continued. "Either he goes, or our project will fall apart!"

As Grant left the office, Rogers leaned back in his chair, wondering how to confront his longtime friend and minority partner Steven Sellers with a smoldering crisis now clearly brought to a head. He knew Sellers was a workaholic, deeply engrossed in the Micro-Tech project, and that he would probably resent the intrusion by Rogers. He knew also that Sellers was having marital problems and that one of his children had just dropped out of college. The timing was not good. Even so, Rogers felt he had to confront the issue head-on. If Grant's warning was to be taken seriously, the stakes were high, and a confrontation could not be postponed. Now was probably as good a time as any. The Micro-Tech software project had fallen five months behind schedule, which was delaying the client's launch of a new laptop computer. Though part of the holdup had been caused by a change in specifications, the project was now subject to a penalty clause.

Walking toward Sellers's office, Rogers began to outline his alternatives. He could buy up Sellers's 17 percent equity and put an end to the immediate crisis. On the other hand, he needed Sellers. Though worried about Sellers's addiction to work, Rogers knew that it was Sellers's single-minded commitment to his job and the firm that had contributed so much to SRI's success. Was Sellers now at the breaking point, he wondered? During the past seven years, they had worked as a team, pulling together a team of bright programmers by buying up a score of small, innovative software houses that needed capital injections. Only recently had Sellers begun to make irrational moves and develop an edgy personal style that seemed to annoy those around him. In fact, his workaholism had all the marks of real psychological dependence, not unlike alcoholism.

It was the first time Sellers's behavior had become a liability. Until now, the two men had made a good team. The introspective and analytical Sellers drew on his vast contacts in the software industry to identify acquisitions, and the outgoing Rogers negotiated the deals. It was a partnership that brought them both fun and profit. Working behind the scenes, performing best under pressure, Sellers acted as the motor, merging new companies into SRI and imposing his will on others to facilitate a clean integration with SRI before moving onto the new acquisition. Though he ruffled feathers, he never stayed long enough with the new units to cause any permanent damage. In fact, Sellers had been invaluable in SRI's acquisition strategy. Now, however, with the acquisition of Micro-Tech, a startup company founded by Grant, things were really starting to go awry.

Sellers understood applications software, but he knew within days of taking over the Micro-Tech project that he was out of his league technically. Grant held the upper hand in this one. Moreover, as the project dragged on, it became clear to everyone else that Sellers was not coping well. He lacked the interpersonal skills needed to lead a longer-term team effort. Distraught with the thought of failure, Sellers began monitoring progress by setting unrealistic targets. When they fell by the wayside, he began pushing Grant's programmers to match his round-the-clock efforts, provoking incidents such as Grant's outburst in Rogers's office.

Rogers slowly walked down the half-darkened corridors and found the lights still on in Sellers's office. "Hey Steve, what's the problem with Grant?" Rogers asked as casually as he could.

A strained and tense Sellers looked up from his terminal and replied, "I've taken the Micro-Tech team off flex-time."

"What?" Rogers asked in stunned disbelief. "That's part of our ethos. Most of these guys are hackers. They spend as much time working on their home computers as they do in the office."

"Maybe so," Sellers replied. "But they're not putting in the lab hours we need to get the project done. I am putting in my hours, and there is no reason to let them cruise in and out as they please."

"Steve, these guys are self-starters. Putting them on a 9-to-5 regime will demotivate them. Are you sure you are making sense? Maybe you need a holiday," Rogers finally said.

"That's just an excuse to take me off the project," Sellers shot back belligerently, jumping up and grabbing his jacket. His face had turned red, and his voice quaked.

"Steve, you're killing yourself with work. What am I going to do with you?" Rogers pleaded.

"I don't know. You tell me," Sellers said, stalking out of the door.

Suppose that you are in Rogers's place. Both Sellers and Grant—and the Micro-Tech project—are important to the organization. How would you resolve this dilemma?

1. What are the sources of stress in this case?
2. What alternatives are available to you as possible solutions to this situation?
3. What are the limitations of each possible solution?
4. Which alternative would you select? Why?

Part Five

Employee and Organization Development

Chapter 18

Careers and Employee Development

The Management Challenge

- To recruit and hire the best employees available for the organization.
- To ensure a good fit between employees and the jobs they are asked to perform.
- To integrate employees into the organization and its culture so they become a part of an effective team.
- To develop employees to their fullest potential through comprehensive career planning and development efforts.
- To recognize diversity among employees and to make use of this diversity for the benefit of both employees and the organization.

CLOSE UP

The Double Edge of Overseas Career Moves

Kendra Davidson seemed to be on the marketing fast track. She joined a large consumer products firm after receiving her MBA from a well-known private east coast university. Within six months, she was made assistant brand manager for a highly visible product. After a year in that position, she was transferred to a smaller product and soon made brand manager of that product. Two years into this position, she was offered the opportunity to go overseas for three years and work as the assistant to the European VP of Marketing. After careful consideration of the nature of the job and the benefit that others pointed out that such a move could have for her career, she accepted the position. Three exciting years later, Kendra returned to corporate headquarters and was promoted to VP of marketing of one of the smaller product divisions. The promotion made her the youngest divisional marketing VPs in the company.

Nathaniel Stewart seemed to be on the management fast track. He joined a large consumer electronics firm after receiving his MBA from a well-known private west coast university. Initially he worked in the new products design group. After being there for about a year, he was promoted to be the product manager of one of the new products that he had championed. Two years later he was offered the opportunity to go overseas and work as the assistant to the VP of operations for the firm's subsidiary in Taiwan. Two of the firm's important products were built in Taiwan and the opportunity seemed like a great career move. Consequently, Nathaniel took the position. Although the products that he work with in Taiwan both sold well and made substantial profits, Nathaniel felt "out-of-sight, out-of-mind" during his time in Taiwan. After his three-year agreement, he returned home only to find that no clear job was waiting for him and he was stuck in a "holding pattern" doing odd assignments for about four months. The position he finally secured was a significant step down from what he had held overseas and included slightly less important responsibilities than the position he had held before he took the job in Taiwan.

Kendra Davidson and Nathaniel Stewart's experiences illustrate the challenges people can encounter during their careers. Just as Kendra and her firm gained from her overseas career move, so too did Nathaniel and his firm lose by what happened as a function of his overseas move. If organizations are to be competitive and prosper they must make the most effective use possible of their human resources. If individuals are to maximize their potential, they must carefully manage their careers and development. That is the topic of this chapter.

THE EMPLOYMENT RELATIONSHIP

The primary emphasis of this chapter is on what may be called the *employment relationship.* By this we mean the nature of the relationship between individuals and their employers—how people see themselves in relation to the organization and what happens to them as a result of their employment in a particular firm. Hence, we are concerned about how both individuals and companies select one another; how companies attempt to integrate or socialize new members; how people develop an implied employment contract; what bonds the individual to an organization; and how the nature of individual-organization relationships changes over the course of a career. More specifically, we shall proceed through the following topics: (1) organizational entry, (2) socialization and employee adaptation, (3) careers in organizations, (4) mentoring, and (5) problems of managing diversity among employees. First, however, we will look a little closer at the basic nature of the employment relationship.

The Psychological Contract

One way to view the employment relationship is as a process of exchange between employees and organizations. This may be referred to as a *psychological contract* in which both parties create mutual expectations of each other that govern their relationship. Ironically, each side is often unaware of the other's expectations and assumes that his or her own view of the exchange is shared by the other party. Included in this psychological contract is a series of legitimate demands (level of output, type of work activities) placed on the individual by the organization. The individual accepts these demands as part of the contract in exchange for receiving valued outcomes (salary, job security) from the organization. Consider the examples in the opening case. What was the implicit contract as viewed by both individuals and the two firms? Were these psychological contracts honored or broken?

Many American companies today face a fundamental conflict with respect to their approach to this contract. This conflict is important because the manner in which companies resolve it can have a dramatic impact on industrial competitiveness. On the one hand, companies, in their search for efficiency and economy, often want to increase their flexibility in the employment, deployment, and disengagement of their work forces. On the other hand, however, these same companies also want to secure increased employee flexibility, discretion, and commitment. Unfortunately, the first objective suggests that companies should avoid making long-term commitments to employees (e.g., lifetime employment), whereas the second objective almost requires such a commitment.[1] How companies resolve this conflict will determine the ultimate quality of their human resources, which, in turn, will affect their long-term survival and effectiveness.

Employee-Organization Linkages

Two general strategies can be identified concerning the manner in which companies attempt to secure employee attachment and participation. In the work of Porter, Tsui, and Pearce, these are referred to as a *contract strategy* and a *mutual investment strategy.*[2] A *contract strategy* involves an agreement— implicit or explicit—between an employee and an employer that specifies exactly what each party will contribute. In exchange for a certain level of job performance, an employee can expect a certain compensation package. For example, when an aerospace company receives a major government contract, it immediately sets out to hire hundreds and sometimes thousands of engineers and technicians to meet the contract. Salaries and benefits are generous, but job security is often absent. When the contract is over, so, too, is the employment of the engineers, unless another contract is received.

Under the contract strategy, job performance is the primary criterion for evaluating employee worth (see Exhibit 18.1). This strategy can be likened to a market situation in which each party contributes specified things to the exchange. Both sides know what to expect. However, either side can terminate

Exhibit 18.1
Two Strategies for Inducing
Employee Involvement

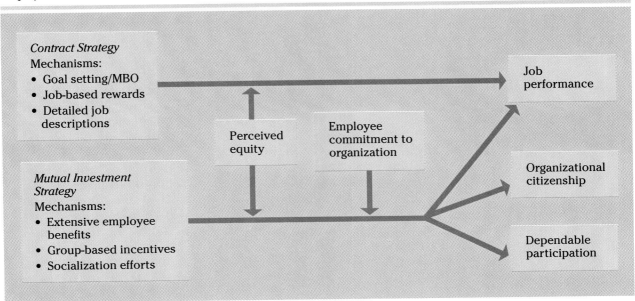

Source: Adapted from L. Porter, A. Tsui, and J. Pearce, "Employee-Organizational Relationships: An Inducement-Contribution Approach," working paper, Graduate School of Management, University of California, Irvine, November 1989, p. 14.

this relationship if the other party violates the contract or a better economic exchange comes along. That is, employers may feel free to lay off employees during slack production times, and employees may feel free to quit when they receive a better job offer. In both cases, one party determines it is in his or her best interest to sever the relationship. Hence, little psychological or moral commitment exists for either party.

In the *mutual investment strategy,* on the other hand, organizations and employees typically seek a broader array of behaviors and commitments (beyond routine job performance and compensation). That is, employers seek individuals who will not only perform but will also participate actively in organizational activities and be good organizational citizens. This is essentially the "whole person" concept that is prevalent in most East Asian companies and many American high-tech firms. Here, the principal focus is on the organization as a whole, not specific job behaviors, and performance evaluation is likely to be based on a broad set of factors that are not limited to job performance. For instance, a company may wish to evaluate an employee's long-range potential to the company, or it may look for employees who serve certain useful roles for the company (e.g., a liaison with a certain group outside the company). As such, the basis for reward distribution is broader, with a greater emphasis on long-term employee development. In exchange, such companies seek employees willing to make a long-term commitment to grow with the company (refer to Exhibit 18.1).

Depending upon which employment strategy an organization adopts, different inducement mechanisms emerge. For example, a contract employment strategy attempts to retain and motivate employees through goal-setting or management-by-objectives, in which rewards are based on individual job performance and the fulfillment of detailed job descriptions (see Chapter 6). The focus of such strategies is to maximize the short-term job performance of the particular individual. Conversely, a mutual investment strategy attempts to gain compliance and motivation by offering extensive employee benefits, rewards based on unit or *group* performance, and socialization efforts to make each employee a team member who is committed to the company. In other words, this strategy stresses collective performance and has a longer-term emphasis.

These efforts, in turn, are moderated by the extent of perceived equity (in the eyes of employees—see Chapter 6) and by organizational commitment (see Chapter 3). That is, for the exchange relationship to work effectively, it has to be seen as being fair. Moreover, for a mutual investment strategy to work, employees must develop a true sense of commitment to the organization. Finally, as shown in the exhibit and discussed above, the outcomes from the mutual investment strategy will tend to be broader than those expected from the contract strategy. That is, although both strategies may lead to increased performance, the mutual investment strategy will also be more likely to lead to both improved organizational citizenship behavior and increased participation.[3]

As we will see below, the choice made by an organization with respect to the manner in which it attempts to retain and motivate its employees has a profound effect on subsequent employee attitudes and behaviors, which ultimately can affect organization-wide effectiveness. To start, let us see how such strategies affect the job and organizational choices made by individuals.

ORGANIZATIONAL ENTRY

For several decades, industrial psychologists have studied employee recruitment and selection processes from the organization's standpoint. These processes constitute a major part of any contemporary text on industrial psychology or human resources management. It is only recently, however, that organization scholars have begun to focus attention on recruitment and selection from the *employee's* standpoint. This study of the manner in which a newcomer moves from outside to inside the organization is an area known as *organizational entry*.[4]

Matching Individuals to Organizations

Organizations are continually involved in matching processes with individuals. Prospective employees bring their skills and abilities to an organization and attempt to match them with the organization's job requirements. In addition, prospective employees also bring a variety of human needs; they are in search of an organization climate in which these needs can be satisfied. In many respects, organizations focus their attention during the recruitment process on the first match (skills and abilities to job requirements), whereas individuals focus on the second match (needs to climate). The end result of these two matching processes determines how satisfied both individuals and organizations are with the choice and how likely each is to want to continue the relationship. Moreover, as shown in Exhibit 18.2, this matching process continues long after the employee joins the organization.[5] In fact, at each stage in an employee's career, some aspect of matching is involved.

The study of organizational entry generally addresses four questions that all relate to this matching process: (1) How do individuals choose organizations? (2) How accurate and complete is the information that prospective employees have about organizations? (3) What is the impact of organizational recruitment on matching individuals and organizations? and (4) What are the consequences of matching or mismatching individuals and organizations? Answers to these questions help managers gain an understanding of the individual's point of view in the recruitment process and allow managers and potential employees to make more informed choices that benefit both.

Choosing an Organization

The most common approach to analyzing how people choose from among various organizations is based on expectancy theory (see Chapter 6). A simplified model of this choice process is shown in Exhibit 18.3, which is adapted from the work of Vroom and Lawler.[6] As this model shows, it is important to distinguish among three stages in the choice process: (1) the relative attractiveness of an organization, (2) the amount of effort directed toward joining the organization, and (3) the actual choice of an organization from among the job offers the individual receives. Hence, attractiveness, effort, and choice refer to the entry process from an individual's point of view.

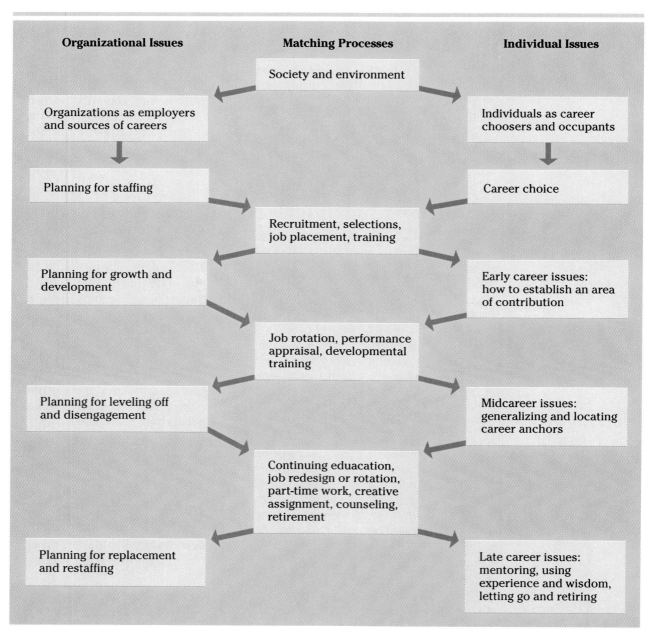

Exhibit 18.2
Matching Individual and
Organizational Needs

Source: Edgar Schein, *Career Dynamics: Matching Individual and Organizational Needs,* © 1978
by Addison-Wesley Publishing Co., Inc., Reading, Massachusetts. Material from pages 4 and
124–160. Reprinted with permission of the publisher.

Stage 1: Attractiveness.   In Stage 1, the relative attractiveness of an organization is determined by a combination of expectations about the characteristics of each organization and valences attached to each of those
characteristics. Vroom studied a group of MBA students as they chose their
first jobs.[7] Students' job expectations and job valences were measured for
each organization being considered. As it turned out, the students' overall

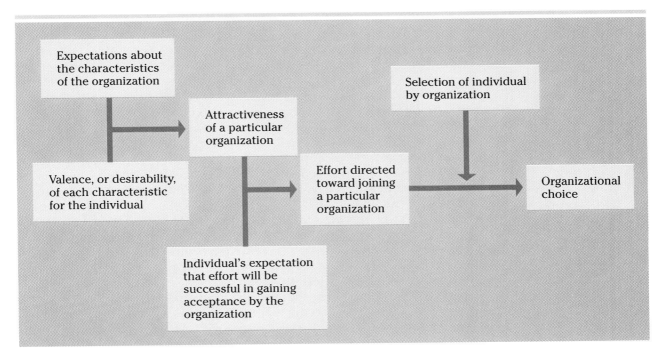

Exhibit 18.3
The Organizational
Choice Process

organizational attractiveness score (expectations × valences) accurately predicted 76 percent of actual job choices. These findings offer strong confirmation of the role of expectancies and valences in choice behavior.

During the information-gathering stage, individuals often ask a number of questions concerning the organization in an effort to gain additional insight for making a decision. These questions commonly cover topics such as the following:

1. How large is the organization's industry, and what are its prospects for growth?
2. What goods and services does it produce?
3. How large is the organization (people, assets, sales volume)?
4. Where does it have other plants or divisions?
5. What are the organization's compensation policies? Performance appraisal practices? Training and development practices?
6. What do people generally like or dislike about the organization?
7. What are the organization's plans for the future?
8. What jobs have top executives held during their careers with the organization?

Stage 2: Effort.   In Stage 2, individuals must determine the amount of energy to devote toward joining an organization. Here, applicants put their best foot forward. The decision to make this effort is influenced by both the attractiveness of the organization and the belief that the effort will in fact be successful in gaining acceptance (that is, a job offer).

Stage 3: Choice.   As a result of this effort, organizations make *their* selections and offer positions to their favored candidates. Once offers have been made, individuals select among alternative offers in Stage 3. Most individuals select the position that appears to offer the greatest attractiveness in either the short or long term.

The model of job choice suggested here is intentionally oversimplified to highlight many prominent aspects of the choice process. Obviously, other factors enter into actual job choice decisions. Some people do not follow anything like a rational or quasi-rational process in their decision but rather take positions almost by caprice (see Chapter 14). Even so, the model is helpful in identifying some of the factors that influence decisions.

Two additional aspects of the organizational choice process need to be mentioned. The first is the cognitive distortions that occur in the decision process. That is, the act of choosing from among job alternatives often causes us to distort our perceptions of the characteristics (and desirability) of the various alternatives. Once we have chosen a particular job (but before we report for work), we often *increase* our perceptions of the chosen job (that is, increase organizational attractiveness) and *decrease* our perceptions of the alternative positions that we did not accept. This is done to justify our choice and to reduce possible dissonance about the decision (see Chapter 3).

However, studies have also shown that once individuals actually join and work in an organization, they become less satisfied with their decision than they were before or immediately after making it.[8] This reality shock occurs as a result of incomplete or inaccurate information people have about the future job. Once they arrive at work, they are confronted with aspects of the job that they either failed to recognize or thought were less important. As a result, satisfaction with their decision diminishes, and propensity to leave increases. In fact, in many industries, a major share of all turnover (often 70 percent or more) occurs during the first year of employment.

Realistic Job Previews

Obviously, many people are led to expect a work environment quite different from what confronts them upon arrival at work. The existence of reality shock raises questions about the accuracy of the information people use in choosing among alternative organizations. How incomplete is this information, and what can be done to increase the accuracy of it?

Several studies indicate that company recruiters tend to give glowing descriptions of jobs to prospective employees rather than balanced descriptions.[9] This is probably done in the hope of attracting desirable candidates in a competitive job market. As a result, however, the inflated expectations of many employees are not met, and the disappointed employees subsequently leave.

There are two important ways in which employee expectations can be met. The first is to increase the positive outcomes experienced by the employee (perhaps through pay increases, better supervision, job enrichment, new office furniture, or increased social activities). This would enhance the likelihood of meeting an employee's inflated expectations. Unfortunately, this is often difficult to accomplish for a variety of reasons. The second approach is to reduce expectations so they more accurately reflect organizational reality. This is done through realistic job previews.

A *realistic job preview* (RJP) attempts to provide prospective employees with accurate job information. When they have been given such information, employees have more realistic initial expectations and can make more informed and appropriate choices. A realistic job preview emphasizes specific facts about the job and presents both the positive and negative aspects. On the basis of these facts, employees are more likely to identify a suitable match between their own needs and those of the organization. In contrast, the traditional approach typically attempts to sell the job and present it in its most favorable light (see Exhibit 18.4).

Several experiments have been done in industry in an attempt to compare the effects of realistic job previews with those of the traditional approach. In the realistic job previews, job information was presented to candidates in either a film about the job, a booklet describing the job, a practice session, or interviews with actual job incumbents. What effect did the previews have? Several benefits were noted:

■ First, contrary to expectations, RJPs did not impair the organization's ability to recruit and hire desired candidates. People were still willing to take the positions, despite less positive impressions.

■ Second, several studies show that RJPs clearly lowered job expectations and created more realistic perceptions of what the actual job would be like.

Exhibit 18.4
A Comparison of Traditional and Realistic Job Previews

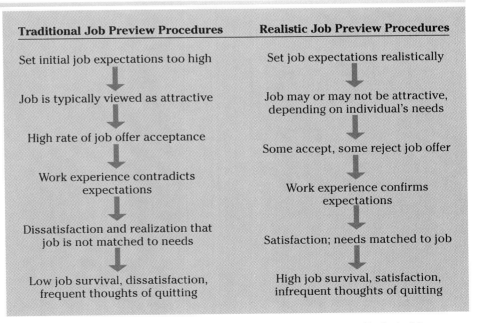

Traditional Job Preview Procedures	Realistic Job Preview Procedures
Set initial job expectations too high	Set job expectations realistically
Job is typically viewed as attractive	Job may or may not be attractive, depending on individual's needs
High rate of job offer acceptance	Some accept, some reject job offer
Work experience contradicts expectations	Work experience confirms expectations
Dissatisfaction and realization that job is not matched to needs	Satisfaction; needs matched to job
Low job survival, dissatisfaction, frequent thoughts of quitting	High job survival, satisfaction, infrequent thoughts of quitting

◼ Third, RJPs led to more positive job attitudes after the initial employment period, as well as fewer thoughts about leaving.

◼ Finally, RJPs consistently led to reduced turnover compared to traditional methods. Employees exposed to realistic job previews in a wide array of work organizations exhibited turnover rates between 10 and 20 percent lower than other employees.[10]

Thus, although realistic job previews should not be seen as a panacea for all organizational ills, they do appear to represent another factor contributing to the overall effectiveness of the organization and its management.

IN PRACTICE
Realistic Job Previews at Nissan-USA

Smyrna, Tenn.—Bookkeeper Phyllis Baines has two minutes to grab 55 nuts, bolts and washers, assemble them in groups of five and attach them in order of size to a metal rack. But she fumbles nervously with several pieces and finishes the task seconds after her allotted time.

"I've got to get a little better at this, don't I?" she frets as she pulls the last of the fasteners out of a grimy plastic tray. Her tester, Harold Hicks, encourages her: "You're close. For the first night, you're probably doing a little better than normal."

It may appear that Mrs. Baines (not her real name) is going through first-night jitters at an adult-school class in home repair. But the 31-year-old department store employee will be devoting 70 hours worth of her nights and weekends over the next few months doing similar exercises, in an effort to land a job at the Nissan Motor Manufacturing Corp. plant here.

Mrs. Baines and about 270 other job seekers are participating in Nissan's "pre-employment" program. In exchange for a shot at highly paid assembly-line and other hourly jobs, and Nissan's promise not to inform their employers, the moonlighters are working up to 360 hours—without pay—being tested and instructed in employment fundamentals by the Japanese auto maker.

"We hope the process makes it plain to people what the job is," says Thomas P. Groom, Nissan's manager of employment. "It's an indoctrination process" as well as a screening tool.

Not all participants are fully satisfied with the program. A candidate who works as a machine adjuster at an envelope factory says that the lack of a job guarantee by Nissan "worries you, because you get your hopes up." And some candidates bemoan the lack of pay for their time.

But many participants feel that the training and experience they receive outweigh any additional obstacles to getting hired. For one thing they get a shot at some of the best paid jobs in the state, and if they don't get hired, they can take the skills they have learned elsewhere. Adds Judy McFarland, a press operator who went through the program in 1983: "It gave me a chance to see what Nissan expected of me without their having to make a commitment to me or to them."[11]

SOCIALIZATION AND EMPLOYEE ADAPTATION

When individuals join an organization, they enter an unknown world filled with new experiences, challenges, and potential threats. This initial employment period is important for both the individual and the organization, because considerable turnover (voluntary and involuntary) occurs during this matching period. Many employees discover that they simply cannot, or do not wish to, handle their assigned jobs. For a variety of reasons they discover, somewhat too late, that a mistake has been made and choose to leave. Others learn to cope, to adapt, even to enjoy their new positions, and they decide to remain.

What causes differences in the reactions of employees? First, many employees simply are not equipped technically to handle the job. Perhaps they cannot master a computer, make decisions, deal with people, or make sales. Under these circumstances, people either seek additional training or leave. In addition to technical factors, however, several psychological factors account for success or failure in adaptation and development. Prominent among these are the related topics of socialization and individualization. Taken together, these two concepts can have a profound impact on employees' abilities to successfully adapt to an organization.

Socialization may be defined as a concerted attempt by one's colleagues and the organization to exert subtle pressures—overt or covert—to shape one into the desired kind of employee. At the same time, individuals attempt to shape the work environment so it meets their own needs. This process is called *individualization*. The continuous interaction of these two processes creates the workplace in which everyone works and lives. Thus, it is important to understand how these processes work.

Socialization is vital to the efficient operation of any work organization. As noted by Schein, "The speed and effectiveness of socialization determine employee loyalty, commitment, productivity, and turnover. The basic stability and effectiveness of organizations therefore depends upon their ability to socialize new members."[12] Without some degree of socialization, employees would diffuse their work efforts, often in conflicting directions, because of disagreements over the major purposes and values of the organization.

Stages in Socialization

The socialization process consists of three stages (see Exhibit 18.5). These stages are as follows:

Stage 1: Anticipatory Socialization.   The first stage in the socialization process, called *anticipatory socialization,* occurs as the individual is about to join the organization. Most individuals enter organizations with preconceptions about the nature of the organization and job. These preconceptions are formed as a result of previous education, work experiences, and contracts with organization members. For instance a dominant attitude taught in many

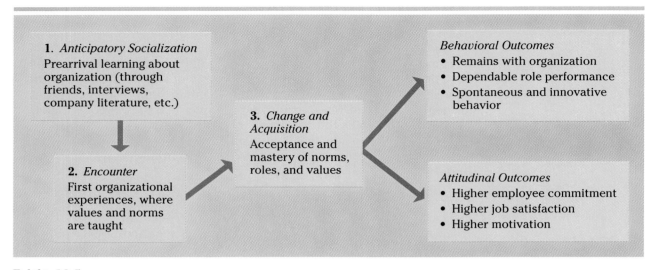

1. *Anticipatory Socialization*
Prearrival learning about organization (through friends, interviews, company literature, etc.)

2. *Encounter*
First organizational experiences, where values and norms are taught

3. *Change and Acquisition*
Acceptance and mastery of norms, roles, and values

Behavioral Outcomes
• Remains with organization
• Dependable role performance
• Spontaneous and innovative behavior

Attitudinal Outcomes
• Higher employee commitment
• Higher job satisfaction
• Higher motivation

Exhibit 18.5
Stages in Employee Socialization

business schools is the need for an efficient, dedicated work force. Hence, many individuals who are exposed to this idea are already well on the way to socialization before actual organizational entry. The anticipatory socialization process consists of an individual accepting the beliefs and values of the group he or she aspires to become a member of. In essence, the person socializes himself in the hope that it may facilitate membership and acceptance by the group or organization. Anticipatory socialization can be seen among students in many professional schools (business, engineering, medicine, law) as they prepare for their careers and develop belief systems that are compatible with that profession.

Stage 2: Encounter.   Once inside the organization, the individual enters the *encounter stage.* He or she encounters other members who exhibit accepted attitudes and behavior. These day-to-day interactions, combined with positive reinforcements for behaving in a similar fashion (and punishment for contrary behavior), condition the individual to accept the status of peers and superiors.

Stage 3: Change and Acquisition.   These initial encounters, with their conditioning and reinforcement properties, ultimately solidify the attitudes and behaviors individuals have learned. Hence, in the *change and acquisition stage,* people develop new self-images more consistent with those of other members. They develop new social relationships, often with members of the same organization. Finally, they develop new values and new modes of behavior. At this point, the individual has been transformed from an outsider into a member.

The success of socialization attempts is influenced by two factors.[13] First, socialization efforts are more successful if individuals are highly motivated upon entry. Individuals who are eager to join a firm, for instance, are more likely to put up with initial discomforts and to be more receptive to company-sanctioned norms and values. In addition, socialization attempts are usually more successful if the organization offers inducements to remain with the organization and comply with its dictates; offering an employee perquisites not offered elsewhere (a private office, a company car) can often entice the individual to remain. Under such circumstances of self-interest, new employees are essentially seduced into willing acceptance of organizational norms and values.

Techniques of Socialization

How do organizations socialize their employees? Several common methods can be identified:

- *Employee selection.* Through the employee selection process, employers and interviewers seek the "right kind of person." This search often translates into a search for individuals who already share common values. This process is closely related to the realistic job preview discussed earlier in the chapter.

- *Training and development.* Once inside the organization, employees participate in a variety of training and development activities, both formal and informal. These expose them to a series of programs designed to instill certain beliefs and values that are desired by the organization. These programs may take the form of new employee orientation, management development workshops, departmental meetings, or simply on-the-job training efforts by a supervisor.

- *Mentoring and apprenticeships.* Mentoring and apprenticeships are other means of socializing employees. Here a senior employee assumes responsibility for socializing a new employee, as noted above. Under this "buddy system," the senior advisor is in an advantageous position to instill in the new employee both technical skills and workplace norms and values. Failure to comply with these efforts can lead to expulsion from the apprentice program, thereby adding significant reinforcing power to socialization attempts.

- *Debasement experiences.* A more dramatic socialization technique is the debasement experience. Here the employee undergoes something that causes him to detach himself from earlier attitudes and to substitute a more humble self-perception, which allows for easier socialization attempts. For example, periodically an old hand or a supervisor will set up a new employee in such a way that the employee fails on a task or is publicly embarrassed. As a result of the experience, the employee is more prone to look up to the supervisor for advice and knowledge.

- *Trial and error.* Finally, socialization often occurs almost by trial and error. Organizations do not control the daily activities of all their employees. They must allow the employees to experience various aspects of the organization and, in the process, learn about them. Although these nonprogrammed efforts may not be as systematic as other methods, they are nevertheless a necessary part of organizational life.

Individualization

The second half of the psychological contract consists of efforts by individuals either to change the workplace to meet their needs or, at the very least, to resist organizational efforts to change the individual. While the organization attempts to socialize individuals to accept its beliefs and values, individuals often respond in ways aimed at nullifying or reducing these attempts and maintaining a certain degree of control over their work life. Efforts to assert individualization can be classified into three broad categories.[14]

Rebellion. At one extreme, an individual may respond to socialization attempts with *rebellion*—open rejection and hostility. This rejection, however, may lead to the individual being dismissed (perhaps as a nonconformist). Alternatively, it could lead to actual change in the organization. More likely, it would result in an attempt by the organization to "co-opt" the rebel and blunt the attack. In any case, the organization must take notice of the individual and the fact that he or she will not likely acquiesce to organizational norms and rules.

Creative Individualism. Toward the middle of the individualization continuum is *creative individualism*. Here, individuals choose to accept the basic aspects of the organization's norms and values but reject the peripheral ones and substitute their own. In essence, this is a compromise position where both parties attempt to make peace—the individual will accept certain aspects of organizational life, and the organization allows room for dissent and unconventional behavior.

Conformity. At the other extreme is *conformity*. Many individuals adapt to organizational life by simply giving up their individuality and conforming to corporate norms. The "organization man" (or woman) is a prime example. However, the personal costs associated with such behavior can be high.

We have seen how individuals and organizations attempt to accommodate one another and create relatively stable situations in which both can survive and prosper. As individuals continue on the job, they come to think more about the nature of their relationship with the organization. Do they agree with the goals and values of the organization? Are they motivated to work hard to help the organization realize these goals? Do they wish to remain with the organization or go elsewhere? Answers to questions such as these focus on the extent to which employees feel a part of the organization. And as noted several times throughout this book, the more employees see their own goals and those of the organization as synonymous, the greater the likelihood that they will wish to remain with the firm and exert high levels of energy on its behalf. In this process, socialization, individualization, and the achievement of an acceptable psychological contract play an essential role.

CAREERS IN ORGANIZATIONS

Employee career patterns vary considerably. Some employees join a particular organization at an early age and remain with that same organization through retirement. Others change jobs—and even vocations—almost at will. Despite these differences, it is possible to develop a portrait of the average pattern by studying career stages. We can do so by asking questions about the way employees become attached to or separated from their employers.

Definition of Career

A *career* may be defined as an "individually perceived sequence of attitudes and behaviors associated with work-related experiences and activities over the span of the person's life."[15] Underlying this definition are four important assumptions:

1. The notion of a career as such does not imply success or failure. A career is viewed as a lifelong series of events rather than an evaluation of how successful someone has been over his or her lifetime.
2. Career success or failure is best judged by the person whose career is being considered, not by the normative opinions of others.
3. A career consists of the events that happen to an individual over time. It is what an individual does and feels at work.
4. A career is best viewed as a process of work-related experiences. These experiences may include a series of promotions within a single company, or they may involve different jobs in varied organizations.

Thus, when we talk about a career, we are in essence referring to a distinct series of positions linked together through time, as experienced by the individual. One way to better understand this concept is to examine what people look for in careers. This can be done by using the concept of career anchors.

Career Anchors

Simply put, *career anchors* are factors that cause people to seek certain types of work; they represent what people look for in jobs. The concept of career anchors was introduced by Edgar Schein of MIT to describe the process by which individuals gravitate toward certain careers. As Schein argues, "Certain motivational, attitudinal, and value syndromes formed early in the lives of individuals apparently function to guide and constrain their entire careers."[16]

Schein identifies at least five primary career anchors that can affect people (see Exhibit 18.6): (1) technical/functional competence, (2) managerial competence, (3) security and stability, (4) creativity/entrepreneurship, and (5) autonomy and independence.

Career Anchor	Characteristics	Typical Career Paths
1. Technical/functional competence	• Excited by work itself • Willing to forgo promotions • Dislikes general management and corporate politics	• Research-oriented position • Functional department management job • Specialized consulting and project management
2. Managerial competence	• Likes to analyze and solve knotty business problems • Likes to influence and harness people to work together • Enjoys the exercise of power	• Vice-presidencies • Plant management and sales management • Large, prestigious firms
3. Security and stability	• Motivated by job security and long-term careers with one firm • Dislikes travel and relocation • Tends to be conformist and compliant to the organization	• Government jobs • Small family-owned businesses • Large government-regulated industries
4. Creativity/ entrepreneurship	• Enjoys launching own business • Restless; moves from project to project • Prefers small and up-and-coming firms to well-established ones	• Entrepreneurial ventures • Stock options, arbitrage, mergers, and acquisitions • General management consulting
5. Autonomy and independence	• Desires freedom from organizational constraints • Wants to be on own and set own pace • Avoids large businesses and governmental agencies	• Academia • Writing and publishing • Small business proprietorships

Exhibit 18.6
Schein's Career
Anchors Model

Source: Adapted from E. A. Schein, *Career Dynamics* (Reading, Mass.: Addison-Wesley, 1978), pp. 124–160. Reprinted from R. Dunham and J. Pierce, *Management* (Glenview, Ill.: Scott, Foresman, 1989), p. 857.

It is generally believed that these anchors serve not only to guide individuals into certain careers in the first place, but also to help pull people back to their original direction when they stray too far from it (hence the term *anchor*). In this sense, they act much like individual needs, as described in Chapter 5. Thus, a person with a strong technical/functional anchor may seek and remain in research or engineering-type jobs, whereas a person with a strong security and stability anchor may seek and remain in a government job or a family business.

The concept of career anchors is useful for managers in helping them understand why people choose the paths they do in occupations and organizations. Moreover, the concept also warns us about the possible difficulties of trying to transfer an employee into a line of work that he or she does not see as central. In short, it helps us improve the accuracy and effectiveness of a company's career planning and development process.

To better understand how career anchors work, you may wish to complete Self-Assessment 18.1. Score it as described in Appendix B.

SELF-ASSESSMENT 18.1
What Are Your Career Anchors?

Instructions: Below is listed a series of statements relating to your career. Answer each item below as truthfully as possible by circling the answer that best describes your agreement or disagreement with the item.

	Strongly Disagree				Strongly Agree
1. Becoming highly specialized in one technical area is very important to me.	1	2	3	4	5
2. I want to rise to a position of senior management within the firm.	1	2	3	4	5
3. I would give up some autonomy in order to stabilize my overall life situation.	1	2	3	4	5
4. The use of my skills in building a new enterprise is important to me.	1	2	3	4	5
5. I want a career that is free of organizational restriction.	1	2	3	4	5
6. I would refuse a promotion rather than move out of my area of expertise.	1	2	3	4	5
7. I would like to reach a position in a firm where my decisions really count.	1	2	3	4	5
8. It is important to me to remain in my present geographic location.	1	2	3	4	5
9. An endless variety of challenges is important to me in a job.	1	2	3	4	5
10. I want a career that provides maximum variety in my work assignments.	1	2	3	4	5
11. It is important to me to be identified by my profession or occupation.	1	2	3	4	5
12. I enjoy supervising people.	1	2	3	4	5
13. I want to work for a company that guarantees job security and good fringe benefits.	1	2	3	4	5
14. The most important thing in a job to me is the ability to create and innovate.	1	2	3	4	5
15. I want a career that gives me considerable flexibility and independence.	1	2	3	4	5

Career Stages

Related to the notion of career anchor is the equally important topic of *career stages*. In many occupations and organizations, it is possible to identify a series of relatively discrete career stages. (Of course, these stages must be presented in a generalized form, and variations on this pattern must be recognized.) In general, we can identify four stages: (1) exploration, (2) establishment, (3) maintenance, and (4) decline. These are shown in Exhibit 18.7.

1. *Exploration.* The *exploration* stage consists of the time period when individuals are completing school and seeking initial employment. (This stage is closely related to the process of organizational entry, which was discussed above.) Here, individuals try to match their needs, abilities, and skills with organizational requirements. This search usually continues throughout the early months on the job, during which individuals question whether the correct job choice was made.

2. *Establishment.* In the *establishment* stage, individuals gain a better understanding of the work environment and organizational demands and strive to establish their worth in the organization. This is also a period when the organization is often carefully evaluating individuals to determine their long-term worth.

3. *Maintenance.* In the *maintenance* stage, individuals have usually entrenched themselves in the organization. In this stage, they frequently experience fairly strong linkages to the organization and often find it difficult if not impossible to leave and go elsewhere. Also during this stage, individuals' performance levels can be expected to vary considerably. Some individuals continue to grow and develop, whereas others begin to stagnate and retreat. Certainly, in terms of wasted employee time and energy, this stage is where the greatest problem lies.

4. *Decline.* Finally, in the *decline* stage, individuals approach retirement. Often, however, physical age does not reflect mental age, and individuals may be capable of contributing far more to the organization than the organization allows.

Throughout this process, individuals typically ask themselves a number of questions relating to their position on the career ladder. The nature and scope of these questions vary considerably depending upon the stage in one's career, as can be seen in Exhibit 18.8.

Exhibit 18.7
Stages in Career
Development

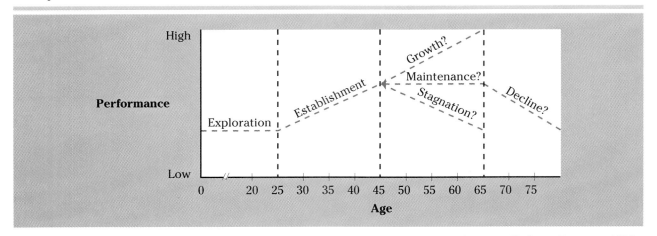

Source: Adapted from D. T. Hall, *Careers in Organizations* (Glenview, Ill.: Scott, Foresman, 1976), p. 57. Used by permission.

Age Group	Career Stage	Career Concerns
15–22	Exploration	• Finding the right career • Getting the appropriate education
22–30	Early career: trial	• Getting the first job • Adjusting to daily work routine and supervisors
30–38	Early career: establishment	• Choosing specialty and deciding on level of commitment • Transfers and promotions • Broadening perspective of occupation and organization
38–45	Middle career: growth	• Establishing professional or organizational identity • Choosing between alternative career paths (e.g., techinical vs. managerial)
45–55	Middle career: maintenance	• Being an independent contributor to the organization • Taking on more areas of responsibility
55–62	Later career: plateau	• Training and developing subordinates • Shaping the future direction of the organization • Dealing with threats to position from younger, more aggressive employees
62–70	Later career: decline	• Planning for retirement • Developing one's replacement • Dealing with a reduced work load and less power

Exhibit 18.8
Concerns of Managers by
Career Stage

Source: Reprinted by permission from H. J. Arnold and D. G. Feldman, *Organizational Behavior* (New York: McGraw-Hill, 1986), p. 548. Based on the work of E. H. Schein, *Career Dynamics: Matching Individual and Organizational Needs* (Reading, Mass.: Addison-Wesley, 1978), pp. 40–46; G. W. Dalton, P. H. Thompson, and R. L. Price, "The Four Stages of Professional Careers: A New Look at Performance by Professionals," *Organizational Dynamics,* 1977, *6,* pp. 19–42; J. Van Maanen and E. H. Schein, "Career Development," in J. R. Hackman and J. L. Suttle, eds., *Improving Life at Work* (Santa Monica, Calif.: Goodyear, 1977), pp. 54–57.

Career Planning and Development

Many contemporary organizations take an active role in developing their employees. In fact, as we saw at the beginning of the book, a hallmark of the human resource management approach is an active effort by managers to identify, develop, and utilize the full human potential of the company's human resources. This approach is consistent with the mutual investment strategy of employee relations discussed earlier in this chapter. In this effort, career development—by both the company and the individual—plays a central role.

The corporation can do many things to facilitate career development. These include the following:

■ *Career counseling.* Either through workshops or one-on-one counseling, employees receive guidance concerning career opportunities throughout the organization and whatever skills they have to exploit these opportunities.

■ *Career pathing.* Some organizations are beginning to plan job changes for employees well in advance in such a way that up-and-coming people get well-planned, broad job experiences. Moved in a logical way, people can use their present skills and can also develop new skills that can be of use to them and the organization over time.

■ *Career information systems.* Organizations make an active effort to post all new job openings so that current employees can apply. In some cases, computers are used to organize job openings systematically so career counselors have ready access to career opportunities.

Human resource planning.   Many companies have developed computerized skill inventories of their employees. When a job opening occurs, all employees who have certain skills can be readily identified (e.g., Who speaks French? Who has an MBA?). In some systems, managers are required to document the efforts they have made to train their subordinates in preparation for promotions.

Training.   In a wide variety of cases, advanced training is used to facilitate career development. This training can be done in house or through external sources; it can also be done informally through workshops and seminars or more formally through degree programs (e.g., in MBA programs).

However they are implemented, career development activities represent an important investment by companies interested in developing their employees so that they can make their maximum contribution over the long term.

International Challenge

IN PRACTICE
Perpetual Careers at Asahi Breweries

It is widely known that Japanese companies have a stronger commitment to lifetime careers than firms in most Western countries. What may be less familiar, however, is the fact that for some Japanese companies, the concept of career goes well beyond lifetime employment. In some firms, employees are considered a part of the organization even after they are dead. Consider Asahi Breweries, in Osaka. Twice each year, the president meets with several other executives of Asahi at a company shrine for deceased employees and reads a company report detailing the firm's accomplishments and financial status. The $4 million shrine contains the names of 673 former employees; it also notes their names, job titles, tenures, and dates of death. These are all meticulously maintained by company officials. At each ceremony, newly deceased employees are added to the list.

Explains a company spokesman, "Workers spend more than half their lives at the company, and we should return their commitment." And employees seem to like the idea. A recent survey at Asahi found that 80 percent of the employees want to spend forever with their co-workers. Says one employee, "I want to leave a footnote showing that I existed in this company."

Although such a practice may seem odd in the West, it makes sense in the group-oriented Japanese society. The practice of honoring and remembering employees is a part of ongoing renewal in Japanese companies and enhances employee loyalty and commitment. And Asahi is not alone in this. In fact, thousands of Japanese firms have such shrines, and most hold annual or semiannual ceremonies recognizing former members of the organizational family. As one executive says, "Our way of thinking is to tie what our employees of the past have done to what our employees today are doing."[17]

MENTORING

A key aspect of getting ahead in any organization is knowing the ropes—that is, understanding both the explicit and implicit norms, rules, criteria for advancement, appropriate behaviors, and so forth that differentiate successful from unsuccessful managers. One way to accomplish this is through the mentoring process. Numerous companies, such as Honeywell, Johnson and Johnson, and AT&T, use mentoring to get new employees off to a good start. Although a mentor relationship can be formed informally between two people, these companies have institutionalized mentors as part of the formal employee development process. This technique has been shown to be particularly effective in integrating women and minorities into careers and positions traditionally held by white males.

The Mentoring Relationship

Briefly, a *mentor* is a senior person within the organization who assumes responsibility for the career development of a more junior person. A mentor is often the employee's immediate supervisor, but this alone does not constitute a mentoring relationship. To be a mentor, there must be a close, long-term relationship between a junior and senior person that focuses on developing the junior person's job skills and career potential. Above all, the mentor is a counselor and guide, helping the new person through the technical, administrative, and political maze that constitutes organizational life. (The term *mentor* derives from Mentor, the wise and trusted counselor in Greek mythology.)

Research by Kathy Kram has identified nine primary functions of mentoring.[18] It should be noted that many of these purposes help the careers of both parties involved in the mentoring relationship. These functions were grouped into the two general categories of *career functions* and *psychosocial functions*. Career functions emphasize providing developmental experiences on the job, whereas psychosocial functions clarify the employee's self-identity and feelings of competence. The five career functions of mentoring include (1) sponsorship, (2) exposure and visibility, (3) coaching, (4) protection, and (5) ensuring challenging job assignments. The four psychosocial functions include (1) role modeling, (2) acceptance and confirmation, (3) counseling, and (4) friendship.

Phases in Mentoring

The mentoring process typically passes through several *phases* as the employee comes to learn more about the organization and refine his or her survival skills.[19] These four phases are shown in Exhibit 18.9. First, there is an *initiation* phase, during which the mentor and the subordinate get to know

Phase	Definition	Turning Points*
Initiation	A period of six months to a year during which time the relationship gets started and begins to have importance for both managers.	• Fantasies become concrete expectations. • Expectations are met; senior manager provides coaching, challenging work, visibility; junior manager provides technical assistance, respect, and desire to be coached. • There are opportunities for interaction around work tasks.
Cultivation	A period of two to five years during which time the range of career and psychosocial functions provided expands to a maximum.	• Both individuals continue to benefit from the relationship. • Opportunities for meaningful and more frequent interaction increase. • Emotional bond deepens and intimacy increases.
Separation	A period of six months to two years after a significant change in the structural role relationship and/or in the emotional experience of the relationship.	• Junior manager no longer wants guidance but rather the opportunity to work more autonomously. • Senior manager faces midlife crisis and is less available to provide mentoring functions. • Job rotation or promotion limits opportunities for continued interaction; career and psychosocial functions can no longer be provided. • Blocked opportunity creates resentment and hostility that disrupts positive interaction.
Redefinition	An indefinite period after the separation phase, during which time the relationship is ended or takes on significantly different characteristics, making it a more peerlike friendship.	• Stresses of separation diminish, and new relationships are formed. • The mentor relationship is no longer needed in its previous form. • Resentment and anger diminish; gratitude and appreciation increase. • Peer status is achieved.

*Examples of the most frequently observed psychological and organizational factors that cause movement into the current relationship phase.

Exhibit 18.9
Phases of the
Mentor Relationship

Source: Kathy E. Kram, "Phases of the Mentor Relationship," *Academy of Mangement Journal,* December 1983, p. 622. Used by permission of the Academy of Management and the author.

one another and begin to develop a close working relationship. Next, in the *cultivation* phase, the range of career and psychosocial functions expands and is nurtured. This is the period during which the junior person in the relationship grows and develops in a quasi-sheltered environment. It is a period when the person "gets his or her wings." In the third phase, called *separation,* the junior person moves into a more autonomous work situation and gains independence from the mentor. Here, the person must stand on his or her own two feet, and, as a result, the mentor relationship begins to diminish. Finally, in the *redefinition* phase, the two individuals either continue to grow apart or, more frequently, redefine their relationship into one of peers or colleagues instead of superior and subordinate. Full independence has been achieved, and the former subordinate must now be recognized as a full-fledged contributor to the organization.

However it is done, mentoring has proven to be an effective way in which to successfully integrate new and valued employees into organizational life. This is especially true for junior managerial personnel who wish to make a career with a particular company but who need continuing counsel during the early years so they are adequately protected and nurtured and grow with the organization. A related way to help integrate new employees into an organization is through a variety of socialization mechanisms, and it is to this subject that we now turn.

MANAGING A DIVERSE WORK FORCE

It was noted in Chapter 1 that the structure of the labor market has been changing rather significantly in recent years and that more change is anticipated. More women and minorities are entering the work force and attempting to move up the career ladder. It is currently estimated that in the United States, 8 percent of all managers, 12 percent of professionals, 18 percent of technicians, and 17 percent of sales representatives are either female or from a minority background.[20] These percentages have increased substantially compared to a decade ago, but many feel that far more progress is needed. That is, despite legislation requiring equal opportunity and affirmative action with respect to under-represented groups, many still refer to a *glass ceiling* in corporations—an invisible barrier on the career ladder above which certain groups of people never seem to pass. For whatever reason, senior management in most corporations continues to be staffed predominantly by white males. Yet by the year 2000, only 32 percent of all people entering the workforce will be white males.

As more companies begin to create greater opportunities for all employees—and to take advantage of a broader array of managerial and employee talents—several special problems emerge that require attention. One of the actions many firms have taken is the training of their employees to work more effectively with a greater diversity of organization members. Because individuals often have preconceived ideas about the abilities or behaviors of a group of people different from themselves, this training often focuses on making employees aware that they carry these stereotypes and then breaking the biases down and replacing them with a more tolerant perspective.

Women in Management

In 1950, women constituted 29 percent of the work force. Of this number, very few held positions of managerial responsibility. By 1990, 46 percent of the work force was female, and 5 percent of managers were women. By the year 2000, it is estimated that women will make up almost 50 percent of the work force.[21] Yet the number of female managers is not expected to increase dramatically, although it will indeed increase. In addition, women who occupy responsible positions consistently earn less than their male counterparts. For instance, a study by the U.S. Department of Commerce reported that salaries for female executives average only 61 percent of salaries for male executives and that females' salaries are 68 percent of males' for professionals and 51 percent for sales representatives.[22] Why? Several reasons can be identified beyond simple job discrimination.

A major study of the pressures facing women in the workplace found that many women face three concomitant pressures that must be dealt with by successful managers.[23] First, there are the normal job requirements that all managers face. There are too many conflicting demands, and there is not enough time, too much competition to get ahead, and so forth. In addition, however, the women who do reach managerial positions soon discover that there is little in the way of support from other women. The paucity of female managers means that women managers are isolated and must exist and succeed in what remains primarily a man's world. This lack of support adds pressure to an already difficult job. And, finally, there is the pressure of home life, where women continue to carry most of the burden. Taken together, these three pressures create a situation in which many women feel that the cards are essentially stacked against them in their efforts to rise.

To overcome these hurdles, women managers often need to rely on different means to get to the top than do men. This was shown in a major study of reasons cited by managers of both genders for their success.[24] As shown in Exhibit 18.10, successful female managers stress the importance of mentors (100 percent), having a good track record (89 percent), and having a desire to succeed (84 percent) far more frequently than do their male counterparts as principal reasons for career success. Hence, keys to success among women managers appear to be an ability to form useful networks among influential persons, consistently high performance, and a strong motivation to succeed. Although such factors may be important for individuals of both genders, these three seem to be particularly important among females.

Regardless of gender, as part of your own self-assessment, you may be curious concerning your own drive for success. If so, complete Self-Assessment 18.2. After you have finished the exercise, see Appendix B for scoring details.

Exhibit 18.10
Important Factors in the Success of Managers

Factor	Percent of Managers Who Feel Factor Is Important	
	Successful Men	**Successful Women**
Having a mentor	55	100
Good job performance	75	89
Desire to succeed	45	84
Ability to manage subordinates effectively	50	74
Willingness to take career risks	15	74
Being a tough and decisive manager	20	68

Source: Data from A. Morrison, R. White, and E. VanVelsor, *Breaking the Glass Ceiling* (Reading, Mass.: Addison-Wesley, 1987).

SELF-ASSESSMENT 18.2
How Important Is Success to You?

Instructions: This questionnaire asks a series of questions concerning how you feel personally about several outcomes. For each item listed below, answer as honestly as you can by circling the most appropriate number.

		Strongly Disagree			Strongly Agree	
1.	When something good happens to me, I often get the feeling that it won't last.	1	2	3	4	5
2.	I usually feel good when I win an argument.	5	4	3	2	1
3.	I seldom tell my friends when I excel at something.	1	2	3	4	5
4.	When my boss or instructor praises my work, I often feel unworthy.	1	2	3	4	5
5.	I like competitive sports and games.	5	4	3	2	1
6.	I have gotten this far in school largely through luck.	1	2	3	4	5
7.	I like receiving praise for a job well done.	5	4	3	2	1
8.	I like to stay in the background on group projects.	1	2	3	4	5
9.	When a project or job is going well, I often feel I will do something to mess things up.	1	2	3	4	5
10.	I think I have a "winning attitude" in my approach to new assignments.	5	4	3	2	1

Dual-Career Problems

Related to the problems facing women in management is the problem of *dual careers*. It is estimated that over 60 percent of all American couples have dual careers outside the home.[25] As a result, each morning during the week, both husband and wife must leave the house for the busy day ahead. Dual careers pose special problems both for the couple and for the companies that employ them. For example, what happens if the husband or wife receives a good job offer in a different geographic region? What happens to the spouse? Similarly, what does a company do if it wants to transfer a manager somewhere, but the manager has an employed spouse? Relocation presents serious problems for everyone concerned.

In addition, what happens to the children of a dual career family? In a traditional family, it was the wife who remained at home with the children. But if she is at work, what happens? Child care can be expensive and in many cases is simply not available. One solution here is what has been called the "Mommy track." And a more recent phenomenon is referred to as the "Daddy track."

IN PRACTICE
Mommy Track, Daddy Track

First there was the Mommy track, the precarious balance that career-oriented women had to make between simultaneously being mothers and managers. A Mommy track represents a situation in which companies provide two different career paths for women: a direct line for those who want to work full time and climb the career ladder steadily, and a Mommy track for those who want to take time off on the way up for family concerns. Although controversial, this concept has gained popularity among companies attempting to accommodate diversity in the workplace.

Now comes the Daddy track, or the male equivalent. Here, male employees are offered an opportunity to take time off from work to help in child rearing. In both cases, the fundamental issue is the same: how does an employee balance the needs of a family with the needs of a career? Children clearly take time and represent a major responsibility. Hence, traditionally, a person had to sacrifice his or her career in support of the family.

Today, many things have changed. First of all, many working women are single parents who could not enjoy the luxury of staying home even if they wanted to. In addition, many women—married or not—simply do not want to let their education and training go to waste; they want to keep their jobs, either because of a career orientation or economic necessity. And, finally, more men today want to assume a more active role in raising their children. As a result, a growing number of men and women are finding innovative ways to have both families and career, and many corporations are beginning to help.

Companies have available to them a number of alternatives in support of valued employees with children. Many companies subsidize (or actually operate) day care centers. Beyond this, some firms, such as Arthur Andersen, offer *alternative career paths*—essentially, a career path for part-time employees. When they wish to, these employees can convert to full-time career paths. Other companies, such as IBM, offer extended leaves of absence (up to three years) to both male and female employees with young children. Still other companies offer flexible work schedules, job sharing, and even telecommuting (see Chapter 9). A few companies have begun offering work-family stress management seminars. Companies today realize that it is increasingly difficult to find and retain highly trained employees. As such, they have taken up the challenge of finding ways to accommodate family needs for both men and women who want to continue to contribute to corporate performance.[26]

PULLING IT ALL TOGETHER

Organizations cannot afford to waste any resources and therefore must design effective career systems that provide the maximum opportunity for the use of human resources and for the development of future talent. Likewise, individuals by understanding the typical career stages and taking proactive steps to evaluate a firm's career system and carefully managing their own career choices can increase the probability of their reaching their full potential.

SUMMARY OF KEY POINTS

- A psychological contract is an employment relationship in which both parties (employee and employer) create mutual expectations of one another that govern the relationship.

- Two general strategies exist for securing employee participation in organizational activities: (1) a contract strategy, in which each party's obligations are clearly recognized; and (2) a mutual investment strategy, in which organizations seek to develop the maximum potential of each employee over the long term.

- Organizational entry refers to the manner in which a new employee moves from outside to inside the organization.

- The organizational choice process consists of (1) the relative attractiveness of an organization to an individual, (2) the amount of effort directed toward joining an organization, and (3) the actual choice of an organization.

- A realistic job preview attempts to provide prospective employees with accurate job information so they can make an informed choice.

- Socialization refers to a concerted effort by one's colleagues and the organization to exert subtle pressures in an effort to shape one's attitudes and behaviors.

- Socialization typically passes through three stages: (1) anticipatory socialization, (2) encounter, and (3) change and acquisition.

- Techniques of socialization include employee selection, training and development, mentoring and apprenticeship, debasement experiences, and trial and error.

- Individualization is the process by which individuals attempt either to shape the organization's environment so it meets their own needs or, at the very least, to resist succumbing to organizational control efforts. Common individualization tactics include rebellion, creative individualism, and conformity.

- A career is an individually perceived sequence of attitudes and behaviors associated with work-related experiences and activities over a person's life span.

- A career anchor is a force that causes people to pursue or remain with certain types of work.

- Career stages typically follow a sequence, including exploration, establishment, maintenance, and decline.

- Corporate efforts in career planning include career counseling, career pathing, career information systems, human resource planning, and training.

- A mentor is a senior person within the organization who assumes responsibility for the career development of a more junior person. Mentors serve a variety of functions focusing on both the career itself and the psychosocial aspects of life within an organization.

■ A glass ceiling refers to an invisible barrier that inhibits career progress of under represented groups within a company.

■ Among the challenges facing contemporary organizations is that of managing an increasingly diverse work force consisting of women, minorities, dual-career families, and so forth. This diversity requires new approaches to traditional management if a company is to adequately utilize its human resources.

KEY WORDS

alternative career path
anticipatory socialization
career
career anchor
career counseling
career information system
career pathing
career planning
career stage
contract strategy
debasement experiences
dual career

employment relationship
fear of failure
fear of success
glass ceiling
human resource planning
individualization
mentor
mutual investment strategy
organizational entry
psychological contract
realistic job preview
socialization

QUESTIONS FOR DISCUSSION

1. What major factors influence a person's choice of an organization? In general, how accurate is the information people have in making this choice?
2. How do realistic job previews differ from traditional ones? What are some of the advantages and disadvantages of RJPs?
3. What is a psychological contract? How does it work?
4. Describe the typical career stages through which most employees pass. How might exceptions to this typical path occur?
5. How do socialization processes work in organizations?
6. What are some of the techniques used to socialize employees?
7. Describe the process of individualization. How do employees attempt to individualize their jobs?
8. Describe the problem facing organizations in terms of employee diversity. What can organizations do to take advantage of this diversity?
9. Discuss the special problems faced by women managers as they attempt to move up the career ladder. What kind of activities or actions might make their progression easier?

NOTES

1. F. Swoboda, "A New Trend in Employment Strategy," *Los Angeles Times,* October 4, 1989, p. IV–10; L. W. Porter, A. Tsui, and J. Pearce, "Employee-Organizational Relationships: An Inducement-Contribution Approach," working paper, Graduate School of Management, University of California, Irvine, November 1989; J. Pfeffer

and J. Baron, "Taking Workers Back Out: Recent Trends in the Structure of Employment," in L. Cummings and B. Staw, eds., *Research in Organizational Behavior* (Greenwich, Conn.: JAI Press, 1988), pp. 257–303.

2. Porter et al., ibid.; R. Mowday, L. Porter, and R. Steers. *Individual-Organizational Linkages: The Psychology of Employee Commitment, Absenteeism, and Turnover.* New York: Academic Press, 1982.

3. Porter et al., op. cit.

4. S. Premack and J. Wanous, "A Meta-Analysis of Realistic Job Preview Experiments," *Journal of Applied Psychology,* November 1985, pp. 706–719.

5. E. Schein, *Career Dynamics: Matching Individual and Organizational Needs* (Reading, Mass.: Addison-Wesley, 1978).

6. V. Vroom, "Organizational Choice: A Study of Pre- and Post-Decision Processes," *Organizational Behavior and Human Performance,* 1966, pp. 212–225; E. E. Lawler, *Motivation in Work Organizations* (Monterey, Calif.: Brooks/Cole, 1973).

7. Ibid.

8. Ibid.

9. Premack and Wanous, op. cit.

10. Ibid.

11. Excerpted from Dale Buss, "Job Tryouts Without Pay Get More Testing in U.S. Auto Plants," *Wall Street Journal,* January 10, 1985, p. 31.

12. Schein, op. cit., p. 2.

13. Ibid; D. Feldman, *Managing Careers in Organizations* (Glenview, Ill.: Scott, Foresman, 1988), Chapter 5.

14. Schein, op. cit.

15. D. Hall, *Careers in Organizations* (Glenview, Ill.: Scott, Foresman, 1976), p. 4.

16. Schein, op. cit., p. 133.

17. M. Brauchli, "Japanese Companies Keep Employees Together—Even the Dearly Departed," *Wall Street Journal,* July 10, 1989, p. B–1.

18. K. Kram, *Mentoring at Work: Developmental Relationships in Organizational Life* (Glenview, Ill.: Scott, Foresman, 1985).

19. Ibid.

20. L. Wynter, "A New Push to Break the Glass Ceiling," *Wall Street Journal,* November 15, 1989, p. B–1.

21. C. Trost, "Firms Heed Women Employees' Needs," *Wall Street Journal,* November 22, 1989, p. B–1.

22. Women Employed Institute, Occupational *Segregation: Understanding the Economic Crisis for Women* (Chicago, 1988).

23. A. Morrison, R. White, and E. VanVelsor, *Breaking the Glass Ceiling* (Reading, Mass.: Addison-Wesley, 1987).

24. Ibid.

25. U. Sakaran, *Dual-Career Families* (San Francisco: Jossey-Bass, 1986).

26. J. Solomon, "Swartz of Mommy Track Notoriety Prods Firms to Address Women's Needs," *Wall Street Journal,* September 11, 1989, p. A-13; E. Ehrlich, "The Mommy Track," *Business Week,* March 20, 1989, pp. 126–134; J. Schachter, "The Daddy Track," *Los Angeles Times Magazine,* October 1, 1989, pp. 7–16.

EXPERIENTIAL EXERCISE 18

Developing Management Potential

A large multinational corporation does extensive business in the Middle East. Company policy requires that middle management employees spend time in one of the overseas offices as part of their career progression. The rationale for this is that to move into top management, managers need experience in dealing with foreign clients, because this aspect of corporate operations contributes over 45 percent of sales and 50 percent of profits. Thus, the path to top management is through the foreign office. The company's clients come from a society where women are treated differently than men, especially in business transactions. They say that each gender has "different roles in society" and that these roles should not be confused. Consequently, the company has not transferred any of its women managers to positions of authority in its foreign operations for fear of losing business. However, the company has attempted to utilize women in domestic operations. It has even initiated an in-house training program for women managers. Even so, to date, no women have advanced into senior management.

On the basis of this dilemma, do the following two-part exercise.

Step 1.   Two groups of about five persons each should be selected from the class. Group 1 is assigned to represent the company in the above case and is responsible for ensuring the continued success of the business, although it cannot ignore the legitimate needs of all its employees. Group 2 is assigned to represent a group of women managers within the company that is concerned about the lack of female executives yet cannot ignore the economic goals of the company. Group 1 and Group 2 will each present an analysis of the case from the assigned perspective. Each group should propose a solution to the conflict, again keeping in mind its own assigned orientation.

Step 2.   Once the two proposed solutions have been presented, Group 1 and Group 2 will negotiate with one another to attempt to reach an acceptable compromise solution that best meets the conflicting goals of the parties involved. The remainder of the class will serve as a panel of judges to determine whether a fair compromise has been reached.

MANAGEMENT DILEMMA 18

Petersen Electronics

Petersen Electronics was founded almost thirty years ago by Benjamin Petersen as a consumer electronics firm. Over the years, the company grew into a successful manufacturer and sales organization, reaching $200 million in sales several years ago. During the past few years, however, growth has been somewhat stagnant.

While the last calendar year was a profitable one, Petersen worries about the long-run stability and potential of his company. In addition, Petersen, now 61, has a second problem: he is approaching retirement age and is unsure of who should take over the management of the company. As he reflects on this dilemma, he is particularly sensitive to the conflicts between some of his highly competent but impatient younger managers, who view some of the older managers as "dead wood," and some of his more experienced managers who view the younger managers as being "unseasoned" and too inexperienced to assume major managerial responsibilities. Many of the younger managers are eager to get ahead and feel that some of the older managers stand in their way, while several older managers are concerned about the lack of respect they receive from the junior members of the firm for their knowledge and their many yeas of real-life work experience.

As Petersen considers his dilemma, three key managers seem to be at the heart of the problem. These include George Briggs, 53, vice president for marketing; Thomas Evans, 34, national sales manager, who reports to Briggs; and Victor Perkins, 39, vice president for personnel.

Petersen's View of the Predicament

"When we started, a handful of people worked very hard and very closely to build something bigger than any of us. One of these people was George Briggs. George has been with me from the start, as have almost all of my vice-presidents and many of my key department heads.

"For the first five years, I did almost all the inventing and engineering work. Tom Carroll ran the plant and George Briggs knocked on doors and sold dreams as well as products for the company.

"As the company grew, we added people, and Briggs slowly worked his way up the sales organization. Eight years ago, when our vice-president of marketing retired, I put George in the job. He has market research, product management, sales, service, and the field sales force (reporting through a national sales manager) under him, and he has really done a first-rate job all around.

"About ten years ago we began bringing in more bright young engineers and MBAs and moved them along as fast as we could. Turnover has been high and we have had some friction between our young Turks and the old guard.

"When business slowed in the early seventies, we also had a lot of competition among the newcomers. Those who stayed have continued to move up, and a few are now in or ready for top jobs. One of the best of this group is Tom Evans. He started with us nine years ago in the sales service area. Later, he spent three years in product management.

"George Briggs got him to move from head of the sales service department to assistant product manager. After one year, George Briggs named him manager of the product management group, and two years later, when the national sales manager retired, George named Evans to the post.

"That move both surprised and pleased me. I felt that Evans would make a good sales manager despite the fact that he had had little direct sales experience. I was afraid, however, that George would not want someone in that job who hadn't had years of field experience.

"I was even more surprised, though, when six months later (a month ago) George told me he was afraid Evans wasn't working out, and asked if I might be able to find a spot for him in the corporate personnel department. While I'm sure our recent upturn in sales is not solely Evans's doing, he certainly seems to be one of the keys. Despite his inexperience, he seems to have the field sales organization behind him. He spends much of his time traveling with them, and from what I hear he has built a great team spirit.

"Despite this, George Briggs claims that he is in over his head and that it is just a matter of time before his inexperience gets him in trouble. I can't understand why George is so adamant. It's clearly not a personality clash, since they have always gotten along well in the past. In many ways, Briggs has been Evans's greatest booster until recently.

"Since George is going to need a replacement someday, I was hoping it would be Evans. If George doesn't retire before we have to move Evans again or lose him, I'd consider moving Evans to another area.

"When we were growing faster, I didn't worry about a new challenge opening up for our aggressive young managers—there were always new divisions, new lines—something to keep them stimulated and satisfied with their progress. Now I have less flexibility—my top people are several years from retirement. And yet I have some younger ones—like Evans, whom I would hate to lose—always pushing and expecting promotion.

"Evans is a good example of this; I could move him, but there are not that many *real* opportunities. He could go to personnel or engineering or even finance. Evans has the makings of a really fine general manager. But I'd hate to move him now. He really isn't ready for another shift—although he will be in a few years—and despite what George claims, I think he is stimulating teamwork and commitment in the sales organization as a result of his style.

"Finally, while I don't want to appear unduly critical of Briggs, I'm not sure he could get the job done in these competitive times without a bright young person like Evans to help him."

Briggs's Account of the Situation

"Before I say anything else, let me assure you there is nothing personal in my criticism of Evans.

"I like him. I have always liked him. I've done more for him than anyone else in the company. I've tried to coach him and bring him along just like a son.

"But the simple truth is that he's in way over his head and showing a side of his personality I've never seen before. I brought him along through sales service and product management and he was always eager to learn. While I couldn't give him a lot of help in those areas (frankly, there are aspects of them I don't yet fully understand), I still tried, and he paid attention and learned from others as well.

"The job of national sales manager, however, is a different story. In the other jobs Evans had—staff jobs—there was always time to consult, to consider, to get more data. In sales, however, all this participative stuff he uses takes too long. The national sales manager has to be able to make quick, intuitive decisions. What's more, like the captain of a ship, he has to inspire confidence in those below him. If the going gets rough, the only thing that keeps the sailors and junior officers from panicking is confidence in the skipper. I've been there and I know.

"Right now, with orders coming in strong, he can get away with all of his meetings and indecisiveness. The people in the field really like him and are trying to keep him out of trouble. In addition, I have been putting in 60 to 70 hours a week trying to do my job and also make sure he doesn't make any serious mistakes.

"I know he is feeling the pressure, too. Despite the fact that he has been his usual cheery self with others, when I call him in to question a decision he has made or is about to make, he gets very defensive. He was never that way with me before.

"I may have lost a little feel for what's going on in the field over the years, but I suspect I still know more about the customers and our sales people than Tom Evans will ever know. I've tried for the past seven months to get him to relax and let the old man help him, but it's no use. I'm convinced he's just not cut out for the job, and before we ruin him I want to transfer him somewhere else. He would probably make a fine personnel director someday. He's a very popular guy who seems genuinely interested in people and in helping them.

"I have talked with Ben Petersen about the move, and he has been stalling me. I understand his position. We have a lot of young comers like Evans in the company, and Ben has to worry about all of them. He told me that if anyone can bring Evans along I can, and he asked me to give it another try. I have, and things are getting worse.

"I hate to admit I made a mistake with Evans, but I plan on seeing Ben about this again tomorrow. We just can't keep putting it off. I'm sure he'll see it my way, and as soon as he approves the transfer, I'll have a heart-to-heart talk with Tom."

Evans's Side of the Story

"This has been a very hectic but rewarding period for me. I've never worked as hard in my life as I have during the last six months, but it's paying off. I'm learning more about sales each day, and more important, I'm building a first-rate sales team. My people are really enjoying the chance to share ideas and support each other.

"At first, particularly with our markets improving, it was hard to convince them to take time to meet with me and their subordinates. Gradually they have come to accept these sessions as an investment in team building. According to them, we've come up with more good ideas and ways to help each other than ever before.

"Fortunately, I also have experience in product management and sales service. Someday I hope to bring representatives from this department and market research into the meeting with regional and branch people, but that will take time. This kind of direct coordination and interaction doesn't fit with the thinking of some of the old-timers. I ran into objections when I tried this while I was working in the other departments.

"But I'm certain that in a year or so I'll be able to show, by results, that we should have some direct contact across department levels.

"My boss, George Briggs, will be one of the ones I will have to convince. He comes from the old school and is slow to give up what he knows used to work well.

"George likes me, though, and has given me a tremendous amount of help in the past. I was amazed when he told me he was giving me this job. Frankly, I didn't think I was ready yet, but he assured me I could handle it. I've gotten a big promotion every few years and I really like that—being challenged to learn new skills and getting more responsibility. I guess I have a real future here, although George won't be retiring for some years and I've gone as high as I can go until then.

"George is a very demanding person, but extremely fair, and he is always trying to help. I only hope I can justify the confidence he has shown in me. He stuck his neck out by giving me this chance, and I'm going to do all I can to succeed.

"Recently, we have had a few run-ins. George Briggs works harder than anyone else around here, and perhaps the pressure of the last few years is getting to him. I wish he'd take a vacation this year and get away for a month or more and just relax. He hasn't taken more than a week off in the nine years I've been here, and for the last two years he hasn't taken any vacation.

"I can see the strain is taking its toll. Recently he has been on my back for all kinds of little things. He always was a worrier, but lately he has been testing me on numerous small issues. He keeps throwing out suggestions or second-guessing me on things that I've spent weeks working on with the field people.

"I try to assure him I'll be all right, and to please help me where I need it with the finance and production people who've had a tough time keeping up with our sales organization. It has been rough lately, but I'm sure it will work out. Sooner or later George will accept the fact that while I will never be able to run things the way he did, I can still get the job done for him."

Perkins's Opinions

"I feel that George Briggs is threatened by Evans's seeming success with the field sales people. I don't think he realizes it, but he is probably jealous of the speed with which Tom has taken charge. In all likelihood, he didn't expect Tom to be able to handle the field people as well as he has, as fast as he has.

"When George put Tom on the job, I have a feeling that he was looking forward to having him need much more help and advice from the old skipper. Tom does need help and advice, but he is getting most of what George would offer from his own subordinates and his peers. As a result, he has created a real team spirit below and around him, but he has upset George in the process.

"George not only has trouble seeing Tom depend so much on his subordinates, I feel that he resents Tom's unwillingness to let him show him how he used to run the sales force.

"I may be wrong about this, of course. I am sure that George honestly believes that Tom's style will get him in trouble sooner or later. George is no doddering old fool who has to relive his past success in lower-level jobs. In the past, I'm told, he has shown real insight and interest in the big-picture aspects of the company.

"The trouble is he knows he was an outstanding sales manager, but I am not sure he has the same confidence in his ability as vice-president. I have seen this time and again, particularly in recent years. When a person begins to doubt his future, he sometimes drops back and begins to protect his past. With more competition from younger subordinates and the new methods that they often bring in, many of our experienced people find that doing their job the way they used to just isn't good enough anymore.

"Some reach out and seek new responsibilities to prove their worth. Others, however, return to the things they used to excel in and try to show that theirs is still the best way to do things. They don't even seem to realize that this puts them in direct competition with their subordinates.

"What do we do about this? I wish I knew! At lower levels, where you have more room to shift people around, you have more options. When the company is growing rapidly, the problem often takes care of itself.

"In this case, I am not sure what I will recommend if Ben Petersen asks my advice. Moving Tom to personnel at this time not only won't help me (I really don't have a spot for him), but it won't help Briggs or Evans either. Moving Evans now would be wasteful of the time and effort we've invested in his development. It may also reverse some important trends Tom has begun in team building within the sales force.

"If Briggs were seven or eight years older, we could wait it out. If the company were growing faster, we might be able to shift people. As things stand, however, I see only one approach as a possibility. And I'm not entirely sure it will work.

"I would recommend that we get busy refocusing Briggs's attention on the vice-president's job and get him to see that there is where he has to put his time and efforts. Perhaps the best thing would be to send him to one of the longer programs for senior executives. Don't forget he is a very bright and experienced person who still has a great deal to offer the company if we can figure out how to help him."

Petersen has agreed to talk with Briggs about Evans tomorrow afternoon. As he thinks about the situation, he wonders what he can do that would be best for the company and everyone concerned.

1. Why do you think the impasse between Briggs and Evans occurred?
2. Should Petersen go along with Briggs's recommendation that Evans be transferred to Personnel? Or should Briggs be sent to an executive program, as Perkins has suggested?
3. In your opinion, what would be the effect of bringing Briggs and Evans together to try to iron out their differences?
4. How would you handle the problem of good employees who have no opportunity to move up in the organization?

Chapter 19

Organizational Change and Development

The Management Challenge

- To know when some form of change within the organization is required or desirable.
- To minimize personal and organizational resistance to planned change efforts.
- To implement organizational innovations where needed by making structural, technological, and personnel changes.
- To understand the specific techniques used in planned organizational change.
- To work with others to bring about continual organizational renewal and development.

CLOSE UP Innovation and Change at Santa Fe Pacific

When we look for examples of a changing, dynamic environment, we tend to look to high-tech electronics firms or aerospace companies; few people think of railroads. Yet, at Santa Fe Pacific, Chairman Robert Krebs is leading a dramatic change effort to transform the traditional railroad into an effective competitor for the year 2000. At the heart of this transformation is a long-term effort to change the basic technology and the way employees think about the company and the industry.

Santa Fe Pacific was a conglomerate that included railroad operations, real estate, and mining operations among others. One of the first major changes made by Krebs was put the non-core operations (i.e., non-freight businesses) up for sale. Next he cut out 3,200 miles of track and kept 8,000 of the most profitable miles. To get closer to his customers, Krebs also eliminated three layers of management. Although these cuts reduced costs, they did nothing to increase revenues. "We needed a product to sell," remarked Krebs. He made a innovative move by linking up with Hunt Transport. Hunt would haul products on its trucks to Santa Fe, which would carry them cross-country. At the other end, Hunt truck would deliver the products right to the final customer. Krebs won Hunt's support by demonstrating that the two could deliver products faster and cheaper working together than either could working alone. This change required a fundamental adjustment in how employees in both businesses viewed themselves, each other, and the transportation industry.[1]

As seen in the example of Robert Krebs at Santa Fe Pacific, the ability to adapt successfully to a changing environment is one of the most important characteristics of effective managers. Such adaptation is not easy, in view of the often conflicting demands of employees and the complex environment facing organizations. Moreover, organizational change must not be random or initiated merely for the sake of change; managers must balance the need for adaptation and innovation with the equally important need for stability and continuity. As Kast and Rosenzweig note:

> Management is charged with the responsibility for maintaining a dynamic equilibrium by diagnosing situations and designing adjustments that are most appropriate for coping with current conditions. A dynamic equilibrium for an organization would include the following:
>
> 1. Enough stability to facilitate achievement of current goals.
> 2. Enough continuity to ensure orderly change in either ends or means.
> 3. Enough adaptability to react appropriately to external opportunities and demands as well as changing internal conditions.
> 4. Enough innovativeness to allow the organization to be proactive (initiate changes) when conditions warrant.[2]

We will conclude this book by examining the subject of change and development in organizations. First we look at the change process in organizations. Included here are several reasons why change is necessary, as well as several reasons why change is often resisted. Next, we consider several change and development mechanisms commonly used in both large and small organizations. Throughout, our emphasis is on managing the change process in such a way that organizations exist in a state of continual renewal and effectiveness.

THE CHALLENGE OF ORGANIZATIONAL CHANGE

The need for organizational change becomes apparent when managers sense that an organization's activities, goals, or values are deficient in some way. When there is a noticeable gap between what an organization is trying to do and what it actually is accomplishing, effective managers move quickly to take positive steps to reduce this disparity. For instance, 20 years ago many scientists and mathematicians—and a great number of college students— considered a slide rule an essential part of their toolkit. The introduction of inexpensive electronic pocket calculators made the slide rule a thing of the past, and one manufacturer of slide rules saw its sales drop 75 percent in just two years. The technology of calculating instruments changed radically, necessitating change in organizations that produced such instruments. Only companies that were aware of trends and began planning early for change were able to maintain their positions in the market. Other companies, such as the one above, either disappeared or moved on to other fields, leaving behind what had been a lucrative market.

The forces necessitating organizational change can be found both inside and outside organizations. If managers are to take a comprehensive view of innovation and adaptation, they must be aware of both types of influence and be able to allow for both in their actions.

External Forces for Change

There are a wide variety of external forces for organizational change that require managerial action (see Exhibit 19.1). These include (1) changes in economic or market conditions, such as a sudden decline in demand for a company's products; (2) changes in product or manufacturing technology, such as the discovery of a less expensive manufacturing process by a competitor; (3) changes in the legal or political situation, such as a new consumer protection law that affects current products or practices; and (4) changes in resource availability, such as an increase in cost or sudden unavailability of a major input, such as oil.

In fact, as Tom Peters noted, the very essence of the traditional business functions (e.g., manufacturing, marketing, finance, MIS [management information systems]) has changed dramatically in recent years, necessitating significant organizational change.[3] These changes are noted in Exhibit 19.2. The external forces for change are increasing, not decreasing, and organizations must respond and adapt if they hope to remain competitive in an increasingly turbulent global environment.

Internal Forces for Change

In addition to these external forces, several factors *within* an organization can also represent important forces for organizational change. These factors include (1) changes in the composition or personal goals of employees, such as the hiring of newer or younger employees with a work ethic different from that of employees with more seniority; (2) changes in job technology, such as the replacement of workers on craft-type jobs by automated

Exhibit 19.1
External and Internal Forces
for Organizational Change

External Forces for Change
- Economic and market changes
- Technological changes
- Legal political changes
- Resource availability changes

The Organization

Internal Forces for Change
- Employee goal changes
- Job technology changes
- Organizational structure changes
- Organizational climate changes
- Organizational goal changes

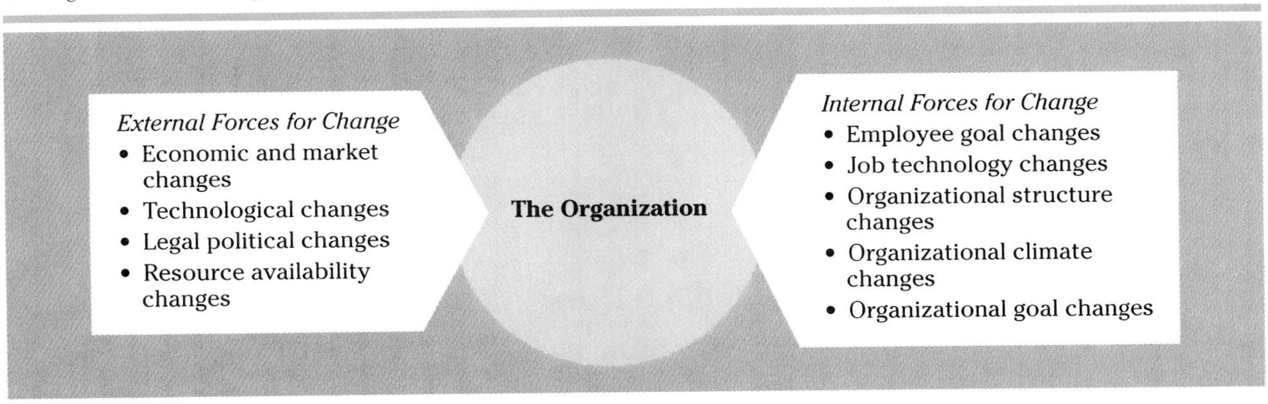

Function	From ...	To ...
Manufacturing	Emphasis on capital and automation; volume and low cost more important than people.	Emphasis on short production runs; fast product changeovers; people, quality, and responsiveness critical.
Marketing	Focus on mass markets and mass advertising.	Segmented markets; small-scale marketing; market creation.
Financial control	Centralized planning and control.	Decentralized, with finance people as members of business teams.
Management information systems	Centralized information control.	Decentralized, with commonly shared information available via computer networks.
Research and development	Centralized; emphasis on large-scale projects; innovation limited to related products and services.	Emphasis on new product creation; portfolio approach with widely decentralized research efforts.

Exhibit 19.2
Recent Changes in
Business Practices

equipment; (3) changes in organizational structure, such as new divisions necessitated by company growth; (4) changes in corporate culture, such as the creation of a climate of distrust, hostility, and insecurity as a result of mass layoffs; and (5) changes in organizational goals, as when goals change because management realizes its initial expectations were too high, too low, or misdirected for some reason.

These forces for change create unstable conditions within organizations and jeopardize goal-directed efforts. When stability and continuity are threatened, organizations must adapt their structure or behavior to ensure long-term growth and survival. Before we consider such change processes, however, we should discuss several reasons why change in organizational settings is often difficult to accomplish.

RESISTANCE TO CHANGE

An important lesson learned by most managers who introduce changes is that resistance to such efforts can be found throughout an organization. The reasons for resistance can be either personal or organizational. Some of the more prominent personal and organizational reasons for resistance are listed in Exhibit 19.3.

Individual Resistance

Employees may resist any effort to change or modify the status quo for a wide variety of reasons. For example, some employees may feel secure under existing conditions and fear that changes will destroy interpersonal relationships or perquisites that have developed through the years. Moreover, some employees may not fully understand the reasons behind a change or how it will affect their own situations; management often fails to adequately explain the reasons behind the change. Group norms may operate to resist any change in work procedures for fear that it will lead to higher output without commensurate rewards or compensation.

In addition, employees—including many managers—who do not identify with or understand the proposed changes often create *passive resistance* and drag their feet in implementation. This reaction often has been cited as a reason for the failure of affirmative action programs that attempt to increase minority or female hiring. Current non-minority employees often are simply indifferent (if not opposed) to the goals of affirmative action and, as a result, simply take no serious action to implement or support such efforts.

It is important to realize that many individual reasons for resisting change are not necessarily overt intentions to interfere with goal attainment. Instead, in many cases, such resistance often results from a fear of the consequences of change and a preference for the known over the unknown.

Organizational Resistance

The nature and character of the organization itself also can influence the extent to which change is accepted. For instance, the prevailing reward structure may favor existing behavior, as when an organization pays salespeople

Exhibit 19.3
Personal and Organizational
Reasons for Resistance
to Change

Personal Sources	**Organizational Sources**
1. Misunderstanding of purpose, mechanics, or consequences of change	1. Reward system may reinforce status quo
2. Failure to see need for change	2. Interdepartmental rivalry or conflict, leading to an unwillingness to cooperate
3. Fear of unknown	3. Sunk costs in past decisions and actions
4. Fear of loss of status, security, power, etc., resulting from change	4. Fear that change will upset current balance of power between groups and departments
5. Lack of indentification or involvement with change	5. Prevailing organizational climate
6. Habit	6. Poor choice of method of introducing change
7. Vested interests in status quo	7. Past history of unsuccessful change attempts and their consequences
8. Group norms and role prescriptions	8. Structural rigidity
9. Threat to existing social relationships	
10. Conflicting personal and organizational objectives	

solely on the basis of total sales and ignores effort and time spent in developing new customers. When various departments see each other as rivals, they may subvert cooperative efforts aimed at change for fear of encroachment on their territory. Managers may consider themselves bound by past decisions and actions because of large investments made previously in a particular product or technology, sometimes preferring to live with past decisions than to admit that a mistake was made or that conditions have changed. In addition, if previous organizational attempts at change were ill-conceived and unsuccessful, employees will lack confidence in the success of any new change efforts.

There are many other reasons for resistance to change, but the important point is that management must be aware of the various sources of this resistance and be able to minimize them. Managers must accurately assess the nature of and need for change and then lay the groundwork for the change by addressing the possible sources of resistance. The manner in which change is implemented is at least as important for success as the actual change itself. With this in mind, we are now in a position to examine the change process in organizations, with particular emphasis on the way planned change is introduced. First, however, consider an example of how organizational resistance continues to stifle the upward mobility of some women.

IN PRACTICE
Defending the Glass Ceiling

For all the talk about diversity, equal opportunity, and utilizing human resources, many American firms continue to resist putting women into positions of top management. As one women executive recently observed, "I don't sense a lot of progress has been made in terms of women moving up in business. That hasn't changed in a decade or more. It's the power structure that doesn't allow women entry." In fact, a quick look at the statistics will reveal that while women make up 46 percent of the total labor force and 41 percent of the lower managerial ranks, they constitute barely 3 percent of senior executives in the U.S.[4]

Why is this? Recent studies suggest a clear gender-related bias in some companies. Overt discrimination clearly exists. However, in other cases, this discrimination may be more subtle. In fact, it may not even be understood by the male exectives keeping women out. The fact is, some male executives either consciously or unconsciously are uncomfortable seeing women assume certain roles or behave in certain ways. While they may agree with equal opportunity intellectually, they often disagree emotionally. In fact, we frequently see an "It's OK for other companies, but not in mine" attitude when the subject of women executives arises. People are not comfortable with change.

Such attitudes keep many highly qualified women from assuming executive roles. In fact, there is a recent trend for gifted women executives to leave Corporate America and start their own companies. Or, as one women put it, "If you can't join 'em, beat 'em!"

PLANNED CHANGE IN ORGANIZATIONS

The ideal organizational change process represents a series of fairly distinct, sequential steps leading from the recognition of the problem to the introduction and execution of the change strategy. Although actual change may be far more complex, it is still possible to show, on a general level, some of the more important steps in the process. The steps in a simplified change process are represented in Exhibit 19.4.

As shown in the exhibit, performance gaps initially emerge because of changes in the environment, structure, technology, or membership of an organization (see box 1). These gaps may take the form of a loss of sales revenue, reduced productivity, or increased absenteeism and turnover. Once a manager recognizes such gaps (box 2), he or she can try to create a climate that is conducive to change (box 3). If sufficient time and effort are invested at the outset in eliminating the causes for resistance, a more open approach to the change process can be taken. Next, a manager diagnoses the extent of the problem (box 4).

On the basis of this analysis, he or she makes recommendations for appropriate adjustments to remedy the situation and eliminate or reduce the performance gaps (box 5). After the implications, costs, and benefits of the alternatives are considered, a decision on a particular change strategy is made and implemented (boxes 6 and 7). Once implementation is complete, the manager can assess how well the strategy reduced the performance gap (box 8). The manager then can take steps to reinforce and maintain the new program as long as it serves the needs of the organization, its members, and its stakeholders.

To see how this process works, consider the following true example. For 20 years, Bendix specialized in designing and manufacturing valves and gauges for aerospace projects. Most of its income came from government contracts. As government funds became scarce, however, the laboratory was

Exhibit 19.4
Basic Change Processes
in Organizations

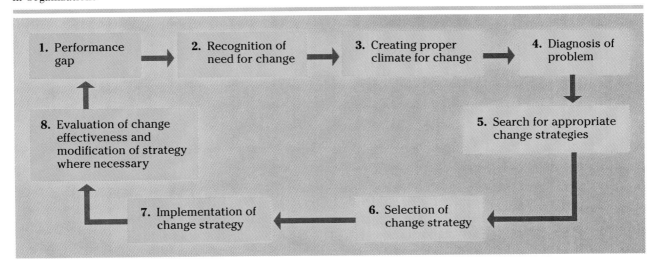

faced with a performance gap. Because it could see no further contracts coming from the government, management recognized the need for change and began laying the groundwork for a shift from aerospace engineering. After diagnosing the situation, management concluded that with minimal organizational disturbance the laboratory's technical expertise could be applied to hardware problems in the automotive industry.

Thus, management shifted the laboratory's goals to providing precision valves and gauges for automobiles instead of space vehicles. Assessment of the change revealed that the process had been carried out with minimal loss of personnel and that the laboratory had sufficient revenues to continue operations in an area in which it had ample expertise. The organization responded to environmental changes by adapting its goals to maintain stability and continuity, thereby enhancing its chances for survival, growth, and development.

STRATEGIES FOR PLANNED CHANGE

The success or failure of change rests not only on accurate identification of the problem and successful reduction of resistance to change but also on the appropriateness of the selected strategy for implementing the change. Understanding the problem is not enough; nor is having employees who are willing to change. Managers must make the right selection among a wide variety of strategies of change. At least three general *strategies* of planned change can be identified. These three approaches differ in their primary target of change and include efforts to change organizational structure, organizational technology, and the employees themselves. Moreover, as noted long ago by Leavitt, these three key approaches interact with more general organizational activities to create conditions that enable organizations to be more effective (see Exhibit 19.5).[5] We will consider each of these three approaches briefly.

Structural Approaches to Change

Changes in an organization's structure can take several forms (see Chapters 10 and 11 for a general discussion of organization structure). Some of the more common techniques include the following:

- Making changes in the design of work to permit more specialization or enrichment.
- Clarifying the job descriptions and role expectations.
- Altering the basis of departmentalization (changing from a functional organization to a department system based on products, for example).
- Increasing or decreasing the span of control and, therefore, the height of the hierarchy.

Exhibit 19.5
Interdependence of
Three Strategies for
Organizational Change

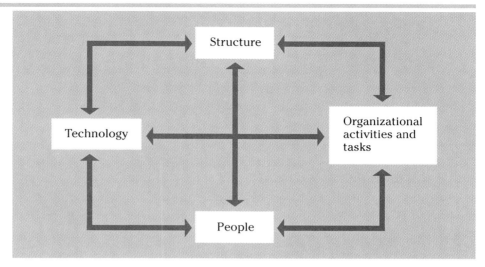

Source: H. J. Leavitt, "Applied Organization Change in Industry: Structural, Technical, and Human Approaches," in W. W. Cooper, H. J. Leavitt, and J. W. Shelly, eds., *New Perspectives in Organization Research* (New York: Wiley, 1964), p. 56. Copyright © 1964 by John Wiley & Sons, Inc. Reprinted by permission.

■ Modifying the organization manual and its description of policies and procedures.

■ Clarifying coordination mechanisms, such as policies and procedures.

■ Changing the power structure (moving from a centralized to a decentralized pattern of authority, for example).

Structural changes are fairly common in organizations. A major purpose of structural change is to create conditions that facilitate and reward goal-directed efforts. For example, a matrix organization (discussed in Chapter 10) may be introduced in a situation in which divergent areas of expertise must be integrated and coordinated for a particular product or project, such as a space satellite. The underlying assumption of this approach is that behavior, performance, and effectiveness are largely determined by the way an organization or work group is structured. A case in point is the large and successful Dutch company of Philips.

IN PRACTICE
Structural Change At Philips

By any measure, Philips is an international success story. Its annual sales of $25 billion make it second only to Matsushita in world sales of consumer electronics. The company is widely known the world over, except in the United States, where its products are marketed under such names as Magnavox, Norelco, Sylvania, and Philco. And yet, Philips was not satisfied with its current level of performance.

Several issues troubled the company. First, although Philips had been innovative in developing new products (such as compact discs, VCRs, etc.), it had been slow to market them effectively. As a result, it had lost markets (most notably to the Japanese) that the company itself had developed. Moreover, its managers had never been seen as particularly aggressive when it came to sales and profits. It was sometimes described as a "gentlemanly company," where style and refinement were often more important than substance and results. And, finally, Philips had grown fat with layers of bureaucratic hierarchies that slowed decision making and action. As a result of these concerns, Philips decided, in 1989, to reorganize the company—to restructure it in such a way that it would become a more flexible, innovative, adaptive organization.

As part of this change, Philips management sold off businesses that did not fit its central strategies. The company decided to concentrate on four related product lines: lighting, consumer electronics, electronic components, and information technology. All four of these areas took advantage of Philips's technological and market strengths. Other businesses that were peripheral to this central expertise—such as defense contracting and home appliances—were eliminated. As a result, the company had a clearer focus for its chief businesses.

Added to this product realignment was a decision to increase managerial decentralization. Each product division became responsible for its own profits, and, as a result, accountability was shifted down to the lowest possible level. Together, these structural changes were designed to make Philips a more marketing-oriented company capable of competing effectively in a global environment.[6]

Technological Approaches to Change

A second general approach to planned change involves alterations in the prevailing *technology*. Research has shown consistently that when the nature of job technology—how we do our jobs—changes, the work environment also changes, although not necessarily for the better (see Chapter 9). Examples of technological approaches to change include the following:

■ Altering the techniques used for doing work in order to change worker-machine relations (this is known as *human factors engineering*).

■ Changing the equipment used in work—for example, by introducing robots or expert systems on an assembly line.

■ Modifying production methods, such as shifting from an assembly line method to an autonomous work group method.

■ Changing engineering processes, such as introducing microprocessors or computers into a product to replace more cumbersome or less reliable mechanical equipment.

The principal assumption underlying technological change is that improved technology or work methods can lead to more efficient operations, increased productivity, and improved working conditions, perhaps through the elimination of more tedious tasks. Consider, however, the introduction of word processors in offices. Many managers were quick to see the potential of word processors. Such computers would allow typists and secretaries to become more efficient and productive, thereby saving the company money and, presumably, offsetting the cost of the equipment. Unfortunately, in many situations no one bothered to ask the typists or secretaries for their opinions of such changes. Because of this, results in many cases were less than expected. Misunderstandings arose over job responsibilities and job procedures, and negative attitudes often resulted. The lesson to be learned here is the importance of involving the employees concerned when attempting to introduce technological change.

IN PRACTICE
Technological Change at UPS

United Parcel Service is a $16.5 billion-a-year company with earnings of more than $765 million per year. This 85-year-old company is consistently ranked at the top of the transportation industry in *Fortune*'s survey of most admired. By any standard of comparison, it is a highly successful enterprise. Why? For one thing, UPS thrives on innovation and change. And for another, it is employee-owned, or, as one employee says, "it is owned by its managers and managed by its owners."

At the heart of UPS's success is the notion that change is a constant. As one vice-president notes, "We like to think that we are constructively dissatisfied most of the time." One aspect of this constant change involves a continual search for ways to bring new technologies to the freight and package delivery service. For instance, when UPS decided to expand its international operations it entered the market with enthusiasm and invested large sums in equipment, personnel, and planes. This investment is starting to pay off. On the ground, UPS continues to experiment with new delivery vans, optical scanning devices for packages, and computerized clipboards that continually monitor the location of each package.

When a new technology works out, UPS seldom has trouble introducing it to its management team, because they share in company ownership and profits. Employee commitment is high, and turnover is low. Employees feel that management is concerned with the company as a whole, and, as a result of this mutual bond, change is far easier. In short, UPS has discovered the secret of making technology work for the company while the company works to capitalize on its technological edge.[7]

People-Centered Approaches to Change

The third approach to change focuses on *individuals*. Strategies aimed at changing people tend to emphasize improving employee skills, attitudes, or motivation. These approaches assume that behavior in organizations and, ultimately, organizational effectiveness are largely determined by the characteristics and actions of the members of the organization. If these people can be changed in some way, it is believed that they will work harder to achieve the organization's goals.

Individual change strategies take many forms, such as introducing personnel training programs in skills, communication effectiveness, decision making, and attitude motivation. They can also take the form of socialization efforts to develop a "company man" or "company woman" (see Chapter 18).

Most such strategies rely on a basic model of individual change that was first advanced by Kurt Lewin and later developed by Ed Schein.[8] The model consists of four basic steps, as shown in Exhibit 19.6:

1. *Desire for change.* Before change can occur, the individual must feel a need for it. This need can result from a perceived deficiency, actual dissatisfaction, or a desire for improvement.
2. *Unfreezing.* As Schein notes, unfreezing occurs when a person's equilibrium is sufficiently disturbed so he or she is motivated to attempt a new pattern of behavior. According to Schein, "This can be accomplished either by increasing the pressure to change or by reducing some of the threats or resistance to change."[9]
3. *Changing.* Changing involves the process by which a person is presented with a new pattern of behavior and adopts the pattern as his or her own. As Schein notes, "This process occurs basically by one of two mechanisms: *(a) identification*—the person learns new attitudes by identifying with and emulating some other person who holds those attitudes, or *(b) internalization*—the person learns new attitudes by being placed in a situation where new attitudes are demanded of him as a way of solving problems which confront him and which he cannot avoid."[10]
4. *Refreezing.* In refreezing, the changed attitudes are integrated into the individual's personality in such a way that they become part of his or her way of thinking.

Although this model is simple, it highlights the basic processes involved in attempts to change people. Managers who are aware of these processes stand a far greater chance of succeeding with planned change attempts than those who ignore the people involved.

You may be interested in your own propensity for or readiness to change. If so, complete Self-Assessment 19.1. Simply indicate the extent of your agreement with each statement. When you have finished, score the instrument according to the procedures outlined in Appendix B.

In conclusion, when one is considering these three approaches to organizational change, the choice of an appropriate technique depends on the nature and character of the problem, the goals of the change, the orientations of the people implementing the change, and the resources available. For instance, if poor communication is seen as a barrier to effective performance, management may decide to make structural changes, such as using a matrix design; this will change reporting procedures and lines of authority, fostering more interaction and exchanges of views and thereby improving communications. On the other hand, management may also simply institute communications training programs to improve both interpersonal

Exhibit 19.6
The Individual
Change Process

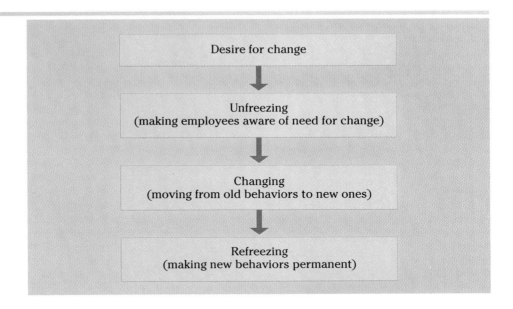

and communications skills. Both of these approaches address barriers to effective communication, though their techniques and underlying assumptions are quite different. The important point is that a primary responsibility of managers is to recognize the need for change in organizations, diagnose the nature and extent of the problems that create this need, and implement the most effective change strategy they can devise. Without such leadership, an organization's ability to respond to both internal and external threats to stability and continuity is greatly diminished, which reduces the organization's ability to operate effectively in the long run.

IN PRACTICE
Continual Self-Renewal at 3M Company

The 3M Company is often cited as one of America's best-managed and most innovative firms. The company employs 6,000 scientists and engineers and makes over 60,000 products. Each year, over 200 new products surface from its 435-acre campus-like headquarters in St. Paul, Minnesota. Annual revenues are in excess of $9 billion, and the company operates in 50 countries.

At the heart of 3M's success is its commitment to research and development. To maintain this commitment, the company must keep its professional staff current and motivated. Nothing ruins an R&D company faster than outmoded technology or outmoded engineers and scientists. At 3M, efforts are continually underway to foster a culture of self-renewal and innovation.

Each scientist and manager at the company is challenged to "keep current." This is done in many ways. For example, all researchers are encouraged to spend 15 percent of their time pursuing pet projects that may have a payoff

SELF-ASSESSMENT 19.1
How Receptive Are You to Change?

Instructions: For each of the items listed below, select the answer that best suits your degree of agreement or disagreement. When you are finished, add up your total points.

		Strongly Agree			Strongly Disagree	
1.	I continually like to try new things.	1	2	3	4	5
2.	I would prefer to have a job that forces me to learn new skills regularly	1	2	3	4	5
3.	I like things just the way they are in my life.	5	4	3	2	1
4.	Life to me is just one new adventure after another.	1	2	3	4	5
5.	For the past several years, I have known exactly what I wanted to do with my life.	5	4	3	2	1
6.	I like to keep all of my things in their proper place.	5	4	3	2	1
7.	My ideal job has clear, fixed requirements that I can count on.	5	4	3	2	1
8.	My friends often tell me that I am adventuresome.	1	2	3	4	5
9.	I see myself changing jobs and careers fairly often in my life.	1	2	3	4	5
10.	I get bored doing the same things over and over.	1	2	3	4	5

for the company in the future. This high-risk and costly strategy—referred to as "bootlegging"—has led to many of 3M's most profitable product innovations, including the popular Post-it™ notes that stick to almost anything. In addition, researchers are encouraged to team up with marketing managers to share information and stay close to the market. In fact, when 3M built its "second headquarters" outside Austin, Texas, it specifically designed the massive facility to "force" people from different parts of the organization to interact.

At 3M, people development is crucial. The company invests considerable sums in a wide variety of individual and organizational change efforts, all directed at maintaining a superior work force. As a result, the company's competitive edge has been maintained. Asked why 3M has remained so effective over several decades, the company president noted two factors: innovation and quality. "These are the tools for staying ahead in our increasingly competitive society."[11]

ORGANIZATION DEVELOPMENT

We have reviewed three general approaches to planned organizational change: changes to structure, technology, and people. These approaches are usually aimed at fairly specific goals within the organization, such as improving employees' achievement motivation through training or improving job efficiency through job redesign. A more integrated approach to change, however, focuses not on one aspect or problem within the organization but on long-term global change and development throughout the organization. *Organization development,* as we will see, is an ongoing and system-wide developmental approach. It seeks to improve both productivity and efficiency on the one hand and the quality of working life on the other.

The topic of organizational development is broad and includes many different and often conflicting approaches. Even so, the following definition of organization development is broad enough to encompass most of the different activities:

> [Organization development is] a long-range effort to improve an organization's problem-solving and renewal processes, particularly through a more effective and collaborative management or organization culture—with special emphasis on the culture of formal work teams—with the assistance of a change agent, or catalyst, and the use of the theory and technology of applied behavioral science, including action research.[12]

Several points emerge from this definition. First, organization development is a problem-solving process used to alleviate threats to organizational survival or well-being or to capitalize on a unique opportunity. Second, its goal is to help the organization renew itself and become more vital. Third, it stresses *collaborative management;* that is, change efforts involve the active participation of all affected parties. Fourth, major organization development efforts are attempts to change an organization's *culture* and *work climate.* Finally, a central aspect of many organization development efforts is *action research.* Action research is the process by which behavioral research findings are collected and then fed back to participants, who discuss the results and use them as a foundation for planned change. Thus, organization development is a mechanism for change that is highly participatory, broad in scope, and evolutionary in design. As such, it truly represents an integrative approach to planned organizational change.

Basic Assumptions of Organization Development

Any approach to change rests on certain assumptions and values espoused by its advocates. Some of the more general assumptions of organization development about what life in organizations should be like, how change should occur, and how individual employees, group relationships, and organizational relationships should work are discussed in the following sections.

Assumptions About Individuals.   Organization development advocates often assume that employees want and need personal growth and fulfillment on the job. They also assume that people generally can contribute more to the organization than they are typically encouraged or allowed to. In other words, organization development assumes that most people are "premotivated" to perform at high levels. Its purpose, then, is to develop a work environment that encourages this motivation and allows employees to realize their full potential within organizations.

Assumptions About Groups.   Organization development practitioners also hold several assumptions concerning the nature of group relations. In many organizations, for example, there is less interpersonal trust and mutual support among group members than is desirable for maximum effectiveness. Organization development holds that leadership responsibilities, instead of being concentrated in one person, can be more widely shared among group members. This emphasizes facilitating group activities and group cooperation; open communication is stressed as a means of securing the active participation of everyone and of rooting out potential problems or conflicts. Advocates also believe that developing an *esprit de corps* among group members will support positive feelings about each other and genuine interest in the welfare of group members.

Assumptions About Organizations.   The third set of assumptions underlying many organization development activities is that change in one part of an organization, such as the marketing department, will necessarily influence and be influenced by other parts, such as engineering or production. As we have said, organization development is a system-wide change effort. In addition, the members of an organization not only are involved in their own groups but also must interact with other groups—hence the emphasis on intergroup relations. Efforts to reduce conflict emphasize *non-zero-sum games;* that is, efforts are made to avoid situations in which someone wins and someone loses. Instead, a search is made for a solution to the conflict that will satisfy all parties. Finally, if organization development is to succeed, it must have the full and active support of top management. This last point cannot be emphasized enough.

Although these assumptions may vary somewhat across situations and organizations, the major thrust of organization development activities can succeed only in environments characterized largely by these values. Organization development is as much a philosophy of change as a technology of change. It assumes that people are open to change and that organizations and their managers are willing to change. Without this willingness, organization development attempts are doomed to failure.

The Organization Development Process

The basic change process used in organization development follows the steps shown earlier in Exhibit 19.4. As a change technology, however, it emphasizes several features not typically found in more focused or narrow efforts. Organization development as a process typically consists of seven rather distinct steps:

1. *Initial diagnosis.* At this stage, fundamental questions are asked: What is the basic problem? Can the problem be solved using organization development techniques?
2. *Data collection.* Data are collected through interviews and questionnaires to verify the initial diagnosis and suggest possible solutions.
3. *Feedback and confrontation.* The findings from the survey are fed back to the participants, discussed, and examined as they relate to the group. Priorities for change are identified.
4. *Planning and problem solving.* Problem-solving groups are established to tackle major problem areas and goals.
5. *Team building.* Conscious efforts are made to develop work groups into cohesive teams rather than isolated individuals who happen to work together.
6. *Intergroup development.* Efforts are made to build and solidify good working relationships among the various teams.
7. *Follow-up and evaluation.* Results are compared with initial goals, and steps are identified to ensure that resulting change sticks. Additional change goals are established when necessary to meet unexpected problems.

The final outcome of this process should be a more cohesive organization with highly integrated work teams, good intergroup relations, less conflict, and greater focus and consensus on organizational goals. Although the results are not always positive, organization development has in many situations contributed to substantial improvements in organizational function. It is because of this, perhaps, that most of the top Fortune 500 companies have adopted some form of organization development activities.

Approaches to Organization Development

Several approaches are available to people interested in organization development. These include survey feedback, process consultation, grid organization development, and team building.

Survey Feedback.   Survey feedback is a relatively straightforward technique in which employees are surveyed, using questionnaires or interviews, and the results are given back to them in an aggregate or summarized form. Next, the employees discuss the meaning of the results. Topics commonly surveyed include the general level of job satisfaction, perceptions of leadership styles, openness of communication, and conflict. As a result of these discussions, training-and-development activities are initiated to solve the problems the survey has identified. This process is shown in Exhibit 19.7.

Process Consultation.   In process consultation, an external agent observes a group at work, assessing such aspects as leadership styles, communication, conflict and cooperation, and decision-making processes. The change agent's observations, when shared with group members, serve as the bases for a discussion concerning ways to improve the situation. The change agent may discover, for example, that decisions are highly centralized—made by the general sales manager, perhaps—but that people far down in the hierarchy

Exhibit 19.7
The Survey
Feedback Process

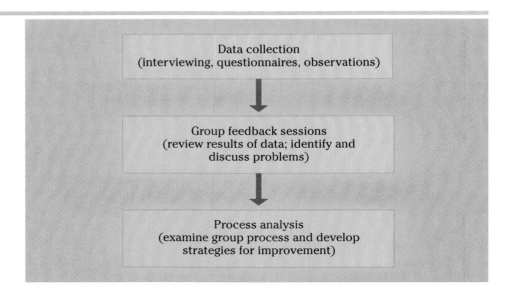

who are seldom consulted, such as sales representatives, have important information bearing on these decisions. As a result, useful information is ignored. Such a conclusion and possible remedies would then be considered.

Grid Organization Development.   An approach that has received considerable attention in recent years is Grid organizational development. This approach was developed by Blake and Mouton and represents one of the more comprehensive and systematic approaches to change.[13] The technique is based on Blake and Mouton's Managerial Grid, which suggests that two key outcome variables are important to organizations: a concern for people and a concern for production. The Grid, shown in Exhibit 19.8, identifies the possible combinations of these two concerns.

In the exhibit, concern for people is plotted on the vertical axis of the Grid, and concern for production is plotted on the horizontal axis. Five major intersections between these two concerns are shown, beginning with what is labeled a 1,1 management style, in which managers show little concern for either people or production. In 1,9 and 9,1 management styles, managers emphasize one concern at the expense of the other. Managers with a 5,5 style attempt to compromise and show sufficient attention to both. The ideal form—a 9,9 management style—emerges when managers are successful in developing highly committed, cohesive, and satisfied work teams that are dedicated to maximum production and organizational effectiveness.

Change agents help managers locate themselves on the Grid. Ideally, this self-evaluation will serve as a starting point for development of a 9,9 manager. The program through which such managers are developed consists of six steps:

■　*Phase 1: Training.* After top management has concluded that Grid organizational development may help solve the organization's problem, key managers attend a week-long seminar to learn the basic concepts of the

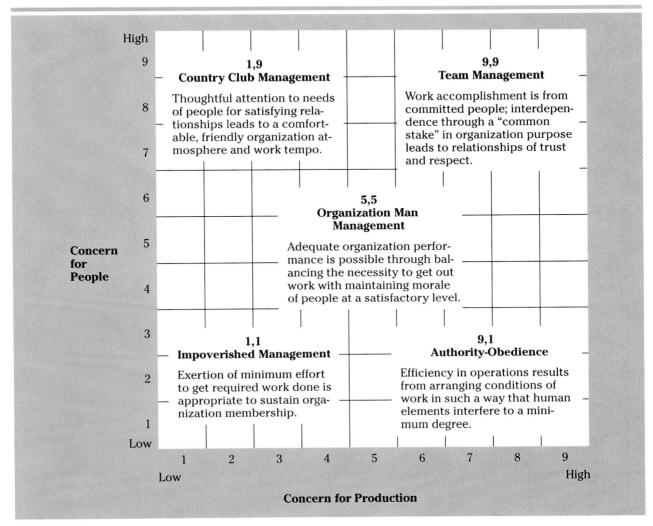

High

9 **1,9**
   Country Club Management
   Thoughtful attention to needs
   of people for satisfying relationships leads to a comfortable, friendly organization atmosphere and work tempo.

                                    9,9
                                    Team Management
                                    Work accomplishment is from
                                    committed people; interdepen-
                                    dence through a "common
                                    stake" in organization purpose
                                    leads to relationships of trust
                                    and respect.

6   **5,5**
            Organization Man
            Management
            Adequate organization perfor-
            mance is possible through bal-
            ancing the necessity to get out
            work with maintaining morale
            of people at a satisfactory level.

Concern
for
People

3 **1,1**
   Impoverished Management
   Exertion of minimum effort
   to get required work done is
   appropriate to sustain organization membership.

                                    9,1
                                    Authority-Obedience
                                    Efficiency in operations results
                                    from arranging conditions of
                                    work in such a way that human
                                    elements interfere to a mini-
                                    mum degree.

Low

Low   1   2   3   4   5   6   7   8   9   High

Concern for Production

Exhibit 19.8
The Managerial Grid®

Source: The Managerial Grid figure from *The Managerial Grid III: The Key to Leadership Excellence* by Robert R. Blake and Jane Srygley Mouton (Houston, Tex.: Gulf Publishing Company, 1985), p. 12. Copyright © 1985. Reproduced by permission.

program. They assess their own managerial styles and work to improve their communication, group problem-solving abilities, and team development skills. Following this seminar, each key manager returns to the organization and attempts to put the program into effect.

■ *Phase 2: Team development.* Managers and their subordinates work together to improve their interrelationship and to develop cohesive teams capable of operating on a 9,9 level.

■ *Phase 3: Intergroup development.* Efforts are made to reduce conflict and increase cooperation in intergroup relations. The goal is for the entire organization to work together and for individual members to help one another work toward organizational goals.

■ *Phase 4: Organizational goal setting.* Once intergroup cooperation is achieved, the organization as a whole can consider what changes are needed in long-term corporate goals. Active participation at all levels is encouraged in the attempt to define what the organization will or should look like in the future.

■ *Phase 5: Goal attainment.* Effort is directed toward making the ideal organization a real one. Concern focuses on removing obstacles to organizational objectives.

■ *Phase 6: Stabilization.* The entire program is evaluated to determine where success has been achieved and where more effort is needed. When necessary, new improvement goals are set to remedy past failures. Finally, the positive outcomes that have been achieved throughout the process are stabilized and secured.

Team Building.   A final approach to organization development that has received widespread attention and support is team building. In team building, the manager attempts to analyze the effectiveness of a work group and help it discover how to work more effectively as an integrated and cohesive team. Methods for team building include discussions with group members about possible barriers to cohesiveness; also included are behavioral techniques, such as sensitivity training, that increase awareness of how other people respond to an individual's behavior in a group setting. A practical approach to team building can be seen in the example of British Petroleum.

International Challenge

IN PRACTICE
Team Building at British Petroleum

When British Petroleum decided to launch a Brussels-based European Finance Center to serve their European offices, they realized the importance of cultural sensitivity training. After all, the new European Finance Center required that 40 people spanning 13 different nationalities work together as a team. Instead of being wary of and eliminating this diversity, BP chose to celebrate it!

Rob Ruijter, a Dutchman, was appointed team leader and manager of the European Finance Center. While he was excited by the uniqueness of this team and project, he also realized that this very uniqueness could lead to disaster. In order to become a close-knit team, each national associate needed to gain the trust and commitment of the others. A veteran of expatriate assignments, Ruijter knew that this diverse group of people needed some support.

Ruijter developed a two-day workshop to provide team members with an awareness of cultural differences and their impact on organizational structure and systems, management style, decision making, and interpersonal behavior. This event was held in Breda in the Netherlands and was based on two theories of human interaction.

The first theory was "red and blue" loop learning, developed by Indrei Ratui. This model suggests that in order to understand another culture, we must first understand our own. Each culture has established an unspoken mode of behavior that it takes for granted. Naturally, when people from different cultures using different frames of reference interact, there is potential for misunderstanding. If people were to compare an unfamiliar event against their own cultural frame of reference, they would gain insight into the differences and how to improve communication.

The second model concerned multicultural team-building. Each culture has a unique understanding of what a team is, how it works, and what are the roles of the leader and follower. For example, French executives consider the authority to make decisions as a right of office and rank. However, managers from the U.K., Scandinavia, and the Netherlands expect decisions to be made on a consultative group basis.

The focus of the workshop was to reveal these national assumptions and build instead what one American consultant, Gary Fontaine, describes as "an international microculture." Using group discussion, communication exercises, and guided negotiation, the team developed a set of guidelines by which they wanted to work. They called these "multi-culture action points."

BP's multicultural team-building workshop was a success in many ways. It brought members of the group together for the very first time. Individuals learned to be more tolerant. They became better listeners. They saw their differences in understanding a problem as a creative challenge. Team members also concluded that while nationals may approach a problem from different angles, they all reach the same point.[14]

A Guide to Successful Interventions

The success of organization development efforts is difficult to assess. Most of the research carried out to evaluate the effectiveness of such interventions has been done by organization development consultants, who have an obvious interest in positive results. Even so, organization development remains a popular form of change. Many managers feel that though imperfect, organization development represents one of the better approaches to planned change in organizations. Efforts can be made to enhance the likelihood of success in organization development interventions. French and Bell[15] have listed eleven such factors:

1. Recognize that the organization has problems.
2. Use an *external* change agent. Internal change agents usually lack necessary experience or expertise and typically have greater political problems in orchestrating serious change.
3. Elicit strong support from top managers for the organization development intervention efforts. Such support is necessary if the efforts are to succeed.
4. Make use of action research. Decisions should be guided by facts, not opinions.
5. Achieve a small success in some part of the organization to motivate employees to participate in the program. A small success indicates that the program can work.
6. Make sure that employees understand what organization development is and is not and that they are aware of why it is being used. In this way, apprehension and resistance to the unknown are reduced.

7. Ensure that change agents do not condescend to managers or employees.
8. Ensure that managers from the personnel department are actively involved. Internal expertise concerning an organization's human resources can be incorporated into the change efforts.
9. Begin to develop internal expertise in organization development. In this way the internal facilitators can assume responsibility from the external change agents in time and assure the continuity of the program.
10. Monitor the results continuously, and be sensitive to deviations from the program or to weakening support for the program.
11. Ensure that valid and reliable measures are taken before and after the intervention to provide an accurate indicator of actual change. Without such data, it becomes virtually impossible to determine whether the efforts were successful.

PULLING IT ALL TOGETHER

Organizational change generally requires that a felt need for change be either externally imposed or internally generated. Even when sufficient motivation for change exists, some resistance to change is nearly inevitable. Thus, successful change efforts require not only a correct analysis of the needed changes but also an identification and analysis of potential resistance to change and the design of an effective change strategy and implementation plan. Given the increasing volatility of the global environment of business, continual organizational change and development are likely to be the rule rather than the exception in the future.

SUMMARY OF KEY POINTS

■ Forces for change can be found both inside the organization and out. Internal forces for change can occur when there are changes in the composition or goals of the work force, job technology, organization structure, organizational climate or corporate culture, or organizational goals. External forces for change can occur when there is a change in economic or market conditions, product or manufacturing technology, legal or political climate, or resource availability.

■ Resistance to organizational change can arise from individual reasons (e.g., misunderstanding the purpose of the change, feeling threatened by the change) and organizational reasons (e.g., interdepartmental rivalry, costs sunk in past decisions).

■ Three types of planned change in organizations can be identified: (1) structural, (2) technological, and (3) people-centered. Each approach focuses on a different target or mechanism for change.

■ The individual or people-centered approach to change involves the process of unfreezing, changing, and refreezing individual attitudes and behaviors.

■ Organization development is an ongoing, systemwide developmental approach to change in which the change effort itself becomes institutionalized within the organization's corporate culture.

■ The organization development process involves initial diagnosis, data collection, feedback and confrontation, planning and problem solving, team building, intergroup development, and follow-up and evaluation.

■ Approaches to organization development include survey feedback, process consultation, team building, and Grid organization development.

■ Successful organizational change efforts typically attempt to recognize problems early in the process, use external change agents, have strong support from top management, and actively involve employees in the entire effort.

KEY WORDS

action research
collaborative management
freezing
Grid organization development
human factors engineering
individual change
non-zero-sum game
organization development
passive resistance
planned change

process consultation
refreezing
resistance to change
structural change
survey feedback
team building
technological change
unfreezing
zero-sum game

QUESTIONS FOR DISCUSSION

1. Describe several external and internal forces for change in organizations? How would such factors be expected to change across organizations?
2. What are some of the more important sources of resistance to change in organizations?
3. What are performance gaps? How do they emerge?
4. Outline a basic change process. What is the role of management at each stage of the process?
5. Distinguish a structural approach to change from a technological approach. Where would each approach be most effective?
6. What is meant by a "people approach" to change? How is it unique?
7. Define *unfreezing*.
8. What is organization development? How does it differ from the approaches described earlier?
9. Outline the organization development approach to change.
10. Define and provide examples of (1) survey feedback, (2) process consultation, and (3) team building.
11. Describe how Grid organization development works. Do you support this approach to organizational change?

NOTES

1. "The Great Train Turnaround," *Business Week,* November 2, 1992, pp. 56–57.
2. F. Kast and J. Rosenzweig, *Organization and Management* (New York: McGraw-Hill, 1974), pp. 574–575.
3. T. Peters, "World Turned Upside Down," *Academy of Management Executive,* 1987, *1,* pp. 231–241.
4. A. T. Segel, "Corporate Women," *Business Week,* June 8, 1992, pp. 74–83.
5. H. Leavitt, "Applied Organization Change in Industry," in W. Cooper, H. Leavitt, and M. Shelly, eds., *New Perspectives on Organization Research* (New York: Wiley, 1964).
6. R. van de Krol, "A Protected Giant Seeks the Bottom Line," *International Herald Tribune,* July 3, 1989, p. B–1.
7. K. Labich, "Big Changes at Big Brown," *Fortune,* January 18, 1988, pp. 56–64.
8. K. Lewin, "Forces Behind Food Habits and Methods of Change," Bulletin of the National Research Council #108, 1947, pp. 35–65; E. Schein, "Organizational Socialization and the Profession of Management," *Industrial Management Review,* 1968, pp. 1–16.
9. Schein, op. cit., p. 62.
10. Ibid.
11. "Keeping the Fires Lit Under Innovators," *Fortune,* March 28, 1988, p. 45.
12. W. French and C. Bell, *Organization Development* (Englewood Cliffs, N.J.: Prentice-Hall, 1973).
13. R. Blake and J. Mouton, *The Managerial Grid* (Houston: Gulf Publishing Company, 1985).
14. R. Neale and R. Mindel. "Rigging Up Multicultural Teamwork." *Personnel Management,* 24(1), pp. 36–39.
15. French and Bell, op. cit.

EXPERIENTIAL EXERCISE 19

Implementing Change

The purpose of this exercise is to learn more about how change is implemented.

As a Group

The class should be divided into groups of four to six persons. Each group will be responsible for designing a plan of action to implement a major change.

Your group has just been informed that your country has engaged in a conventional war that appears will last for more than one year. Government officials feel that it must get its citizens to reduce their consumption of traditional beef products and increase their consumption of non-traditional beef products such as cow's tongue in order to have sufficient supplies for the troops.

As a group, you should do the following (40 minutes):

1. Identify the groups of constituents who need to be involved in the change. What role should each group play in the change?
2. On the basis of the materials discussed in this chapter, develop a plan of action for implementing the change. How would you do it, and what timetable would you use?

3. What possible sources of resistance to the change can you identify? Why might each of these sources resist the change?
4. What steps would you take to minimize resistance to the change?

As a Class

When each group has finished, the class should convene as a whole and hear and compare the various plans of action. In comparing the plans, consider the following:

1. How similar are the various plans of action?
2. Are the plans realistic? What might make them more realistic?
3. What do you think are the chances that the plans can be successfully implemented within the prescribed time limit? Why?

MANAGEMENT DILEMMA 19

Sunflower Incorporated

Sunflower Incorporated is a large distribution company with over 5,000 employees and gross sales of over $550 million (1992). The company purchases salty snack foods and liquor and distributes them to independent retail stores throughout the United States and Canada. Salty snack foods include corn chips, potato chips, cheese curls, tortilla chips, and peanuts. The United States and Canada are divided into twenty-two regions, each with its own central warehouse, salespeople, finance department, and purchasing department. The company distributes national as well as local brands, and packages some items under private labels. Competition in this industry is intense. The demand for liquor has been declining, and competitors like Procter & Gamble and Frito-Lay develop new snack foods to gain market share from smaller companies like Sunflower. The head office encourages each region to be autonomous because of local tastes and practices. In the Northeast United States, for example, people consume a greater percentage of Canadian whisky and American bourbon, while in the West they consume more light liquors such as vodka, gin, and rum. Snack foods in the Southwest are often seasoned to reflect Mexican tastes.

Early in 1992, Sunflower began using a financial reporting system that compared sales, costs, and profits across company regions. Each region was a profit center, and top management was surprised to learn that profits varied widely. By the end of the year, the differences were so great that management decided some standardization was necessary. Managers believed that highly profitable regions were sometimes using lower-quality items, even seconds, to boost profit margins. This practice could hurt Sunflower's image. Other regions were facing cutthroat price competition to hold market share. National distributors such as Frito-Lay, Borden, Nabisco, and Procter & Gamble (Pringles) were pushing to increase market share by cutting prices and launching new products.

As these problems accumulated, Joe Steelman, president of Sunflower, decided to create a new position to monitor pricing and purchasing practices. Loretta Williams was hired from the finance department of a competing organization. Her new title was director of pricing and purchasing, and she reported to the vice-president of finance, Peter Langly. Langly gave Williams great latitude in organizing her job, and encouraged her to establish whatever rules and procedures were necessary. She was also encouraged to gather information from each region. Each region was notified of her appointment by an official memo sent to the 22 regional directors. A copy of the memo was posted on each warehouse bulletin board. The announcement was also made in the company newspaper.

After three weeks on the job, Williams decided that pricing and purchasing decisions should be standardized across regions. As a first step, she wanted the financial executive in each region to notify her of any change in local prices of more than 3 percent. She also decided that all new contracts for local purchases of more than $5,000 should be cleared through her office. (Approximately 60 percent of items distributed in the regions were purchased in large quantities and supplied from the home office. The other 40 percent were purchased and distributed within the region.) Williams believed that the only way to standardize operations was for each region to notify the home office in advance of any change in prices or purchases. She discussed the proposed policy with Langly. He agreed, so they submitted a formal proposal to the president and board of directors, who approved the plan. The changes represented a complicated shift in policy procedures, and Sunflower was moving into the peak holiday season, so Williams wanted to implement the new procedures right away. She decided to send a telex to the financial and purchasing executives in each region notifying them of the new procedures. The change would be inserted in all policy and procedure manuals throughout Sunflower within four months.

Williams showed a draft of the telex to Langly and invited his comments. Langly said the telex was a good idea but wondered if it was sufficient. The regions handled hundreds of items, and were used to decentralized decision making. Langly suggested that Williams ought to visit the regions and discuss purchasing and pricing policies with the executives. Williams refused, saying that such trips would be expensive and time-consuming. She had so many things to do at headquarters that trips were impossible. Langly also suggested waiting to implement the procedures until after the annual company meeting in three months, when Williams could meet the regional directors personally. Williams said that this would take too long, because the procedures would then not take effect until after the peak sales season. She believed the procedures were needed now. The telexes went out the next day.

During the next few days, replies came in from seven regions. The managers said they were in agreement with the telex, and said they would be happy to cooperate.

Eight weeks later, Williams had not received notices from any regions about local price or purchase changes. Other executives who had visited regional warehouses indicated to her that the regions were busy as usual. Regional executives seemed to be following usual procedures for that time of year. She telephoned one of the regional managers, and discovered that he did not know who she was, and had never heard of the position called director of pricing and purchasing. Besides, he said, "We have enough to worry about reaching profit goals without additional procedures from headquarters." Williams was chagrinned that her position and her suggested changes in procedure had no impact. She wondered whether field managers were disobedient or whether she should have used another communication strategy.

On the basis of this case, how would you respond to the following?

1. Using the model of planned organization change in the text, describe the incident in the case.
2. What type of change is being proposed? How would you implement this change?
3. Do you believe the innovation has been successful? If not, what should have been done?

Source: R. Daft, *Organization Theory and Design* (St. Paul: West Publishing, 1989), pp. 341–343. Copyright 1989 by West Publishing Company. All rights reserved. Reprinted by permission.

A

Scientific Method in Organizational Research

Students of management often complain about "theoretical" or "abstract" approaches to a subject; they argue instead in favor of "relevant" and "applied" approaches. The feeling is that there usually exist two distinct ways to study a topic, and from a managerial standpoint, a focus on application is the preferred way. Serious reflection about this problem may suggest a somewhat different approach, however. Consider the following situation.

As a personnel manager for a medium-sized firm, you have been asked to discover why employee turnover in your firm is so high. Your boss has told you that it is your responsibility to assess this problem and then to offer suggestions aimed at reducing turnover. What will you do? Several possible strategies come to mind:

- Talk with those who have quit the organization
- Talk with those who remain
- Talk to the employees' supervisors
- Consult with personnel managers in other companies
- Measure job satisfaction
- Examine company policies and practices
- Examine the jobs where most turnover occurs

None of these actions will likely be very successful in helping you arrive at sound conclusions, however. Talking with those who have left usually yields a variety of biased responses by those who either want to "get back at" the company or who fear that criticism will negatively affect their chances for future recommendations. Talking with those still employed has similar problems: why *should* they be candid and jeopardize their jobs? Talking with supervisors will not help if they themselves are the problem. Asking other personnel managers, while comforting, ignores major differences between organizations. Measuring job satisfaction, examining company policies, or examining the jobs themselves may help if one is fortunate enough to hit upon the right problem, but the probability of doing so is minimal. In short, many of the most obvious ways a manager can choose to solve a problem may yield biased results at best, and possibly no results at all.

A more viable approach would be to view the situation from a research standpoint and to use accepted methods of scientific inquiry to arrive at a solution that minimizes biased results. Most of what we know about organizational behavior results from efforts to apply such methods in solving organizational problems (e.g., How do we motivate employees? How do we develop effective leaders? How do we reduce stress at work?). An awareness of the nature of scientific inquiry is useful for understanding how we learned what we know about organizations as well as in facilitating efforts to solve behavioral problems at work.

THEORY BUILDING IN ORGANIZATIONS

Briefly stated, a *theory* is a set of statements that serves to explain the manner in which certain concepts or variables are related. These statements result both from our present level of knowledge on the topic and from our assumptions about the variables themselves. The theory allows us to deduce logical propositions, or hypotheses, that can be tested in the field or laboratory. In short, a theory is a technique that helps us understand how variables fit together. Their use in research and in management is invaluable.

Uses of a Theory

Why do we have theories in the study of organizational behavior? First, theories help us *organize* knowledge about a given subject into a pattern of relationships that lends meaning to a series of observed events. They provide a structure for understanding. For instance, rather than struggling with a lengthy list of factors found to relate to employee turnover, a theory of turnover might suggest how such factors fit together and are related.

Second, theories help us to *summarize* diverse findings so that we can focus on major relationships and not get bogged down in details. A theory "permits us to handle large amounts of empirical data with relatively few propositions."[1]

Finally, theories are useful they *point the way* to future research efforts. They raise new questions and suggest answers. In this sense, they serve a useful heuristic value in helping to differentiate between important and trivial questions for future research. Theories are useful both for the study and management of organizations. As Kurt Lewin said, "There is nothing so practical as a good theory."

What Is a Good Theory?

Abraham Kaplan discusses in detail the criteria for evaluating the utility or soundness of a theory.[2] At least five such criteria can be mentioned:

1. *Internal consistency.* Are the propositions central to the theory free from contradiction? Are they logical?
2. *External consistency.* Are the propositions of a theory consistent with observations from real life?
3. *Scientific parsimony.* Does the theory contain only those concepts that are necessary to account for findings or to explain relationships? Simplicity of

presentation is preferable unless added complexity furthers understanding or clarifies additional research findings.

4. *Generalizability.* In order for a theory to have much utility, it must apply to a wide range of situations or organizations. A theory of employee motivation that applies only to one company hardly helps us understand motivational processes or apply such knowledge elsewhere.

5. *Verification.* A good theory presents propositions that can be tested. Without an ability to operationalize the variables and subject the theory to field or laboratory testing, we are unable to determine its accuracy or utility.

To the extent that a theory satisfies these requirements, its usefulness both to researchers and managers is enhanced. However, a theory is only a starting point. On the basis of theory, researchers and problem solvers can proceed to design studies aimed at verifying and refining the theories themselves. These studies must proceed according to commonly accepted principles of scientific method.

SCIENTIFIC METHOD IN ORGANIZATIONAL BEHAVIOR RESEARCH

Cohen and Nagel suggested that there are four basic "ways of knowing."[3] Managers and researchers use all four of these techniques: tenacity, intuition, authority, and science. When managers form a belief (e.g., a happy worker is a productive worker) and continue to hold that belief out of habit and often in spite of contradictory information, they are using *tenacity.* They use *intuition* when they feel the answer is self-evident or when they have a hunch about how to solve a problem. They use *authority* when they seek an answer to a problem from an expert or consultant who supposedly has experience in the area. Finally, they use *science*—perhaps too seldom—when they are convinced that the three previous methods allow for too much subjectivity in interpretation.

In contrast to tenacity, intuition, and authority, the scientific method of inquiry "aims at knowledge that is *objective* in the sense of being intrasubjectively certifiable, independent of individual opinion or preference, on the basis of data obtainable by suitable experiments or observations."[4] In other words, the scientific approach to problem solving sets some fairly rigorous standards in an attempt to substitute objectivity for subjectivity.

The scientific method in organizational behavior consists of four stages: (1) observation of the phenomena (facts) in the real world; (2) formulation of explanations for such phenomena using the inductive process; (3) generation of predictions or hypotheses about the phenomena using the deductive process; and (4) verification of the predictions or hypotheses using systematic, controlled observation. This process is shown in Exhibit A.1. When this rather abstract description of the steps of scientific inquiry is shown within the framework of an actual research study, the process becomes much clearer. A basic research paradigm is shown in Exhibit A.2. In essence, a scientific approach to research requires that the investigator or manager first recognize clearly what research questions are being posed. To paraphrase Lewis Carroll,

Exhibit A.1
A Model Depicting the
Scientific Method

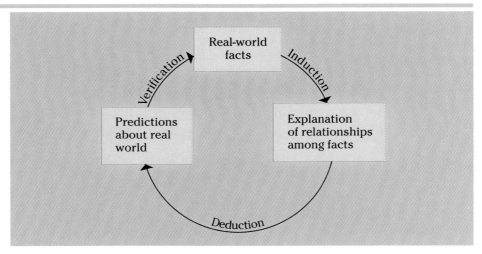

Source: E. F. Stone, *Research Methods in Organizational Behavior* (Glenview, Ill.: Scott, Foresman and Company, 1978), p. 8. Reprinted by permission.

Exhibit A.2
A Model of the Empirical
Research Process

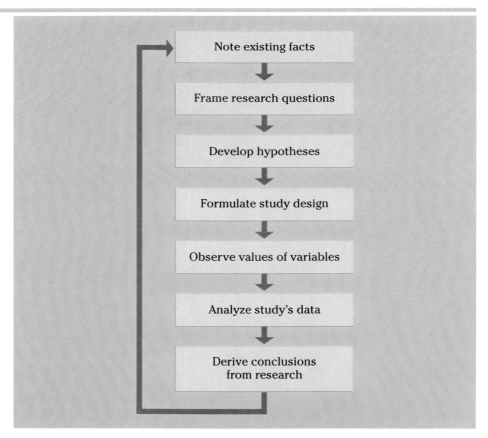

Source: E. F. Stone, *Research Methods in Organizational Behavior* (Glenview, Ill.: Scott, Foresman and Company, 1978), p. 17. Reprinted by permission.

if you don't know where you're going, any road will take you there. Many managers identify what they think is a problem (e.g., turnover) only to discover later that their "problem" turnover rate is much lower than that in comparable industries. Other managers look at poor employee morale or performance and ignore what may be the real problem (e.g., poor leadership).

On the basis of the research questions, specific hypotheses are identified. These hypotheses represent best guesses about what we expect to find. We set forth hypotheses to determine if we can predict the right answer so we can select a study design that allows for a suitable testing. On the basis of the study design (to be discussed shortly), we observe the variables under study, analyze the data we collect, and draw relevant conclusions and management implications. When we follow this process, the risks of being guided by our own opinions or prejudices are minimized, and we arrive at useful answers to our original research questions.

BASIC RESEARCH DESIGNS

Although a detailed discussion of the various research designs is beyond the scope of this Appendix, we can review several common research designs that have been used to collect data in the study of people at work. Specifically, we will examine five different research designs that are frequently used to study behavior at work: (1) naturalistic observation, (2) survey research, (3) field study, (4) field experiment, and (5) laboratory experiment. In general, the level of rigor of the design increases as we move from naturalistic observation toward laboratory study. Unfortunately, so do the costs, in many cases.

Criteria for Evaluating Research Designs

Before examining the five designs, it will be helpful to consider how a researcher selects from among the various designs. Clearly, no one strategy or design is superior in all cases. Each has its place, depending upon the research goals and the constraints placed on the research.

However, when choosing among the potential designs, researchers generally must consider several things. For example, does the design require that you *specify hypotheses* a priori? If you specify appropriate hypotheses and are able to confirm them, then you can predict behavior in organizations. As a manager, being able to predict behavior in advance allows you to intervene and make necessary changes to remedy problem situations. The ability to accurately predict behavior is clearly superior to simply being able to explain behavior after the fact.

Other factors to examine are the *method of measurement* and the *degree of control* to be used. Does the method of measurement use qualitative or quantitative measures? Although qualitative measures may be useful for generating future hypotheses, quantitative measures add more perceived rigor to results. Also, if you are interested in demonstrating causal relationships, it is necessary to have a high degree of control over the study variables. You must be able to manipulate the primary study variable to determine the results of this manipulation while at the same time keeping other potentially contaminating variables constant so they do not interfere in the results.

In addition, a researcher must know to what extent he or she can generalize the results from the study to apply to other organizations or situations. Results that are situation-specific are of little use to managers. *External validity* is of key importance. And, of course, in practical terms, how much is it going to cost to carry out the study and discover a solution? *Cost* can be measured in many ways, including time and money.

The analysis of the previous five criteria provides insight concerning the *overall level of rigor* of the research design. The more rigorous the design, the more confidence one has in the results. This is because more rigorous designs typically employ more accurate measures or interventions and attempt to control for contaminating influences on study results. With this in mind, we can now consider various research designs.

Naturalistic Observation

Naturalistic observations represent the most primitive (least rigorous) method of research in organizations. Simply put, *naturalistic observations* represent conclusions drawn from observing events. At least two forms of such research can be identified: (1) authoritative opinions and (2) case studies.

Authoritative opinions are the opinions of experts in the field. When Henri Fayol wrote his early works on management, for example, he was offering his advice as a former industrial manager. On the basis of experience in real work situations, Fayol and others suggest that what they have learned can be applied to a variety of work organizations with relative ease. Other examples of authoritative opinions can be found in Barnard's *The Functions of the Executive,* Sloan's *My Years with General Motors,* and Peters and Waterman's *In Search of Excellence.* Throughout their works, these writers attempt to draw lessons from their own practical experience that can help other managers assess their problems.

The second use of naturalistic observation can be seen in the *case study.* Case studies attempt to take one situation in one organization and to analyze it in detail with regard to the interpersonal dynamics among the various members. For instance, we may have a case of one middle manager who appears to have burned out on the job; his performance seems to have reached a plateau. The case would then review the cast of characters in the situation and how each one related to this manager's problem. Moreover, the case would review any actions that were taken to remedy the problem. Throughout, emphasis would be placed on what managers could learn from this one real-life problem that can possibly relate to other situations.

Survey Research

Many times, managers wish to know something about the extent to which employees are satisfied with their jobs, are loyal to the organization, or experience stress on the job. In such cases, the managers (or the researchers) are interested mainly in considering quantitative values of the responses. Questionnaires designed to measure such variables are examples of *survey research.* Here we are not attempting to relate results to subsequent events. We simply wish to assess the general feelings and attitudes of employees.

Surveys are particularly popular with managers today as a method of assessing relative job attitudes. Hence, we may make an annual attitude survey and track changes in attitudes over time. If attitudes begin to decline, management is alerted to the problem and can take steps to remedy the situation.

Field Study

In a *field study,* the researcher is interested in the relationship between a *predictor* variable (e.g., job satisfaction) and a subsequent *criterion* variable (e.g., employee turnover or performance). Measures of each variable are taken (satisfaction, perhaps through a questionnaire, and turnover, from company records) and are compared to determine the extent of correlation. No attempt is made to intervene in the system or to manipulate any of the variables, as is the case with experimental approaches.

To continue the simple example we began with, a manager may have a hypothesis that says that satisfaction is a primary indicator of employee turnover. After measuring both, it is found that there is a moderate relationship between the two variables. Hence, the manager may conclude that the two are probably related. Even so, because of the moderate nature of the relationship, it is clear that other factors also influence turnover; otherwise, there would be a much stronger relationship. The manager concludes that, although efforts to improve job satisfaction may help solve the problem, other influences on turnover must also be looked at as well, such as salary level and supervisory style.

Field Experiment

A *field experiment* is much like a field study, with one important exception. Instead of simply measuring job satisfaction, the manager or researcher makes efforts to actually change satisfaction levels. In an experiment, we attempt to manipulate the predictor variable. This is most often done by dividing the sample into two groups: an experimental group and a control group. In the experimental group, we intervene and introduce a major change. Perhaps we alter the compensation program or give supervisors some human relations training. The control group receives no such treatment. After a time, we compare turnover rates in the two groups. If we have identified the correct treatment (that is, a true influence on turnover), turnover rates would be reduced on the experimental group but not in the control group.

In other words, in a field experiment, as opposed to a field study, we intentionally change one aspect of the work environment in the experimental group and compare the impact of the change with the untreated control group. Thus, we can be relatively assured that the solution we have identified is, in fact, a true predictor variable and is of use to management.

Laboratory Experiment

Up to this point, we have considered a variety of research designs that all make use of the actual work environment, the *field.* In this last design, *laboratory experiments,* we employ the same level of rigor as that of the field experiment and actually manipulate the predictor variable, but we do so in an artificial environment instead of a real one.

We might, for instance, wish to study the effects of various compensation programs (hourly rate versus piece rate) on performance. To do this, we might employ two groups of business students and have both groups work on a simulated work exercise. In doing so, we are simulating a real work situation. Each group would then be paid differently. After the experiment, an assessment would be made of the impact of the two compensation plans on productivity.

Comparing Research Designs

Now that we have reviewed various research designs, we might wonder which designs are best. This is not an easy call. All designs have been used by managers and researchers in studying problems of people at work. Perhaps the question can best be answered by considering the relative strengths and weaknesses of each, on the basis of our earlier discussion of the criteria for evaluating research designs (see Exhibit A.3). We should then have a better idea of which design or designs would be appropriate for a particular problem or situation.

Specification of Hypotheses in Advance. It was noted earlier that the ability to specify a priori hypotheses adds rigor to the study. In general, hypotheses are not given for naturalistic observations or survey research. These two techniques are used commonly for exploratory analyses and for identifying pertinent research questions for more rigorous future study. On the other hand, the remaining three designs (field study, field experiment, and laboratory experiment) do allow explicitly for a priori hypotheses. Hence, they are superior in this sense.

Exhibit A.3
A Comparison of Various Research Designs

Research Design	A Priori Hypotheses	Qualitative vs. Quantitative Measures	Control	External Validity	Cost	Overall Level of Rigor
Naturalistic observation	No	Qualitative	Low	Low	Low	Low
Survey research	No	Qualitative and quantitative	Low	High	Low	Medium
Field study	Yes	Quantitative	Medium	High	Medium	Medium
Field experiment	Yes	Quantitative	High	High	High	High
Laboratory experiment	Yes	Quantitative	High	Low	High	High

Note: This table represents general trends; exceptions can clearly be identified

Qualitative Versus Quantitative Measures.   Naturalistic observations typically involve qualitative data, whereas field studies and both forms of experiment typically involve quantitative data. Survey research most often provides for both. Hence, if it is important to collect hard data concerning a problem (e.g., what is the magnitude of the relationship between satisfaction and turnover?), quantitative designs are to be preferred. On the other hand, if one is more concerned about identifying major reasons for turnover and little prior knowledge about the problem exists, qualitative data may be preferred, and survey research may be a better research strategy. The selection of an appropriate design hinges in part on the intended uses for the information.

Control.   As noted earlier, control represents the extent to which potentially contaminating influences can be minimized in a study. Clearly, experimental procedures allow for better control than do nonexperimental ones. The researcher or manager can systematically structure the desired work environment and minimize irrelevant or contaminating influences. As a result, conclusions concerning causal relations between variables can be made with some degree of certainty. Where it is not possible to secure such high control, however—perhaps because the organization does not wish to make a major structural change simply for purposes of an experiment—a field study represents a compromise design. It allows for some degree of control but does not require changing the organization.

External Validity.   The question of external validity is crucial to any study. If the results of a study in one setting cannot be applied with confidence to other settings, the utility of the results for managers is limited. In this regard, survey research, field studies, and field experiments have higher levels of external validity than naturalistic observations or laboratory experiments. Naturalistic observations are typically based on nonrandom samples, and such samples often exhibit characteristics that may not allow for transfers of learning from one organization to another. A clear example can be seen in the case of a small company in which the president implemented a unique compensation plan that proved successful. It would be impossible to predict whether such a plan would work in a major corporation, because of the different nature of the organizations. Similarly, there is some question about how realistic a work environment is actually created in a laboratory situation. If managers are to learn from the lessons of other organizations, they should first learn the extent to which the findings from one kind of organization are applicable elsewhere.

Cost.   As one would expect, the quality of information and its price covary. The more rigorous the design (and thus the more accurate the information), the higher the cost. Costs can be incurred in a variety of ways and include actual out-of-pocket expenses, time invested, and residue costs. The organization is left with the aftermath of an experiment, which could mean raised employee expectations and anxieties, as well as the possibility of disillusionment if the experiment fails. It should be noted that, in survey research, a large amount of general information can be gathered quickly and cheaply.

Overall Level of Rigor.   In summary, then, the real answer to the question concerning which strategy is best lies in the degrees of freedom a manager has in selecting the design. If an experiment is clearly out of the question (perhaps because one's superior doesn't want anything altered), a field study may be the best possible strategy, given the constraints. In fact, field studies are often considered a good compromise strategy in that they have a medium amount of rigor but are also fairly quick and inexpensive. On the other hand, if one simply wishes to take an attitude survey, survey research is clearly in order. If one is not allowed to do anything, authoritative opinions from others may be the only information available. However, if constraints are not severe, experimental methods are clearly superior in that they allow for greater certainty concerning major influences on the criterion variable and on the problem itself.

NOTES

1. M. E. Shaw and P. R. Costanzo, *Theories of Social Psychology* (New York: McGraw-Hill, 1970), p. 9.
2. A. Kaplan, *The Conduct of Inquiry* (San Francisco: Chandler, 1964).
3. M. Cohen and E. Nagel, *An Introduction to Logic and Scientific Inquiry* (New York: Harcourt, Brace and Company, 1943). See also E. Lawler, A. Mohrman, S. Mohrman, G. Ledford, and T. Cummings, *Doing Research That Is Useful for Theory and Practice* (San Francisco: Jossey-Bass, 1985).
4. C. G. Hempel, *Aspects of Scientific Explanation* (New York: The Free Press, 1965), p. 141.

Scoring Keys for Self-Assessment Exercises

Appendix B contains the scoring procedures and interpretations for the various Self-Assessment exercises found throughout the book. These exercises are designed to provide students with an appreciation for the study of management and organization behavior. This is done through active learning—that is, by allowing students to respond to various instruments and questionnaires relating to the subject matter. In this way, it is hoped that students can better understand the subject matter. Students are advised, however, that these instruments are imprecise, and results are sometimes open to divergent interpretations. Thus, caution is in order in interpreting these results; the instruments are provided in this text for purposes of illustration only.

Self-Assessment 2.1: What Is Your Locus of Control?

This instrument measures your locus of control, as described in Chapter 2. After completing the instrument score it by assigning a "0" to any *A* you selected and a "1" to any *B*. Then add up your total score, and compare it to these norms:

> 1–3 = an *external* locus of control
> 4–5 = a *balanced* locus of control
> 5–7 = an *internal* locus of control

See chapter details for a discussion of the meaning of these results.

Self-Assessment 2.2: Which Values Are Most Important to You?

This instrument is intended as an informal measure of instrumental and terminal values. There are no right or wrong answers here. This is simply a chance for you to see what your value structure looks like. Simply examine the pattern of responses you made for both sets of values. What did you learn about yourself? Which values are most important to you?

Self-Assessment 3.1: Can You Understand This Passage?

See Note 5 at the end of Chapter 3 for the answer.

Self-Assessment 3.2: How Do You Feel About Women Executives?

This questionnaire asks ten questions concerning people's attitudes toward women in managerial positions. To score this instrument, add up your score and compare the results to a national sample:

> 10–21 = an unfavorable attitude concerning women as managers
> 22–38 = a neutral attitude toward women as managers
> 39–50 = a favorable attitude toward women as managers

What did you learn about yourself on the basis of this exercise?

Self-Assessment 3.3: Are You Satisfied with Your Job?

This questionnaire is part of the Minnesota Satisfaction Questionnaire. Two scales are used here, one for satisfaction with the level of personal recognition you receive and one for satisfaction with pay or salary. To score this questionnaire, add up your results (separately) for questions 1–5 and 6–10. Remember: items 1–5 refer to your satisfaction with the amount of recognition you receive on the job, whereas items 6–10 refer to your satisfaction with the compensation. For both factors, scoring norms are as follows:

> 5–10 indicates low satisfaction
> 11–19 indicates moderate satisfaction
> 20–25 indicates high satisfaction

How did you do on each factor? If you were the manager of this group, what would you do to improve such scores for your co-workers?

Self-Assessment 4.1: Designing Your Own Behavioral Self-Management Program

The key to this exercise is to see if you understand how to put the concepts of behavioral self-management (BSM) into practice. Did you identify a specific problem that lends itself to the BSM approach? Does your own BSM program follow the procedures outlined in the text? What were the major problems you encountered when you tried to apply your program? And, finally, did the program work? What did you learn about yourself from this exercise?

Self-Assessment 5.1: Where Are You in the Need Hierarchy?

This instrument follows Alderfer's ERG theory of needs, as described in Chapter 5. To score your questionnaire, first add up your point totals for items 2, 5, 8, and 11; this is your *growth* need score. Next, add up items 1, 4, 7, and 10; this is your *relatedness* need score. Finally, add up items 3, 6, 9, and 12; this is your *existence* need score. Which need received the highest point total? This score will tell you which need level you feel is most important to you at this time. Again, remember that there are no right or wrong answers. How did you do? What did you learn about yourself and about the need hierarchy concept?

Self-Assessment 5.2: Which Needs Are Most Important to You?

This questionnaire measures four of Murray's manifest needs: achievement, affiliation, autonomy, and power. Remember, the theory underlying these needs argues that these needs are not arranged in a hierarchy (see text). You can determine your results by adding up your point totals as follows. Items 1–5 relate to need for *achievement;* add up your scores on these five items. (Remember that some of the items are reverse numbered; use the number that you circled.) Next, repeat this process for items 6–10 for need for *affiliation,* items 11–15 for *autonomy,* and 16–20 for *power.*

Norms for each of the needs are as follows:

5–12 points indicates that your need strength is relatively low
13–20 points indicates that your need strength is moderate
21–25 points indicates that your need strength is relatively high

Compare your four scores to develop a *needs profile* for yourself. How does it look? On the basis of these results, what kind of job or work environment would be most suitable for you? What kind of job or work environment would be most unsuitable for you? Why?

Self-Assessment 6.1: How Fair Is Your Employer?

This questionnaire is designed to measure your assessment of the relative fairness of your employer. To score it, add up your total score.

If you got 26–35 points, you view your organization as very fair and equitable.
If you got 15–25 points, you view your organization as moderately equitable.
If you got 5–14 points, you view your organization as being largely inequitable or unfair.

How did you do? Would other employees of this same organization have similar assessments? Why, or why not? If you were the manager of this organization, what kind of things would you do to improve this situation? When you have finished your own results, it might prove interesting to compare your results with those of other students in your class to see how they assess their own employers.

Self-Assessment 6.2: What Do You Want Most in a Job?

This exercise allows you to rank-order ten possible job outcomes. You are asked, in essence, to assign a valence to each of the outcomes—that is, how important is each to you? There are no correct answers. Rather, the exercise is designed to allow you to consider what you want from your present or future job. What did you learn from this exercise? Are your rankings similar to those of your fellow students?

Self-Assessment 7.1: How Would You Rate Your Supervisor?

This exercise, which has no right or wrong answers, asks you to evaluate the performance of your current or former boss. Because it is usually the boss who gets to rate the subordinate, this should be an interesting experience. When you have finished, show your appraisal to a friend, and explain (defend) your assessment. Are there any rating biases in your appraisal? If so, where? Is this a fair appraisal? Why? How would other co-workers evaluate the same boss?

Self-Assessment 7.2: How Much Feedback Are You Getting from Your Job?

This exercise gives you an opportunity to analyze feedback patterns for your current or previous job. Add up your four scores corresponding to the four types of job-related feedback:

> Corrective feedback (add up items 1–3)
> Positive supervisory feedback (items 4–6)
> Positive co-worker feedback (items 7–9)
> Self-administered feedback (items 10–12)

When you have finished, examine the results. Where did you get the most feedback? Where did you get the least feedback? You may wish to share your results with your friends to see the differences. If you were the supervisor, what would you do differently to ensure that your subordinates were performing well? Why?

Self-Assessment 8.1: How Do You Behave in a Group?

This questionnaire asks you to describe your own behavior within a group setting. To score the instrument, add up your scores as follows for the three categories of behavior (see text):

> Task-oriented behavior (add up items 1–4)
> Relations-oriented behavior (items 5–8)
> Self-oriented behavior (items 9–12)

Examine the resulting pattern in your answers. As usual, there are no correct or incorrect answers. Instead, this is an opportunity to see how you describe your own role-related activities in a group. What did you learn about yourself? How does your role in a typical group differ from those of other individuals?

Self-Assessment 8.2: How Effective Is Your Work Group?

This instrument measures the relative effectiveness of a group to which you belong. Count the number of times you answered "mostly yes." The larger the number, the more productive and satisfied the group members should be. There are no norms for this exercise, so you might wish to create your own norms by comparing scores among your classmates for the various groups to which they belong. Look at the range of scores, and then describe the characteristics of each group. Are there any common characteristics that distinguish the groups with the highest scores? The lowest scores? Why do these differences occur?

Alternatively, you might use this questionnaire to compare groups to which you belong. If you were the leader of one of these groups, what would you do to make the group more effective? Why hasn't this been done already?

Self-Assessment 9.1: The Job Diagnostic Survey

This instrument, developed by Hackman and Oldham, is commonly used to assess the extent to which a job is enriched. It also measures an individual's motivating potential score (MPS) on the basis of the actual job. You were asked to select a present or past job (part- or full-time) and complete the questionnaire. Scoring instructions are included in the exercise itself. When considering your results, you should know that the *national average* for the MPS is 128. How did you do? If you were the supervisor or manager, what would you suggest as a way to enrich this job so it is more challenging and rewarding? Are these suggestions realistic? Why?

Self-Assessment 10.1: What Is Your Bureaucratic Orientation?

This exercise examines one's tendency toward bureaucracy. To score it, give yourself 1 point (each) if you *agreed* with questions 1, 2, 4, 7, 8, 10, 11, 14, 16, 18, and 19. Give yourself 1 point (each) if you *disagreed* with questions 3, 5, 6, 9, 12, 13, 15, 17, and 20. Now sum your score.

> If you received a *high* score (15 or over), you would probably enjoy working in a bureaucracy or highly structured work environment.
>
> If you received a *low* score (5 or lower), you would probably be very frustrated working in a bureaucracy.

How did you do? On the basis of this information, identify several types of job or organization where you think you would succeed. Now identify several where you think you would be less successful. What primary characteristics differentiate the jobs in your first category from those in the second? Explain.

Self-Assessment 11.1: Do You Work in a Mechanistic or an Organic Environment?

This questionnaire measures the extent to which a particular work environment is mechanistic or organic. You are asked to describe both the company (in Part 1) and the company's environment (in Part 2). When you have finished, add up the total number of points in Part 1.

> If your score is 8–24, the organization is relatively *mechanistic*.
>
> If your score is 25–39, your organization yields a mixed orientation.
>
> If your score is 40–56, your organization is relatively *organic*.

Now compare these results with your description of the environment in Part 2. Is there a good match? (You might wish to refer again to the text to make sure you understand possible variations in the environment.) If so, why? If not, what do you see as the future of this organization? If you were in charge of this organization, what might you do differently to develop a better match? Why hasn't this already been done by the present leader?

Self-Assessment 12.1: What Is Your LPC?

This instrument was designed by Fiedler to measure one's "least preferred co-worker" (or LPC). You were asked to describe your least favored co-worker with whom you have worked at some time. To score the LPC, simply add up the numeric values.

> If your score is 73 or above, you are classified as a *high LPC* person (relationship-oriented).
>
> If your score is 63 or below, you are a *low LPC* person (task-oriented).

A score between 64 and 72 is classified as a *middle LPC* score, meaning that you exhibit characteristics of both high and low LPC.

Remember, there are no correct or incorrect answers. Do you think your score is an accurate description of yourself? How would you describe your own leadership style? Would your co-workers or friends agree with your assessment of your own leader style? Given this assessment, what type of group or organization do you feel you would be best suited for? Why?

Self-Assessment 13.1: What Is Your Interaction Involvement?

This exercise looks at your interaction involvement (see text). To score it, add up your three scores as follows:

Responsiveness (add items 1–3)
Perceptiveness (add items 4–6)
Attentiveness (add items 7–9)

Norms for *responsiveness* and for *attentiveness* are 3–6 = high; 7–10 = moderate; and 11–15 = low. Norms for *perceptiveness* are 3–7 = low; 8–11 = moderate; and 12–15 = high. How did you do? Please note which aspect of interaction you were strongest (and weakest) in.

Self-Assessment 13.2: How Effective Is Your Organizational Communication?

To assess your relative effectiveness in organizational communication, add up the answers to the six items.

If you scored 25–30, your communication at work is very effective.
If you scored 13–24, your communication is moderately effective.
If you scored 6–12, your communication is very ineffective.

How did you do? How did your friends do? How might you do things better in the future?

Self-Assessment 13.3: What Are Your Listening Skills?

This ten-item instrument assesses your relative degree of attentiveness when listening to or talking with others. To score the instrument, add up the numbers you circled.

If you received a score of 10–25, you have "poor" listening skills.
If you received a score of 26–39, you have "average" listening skills.
If you received a score of 40–50, you have "superior" listening skills.

Why do you think you received the score you did? Do you feel this is an accurate reflection of your attentiveness when talking with others? Why, or why not? What might you do to improve your listening skills?

Self-Assessment 14.1: How Participative Is Your Boss?

This exercise asks you to rate your boss (on a current or previous job) on the extent to which he or she is (was) participative. When you are finished, add up your score, and compare it with the following norms:

> 10–20 = low participation
> 21–43 = moderate participation
> 44–50 = high participation

How participative is your boss? Compare your results with those of your friends who have different types of jobs and different supervisors. Where does your boss stand? If you were the supervisor in your group, would you do anything differently with respect to the amount of employee involvement you allowed? If so, what? Why?

Self-Assessment 14.2: How Would You Make This Decision?

This exercise is based on the research of Vroom, Yetton, and Jago on the decision-making styles of various leaders. It asks you to use the normative model and its decision tree to determine how best to make the decision. Following the decision tree in Exhibit 14.10, we see the following analysis:

QR: *How important is the technical quality of this decision?*

Answer: Technical quality is not a factor here, because the case notes that all candidates for the assignment are equally qualified. Performance quality would remain the same no matter who is selected. Thus, the answer to QR is "low."

CR: *How important is subordinate commitment to the decision?*

Answer: In view of the importance of the assignment to the company and the fact that no one wishes to go, commitment to the decision must be "high." To keep the group effective, members have to know that the selection decision was fair, and they have to support the decision. Thus, the answer to CR is "high."

CP: *If you were to make the decision by yourself, is it reasonably certain that your subordinates would be committed to the decision?*

Answer: The answer to this depends upon the extent to which your subordinates trust you to make a "fair" decision. That is, because no one wants to be selected, if you are not universally trusted and seen as operating on behalf of the group—that is, a "no" for CP— a participative (GII) decision style would be best. This would ensure that all members had an opportunity to get involved in this distasteful decision. On the other hand, if you were universally trusted, your subordinates would probably feel comfortable allowing you to make a unitary (AI) decision, because they would fully expect you to make a decision that is both impartial and in the best interests of the group as a whole. Thus, your decision analysis leads you toward the lower right-hand side of the decision tree, either to the GII or the AI, depending upon the answer to the CP (commitment probability) question.

Self-Assessment 14.3: Are You a Victim of Groupthink?

This instrument examines the extent to which a group to which you belong has experienced groupthink. First, add up your total points.

> If you got 8–16 points, your group is *low* on groupthink; that is, your group is not unduly affected by those factors that characterize the groupthink phenomenon.
> If you scored 17–31 points, your group is experiencing *moderate* groupthink tendencies.
> If you scored 32–40 points, your group is experiencing *high* groupthink tendencies.

If you wish, you can apply this exercise to several different groups to which you belong, or you can compare your results with those of your classmates. What do you see in your results? What might you have done to reduce the level of groupthink in any of these groups?

Self-Assessment 15.1: What Are Your Bases of Power?

This instrument examines the five bases of power discussed in Chapter 15. When you have finished the questionnaire, add up your scores for each scale as follows:

> Referent power (add items 1–3)
> Expert power (add items 4–6)
> Legitimate power (add items 7–9)
> Reward power (add items 10–12)
> Coercive power (add items 13–15)

To interpret these results, consider the following:
A score of 3–6 points indicates a weak power base on a particular scale.
A score of 7–11 points indicates a moderate power base.
A score of 12–15 points indicates a strong power base on a particular scale.

On the basis of this, what does your power profile look like? Does this seem like an accurate reflection of your actual situation? If you wished to change your power bases, which bases would you change? How would you try to change these bases?

Self-Assessment 15.2: How Political Are You?

This questionnaire is designed to measure your political behavior. You have been asked to answer "true" or "false" to the ten questions. When you have finished, consider the following. According to the author of this instrument, if you answered "true" to almost all of the questions, you should consider yourself a confirmed politician. (This is not meant to be a compliment.) If you answered "false" to questions 5 and 6, which deal with deliberate lies and uncharitable behavior, you have shown yourself to be a person of high ethical behavior. Finally, if you answered "false" to all or almost all of the questions, you are not considered a politician; rather, you are a person who rejects manipulation, incomplete disclosure, and self-serving behavior. On the basis of this instrument, how political are you? How political are your friends? On the basis of this response, what have you learned about the role of political behavior in organizations? What implications follow from these results concerning your future management style? Why?

Self-Assessment 16.1: What Is Your Approach to Conflict Resolution?

In this exercise, there are no right answers. Instead, you are simply asked to describe your own approach to conflict resolution. To do this, score the instrument as follows:

> Competition (add items 1–3)
> Collaboration (add items 4–6)
> Compromise (add items 7–9)
> Avoidance (add items 10–12)
> Accommodation (add items 13–15)

Now, compare the relative strength of your preferences for each of the five conflict resolution modes. The larger your score on a particular scale, the more you favor this mode of resolution. What patterns do you see in this analysis? Are there any substantive differences between you and your friends in your approach to conflict resolution? Why? What did you learn about yourself as a manager?

Self-Assessment 17.1: How Stressful Is Your Job?

To score this instrument, first add up your score.

> If you scored 10–18 points, you see yourself as having a normal amount of stress.
> If you scored 19–38, you feel that stress is becoming a problem.
> If you scored 39–50, you feel that stress is a serious problem for you on this job.

Where did you score on this instrument? Does this seem like an accurate description of the real situation? On the job you describe, what kind of things might you do to reduce the stress levels?

Self-Assessment 17.2: Are You a Type A?

This instrument is somewhat complicated to score. Follow the following instructions carefully:

> *Time urgency.* Time urgency reflects one's race against the clock, even when there is little reason to hurry. It is measured by the following items: 1, 2, 8, 12, and 14. For each *A* or *B* answer you gave on these questions, give yourself one point. Put the total number on the line at the left.
>
> *Inappropriate aggression and hostility.* This dimension reflects excessively competitive behavior and frequent displays of hostility. It is measured by items 3, 4, 9, and 10. Give yourself one point for each *A* or *B* you received on these items, and record your total at the left.
>
> *Polyphasic behavior.* This is the tendency to undertake several activities simultaneously at inappropriate times. As a result, individuals often end up wasting time instead of saving it, which leads to wasted energy. This factor is measured by items 6 and 11. Every *A* or *B* answer yields one point. Again, put your total points at the left.
>
> *Goal directedness without proper planning.* This refers to a tendency for individuals to rush into work without knowing how to accomplish the desired result. Consequently, incomplete work and errors are likely to occur. This factor is scored by items 5 and 7. Each *A* or *B* yields one point; put the total to the left.
>
> *Total score*

If you received a total score of 5 or greater, you may possess some of the basic components of the Type A personality. How did you do? If you received a high score, what kinds of things should you do to reduce the stress level here?

Self-Assessment 17.3: How Stable Is Your Life?

This instrument attempts to assess your rate of life change; that is, how much activity and change do you currently have that may cause stress? To score it, add up the points or units assigned to the various life changes you experienced during the year (for example, put down 73 points for a divorce, 11 for Christmas, etc.).

> If your total score is less than 150, available research suggests that you should remain reasonably healthy during the coming year.
>
> If you scored 150–300, there is a 50 percent chance that you will experience illness during the coming year.
>
> If you scored over 300, there is a 70 percent chance of impending illness.

Remember in evaluating your results that a high score does not automatically mean illness; rather, it means that your odds of illness are statistically higher than those with lower scores. Where did you score? Is this a reasonable description of your current situation? If so, what actions might you take to reduce your rate of risk?

Self-Assessment 17.4: Are You Suffering from Burnout?

This instrument measures your self-perceptions concerning burnout. To score it, add up the number of times you checked "mostly true." If you answered "mostly true" to seven or more of the questions, you may be suffering from burnout. If you received a high score, consider what specific actions you might take to reduce the level of burnout?

Self-Assessment 18.1: What Are Your Career Anchors?

This exercise will give you five scores relating to the five career anchors discussed in the chapter. Score the exercise as follows:

Technical/functional competence (items 1, 6, and 11)
Managerial competence (items 2, 7, and 12)
Security and stability (items 3, 8, and 13)
Creativity/entrepreneurship (items 4, 9, and 14)
Autonomy and independence (items 5, 10, and 15)

For each factor, the higher the score, the stronger the particular anchor. Which anchors are stronger for you? Which are weaker? What implications follow from these results for you and your career? You may wish to discuss these results with your friends to see how the concept of career anchors relates to their career choices, too.

Self-Assessment 18.2: How Important Is Success to You?

This exercise looks at your self-perceptions concerning success. Specifically, it focuses on how you feel if you win or if you lose. To score this exercise, first add up your point total.

If you received 10–22, you have a fairly strong need for success; you like to win. In fact, many such people demonstrate a strong *fear of failure;* they hate losing and have an internalized fear that they may not succeed. This anxiety often causes people not to try on a task unless they feel confident that they have a reasonably good chance of success. Is this you?

If you scored 23–35, you have a moderate need for success; you fall in between the two other groups.

If you scored 36–50, you tend to have what is called a *fear of success;* that is, you may be apprehensive about possible negative outcomes associated with success (as opposed to failure). You may feel unworthy about winning or uncomfortable with public recognition of your accomplishments. Such people often think that success is to be avoided.

How did you score on the self-assessment? What can you learn from this exercise that can help you with your own career success?

Self-Assessment 19.1: How Receptive Are You to Change?

This exercise focuses on your receptivity or openness to change. Some people like continual change in their lives and view each change as a new adventure. Others are more comfortable with the status quo and with continuity; they would prefer to see less change. In fact, they may be suspicious of change. To see how you did on this exercise, add up your total score. Then consider the following categories:

A score of 10–20 indicates high receptivity to change.
A score of 21–39 indicates a modest receptivity to change.
A score of 40–50 indicates a low receptivity to change.

As usual, there are no correct or incorrect answers; differences across people are natural. How did you do on this exercise? Do you agree with the findings? What lessons can you learn from this exercise that may improve your abilities as a manager?

Text Credits

Name Index

Subject Index